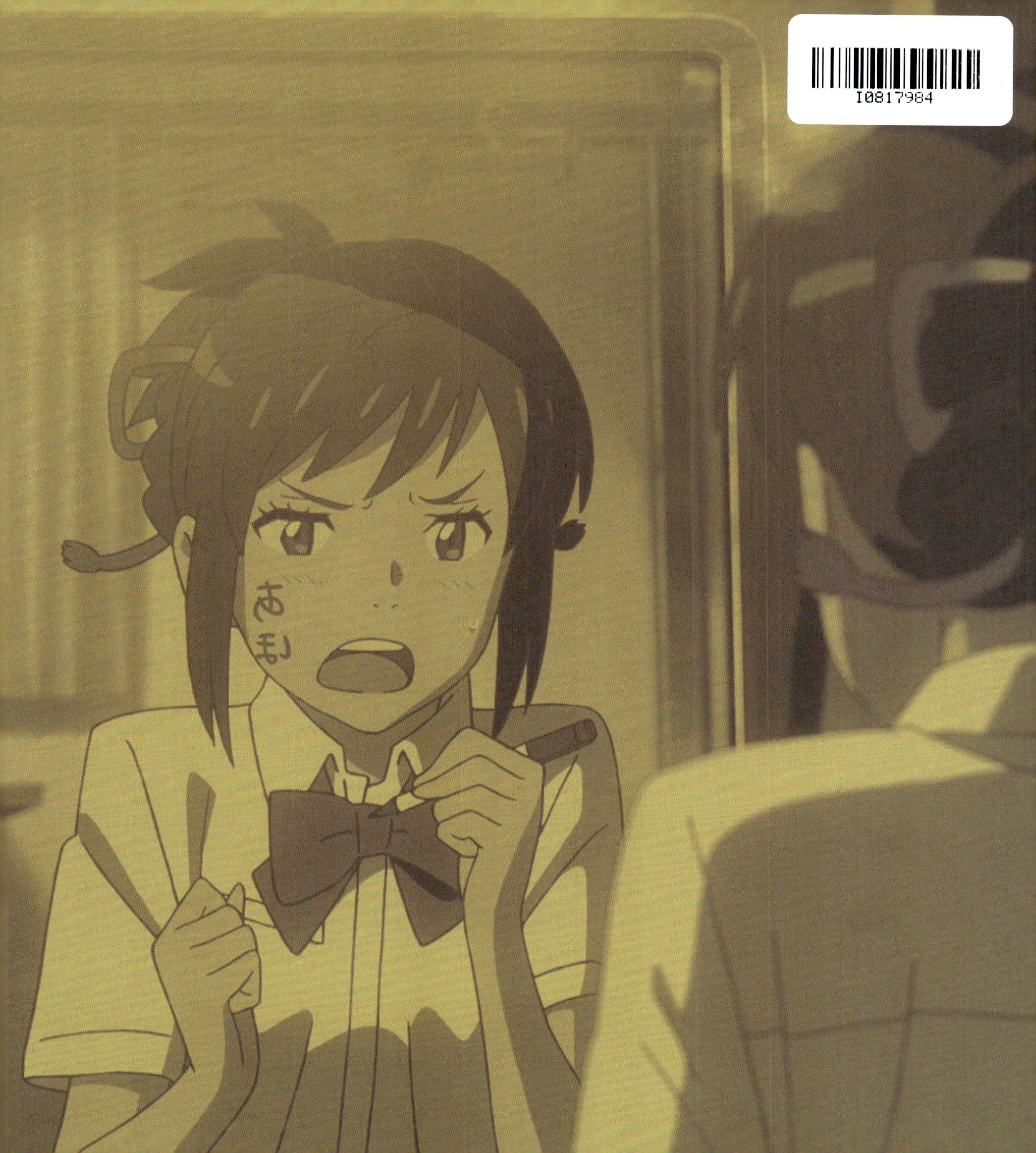
あほ

100 YEARS OF ANIME

MATTHIEU PINON
PHILIPPE BUNEL

88 1983 TO 1995 THE THREE MEDIA

142 1996 TO 2017 THE DIGITAL ERA

Introduction

In 2016, the animated film *Your Name.* became the biggest overseas Japanese film of all time, and the ambassador of an industry worth nearly ¥2,000 billion ($13.7 billion). We've come a long way since the first historically dated animated film in 1917! A simple comparison between the starting point and the ending point in *100 Years of Anime* is all it takes to see that retracing those hundred years is far more complex than the title suggests.

Anime has become a part of global pop culture. Many new fans emerged with the new millennium and the advent of the internet, evidenced by the roughly 250,000 people who visited the Japan Expo in Villepinte, France, in July 2019. These fans have learned the anime codes and know its universally themed works inside and out. On the other hand, titles deeply rooted in Japanese culture and avoided by international publishers and distributors did not reach them. You just need to stand in the lobby of the Fuji TV headquarters in Tokyo to see this in action—as tourists rush to the temporary exhibitions of the channel's latest hit anime series, Japanese families pose in front of the permanent statue of Sazae-san, star of the series that has been following the daily life of a typical Japanese housewife for more than half a century.

Unraveling one hundred years of animation means dispelling this misunderstanding. To do this, we have focused on the general public, to whom this book is dedicated first and foremost. Enlightened amateurs and even enthusiasts need not worry—although they will probably have mastered some of the basics and jargon of this medium, they will also find a wealth of stories and information! All the more as animation has changed, generation after generation, over the last century. Children's stories in the 1960s differ from contemporary titles but maintain the same intergenerational appeal, just as the artistic paths of leading directors such as Osamu Tezuka, Rintaro, Hayao Miyazaki, Katsuhiro Ōtomo, Hideaki Anno, and Makoto Shinkai diverged, despite their common foundation. These stories continue to appeal to teenagers and sexagenarians alike.

With this in mind, of the many options offered by the multifaceted evolution of this medium over the course of a century, we have chosen the one that everyone has experienced: technological progress, from silent movies to the internet through television and the VCR, a crucial player in the expansion of anime. However, the desire for accessibility comes up against the `need to respect the field to which this book is dedicated—major works in the development of "Japanimation," as international fans have called it, must be cited in their original language. Seemingly paradoxical, our choice of title names was logically dictated by our approach.

A work will appear first in italics by its Japanese title, followed by its English or international title in parentheses where applicable. We will use that second title throughout the book to avoid overloading it with Japanese terms and make it as easy to read as possible. Thus, *Shingeki no Kyojin* (*Attack on Titan*) and *Sen to Chihiro no Kamikakushi* (*Spirited Away*) will then appear as *Attack on Titan* and *Spirited Away*, which is not the case for many titles, like *Dragon Ball*, *Akira*, and *Pokémon*. There are a few instances, particularly in the first part of the book, of works with no official translation. In those cases, we suggest a literal and unofficial translation denoted by an asterisk.

Because art is the essence of anime, we have used substantial iconography to illustrate our remarks. The further back in time we went, the more the iconographic spring dried up, which is why some older visuals are of a much lower quality than today's HD standards. Nevertheless, we're counting on your understanding to get past this, because our primary goal is to enable every reader to associate a title with a visual.

The written word is still the best tool for developing such a rich theme in depth, but it cannot convey the emotions aroused by these audiovisual productions. However, in the age of multimedia and the internet, all it takes are a few clicks to legally access a catalog that has continued to grow and diversify over a century. At the end of each crucial period in our journey through time, we will give you a selection of twelve works synthesizing the major trends of the era, a summary that is representative, if not qualitative.

Now you're ready to immerse yourself in a century of artistic, technical, economic, international, and cultural evolution.

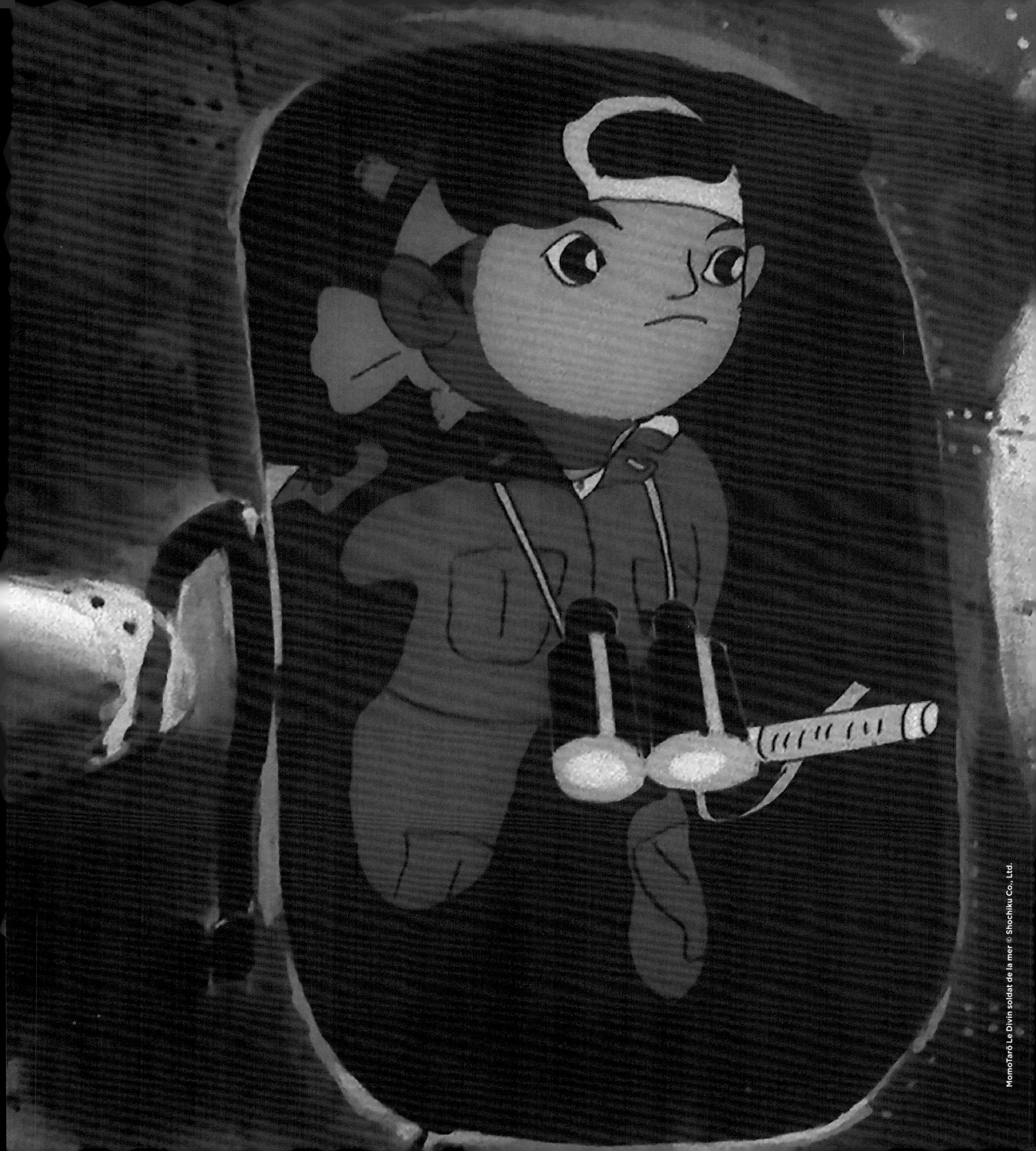

MomoTarō Le Divin soldat de la mer © Shochiku Co., Ltd.

1917 TO 1957 BLACK AND WHITE FILM

Early stages and first pitfalls

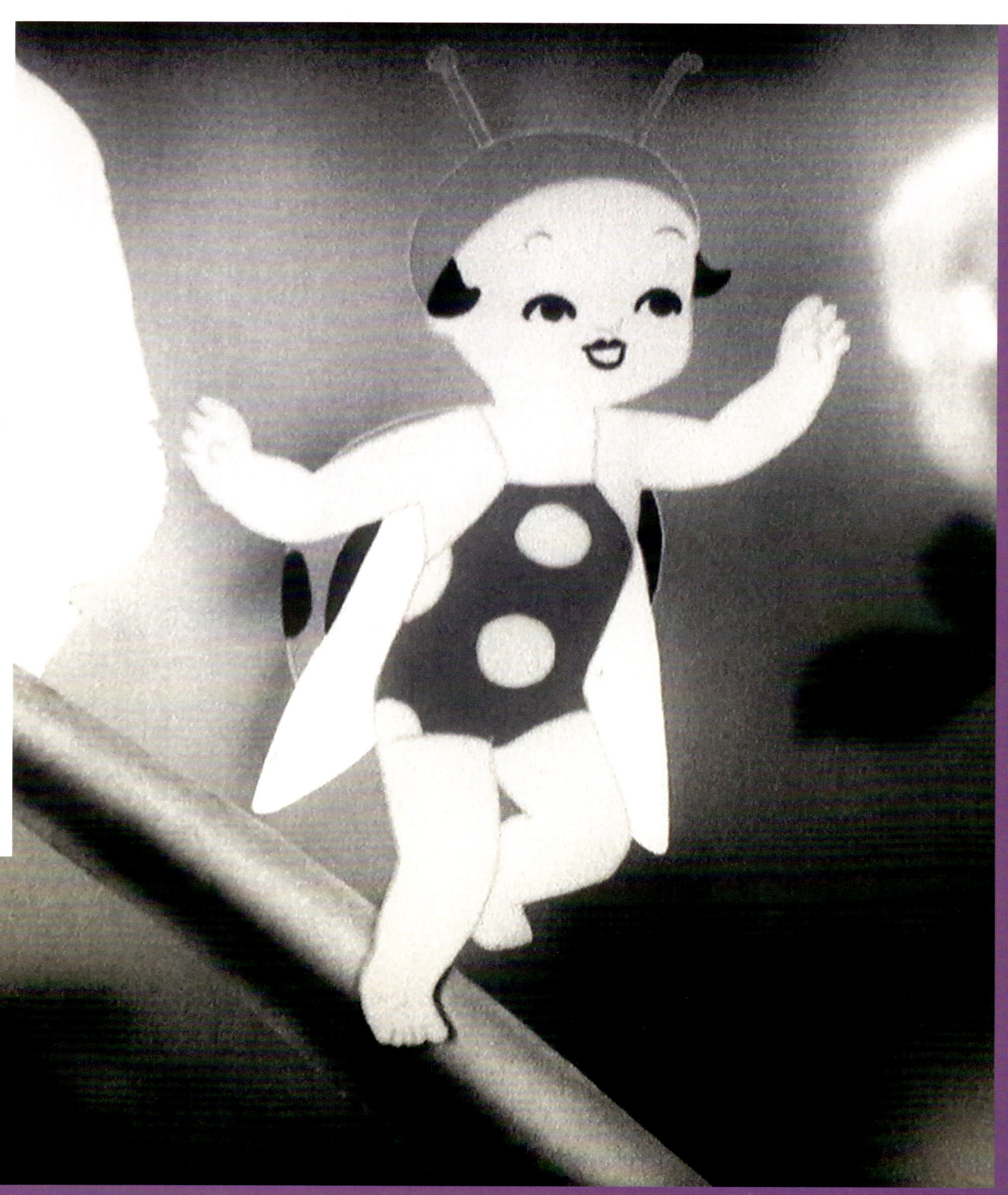

Kumo to chūrippu © 1943 Shochiku Co. Ltd.

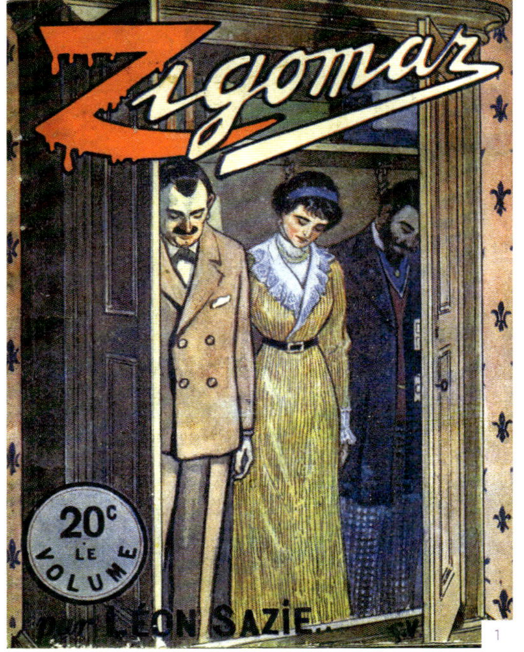

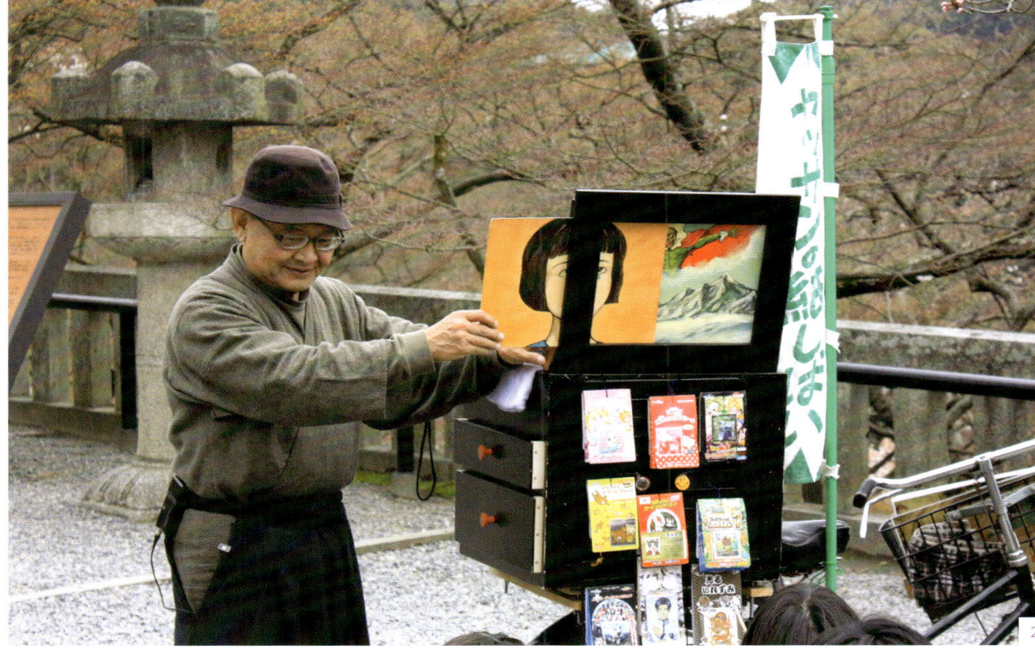

1
1912
Zigomar

2
A *kamishibai* storyteller

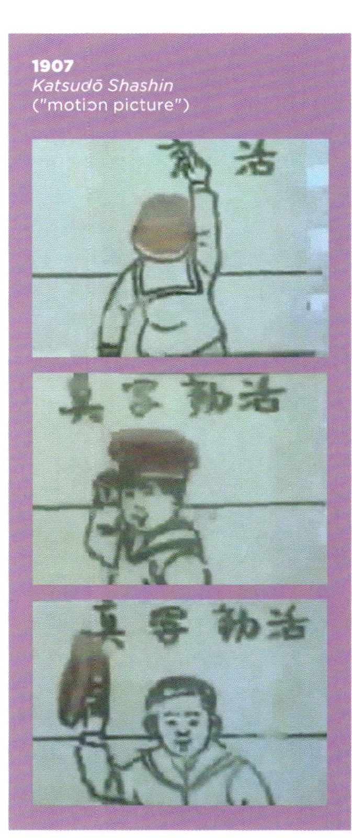

1907
Katsudō Shashin
("motion picture")

First explorations, first setbacks

FERTILE GROUND

Japanese animation, now commonly called **anime**, needed rich and dynamic soil in order to take root. Japan underwent many far-reaching reforms after the Boshin Civil War (1868 to 1869) under the reign of Emperor Meiji, who had just died in 1912. Two centuries of isolationism (1641 to 1853) had come to an end! By supporting the Allies against the German navy in the Pacific and Indian oceans, Japan entered the international scene and picked up a few colonies along the way. For half a century, the Japanese had been discovering Western technological innovations, including the magic lanterns that foreshadowed cinema.

The first Japanese models consisted of a wooden frame, two lenses, and very thin plates of painted glass and were so fragile that they did not survive the ravages of time. This entertainment quickly became popular with younger generations, who saw it as a technological extension of the traditional *kamishibai*. Literally "paper theater," *kamishibai* tells a story by scrolling through drawings in a frame one by one. The show was officially free but was actually offered only to children who bought treats from the traveling storyteller carrying his equipment by bicycle—the luggage rack served as a backdrop for the theater. These street shows, which saw the emergence of the pioneers of **manga** (Japanese comic books), also heavily influenced early animation experiments. The instability of Japanese cinema, still searching for its own identity, did not help the medium's development.

The first of the two main factors for this upheaval was the release of a film in early twentieth-century Japan. The *benshi*, or master of ceremonies, explained the technological principles of cinema to the audience

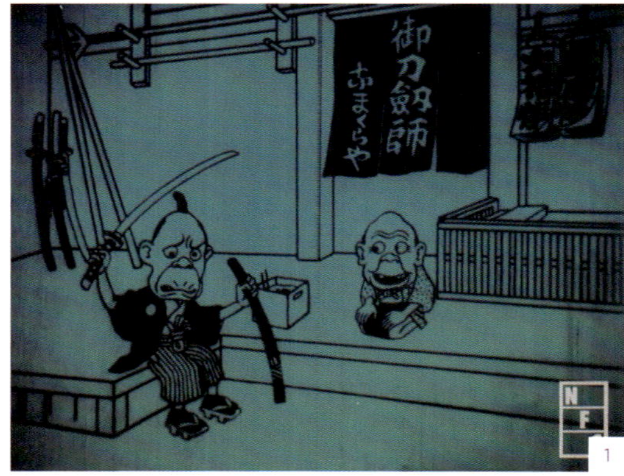

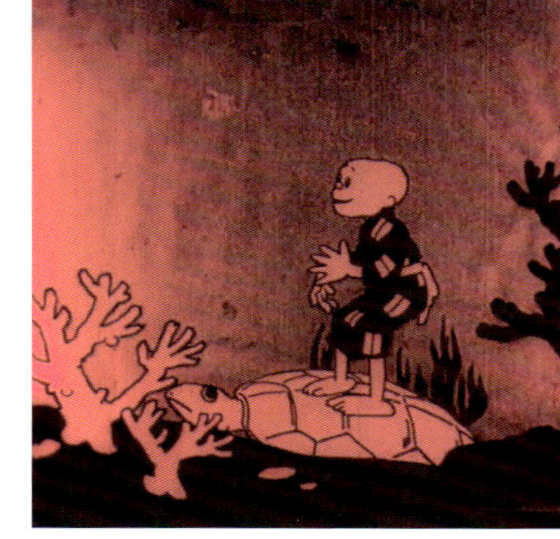

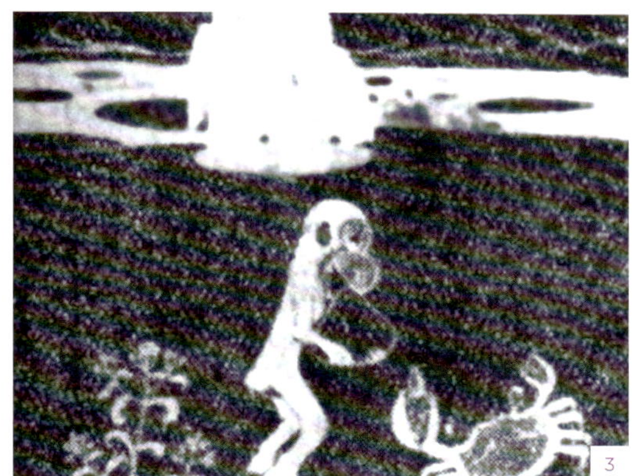

1
1917
Hanawa Hekonai Meitō no Maki (Hanawa Hekonai: A New Sword Chapter)

2
1918
Urashima Tarō

3
1917
Saru Kani Kassen (The Battle of the Monkey and the Crab)

in front of the screen and then voiced the characters in the film, which were still silent at the time. They were true stars of the show, capable of transforming a flop into a masterpiece (and vice versa) and were often featured front and center on movie posters! In the 1910s, a group of young artists came together under the banner of the *Jun Eiga-geki Undō* (Pure Film Movement) to breathe new life into Japanese cinema, which until then had been confined to filmed theater, including traditional Kabuki plays where female characters were still played by men. This movement echoed what was found on the international stage, overshadowing the role of the smooth-talking *benshi*. The profession fell into decline and did not survive a law issued in 1917 restricting its role.

The second factor was governmental control over a growing medium. In 1912, the French series *Zigomar* created quite the scandal—choosing a criminal as the hero; what an example for the youth! Governmental decrees closely followed, monitoring all cinematic production aimed at children. With the sector having become too risky and not profitable enough, it was reduced to a bare minimum in studios. This is the troubled context in which the first Japanese cartoons appeared. Or rather, the oldest precisely dated archives to be found while awaiting future discoveries. In 2004, Natsuki Matsumoto found a film strip of fifty hand-painted frames showing a three-second animation sequence. Though all the necessary equipment was technically available in 1907, there is nothing to suggest that *Katsudō Shashin* was not produced later.

In its drive for internationalization, the Pure Film Movement had reintroduced text boxes into films, to the detriment of the *benshi*. Two rivaling major studios at the time, Nikkatsu and Tennenshoku Katsudō Shashin (aka Tenkatsu), introduced the new intertitle designer role, opening the door to the pioneers of animation. The first Western attempts in this new medium of expression had reached Japan, notably through the works of Émile Cohl, as historians currently consider Cohl's 1912 *Les Exploits de Feu-Follet* (*The Exploits of Will-o'-the-Wisp**) to be the first foreign animated cartoon (without interruption or interaction with live scenes). Fascinated by this work, three talented young men were on their way to becoming "the fathers of anime": Ōten Shimokawa, Seitarō Kitayama, and Junichi Kōuchi.

THE THREE FATHERS OF ANIME

Ōten Shimokawa (1892 to 1973) was already known for his comics in the satire magazine *Tokyo Puck*. He was just twenty-six years old when Tenkatsu hired him to make an animated short film inspired by one of his characters, Imokawa Mukuzō. At no point did the artist, who knew nothing about filmmaking, realize that Émile Cohl had drawn in black ink on white paper and used negatives to get white outlines on a black background for *Fantasmagorie*. Shimokawa patiently drew with chalk on a blackboard, photographed the image, erased it, and redrew the parts he wanted to animate before taking another photo, using ink directly on the film to remove any defects! This titanic effort resulted in the April 1917 release of *Imokawa Mukuzō Genkanban no Maki* (*Imokawa Mukuzō the Doorman**), considered to be the first professional cartoon in history. But here again, the sources are vague and contradictory; the only magazine specialized in Japanese cinema at the time, *Kinema Record*, states that the first screening of a cartoon took place in January 1917, without specifying the title.

Records show that Shimokawa worked intensely on five short films for Tenkatsu in 1917. With the help of his assistant, Masaru Shibata, he experimented with various technology to improve his shots, which included creating many copies of the same background to which he added his moving characters. Nevertheless, he threw in the towel at the end of the year—animation was not profitable, especially when considering the physical investment involved. Rather than wearing out his eyesight, Shimokawa went back to more lucrative activities, like political cartoons, especially since the Tennenshoku Katsudō Shashin company was not in the best shape. The studio, whose name literally meant the "Natural Color Moving Picture Company," had not only experimented in animation, but also in the Kinemacolor process, which was extremely expensive to produce. With its finances in the red, Tenkatsu resolved to shift toward more classic films to stand up against its great rival, Nikkatsu, where a certain Seitarō Kitayama worked.

A watercolorist by training, he joined the studio in 1916 for purely financial reasons. He was responsible for the intertitles, which he gradually embellished with very simple graphic effects such as blurring, pixilation, and superimposed text on images. These sequences of a few short seconds were a major asset to Nikkatsu's open struggle against the prevailing *benshi*, launched by the Pure Film Movement. Outside his working hours, the young man, who had discovered animation through American cartoons, was striving to understand and reproduce the techniques using the studio's equipment. He used cutout animation for his first film, *Saru Kani Kassen* (*The Battle of the Monkey and the Crab**), released on May 20, 1917. Although in form he used the current trend of intertitles that had taken over the *benshi*'s role, the story itself was inspired by a fourteenth-century legend. His film was highly successful, and Kitayama was called before the head of Nikkatsu, who had found a loophole in the government's surveillance system.

By explaining to Japanese children the disastrous consequences of bad behavior in the moralistic tone of a fable, they were free to feature utter scoundrels who were always punished in the end. Nikkatsu pushed the idea and obtained grants to produce a series of educational films for the general public to be created by Seitarō Kitayama himself. Surrounded by a team of artists who were painters by trade, including Sanae Yamamoto, Kitayama directed twenty-two short films in 1917 (ten) and 1918 (twelve) detailing the pitfalls along the path of a mail carrier and the future profits brought by the public savings bank. A striking detail was that his adaptation of the traditional *Momotarō* tale was fully subtitled, for the express purpose of exporting it.

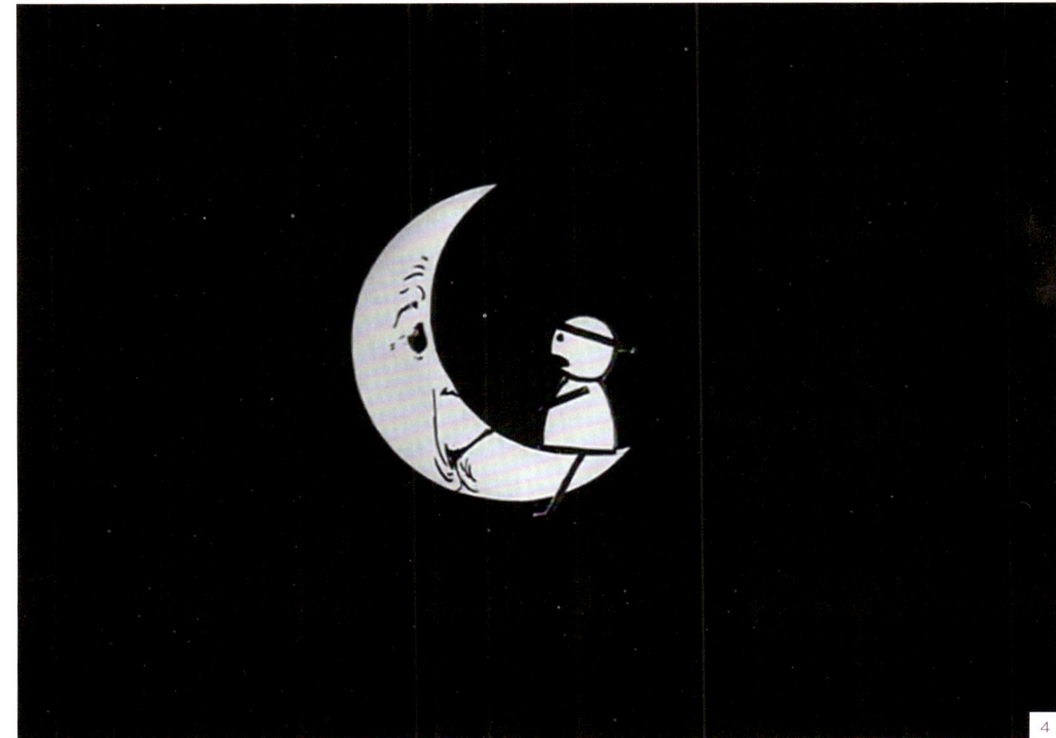

4

4
—
1912
The Exploits of Will-o'-the-Wisp

1917
Hanawa Hekonai Meitō no Maki (Hanawa Hekonai: A New Sword Chapter)

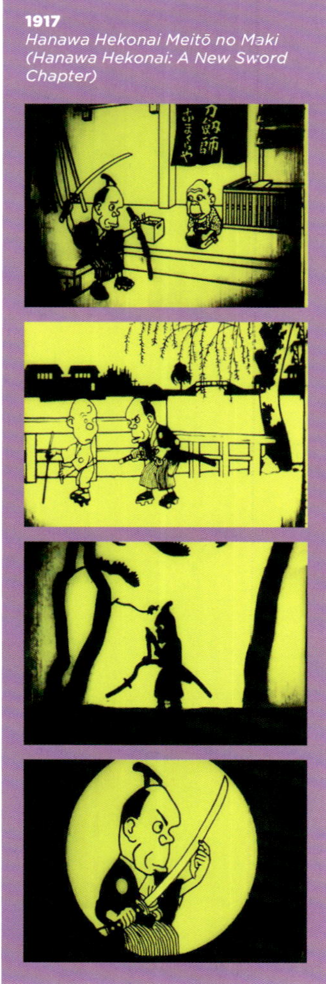

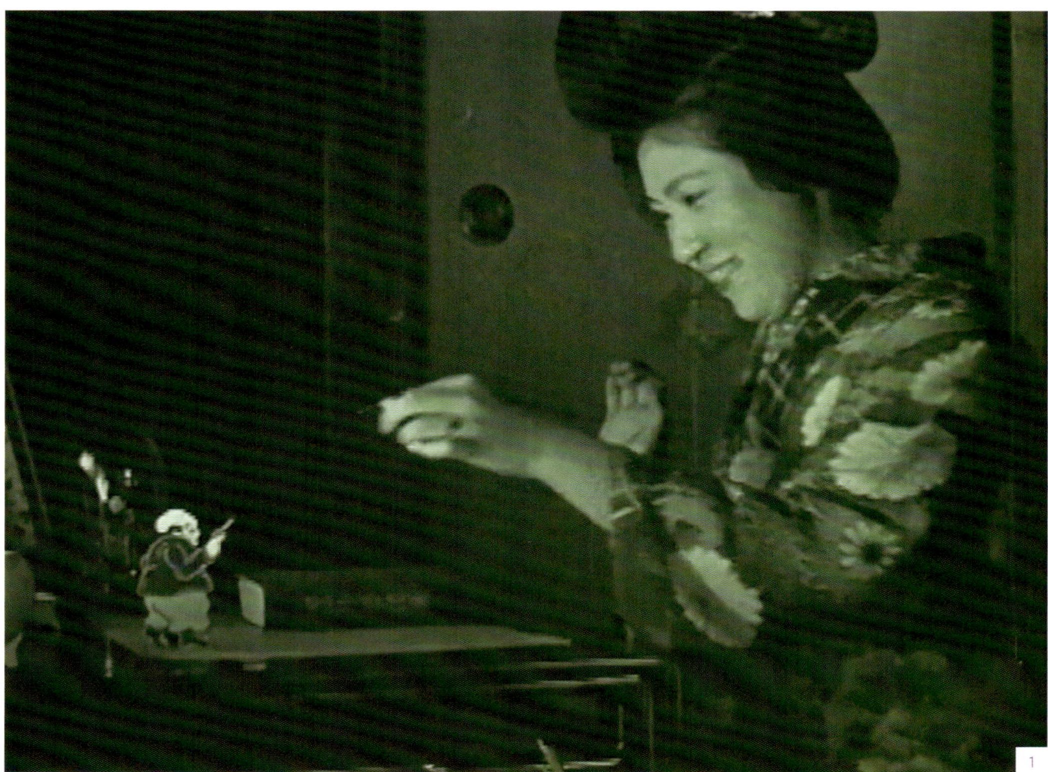

1
1924
Kemurigusa monogatari (A Story of Tobacco)*

The new medium was gaining popularity and proving far more lucrative than a salary of an intertitle worker. Better yet, the messages conveyed by these two- to three-minute films were taking root in the public's mind, and the government wanted to invest in them even more. In 1921, Kitayama left Nikkatsu to found his own animation studio, Kitayama Eiga Seisakusho (Kitayama Movie Factory). This artistic trailblazer was exploring a brand-new industry, paving the way for the third father of Japanese animation, Junichi Kōuchi.

Kōuchi, like Shimokawa, got his start at the satire magazine *Tokyo Puck* and was recruited in 1916 by a third production company, Kobayashi Shokai, founded two years earlier by a defector from Tenkatsu. His film *Hanawa Hekonai Meitō no Maki* (*Hanawa Hekonai: A New Sword Chapter*), first projected on June 30, 1917, is currently the oldest precisely dated archive ever found. The short, two-minute film has impressively detailed drawings, with some of the clothing patterns experimenting with grayscale. The comical adventure of a samurai who bought a secondhand sword that turned out to be brand-new was a godsend for *benshi*, who accentuated the caricaturist's dark humor.

A little too dark. The title alone for *Chamebō: Kūkijū no Maki* (*Playful Boy's Air Gun**) immediately drew the government's wrath. Facing censorship, the already financially troubled company went bankrupt at the end of 1917, leaving just enough time for Kōuchi to produce a third short film, *Hanawa Hekonai Kappa Matsuri* (*Hekonai Hanawa at the Kappa Festival**). At thirty years old, the artist returned to press illustrations before following Kitayama's example five years later, founding Sumikazu Eiga Sosakusha (Sumikazu Film Studio) in 1923.

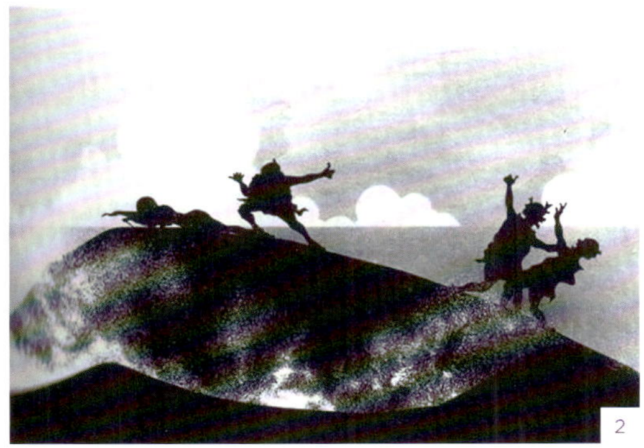

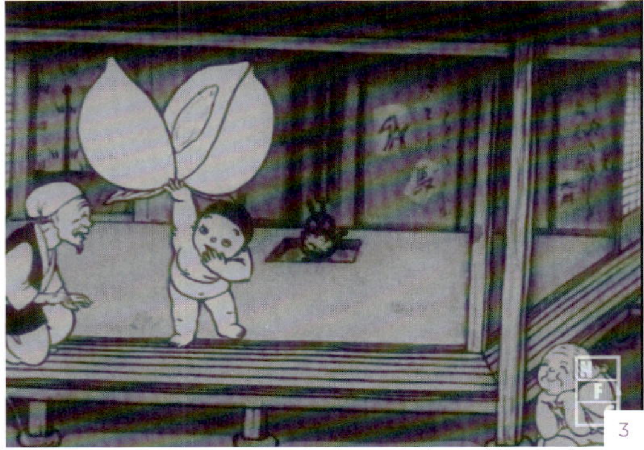

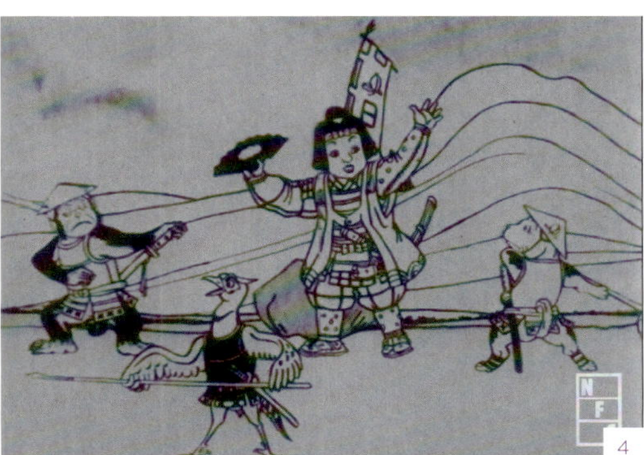

2
1927
Kujira
(The Whale)

3 and 4
1928
Nihon-ichi no Momotarō (Momotarō the Undefeated)

1: *Kemurigusa monogatari (A Story of Tobacco)* **2:** *Kujira (The Whale)* **3 and 4:** *Nihon-ichi no Momotarō (Momotarō the Undefeated)* **Panels:** *Hanawa Hekonai Meitō no Maki (Hanawa Hekonai: A New Sword Chapter)*

THE BEGINNINGS OF A NEW INDUSTRY

These fragile new companies benefited from a new government decision supporting animated cinema at the same level as live cinema. In addition to numerous film commissions by the government, studios earned income from advertising contracts—some short films were screened exclusively during promotional events organized by confectioners. At no time did these pioneers set out to create artistic works; their films were at best entertaining. The creative stages were so time-consuming that it seemed inconceivable to develop a plot longer than three minutes.

Over time, a production line was set up, enabling animation at sixteen frames per second, but the teams were still restricted by technology. Drawing tables that were illuminated from the inside appeared on scene, but artists could only work in daylight until 5 p.m. when the electricity was turned on for the night! Shots were done using a machine whose frame resembled a bunk bed. The camera was controlled by one operator at the top, while the second operator worked three feet lower placing a drawing under a glass plate and replacing it with a new drawing for each shot.

Discontent gradually grew at Kitayama Studios, where the boss kept the lion's share of revenue. Like a Walt Disney (or later, an Osamu Tezuka), the director also established himself as a ruthless businessman, a captain wielding an iron fist on this expedition into *terra incognita*. Under his leadership, Kitayama Studios produced one cartoon per month and was preparing to make a film longer than five minutes in 1923.

But everything collapsed on November 1, 1923. At 11:58 a.m., the Kanto earthquake hit, ravaging Tokyo and its surroundings. Not only did it devastate the infrastructure, but the quake knocked over stoves all over the city, setting off fires across the capital. The first Japanese cartoons went up in smoke in the apocalyptic setting of a Tokyo in flames.

Production companies moved their studios to Kansai. Seitarō Kitayama saw it as a possibility for expansion. He figured that with government aid, he could operate a new studio in Osaka while entrusting the reconstruction and management of the Tokyo facility to his faithful assistant Sanae Yamamoto. It wasn't long before the discord that had long been building exploded in 1925 in the boss's absence. His former assistants jumped ship one by one to found their own production companies, starting with Yamamoto. With only the experience of the three fathers of Japanese animation to guide them, a new generation of artists once again prepared to set out in uncharted territory.

Renewal and technological advancements

THE NEXT GENERATION

Despite the tragedy that struck the capital leaving 100,000 dead and 40,000 missing, the rest of the country continued to live and have fun. The anime industry, which had just ground to a halt, was picking up again thanks to public funding. After directing his first film, *Usagi to Kame* (*The Tortoise and the Hare*), in his mentor Kitayama's studio in 1924, Sanae Yamamoto spread his wings to fly on his own. In 1925, he founded Yamamoto Manga Seisaku-jo (Yamamoto Image Company) where he produced *Ubasute Yama* (*The Mountain Where We Abandon the Elderly**). His 1928 adaptation of the traditional tale *Nihon-ichi Momotarō* (*Momotarō the Undefeated**), commissioned by the Ministry of Education, was impressive. The eleven-minute film layered horizontal and vertical tracking shots, offered detailed grayscale backgrounds, and played with the diaphragm aperture at transitions. Paired with a talented *benshi*, *Nihon-ichi no Momotarō* is the best representation of a Japanese animation that was finally coming into its own, ten years after its debut.

With his government-commissioned films, Sanae Yamamoto was following in the footsteps of his teacher (and now rival), Kitayama. Likewise, Noburō Ōfuji was making a name for himself by perpetuating the caustic style of Junichi Kōuchi, who had taken him under his wing. Ōfuji founded the *Jiyu Eiga Kenkyusho (Institute for Independent Film)* studio in 1925, where he made a pastiche of Douglas Fairbanks's *Thief of Baghdad* called *Baghdad-jo no Tozoku* using cutout animation. Despite the poor image quality, viewers savored the details and patterns of the traditional *chiyogami* paper with which Kōuchi created the characters and settings in *Urashima Tarō* in 1928.

The director continued experimenting and created *Kujira* (*The Whale*) in 1927, a short Chinese shadow-puppet film inspired by German silhouette animation. The resolutely adult tale was a sharp contrast to the typical lighthearted productions: after a shipwreck, a samurai, a merchant, a sailor, and a woman are swallowed by a whale. Once expelled onto his back, the three men fight to win the heart of the beautiful woman. Punished by the God of the Seas, they drown while the woman continues her journey.

Ōfuji broke not only artistic and screenwriting norms, but technical ones, too. He was one of the first to experiment with color by tinting the film for *Osekisho* (*At the Border Checkpoint*), even if the end result was a film in black and pink. By using several glass plates spaced apart for the backgrounds, he foreshadowed the multiplane cameras of the future. Even better, in 1928 he shot the first music video in Japanese history, *Kuro Nyago* (*The Black Cat*). The three-minute jazz animation featured a tomcat singing and dancing before inviting his sidekicks and then humans along to join the party and played synchronously with a 78 rpm record!

1929
Kobu-Tori
(The Stolen Lump)

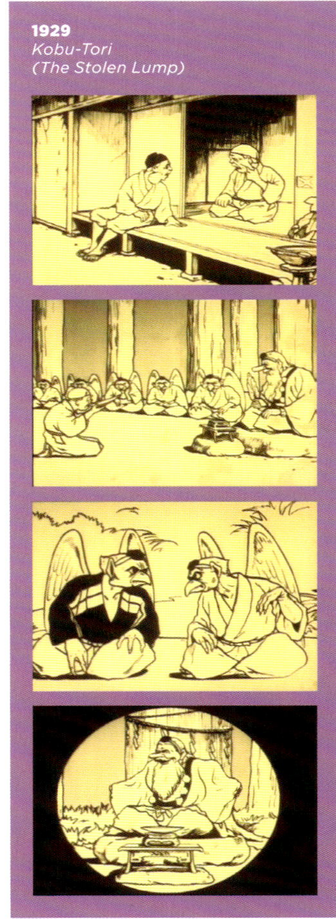

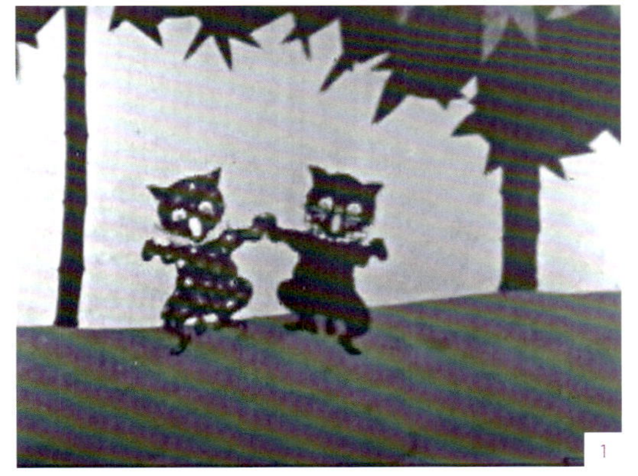

1

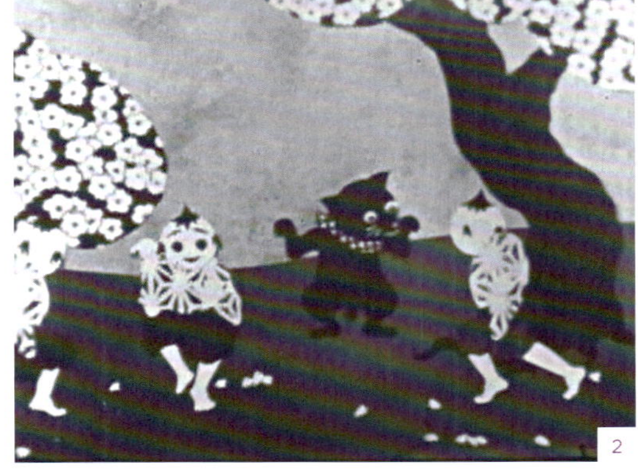

2

1 and 2
1929
Kuro Nyago
(The Black Cat)

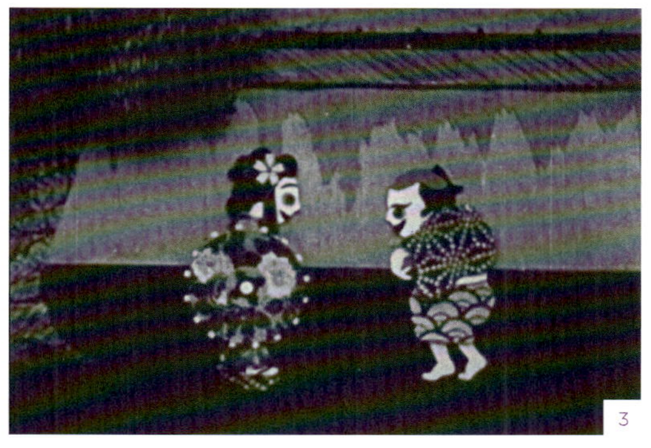

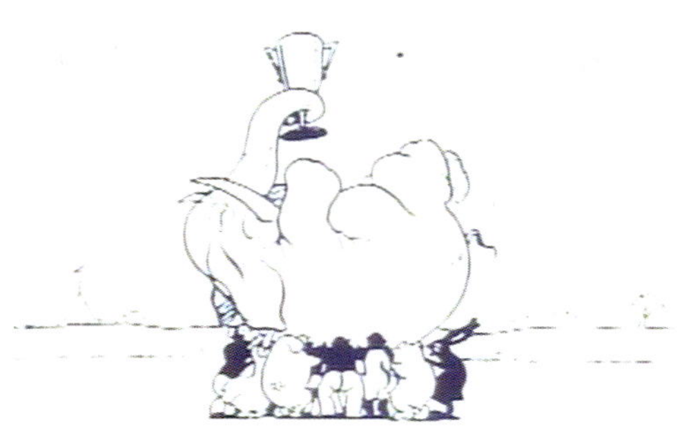

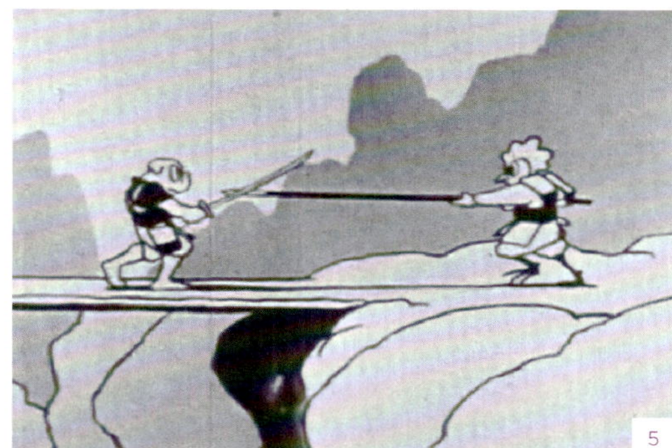

3
1926
Baghdad-jo no Tozoku (The Burglars of Baghdad Castle)

4
1928
Dōbutsu Olympic Taikai (Animal Olympic Games)

5
1930
Komori (The Bat)

THE FIRST LEGENDARY DUO

Other technical developments appeared, notably those of Yasuji Murata, who also got his start by writing subtitles on American reels imported by Yokohama Cinema Shokai. Thanks to his longtime friend Sanae Yamamoto, who was still working at Kitayama, he learned the basics of animation and created a new version of *The Battle of the Monkey and the Crab* in 1927. He produced many short films over the next ten years, including *Hana Saka Jiji* (*The Old Man Who Made Dead Trees Bloom**), a bittersweet fable in which an old man suffers the dirty tricks of a jealous neighbor, and *Dōbutsu Olympic Taikai* (*Animal Olympic Games**).

In 1934, Murata cut characters' body parts out of thin paper and attached them at the joints with pins for *Tsuki no miya no ōjosama* (*Princess of the Moon Shrine**). Not only did this innovation make the shots easier, but the final animation was more fluid. After bringing to the screen one of the era's greatest manga stars, the clumsy black dog Norakuro, in *Osaru no Taigyo* (*The Monkey's Big Catch**), Yasuji Murata left Yokohama Cinema Shokai in 1937. He worked for various studios before opening Murata Seisakusho in 1956.

Any conversation about Yasuji Murata must involve Chūzō Aochi, his best business partner. They were each equally involved in the production process, even if their respective roles were quite distinct—Aochi dealt with the script while Murata did the drawings and animation of their funny stories. Their productions rivaled *rakugo* theater, a style of live comedy that appeared on scene in the seventeenth century and was still popular at the time. Their works include *Komori* (*The Bat*) in 1930, which explains the shame that pushes bats to hide during the day and only go out at night, and *Kobu-Tori* (*The Stolen Lump*), a 1929 gem. In this story, an old man finds himself in the middle of a *tengu* party and mingles with the mythological creatures who, to thank him for his good humor, remove the lump from the left side of his neck. He recounts his good fortune to a friend, afflicted with a lump on his right side, who tries his own luck by posing as the old man. When the *tengu* discover his deception, they punish him by giving him the lump they had taken from his friend. Murata's detailed drawings, close to traditional prints and engravings, were enhanced by the film's subtle yellow tint.

The last big name in the group of young talent breathing new life into Japanese animation is Kenzō Masaoka. Born in Kansai where he studied Western painting, the young artist benefited from the film studios' relocation to his region after the 1923 earthquake. He joined Nikkatsu Uzumasa Studio in Kyoto in 1929, where he worked in the educational films department and directed his first film, *Nansensu Monogatari Daīppen, Sarugashima* (*Nonsense Story, Volume 1: Monkey Island**). The film was so successful that in 1932 Masaoka needed to create a sequel!

Starting back at square one, the anime industry gained new momentum but now had a new competitor: American cartoons. Disney and the Fleischer brothers' films were already profitable at home, so they could be sold abroad at a competitive price, much lower than the cost of a Japanese production. The 1930s brought new American icons to Japanese screens, such as Mickey Mouse, Betty Boop, and Popeye. Above all, the 1930s had the Japanese public demanding national productions at the same artistic and technical level, which meant sound!

NEW TECHNOLOGIES, NEW PERSPECTIVES

The new decade was an awkward transitional period for Japanese animation—most of the production patterns still in use today were solidified by the end of the 1930s. But to get there, this new art needed to go through its adolescent crisis. By turning to new technologies, it learned to throw off the shackles of yesteryear and stand on its own.

The first of these advances, probably the most obvious to the public, was the advent of sound films. Whether through a synchronized record disc or an optical track added along the film strip, musical interludes and prerecorded dialogues were established as the new norm for modern theaters, much to the detriment of the *benshi*. The showmen were in their last hour, and their strike in 1932 was not enough to recover. The profession would disappear before the end of the decade, with disastrous consequences: director Akira Kurosawa's older brother Heigo died in 1933, having found no more *benshi* jobs to pay his bills.

Noburō Ōfuji in particular thrived in sound film. Following *The Black Cat*'s success, he directed another hit, this time foreshadowing karaoke fifty years before its debut with *Mura Matsuri* (*Village Festival**) in 1930 and *Haru no Uta* (*Spring Song**) in 1931, both of which had the lyrics written over the animation. However, synchronization problems (the disc spinning too fast or slow) turned off spectators, especially as they were hearing the song for the first time. Ōfuji bounced back later in 1931 with *Kokka Kimigayo*, the Japanese national anthem, whose story he summarized in three minutes using articulated paper cutout characters.

That same year, Shochiku produced the first sound film in the history of Japanese cinema, *Madam to Nyōbō* (*The Neighbor's Wife and Mine*), directed by Heinosuke Gosho. The studio wanted to continue in this vein and poached Kenzō Masaoka from its rival Nikkatsu to make animated sound films. Along with his student Mitsuyo Seo, Gosho directed *Chikara to Onna no Yo no Naka* (*In the World of Power and Women**) in 1933. This comedy focused on a mother's anger at discovering her husband's affair with his secretary and marked a turning point in the animation industry.

By paving the way for sound animation, the short film also created a new profession! *Benshi* gave way to *seiyū*, voice actors. Though they were no longer in the spotlight, they nevertheless became stars in their own right, and their names were used to promote films—a practice we still use today. In addition to this economic revolution and the enhanced immersive experience for viewers, *In the World of Power and Women* also shook things up for anime behind the scenes.

The boulevard comedy was the first work entirely filmed using celluloid. The transparent sheets of plant cellulose, patented in 1914, made the animators' work a whole lot easier. They were perforated in the same places, so they could be stacked to offer unparalleled precision in positioning the drawings in relation to one another. Best of all, by dipping them in an acid bath, they came out as good as new! Masaoka, won over by this innovation, abandoned cutout animation and founded his own studio in 1933, Masaoka Eiga Bijutsu Kenkyusho, which he inaugurated with *Kaguya Hime* (*Princess Kaguya*), a traditional tale. With the support of a passionate team, he flooded the market over the next two years (five films in 1934, four in 1935) before his studio became overwhelmed by celluloid's expensive price tag and was bought out. Each of his productions received enthusiastic praise from critics and audiences alike.

Chagama Ondo (*Dance of the Teakettles*) surprised viewers with smooth animation across multiple elements. The opening scene set the tone, with *tanuki* dancing to music, twirling in the air, and then crashing into a spider's web. Folklore tells that these *tanuki*, Japanese raccoon dogs, are shape-shifters, and the six-minute film shows a series of their comical transformations!

1
1933
Chikara to Onna no Yo no Naka (In the World of Power and Women)

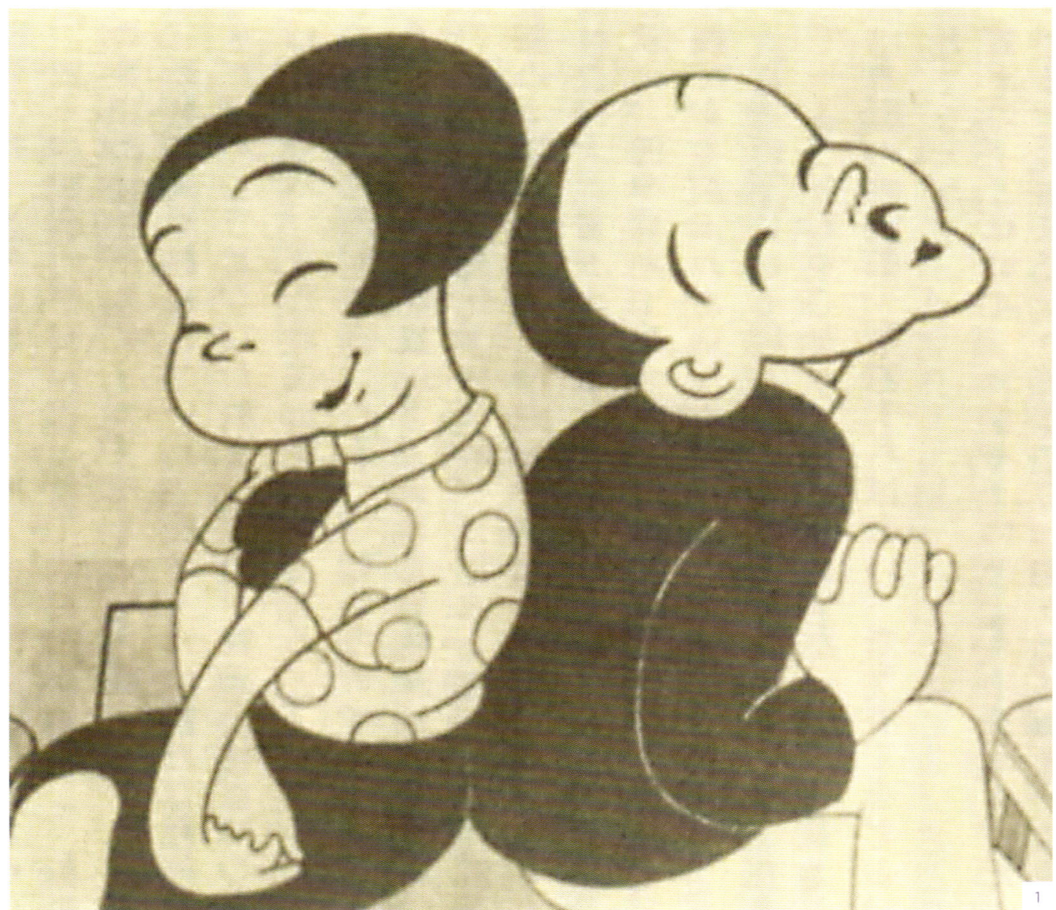
1

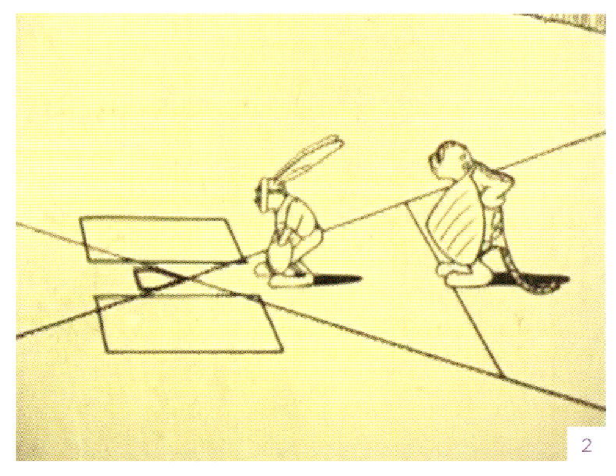
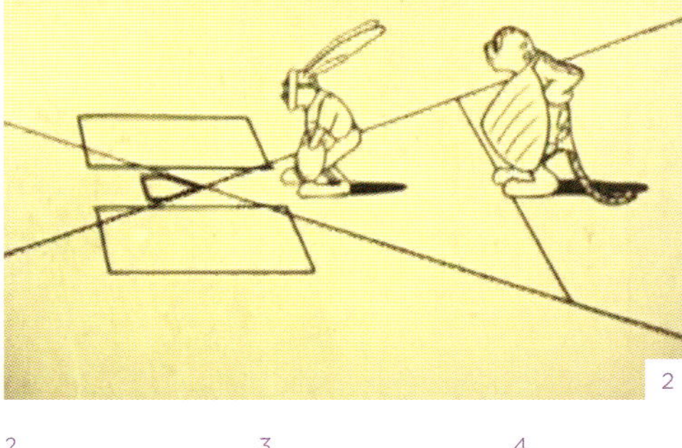
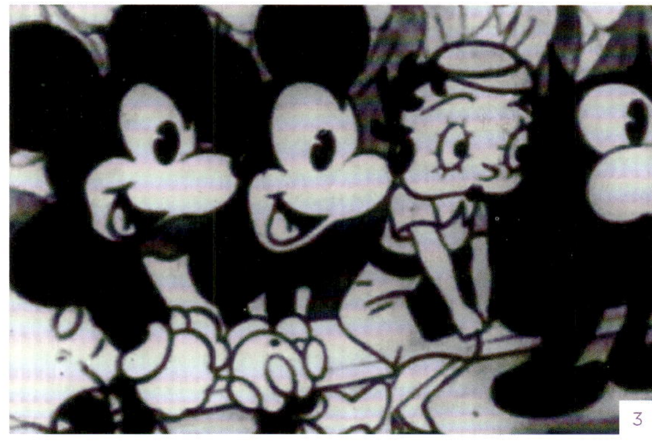
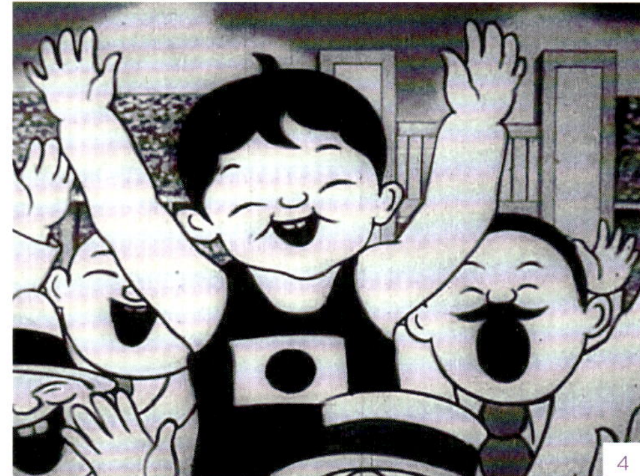

2
1931
Oira No Yaku (Our Baseball Game)

3
1936
Mabō no Dai Kyōsō (Mabō's Big Race)

4
1936
Mabō no Tokyo Olympic Taikai (Mabō's Tokyo Olympics)

THE AMERICAN WAY, CARTOON EDITION

Masaoka earned the nicknames "Japanese Méliès" and "Japanese Disney." His productions were on the same level as Uncle Walt's *Silly Symphonies*, with musical surprises, slapstick jokes, and anthropomorphic animals as heroes in most cases. American cartoons delighted the public, and their more advanced production methods meant that they were a source of both rivalry and inspiration for Japanese animators. In his 1935 *Mori no Yakyū-dan* (*The Forest Baseball Team**), Kenzō Masaoka even included images of Mickey, Minnie, and Betty Boop as spectators in the stands.

These iconic characters made another unofficial cameo in *Mabō no Dai Kyōsō* (*Mabō's Big Race*) in 1936. This ninety-second film was produced at Satō Eiga Seikashu-sho, a studio founded by Kinjirō Satō, who learned the ropes of the profession from his older brother, Kiichirō Kanai, a former assistant of Seitarō Kitayama. Mabō continued to endear himself to audiences through his adventures across twelve films, which took an anti-American turn with the growing world conflict.

In the meantime, the young hero continued his athletic endeavors in a second installment, *Mabō no Tokyo Olympic Taikai* (*Mabō's Tokyo Olympics**). Athletics had clearly become established as the new theme of choice for Japanese cartoons. Not only were sports an ideal pretext for making animals perform amusing antics, but they were also a hot topic throughout the country.

After a timid foray into the 1912 Olympic Games, Japan became passionate about the event, which ignited their warrior spirit in a less aggressive way than traditional martial arts, such as judo, which would go on to be modernized shortly thereafter. Filmmakers couldn't pass up this cinematic manna! A popular success of the 1920s were *wakamono sports eiga* (youth sports films), which logically lent themselves to animation with the bulk of their production being done at each Olympiad (1928, 1932, and 1936). By borrowing narrative codes (animal musicals) and mascots from Hollywood productions, Japanese animators thought they would catch up with Uncle Sam. But it was a wasted effort—in 1932, Disney Studios produced the first color cartoon, *Flowers and Trees*. The Japanese, who had shown themselves to be undeniably behind in terms of technology, also needed to abandon their first methods of colorization, now obsolete. They could no longer tint the film as Noburō Ōfuji had done because it deteriorated the transparency of the optical soundtrack, thus harming the film's sound quality.

Some attempts appeared here and there, particularly at J.O. Studios where the team applied red, blue, and yellow paint directly to the film. But their efforts were in vain because the films were still projected in black and white. At any rate, it was inconceivable to continue the extremely costly attempts at colorization during this period of scarcity, between the 1929 economic crisis and the impending global conflict. Nevertheless, Japanese animation continued to progress and gain in scope thanks to the latest technological innovation, which had far-reaching consequences . . .

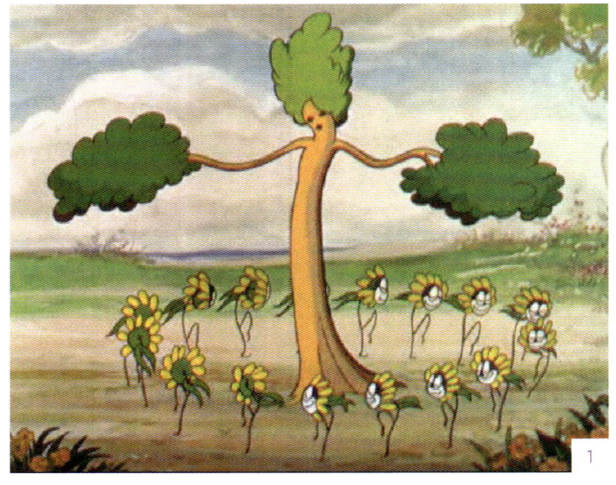

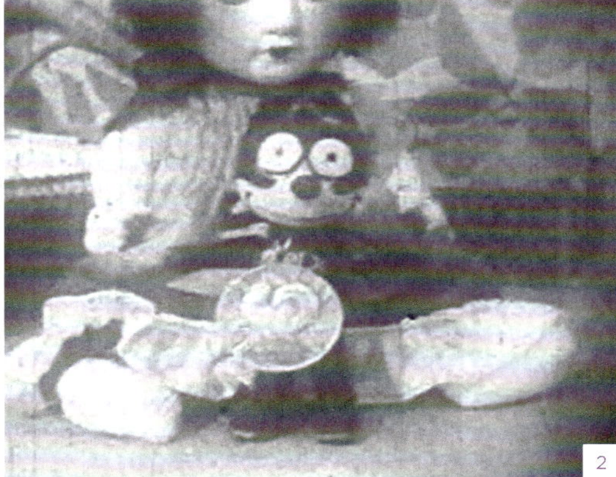

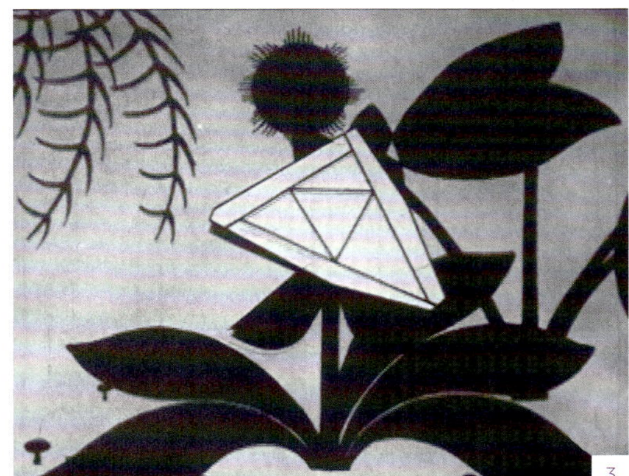

1
1932
Flowers and Trees

2
1932
Felix no Meitantei (Detective Felix in Trouble)

3
1935
Propagate

ANIMATION FOR ALL

Miniature cameras and projectors, which had arrived on the scene in Europe in the 1920s, made their appearance in Japan. The Pathé-Baby and other Kodascopes, though extremely expensive at first, became popular as the 1930s approached. Young Osamu Tezuka would see his first cartoons on the family projector. On studio outskirts, small groups of enthusiasts came together and bonded over modest amateur productions.

Shigeji Ogino devoted his life to the 9.5 mm format, having produced more than 400 short films over four decades. He began by putting together a stop-motion detective story with a disproportionate doll and a figurine of Felix the Cat (without permission) in *Felix no Meitantei* (*Detective Felix in Trouble**), before turning to abstract animation with *Propagate* and *An Expression* in 1935.

Eighty years before YouTube, these portable cameras became the new weapon of opposition. In 1925, the government passed a law seeking to muzzle the communism that had been expanding since the creation of the USSR in 1922. The law said that anyone who joined a movement criticizing private property or national identity would be liable to ten years in prison. That was all it took for the Proletarian Film League of Japan (*Nihon Puroretaria Eiga Dōmei*), or Prokino, to emerge. It rarely produced fiction because the organization was first and foremost about bearing witness, camera in hand, to the working conditions inside mines and factories. Or to broadcast information withheld by the government and news of Stalin.

However, these leftist documentary compilations were missing a little something to give the underground screenings a real cinematic feel—an opening cartoon! Thus, short films appeared, some more than twenty minutes long, such as *Entotsuya Perō* (*Perō the Chimney Sweep**), inspired by Charles Perrault's version of *The Shepherdess and the Chimney Sweep*. Made using puppets like Chinese shadow theater, the 1930 film's parable is crystal clear: tasked with monitoring the starving masses pressing in on his village, Pero watches with horror as the army leads an assault causing civilian carnage, leaving him forever disgusted with imperialism. They crossed the line in 1931 with *Dorei Sensō* (*Slave War**) by Hakusan Kimura, a collaborator of Seitarō Kitayama and Kenzō Masaoka, in which the bourgeois were represented by pigs in suits exploiting Chinese labor. Each reel was tracked by the police, and the risks became too great for Prokino, which abandoned animation before slowly dying out in 1934.

Despite its brevity, this period served as a springboard for new talent. Mitsuyo Seo, the director of *Dorei Senso*, spent twenty-one days in prison in 1931 for his allegory in which a bird describes a Utopian society to an amazed child. The sweet irony is that he became one of the leaders of propaganda filmmaking, led by the same government, just a few years later. The global conflict was getting closer and closer, and tensions with the United States were on the rise.

1931
Kokka Kimigayo (The National Anthem: His Majesty's Reign)

4
1931
Sora no Momotarō (Momotarō in the Sky)*

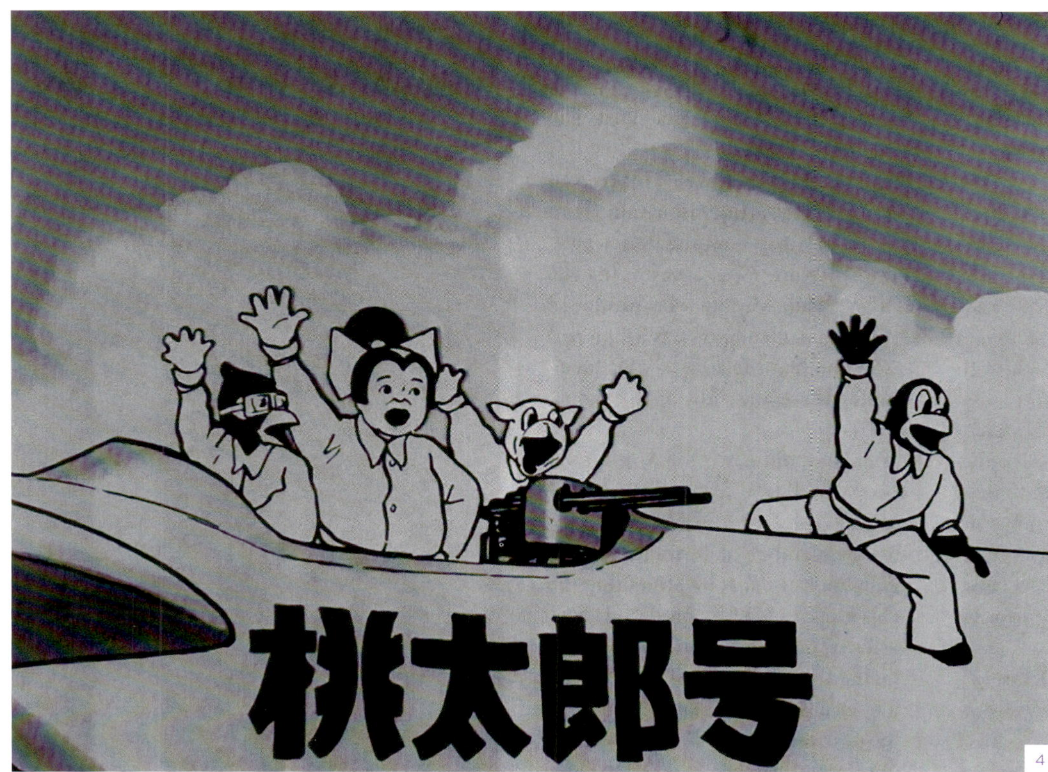

4

Propaganda in animation

FOLKLORE: THE FACE OF NATIONALISM

The Meiji Era (1868 to 1912) propelled Japan from feudalism to industrialism. But the country's obsession with security and lack of raw materials led Japan to develop an expansionist policy.

Japan became an important world power following World War I, and after signing the Treaties of Paris and Versailles, it signed the Washington Treaty regulating its navy. But many Japanese politicians and military members took offense at their country's unfavorable treatment. Japan began to experience a sharp rise in nationalism, creating an aversion to Western powers. In 1929, the Great Depression led the country to take refuge in fascist ideology. The 1930s became the stage for sovereign indoctrination, ensured by censorship and the gradual spread of propaganda within the country, along with the removal of foreign cultures that had become anchored in Japanese daily life over the past few decades. In 1928, the short *Mikuni no Tame Ni* (*For the Kingdom*) by Hakusan Kimura advocated the imperial military's invincibility during the Russo-Japanese War of 1904, sparking the Shōwa government's (1926 to 1989) desire to establish nationalist values in popular entertainment. But it was when Japan invaded Manchuria in 1931 that the army began gradually imposing itself on the film industry, ordering the great directors to create government-sponsored films. Yasuji Murata transformed a folklore hero into a national icon in *Sora no Momotarō* (*Momotarō in the Sky**) and and then again in 1932 in *Umi no Momotarō* (*Momotarō's Underwater Adventure**). This is how propaganda publicly monopolized Bushido code to glorify soldiers.

As for Noburō Ōfuji, he produced *Kokka Kimigayo* (*The National Anthem: His Majesty's Reign*) with a great deal of Shinto symbolism. By adapting the *kojiki*, a collection of legends about the divine creation of Japan, he reminded people of the empire's direct link to the gods, with the imperial family having descended from the Sun Goddess Amaterasu.

One of the greatest figures used in Japanese indoctrination was undoubtedly Norakuro, the protagonist of Suihō Tagawa's eponymous manga. The manga, originally published shortly after the start of the war in Manchuria, narrates the military journey of an orphan black dog who is as clumsy as he is brave. Tagawa's aim was educational, drawing inspiration from his experience in the army in the early 1920s. He

1: Flowers and Trees *© 1932 Disney.* **2:** Felix no Meitantei *© Shigeji Ogino.* **3:** Propagate *© Shigeji Ogino.* **4:** Sora no Momotarō *© Yokohama Cinema Shokai.* **Panels:** Kokka Kimigayo *© Chiyogami Eiga-sha.*

revisited discipline and strategy with enough humor to captivate the nation's youth. Tagawa explained the different levels of command and encouraged people to embark on a military career with his protagonist, who regularly rose through the ranks.

Norakuro was very popular with children at school, making it possible to bring discussion about the war into homes in an uncomplicated way—the enemies in the story are pigs representing the Chinese. It was also Yasuji Murata who produced the manga's first animated adaptations. With no real technical feats, the comical series was well loved and continued under the leadership of the young Mitsuyo Seo.

Seo was a promising animator for *In the World of Power and Women* and left Kenzō Masaoka's studio to join the Tokyo-based firm Nihon Manga Kenkyu-jo. A former member of Prokino, he was now participating in the war effort by promoting the imperial army in his films. In 1934, he produced *Osaru no Sankichi: Totsugeki-tai* (*Sankichi the Monkey: The Storm Troopers**) denouncing the cowardice of the Russian army, personified by drunken polar bears.

As clashes intensified with the Russians and Chinese on the borders of Manchukuo (a Japanese puppet state established in Manchuria) and resentment against America grew, the government was placing more and more pressure on film studios.

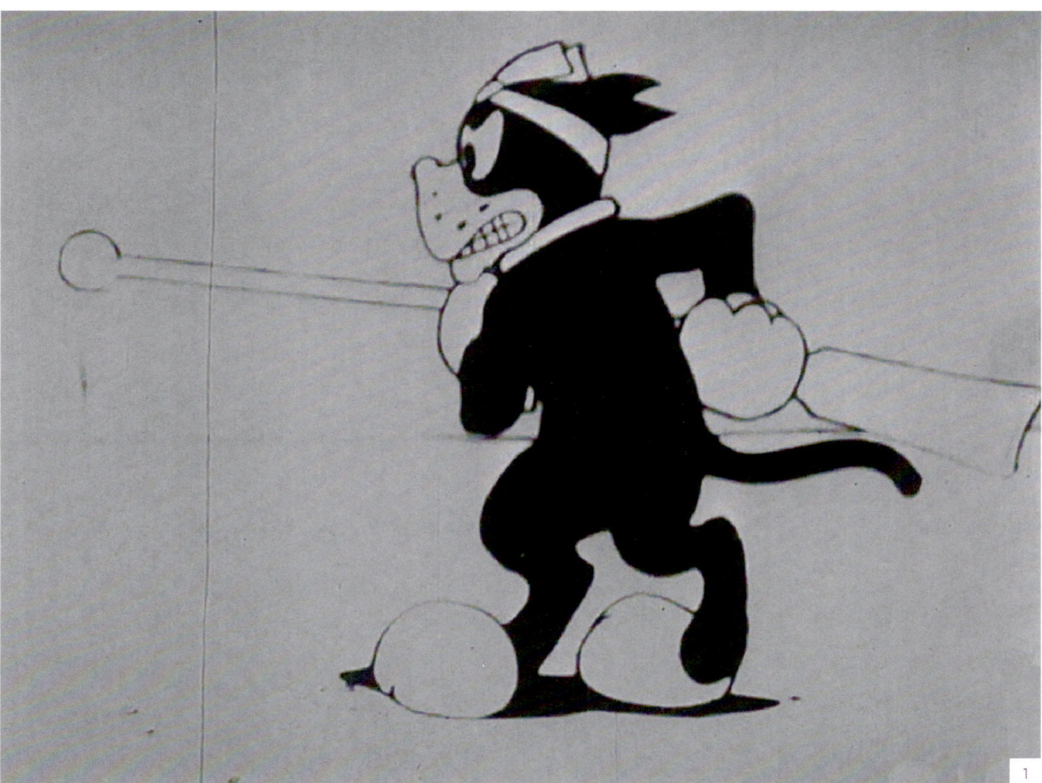

1
1933
Norakuro Gocho (Corporal Norakuro)

1936: THE TIPPING POINT

On February 26, 1936, ultranationalists attempted a coup d'état to restore imperial omnipotence and Japan's independence from the international community. The murderous putsch, reminiscent of the League of Blood incident on May 15, 1932, caused controversy that risked splitting the country in two. Taking advantage of the confusion, the army seized more political power and imposed greater censorship, as well as more drastic control over citizens' political activity. The Ministry of Internal Affairs created the Information and Propaganda Committee, which was much more involved in the press and entertainment industries.

In 1936, filmmakers were torn between adapting popular stories and legends or creating nationalist films. Even the prolific Yasuji Murata made only one short film that year, leaving it to others to deal with propaganda films such as *Osaru no Kantai* (*The Monkey Fleet*), in which the Japanese went to war against an octopus army. Before drastically curtailing his involvement in cinema, Murata directed *Izakaya no Ichiya* (*Over a Drink*). The film's social dimension was astonishing; it denounced the absurdity of the prevailing xenophobia when two samurai from a bygone era almost kill the protagonist, thinking he is a foreigner. Like many of his colleagues, Murata admired American animation, which he demonstrated in a long battle scene with several skeletons, a reference to *The Skeleton Dance* (1929), the first short in Disney's *Silly Symphonies*.

Aware that American culture had influenced Japanese audiences and creatives since the 1920s, the government decided to use Western animation styles to convey its messages to the people. The cartoonish style became more assertive in much less subtle films. This is the case for experienced director Sanae Yamamoto's *Oira no Hijouji* (*My Big Emergency*), which depicts an island being bombed by a so-called demonic army. Boosted by a comfortable budget, the short film is technically superior to the Japanese standards of the time. Yamamoto delivered a whirlwind film and even varied the environments by staging a nighttime counterattack.

In parallel with the announcement of the release of Japan from the Treaty of London (following the Treaty of Washington), the short film *Ehon 1936-nen* (*Picture Book 1936*) by Takao Nakano and Yoshitsugu Tanaka was made in 1934 at J.O. Studios but only aired in 1936. It also depicts a small, peaceful island being invaded by an evil army, this time commanded by a Machiavellian mouse that looks like Mickey. The pacifist characters are reminiscent of Fleischer or Disney productions, both in the animation of their dismembered bodies and in the design of the protagonists, one of whom bears a striking resemblance to Felix the Cat. In the film, "1936" looms in the sky like a threatening date. America represented a clear danger that must be fought. To do so, the underdogs called upon the great figures of Japanese folklore, such as Momotarō, the Peach Boy; the Golden Boy, Kintaro; Issun Boshi, a Japanese Tom Thumb; the warrior monk Benkei; and the flute-playing samurai Ushiwaka. Together they banished the invader so peace could flourish.

The Japanese now had their team of superheroes, whom J.O. Studios brought back in Kon Ichikawa's film *Shinsetsu Kachi Kachi Yama* (*New Kachi Kachi Mountain**). The future live-action film director, who criticized the absurdity of nationalist doctrine in *The Burmese Harp* and *Fires on the Plain*, adapted the popular folktale *Kachi Kachi Yama*. Ichikawa transposed the famous duel between a *tanuki* (raccoon dog) and a hare into an armed conflict, where Dangonosuke (a cross between Mickey and Momotarō) fights with the other Japanese Avengers to make a difference.

The film's assembly of elites was a response to the rise of eugenics, which came close to Nazi fundamentalism, in this allegory of the Japanese army's purity. This was how stories could assert the genetic superiority of their patriotic and legendary heroes. Japan aligned itself more closely with Germany that year, sending a delegation of 153 athletes to the 1936 Summer Olympics in Berlin and signing the Anti-Comintern Pact.

YOUNG MINDS TO MOLD

In 1937, the Second Sino-Japanese War was declared. The concept of *Kokutai* was officially promulgated, designating the political system based on the emperor's divine right and justifying the notion of fighting blindly for the country. Censorship was on the rise and anime production declined. On October 1, 1939, the government passed the Film Law. From this point on, films could only reflect the national conscience. This law came on the heels of the National Mobilization Law, enabling Japan to operate a wartime economy, which included nationalizing strategic industries and controlling the media. The press was heavily censored and finally stripped of its freedom in 1941, before being fully centralized in 1942. Meanwhile, Japan joined the Axis powers by signing the Tripartite Pact in 1940, and the American government ended the treaty of commerce in 1941, issuing an embargo on exports to Japan. Five months later, Japan launched a surprise attack on the naval base at Pearl Harbor, pulling the United States into World War II.

Film projects became subject to state control before they were even produced. Creative freedom was vastly diminished as filmmakers could not refuse government orders. However, the higher budgets allocated by the state allowed some production companies to expand and new ones to be created, while at the same time helping animation techniques to evolve.

After he left J.O. Studios, Kenzō Masaoka created the Nihon Dōga Kenkyu-jo studio in 1939, working with Shochiku to rebuild a strong team. He employed former colleagues, including animator Masao Kumagawa, who had worked with him since his first animated films. Masaoka understood that if he wanted his stories to be accepted, he must not go against the current doctrine and decided to adapt other great classics of Japanese culture. He directed *Benkei tai Ushiwaka* (*Benkei vs. Ushiwaka*), the studio's first production, in 1939. The story is about samurai loyalty and pride, so Masaoka did not need to transform the traditional tale to serve propaganda.

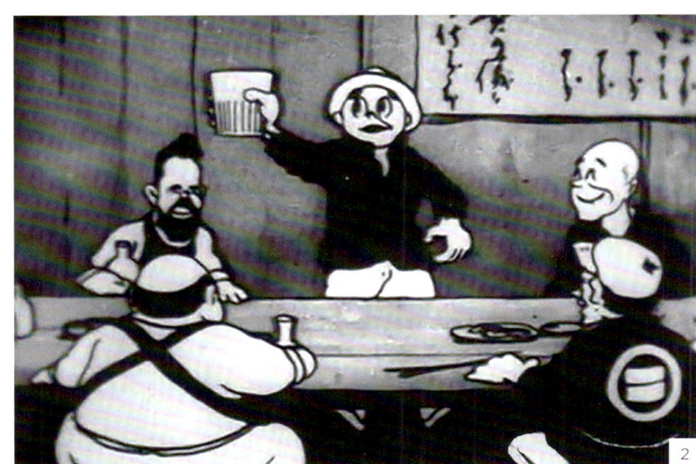

2

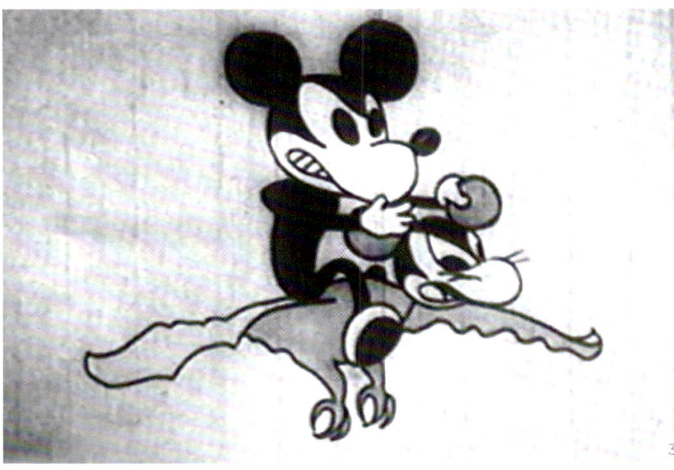

3

2
—
1936
Izakaya no Ichiya (Over a Drink)

3
—
1934
Ehon 1936-nen (Picture Book 1936)

It was an ambitious production—he used superimposed celluloid (cels) to create more dynamic tracking shots, with scenery scrolling at different speeds for a more realistic rendering.

While Japanese men were being sent away to fight, the Ministry of Education was commissioning films aimed at kindling a fighting nationalist spirit in children who were not yet old enough to enlist. For filmmakers, they were an alternative to indoctrinating, pro-war films. When Masaoka made a new adaptation of *Shin Saru Kani Kassen* (*The Battle of the Monkey and the Crab*), he toned down the original, rather morbid, tale for children. Only the Japanese flags proudly waved by the kind victors at the end of the film served as a reminder of how unavoidable the patriotic message was. In other productions, it became a code of good conduct or even a set of house rules. This can be seen in *Dōbutsu Tonarigumi* (*The Animal Neighborhood Community**), in which Masao Kumagawa deals with *Tonarigumi*, a civil defense and fire prevention militia. He directed *Kangaroo no Tanjōbi* (*Baby Kangaroo's Birthday Surprise*) that same year, depicting the daily life of a housewife raising her brood of youngsters alone. With the father figure absent, the children have to stick together and help their mother accomplish her many tasks. This includes protecting the home from a nasty wolf straight out of Tex Avery's cartoons. Similarly, Sanae Yamamoto's film *Namake Gitsune* (*The Lazy Fox**) advocates hard work in the fields and the importance of crop storage. The brave farmers fight as one to prevent an idle, sneaky fox from stealing their provisions. Wagorō Arai's *Ochō Fujin no Genso* (1940), an adaptation of Giacomo Puccini's *Madame Butterfly*, reiterates the warning about the profiteering and manipulative "inferior race" with the story of a Japanese woman who dies by suicide to regain her honor, tarnished by her husband, an American soldier.

The absurd humor and Disney-like animation in some films allowed for stronger images without shocking young audiences. *Ahiru Rikusentai* (*The Quack Infantry Troop**), directed by propaganda filmmaker Mitsuyo Seo, depicts a pond war in which frogs clash with ducks. The conflict begins when a revenge bombing becomes a real, armed, and bitter battle. Although the imagery of child warriors may have been striking, they were still neighboring peoples who faced an even greater danger. Their reconciliation in the end was a welcome change from the punishments usually inflicted on vile wolves and foxes. With this unifying film, Seo brought out a certain sensitivity to nature, which he repeated the following year with *Ari-chan* (*Arichan the Ant**), another commission from the Ministry of Education.

1
1936
Shinsetsu Kachi Kachi Yama (New Kachi Kachi Mountain)*

2
1939
Benkei tai Ushiwaka (Benkei vs. Ushiwaka)

3
1946
Ochō Fujin no Genso (Madame Butterfly)

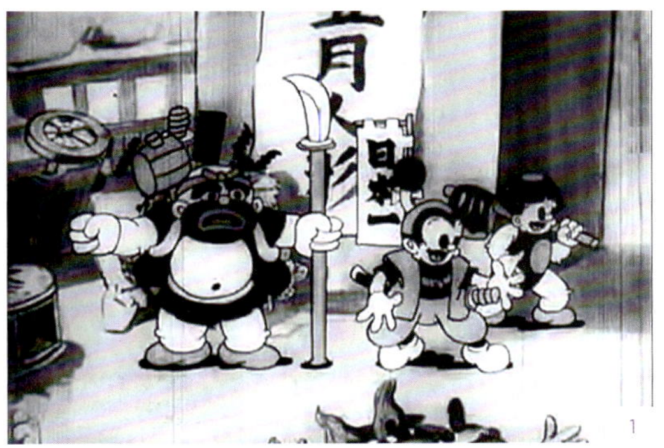
1

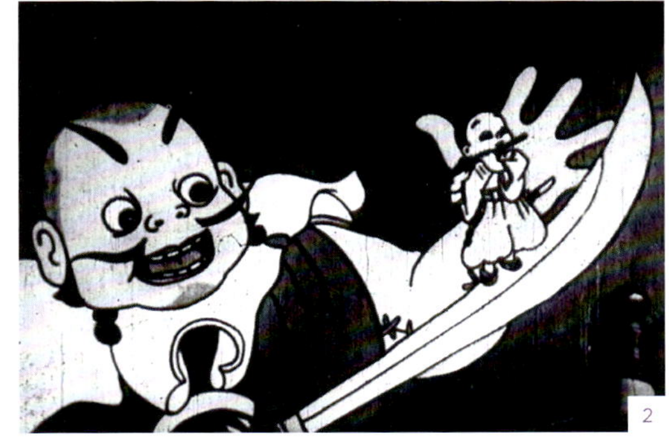
2

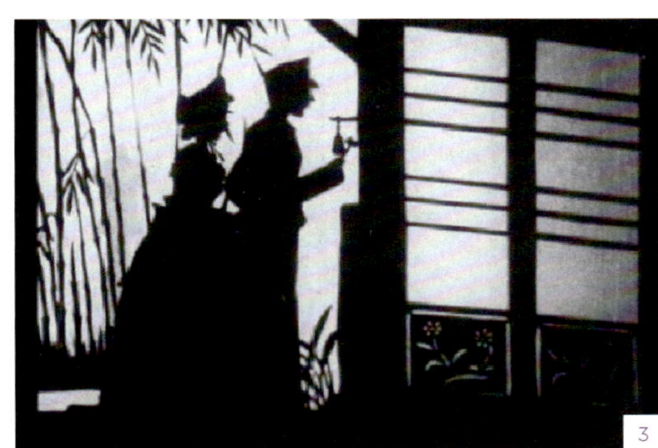
3

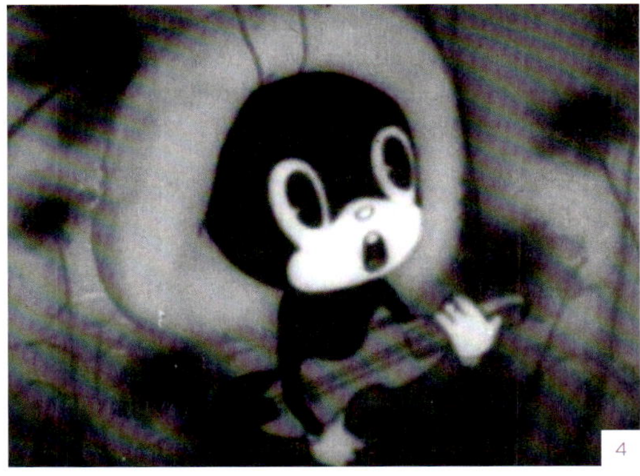
4

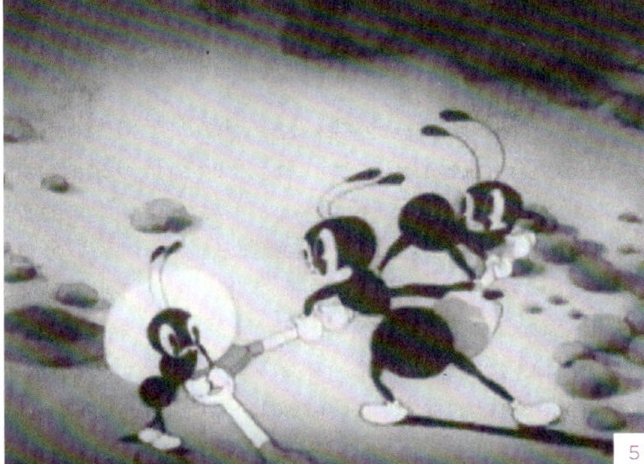
5

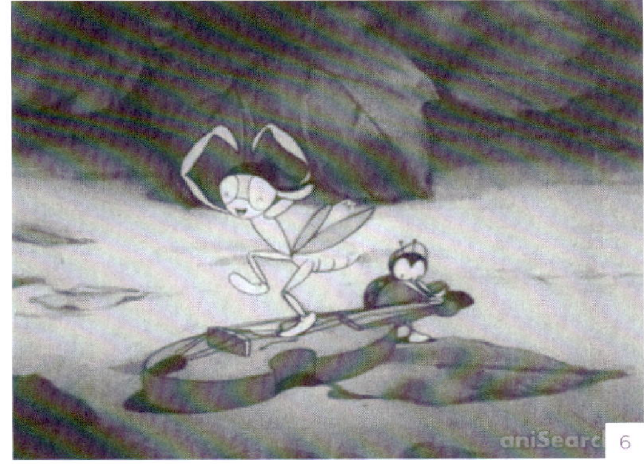
6

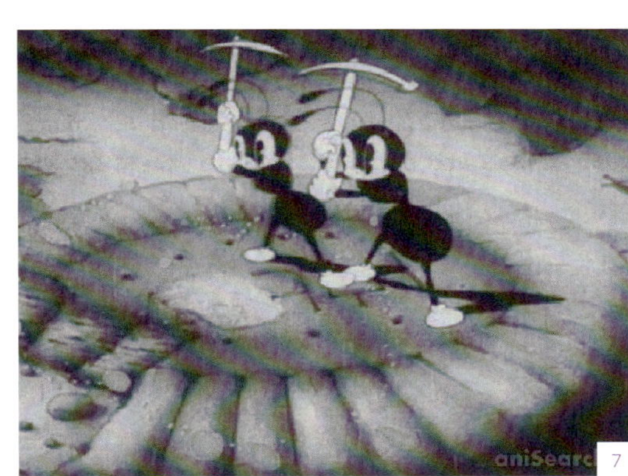
7

1943
Kumo to Chūrippu
(The Spider and the Tulip)

FLOWERS AMID BOMBINGS

The short musical film *Ari-chan* (*Arichan the Ant*) stands out in the era's audiovisual landscape. It follows an ant's journey through nature and closely resembles *The Grasshopper and the Ants* in *Silly Symphonies* (1934). For its animation, Mitsuyo Seo called on young Tadahito Mochinaga, an artist specializing in stop-motion and scenery. Mochinaga was also a great Disney admirer and became the first to use the multiplane camera in Japan. This process, invented in Mickey's studio, involved placing cels at varying heights to create a more realistic depth of field. The camera could then adjust its focus, and the cels could be moved independently. The benefit of this technique was all the more important, as flora was sharing the leading role with the ant in this film. Mochinaga mainly used the multiplane camera for still shots and horizontal pans, a technique that really came into its own with forward and backward tracking shots. This method added an energetic quality to the film, accompanied by a wonderfully synchronized score by Tadashi Hattori.

Arichan the Ant amazed audiences, and the Ministry of Education commissioned *Kumo to Chūrippu* (*The Spider and the Tulip*) from Kenzō Masaoka, which was released in 1943. It took eight months to produce the fifteen-minute short film telling the story of a ladybug who finds refuge in a tulip from its spider predator. Masaoka made more intensive use of the multiplane camera, seeking to free himself from the technical constraints of animation. The viewer is completely immersed in the universe of the tiny beings, as the complex camera movements making the scenery seem gigantic. Masaoka took great care with the different spider web effects and the rain, adding to the realism of this melodious work.

Arichan the Ant and *The Spider and the Tulip* represent both true technical achievement and impressive creative freedom in a world where government funding for entertainment was primarily for the war effort.

4 to 7
1941
Ari-chan (Arichan the Ant)

PRO-WAR FILMS

Propaganda was affecting animators around the world, whether in Germany, Russia, or the United States. Cinema was a modern means of mass manipulation that each country exploited in its own way. Unlike Japanese animation, American animated films were very specific when they evoked the enemy. Popeye, Superman, and Daffy Duck fought against extreme caricatures of the Japanese, sporting slanted eyes, big teeth, and a sly laugh. Even the titles were telling, like the "Japoteurs" episode of *Superman* and "You're a Sap, Mr. Jap" in *Popeye*. When Donald took out an entire enemy base in *Commando Duck* (1943), there was no room for interpretation; the message was loud and clear—animation was a true outlet. In Japan, symbolism prevailed over slapstick, emphasizing national purity rather than ridiculing the enemy. Unlike American films, Japanese shorts were not trying to meet standards established by the studios. Each film was more of an independent short than an episode, even when characters from folklore or manga were developed as part of a series. That is how Mabō, renowned for his performance in the Olympic Games, became the famous conqueror Toyotomi Hideyoshi in *Mabō no Kinoshita Tokijirō* (*Mabō as Kinoshita Tokijirō*,* 1938), echoing expansionist policy. He went on to advocate mobilization and bravery in combat in a dozen films.

The *Fuku-chan* series directed by Kenzō Masaoka in Shochiku's animation department became a big name on screen. Ryūichi Yokoyama's manga hero enthralled children like Norakuro had done and became a mascot of propaganda. The series culminated in 1944 with Tadahito Mochinaga's *Fuku-chan no Suisenkan* (*Fuku-chan's Submarine**). It showcased the Japanese navy by recounting the daily life of a submarine crew, but the film stands out due to its length—it was over thirty minutes long, a response to the imperial navy's need to compete with foreign feature films. While *Snow White and the Seven Dwarfs* (1937) and *Fantasia* (1940) weren't released until much later in the Land of the Rising Sun, it was *Princess Iron Fan* (1941), a sixty-five-minute film by the Wan brothers, that alarmed the Japanese government. Not only was it the first Chinese feature-length film, but it was also the first Asian feature film!

The government quickly ordered grand military on-screen adventures. In 1943, Noburō Ōfuji, who had directed several shorts promoting the Japanese air and naval forces since the start of the war, was asked to direct *Hawai Mare Oki Kaisen* (*The War at Sea from Hawaii to Malaya**), a film that depicted the great victorious invasion of Malaysia on December 8, 1941. For this twenty-six-minute film, Ōfuji once again took out the silhouettes that he had traded in for more Americanized visuals in his previous propaganda films. Even with his intense naval fight scene, the big hit of the year was the return of the Peach Boy, Momotarō.

1
1944
Fuku-chan no Suisenkan (Fuku-chan's Submarine)

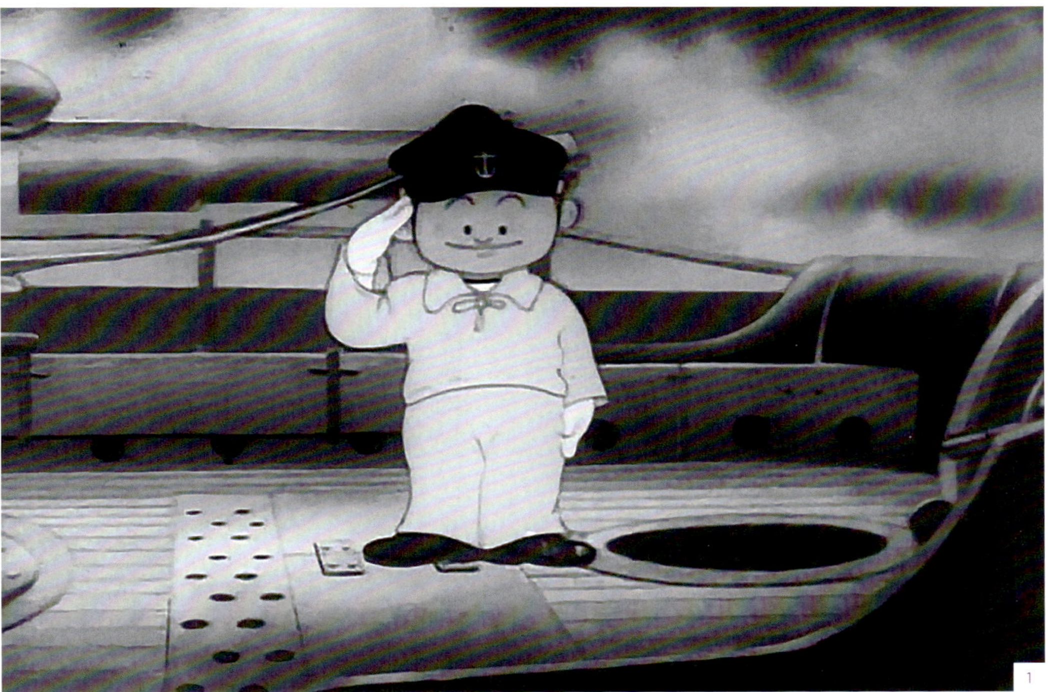

1

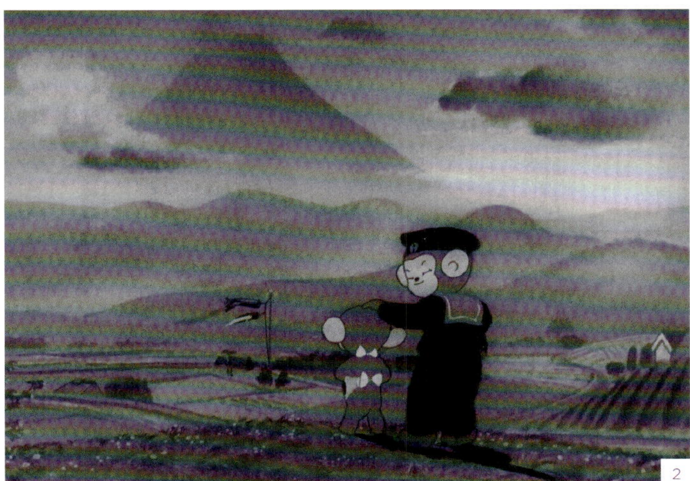

2

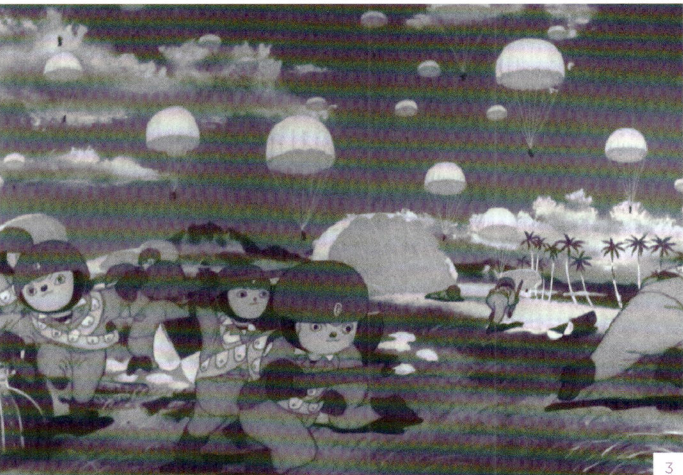

3

2 and 3
1945
Momotarō: Umi no Shinpei (Momotarō: Sacred Sailors)

MOMOTARŌ, ASIA'S HERO

Mitsuyo Seo, now working with Shochiku, took on an extremely ambitious order: *Momotarō no Umiwashi* (*Momotarō's Sea Eagles*). In this thirty-seven-minute film (a national record), he showed a naval assault led by General Momotarō. Despite support from his friend Tadahito Mochinaga, Mitsuyo Seo had great difficulty directing the film. It had a lower budget, a tight deadline, and a severe lack of cels, to the point that they needed to be washed and reused several times at the risk of warping it and altering its transparency. Seo decided to work with a maximum of two superimposed cels (forcing him to have many drawings per sheet) and delivered the film on time. It was a huge success in Japan and the imperial colonies, marking the apogee of propaganda films. In this interpretation of the attack on Pearl Harbor, the legendary icon Momotarō, now perfectly assimilated to modern warfare, isn't the ultimate hero—it is the cute little animal soldiers manning heavily armed vehicles. Their surprise offensive defeats their enemies who have no choice but to flee. It's no surprise to see the face of Brutus (Popeye's enemy) illustrating the American cowardice. The film's aggressive tone was justified by a desire to purify the world , a sentiment echoed two years later in its sequel *Momotarō: Umi no Shinpei* (*Momotarō: Sacred Sailors*).

This time, the Imperial Japanese Navy commissioned Mitsuyo Seo, in collaboration with Shochiku, to direct a film showing that the Japanese Empire could end the war. Now it was time to talk about peace, like Disney's *Fantasia*. Seo combined militarism with the lyricism of *Arichan the Ant* to create *Momotarō: Sacred Sailors*, Japan's first animated feature, lasting seventy-four minutes. The film was less radical than his previous one and took the time to introduce the characters in their home villages, where life was good and war heroes were adored. He had a noticeable propensity for wanting to educate others, whether in the classroom where children learn to read or on the front. Both films crystallized the message conveyed throughout propaganda, from Yasuji Murata's first use of Momotarō in 1931, through the productions of J.O. Studios, where folklore heroes joined forces to defend the animals: Japan is the great unifier of Asia and leads the peoples (symbolized by the different animal races) toward an ultimate struggle for peace. When the proud warrior Momotarō forced his opponents to surrender, Seo showed the fantasy of a total capitulation, with unyielding Japanese values undermining any form of unhealthy negotiation. Though still far from Disney's luxurious color productions, *Momotarō: Sacred Sailors* surpassed its prequel on all technical levels. The film was released in April 1945, five months before the Japanese surrender. It was a beautiful way to end the propaganda period, but did not achieve the expected success due to the desertion of the big cities. After Shochiku's animation department was bombed, the film quickly fell into oblivion under the American occupation. It was found in 1984 in a Shochiku warehouse.

Osamu Tezuka later explained that when he was a child, reading manga such as *Norakuro* and *Fuku-chan* inspired him to become an artist, and watching *Momotarō: Sacred Sailors* made him want to create animation. Films such as *Arichan the Ant* and *The Spider and the Tulip* must have surely awakened his great passion for insects.

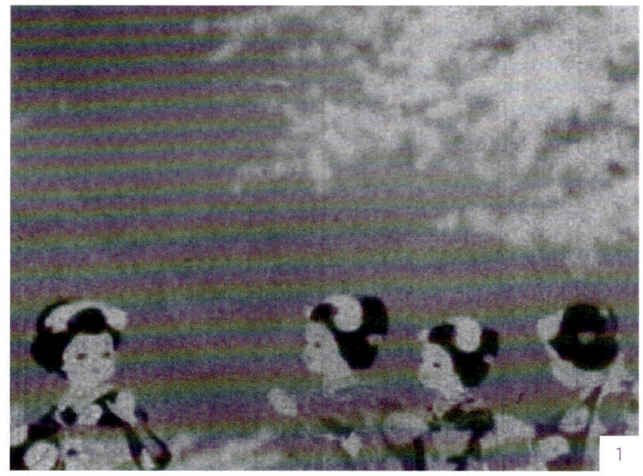

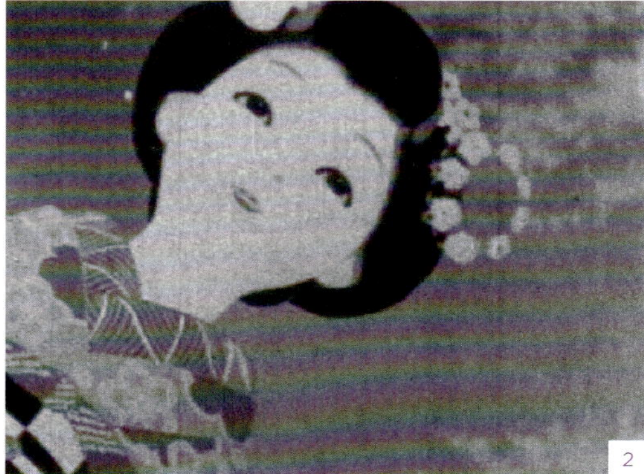

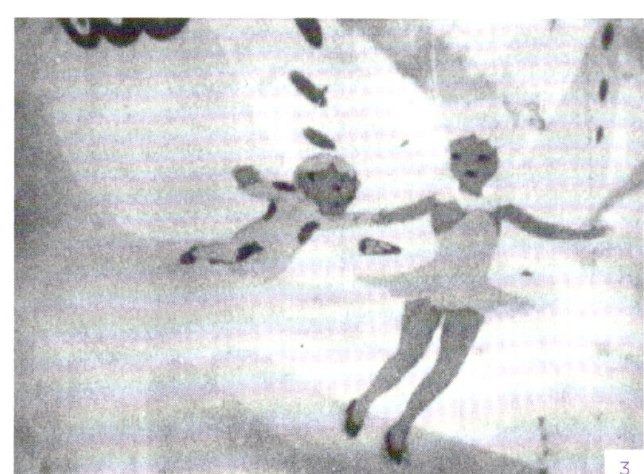

1 to 3
1946
Sakura
(Cherry Blossom)

Postwar: The dawn of modernism

A DIFFICULT RENEWAL

After a succession of military failures hidden from the people and two nuclear bombs dropped on Hiroshima and Nagasaki, Japan surrendered in September 1945. Though it was now possible to walk the streets without fear of bombardment, the postwar period was synonymous with dishonor for the people, emphasized by the occupation of General MacArthur's American troops. Japan was struggling to recover—cities were in ruins, famine was gradually setting in, the Japanese in Asia were repatriated, and the people needed to turn away from the nationalist regime toward democracy.

Under these chaotic circumstances, and as agreed with the American administration, Sanae Yamamoto and Kenzō Masaoka, joined by Yasuji Murata and Masao Kumagawa, created the Shin Nihon Dōga-sha company in November 1945. It was a sizable studio with around a hundred employees. Such a venture was accepted by the occupation authorities mainly because it allowed authors and animators to be united within a single entity rather than having dozens of small, scattered studios.

Masaoka got the ball rolling in 1946 with the film *Sakura* (*Cherry Blossom*). In keeping with *The Spider and the Tulip*, the short film depicts the awakening of spring with butterflies celebrating the cherry tree blossoms. Although it was made with salvaged material, including used cels, the film was a tribute to peace, enhanced by the characters' graceful movements, the musical piece *Invitation to the Dance* by German composer Carl Maria von Weber (1786 to 1826), and particularly innovative framing. The film was finished in the spring of 1946 when the emperor had just renounced his divinity, stripping him of the legendary status of Japan's founding myths, and the Supreme Allied Commander had burned more than two hundred films deemed propaganda or nationalist. Toho was responsible for distributing the short film, but the company, which specialized in war films like Akira Kurosawa's *The Most Beautiful* (1944), was under pressure from the new regime to change its style. Shown in a private screening, the film's traditional imagery was a reminder of pro-nationalist films. Chrysanthemums evoked Japan's imperial seal, just as Mount Fuji was likened to its power. The company, believing the film was against the new censorship policy, decided not to distribute *Sakura*.

That same year, Kumagawa directed *Maho no Pen* (*The Magic Pen*), in which a little boy wandering through the ruined countryside creates drawings that come to life, covering the destroyed landscape with huge modern constructions. Although poetic, the film left no room for interpretation, flattering the new occupying regime. The doll that offered the pen to the child symbolized the American aid needed to rebuild the now orphaned country—he even thanks her in English. This collaboration is found in many later works, including Masaoka's *Tora-Chan* series and Tokio Kuroda's *Grlliver Funtouki* (*Gulliver's Great Activities*, 1950). In the latter, the Western giant helps the people while developing trade. Films now needed to demonstrate the country's willingness to move forward. They no longer borrowed only animation techniques from overseas, but themes, too. Their great folktales were too closely linked to the empire's recent eugenic ideology, and they disappeared in favor of pro-modernist family stories showing a Westernized way of life.

The new administration commissioned numerous educational films, which developed into a solid market. It was divided between the three major companies (Toho, Daei, and Shochiku), as well as the highly esteemed Kenzō Masaoka's Nihon Manga Eiga-sha company. Toho, which launched its animation division with help from Masaoka, who trained its staff, decided to create an educational film division (Tōhō Kyōiku Eiga-bu). The teams expanded, but the company soon faced a financial crisis (there was even talk of a "personnel purge") that led the studio to split in two, creating Shintōhō in 1951.

Mitsuyo Seo made his great comeback during this period of turmoil. In 1948, after the release of Fleischer Studios' *Gulliver's Travels* (the first Western feature film distributed in Japan), Toho's new director Tetsuzō Watanabe was convinced that it was possible to make a feature-length film that the public would pay to see, rather than investing in shorts that mainly served as an introduction. Seo still had a good technical reputation from the *Momotarō* films. He was asked to direct *Osama no Shippo* (*The King's Tail**), an excessive production that required more than 100,000 cels, which Toho wanted to distribute to its cinema network. But the former leftist activist's work alarmed Watanabe, who saw it as a film with communist values, in total opposition to the Soviet containment imposed by the United States since 1947. What could have been the second Japanese feature film was not released in the end—a failure so great that it forced Seo out of animation to become a children's book illustrator.

1947
Sute Neko Tora-chan (Tora-chan the Abandoned Kitten)

4

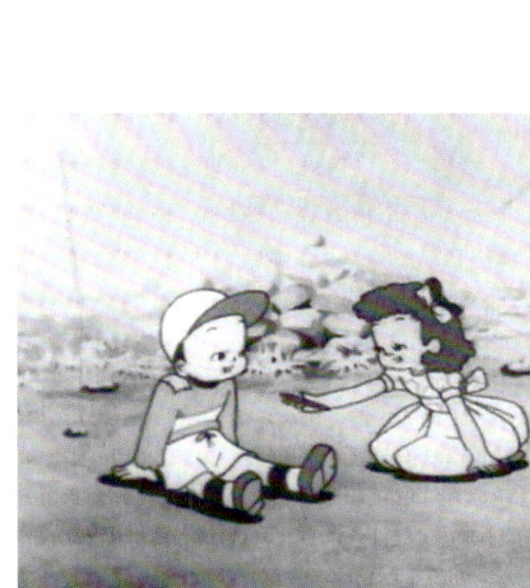

5

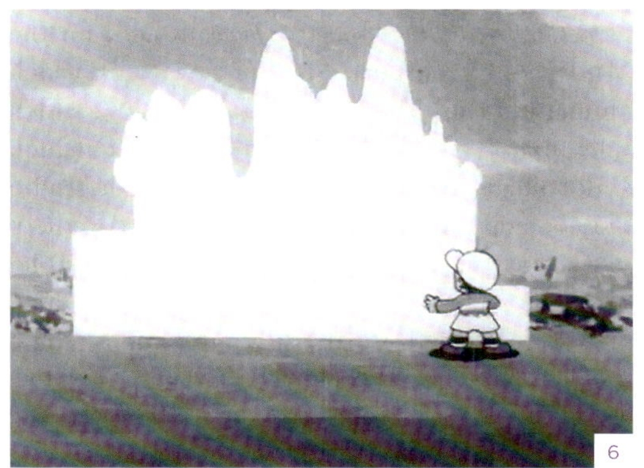

6

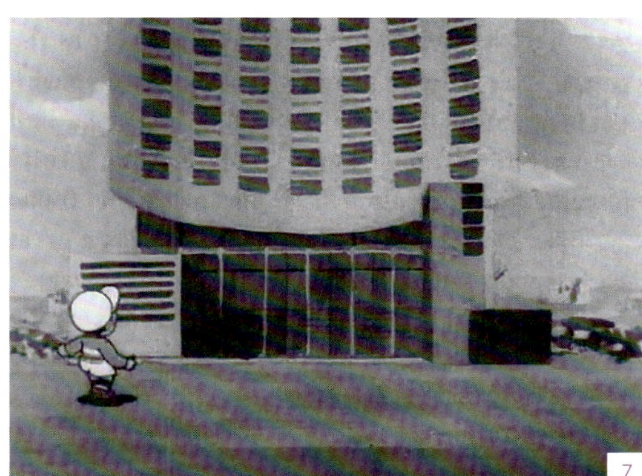

7

4 to 7
1946
Maho no Pen (The Magic Pen)

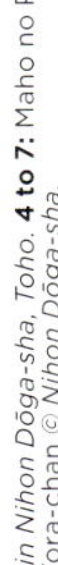

1 to 3: Sakura © *Shin Nihon Dōga-sha, Toho.* **4 to 7:** Maho no Pen © *Shin Nihon Dōga-sha.*
Panel: Sute Neko Tora-chan © *Nihon Dōga-sha.*

1948
Tora-chan to Hanayome (Tora-chan and the Bride)

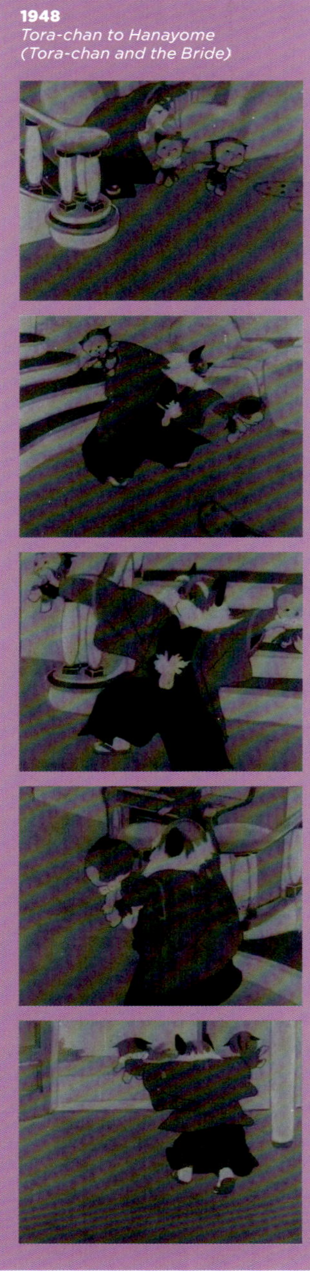

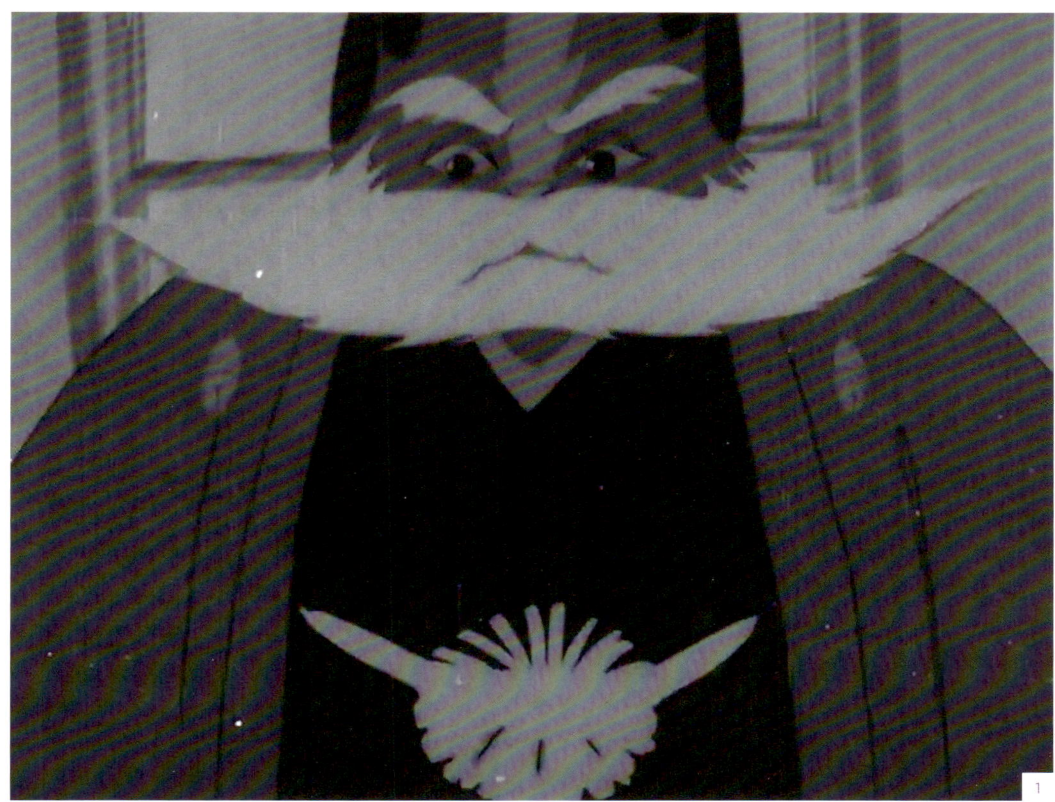

1
1948
Tora-chan to Hanayome (Tora-chan and the Bride)

FROM NIHON DŌGA-SHA TO TOEI DŌGA

Yamamoto and Masaoka, seeing that Toho was gradually absorbing their studio, moved to Shinjuku in 1947 to open a more independent company: Nihon Dōga-sha. The studio intended to separate the social aspect from the creative aspect. Masaoka directed *Sute Neko Tora-chan* (*Tora-chan the Abandoned Kitten**) in 1947, distributed by Toho. It is the touching story of a kitten who joins a family, another of the postwar era's abundant messages of hope. Along with his cinematographer Taiji Yabushita, Masaoka shot at twenty-four frames per second, creating a fully animated film. The film's fluid movements and frame stability made it extremely modern. It was a great success, and a sequel was commissioned right away.

In *Tora-chan to Hanayome* (*Tora-chan and the Bride**), the heroes from the first film must delay their traditionalist grandfather, who disapproves of a Western family marriage. Finally, the grumpy grandpa realizes the benefits of mixing cultures, announcing that "times are changing." With this scenario taking place almost exclusively in one setting, Masaoka wanted his frames to move more freely in space. His team undertook the colossal work of redrawing each scene frame by frame to vary the camera angles and create circular movements.

When Masao Kumagawa joined Masaoka at the Tokyo studio, he directed *Poppoya-san: Nonki Ekichou* (*The Carefree Station Manager Poppoya-san**) for the Ministry of Transport. Another success on which animator Yasuji Mori made his debut, and which immediately led to the commission of a sequel. Unfortunately, and despite the fact that the studio did not stop producing shorts, the success of these two series put Nihon Dōga-sha in jeopardy. Toho urged Masaoka to release a third *Tora-chan*, which he did, though with difficulty due to ophthalmic problems. The resulting film fell short of the first two as Masaoka was forced to leave the studio before the end of production. Additionally, a financial dispute between the studio and the Ministry of Transport concerning the payment for the second *Poppoya-san* animation greatly weakened the company. Kumagawa left the studio, in turn, moving on to magazine illustration.

In order to avoid bankruptcy, Nihon Dōga-sha merged with Toho's animation divisions in 1952 to create Nichido Eiga-sha. Sanae Yamamoto was still in charge, but Yasuji Mori and Taiji Yabushita became the new leading duo. Nichido produced several educational shorts, such as *Kappa Kawatarō* (1954) and *Ko usagi Monogatari* (*Story of the Little Rabbit*,* 1954), but even though it was the largest animation studio in Japan, competition (mainly Western) was causing it new financial difficulties. In 1955, Toei, a new firm in the audiovisual market, commissioned the film *Ukare Violin* (*The Merry Violin**) from Nichido. The following year, Taiji Yabushita directed two shorts, including *Kuroi Kikori to Shiroi Kikori* (*The Black Woodcutter and the White Woodcutter**), a beautiful color film showing creative potential that did not escape Toei.

Convinced that the animation market was strong and that it could compete with the United States if only it had the means, the major studio created its animation department in 1956, integrating Nichido into the company. Toei Dōga studio was born.

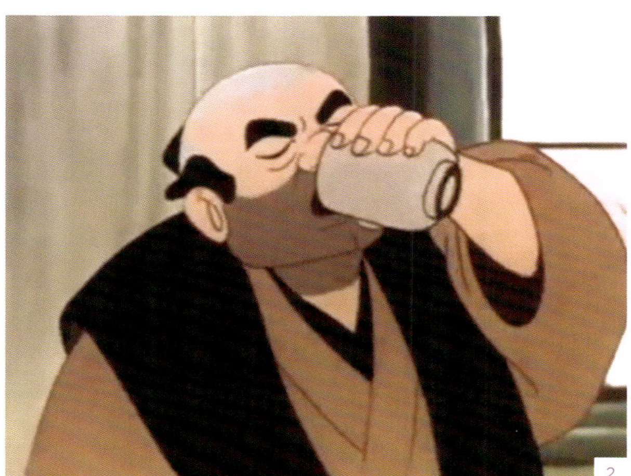
2

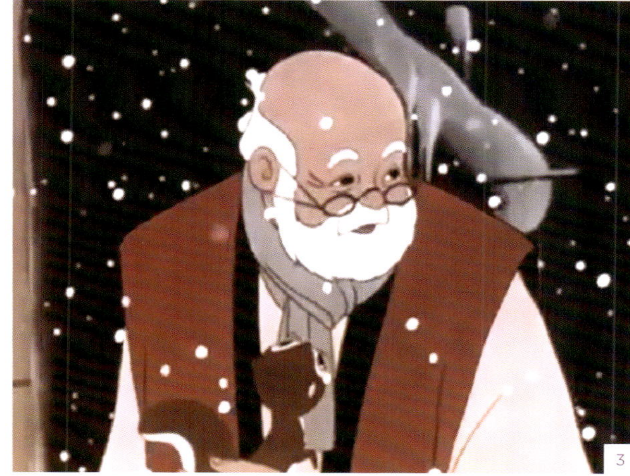
3

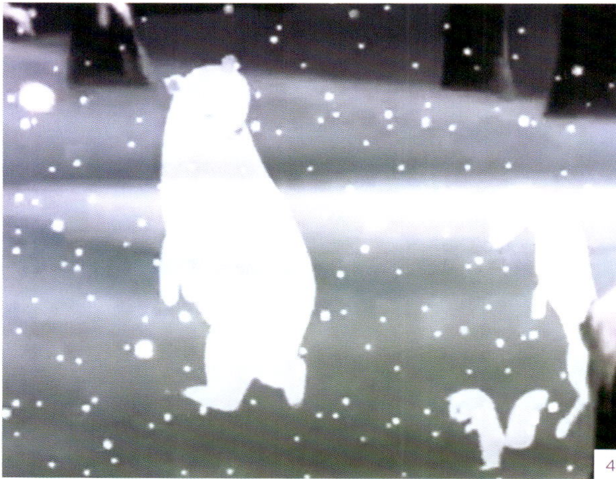
4

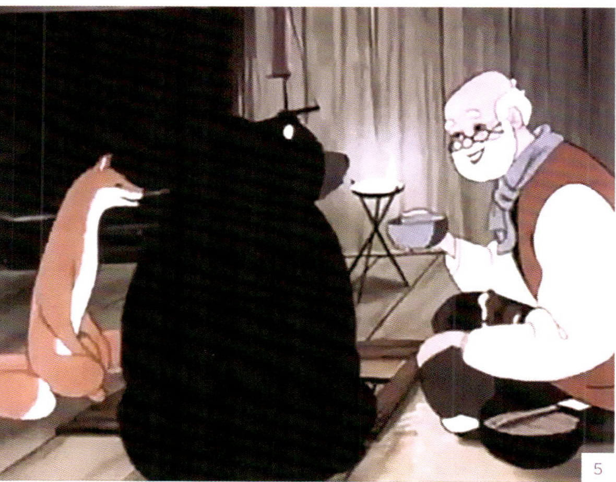
5

2 to 5
1956
Kuroi Kikori to Shiroi Kikori (The Black Woodcutter and the White Woodcutter)*

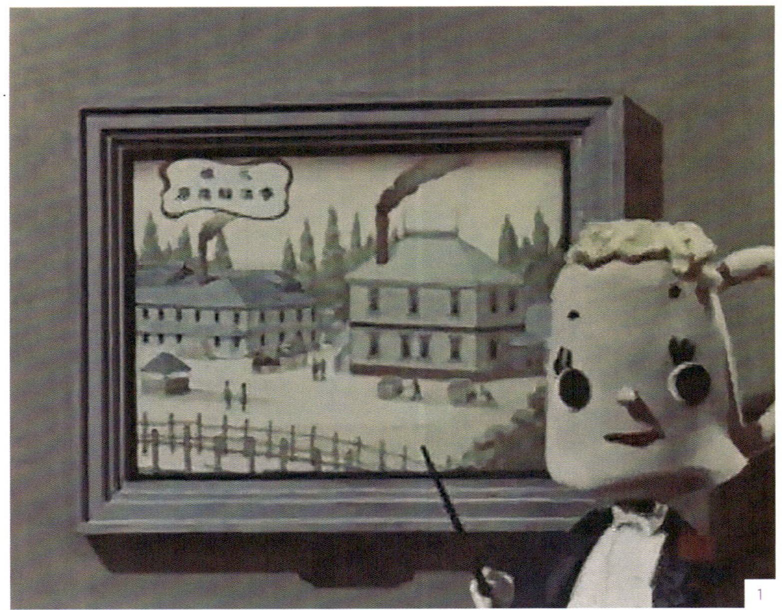

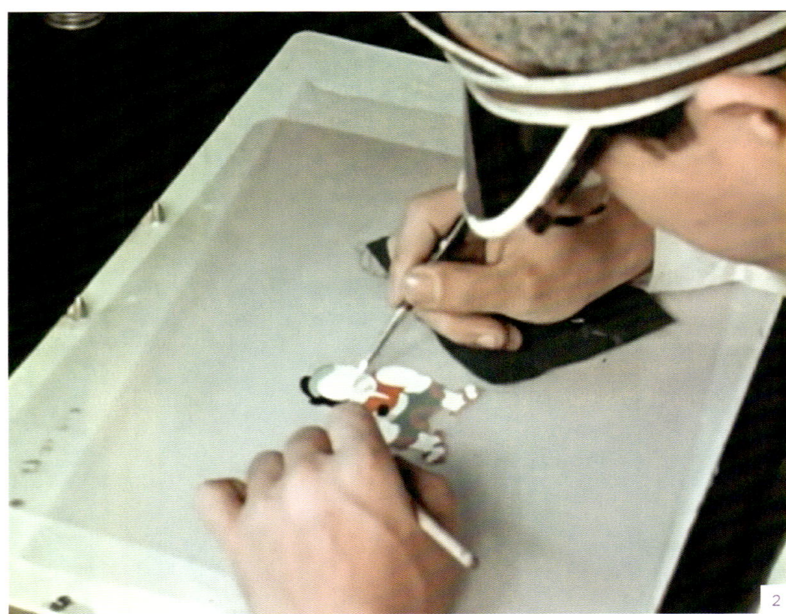

1
1956
Beer Mukashi Mukashi (Beer, Those Were the Days)

2
1937
Katsura Hime
Noburō Ōfuji, a documentary on the creation of a color cartoon

TELEVISION, A NEW MARKET

American culture had flooded Japan throughout the occupation, and Japan launched an industrialization based on the capitalist model. Hand-in-hand evolution with the Americans was a reality, supported by the persistent fantasy of catching up with Western modernism. At the end of the occupation in 1952, the Japanese were once again accustomed to seeing Western films, and had just discovered luxurious animated feature films, such as *Gulliver's Travels*, *Snow White and the Seven Dwarfs*, *Pinocchio*, and *Bambi*.

There was no denying it: Japan was lagging far behind in film in terms of both format length and color standardization. And Japanese studios were not powerful enough to compete with the American colossus.

In 1953, the Japanese finally had their first television channel, NHK, modeled after the BBC, which had held a monopoly in the United Kingdom for nearly seventeen years. However, competition from new channels soon followed, creating a whole new market for audio production companies. As advertising needs grew, animation studios were called upon by communication companies such as Dentsu to add eye-catching images to TV commercials. In 1956, Toei Dōga made this its specialty before moving into its own premises a year later, as did Yasuji Murata who founded his own production company, Murata Seisakusho. Stop-motion experts Tadahito Mochinaga and Kihachirō Kawamoto created MOM Production (1960) and Shiba Productions (1958) to target the booming advertising market. This led to commercials for brands such as Suntory (whisky) and Mitsuwa Sekken (Mitsuwa soup). The animations were no longer aimed at children, which offered a new range of narrative and graphic possibilities. This allowed *mangaka* (manga artist) and director Yōji Kuri to create his own studio in turn, specializing in NHK's *Minna no Uta* (*Songs for Everyone*) interstitial television show.

Asahi Production went as far as producing an advertising short shown in theaters about the history of beer, *Beer Mukashi Mukashi* (*Beer, Those Were the Days*, 1956). Several animation techniques were used in the twelve-minute film, which recalled that, without Commodore Perry's threatening black ships forcing the country to open its doors in 1853, the Japanese could not enjoy this beverage. Several independent artists worked on the short written by Tadasu Iizawa, notably Tadahito Mochinaga and even the untouchable Noburō Ōfuji.

ART FILMS, THE ALTERNATIVE

Though Masaoka and his team had long sought to be independent, their style had always been inspired by American films, and their ambition required the support of major studios such as Shochiku and Toho. However, after the occupation, Taiji Yabushita and Yasuji Mori gradually oriented their scenes toward a more classical style borrowed from prints.

During the postwar period, some independent animator-directors proved to be an alternative to Western standardization. Mochinaga, repatriated to Japan after a long career in China and the state of Manchukuo, developed the Animagic technique to make short stop-motion films. Thus *Uriko-hime to Amanojaku*, commissioned by Dentsu in 1955, and *Go-hiki no Kozaru-tachi* retained the traditional spirit of *bunraku* (puppet theater), while showcasing the evolution of film through camera movements and aerial animations.

But Noburō Ōfuji was the director who really distinguished himself during this tumultuous transitional period when studios were continually being created, merging, and collapsing. He was present before, during, and after the war and continued to produce many films at his Chiyogami Eiga-sha studio. In 1946, he directed *Kumo no Ito*, an intense adaptation of Ryūnosuke Akutagawa's *The Spider's Thread*, in which a man tries to escape hell with the help of a spider. The film was more subtle than *The Magic Pen* produced the same year, which also evoked the theme of outside aid, and preserved Ōfuji's trademark style, using silhouette animation and colorfully patterned *chiyogami*. He dared to approach Buddhism in this short film while competing productions were moving away from any religious symbolism. But Ōfuji discussed redemption first and foremost, and two years later, he directed a film about Buddha's life, *Shaka*, which he didn't finish until 1961. Theology was at the center of his latest works, confirming his obsession with the *kojiki*, to which he devoted five films in addition to his first adaptation in 1931.

In the meantime, he adapted to trends as he did during the war, offering a poignant vision of *Yuki no Yoru no Yume* (*Dream of a Snowy Night*, 1947), whose misery reminded viewers of Japan's current state, and directed mainstream films such as his adaptation of *Ali Baba and the Forty Thieves*, called *Dangobei Torimonochō: Hirake Goma no Maki*, in 1952. But, ultimately, his personal and experimental films were the biggest successes outside Japan. In 1952, he produced a version of his flagship film *The Whale* in Konicolor, which brought him to the Cannes Film Festival. The exoticism of Ōfuji films was attractive to the West, and his fascinating *Yūreisen* (*The Phantom Ship*, 1956), made of Fujicolor cellophane, even made it to the Venice Film Festival.

Ōfuji was a pioneer in colorization, having shot a film in Cinecolor in 1929 and codirected the documentary *Katsura Hime* on the creation of an animated cartoon in 1937, before directing *Hana to Cho* (*The Flower and the Butterfly**) in 1954. It was an immersion in celluloid flora, as his colleagues Mitsuyo Seo and Kenzō Masaoka had done, but this time in color.

Unlike Sanae Yamamoto, who also got his start in the 1920s but had always been inspired by American animation, followed by Murata, Seo, and Masaoka, Noburō Ōfuji was one of the few artists to establish his own themes and original graphic style. His impact on animation was so great that there is an annual prize named after him that has been awarded to an animated film since 1962. When he died in 1961, he made way for a new generation of independent artists, such as Yōji Kuri and Kihachirō Kawamoto. However, their films would have a hard time finding their place in the audiovisual landscape, which was being invaded by an intense level of production by the future major studios.

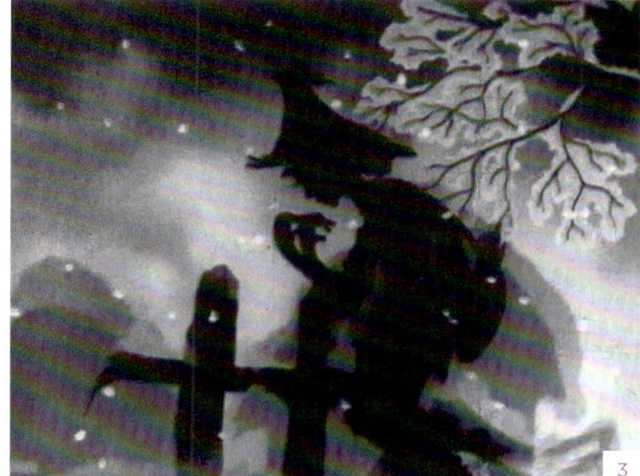

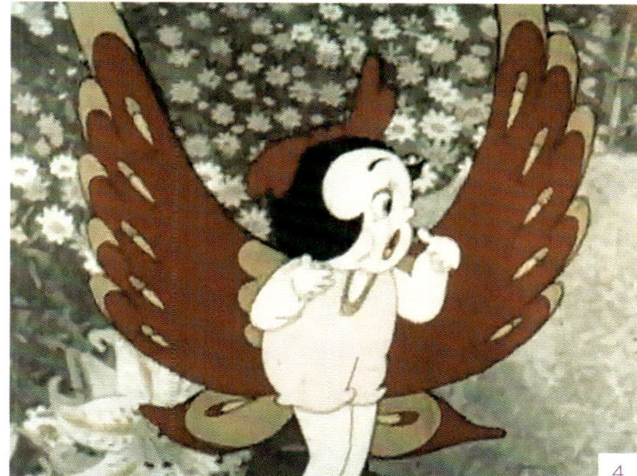

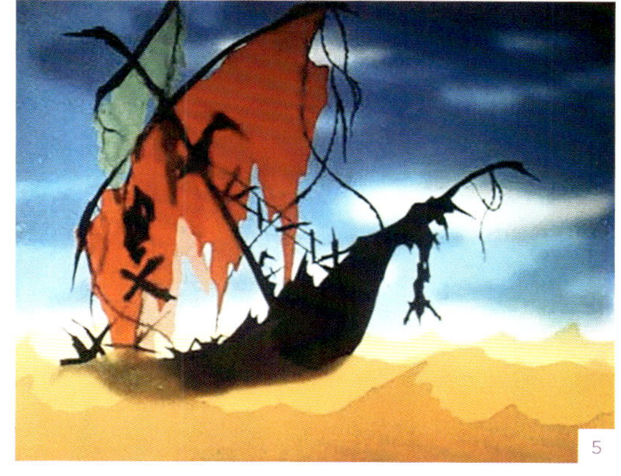

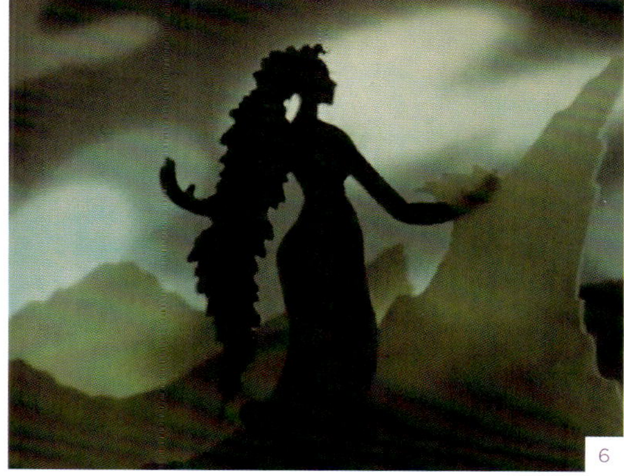

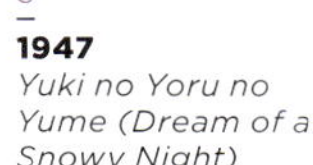

3
1947
Yuki no Yoru no Yume (Dream of a Snowy Night)

4
1952
Kujira (The Whale)

5
1954
Hana to Cho (The Flower and the Butterfly)*

6
1956
Yūreisen (The Phantom Ship)

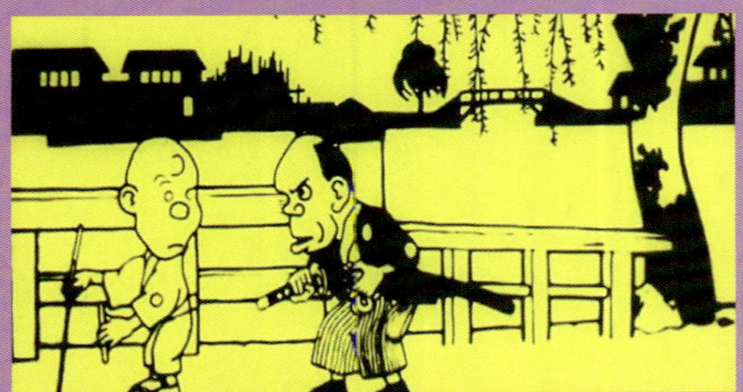

HANAWA HEKONAI MEITŌ NO MAKI

Hanawa Hekonai: A New Sword Chapter
Year: 1917
Category: Film
Director: Junichi Kōuchi
Animation Studio: Kobayashi Shokai

AT A GLANCE:
Though there may likely be older examples of animation, this short film is the oldest precisely dated archive to have survived intact.

YOU MAY ALSO LIKE . . .
Urashima Taro from 1918, one of rival Seitarō Kitayama's few films to be seen.

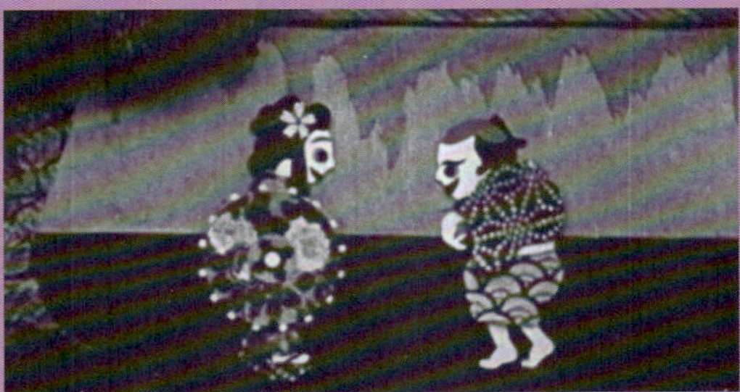

BAGHDAD-JO NO TOZOKU

The Burglars of Baghdad Castle
Year: 1926
Category: Film
Director: Noburō Ōfuji
Animation Studio: Jiyu Eiga Kenkyusho

AT A GLANCE:
Animators experiment with patterned-paper cutout animation in this epic film, which has abundant imagery and even features camera movements.

YOU MAY ALSO LIKE . . .
Noburō Ōfuji's iconic film *The Whale.*

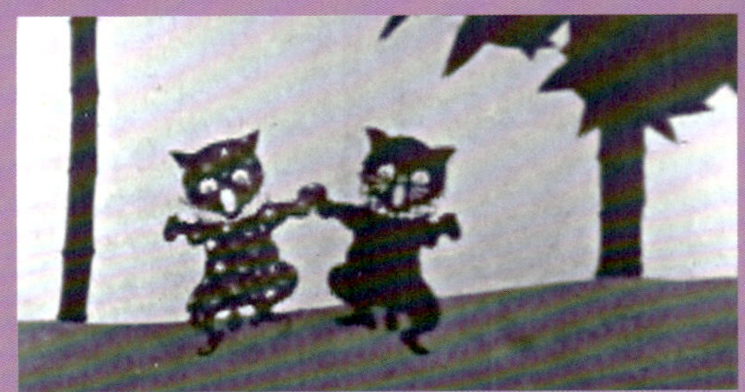

KURO NYAGO

The Black Cat
Year: 1928
Category: Film
Director: Noburō Ōfuji
Animation Studio: Jiyu Eiga Kenkyusho

AT A GLANCE:
This was the first Japanese animated musical video, with karaoke-style lyrics synchronized to the music.

YOU MAY ALSO LIKE . . .
The dragon dance in *Mura Matsuri* by the same director.

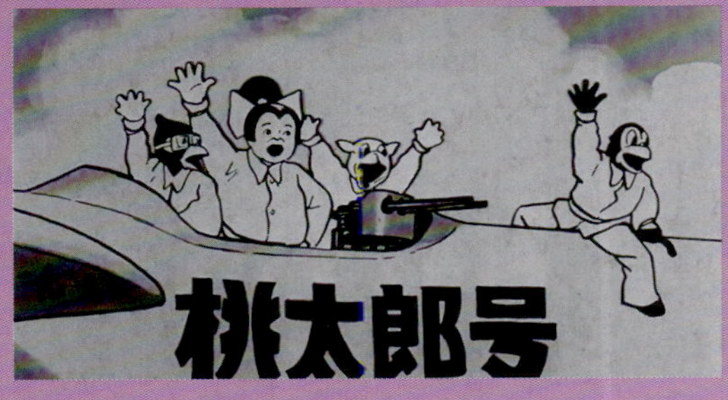

SORA NO MOMOTARŌ

Momotarō in the Sky
Year: 1931
Category: Film
Director: Yasuji Murata
Animation Studio: Yokohama Cinema

AT A GLANCE:
Folklore hero Momotarō is used for nationalist purposes, featured as an airplane pilot accompanied by his fairy-tale acolytes.

YOU MAY ALSO LIKE . . .
Momotarō's Underwater Adventure, in which the hero pilots a submarine and takes on a great white shark with his sword. *Kamishibai Kintaro,* another legendary hero's tale by the same director.

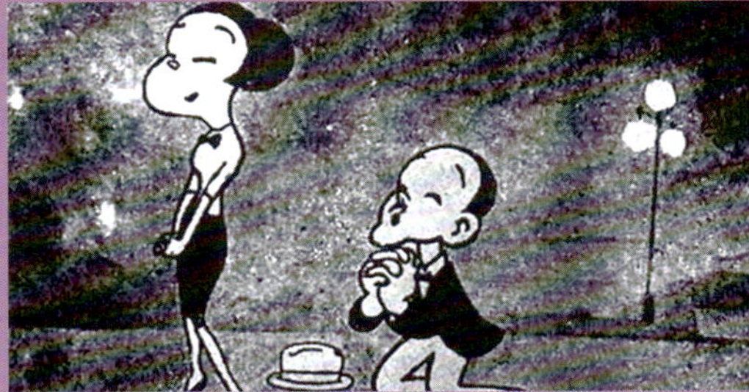

CHIKARA TO ONNA NO YO NO NAKA

In the World of Power and Women
Year: 1933
Category: Film
Director: Kenzō Masaoka
Animation Studio: Shochiku

AT A GLANCE:
A smooth-talking technical revolution that ushered in the era of both cel animation and sound cartoons!

YOU MAY ALSO LIKE . . .
*Monkey Island** by the same director, a twenty-seven-minute film that combines multiple points of view. *Taro's Train* by Yasuji Mori, which alternates between live shots and animation.

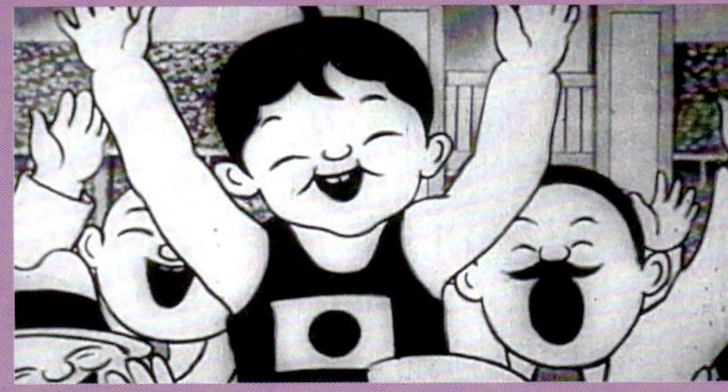

MABŌ NO DAI KYŌSŌ

Mabō's Big Race
Year: 1936
Category: Film
Director: Kinjirō Satō
Animation Studio: Satō Eiga Seikashu-sho

AT A GLANCE:
Mabō became the first recurring hero in a series of films and quickly turned into an emissary of propaganda during the war.

YOU MAY ALSO LIKE . . .
Adaptations of the manga *Norakuro,* the famous brave and clumsy dog who battles the bears of the north, or *Fuku-chan,* another mischievous hero adored by children.

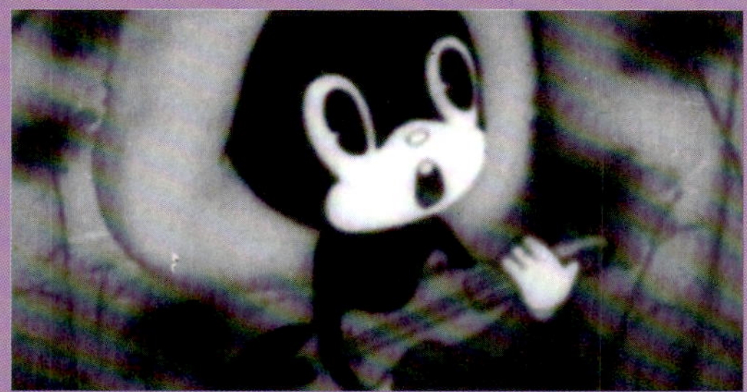

ARI-CHAN

Arichan the Ant
Year: 1941
Category: Film
Director: Mitsuyo Seo
Animation Studio: Geijutsu Eigasha

AT A GLANCE:
This poetic film gives no hint of the propaganda period in which it was made. It was the first Japanese film to use the American concept of the multiplane camera, which was used until the end of the century.

YOU MAY ALSO LIKE . . .
The Spider and the Tulip, which goes beyond *Arichan* with detailed and realistic drawings, complex movements, and depth of field never before seen in the Land of the Rising Sun.

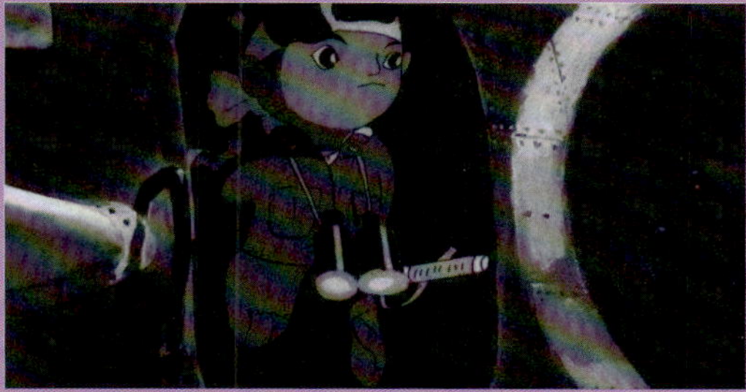

MOMOTARŌ UMI NO SHINPEI

Momotarō: Sacred Sailors
Year: 1945
Category: Film
Director: Mitsuyo Seo
Animation Studio: Shochiku

AT A GLANCE:
This film is the ultimate propaganda cartoon. Sponsored by the Ministry of Animation, *Sacred Sailors* brings animation to feature film.

YOU MAY ALSO LIKE . . .
Momotarō's Sea Eagles, a defense of the attack on Pearl Harbor that was shown before the feature film. J.O. Talkie's 1936 attack films bringing together different folklore heroes.

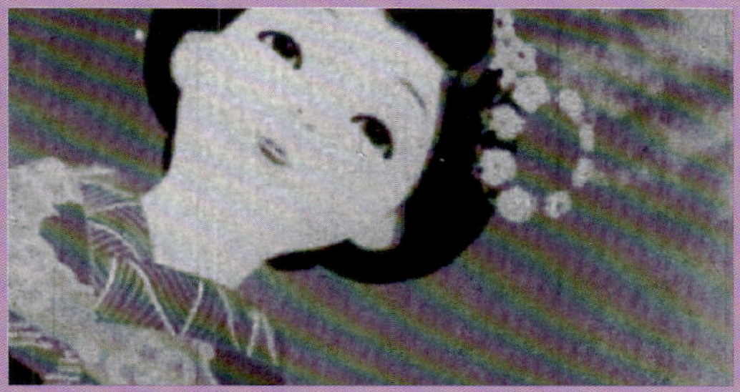

SAKURA

Cherry Blossom
Year: 1946
Category: Film
Director: Kenzō Masaoka
Animation Studio: Shin Nihon Dōga-sha

AT A GLANCE:
Cinema is rebuilt after the war and Masaoka creates an optimistic film celebrating the arrival of spring.

YOU MAY ALSO LIKE . . .
Nine years later, Noburō Ōfuji attempted this poetic experience in color with *The Flower and the Butterfly*.*

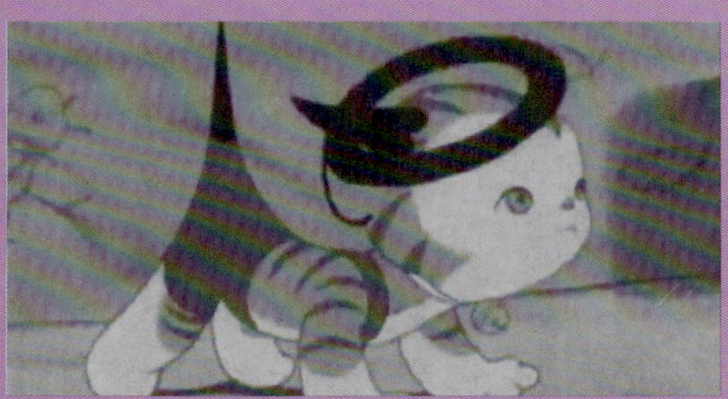

SUTE NEKO TORA-CHAN

Tora-chan the Abandoned Kitten
Year: 1947
Category: Film
Director: Kenzō Masaoka
Animation Studio: Nihon Dōga-sha

AT A GLANCE:
This animation encourages children to support the great work of rebuilding a battered Japan after the war.

YOU MAY ALSO LIKE . . .
The culture clash in the second *Tora-chan*, in which a conservative grandfather disapproves of a Western marriage. The glorification of the American support was essential for modernization in *The Magic Pen*.

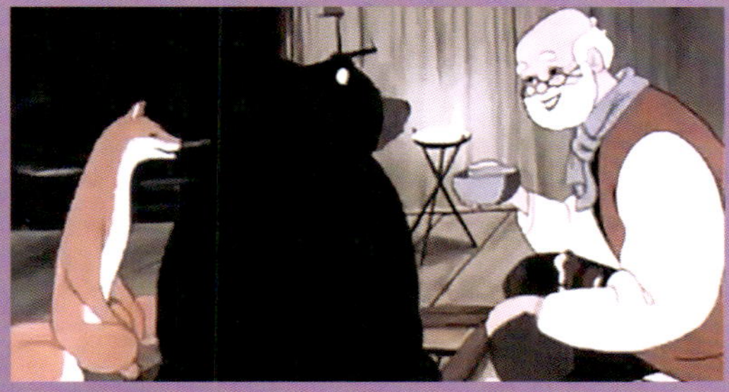

KUROI KIKORI TO SHIROI KIKORI

The Black Woodcutter and the White Woodcutter
Year: 1956
Category: Film
Director: Taiji Yabushita
Animation Studio: Nichido Eiga-sha

AT A GLANCE:
Nichido's last film, in which director Taiji Yabushita and animator Yasuji Mori perfected a graphic style that became the hallmark of Toei Dōga studio.

YOU MAY ALSO LIKE . . .
Kitty's Graffiti and *Kitty's Studio*, Toei Dōga's first two short films.

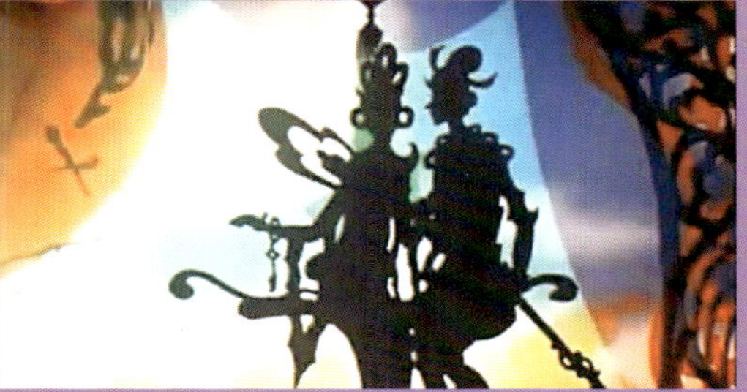

YŪREISEN

The Phantom Ship
Year: 1956
Category: Film
Director: Noburō Ōfuji
Animation Studio: Toei Kyoto

AT A GLANCE:
Presented at the Venice Film Festival, this film revealed Japanese animation on the world stage, prepared to rival the industry leader, the United States.

YOU MAY ALSO LIKE . . .
Ōfuji's remake of *The Whale*, a 1953 Cannes Film Festival selection.

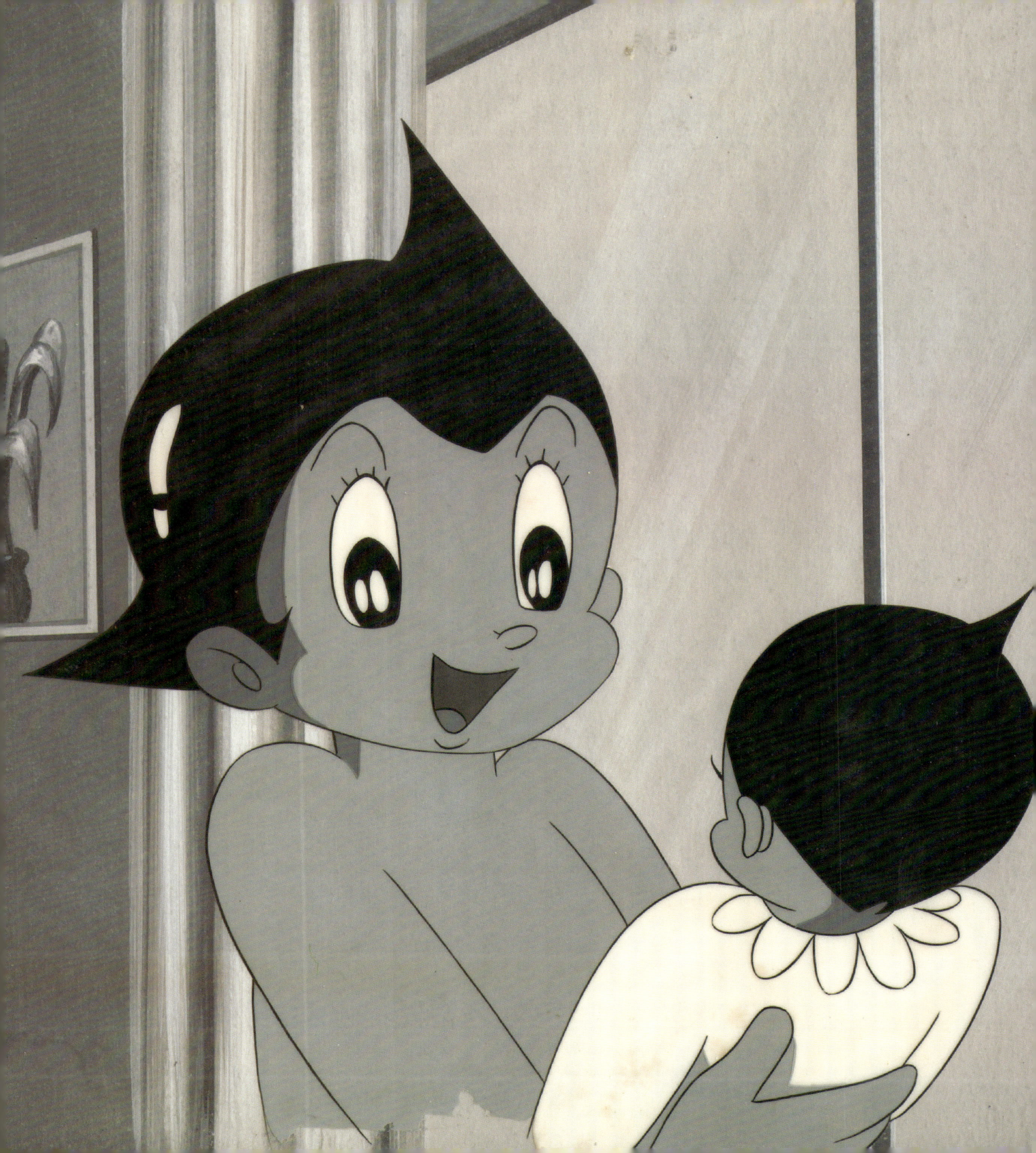

1958 TO 1982
COLOR FILM AND TELEVISION

Detail view: Astro Boy. *Original production celluloid showing Astro carrying his brother © 1963 Osamu Tezuka, Mushi Productions. THE ART OF ANIME cultural exhibition, Spacher Vogler Collection © Tezuka Productions.*

Industrial animation

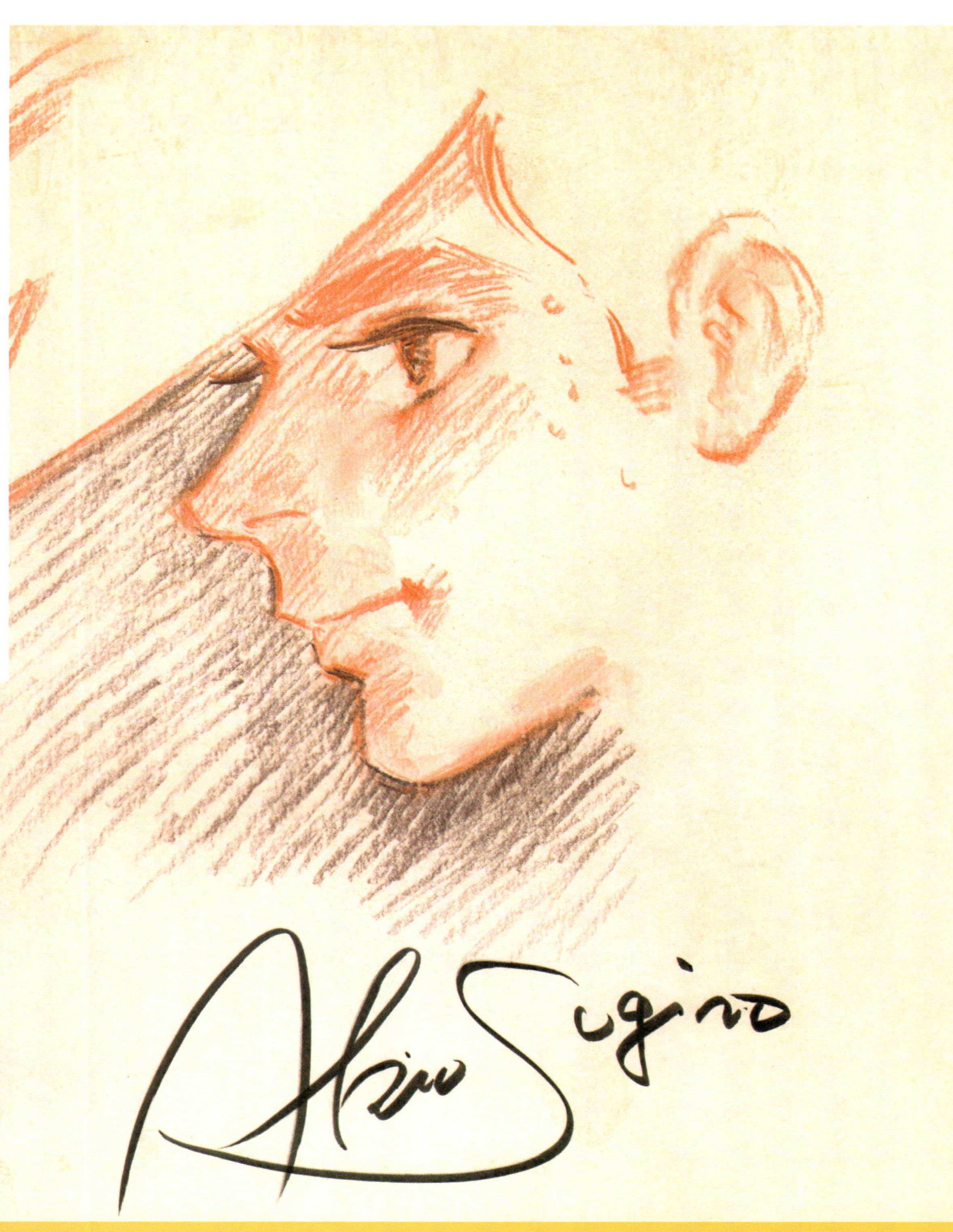

Detail view: Ashita no Joe. *Original illustrated autograph by Akio Sugino © 1971 Tetsuya Chiba, Tokyo Movie Shinsha. THE ART OF ANIME cultural exhibition, Spacher Vogler Collection.*

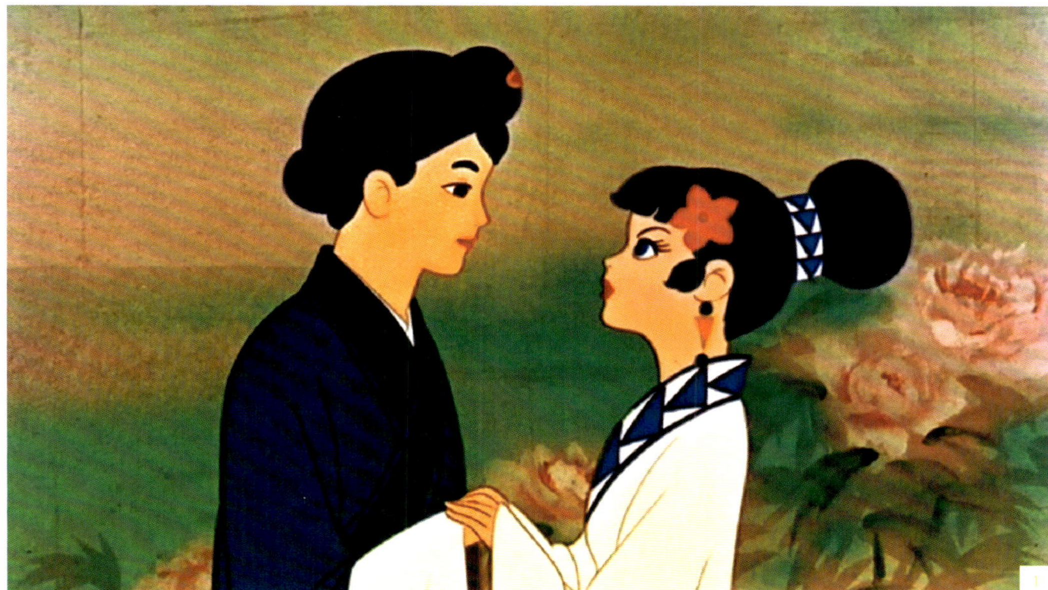

1
1958
Hakujaden
(The Tale of the White Serpent)

1958
Hakujaoen
(The Tale of the White Serpent)

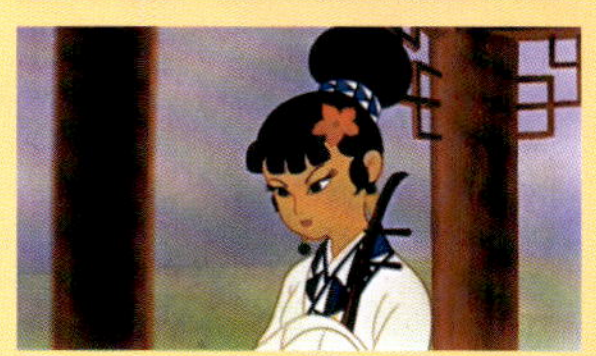

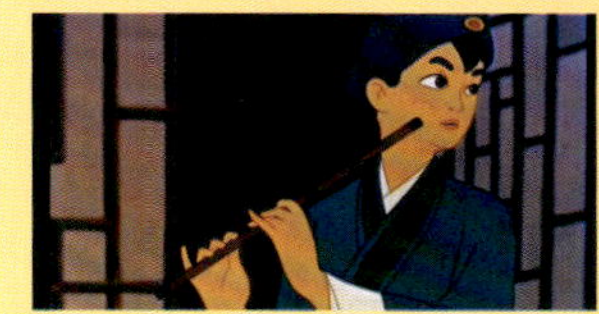

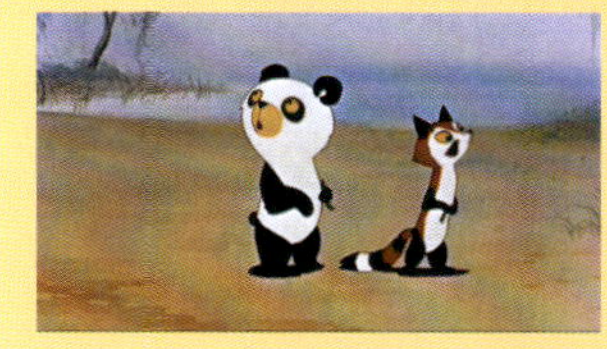

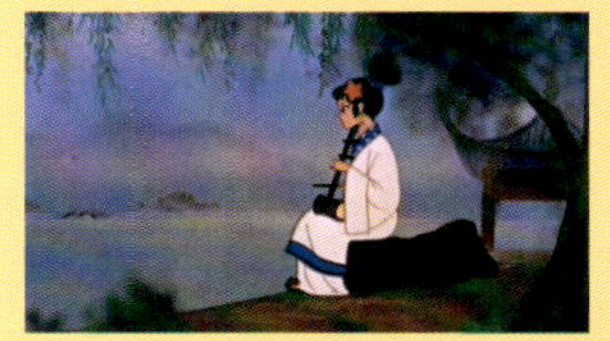

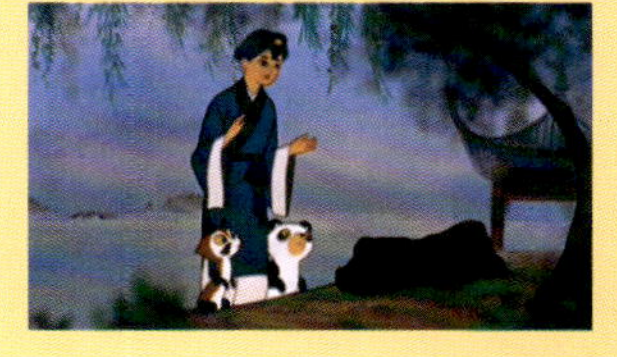

Film, a new economic model

TOEI DŌGA: ANIMATION'S SECOND WIND

At the head of the Toei company, and thus Toei Dōga, Hiroshi Ōkawa aimed to rival the luxurious American animated feature films that had flooded the Japanese market. From that point on, he based his economic model on Disney's—adapting international works of literature for musical films intended for the general public. This desire lined up with the former Nichido studio's artistic team, where director Taiji Yabushita and animators Yasuji Mori and Akira Daikubara had always been inspired by Disney productions when creating their animations. Yabushita's short films *Ukare Violin* and *Kuro Kikori to Shiroi Kikori* introduced a new style, where offset character animation was the perfect evolution of the graceful movements in the films by his mentors, Kenzō Masaoka and Masao Kumagawa. Father figure and perfectionist Sanae Yamamoto's valuable experience also shaped the studio's next productions.

The new generation made its mark in 1958 with *Hakujaden* (*The Tale of the White Serpent*), the first feature-length Japanese animation in color. The film was inspired by a popular Chinese legend, which allowed Ōkawa to more easily export it despite China's and Korea's persistent resentment toward Japan. His choice to adapt this tale was especially astute as he could piggyback on the release of *Byaku Fujin no Yoren* (*The Legend of the White Serpent*), a highly successful 1956 Sino-Japanese coproduction. Directed by Taiji Yabushita (also the scriptwriter) and Kazuhiko Okabe, this film was the Japanese response to *Snow White and the Seven Dwarfs*. The delicate human traits animated by Daikubara and numerous backgrounds recalled traditional Chinese paintings, which the studio tested out in the short film *Yumemi Douji* (1958). Like in *Snow White*, the characters were animated

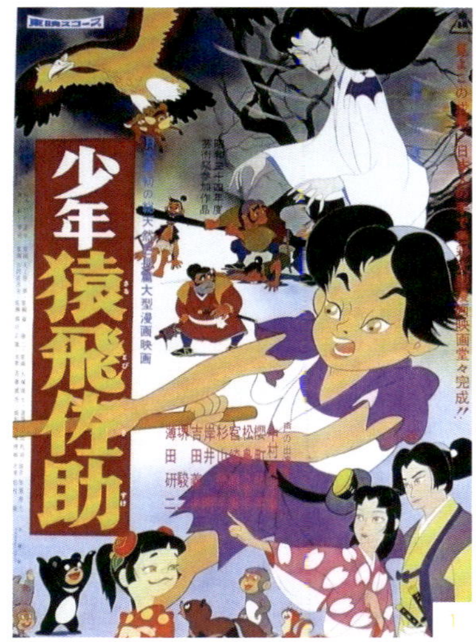

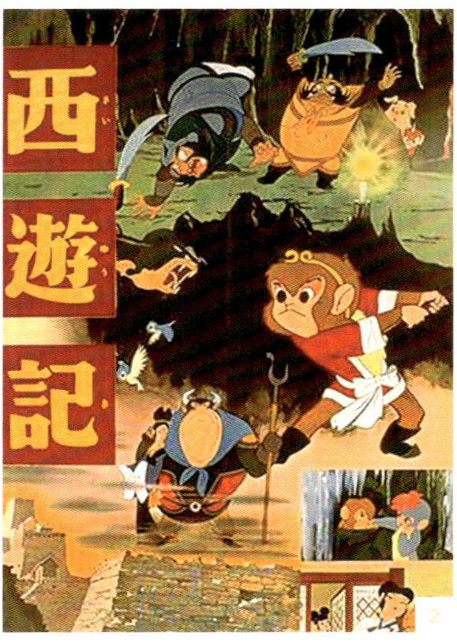

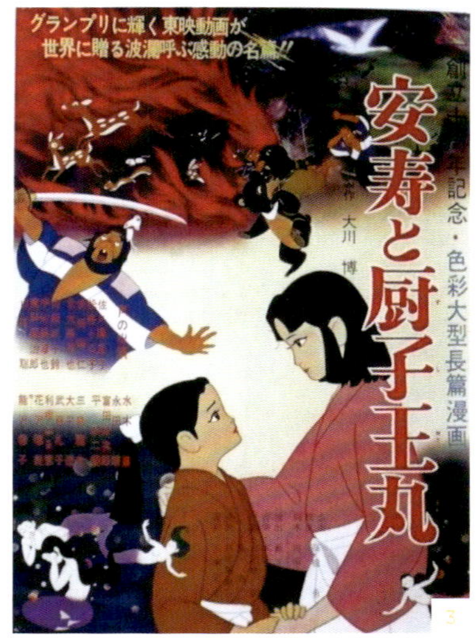

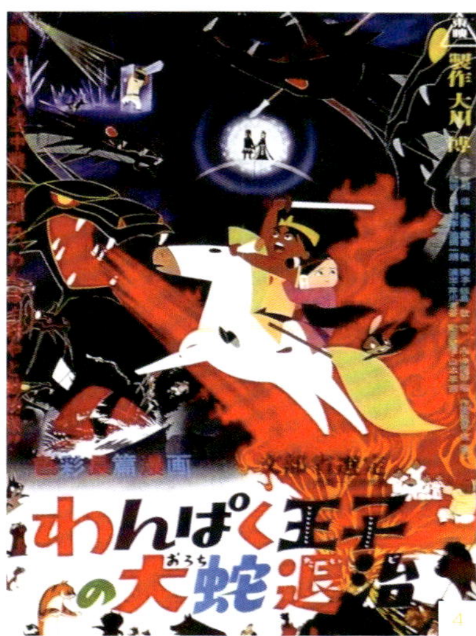

1
1959
Shōnen Sarutobi Sasuke (Magic Boy)

2
1960
Saiyuki (Alakazam the Great)

3
1961
Anju to Zushiomaru (The Littlest Warrior)

4
1963
Wanpaku Ōji no Orochi Taiji (The Little Prince and the Eight-Headed Dragon)

using rotoscoping, a process of filming live actors and copying their movements to get a more fluid and realistic rendering. Still drawing inspiration from Disney, Yabushita and Mori added many animals to captivate the youngest viewers. It was also their strong suit, as they had created mainly anthropomorphic heroes. They directed two short films within Toei Dōga between 1957 and 1959, *Koneko no Rakugaki* (*Kitty's Graffiti**) and *Koneko no Studio* (*Kitty's Studio**), which revisited their passion for moving images, as a tribute to the term *dōga* ("moving pictures") popularized by Kenzō Masaoka. These animals became a recurring theme in the many films that followed the huge success of *The Tale of the White Serpent*, which won the Mainichi Film Award.

The gamble paid off and Toei established a new rhythm of producing one fully animated feature film per year. In 1959, the studio adapted popular ninja stories with *Shōnen Sarutobi Sasuke* (*Magic Boy*), allowing the studio to combine its narrative tradition with its international target. The film was shot in CinemaScope, a wide screen requiring larger, more detailed drawings, whereas *The Tale of the White Serpent* had used the 1.33:1 ratio standardized by previous productions. This format gave the film a certain prestige (which Disney brought to animation with *Sleeping Beauty* in 1959) and the studio kept it for its next animated films. The following year, Toei Dōga adapted Osamu Tezuka's manga *Saiyuki* (*Alakazam the Great*), another hit that was a return to Chinese legend. Both films featured characters with special powers—the ninja Sasuke walking up walls and the monkey Goku flying around on a cloud with his magical staff. Toei Dōga opened the door for works for boys (*shōnen*), heralding the future *Dragon Ball* (1984) and *Naruto* (1999) series.

Next came *Anju to Zushiomaru* (*The Littlest Warrior*, 1961), based on Ogai Mori's novel (which Akira Kurosawa had adapted in 1954 in *Sansho the Bailiff*); *Arabian Night: Sindbad no Bōken* (*Arabian Nights: The Adventures of Sinbad*, 1962); and the epic *Wanpaku Ōji no Orochi Taiji* (*The Little Prince and the Eight-Headed Dragon*, 1963). Yasuji Mori was credited as the first animation director in Japan in the latter film, supervising the animators to achieve greater graphic consistency.

These productions, still led by Sanae Yamamoto, gradually explored the possibilities offered by modern animation techniques, considerably narrowing the technical gap between Japanese and American films while maintaining their distinct style. Above all, they served as training for many directors who became extremely prolific, such as Yūgo Serikawa, Yoshio Kuroda, and Isao Takahata, as well as star animators like Gisaburō Sugii, Yōichi Kotabe, Yasuo Ōtsuka, and Hayao Miyazaki. Thus began Toei's golden age in animation cinema with successful films winning numerous festival awards. The studio had managed to create a thriving industry to which numerous artists gravitated, both those who were already established and apprentices. Its internal training and competitions facilitated the artists' professional growth and allowed them to level up both artistically and economically. However, this excitement was quickly overtaken by many difficulties . . .

OBSTACLES AND TRANSFORMED PRODUCTIONS

At the beginning of the 1960s, the television market gradually eclipsed new cinema releases, especially when anime took its place on the small screen in 1963. The democratization of this new medium and the many new TV productions were gradually emptying movie theaters and endangering feature film projects. To counter the competition, Toei reacted by developing a separate television division and in 1964 created the Toei Manga Matsuri—three annual festivals that took place over school vacations (spring, summer, and winter) in several cities simultaneously. These events were an opportunity to bring a young audience back into theaters with premieres, montages of exclusive television episodes, and the sale of highly limited merchandise. They were so successful that the lucrative events become fundamental for the firm. In 1965, Toei Dōga used the festival to promote its new major animated film, *Garibā no Uchū Ryokō* (*Gulliver's Travels Beyond the Moon*), in which Taiji Yabushita tried his hand at science fiction, another way to compete with television heroes.

Competition was forcing the studio to work twice as hard, increasing social conflicts, and causing the workers' union to lobby for better working conditions and wages. In its midst, Takahata, Miyazaki, and Ōtsuka were closer to starting work on the 1965 feature film *Taiyō no Ōji Horusu no Daibōken* (*The Great Adventure of Horus, Prince of the Sun*). The project was inspired by screenwriter Kazuo Fukazawa's puppet play based on Ainu folklore. The trio was met with higher-ups who wanted to target a wide audience, greatly slowing down production. The film was finally released in 1968 but failed to draw in a big audience despite a more mature storyline and groundbreaking animation sequences. The film featured a particularly innovative representation of the sea animated by Yōichi Kotabe. He reused these aquatic movements in 1971 in *Dōbutsu Takarajima* (*Animal Treasure Island*), in which water became a main character. *The Great Adventure of Horus, Prince of the Sun* was in line with *Shōnen Jakku to Mahōtsukai* (*Jack and the Witch*, 1967), which retold the English legends of Beowulf and Jack (a recurring name given to intrepid heroes like Tarō in Japan), where children and other animals were kidnapped and transformed into monsters. Horus and Jack were characters at the center of darker, more realistic themes.

Trends were changing, and young viewers were no longer looking for graceful movements so much as powerful images, just as science fiction was becoming more popular than classic tales, as seen in the two successful adaptations of Shotaro Ishinomori's *Cyborg*

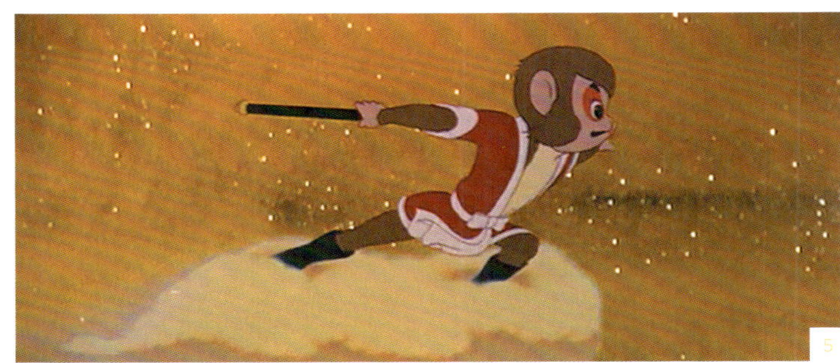

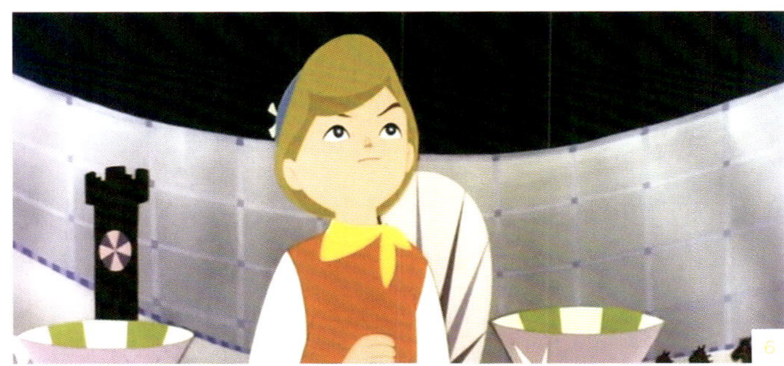

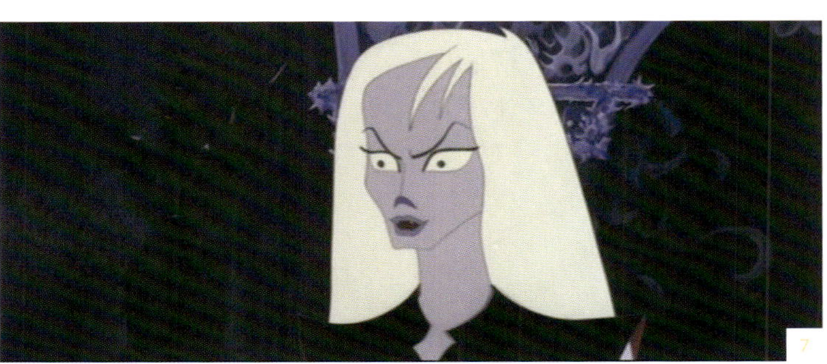

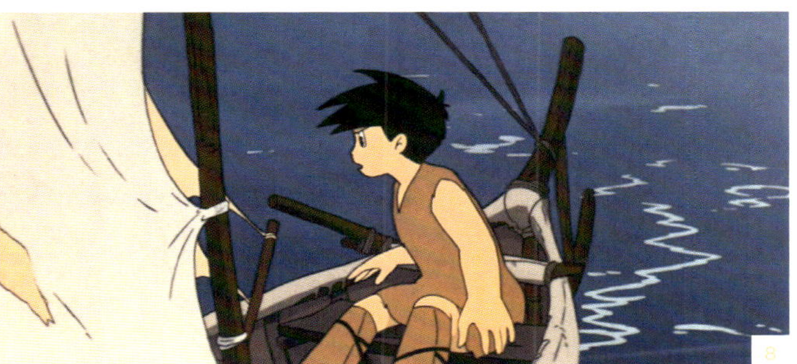

5
—
1960
Saiyuki (Alakazam the Great)

6
—
1965
Gariba no Uchû Ryokō (Gulliver's Travels Beyond the Moon)

7
—
1967
Shonen Jakku to Mahô-tsuka (Jack and the Witch)

8
—
1968
Taiyō no Ōji Horusu no Daibōken (The Great Adventure of Horus, Prince of the Sun)

009 manga in 1966 and 1967. Although the animation quality of the two-part work was far below the productions to which the studio's audiences were accustomed, director Yūgo Serikawa understood that it was time to opt for more dynamic editing and close-ups that showed off the stylized heroes. Toei set out to conquer the world of science fiction and placed Ishinomori at the forefront. The author brought to the studio his suspense stories, in which heroes must confront gangs and other cataclysmic threats, like *Soratobu Yūreisen* (*Flying Phantom Ship*, 1969), in which a robot destroying the city is only the start to a greater conspiracy.

TELEVISION MOVIES

Toei continued its focus on literary classics for its major annual films until 1971, the year producer Hiroshi Ōkawa died. The studio freely adapted works like *Andersen Monogatari* (*The World of Hans Christian Andersen*, 1968), *Nagagutsu o Haita Neko* (*The Wonderful World of Puss 'n Boots*, 1969), *Chibikko Remi to Meiken Kapi* (*Little Remi and Famous Dog Capi**), and *Dōbutsu Takarajima* (*Animal Treasure Island*) by Hans Christian Andersen, Charles Perrault, Hector Malot, and Robert Louis Stevenson. Following the great success of *The Wonderful World of Puss 'n Boots*, Toei Dōga produced two sequels in 1972 and 1976, and made the feline musketeer the company mascot. Pero the cat was a cowboy in the American West, a traveler going around the world in eighty days, and more.

But the competition was increasingly fierce, and television won the day, forcing Toei Dōga to drastically reduce its production of original feature films from 1971 onward, much to the dismay of the many teams involved. The studio went on to fire a large percentage of its workforce following a major strike in 1972 and then hired contract workers paid by the drawing. To limit costs, part of the production was also outsourced, both to subcontractors within the city, such as the recent Nippon Sunrise studio founded in 1972, and abroad, especially to South Korea. Many artists left the studio, including Kotabe, Miyazaki, and Takahata, who together created A-Prod, and Yasuji Mori, who joined Nippon Animation.

Cinema inevitably became a by-product of television, and Toei decided to adapt its popular television series into feature films. The artistic stakes were much lower, with production teams happy to create one lavish episode or a story where various heroes meet up (*Mazinger Z vs. Devilman*, 1973). This extension from the small to the big screen was a success, supported by Toei's festival presence. The studio still adapted some classics in the 1970s, from *Alibaba to Yonjūppiki no Tōzoku* (*Ali Baba and the Forty Thieves*, 1971) to *Tatsu no ko Tarō* (*Taro the Dragon Boy*, 1979) and *Andersen Dōwa: Ningyo Hime* (*Hans Christian Andersen's The Little Mermaid*, 1975), but they were less an expression of the studio's identity than nostalgic productions of an old dream. Toei Dōga was gradually moving away from the artistic model inspired by Disney's works, which had also influenced many other studios . . .

1
1966
Cyborg 009

2
1969
Soratobu Yūreisen (Flying Phantom Ship)

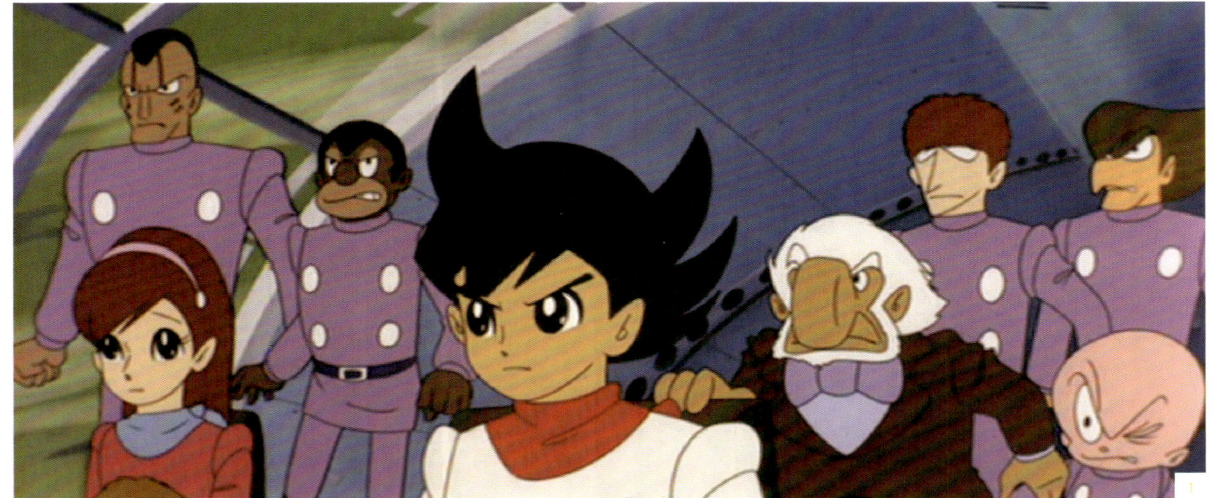

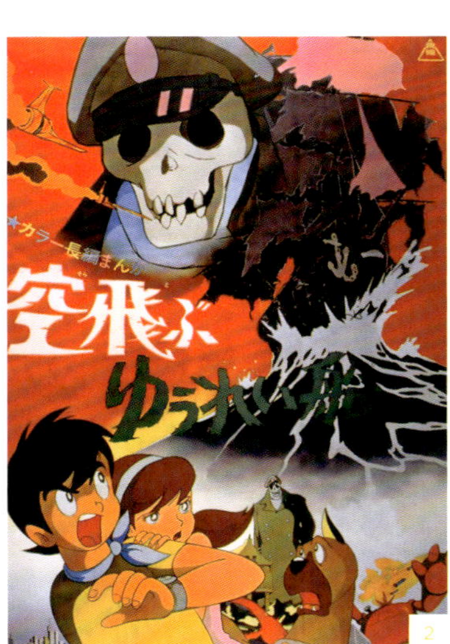

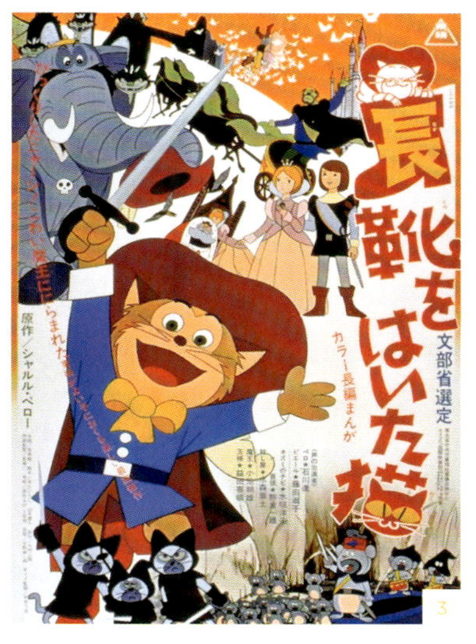

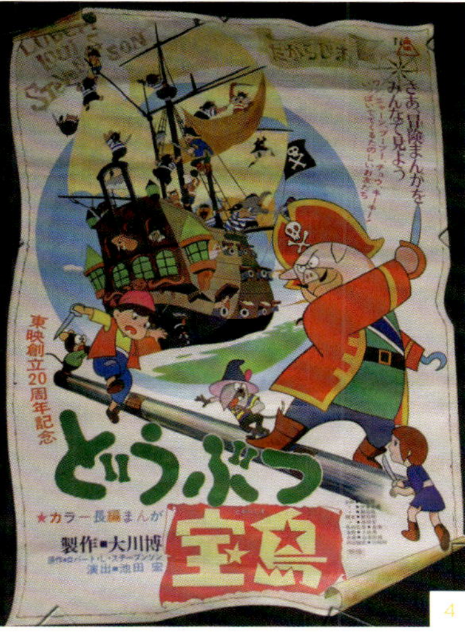

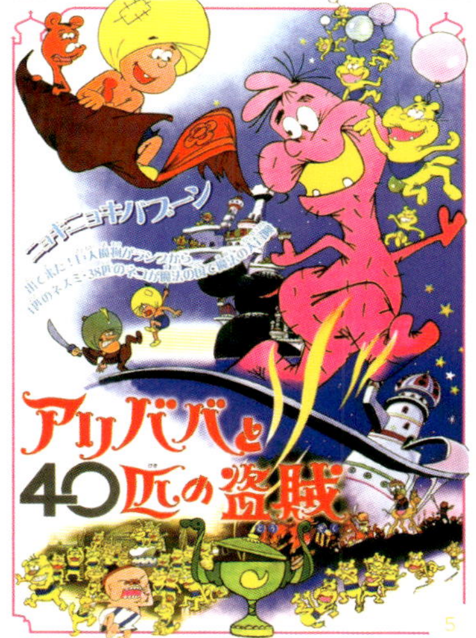

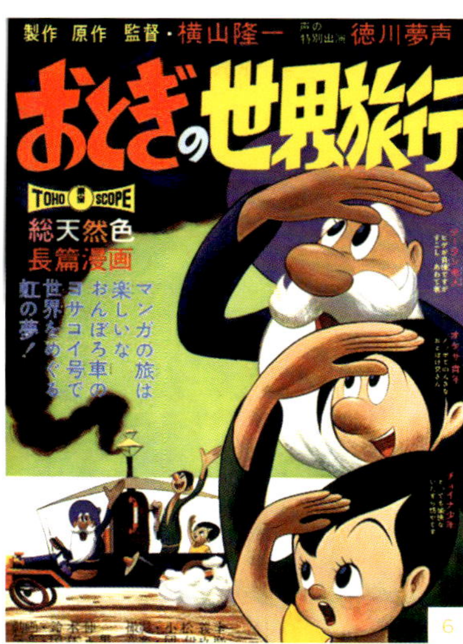

3
1969
Nagagutsu o Haita Neko (The Wonderful World of Puss 'n Boots)

4
1971
Dōbutsu Takarajima (Animal Treasure Island)

5
1971
Alibaba to Yonjūppiki no Tōzoku (Ali Baba and the Forty Thieves)

6
1962
Otogi no Sekai Ryoko (Otogi's Voyage Around the World)*

1: Cyborg 009 © *1966 Ishinomori, Toei Animation.* **2:** Soratobu Yūreisen © *1969 Toei Animation Ltd.* **3:** Nagagutsu o Haita Neko © *1967 Toei Animation Ltd.* **4:** Animal Treasure Island *(Dōbutsu Takarajima)* © *1971 Toei Animation Ltd.* **5:** Alibaba to Yonjūppiki no Tōzoku © *1971 Toei Animation Ltd.* **6:** Otogi no Sekai Ryoko © *Otogi Productions, Toho.*

YOKOYAMA AND TEZUKA: *MANGAKA* FILMMAKERS

Another studio sprang up in direct competition to the creation of Toei Dōga—Otogi Production ("Fairy-Tale Productions"). After meeting Walt Disney and visiting his studios for a feature he was filming in the United States for Mainichi, *mangaka* Ryūichi Yokoyama (author of *Fuku-chan*) directed the twenty-five-minute short *Onbu Obake* (*Piggyback Ghost**, 1955). He created Otogi Pro studio in 1956 out of his desire to get closer to the Disney model and directed *Fukusuke* the following year. Yokoyama was backed by Toho's distribution network and held various positions despite his limited experience in the animation world. Although the film's craftsmanship was below Nichido's standards, *Fukusuke* won the Blue Ribbon Award as well as an award at the Mainichi Film Awards. The manga artist's animation studio became an alternative to the productions of auteur director Noburō Ōfuji and those of animation giant Toei Dōga, which attracted young artists such as Eiichi Yamamoto. The team grew, and Yokoyama's artisanal, even amateur, methods began to improve. Although the *mangaka* had a thorough knowledge of the various trades in the world of animation, he wasn't particularly organized and didn't use any real quality control on the work he produced. When he got started, Yokoyama directed *Hyotan Suzume* (*Sparrow in the Gourd*, 1959), which allowed him to complete an old, abandoned project, and then *Otogi no Sekai Ryoko* (*Otogi's Voyage Around the World**), a feature film combining several shorts. His team was heavily invested in the anthology that was meant to rival Toei's productions. Unfortunately, Toho didn't find it commercial enough, and it wasn't released until 1962 at the same time as the box office hit *King Kong vs. Godzilla*. The film's obvious failure forced Yokoyama out of cinema, and he turned to television production.

In a similar pattern of Disney-worship, the famous *mangaka* Osamu Tezuka, who popularized *story manga* with *Shin Takarajima* (*New Treasure Island*) and *Tetsuwan Atom* (*Astro Boy*), also wanted to open his own animation studio. His love of cinema led him to work alongside Yokoyama, whom he respected and envied, and then to take an active part in Toei's adaptation of his own manga, *Saiyuki*. It was an unpleasant experience with a grueling schedule (he continued working on his manga at the same time), and he had to make many concessions during production. However, he learned teamwork and the different stages of production, which strengthened his desire to create animation. In 1962, he founded Mushi Production, where he directed *Aru Machikado no Monogatari* (*Tales of a Street Corner*) with Eiichi Yamamoto, whom he had poached from Otogi Pro. This experimental anti-militarist, even anti-conformist, film led the author to question artistic freedom, which was being destroyed by the industry and politics. To screen his film, Tezuka organized a double feature with a unique second act—the pilot of *Tetsuwan Atom* (*Astro Boy*), a TV series that would revolutionize the anime industry.

While Tezuka was making a name for himself on the small screen, he was also making several short films of his own, allowing him to experiment further. Then, in 1969, while the studio was trying to gain new audiences, he and his colleague Eiichi Yamamoto set about making a feature film for adults: *Senya Ichiya Monogatari* (*A Thousand and One Nights*), the first erotic anime. Tezuka offered a patchwork of the oriental collection, an eclectic work that played on current trends (Jean-Paul Belmondo's face for the hero, rock music, and more) while retaining the quirky, anachronistic humor of the author's manga. Production was tedious, and the film became a 128-minute saga. However, its success in theaters allowed the artistic duo to produce a second feature film: *Cleopatra*. The eccentric biopic was the perfect continuation of *A Thousand and One Nights*, with a more pronounced sensuality and a surprising contribution from science fiction that gave Tezuka the opportunity to blend visual techniques once again. In 1973, Yamamoto directed *Kanashimi no Belladonna* (*Belladonna of Sadness*) based on an essay by Jules Michelet. It was a more conceptual film, and the partial drawings accentuated the erotic overtones. Although independent of one another, these experimental features form a trilogy called *Animerama*, which extended the possibilities of animation, up to that point limited to children's productions. But *Cleopatra*'s moderate success, coupled with *Belladonna*'s commercial failure, demonstrated that the public wasn't ready for animated works designed exclusively for adults, and that cinema had undoubtedly been eclipsed by television.

Though animation was still a genre in its own right, known as *manga eiga* (cartoon films), it was most popular on television, thus establishing *terebi manga* (television manga).

1
1969
Senya Ichiya Monogatari (A Thousand and One Nights)

2
1970
Cleopatra

3
1973
Kanashimi no Belladonna (Belladonna of Sadness)

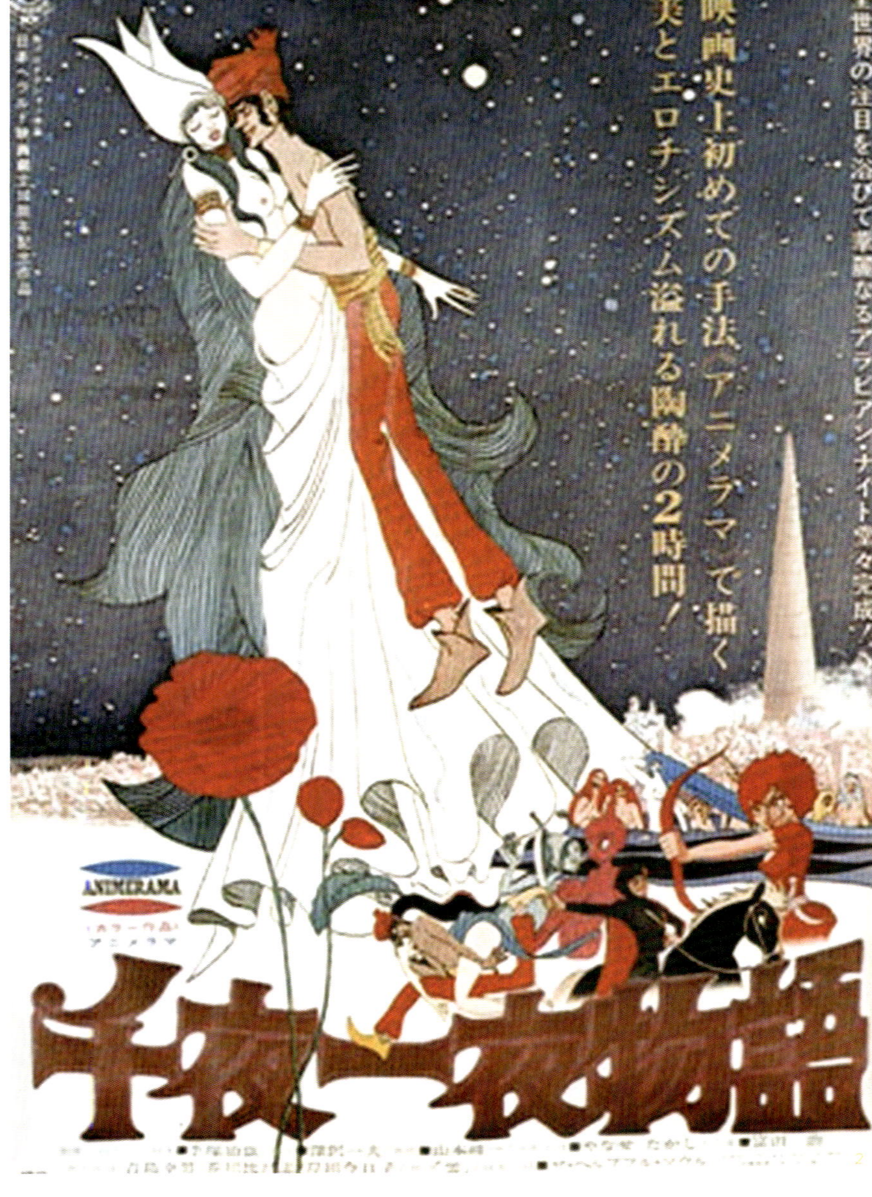

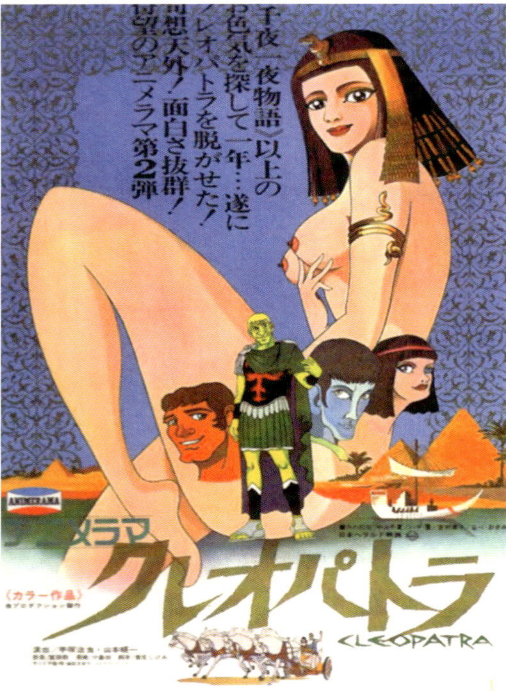

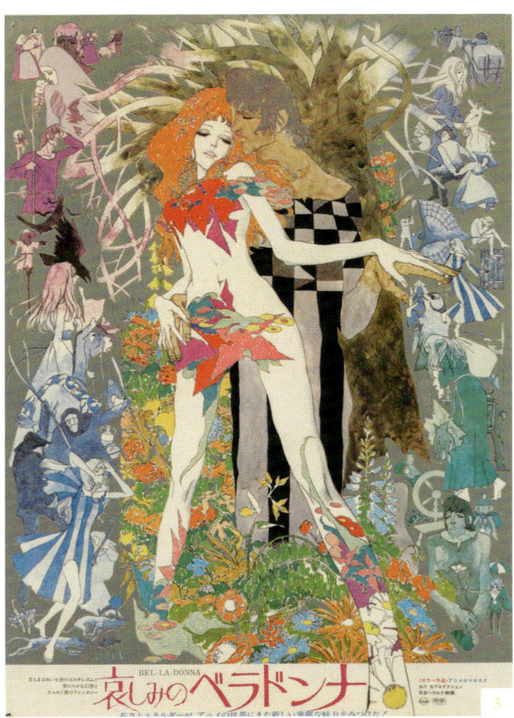

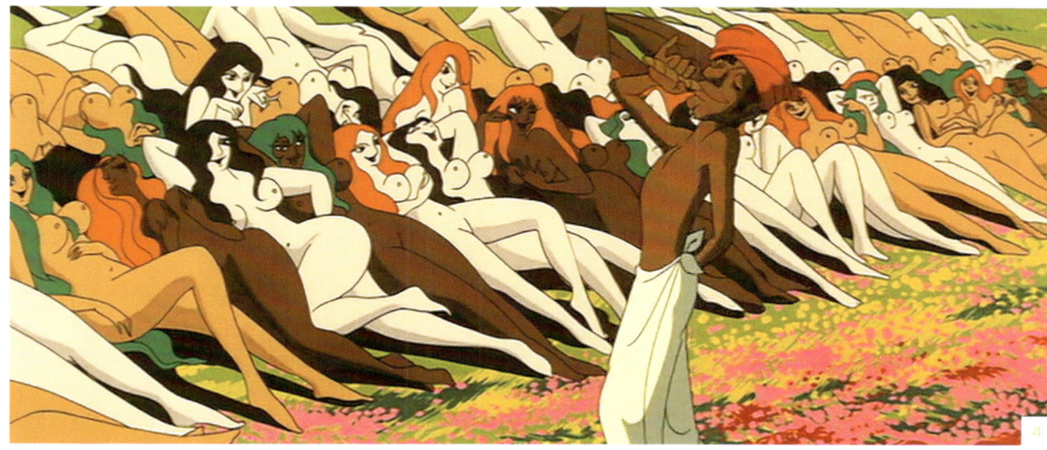

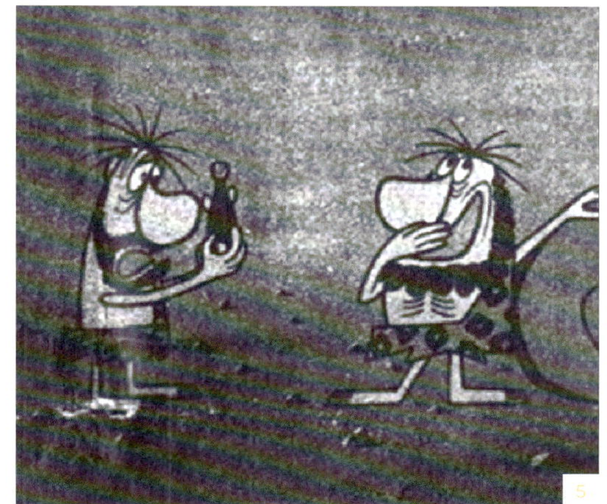

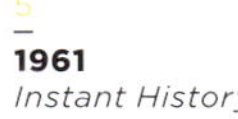

4
1969
Senya Ichiya Monogatari (A Thousand and One Nights)

5
1961
Instant History

New medium, new methods

SMALL SCREEN, BIG ADVENTURES

When the public channel NHK was launched on February 1, 1953, Japan was lagging behind colossally in television (RDF, the ancestor of RTF, had come about in 1945 in France). Despite being dead last, it progressed so quickly that it surpassed the rest of the developed world! Just a few months after NHK, its first private competitor, Nippon TV, appeared on scene in August 1953, backed by the media group Yomiuri Shimbun. In April 1955, the owners of the *Mainichi Shimbun* newspaper launched the Tokyo Broadcasting System (TBS).

In 1958, the Eiffel Tower–inspired Tokyo Tower was completed; at 1,092 feet (333 meters) high, the communications antenna is unmissable. By 1959, the Japanese already had the choice between six channels! Only two were public (NHK and its educational version, NHK E). The other four were private broadcasters held by well-established media corporations, with the success of Nippon TV and TBS prompting the owners of the daily newspapers *The Asahi Shimbun* and *The Sankei Shimbun* to launch TV Asahi and Fuji TV, respectively. Last, but not least, Tokyo TV (in association with the daily *Nihon Keizai Shimbun*) was launched in 1964, and these broadcasters would define the television landscape for decades. The growing supply of channels met with massive demand. Sales were soaring—between 1957 and 1967, an average of two million households got a television set every year. That number went from six to nine million in 1961 alone due to the arrival of color TV in 1960, slashing prices for black-and-white receivers. Technological innovation was without a doubt the highlight of the decade. In the 1950s, families dreamed of the "three sacred treasures": a black-and-white TV, a washing machine, and a refrigerator. In the 1960s, it was the three Cs—car, cooler (air conditioner), and color TV. Between 1959 (the wedding of the Crown Prince) and 1964 (the Tokyo Olympics), the number of households with a TV went from 55 to 95 percent!

Movie producers began referring to the exponentially popular device as the "brown screen." Forty years after its debut in dark theaters, Japanese animation was once again taking tentative first steps in this new medium. Its first foray into television was the cartoon *Mogura no Adventure* (*Mole's Adventure*), broadcast in monochrome on NTV on October 15, 1958. Despite being shown in black and white, the nine-minute short narrating the lunar expedition of an intrepid mole was made entirely in color!

The first recurring cartoon was Ryūichi Yokoyama's *Instant History* on Fuji TV starting in May 1961. The three-minute historical short mixed the animated hero with real footage and photographs of events that had occurred on the same day in the past. Yokoyama used the database from the *Mainichi Shimbun* newspaper, which was publishing his manga *Fuku-chan*, to create 312 episodes. A recycled montage was broadcast weekly from 1962 to 1964 called *Otogi Manga Calendar* on TBS, a channel controlled by the newspaper, which thus earned quite the return on investment.

THE BIRTH OF AN ICON

The manga *Astro Boy*, which debuted in 1952, made Osamu Tezuka a manga star. In 1959, Toei, who had employed him to work in its animation division, obtained the rights to his manga to adapt a television series. It was unimaginable to produce half an hour of animation every week, so the regional channel MBS broadcast a live-action version from Osaka, Tezuka's hometown. The blurry image quality barely masked the ridiculous costumes, but the love story between manga and the "brown screen" had finally blossomed.

Released from his contract with Toei, Tezuka founded Mushi Production in 1961 to develop his own vision of animation for television. While his studio was being built, he explored a little more behind-the-scenes in television through a partnership with NHK. Each week, alongside a chapter of its *Fushigi na Shōnen* (*Wonder Boy*) manga, the channel broadcast a new episode of the TV series adaptation. As easy as it was for a *mangaka* to pass off the idea of a hero who could freeze time, producing a live-action series was a different story. And the stakes were even higher because it was broadcast live! Resourcefulness was a must in audiovisual productions whose special effects were limited by the absence of postproduction. High viewer ratings and comic book sales confirmed that manga and television were a match made in heaven.

The construction of Mushi Production was completed in April 1962. Now alone at the helm and master of his *Astro Boy* creation, Tezuka wanted to make it the first weekly anime series. According to calculations by his right-hand man, Eiichi Yamamoto, achieving such a feat at Toei's high standards would require five times as many animators as there were in Japan, and the costs would be so high that no channel would be able to buy the finished product. It seemed like an impossible bet, both technically and financially, but Tezuka wanted to be the first to do it. In eight months.

The only way to achieve this was to sacrifice the most expensive step in financial and human terms—animation. Forgotten was full animation at twelve or even twenty-four frames per second, which Toei needed to compete with Disney. For *Astro Boy*, they lowered the standard to eight, and even six frames per second. But this method, while obvious, was far from sufficient. Tezuka and his team developed many other techniques to limit the most time-consuming stage of production as much as possible.

Why create movement when you can create the illusion of movement? In transportation scenes, and especially when Astro was flying, they just scrolled the scenery behind the cel to make the viewer believe it was moving. If a character was walking, they could just loop a simple one- to two-step animation. The two methods combined saved many seconds, if not minutes. In that same vein, a simple zoom on a motionless character's facial expression (usually surprise or fear) cost less than animating its complete reaction.

When Tezuka asked for "limited animation," he wasn't talking about limiting only time but space as well. Only the essential actions needed to be animated—if a person waved a greeting, his arm moved and nothing else! The process was particularly effective during dialogue scenes, where only the mouth and eyes moved on close-up faces, essentially a shot-reverse shot. Editing was equally tight; the longer a shot, the more likely it was to be complicated.

Mushi Production was also inspired by Hanna-Barbera studios, whose *The Flintstones* (1960) and *The Jetsons* (1962) delighted children to the same extent that they displeased Japanese professionals. As production progressed, each sequence was duly indexed and archived on gigantic shelves that took up all the walls of the studio. It quickly became possible to draw from this ever-growing bank of images and recycle the cels in episode after episode. All they needed to do was change the background to reuse Astro's launch scenes as often as they wished. Although it meant that each sequence to be reused

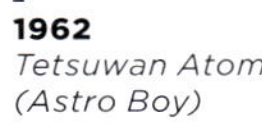

1
1962
Tetsuwan Atom (Astro Boy)

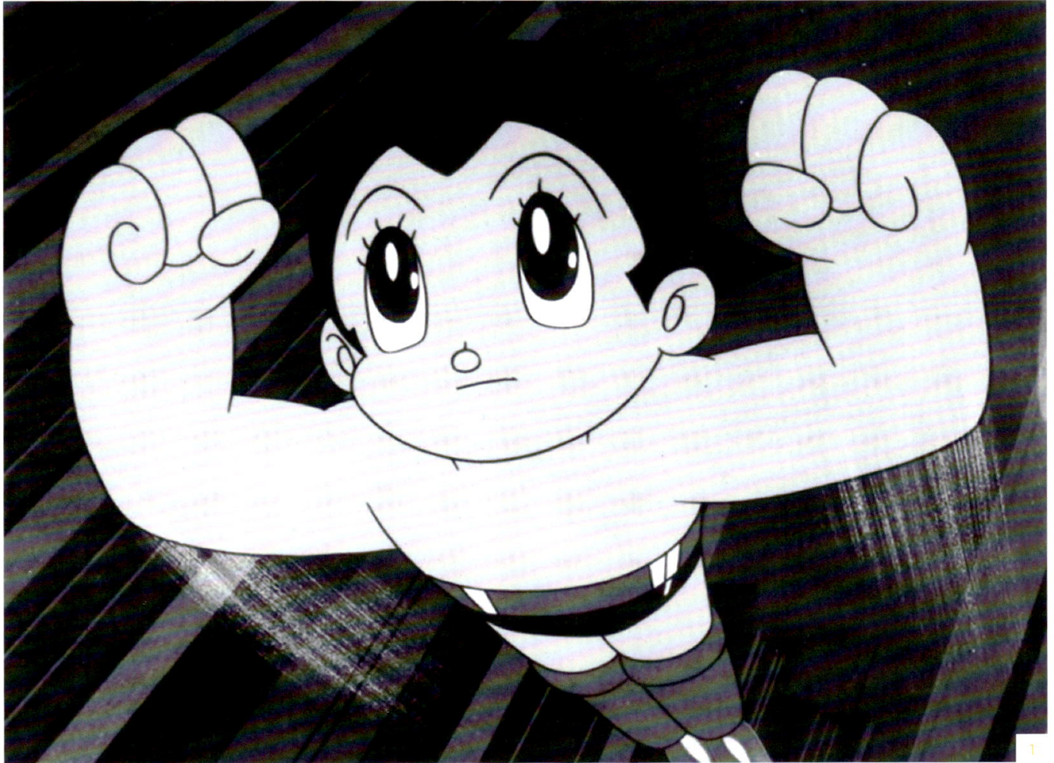

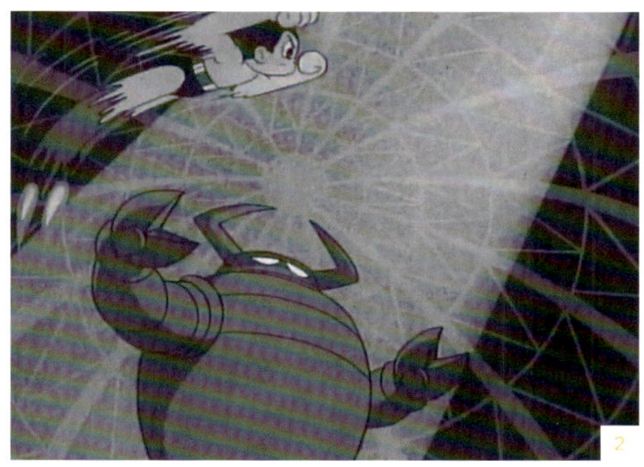

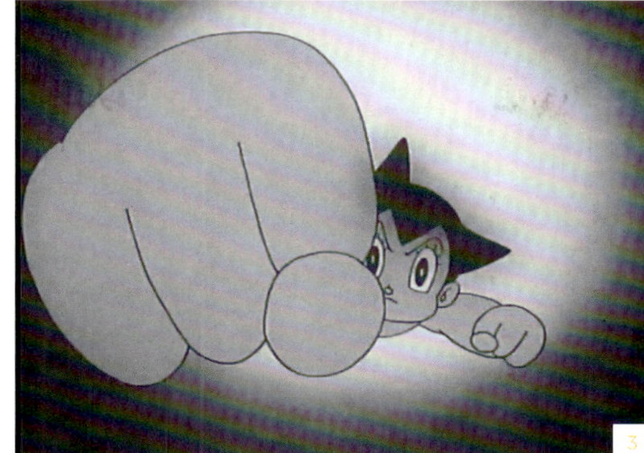

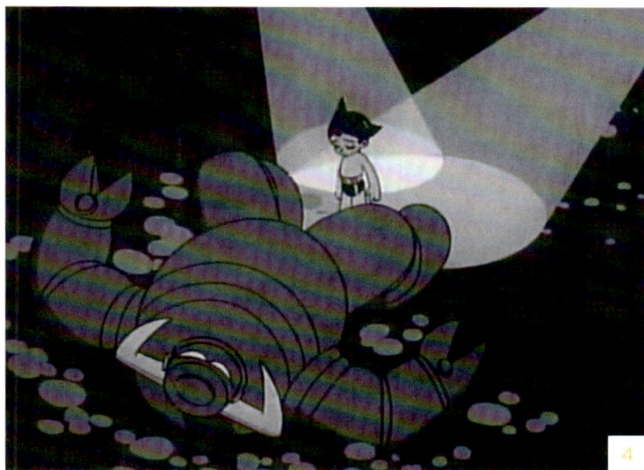

2 to 4
1962
Tetsuwan Atom
(Astro Boy)

needed to be top-quality, the technique bore fruit in just a few weeks. A rumor went around the industry that later became urban legend: it only took a thousand new cels to create an entire episode of *Astro Boy*!

Tezuka was finally putting all his experience in the audiovisual field to good use. During his years at Toei, he had learned the importance of the storyboard in production and prioritized this preliminary stage in animation. Some episodes didn't have a script at all, simply a detailed storyboard as a basis for the show. Tezuka also took advantage of a trick he learned behind the scenes of *Fushigi na Shōnen*—the importance of sound. In the live-action series, he could just add birdsong or horn sounds on a still frame of empty scenery to bring it to life and for the viewer to know that the scene was moving on. The director placed particular importance on Mushi Production's sound department, which had the complicated task of creating futuristic sound effects for his sci-fi show.

FOR A FEW YEN MORE . . .

The studio staff was quickly overwhelmed by the scale of the task. Mushi Production had no choice but to outsource; however, the workload was so great that partner studios were soon at capacity and called other providers in turn. Across the capital, thousands of animators worked for their employers during the day and when night fell, they freelanced for *Tetsuwan Atom*, which they nickname *Tetsu-ya Atom* ("Sleepless Nights Atom"). And all that labor needed to be paid for! The final cost of a twenty-six-minute episode was estimated at ¥2.5 million, or ¥100,000 per minute of animation—no one in the profession could have imagined such a low rate. Yet it was far too expensive for broadcasters.

The television economic system that was quickly set up in the early days of the "brown screen" is still in use today: an advertising and communication company (Dentsu being probably the most famous) bought a time slot from a TV channel and filled it with programming of its choice—an investment made profitable by the sale of commercials. Mannensha, which had already spent half a billion yen to reserve a weekly one-hour slot on Fuji TV, didn't want to invest the same fortune in Tezuka's series. Accountants

1962
Tetsuwan Atom
(Astro Boy)

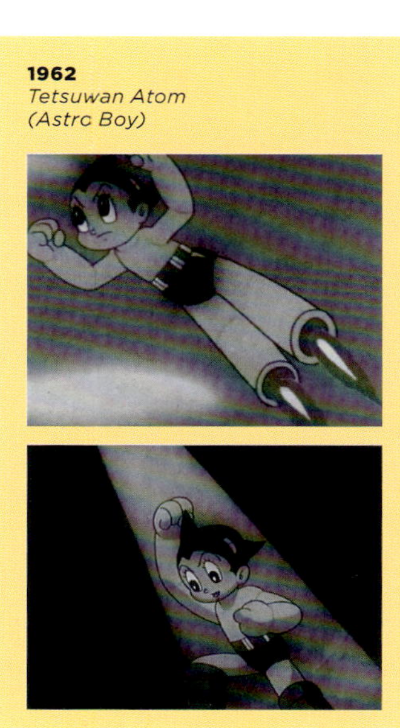

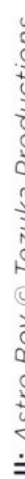

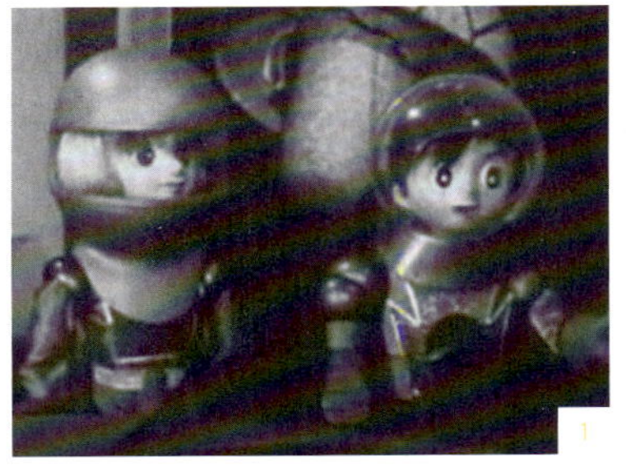

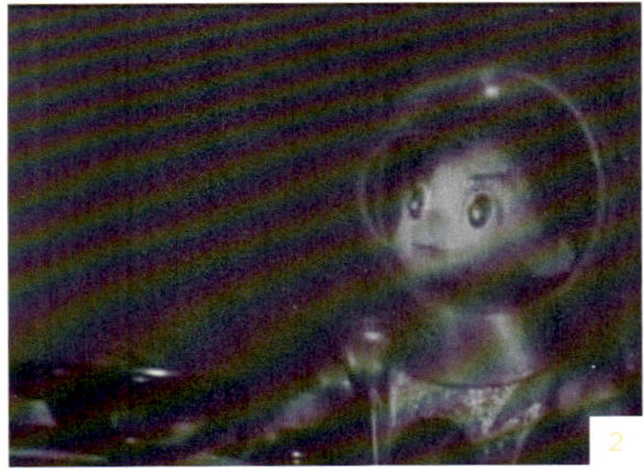

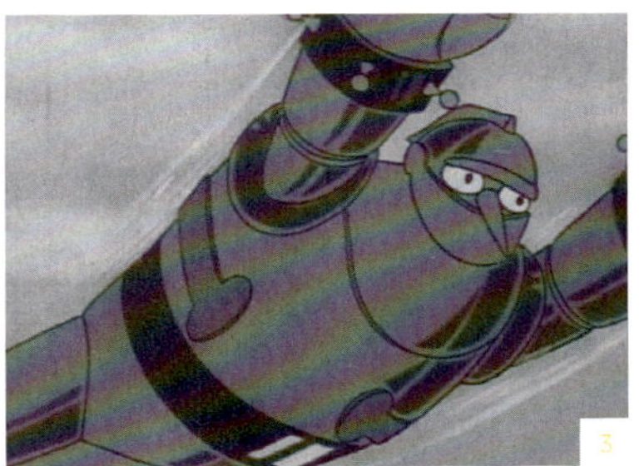

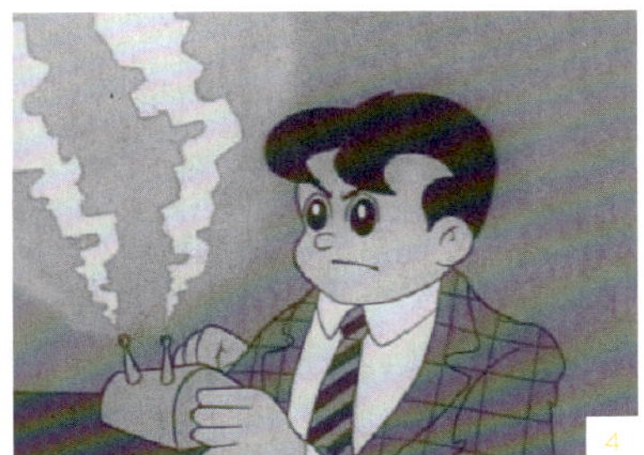

1 and 2
1963
Ginga Shōnen Tai (Galaxy Boy Troop)

3 and 4
1963
Tetsujin 28-go

based their calculations on the costs of a live children's program at the time, about ¥600,000 for a thirty-minute episode, and a tiny sum for imported American designs (after all, that art had already been paid off in its country of origin). According to them, production costs should be lower since animation only required drawings. Thus, Mannensha offered to buy each episode from Mushi Production for ¥300,000—a mere ¥10,000 per minute of animation—which was worth ten times more!

In his search for sponsors, Tezuka took advantage of a market war between confectionery companies. Because its rival Morinaga refused to support *Astro Boy*, Meiji was ready to invest in Tezuka's gamble. A meeting was held between the heads of Mushi Production, Fuji TV, Mannensha, and Meiji, foreshadowing the production committees on which the entire contemporary anime industry is based. Tezuka set the price of an episode at a sum slightly over ¥500,000. How much exactly? It's hard to say; Tezuka himself gave different amounts in future interviews. One thing was certain—at such a low price, the competition would have a hard time keeping up.

THE CATHODIC GOLD RUSH

The first episode of *Astro Boy* was broadcast on Fuji TV on January 1, 1963, with a staggering 27.4 percent audience rating. Tezuka's legitimate pride was quickly overtaken by the harsh reality. Even though he had sacrificed his copyright and minimized the shortfall through merchandise sales, Tezuka lost half his stake; by the time the credits rolled, over a million yen had been drained from a dying cash flow. There were four episodes left in stock at Mushi Production, and just enough financing for one more, even though the series was supposed to run all year long.

The answer came from the United States. The check from NBC, which bought the rights to the series under the title *Mighty Atom*, allowed Tezuka to keep going . . . at the cost of a few concessions. To broadcast his show in the United States, he needed to rework some scenes deemed too shocking for a young audience, such as an evil scientist performing surgery on animals to turn them into robots. Thanks to the foreign capital, *Astro Boy* could continue broadcasting, much to the delight of the Japanese. It lasted four years in all, with its 193rd and final episode on December 31, 1966. It was a marathon that finished off the entire Tezuka team, some literally falling from exhaustion during production! The show is forever a part of Japanese pop culture's DNA, and its song still plays at the train station in Takadanobaba, the Tokyo district where Mushi Production's headquarters were located.

Despite everything, *Astro Boy* was a financial loss, and to replenish its coffers, Mushi Production concurrently produced a show inspired by another Tezuka manga: *Ginga Shōnen Tai* (*Galaxy Boy Troop*), a puppet series heralding *Thunderbirds*. The boss didn't have enough time to supervise everything! He needed to return to his drawing board to create more manga, and therefore income, to immediately inject back into his animation company, which was leaking cash from all sides. "If manga is my wife, then animation is my mistress," the pioneer liked to recall with humor. On the other hand, he took the arrival of competition lured in by the new financing tactic much more seriously. At the end of 1963, two new contenders showed up in territory previously monopolized by Tezuka.

The first blow was all the more violent as *Tetsujin 28-go* was broadcast on the same channel, Fuji TV, starting on October 20. Adapted from Mitsuteru Yokoyama's manga, the series made a clear distinction between the gigantic, superpowerful robot, Tetsu-jin 28, and the young boy who remotely controlled it, Shotaro Kaneda, in contrast with Astro's characters, who who merged the two. This forebearer of *Goldorak* and *Akira* lasted ninety-three episodes, a success for its creator, Television Corporation of Japan (TCJ), which had thus far been producing animated commercials. Determined to keep up the momentum, TCJ also adapted the manga *Eightman*, whose first

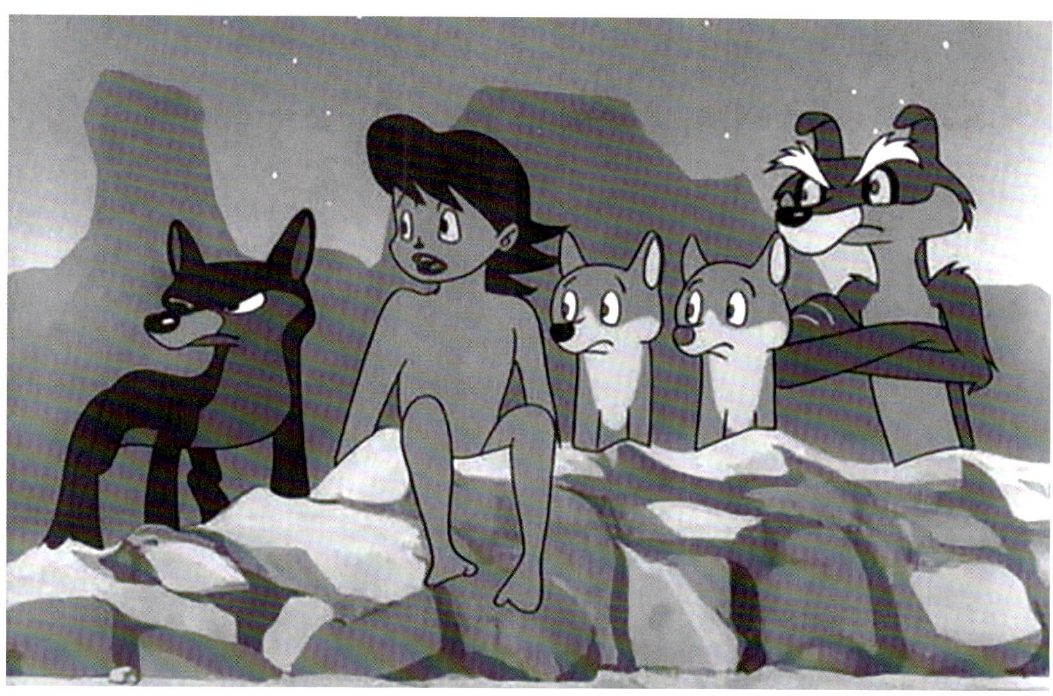

5
1963
Ōkami Shōnen Ken (Wolf Boy Ken)

episode aired on November 7 on TBS. Its cyborg hero, who recharged with energy cigarettes to fight the criminal underworld, targeted an older audience without leaving the popular sci-fi realm.

Toei studios took a different approach to the small screen. Broadcast on November 5, 1963, its series Ōkami Shōnen Ken (*Wolf Boy Ken*) played the quality card to stand out. First, in terms of content—the show, although strongly influenced by *The Jungle Book*, began as an original screenplay that did not come from a manga, unlike its competition. Next, in terms of form, it used an increased number of images per second. Toei's signature in film production, fluid animation, also needed to be in the studio's TV shows. Consequently, the eighty-six episodes of *Wolf Boy Ken* were entrusted to directors renowned for their perfectionism, including Isao Takahata. Toei also indulged in some self-promotion by showing an episode in theaters as a prelude to its December 1963 feature film *Wanwan Chūshingura*, the last one to have been storyboarded by Tezuka himself.

Nevertheless, the production company was struggling and had been dealing with union demands for the past three years as employees, especially women, were fed up with their working conditions. The salary for the same position could be double or even triple the amount depending on an employee's education or gender. As one can imagine, men, particularly single men, had the advantage. During "killer weeks," they spent sleepless nights in the studio, whereas women and married men returned home by the last train. Some high-ranking positions (animation, storyboard, direction) were even out of the question for female employees.

Beyond these gender-based inequalities, everyone was calling for the same improvements. During clandestine meetings in bars, over greasy kebabs and lukewarm beers, the movement's leaders drew up their list of demands: harmonize wages, receive dinner during all-nighters, screen dailies during working hours instead of during breaks, and so on. With Japan in the grip of violent social tensions at the start of the decade, Toei artists went on strike in 1961. They handed out pamphlets for two hours a day explaining the dark underbelly of the animation world to passersby.

A few concessions from management stemmed the crisis for a while, but it wasn't long before one big name after another abandoned the Toei ship. The grass really was greener at neighboring studios! Tezuka, ready to do anything to keep his monopoly, offered golden opportunities to Toei's resigning employees, despite his finances being in the red. A genius artist but a poor manager, he offered the young artist Rintaro double his salary to join Mushi Production. This talent drain was even more pronounced given the situation of an industry turned completely upside down by *Astro Boy*.

With the outsourcing created by the Tezuka series, animation studios had sprung up throughout the capital, all working from the same playbook: they carried out part of the work assigned to them while training their new recruits and passed the rest on to other service providers. The need for new blood was constant because, over time, exhausted animators needed to take life-saving time off. There were not enough competent workers, and studios were doing anything necessary to have the best staff possible. Fortunately for studios, the massive rural exodus taking place at the time (Tokyo's population rose from eight million in 1956 to ten million in 1963) provided them with the much-needed workforce. Headhunters used every technique they could to recruit new talent who could hypothetically keep up the unsustainable pace. Dressed to the nines, the handsome young men from each company lined up at bus terminals to seduce provincial girls who had just disembarked, taking them not to their beds but to a drawing table. But the animation bubble also attracted a host of clever characters whose talents were far removed from their salary demands—by the time they were found out, they had already made their fortunes!

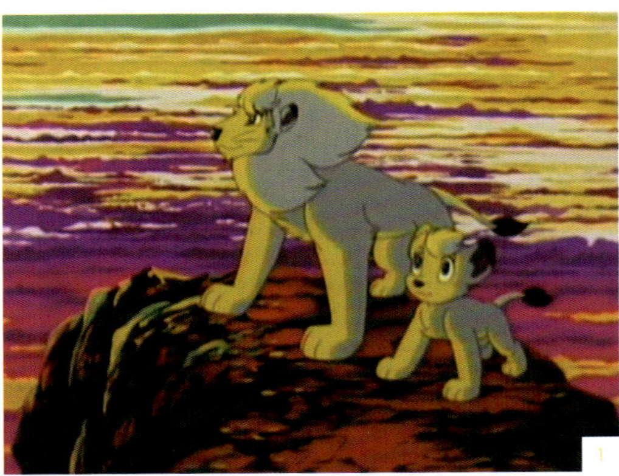

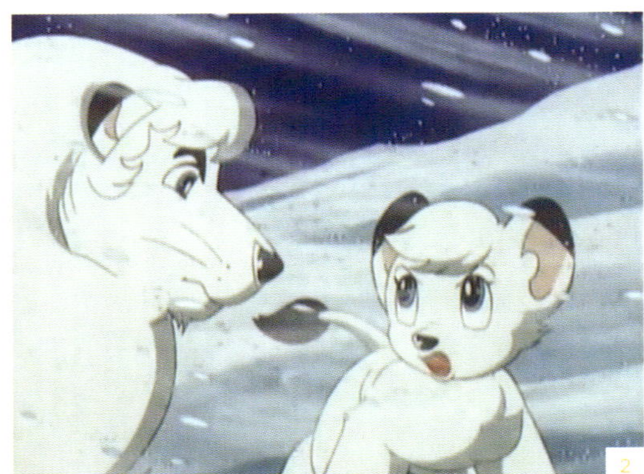

1 and 2
1950
Jungle Taitei (Kimba the White Lion)

AND THEN THERE WAS COLOR . . .

Tezuka was well aware that this fierce competition was still only in its infancy. At this rate, his productions would soon be drowned out by the masses. That was out of question for his ego! He still needed to be innovative to dominate the industry, and Tezuka was preparing his reaction in the utmost secrecy—the transition to color! Not only was the Japanese market developing, but the United States in particular, which had bought the broadcasting rights under the title *Mighty Atom*, wanted a color series.

And so, he chose his best team members for an experiment on episode 54 of *Astro Boy*. Broadcast on January 4, 1964, the episode reached an audience of 40.3 percent! Across the country, children's jaws dropped at the technical prowess, whereas professionals were pulling out their hair. The crossover episode introduced the heroes from *Number Seven*, another Tezuka manga, likely to become the studio's first color production.

The idea was quickly abandoned because the short comic could only give rise to three episodes. But above all, the American channel NBC had set its sights on broadcasting *Jungle Taitei* (*Kimba the White Lion*), an animal manga published by Tezuka between 1950 and 1954, which follows the journey of a young lion from childhood to his accession to the jungle throne. However, the advance on rights (which finally bailed out *Astro Boy*'s debts) was only paid under strict conditions. This time, American investors had read the original manga and demanded a politically correct adaptation: no Black person could play the role of the villain, no human could mistreat an animal, and so on. The biggest constraint was on the structure of the series—the episodes needed to be independent to allow for random broadcasting. To better focus on this new challenge, Mushi Production entrusted almost all of *Astro Boy*'s production to the booming market of subcontracting studios.

So much for the young lion's rite of passage! The fifty-two episodes of *Kimba the White Lion*, directed by Rintaro and broadcast on Fuji TV starting on October 6, 1965, only dealt with the lion's childhood and was a huge success in both Japan and in the United States. It is said that the series strongly inspired Disney's *The Lion King* thirty years later. Tezuka adroitly copied

Toei's methods of promoting its TV productions in movie theaters. He asked director Eiichi Yamamoto to put together the best footage for a twenty-two-minute best-of episode that was shown in cinemas before the feature film.

With *Kimba the White Lion*, Mushi Production had jumped into the ring. The advance on rights had paid off the *Astro Boy* deficit, but producing *Kimba* had generated new debt. To pay it off, the studio needed the advance on the next title, the production of which once again drained the cash flow in a never-ending cycle. Tezuka's main mistake was relying on the market in his early days as a *mangaka*, when baby boomers had flocked to his series and any related merchandise! The brief spike in birth rate was now a thing of the past, and since the number of children was limited, sales had plateaued.

The competition, momentarily caught off guard, needed to catch up technologically by switching to color, and, above all, build bridges with the United States. Some American production companies were subcontracting their animation to Japan due to its expertise in the field in response to soaring demand. One such company was Rankin/Bass (named after its founders), specializing in seasonal and holiday TV movies. Its *Rudolph the Red-Nosed Reindeer*, released in 1964, gets more profitable when rebroadcast each Christmas! Although their names don't appear in the credits (or were horribly misspelled), animators specializing in stop-motion such as Tadahito Mochinaga and his studio MOM Productions, opened the financial floodgates on the other side of the Pacific, which did not run dry for another thirty years.

The great expansion

NEW CHALLENGERS, NEW PERSPECTIVES

Created in 1966 by Mitsuteru Yokoyama, *Mahōtsukai Sally* (*Sally the Witch*) sums up these two new trends. The sitcom *Bewitched* had obviously influenced the character of Sally, princess of the Magic Kingdom who wished to stay on Earth incognito and, without warning, the series went from black and white to color in the eighteenth episode! Toei was targeting a more female audience with *Sally the Witch*, to stand out from the competition in the now-saturated boys' market. Having started out as simple service providers, many studios were now big enough to offer their own animation philosophy, turning the television landscape upside down.

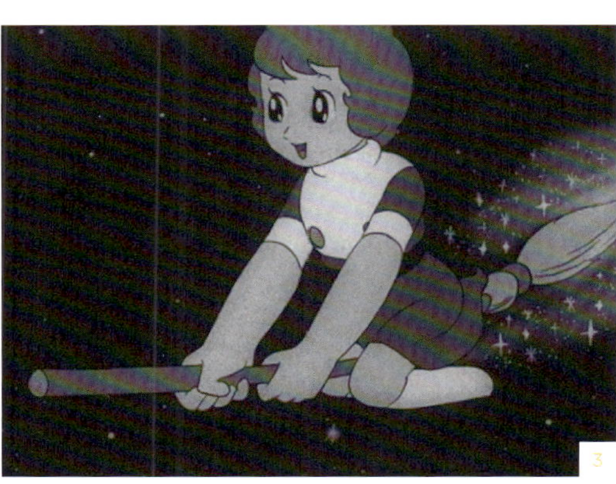

3

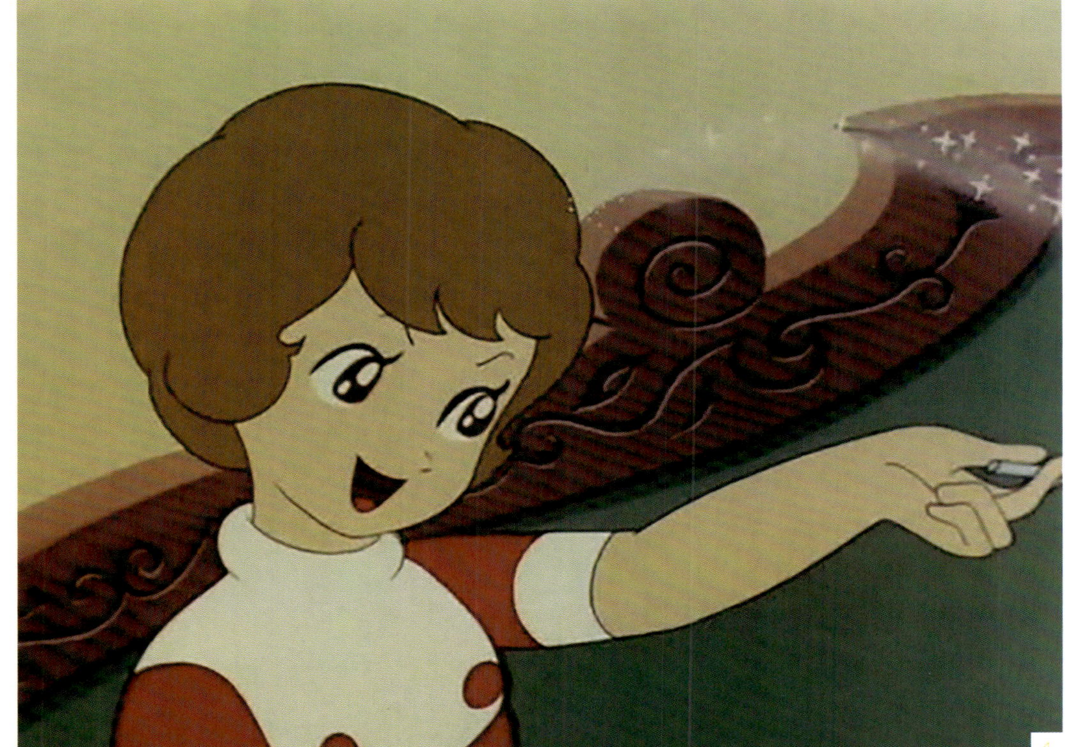

4

3 and 4

1966
Mahōtsukai Sally (Sally the Witch)

A puppeteer by training, Yutaka Fujioka was convinced that cartoon animation was close to his art and that it would be easy for him to adapt to this flourishing new market. When Fuji TV commissioned an adaptation of Tezuka's *Big X* manga in 1964 from its usual partner, TCJ had to decline the contract, already overwhelmed by *Tetsujin 28-go* and *Eightman*. Fujioka seized the opportunity and founded Tokyo Movie Shinsha (TMS) to respond to the call for tenders. The result, though technically mediocre, was a resounding flop. Because it was unthinkable to train the whole staff and fall months behind, Fujioka had no choice but to recruit experienced professionals. He did so at A Production, where he created a satellite studio for the many animators who had left Toei to adapt the manga whose rights had been reacquired by TMS. The production company needed to stand out by going beyond the realm of science fiction and into comedy! It set its sights on *mangaka* Fujiko Fujio's hit duo *Obake no Q-Taro* (1965), *Casper the Friendly Ghost*'s Japanese counterpart, and *Perman* (1967), a parody of *Superman*.

The three Yoshida brothers who worked in manga also understood how lucrative the TV business could be, in more ways than one. When they weren't under contract drawing comics based on live shows, they were selling the rights to their own manga for TV adaptations, enough so that they developed special relationships with different broadcasters over time. When Toei offered Tatsuo Yoshida, the eldest brother, a contract to adapt his manga *Uchuu Ace* (*Space Ace*), strongly inspired by *Astro Boy*, he refused flat out—he did not agree with his merchandising percentage. He and his brothers, Kenji and Toyoharu, went on to found Tatsunoko Production, a company that allowed them to exploit one license across several media, including manga, television, and merchandising.

Tatsunoko hit the jackpot in 1967 with its first color-TV production about automobile racing. With his gadget-studded cars and impossible courses, *Mach GoGoGo* became a true phenomenon with children in both Japan and America. It aired the following year in the United States as *Speed Racer*, up against Hanna-Barbera's *Wacky Races*. Whereas both series focused on outlandish races between improbable race cars, the Japanese production's more serious tone far outshone Dastardly and Muttley's comedy. *Speed Racer* was even given a psychedelic makeover by the directors of *The Matrix* in 2008, forty years later. Nevertheless, the studio chose not to capitalize on *Mach GoGoGo*, turning instead to the newest trend: comedy. Tatsunoko followed in the footsteps of TMS by creating shows for young children about the adventures of a pet monster (*Oraa Guzura Dado*, 1967) and a prehistoric man who inadvertently teleported into our time (*Dokachin*, 1968).

The origins of Studio Zero can be traced back to the mid-1950s, shortly before the advent of television sets. At that time, Osamu Tezuka was starting out in his career and had just moved to a second-rate boardinghouse in Tokyo. Young artists who worshipped this "God of Manga" came from all over the country and settled in the tiny studio apartments of Tokiwa-sō, where they stayed until the early 1960s, despite their mentor's departure. Driven by the same passion as Tezuka, his former disciples, linked by their years in a shared living space and now recognized *mangaka* themselves, also took up animation through their collective studio, Studio Zero.

They chose to adapt to the screen a comedy manga by one of the members, Fujio Akatsuka. In 1966, the *Osomatsu-kun* sextuplets were a huge hit with children, to the point of alarming their parents. Usually, comedies for young audiences contained an imaginary element—a ghost, a monster, a Neanderthal man—but this time the jokes were rooted in real life, sometimes turning to mischief, and risked inspiring young viewers to attempt these pranks. That was all it took for the Parent Teacher Association to label *Osomatsu-kun* the worst television program of the era, giving it unintended publicity and making children even more eager to watch a series forbidden by their parents.

1 to 3
1966
Osomatsu-kun

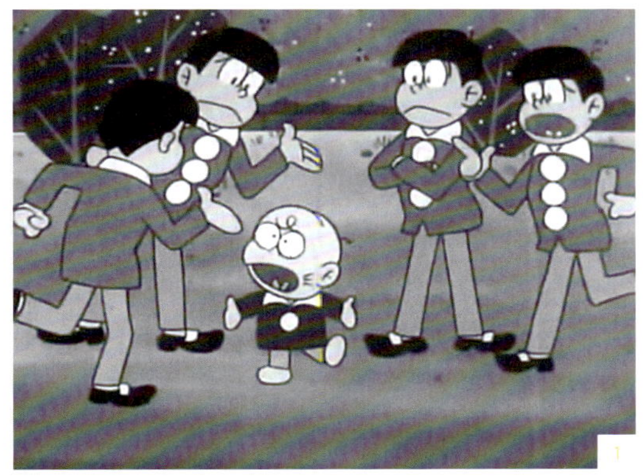
1

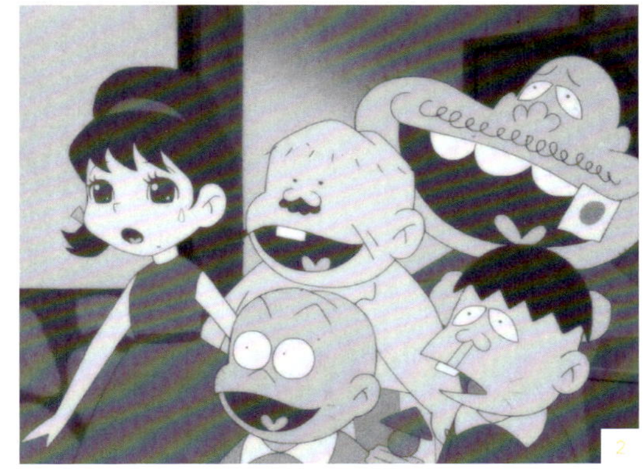
2

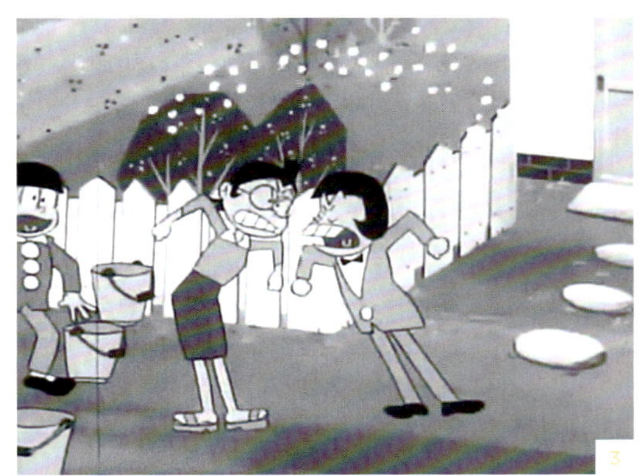
3

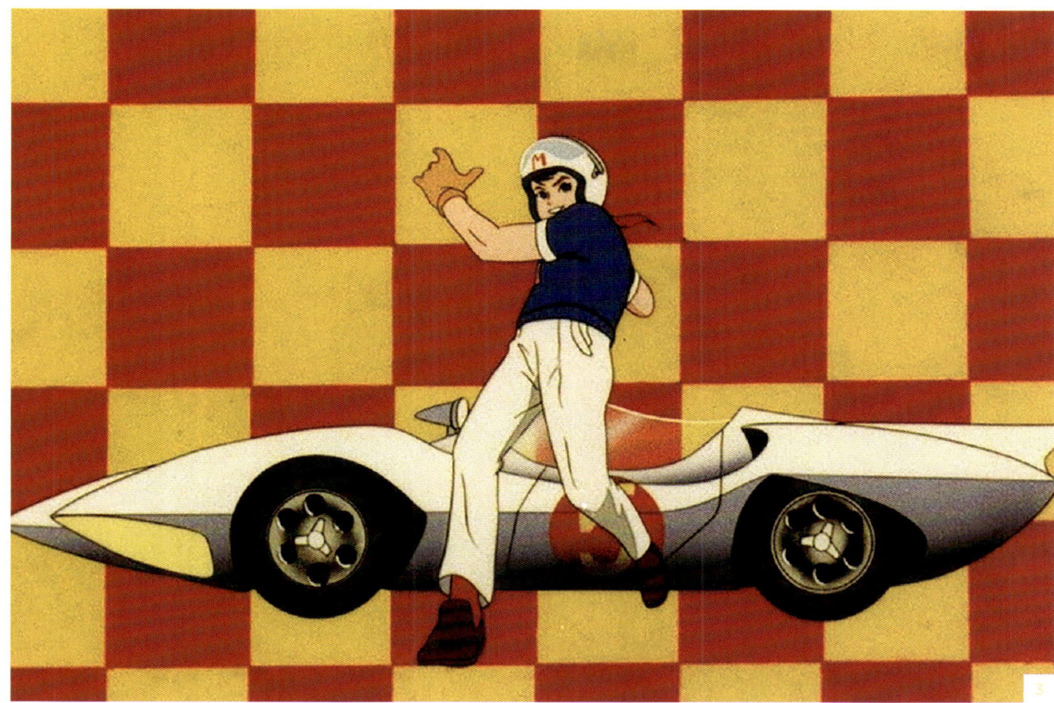

3

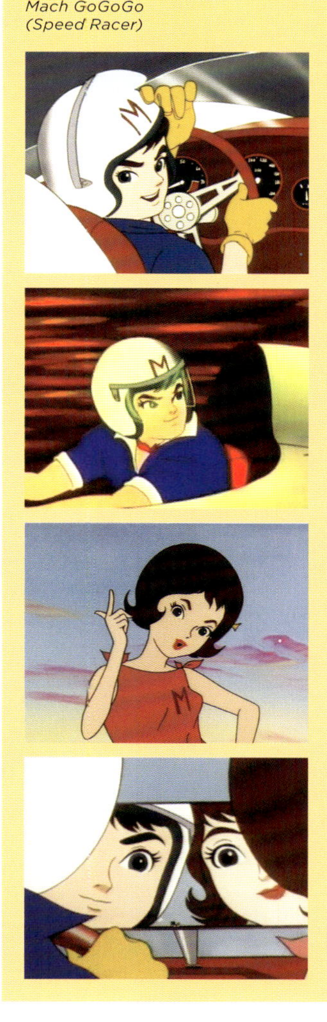

1968
Mach GoGoGo (Speed Racer)

3
1968
Mach GoGoGo (Speed Racer)

FORMER PIONEERS WERE STRUGGLING

The mastermind behind Studio Zero's creations was struggling much more—Tezuka's disastrous management on the money pits that were *Astro Boy* and *Kimba the White Lion* had put Mushi Production in the red. But beyond that, at the end of the 1960s, a new genre of manga appeared: *gekiga*. The decade had been marked by violent conflicts between a conservative government and the alliance between workers' and students' unions. The children of the 1950s were now in their twenties and no longer satisfied with the straightforward adventures in story manga; they wanted darker, social stories, anchored in the daily life of the proletariat.

Having fallen into obsolescence, Tezuka was going through the greatest artistic crisis of his career. And, so, he abandoned TV animation to focus solely on his drawing board and worked nonstop on adult manga in order to reclaim his throne. The godfather of the first weekly series in both black and white and then color had nothing left to prove on the small screen. Now that he was targeting an adult audience, he opted for film productions.

Of all the apostles of the "God of Manga" from the Tokiwa-sō boarding house, Shotaro Ishinomori was the one who followed in Tezuka's footsteps. First, for his enormous production in the manga industry—he earned the nickname "King of Manga" and set the Guinness World Record as the comic book author with the most published series, for a total of 128,000 pages (compared to Tezuka's 150,000)—but also for having established the grammar of a form of television entertainment that is still very much alive today.

Having grasped the new *gekiga* trend better than Tezuka, in 1970 he published *Skull Man*, a 100-page story whose main character was probably the first antihero in manga history, ready to sacrifice innocent people in his thirst for revenge on his parents' killers. At Toei's request, he toned down his basic material to create *Kamen Rider*, whose motorcycle hero fights against the terrorist group Shocker who had turned him into a cyborg. Debuted in 1971, the live-action series generated thirty sequels over the next half century and is still popular today.

Tokusatsu (special effects), a trend that appeared with *Ultraman* in 1966, offered Ishinomori a new field of expression. In 1975, he introduced a new subgenre, the *super sentai*, in which five fighters in different-colored outfits fight against evil using vehicles that combined to form a giant robot in *Himitsu Sentai Gorenger*, the illustrious ancestor of the *Power Rangers*. The licenses were constantly renewed due to a well-honed production system (a different monster every week, experienced stuntmen from action films, and so on), which allowed Toei to regain its footing after its animation department's talent had walked out.

The real tour de force of the King of Manga went completely unnoticed in the eyes of the general public: reconciling the animation industry's oldest enemies! Started in 1966, Ishinomori's manga *Sabu to Ichi Torimono Hikae* (*Sabu and Ichi's Detective Stories*) tells the tales of a young detective's police investigations accompanied by a blind master swordsman, which became a TV series coproduced by Toei and Mushi in 1968. Studio Zero, of which Ishinomori was one of the cofounders, served as neutral ground for producing the fifty-two episodes under the direction of none other than Rintaro, one of the leaders of the 1961 Toei strike.

Grateful to Ishinomori, Toei decided to create an animated adaptation of his *Cyborg 009* series, whose heroes with different skills and nationalities offered a more complex subplot than ever before. They tested the waters first with two feature films in 1968. The production company's newest television series was *GeGeGe no Kitarō*, a horror-comedy featuring *yōkai*, creatures from Japanese folklore. Launched in January 1968, the series based on Shigeru Mizuki's manga sparked sequels and remakes for the next fifty years, all sharing the same theme song, a melody and lyrics familiar to all generations of Japanese people.

AUDIO AND VISUAL

Following Tezuka's *Astro Boy* example, studios attached great importance to sound when producing an animated series. There was an economic argument in addition to the technical advantages because a theme song quickly brought in additional income. First introduced in 1948, microgroove technology was enhanced by stereophonic sound at the end of the decade. Only wealthy music-lovers could regularly buy new records to play on their expensive stereos, like Tezuka, who turned the volume up to max and played the role of the DJ so the Mushi Production team could work to music.

Referred to as a **sonosheet** in Japan, the flexi disc is, as its name suggests, a flexible vinyl record of lower quality (and above all, lower cost) than the 33 rpm, requiring only a rigid support to be added to the turntable. Founded in 1959, the daily *Asahi Shimbun*'s subsidiary, Asahi Sonopress, added a flexi disc to its monthly magazine *Sonorama*, featuring current news, analyses of social issues, and detective stories. With the emergence of television, Asahi Sonopress diversified its product range, offering the theme songs of animated and *tokusatsu* series in magazines for younger readers.

Competition swooped in to fill this unexpected niche, but despite the significant increase in animated productions, the selection of songs was still limited. Soon, all sound magazines featured almost identical playlists on their bonus sonosheets. In 1966, Asahi Sonopress began working in hard vinyl and renamed itself Asahi Sonorama, after its flagship magazine. The investment enabled the company to survive the crisis that hit a market too quickly saturated—now adorned with colorful labels, the sonosheets, renamed punch sheets, were recorded in stereo. On the other hand, the disappearance of the children's book and record market proved fatal to the company in the 1980s.

As intense as it was ephemeral, the sonosheet fad created a new industry: *anison*, a portmanteau of "anime" and "song." The industry's greatest representative, Ichirou Mizuki, made his debut in 1971. When he created the opening song for *Genshi Shōnen Ryu* (*Ryu, the Cave Boy*), the twenty-three-year-old didn't realize he was recording the first theme song in a career of over 1,200! During the 1970s, his was a key name in major productions, as was Mitsuko Horie's, a singer who made her debut with the *Kurenai Sanshirō* (*Judo Boy*) theme in 1969, when she was only

1968
GeGeGe no Kitarō

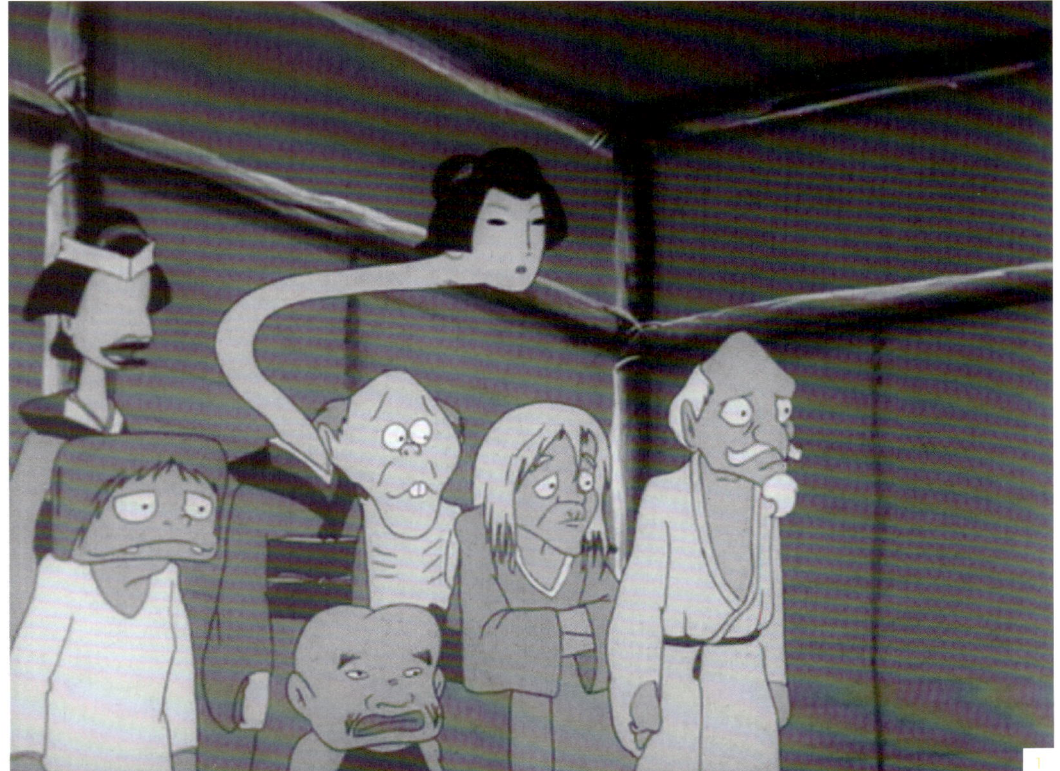

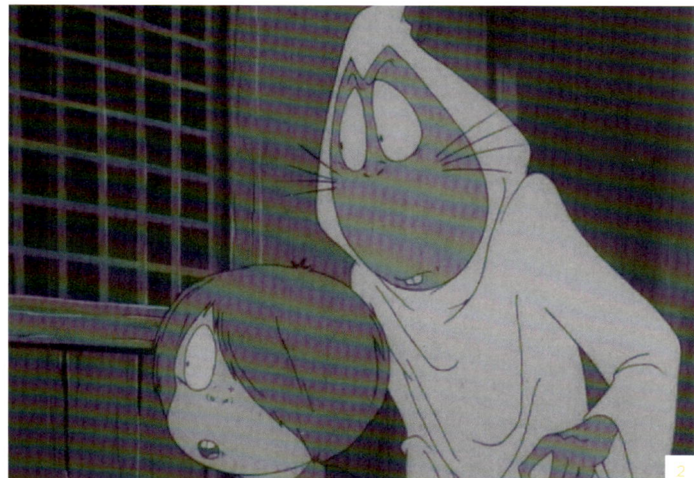

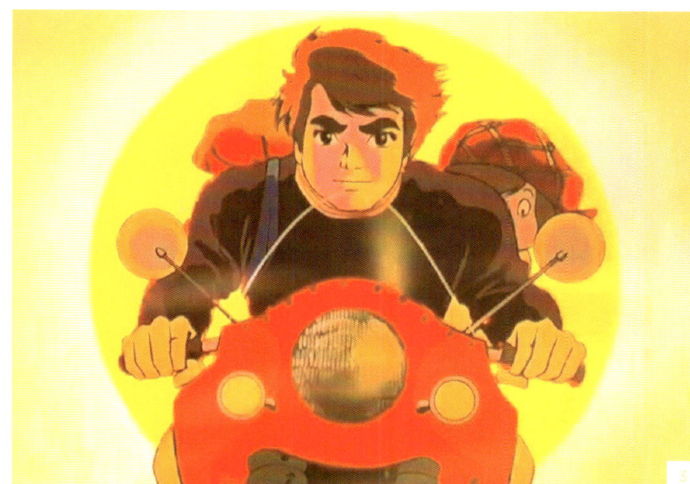

2
1968
GeGeGe no Kitarō

3
1969
Kurenai Sanshirō (Judo Boy)

twelve years old. The duo was nicknamed the "King and Queen of *Anison*."

Other voices would become familiar to viewers—without actors to voice their dialogues, animated characters would have stayed desperately silent! In the beginning, with no original programming, the channels broadcast mostly American live-action or animated series subtitled in Japanese. Held back by tacit agreements with their production companies, cinema and television actors couldn't dub these broadcasts!

The channels turned to theater actors (especially of the *rakugo* genre) and radio actors, whose voices had become essential. The first real star in the profession, Nachi Nozawa (the voice actor to dub Alain Delon, Robert Redford, and Bruce Willis), credited in *Astro Boy* and *Wolf Boy Ken*, was the recognizable voice in the main productions of the 1960s. All these actors, who had not foreseen this career change, gave rise to an industry that came into its own at the end of the 1970s.

THE SPORTS BOOM

After venturing out of science fiction, TMS continued exploring new avenues in 1968 with *Kyojin no Hoshi* (*Star of the Giants*), a baseball manga written by Ikki Kajiwara and illustrated by Noboru Kawasaki. The comic, written two years earlier, narrates the journey of Hyuma, a young pitcher dreaming of becoming as famous as his father, whose career was interrupted by an injury during World War II. With his Spartan training under the aegis of an inflexible master, the series recaptures the martial and virile spirit of the warrior's way, transcending personal investment to victory.

Father and son reunite in the anime, which features enhanced actions never seen before thanks to the innovative effects used by director Tadao Nagahama. The viewer follows the ball as it visually changes from the high-speed throw all the way to the bat, sees brutal flashbacks that prolong the suspense at crucial moments, and hears sound effects punctuate the climax of the action. In fact, an entire twenty-five-minute episode was devoted to just one pitch resulting in a home run, an action that lasts a minute at most in real life; it was a lesson in time dilation that would be found in the majority of boys' shows to come.

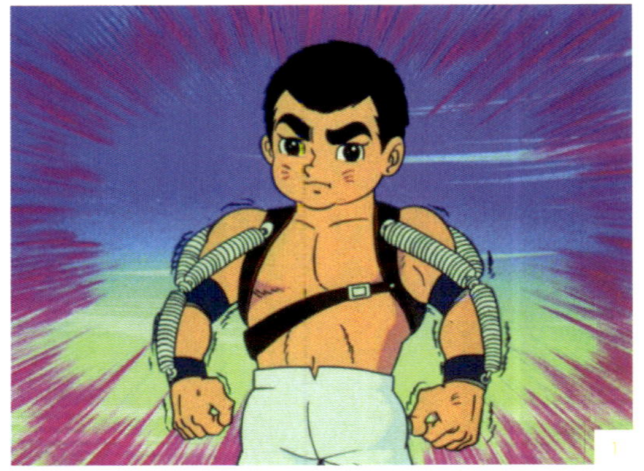

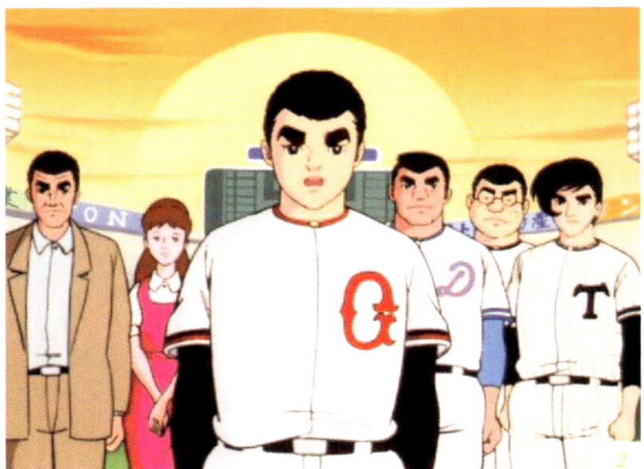

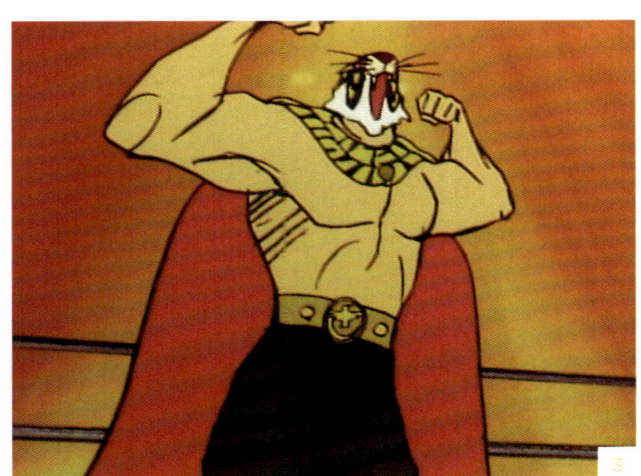

1 and 2
1968
Kyojin no Hoshi (Star of the Giants)

3
1969
Tiger Mask

TMS continued in this direction at the end of 1969. While Toei was offering the female audience a new **magical girl** with *Himitsu no Akko-chan*, TMS was giving them a sports anime, *Attack No. 1*, inspired by the Japanese volleyball players at the 1968 Olympics who took home the silver medal. Here again the message was stretching beyond one's limits, but it emphasized the team aspect more than *Star of the Giants*.

Toei jumped into the ring in 1969 with *Tiger Mask*, capitalizing on the popularity of wrestling, which had been a hit since wrestler Rikodōzan's creation of an official league fifteen years earlier. Hiding his identity behind a tiger mask in the ring, Naoto Date fights against a villainous wrestling organization in epic matches where forced perspective and crosshatched shading accentuated realistic armlocks, throws, and other choke holds. This aesthetic evolution forced Toei to sacrifice its signature fluid animation for the first time and follow the criteria for limited animation, focusing on the impact of key poses.

Like *Star of the Giants*, *Tiger Mask* was also adapted from an Ikki Kajiwara manga, and the series owed its success to its societal aspect (the hero finances the orphanage where he grew up with his winnings), in line with the growing popularity of *gekiga*. With two levels of interpretation, young children liked *Tiger Mask* for its intense fight scenes as much as teenagers enjoyed the hero's guiding principles. Multiple generations happily came together around the turntable to listen to the soundtrack by Shunsuke Kikuchi. The composer would go on to become inextricably linked to Toei's epic hits, from *Goldorak* to *Dragon Ball*.

Tatsunoko went in the same direction with *Kurenai Sanshirō* (*Judo Boy*), a 1969 adaptation of the manga by Ippei Kuri, Toyoharu Yoshida's pen name. This time, the hero called upon a typical Japanese martial art in pursuit of his father's one-eyed assassin. Although jujitsu was central to the series (guaranteeing a weekly fight scene), *Judo Boy* was more action-oriented, as seen through his motorcycle chases, a vehicle that was coming back into favor in Japan. The series also attracted two audiences: children, who saw themselves in Kenbo, an orphan boy sidekick accompanying the hero with his dog; and older viewers who dreamed of knocking their adversaries to the ground with a well-placed *atemi* blow before strolling into the setting sun.

On its last legs after its failed films, Mushi Production had no choice but to jump on the bandwagon and adapted a manga scripted by Ikki Kajiwara. Illustrated by Tetsuya Chiba since 1968, *Ashita no Joe* tells the tale of a street orphan, Joe Yabuki, who rises to the boxing ring from the Tokyo's dark underbelly, against the backdrop of riots that had been stirring the capital for almost ten years. Osamu Tezuka's young protégé had been working at Mushi Production since 1963, directing his first film, *Ashita no Joe*, in 1970, at just twenty-seven years old. Far from the simplicity of *Astro Boy*, *Ashita no Joe* marked the beginning of a major career in animation's history, but especially in Mushi Production's swan song…

ANIMATION FOR ALL: REACHING A WIDER AUDIENCE

In the early 1970s, the anime market expanded further and began breaking into other categories, creating a show to meet the expectations of each member of the Japanese model family. Intended for the adult male audience, the picaresque adventures of *Lupin III* were produced in 1971 at A Productions for TMS, with Hayao Miyazaki and Isao Takahata directing half of the episodes. The unofficial grandson of Maurice Leblanc's famous burglar delighted viewers with deception, chase scenes, shootouts, and femmes fatales.

At Toei, Go Nagai was also evoking viewers' Eros and Thanatos. The young, prolific artist had been shaking up the manga industry since 1968 by exploring new genres. Inspired by Dante, the gothic horror *Devilman* was toned down for its broadcast in 1972 but was still a milestone in fantasy anime. The following year, *Cutie Honey*, his flirtatious reinterpretation of the magical girl story, playfully called to Eros right from the start with its theme song: "She's a fashionable girl with a nice little bum."

Mothers, on the other hand, wouldn't miss their Sunday episode of *Sazae-san* for anything in the world! She was an incarnation of the typical Japanese woman created by Machiko Hasegawa, whose *yonkoma* (four-panel comics) inspired by daily life appeared in *The Asahi Shimbun* newspaper between 1946 and 1974. The humorous critique of postwar society became a chronicle of Japan's booming economy when it appeared on television on October 5, 1969. Since then, the TCJ series has been broadcast weekly on Fuji TV with more than 7,800 episodes—a world record and proof of Sazae's popularity.

Going even further, the dim-witted, easygoing father in *Tensai Bakabon*, forefather of Homer Simpson, desecrated the husband's authority. Produced in 1971 at TMS, this scathing satire about Japanese daily life was taken from a manga by Fujio Akatsuka; the same author parents decried five years earlier for *Osomatsu-kun* now made them scream with laughter! Under the guise of humor, the two series, glorifying the housewife and ridiculing the working husband, paved the way for upcoming feminist titles.

Children had their animal series, which didn't necessarily mean a happy ending. Many tears were shed in 1970 for the orphan honeybee Hatchi searching for his mother in *Konchu Monogatari: Minashigo Hutch* (*The Adventures of Hutch the Honeybee*),

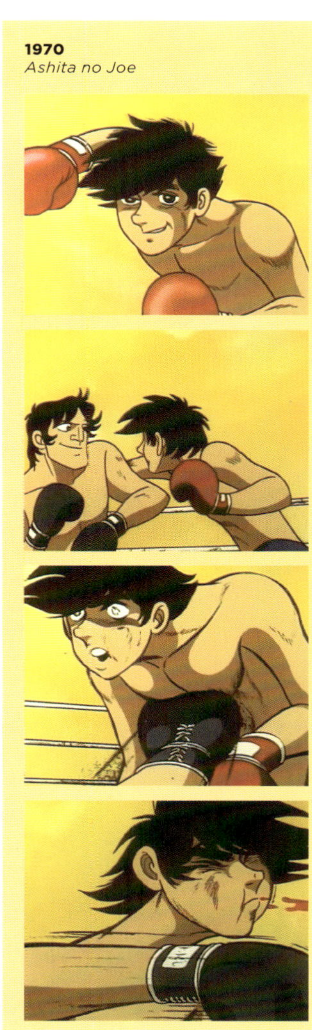

1970
Ashita no Joe

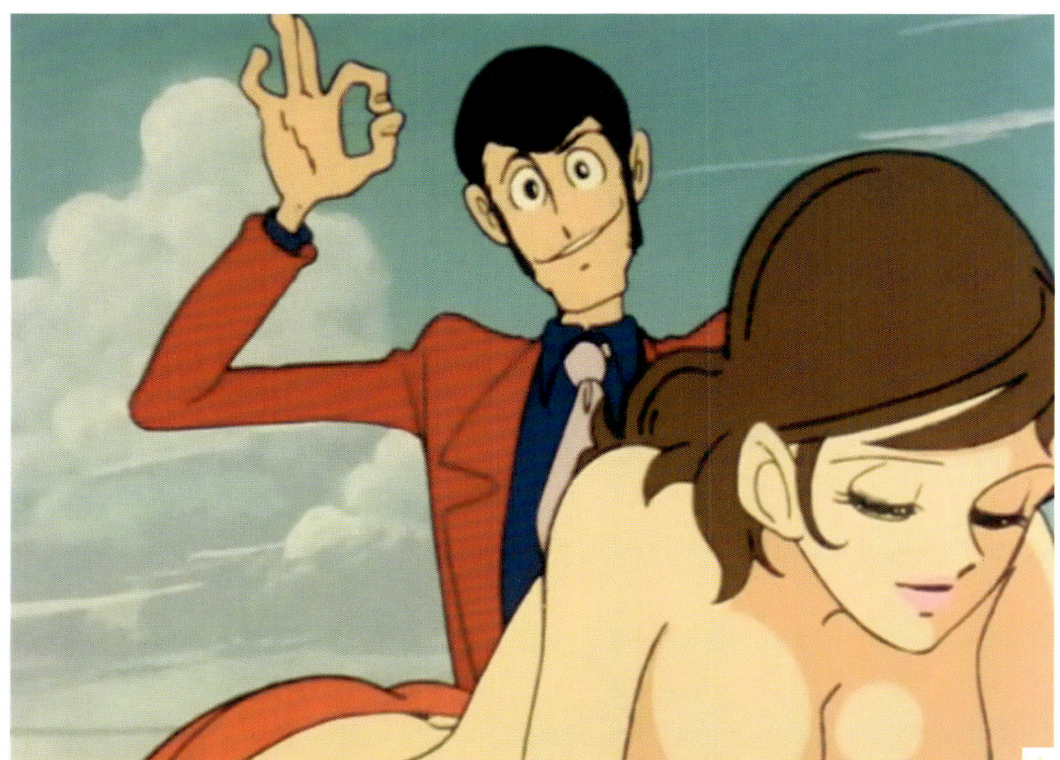

4
—
1971
Lupin III

1973
Cutie Honey

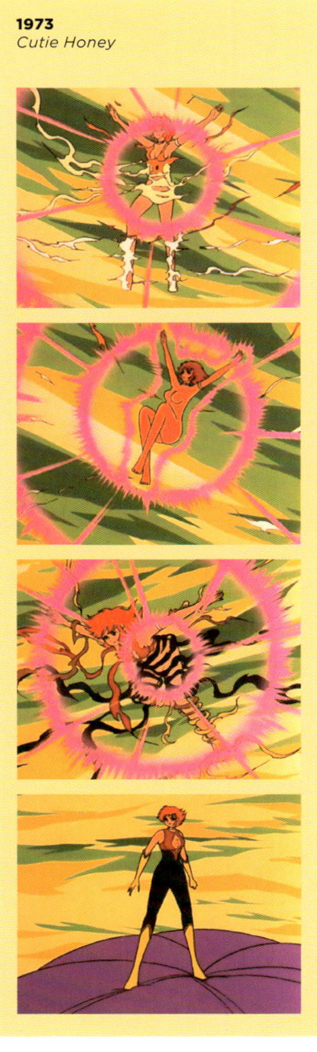

1
1969
Sazae-san

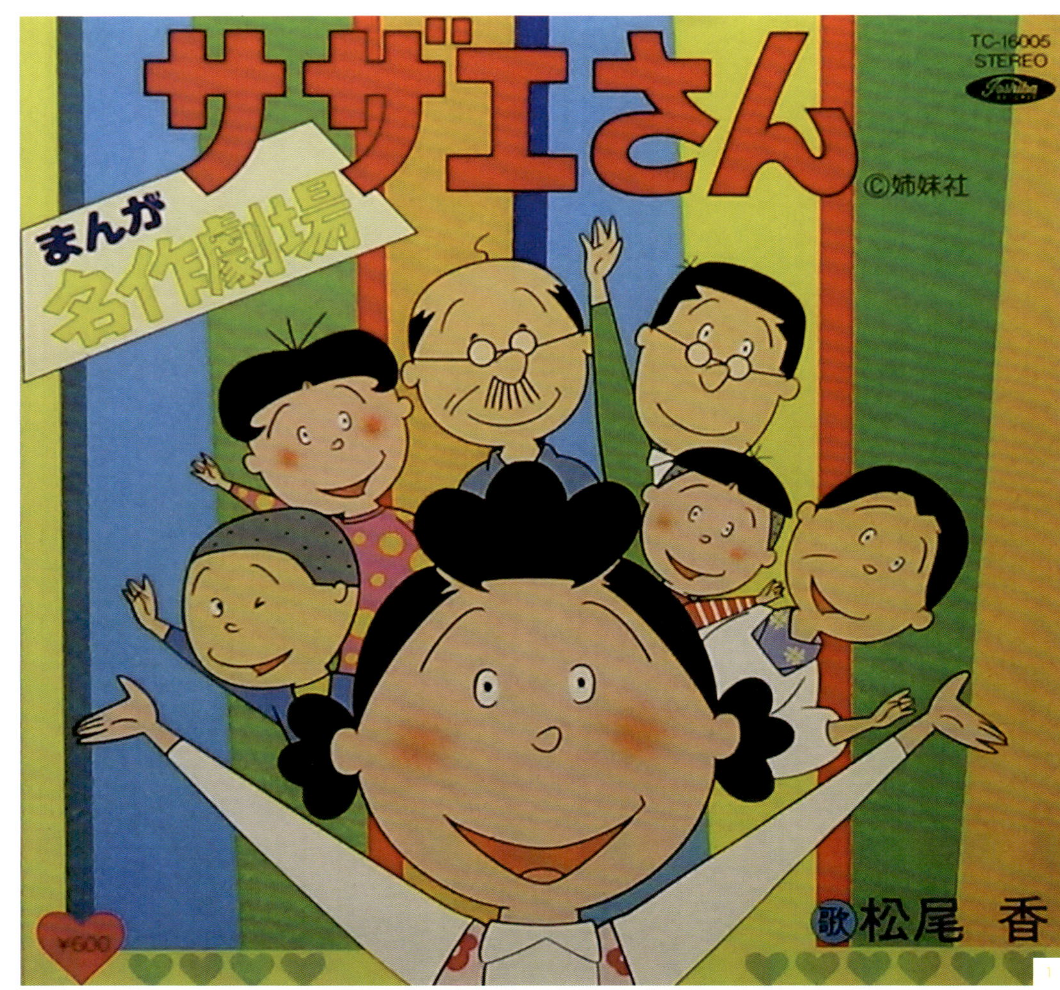

and in 1973, when the frog *Demetan Croaker* narrowly escaped predators. In addition to these two original titles, Tatsunoko also produced a five-episode version of *Pinocchio* in 1972 to keep its grip on the children's audience it had won over with comedies in the late 1960s.

The gentler countryside adventures of *Yama Nezumi Rokki Chakku* (*Fables of the Green Forest*) were adapted from children's novels by Zuiyo Eizo studio. However, drawing on children's literature, which would be a breeding ground for the young studio founded in 1969, was not without risk. Moomin, the Finnish novel heroes, were now the part of a cross-border dispute. For daring to change one of the character's names in 1969, TMS was stripped of the production rights, subsequently taken over by Mushi Production, which survived a little longer with a new version in 1972.

STABILIZING THE TARGET AUDIENCE

This expansion beyond the target audience (eight-to fifteen-year-olds) can be explained by the democratization of television, but it also reflects the evolution of the manga market, which had been booming for the past decade. The links between magazines and TV, which had been multiplying and diversifying steadily throughout the 1960s, underwent a sudden mutation that began at its roots, with series aimed at young boys.

Since 1959, boys had had the choice between two weekly magazines for reading about their heroes' adventures: *Weekly Shōnen Sunday* (Shogakukan) and *Weekly Shōnen Magazine* (Kodansha). The arrival in 1968 of Shueisha's *Shōnen Jump* shook things up. Young, dynamic, and provocative, it quickly encroached on the territory of its outdated predecessors. Go Nagai was one of the drivers of this success and stood out by crossing the line of decency;

his manga *Harenchi Gakuen* (*Shameless School**) was one of the PTA's first targets, along with *Osomatsu-kun*. Previously known for unscrupulously integrating sex and violence into his work (*Devilman* and *Cutie Honey*), Go Nagai became the father of a new genre: the super robot. In *Mazinger Z*, the hero pilots his robot from the inside, shouting the name of each attack that the metal giant uses on his opponent in a man-machine fusion yet unseen in manga or on TV. Despite its repetitive nature, Toei's 1972 series won over young viewers and generated huge amounts of merchandising. This fruitful partnership marked the start of a long collaboration between the animation company and Shueisha, which would provide Toei with its biggest franchise rights in the coming years, from *Dragon Ball* to *One Piece*.

Instead of a total revolution like *Mazinger Z*, Tatsunoko chose to recycle the successful ingredients of the *tokusatsu* series to jump back into the race: five archetypal heroes (the young leader, the bad boy, the girl, the strong one, the brain), each with their own vehicle (more merchandising!), who face the "monster of the week." The science ninja team in *Kagaku Ninjatai Gatchaman* would leave the small screen in 1974 after only 105 episodes. That same year saw the beginning of a founding myth, *Uchū Senkan Yamato* (*Space Battleship Yamato*), the space epic about a ship named after the powerful Japanese battleship from World War II. The series crystallized Japan's state of mind, which had returned to its glorious past twenty years after the American occupation, while also projecting into the future with the emergence

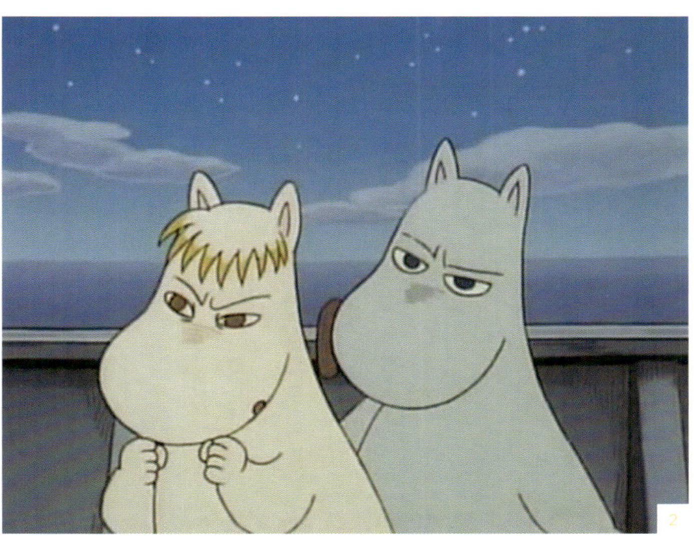

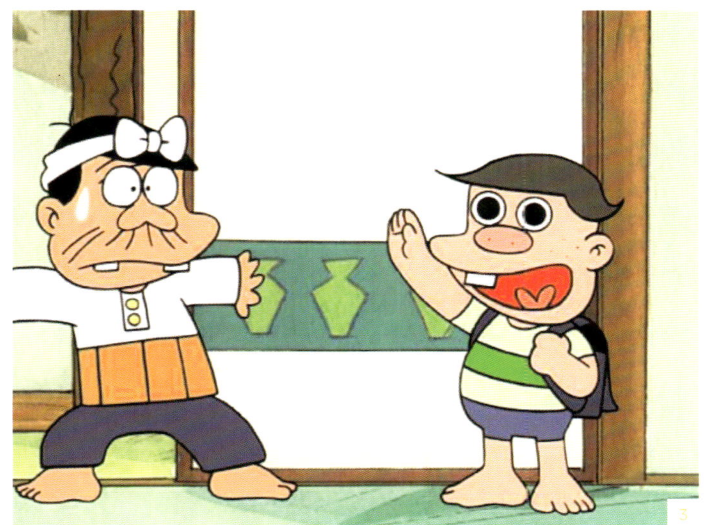

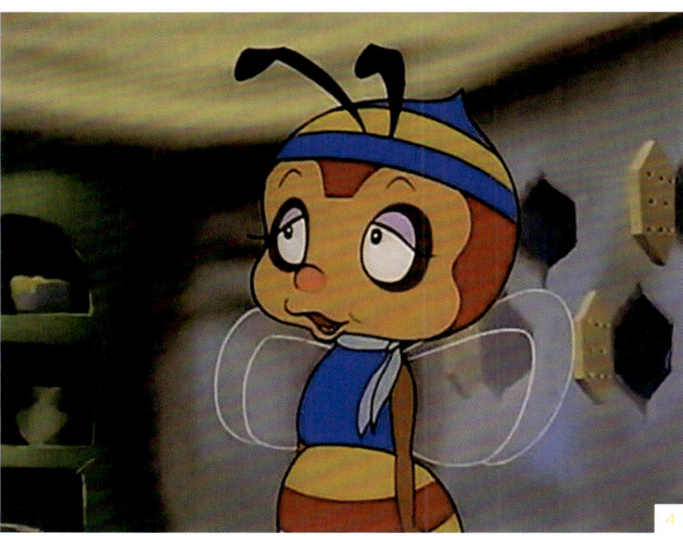

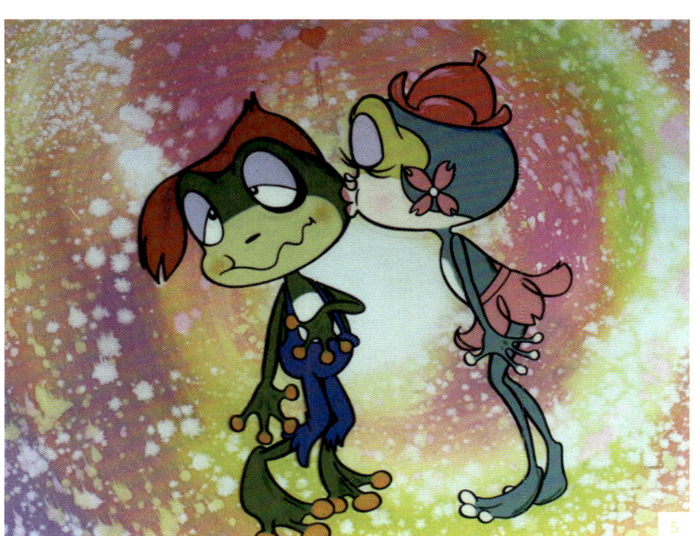

2
—
1969
Tanoshii Moomin Ikka (Moomin)

3
—
1971
Tensai Bakabon

4
—
1970
Konchu Monogatari: Minashigo Hutch (The Adventures of Hutch the Honeybee)

5
—
1973
Kerokko Demetan (Demetan Croaker, the Boy Frog)

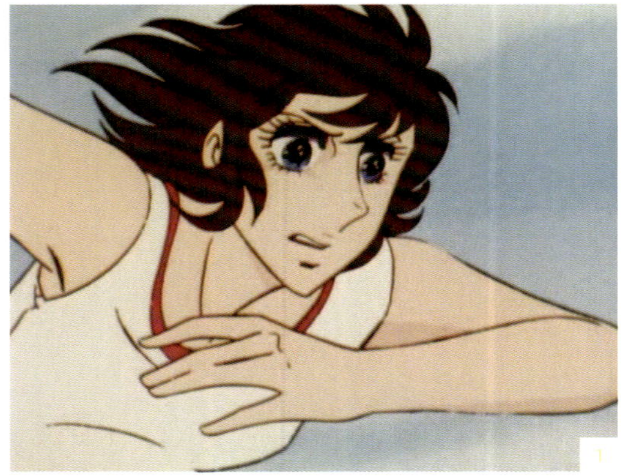

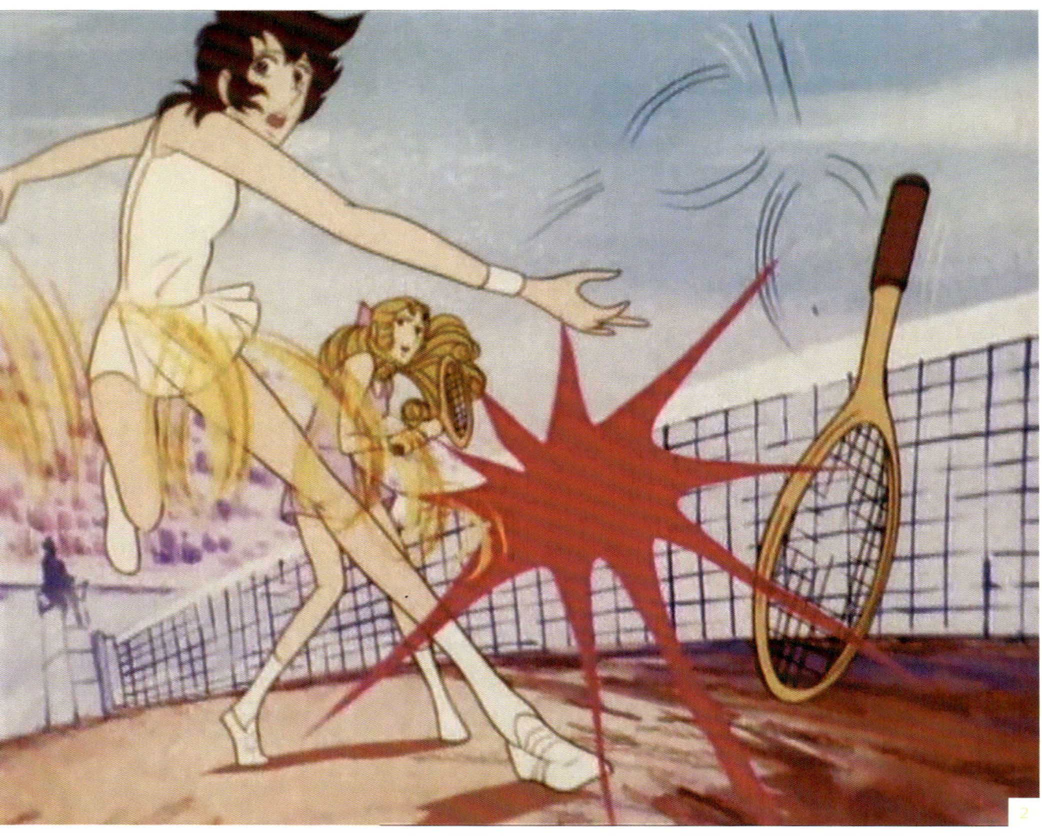

1 to 3
1973
Ace o Nerae!
(Aim for the Ace!)

of microprocessors, the spearhead of its economy for years to come. After falling out of favor for a short time, science fiction was bringing schoolboys back together in front of the TV.

LEARNING TO TALK TO GIRLS

Girls, on the other hand, were not getting the same creative new shows. Production companies were far from neglecting this lucrative market, but mainly for the merchandising revenue generated by magical girl series (Toei's specialty) like *Mahōtsukai Chappy* in 1972 and *Majokko Megu-chan* (*Meg the Witch*) in 1974. They also had their own sports series, like the thrilling *Ace o Nerae!* (*Aim for the Ace!*) directed in 1973 by Osamu Dezaki, former protégé of Tezuka, who left for TMS. Despite their starry eyes and lanky appearance, the show's tennis players were as passionately invested in their matches as their male counterparts.

Anime for girls was really just a gendered reflection of the universal themes already present in titles for boys, like transforming into superheroes or surpassing one's limits. Studios accustomed to dipping into *shōnen* manga (manga for boys) for content did not have the same diversity in *shōjo* manga (manga for girls), thus far created mainly by

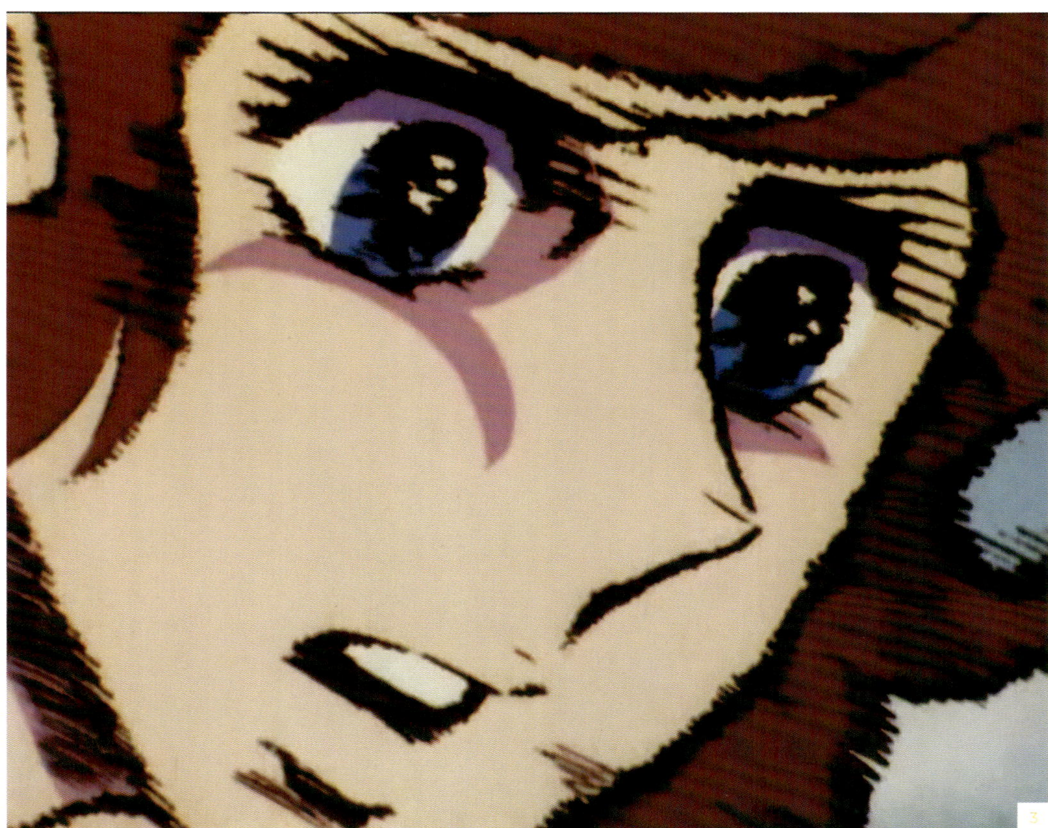

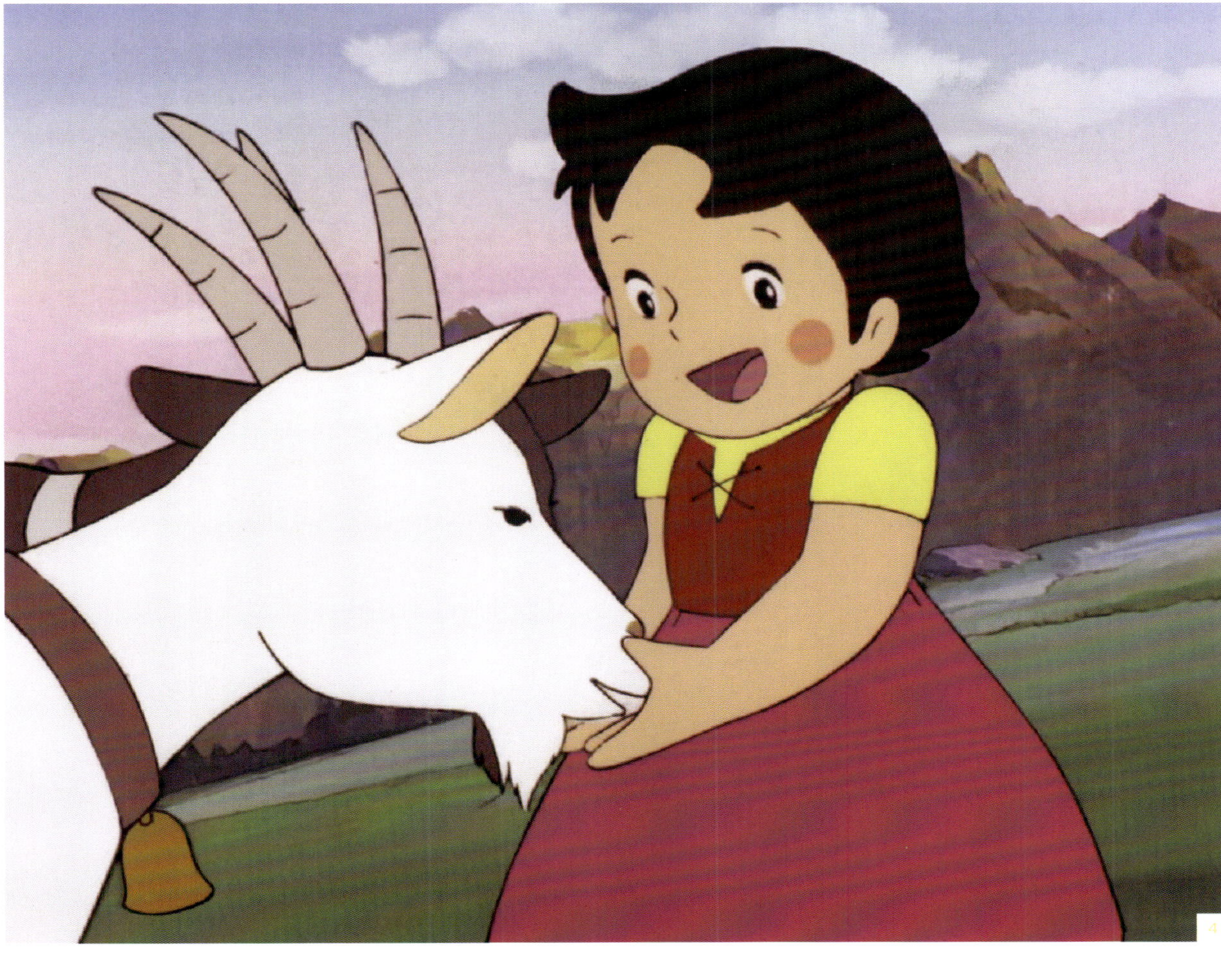

1974
Alps no shōjo Heidi
(Heidi, Girl of the Alps)

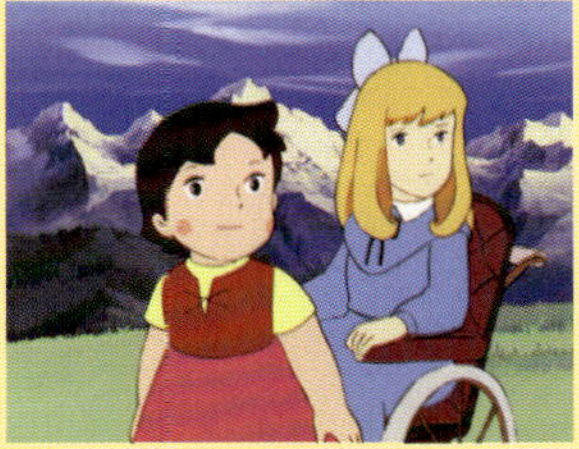

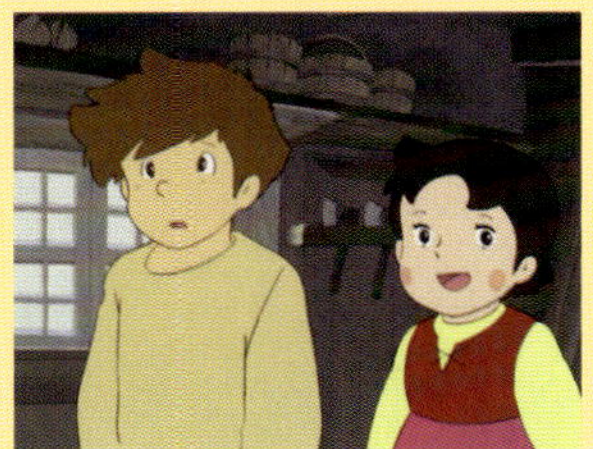

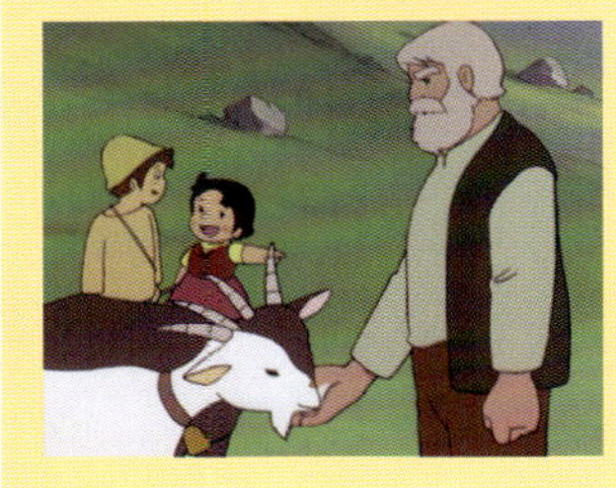

4
—
1974
Alps no shōjo Heidi (Heidi, Girl of the Alps)

men. The feminization of the profession expanded in the early 1970s, tackling themes their female readers dreamed of, but production companies never adapted, such as school romance. As for *shōnen-ai*, a subgenre focused on budding gay love between androgynous young men, it was still inconceivable to bring it to the screen.

These distinct markets also influenced the content of stories for boys, where female characters were present to make the male characters look good, reduced to damsels in distress, or missing altogether. This made it difficult for girls to identify with animated series for boys. Although the series was not specifically intended for girls, they wholeheartedly welcomed in 1974 *Alps no shōjo Heidi* (*Heidi, Girl of the Alps*), a young girl they could identify with.

The ratings duel between *Heidi* and *Yamato* (both titles peaked at 15 percent) symbolized the two opposing directions that would define the anime market for the decade to come. A market finally freed from Tezuka's shadow after the bankruptcy of Mushi Production in 1973. Following the studio's demise, the former employees set out to create their own companies—new, better-organized animation machines designed for an industry that was finally finding its cruising speed.

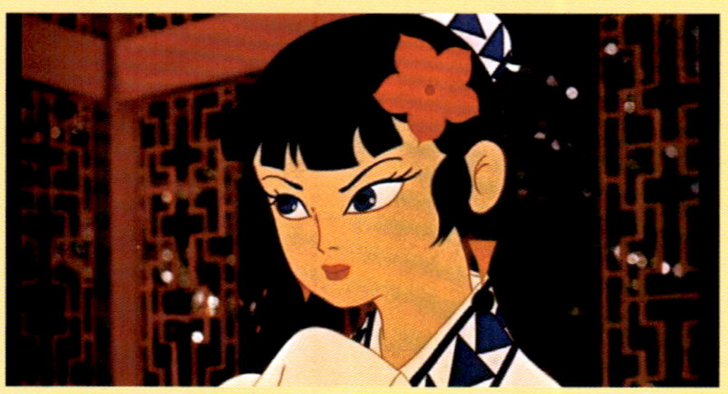

HAKUJADEN

Tale of the White Serpent

Year: 1958
Category: Film
Director: Taiji Yabushita
Animation Studio: Toei Dōga

AT A GLANCE:
The first anime feature film in color. By adapting a famous Chinese legend, Toei was inspired by the Disney model to conquer international markets.

YOU MAY ALSO LIKE . . .
Magic Boy or *Taro the Dragon Boy* exploring Japanese folklore. *Saiyuki*, from Osamu Tezuka's manga revisiting a great classic of Chinese literature.

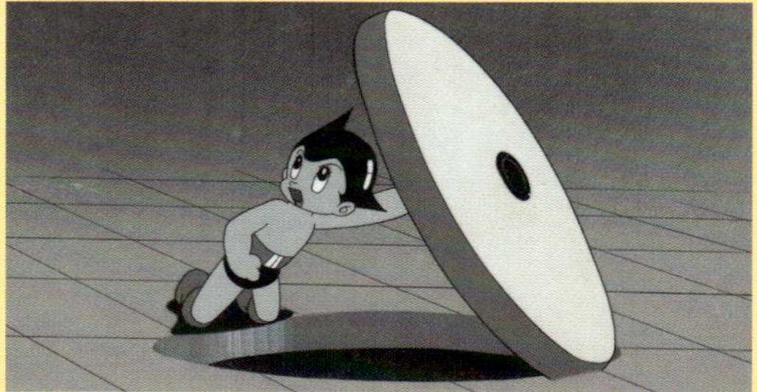

TETSUWAN ATOM

Astro Boy

Year: 1963
Category: TV
Director: Osamu Tezuka
Animation Studio: Mushi Production

AT A GLANCE:
By creating the first weekly anime series, Osamu Tezuka imposed a pace of work and technical processes that regulated television productions.

YOU MAY ALSO LIKE . . .
The man-machine relationship in *Tetsujin 28-go*, in which a young boy remotely pilots a giant robot, and *Cyborg 009*, which has multiple cyborg heroes with special powers.

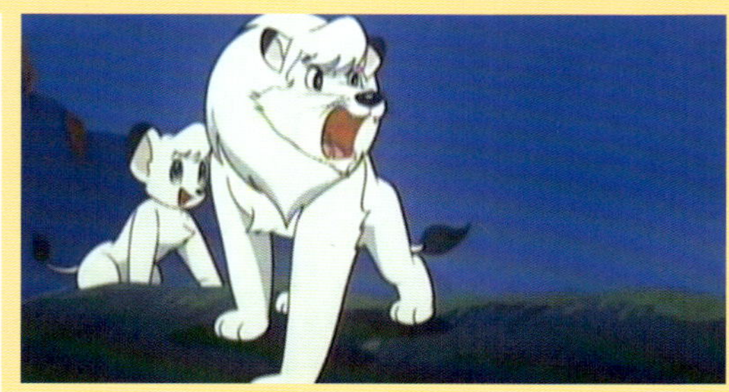

JUNGLE TAITEI

Kimba the White Lion

Year: 1965
Category: TV
Director: Eiichi Yamamoto
Animation Studio: Mushi Production

AT A GLANCE:
Mushi Production revolutionizes Japanese TV once again by creating the first anime series in color for this new large-scale adaptation of a manga by Osamu Tezuka.

YOU MAY ALSO LIKE . . .
Wolf Boy Ken, an original series inspired by *The Jungle Book*. *The Adventures of Hutch the Honeybee* and *Demetan Croaker, the Boy Frog*, two animal series for children that contain difficult and sometimes cruel themes.

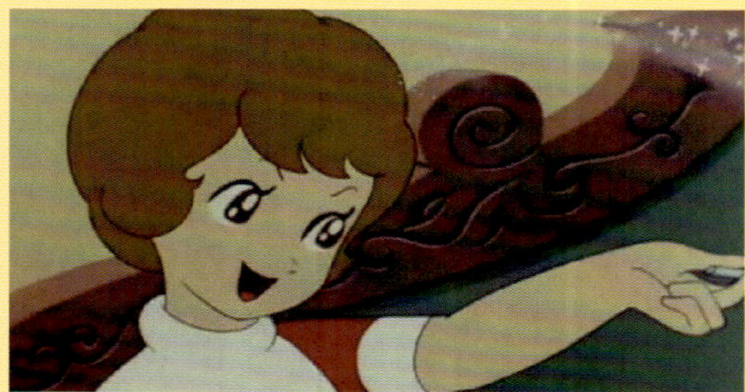

MAHŌTSUKAI SALLY

Sally the Witch

Year: 1966
Category: TV
Director: Toshio Katsuta
Animation Studio: Toei Dōga

AT A GLANCE:
An early example of a genre originally intended for female audiences, with the magical girl going on to become a pillar in anime. Humor and kindness take center stage in this colorful series inspired by *Bewitched*.

YOU MAY ALSO LIKE . . .
Toei held a monopoly on the magical girl genre until the end of the 1970s, from Akko the shape-shifter in *Himitsu no Akko-chan* to *Lalabel* the comical magician to Mako the Little Mermaid in Toei's rendition of Andersen's tale.

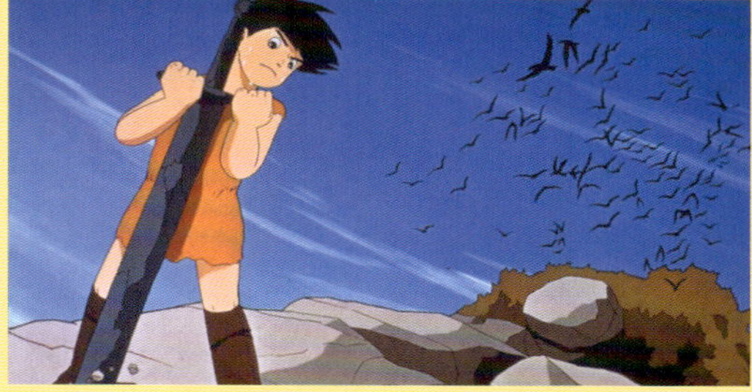

TAIYŌ NO ŌJI HORUSU NO DAIBŌKEN

The Great Adventure of Horus, Prince of the Sun

Year: 1968
Category: Film
Director: Isao Takahata
Animation Studio: Toei Dōga

AT A GLANCE:
With the support of animators Hayao Miyazaki and Yōichi Kotabe, Isao Takahata created a dark, mature first feature film, breaking away from Toei Dōga's policy of focusing on young audiences.

YOU MAY ALSO LIKE . . .
The Little Prince and the Eight-Headed Dragon, an epic saga with a monumental final battle. *Jack and the Witch*, a disturbing adventure inspired by Anglo-Saxon folklore.

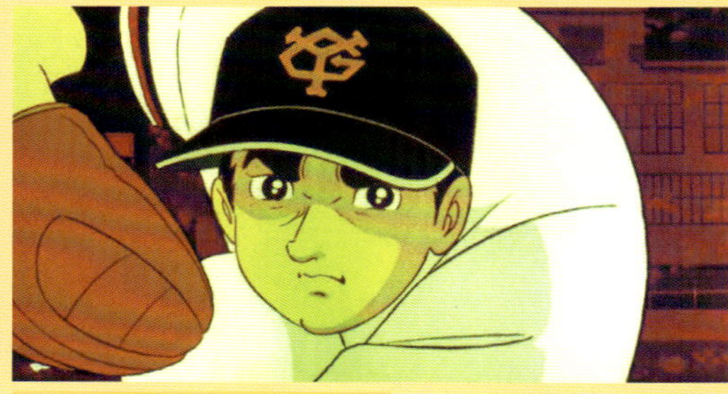

KYOJIN NO HOSHI

Star of the Giants

Year: 1968
Category: TV
Director: Tadao Nagahama
Animation Studio: Tokyo Movie Shinsha

AT A GLANCE:
The start of the professional sports craze in animation. TMS used Japan's love for baseball to establish itself as a leader in the field.

YOU MAY ALSO LIKE . . .
The fiery car races in *Speed Racer*. The fierce boxing training of a young inner-city delinquent in *Ashita no Joe*. The many baseball games in *Dokaben*.

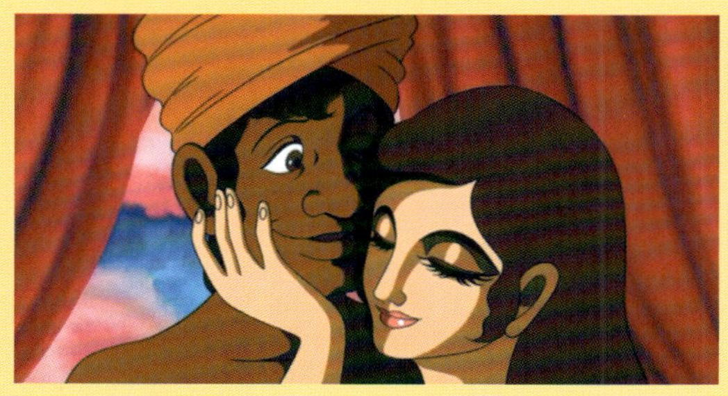

SENYA ICHIYA MONOGATARI

A Thousand and One Nights

Year: 1969
Category: Film
Director: Eiichi Yamamoto
Animation Studio: Mushi Production

AT A GLANCE:
Wishing to gain an adult audience, the Tezuka-Yamamoto duo created the first erotic anime film. It's a comical adventure that interweaves tales from the famous oriental collection.

YOU MAY ALSO LIKE . . .
The comedy-tragedy pair *Cleopatra* and *Belladonna of Sadness*, the two other naughty tales in Mushi Production's experimental collection *Animerama*.

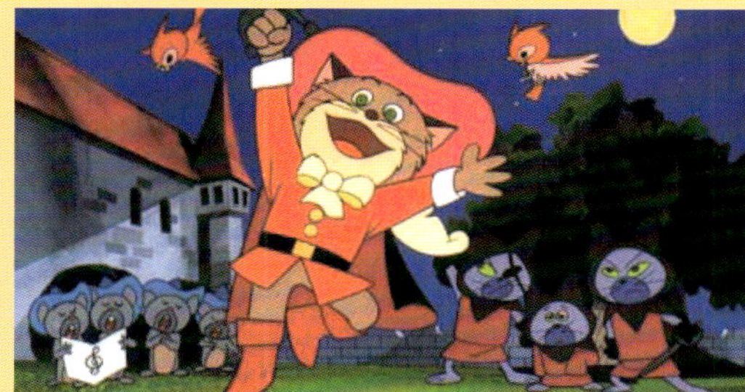

NAGAGUTSU O HAITA NEKO

The Wonderful World of Puss 'n Boots

Year: 1969
Category: Film
Director: Kimio Yabuki
Animation Studio: Toei Dōga

AT A GLANCE:
Following the success of Toei Dōga's sixteenth feature film, the feline hero became the studio's mascot. Inspired by *The Shepherdess and the Chimney Sweep*, Hayao Miyazaki stood out by animating the final chase scene.

YOU MAY ALSO LIKE . . .
Animal Treasure Island, an anthropomorphic adaptation of Stevenson's novel. *Ali Baba and the Forty Thieves*, a cartoon version of the Persian tale.

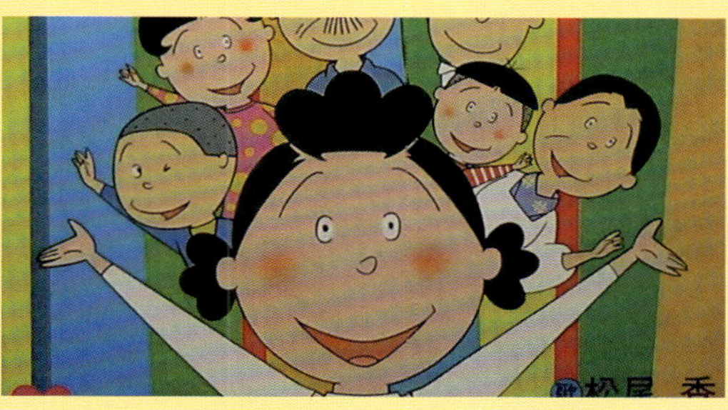

SAZAE-SAN

Sazae-san

Year: 1969
Category: TV
Director: Hiromitsu Morita
Animation Studio: Eiken

AT A GLANCE:
This social satire featuring Sazae Fugata and her family has been a staple in Japanese households every week for almost fifty years. The animated series is the longest ever produced.

YOU MAY ALSO LIKE . . .
The sardonic father-son duo in *Tensai Bakabon* and the six rascals in *Osomatsu-kun*. Japanese traditions take a beating in these two series filled with blunders and foolishness!

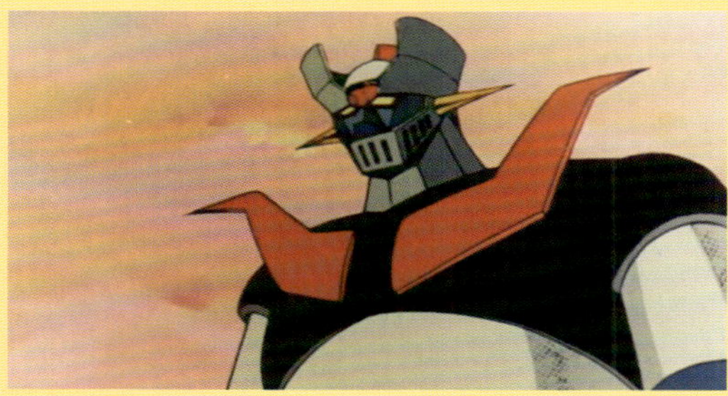

MAZINGER Z

Mazinger Z

Year: 1972
Category: TV
Director: Tomoharu Katsumata
Animation Studio: Toei Dōga

AT A GLANCE:
With its giant robot piloted from the inside by a human, *Mazinger Z* kicks off the golden age of super robots and established Go Nagai as the new forger of superhero science fiction at the Toei studio.

YOU MAY ALSO LIKE . . .
The successors *Getter Robo* and *Goldorak*, by the same author. The progressive competitors from Sunrise, such as the mystical *Brave Raideen* or the tragic *Zambot III*.

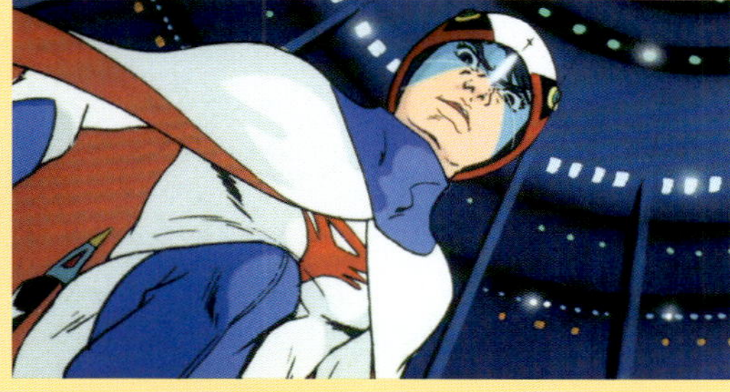

KAGAKU NINJATAI GATCHAMAN

Science Ninja Team Gatchaman

Year: 1972
Category: TV
Director: Hisayuki Toriumi
Animation Studio: Tatsunoko Production

AT A GLANCE:
Anime's resounding response to the wave of superheroes in live-action series. As a twist of fate, this multicolored hero team would serve as the formula for *super sentai*.

YOU MAY ALSO LIKE . . .
Hurricane Polymar's high-speed tactics. The battles between Machiavellian robots and the cyborg *Casshan*. Burlesque time-travel in *Time Bokan*. The *Cyborg 009* remake.

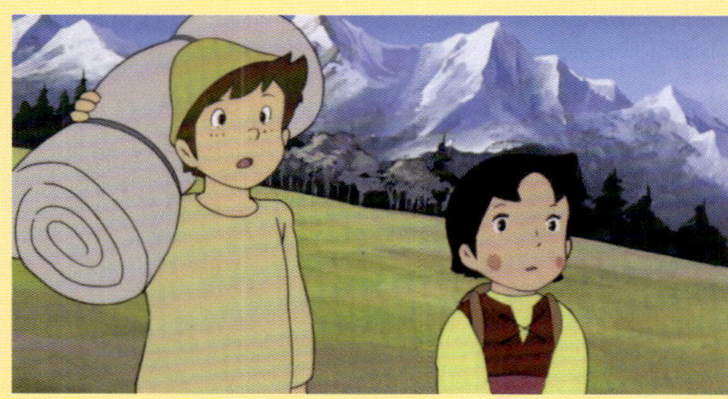

ALPS NO SHŌJO HEIDI

Heidi, Girl of the Alps

Year: 1974
Category: TV
Director: Isao Takahata
Animation Studio: Nippon Animation

AT A GLANCE:
The first *World Masterpiece Theater* (*WMT*) series. Isao Takahata depicts the laborious journey of an orphan with striking realism using **layout**, a technical revolution.

YOU MAY ALSO LIKE . . .
Anne of Green Gables and *Pollyanna*, *WMT* presentations with clever orphan heroines. *Laura, the Prairie Girl*, the story of the Ingalls family using *Heidi*'s original designs.

The new market

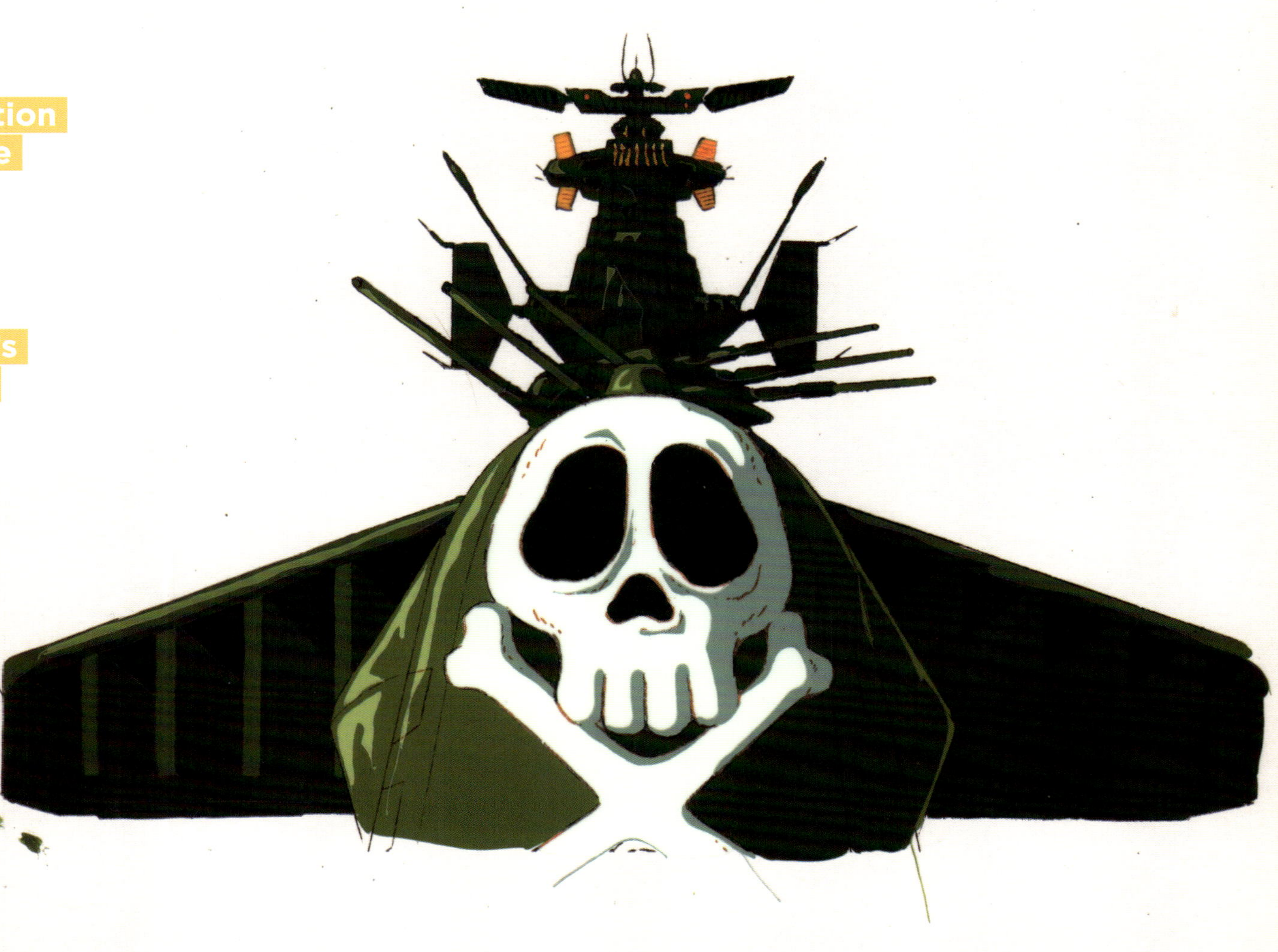

Detail view: Arcadia of My Youth: Endless Orbit SSX. *Original production cel from the opening credits © 1982 Leiji Matsumoto, Toei Animation. THE ART OF ANIME cultural exhibition, Spacher Vogler Collection.*

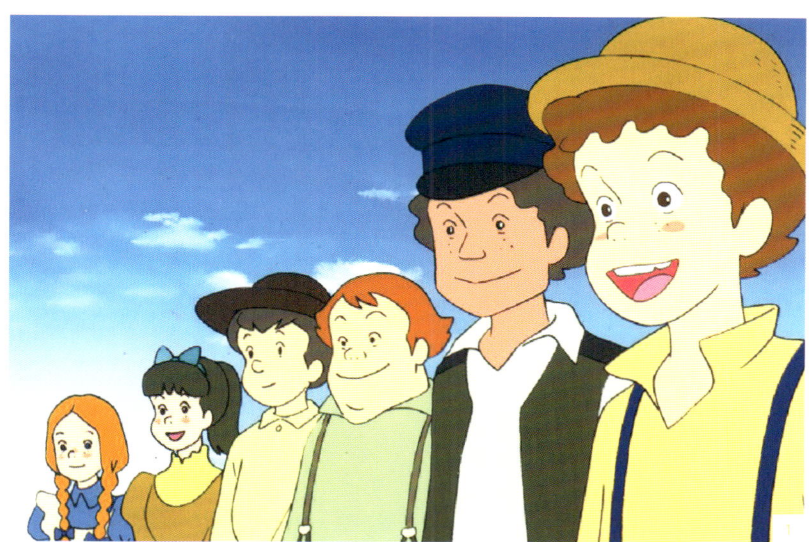

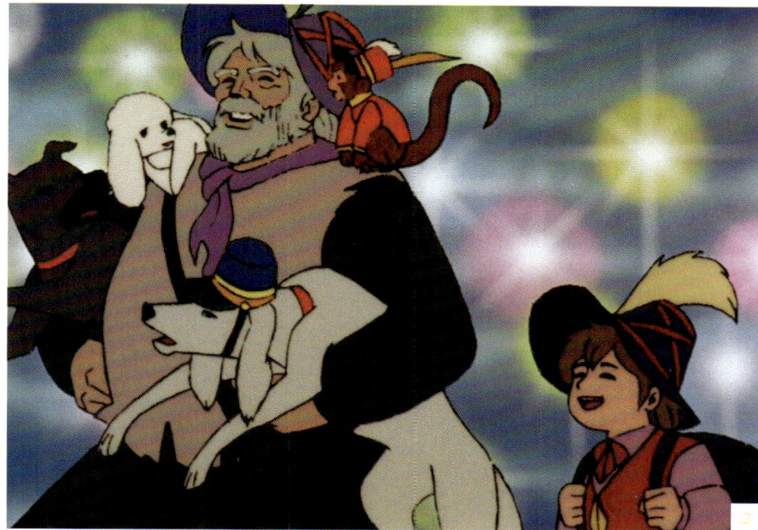

1
1980
Tom Sawyer no Bōken (The Adventures of Tom Sawyer)

2
1977
Ie Naki Ko (Nobody's Boy: Remi)

An established market

THE NEXT GENERATION

The collapse of Mushi Production did not stop the "God of Manga" from pushing forward in animation; he simply created a new studio out of the organization in charge of the rights to his creations, Tezuka Productions. But this marked the end of a golden era for its employees, who lost a grueling but well-paid job. Rintaro and Osamu Dezaki, now established directors, founded Madhouse in 1972 with two other former Mushi Production employees. The first, young artist Yoshiaki Kawajiri, was only twenty-two when Dezaki noticed him on *Ashita no Joe* and brought him on as a key animator and later animation director. The second was Masao Maruyama, given the role of producer, who drew on his experience with Tezuka. He kept the best of what he had learned, having also worked on the artistic part of Tezuka's productions, but eliminated the mistakes, notably his calamitous management.

Before the young company could achieve any other ambition, it first needed to build up its cash flow. The method was simple: the two directors worked as freelancers on other studios' series, logically attracting animation subcontractors to Madhouse. Osamu Dezaki worked mostly with TMS (*Ace o Nerae!*), and Rintaro used his past contacts at Studio Zero (*Hoshi no Koe*) and Toei (*Jetter Mars*). In September 1972, another group of animators trained at Mushi Production, including Yoshiyuki Tomino, founded the Sunrise Studio. United by the same passion, robot and vehicle design, they began by subcontracting on Toei's great wave of post-*Mazinger Z* sci-fi series. Like their colleagues at Madhouse, the thirty-somethings had learned from Tezuka's successes and mistakes and ran their business as sensible technicians and managers. Having come from the same company, the two new organizations didn't hesitate to team up. For Sunrise in 1975, Rintaro directed *Wanpaku Omukashi Kum Kum* (*Kum Kum*) about the adventures of mischievous cave boys. The story was adapted from a manga by Yoshikazu Yasuhiko, better known for his *Space Battleship Yamato* storyboards.

Throughout the decade, rival studios would adapt to this industry transformation: the time for exploration was over, and now it was time for exploitation! TV Asahi bought A Production, abandoned by TMS, to make it an independent company. Renamed Shin-Ei Dōga in 1976, it

1975
Wanpaku Omukashi Kum Kum (Kum Kum)

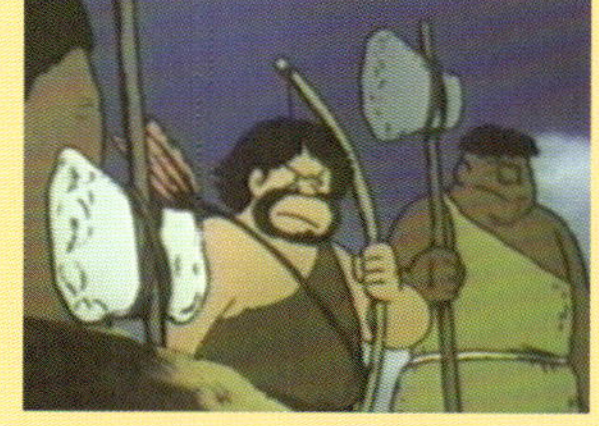

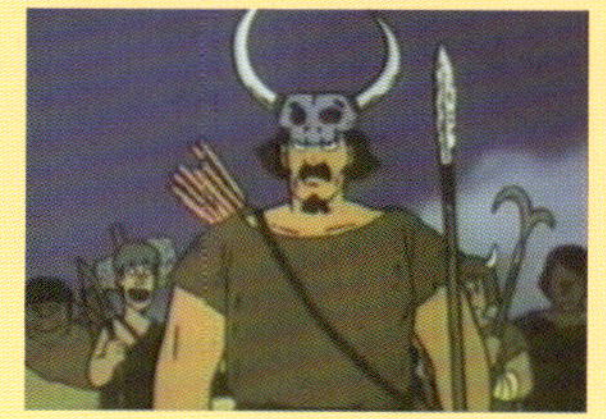

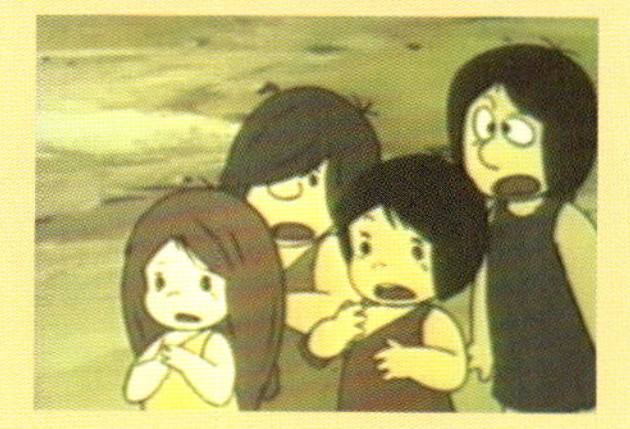

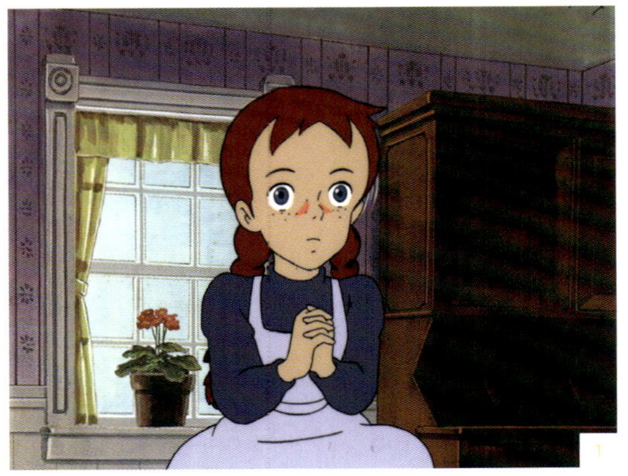

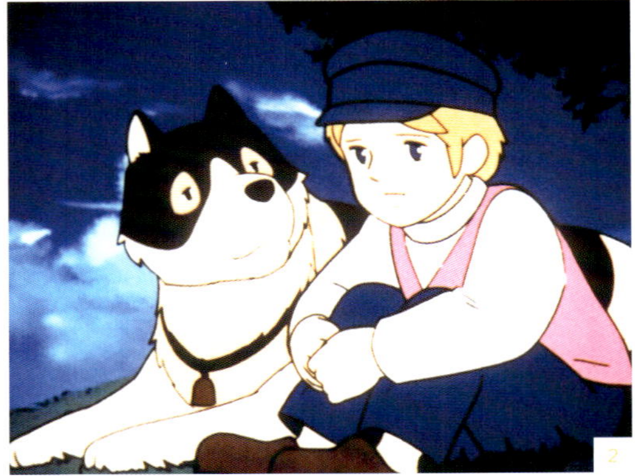

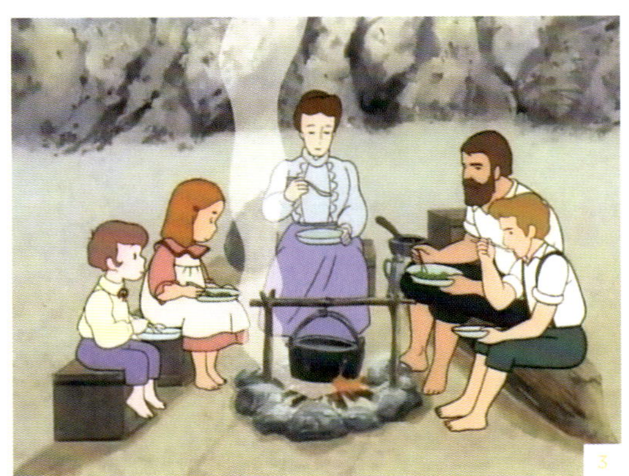

1
1979
Akage no Anne (Anne of Green Gables)

2
1975
Flanders no Inu (The Dog of Flanders)

3
1981
Kazoku Robinson Hyōryūki Fushigi na Shima no Furōne (The Swiss Family Robinson: Flone of the Mysterious Island)

specialized in cartoons for the youngest viewers. Similarly, reforms within TCJ forced the studio to change its name to Eiken in 1969, a change that would not be seen in the credits until 1973.

Kōichi Motohashi seized this opportunity to leave Eiken and go it alone. With his studio Zuiyo Eizo, he wanted to prove that a TV series could be a work of art and not simple entertainment intended to sell advertisements and merchandising. This countercurrent decision allowed him to recruit a trio of ex-unionists from Toei: Isao Takahata, Hayao Miyazaki, and Yōichi Kotabe, rebels who were fiercely attached to their freedom of artistic expression. The studio specialized in adapting children's novels, producing a series based on Johanna Spyri's *Heidi*.

Any and all means were used to create a work that would stand the test of time, starting with a scouting trip to Switzerland for the artistic team; in addition to Takahata, Miyazaki, and Kotabe, Yoshiyuki Tomino, the sci-fi champion, worked on the storyboard. When they returned, they blew up the celluloid budget for optimal animation and forced the animators to rework every sequence that didn't meet their expectations. Despite the constraints, the team kept its deadlines but caused Fuji TV many a cold sweat—throughout the broadcast year, every episode was delivered at the very last second.

Perfectionism and intransigence paid off. It was a huge hit in Japan, and *Heidi* was already headed around the globe to Europe and South America. Between foreign TV rights and merchandising, Zuiyo Eizo recouped the staggering costs of producing the 52 episodes. But the company was too ambitious and couldn't make ends meet for the 104 episodes of its new series, *Maya the Honey Bee*. Thanks to a clever business plan, Zuiyo Eizo sacrificed its administrative branch but saved the animation studios, which carried on under a new name: Nippon Animation.

ANIMATION CLASSICS

Starting with *Heidi*, the 7:30 slot on Sunday evenings on Fuji TV was reserved for a Nippon Animation collection, *Sekai Meisaku Gekijō*, internationalized as *World Masterpiece Theater*, until 1997. Every year, a great children's literature classic was adapted with the same aim: to become a timeless work of art based on its quality. The first two set the tone—Nello and his dog Patrache, the hero in *Flanders no Inu* (*The Dog of Flanders*, 1975) die in a church in the final episode, whereas *Haha o Tazunete Sanzenri* (*3000 Leagues in Search of Mother*, 1976) narrates the epic journey of a young boy who is looking for his mother from Italy to Argentina. During production of *3000 Leagues in Search of Mother*, Takahata's and Miyazaki's artistic differences led Miyazaki to walk out at episode 15. However, the quarrel was soon forgotten, and they were together again for *Akage no Anne* (*Anne of Green Gables*) in 1979.

The *World Masterpiece Theater* franchise was not all heartbreaking tearjerkers. It also adapted adventure stories: school-skipping *Tom Sawyer* (1980), shipwrecked survivors in *Kazoku Robinson Hyōryūki Fushigi na Shima no Furōne* (*The Swiss Family Robinson:*

Flone of the Mysterious Island, 1981), Australia's discovery by settlers in *Minami no Niji no Lucy* (*Lucy-May of the Southern Rainbow*, 1982), and so on. Nippon Animation continued to draw from classics for series outside the Sunday slot, such as *Sinbad* (1975) and *Pinocchio* (1976). Miyazaki was entrusted with a novel by Alexander Key, which became his directorial debut *Mirai shōnen Conan* (*Future Boy Conan*) in 1978. The series contained themes that were dear to him—ecology, pacifism, and flying buildings.

In a few years, Nippon Animation had established itself as the undisputed leader in a field that the competition now avoided. However, Osamu Dezaki's 1977 adaptation of Hector Malot's novel *Ie Naki Ko* (*Nobody's Boy: Remi*) was outstanding. Jointly produced by TMS and Madhouse, the series was not based on realistic animation but rather expressionist framing enhanced by unprecedented depth and speed effects with a multiplane camera. Above all, it confirmed the artistic symbiosis between the director and **character designer** Akio Sugino, which began in 1970 at Mushi Production with *Ashita no Joe*. The duo jumped back into the ring in 1980 for a sequel to the boxing series, produced at TMS this time. Convinced by the show's success, Dezaki and Sugino left Madhouse to found Studio Annapuru, a decision precipitated by a memorable turn of events in the now mature and finally exploitable girls' cartoon sector.

GIVE THE GIRLS A TURN!

The feminist wave of the early 1970s upset the *shōjo* manga market. They were now women who spoke directly to female readers, whose expectations they knew from having been young girls themselves. Toei got the ball rolling by adapting a *shōjo* manga by Yumiko Igarashi and Kyoko Mizuki. Following the life of an American orphan from ages ten to eighteen, *Candy Candy* is a melodrama on par with *Gone with the Wind*, but 100 percent Japanese! From 1976 to 1979, the blonde girl and her raccoon (missing from the original manga) captivated Japanese women across 115 episodes, upsetting the codes of cartoons for girls. So much revenue was generated that an argument broke out between artist Igarashi and scriptwriter Mizuki, forever freezing the video rights to the series!

Just months after the end of *Candy Candy*, *Versailles no Bara* (*The Rose of Versailles*) began, a flamboyant feminist manifesto from Riyoko Ikeda's manga. Born a

1978
Mirai shōnen Conan (Future Boy Conan)

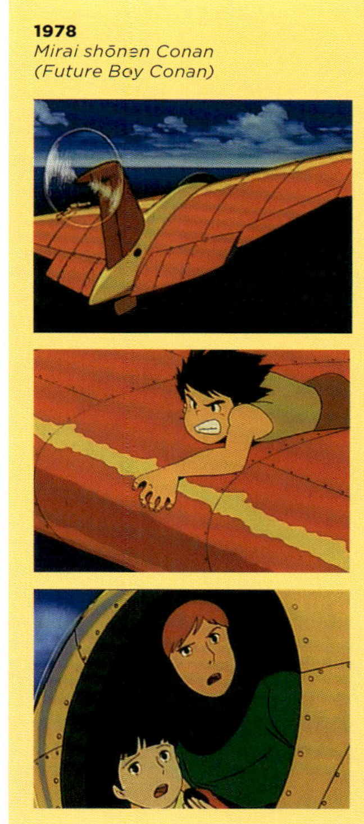

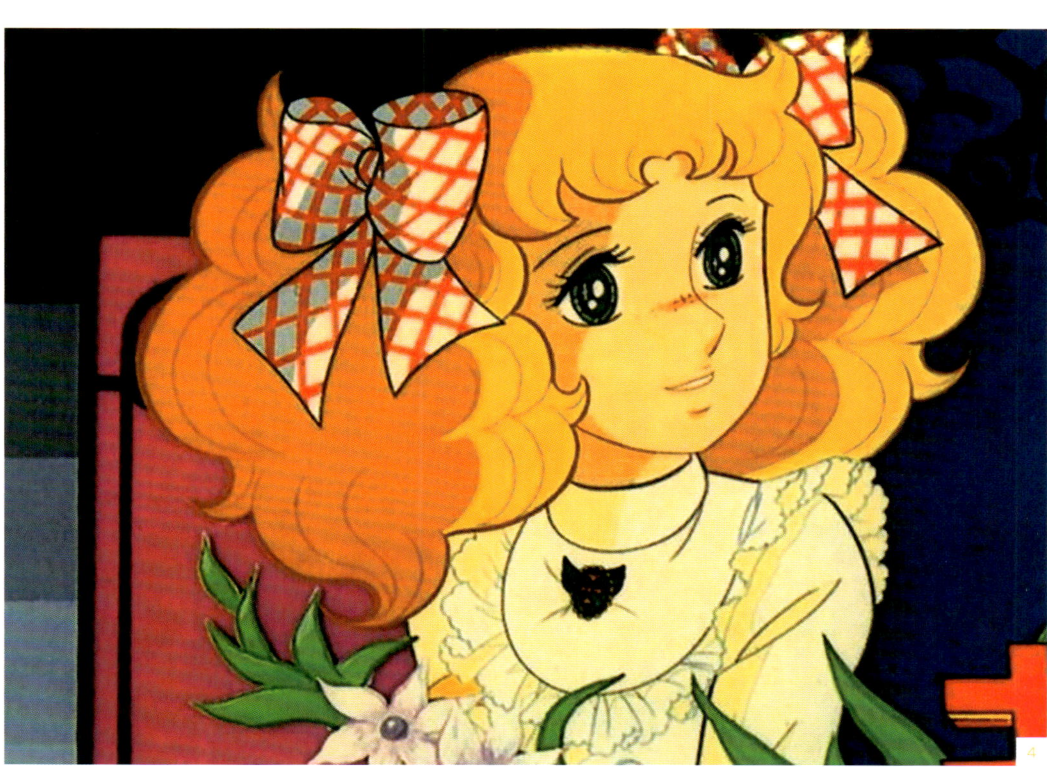

4
1976
Candy Candy

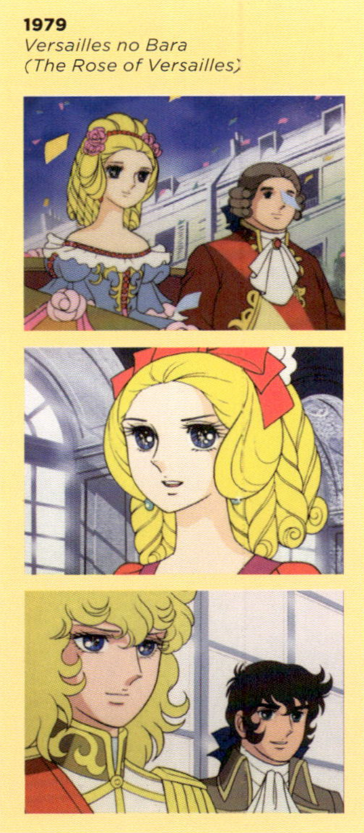

1979
Versailles no Bara
(The Rose of Versailles)

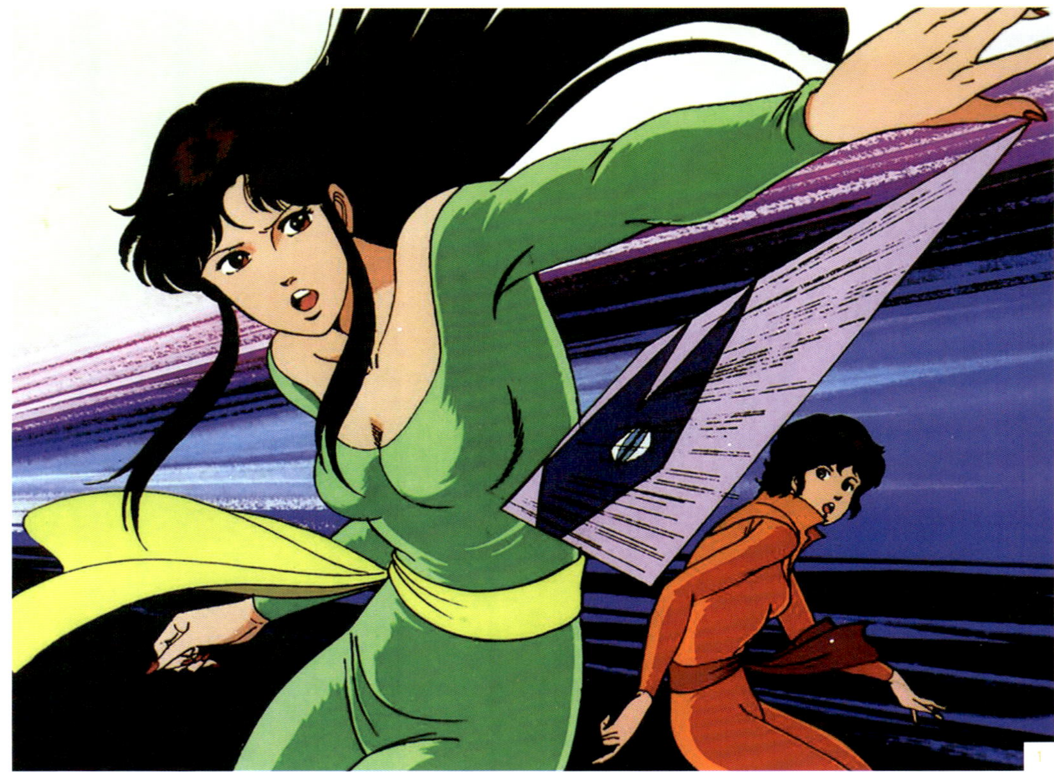

1983
Cat's Eye

girl, Oscar François de Jarjayes was raised as a boy and began a brilliant military career, becoming captain of the guard for Queen Marie Antoinette. Against the backdrop of a fantasized French Revolution, the series reflected the desire of women in the 1970s to access positions that were previously off-limits, both literally and figuratively.

To draw the characters and supervise their animation, the experienced Akio Sugino brought on Shingo Araki and Michi Himeno, who began collaborating on *Cutie Honey* in 1973. Since their studio had opened in 1974, Araki Production brought together eight skilled artists who had been adapting series for both boys and girls—Araki or Himeno had the last word, depending on the target audience. Already known for the refined designs in the 1975 series *UFO Robot Grendizer* (*Goldorak*), the Araki-Himeno duo built its reputation on *The Rose of Versailles*, proof that women were equally competent in key positions.

From the beginning of production, the tension was palpable between director Tadao Nagahama and Reiko Tajima, who voiced the heroine. Women had real power, and she managed to get him fired! Akio Sugino called his lifelong friend Osamu Dezaki for help, who took over the reins at the nineteenth episode and left even more room for the Araki-Himeno team. The noticeable increase in quality midway through the forty-episode series made *The Rose of Versailles* a social phenomenon, whose theme song is still all the rage in karaoke today.

Even *shōnen-ai*, still unwelcome on the small screen a few years earlier, ended up on TV under the guise of humor. Since 1978, Mineo Maya had parodied these gay love stories in his manga *Patalliro!* in which he made one of the characters pregnant. That particular joke was removed from the animated adaptation produced by Toei in 1982; it was important not to shake up the Japanese too much—they had already made great strides in creating entertainment for female audiences. *Cat's Eye*, a 1983 adaptation of Tsukasa Hōjō's manga, was the tipping point: Inspector Toshio, played for a fool by three thieves in skintight suits, has no idea that they are his fiancée, Hitomi, and her two sisters! The series not only gives prominence to the female characters (Cat's Eye and

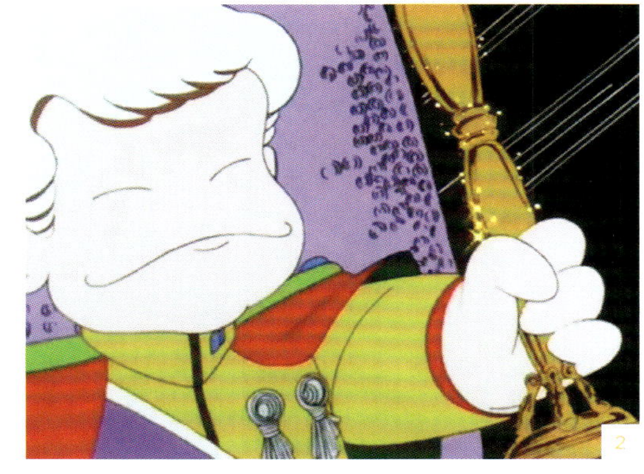

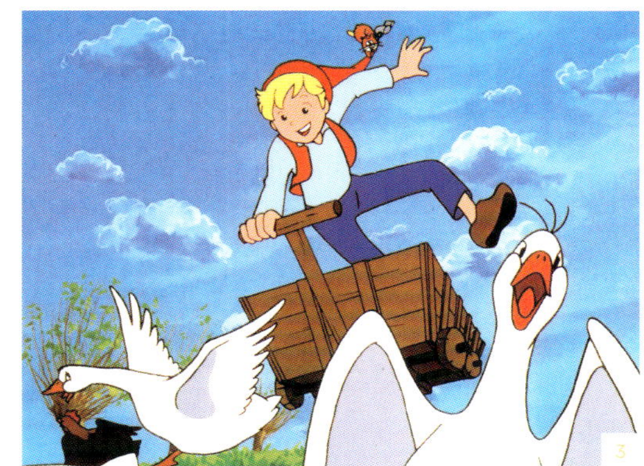

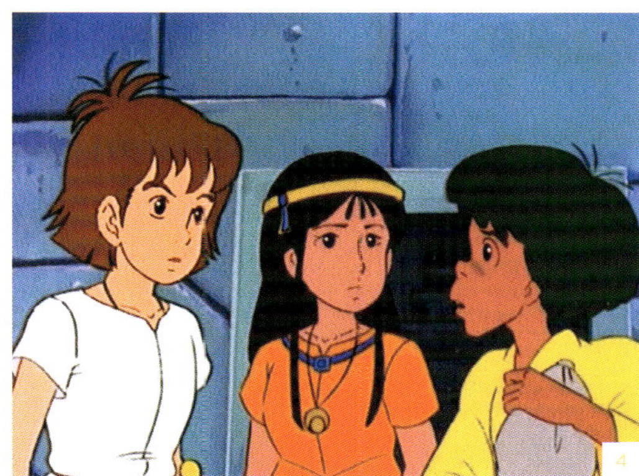

2
—
1982
Patalliro!

3
—
1980
Nils no Fushigi na Tabi (The Wonderful Adventures of Nils)

4
—
1982
The Mysterious Cities of Gold

their rival Inspector Mitsuko Asatani), but between the hero's candor and her superior's hot temper, it also makes a mockery of men!

Symbolizing this shifting mentality, magical girls made their comeback in the early 1980s. Now they physically transformed to become adults. Through them, little girls experienced "big girl" stories, whether it was the versatile heroine in *Mahō no Princess Minky Momo* (*Magical Princess Minky Momo*, 1982), the singer in *Mahō no Tenshi Creamy Mami* (*Magical Angel Creamy Mami*, 1983), or the magician in *Mahō no Star Magical Emi* (*Magic Star Magical Emi*, 1985).

GOING INTERNATIONAL

Those last two titles came from Studio Pierrot, founded in 1979 by former Tatsunoko animators, who disagreed with the direction the studio took after the death of its founding president, Tatsuo Yoshida, in 1977. Among them, *Gatchaman* director Hisayuki Toriumi convinced his disciple Mamoru Oshii to join the adventure. On behalf of NHK (only a public channel dared to take this on), the studio started in on Nippon Animation's guarded territory: the adaptation of children's books. In addition to *Nils no Fushigi na Tabi* (*The Wonderful Adventures of Nils*) in 1980 and *Spoon Obasan* (*Mrs. Pepper Pot*) in 1983.

Anime was being exported more and more, especially to the European market. As channels multiplied in countries with different languages, they needed content for their children's programming, and producing a series cost much more than purchasing a turnkey series already broadcast in Japan, that only needed to be dubbed. In France, *Candy Candy* and *Goldorak* were the pioneers of this long-term trend. Faced with such a phenomenon, young enthusiasts Jean Chalopin and Bernard Deyriès proposed a partnership with TMS: *Ulysses 31*, a space opera remake of Homer's *Odyssey* broadcast in 1981.

It was a win-win! The French benefited from the unparalleled expertise of the Japanese, who in turn would have unparalleled working conditions. Not only were teams given two weeks instead of one to produce an episode, but they were also invited to express their artistic suggestions! The Araki-Himeno duo had free rein to express their style creating Yumi, an alien traveling with Ulysses and Telemachus.

The French company DIC Audiovisuel, already the European leader in animation, became a global leader by teaming up with the Japanese once again for *The Mysterious Cities of Gold* in 1982. Although missing from the credits, it was coproduced by Studio Pierrot and came about using the same innovative technology that was crucial in breaking down international barriers for *Ulysses 31*: the fax machine! Assistants spent their days next to the machine, which required eight minutes to transfer a shakily outlined drawing. The drawing then needed to be smoothed back out by the animators, a process that created a source of discontinuity in the designs over the episodes.

The start of Toei's American adventure, on the other hand, was much more pragmatic. When toy giant Hasbro discovered Takara's transformable robots Microman and Diaclone, it proposed a global partnership to its Japanese counterpart. To encourage American children to buy these toys, renamed Transformers, they needed an animated series! Takara suggested its longtime collaborator Toei, which provided the company with profitable merchandising rights—the success of *Transformers* would make the studio the preferred contact for American investors in the 1980s.

Nippon Animation collaborated mostly with Germany and Spain. After *Chiisana Viking Vicky* (*Vicky the Viking*) in 1974 and a new season of *Mitsubachi Māya no Bōken* (*Maya the Honey Bee*) in 1980, the studio coproduced *Fushigi no Kuni no Alice* (*Alice in Wonderland*) in 1983, a fifty-two-episode series based on Lewis Caroll's novel, for the German market. Working with BRB Internacional's studios in Madrid, it also created animal retellings of the classics *Wan Wan Sanjushii* (*Three Musketeers*) in 1981 and *Anime 80-Kakan Sekai Isshu* (*Around the World with Willy Fog*) two years later.

LAUGHTER COSTS NOTHING AND PAYS OFF IN SPADES

Despite its magical girl productions and collaboration abroad, Studio Pierrot's crowning achievement was its adaptation of a phenomenal manga, *Urusei Yatsura* by Rumiko Takahashi. Beginning on October 14, 1981, Pierrot combined its know-how with Mamoru Oshii's directing talent for the first 106 episodes. The high-energy comedy (the bikini-clad Lamu calls her bawdy, lazy human husband to order using electric shocks) draws from both Japanese folklore and science fiction, and reflects the flamboyant, no-holds-barred Japan in the 1980s.

1981
Urusei Yatsura

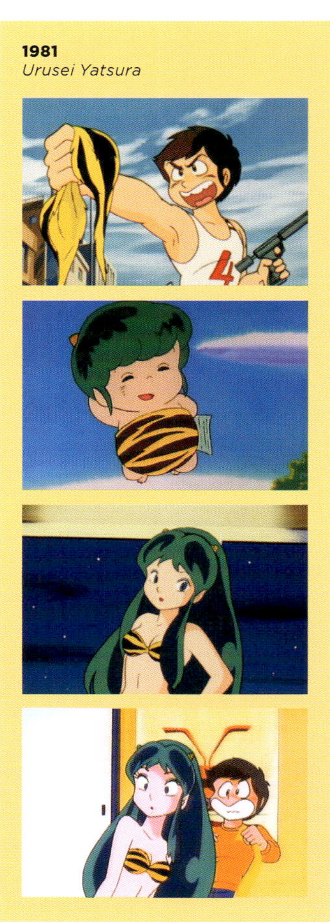

1 – **1981** *Anime 80-Kakan Sekai Isshu (Around the World with Willy Fog)*

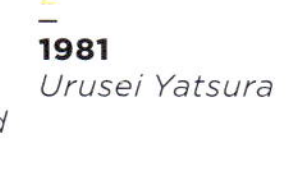

2 – **1981** *Urusei Yatsura*

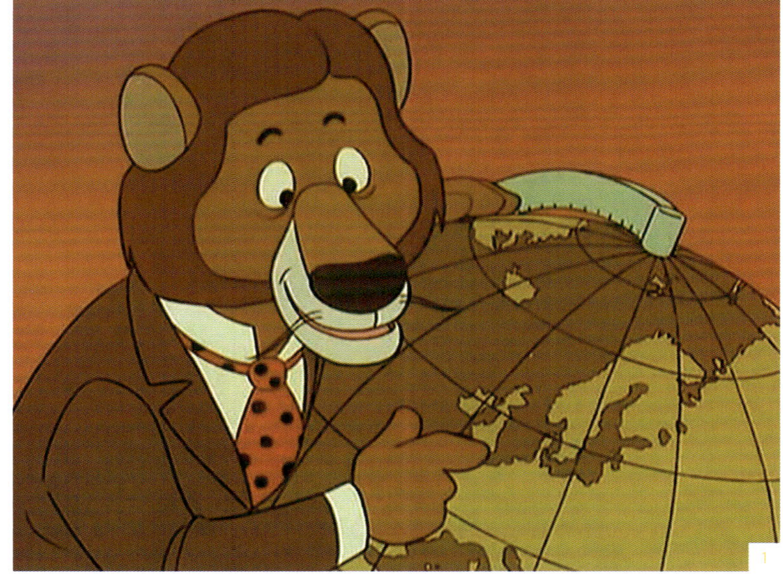

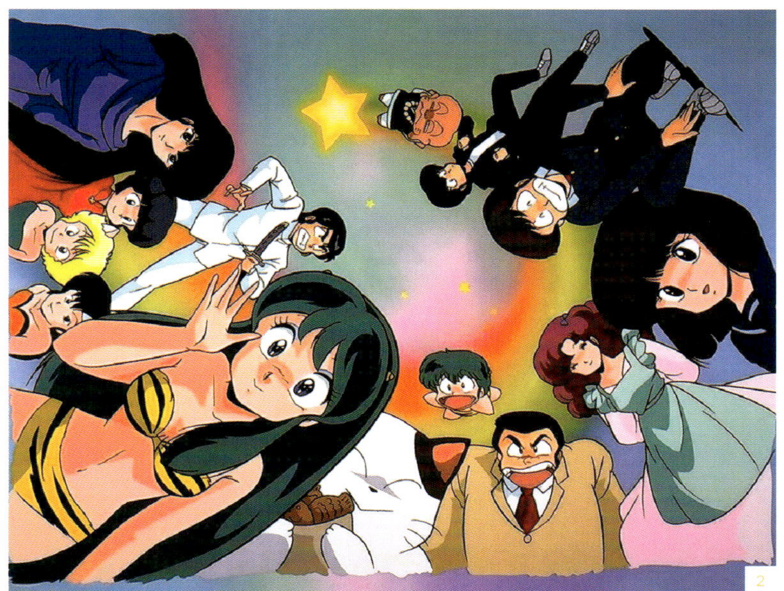

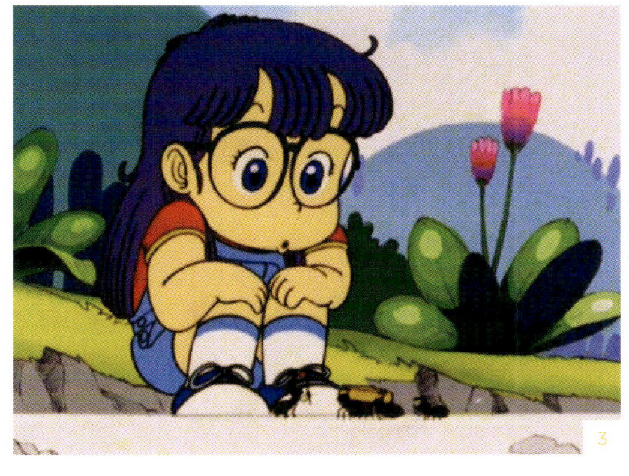

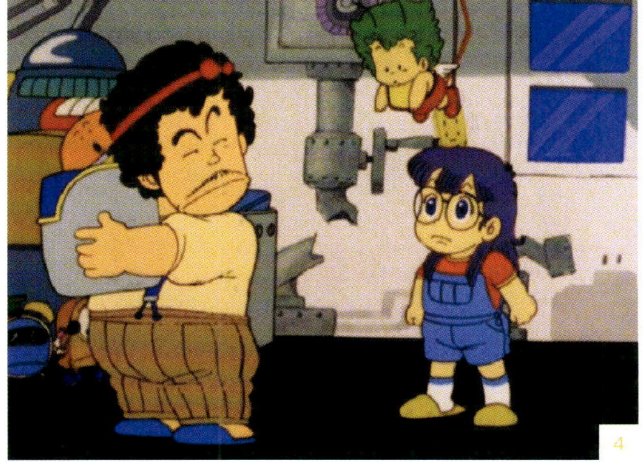

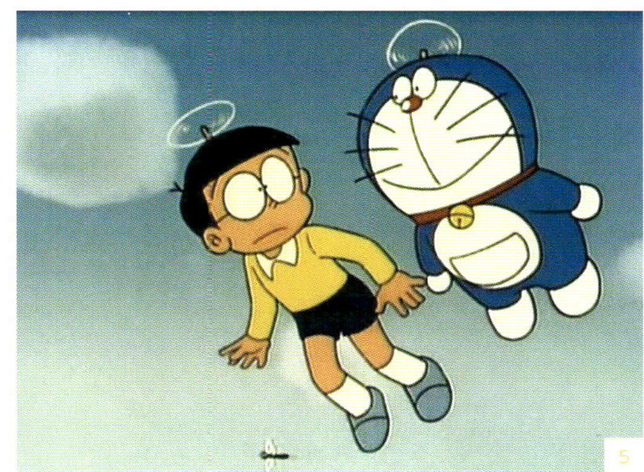

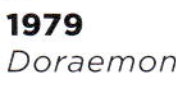

3 and 4
1981
Dr Slump to Arale-chan (Dr Slump)

5
1979
Doraemon

In the midst of incredible economic growth, Japan wanted to have fun! The 3Cs of the 1960s gave way to the 3Js of Japanese desire: *juweru* (jewelry), *jetto* (travel abroad by plane), and *juttaku* (house). Televisions were set up in every home, even in multiple rooms, and served primarily as entertainment, with animation adapting to demand. *Dr. Slump: Arale-chan* (*Dr. Slump*) is packed with childish humor, exemplified by one of the Penguin Village characters, Unchi-kun, known as Poop Boy in English. This echoes the nonsense in *Urusei Yatsura* in 1981, as both series were broadcast for five years during the same period. The initial collaboration between Toei and *mangaka* Akira Toriyama on these series would serve as the foundation for *Dragon Ball*'s phenomenal success a few years later.

The studio went even further in 1983 with *Kinnikuman*, adapted from Yudetamago's homonymic manga, in which the main character, whose name translates to Muscleman, discovers that he is a superhero from the planet Kinniku and finds himself in wrestling tournaments with contenders to the throne. Far from the conventionalism in *Tiger Mask*, these fights were an excuse for zany antics and terrible puns that delighted audiences for 137 episodes.

Wiser, more moralistic humor continued to flourish. Ten years after *Sazae-san*, another icon took its permanent place on TV: *Doraemon*, the blue robotic cat from the future. Having already been adapted in black and white in 1973, Fujiko Fujio's manga hero embarked on a 1,787-episode marathon on April 2, 1979. The series got a reboot after a brief pause in 2005, and the new version (featuring an all-new voice cast) is still going today. With its unchanging story arc (to solve his friend Nobita's problems, Doraemon gives him incredible gadgets, a tactic that always backfires on the boy), the series has become an intergenerational classic and a goose that laid the golden egg for Shin-Ei.

With aliens, an android girl with superhuman strength, and a robotic cat with futuristic gadgets, the sci-fi market was booming, and its space operas lent themselves particularly well to comedy. Especially if they had a touch of action, like in movies with Jean-Paul Belmondo, the French actor from which Buichi Terasawa drew inspiration for the hero in his manga *Cobra*. Cobra, voiced by Alain Delon's Japanese voice actor, Nachi Nozawa, adventures from planet to planet, wiping out his opponents with the weapon embedded in his arm, a smile, and a cigar in his mouth. Overseen at TMS by Dezaki and Sugino in 1982, *Space Cobra*'s picaresque adventures captured the free spirit of the times, enhanced by its funky soundtrack by Kentaro Haneda. The composer became a fixture on the small screen that same year with *Chōjikū Yōsai Macross* (*Super Dimension Fortress Macross*).

SPEAKING OF LOVE

The era of channels having only American shows to broadcast had passed. The national production of live-action and animated series called for original soundtracks (OST) and generated a new market, driven by the democratization of 33 and 45 rpm records. Kitty Music Corporation, a branch of Polydor and Universal founded in 1972, specialized in producing the soundtracks for live television **dramas** before turning to movies in 1979. For its first foray into the world of animation, the company renamed itself Kitty Films and managed the budget for *Urusei Yatsura*.

The success of the series was the result of the combined efforts of Studio Pierrot and Kitty Films, which became a privileged partner for future Rumiko Takahashi manga adaptations. The manga artist was also a champion of sales and showed the highlight of Shogakukan's weekly *Shōnen Sunday* to her friend and colleague Mitsuru Adachi. The two artists succeeded at the formidable task of reaching both boys and girls in a market that was increasingly divided into sectors. But Takahashi chose the universality of absurd, burlesque humor, whereas Adachi opted for another realm common to both sexes: feelings. Kitty Films was tasked with adapting Adachi's manga *Miyuki* in 1983, a love triangle between Masato and two young girls (including his half sister, whom he finds after six years of separation).

The series was directed by Mizuho Nishikubo, who worked with Dezaki and Sugino on *The Rose of Versailles* and *Ashita no Joe 2*. It broke new ground in romantic comedy, which expanded on television in the second half of the 1980s, five years behind the manga industry.

Toei followed suit by adapting Mitsuru Miura's *shōjo* manga *The Kabocha Wine*, featuring the daily life of a mismatched high school couple—Natsumi is much taller than her boyfriend, Shunsuke! To draw ninety-five episodes from the pitch, which had more depth than it seemed, the studio gave the series to a mainstay of animation, Kimio Yabuki, who had directed *Wolf Boy Ken*. The production company diversified its offerings by selecting a manga by Kaoru Tada published by their privileged partner, Shueisha, in which a young girl closely watched by her father flirts with rock'n'roll stars.

At the height of her glory, Mitsuko Horie didn't just sing the theme song for *Aishite Night* (*Love Me, My Knight*, 1983), she also voiced the heroine torn between the singer and the keyboardist of Bee Hive. Naive and sappy, the series amplified the strange feelings that trouble teenage viewers like a sound box and plunged them into the fantastical world of show business. Bee Hive's look and their colorful hairstyles referred directly to the *visual kei* scene that was emerging in Japan. And once again, it was all about the music! Toei called on a very young composer, Joe Hisaishi, to create real songs for the fictional band.

These contemporary teen romances coexisted with flamboyant "old-fashioned" shows. Yumiko Igarashi, the artist who illustrated *Candy Candy*, joined forces with screenwriter Mann Izawa to tell the incomparable tale of Georgie, an orphan taken in by a farmer at birth. When she discovers that she has no blood ties with her brothers, Abel and Arthur, she flees in search of her origins with a bracelet as her only clue, rather than face her conflicting emotions. To stack the odds for success in its favor for the 1983 broadcast, TMS commissioned the music for *Lady Georgie* from Takeo Watanabe, the composer for *Candy Candy*! This was further proof of the importance of original soundtracks to a series' success.

STAYING THE COURSE

The expanding genres in anime reflected the upheaval in the manga industry over the decade. Nevertheless, while studios were successfully exploring new storytelling horizons, they didn't forget the fundamentals on which they had built their success, starting with sports. Baseball was obviously king, as proven once again by the 1983 series *Nine*. This marked the beginning of a collaboration between Mitsuru Adachi and Group TAC, a company finally taking off fifteen years after it was founded in 1968 by former Mushi Production staff.

Other team sports were also making the small screen. True to form, Tatsunoko was the first to venture into another flagship sport from the United States—basketball—with *Dash Kappei*, a 1981 adaptation of Noboru Rokuda's manga. However, Toei Animation won the first victory in this new competition with *Captain Tsubasa* in 1983, adapted from Yōichi Takahashi's phenomenal manga. The 128-episode series describes the journey of Tsubasa Oozora, a gifted soccer player, from his first practice ever to the start of his professional career in Brazil. A precursor of the epic series to follow, *Captain Tsubasa* became the new foundation for sports anime.

But the TV animation industry remained primarily focused on the genre in which it was born—science fiction. Emancipated, experienced, and well established in companies that were both financially and technologically equipped, the new generation was determined to express its vision of a distant future, unaware that it was shaping the near future of animation.

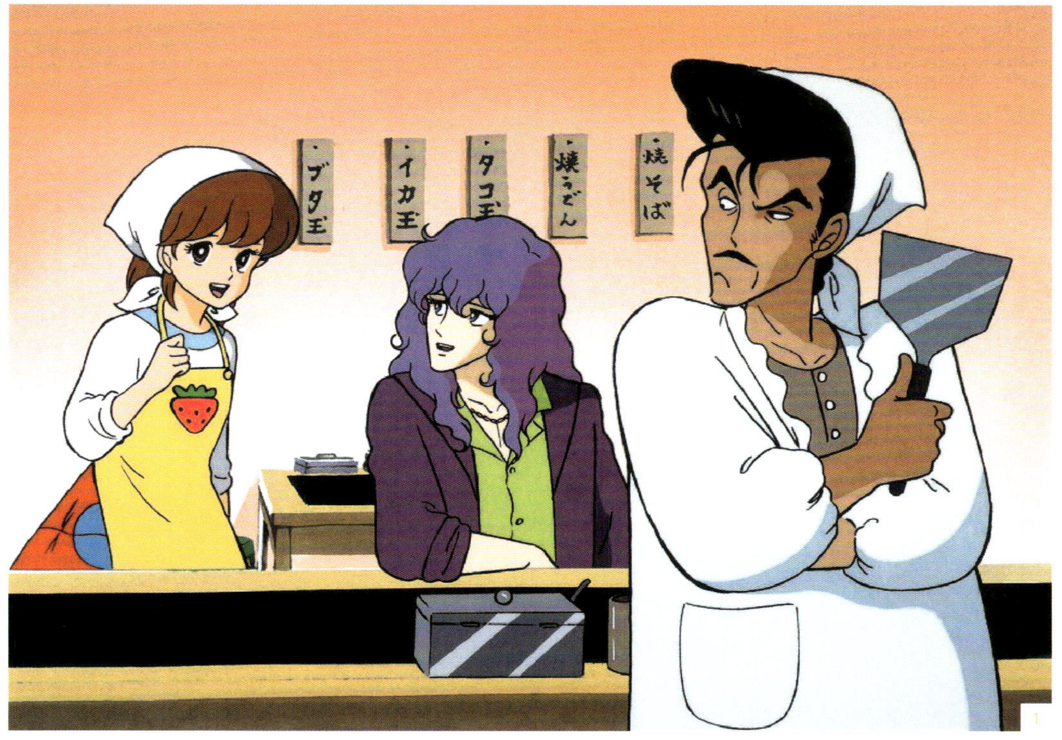

1
1983
Aishite Night (Love Me, My Knight)

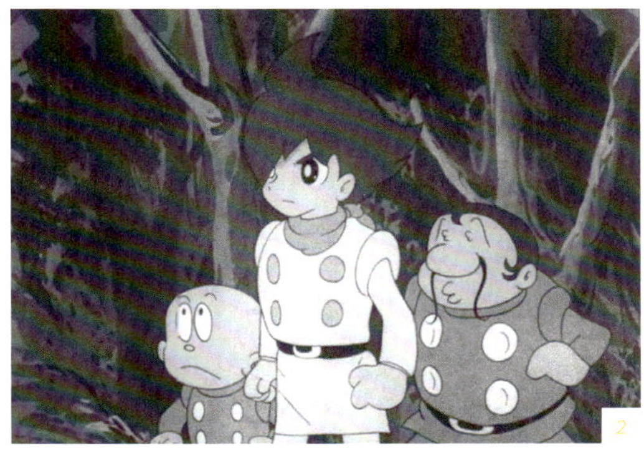
2

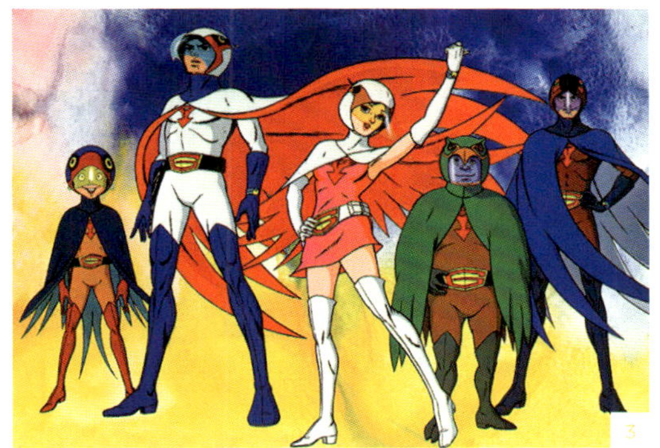
3

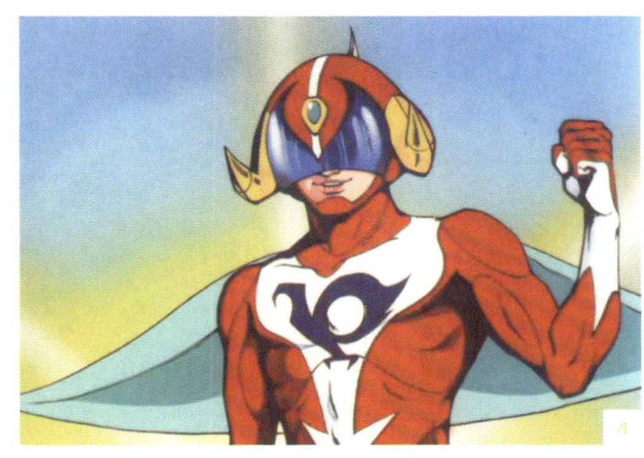
4

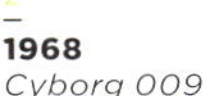

The consecration of science fiction

GATCHAMAN AND THE ERA OF MULTICOLORED SUPERHEROES

From the *Astro Boy* series to the *Cyborg 009* films, by way of *Big X*, *Space Ace*, *Galaxy Boy Troop*, *Eightman*, and *Tetsujin 28-go*, the Japanese were increasingly fascinated by futuristic stories in which robotics and space travel symbolized technological expansion. Anime jumped on the trend that had already been introduced by the overflowing production of American sci-fi films since the 1950s, such as *Forbidden Planet* and *When Worlds Collide*, as well as Toho's many feature films. Ishirō Honda, creator of *Godzilla*, established himself as a master of monster movies and science fiction. The 1957 film *The Mysterians* featured a giant robot and aliens clad in precise, telltale colors. Although Honda had already placed Japan in the UN in *The Mysterians*, he really glorified his country in 1959 in *Uchū Daisensō* (*Battle in Outer Space*), an edgy space action film in which the Land of the Rising Sun is a leader in scientific research. And why stop there when they could "lend" the dreadful superstar monsters Rodan and Godzilla to help aliens in *Kaiju Daisensō* (*Invasion of Astro-Monster*, 1965)? Gigantism and technology became the symbols of exponential economic growth.

When *Ultraman* came to television in 1966, it was a revolution! Tsuburaya Productions modernized the concept of a giant superhero who defends the country against weekly attacks by huge monsters. The new show was in color, whereas its predecessor *Ultra Q*, a *kaiju* (giant monster) series released shortly before, was still in black and white. One of the country's most popular icons was born, and the shadow of *tokusatsu* fell across the world of television. The pace of these pyrotechnic productions was intense. The following year, Toei responded with the cosmic *Captain Ultra*, an adaptation of Edmond Hamilton's Captain Future novels. *Kamen Rider* followed in 1971, a tenacious rival for *Ultraman* whose stories could also be read in Shotaro Ishinomori's manga, which he published in parallel.

Anime's response to this tsunami of superheroes was to add many main characters within the same team. The success of the two *Cyborg 009* films prompted Toei Dōga to adapt Ishinomori's manga to television in 1968. Although it was black and white, the series stood out for the energy brought by this cyborg team. But animation revolutionized the concept of the superhero in 1972 with *Science Ninja Team Gatchaman*.

Tatsunoko Production produced series of all genres in the 1960s, but it also sought the most effective ways to meet deadlines and keep pace. The studio very quickly assimilated the xerography technique, which transferred the animators' drawings directly onto the screen, bypassing the celluloid inking process. This process, created for Disney's *101 Dalmatians* and used for the first time in Japan for *Star of the Giants* (1968) by TMS, saved considerable time while reducing costs. It allowed Tatsunoko Production to create *Animentary: Ketsudan* in 1971, a documentary series on the Pacific War with highly

2
1968
Cyborg 009

3
1972
Kagaku Ninja-tai Gatchaman (Science Ninja Team Gatchaman)

4
1974
Hurricane Polymar

1972
Kagaku Ninjatai Gatchaman (Science Ninja Team Gatchaman)

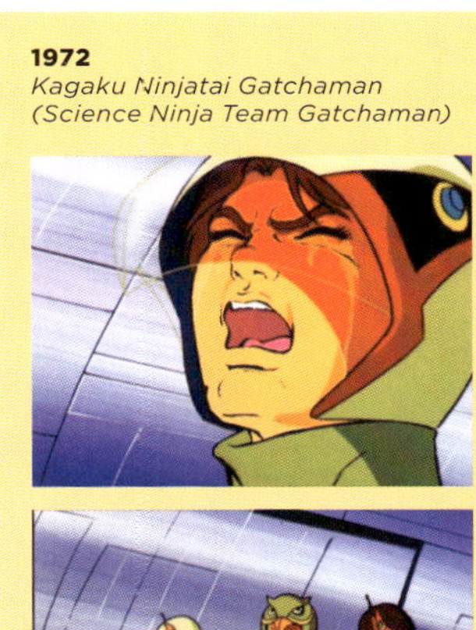

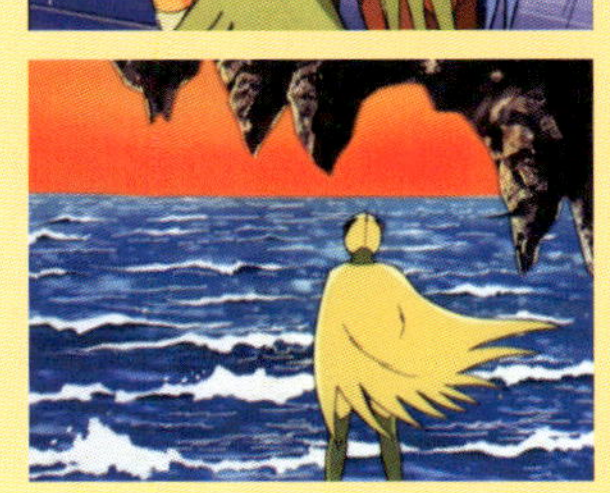

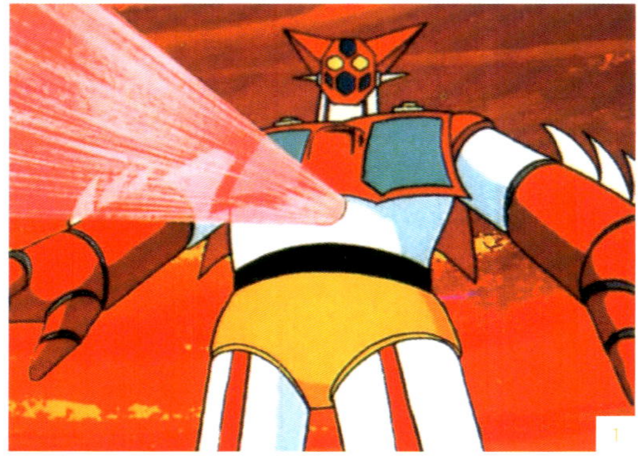

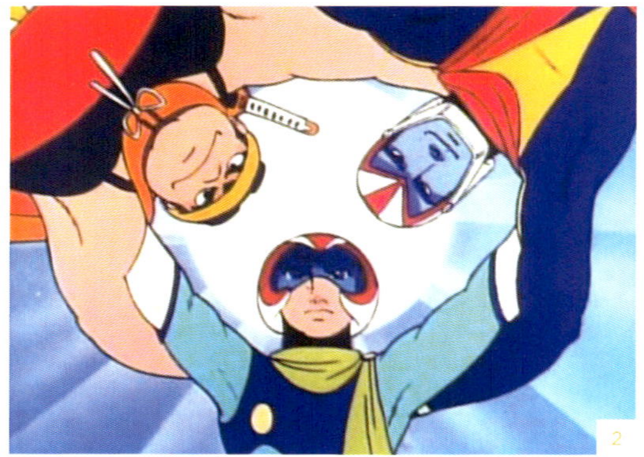

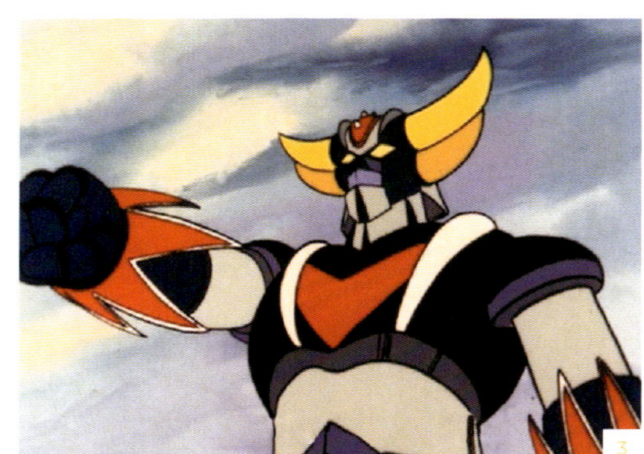

1 and 2
1974
Getter Robo

3
1974
UFO Robot Grendizer (Goldorak)

detailed drawings of military vehicles, in which the first credited instances of a **mecha** (mechanics) **designer** appear.

This was the dynamic when the studio spread its wings with *Kagaku Ninja-tai Gatchaman* (*Science Ninja Team Gatchaman*) in 1972. The formula they used for the original series broadcast on Fuji TV was infallible: a team of five superheroes with secret identities, different colors, and different powers, fighting against robot monsters using ships and gadgets. Unlike *Cyborg 009*, the costumes in *Gatchaman* were an integral part of the characters, giving audiences the transformation scenes they loved while being profitable for Tatsunoko Production because they could reuse the same shots in multiple episodes. The studio won on all fronts since Japanese children didn't just want to watch the episodes, they wanted to re-create them with the many merchandising spin-offs. The *Gatchaman* concept was repeated many times and even standardized the *super sentai* subgenre (*Gorenger*, *Bioman*, and so forth). Meanwhile, Tatsunoko capitalized on the series' success to further stand out in superhero realm with many new shows, including *Casshan* (1973), *Hurricane Polymar* (1974), *Tekkaman, the Space Knight* (1975), *Yatterman* (1977), and the sequels *Gatchaman 2* (1978) and *Gatchaman F* (1980). The studio had forged its own identity.

A few months after the first episode of *Gatchaman* aired in 1972, another superhero arrived on scene to shake things up for the viewers of Fuji TV. It was made of Super Alloy Z, and its size was likely to eclipse its competitors . . .

SUPER ROBOTS: TOEI'S COMEBACK

In its 1972 economic comeback, Toei Dōga saw a perfect strategy for establishing its own superheroes in the work of *mangaka* Go Nagai. The studio adapted Nagai's *Devilman* manga by toning down the apocalyptic story to better compete with the new *Ultraman* series. Stripped of its frightening features, the demon was now taller than buildings to keep up with the giant hero trend. At the end of the year, Toei adapted *Mazinger Z*, Go Nagai's new manga that had just been released in the famous magazine *Weekly Shōnen Jump*. Its TV success quickly made people forget the poor animation in *Astroganger*, the first super robot series in color three months earlier. Go Nagai's concept had quite the appeal—unlike in *Tetsujin 28-go* where the robot was controlled remotely, *Mazinger Z* integrated pilot and machine. To do so, young rebel Koji Kabuto flies an aircraft that connects to the giant's head. From atop his robot, Koji is the brain enabling the machine to confront evil Dr. Hell's monster machines. Mazinger Z became the allegory for a highly performing national defense and Japan's industrial, scientific, and technological power.

While Toho followed in Toei's footsteps by holding its own annual festival, the Toho Champion Matsuri, which started in 1969, the studio also created a contest asking children to draw a hero who would be featured in the next giant monster film (*kaiju eiga*): *Godzilla vs. Megalon*. Selected to appear alongside the radioactive monster, now reduced to child-friendly entertainment, the character who would become Jet Jaguar, who looked like a cross between Ultraman and Mazinger Z.

With ninety-two episodes of *Mazinger Z*, toy manufacturers rubbed their hands together in anticipation as children raved about their new hero's super attacks and the different creatures in the repetitive episodes. The serialized formula of the "monster of the week" didn't seem to bother anyone—quite the contrary, because the giant robots of Go Nagai and his friend Ken Ishikawa appeared year after year in *Great Mazinger*, *Getter Robo*, *Getter Robo G*, and *UFO Robot Grendizer* (*Goldorak*). Even though these

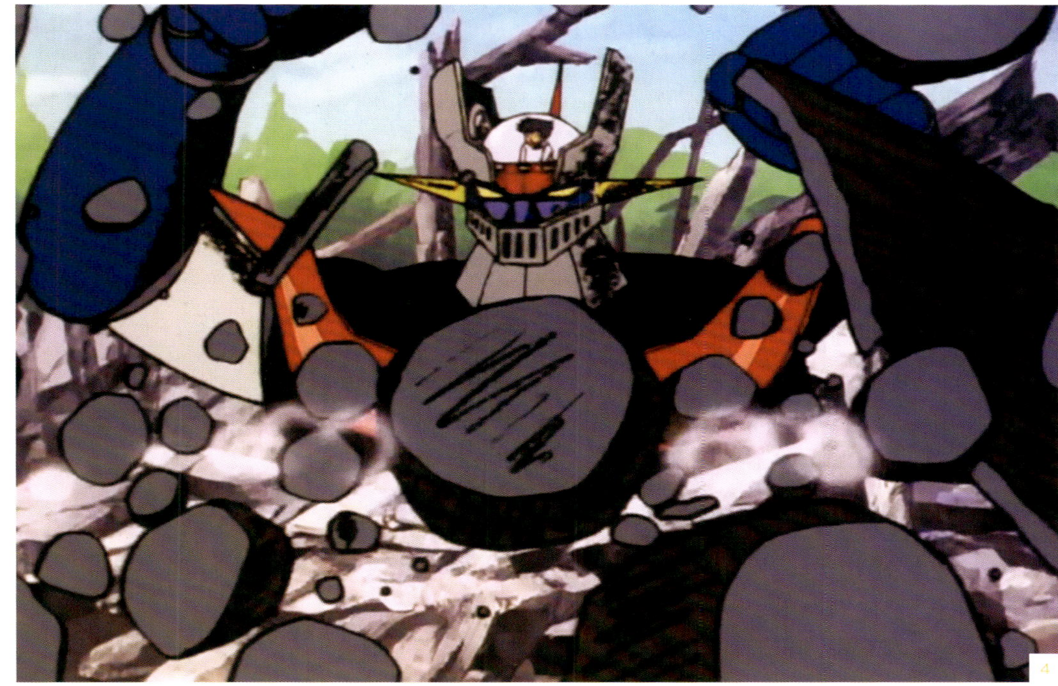

4
—
1972
Mazinger Z

series had guaranteed and often fierce fight scenes, they downplayed the great violence in the manga to appeal to a wider audience. Various connections between series and other robot matchups in film productions kept fans coming back for more hero one-upmanship. However, even though he was part of a great team in the *Mazinger* series, Koji Kabuto was merely a secondary character in *Goldorak*, strongly displeasing Japanese audiences who had begun to sanctify their fictional icons. The series was the only one not to have a sequel. After *Goldorak* aired, the time slot that had gotten Japan accustomed to Go Nagai's work was filled by a new Toei robot series: *Planetary Robot Danguard Ace* by Leiji Matsumoto, known for his space series *Uchū Senkan Yamato* (*Space Battleship Yamato*, 1974).

The super robot theme was overexploited, as became customary for fashionable genres in the 1970s, to the point that Toho produced the diptych *Godzilla vs. Mechagodzilla* (1974 and 1975) to respond to the public's fascination with these colossal machines. Animated series multiplied quickly as well, doubling down on creative efforts to make an impression and sell even more toys. Gone were the days when Osamu Tezuka speculated on the toy market to invest in new projects; now it was the makers of plastic robots and spaceships that created the series. Titles didn't stand out for their standardized storylines, but for their high-performance machines. The robot was the superstar of the show, its abilities and different attacks needed to ring out from playgrounds. Thus, three pilots combined their aircrafts to create Getter Robo, itself convertible into three positions. The robot Gaiking had a head forming its core and was made up of three parts coming together to become a huge flying dragon. As for Kotetsu Jeeg, this robot was entirely composed of smaller parts. Toei even managed to ride the latest *super sentai* trend with its series *Chōjin Sentai Baratakku* (*Balatack*). The sky was the limit for these series that charmed financiers and advertisers with their economic potential.

SUPER ROBOTS: FROM *ASTROGANGER* TO *GUNDAM*

Although Toei dominated the super robot market, other studios were making their presence felt, for better or for worse. Knack Production, created in 1967 by former employees of Mushi Production and Toei Dōga, was prolific despite having animation quality well below that of its competitors. Its *Astroganger* series (1972), shortly predating the broadcast of *Mazinger Z*, depicts a robot made of living metal that can talk and fuse with Kentaro, the young hero. The sequence of poorly interwoven still shots and scarcity of movement became a disappointing trademark of the studio, which heavily relied on eye-catching drawings. Even when Go Nagai was involved, such as in *Groizer X* (1976) and *Psycho Armor Govarian* (1983), the motionless images did no credit to the series' original concepts. In 1974, Knack Production created a superhero whose technical aspects and writing were so cheesy that *Chargeman Ken!* became a cult classic at its own expense. Despite everything, the studio was very successful internationally.

Also made up of former Mushi Production employees, Sunrise Nippon was established in 1979 and quickly specialized in producing super robot series. It started by subcontracting shows for various companies such as *Yūsha Raideen* (*Brave Raideen*, 1975) by Tōhokushinsha Film. Directed by Yoshiyuki Tomino and Tadao Nagahama and written by Sōji Yoshikawa, this series was the first to give the title robot mystic rather than sci-fi origins. It also has more touching characters, especially because the robot itself has feelings. Above all, the series enabled the Popy toy company to design the first toy robot.

The great success of *Brave Raideen* allowed Tadao Nagahama and Yoshiyuki Tomino to take the reins of the decisive series at Sunrise Nippon. Nagahama directed *Chōdenji Robo Combattler V* (1976), a coproduction with Toei that would lead to two other series: *Chōdenji Machine Voltes V* (1977) and *Tosho Daimos* (1978), making up the *Robot Romance Trilogy*. The three titles are independent of one another, but they are linked by a theatrical, dramatic treatment of the story and characters. Sunrise Nippon had positioned itself as an alternative to help this sci-fi subgenre mature, as confirmed by the first series produced entirely by the studio and directed by Tomino.

In *Muteki Chōjin Zambot 3* (*Invincible Super Man Zambot* 3, 1977), Sunrise produced an original series that used the concept of different pilots within the same machine, as well as the bright colors of Toei's robots. Although it was still a serialized production, author and director Yoshiyuki Tomino also featured ambiguous characters—heroes were part of the same family, implying less archetypal relationships. Despite the common structure in each episode, Tomino and his scriptwriter Sōji Yoshikawa had fun with the shots in the super robot series. The director continued building momentum the next year with *Muteki Kōjin Daitān 3* (*Invincible Steel Man Daitarn* 3). The hero, Haran Banjo, is an unlikely cross between billionaire vigilante Bruce Wayne (*Batman*) and charming spy James Bond, accompanied by two voluptuous women, a feisty boy, and a butler who is an expert pilot. Senseless absurdity was paired with intense drama in *Zambot 3*, and Tomino thumbed his nose at the subgenre with extremely dark final episodes to emphasize its obvious saturation. This revealed his intention to break with codes, which he set out to do in 1979 with *Gundam*, marking the next major turning point for anime after *Astro Boy* and *Mazinger Z*.

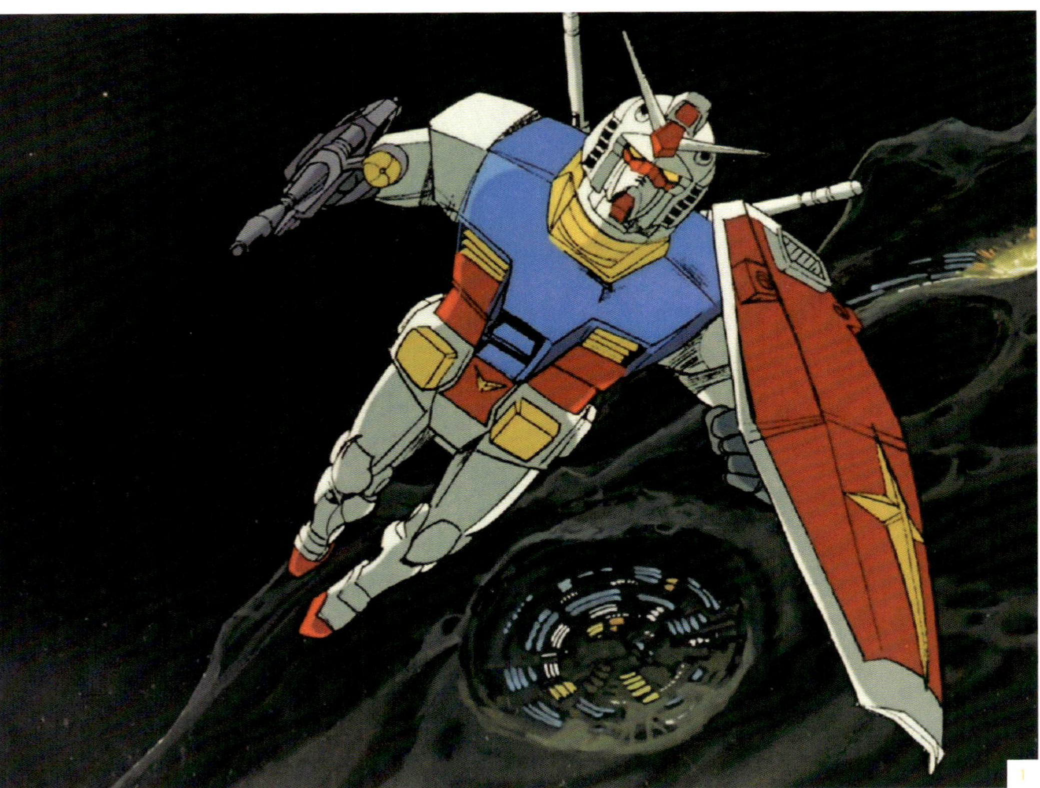

1979
Kidō Senshi Gundam (Mobile Suit Gundam)

GUNDAM: META MECHA

In 1979, Sunrise Nippon solidified anime with two extremely ambitious projects led by directors Ryōsuke Takahashi and Yoshiyuki Tomino, who became the studio's key figures. Takahashi proposed a new adaptation of *Cyborg 009*, coproduced by Toei, who had the audiovisual rights. While author Shotaro Ishinomori participated in the first few episodes, Takahashi and screenwriter Sōji Yoshikawa were then entirely free to create a more complex story. In tune with the times, it touched upon the oil crisis, the energy crisis, and various prejudices. The dynamic series was made up of long story arcs, allowing the series to progressively break free from the formulaic structure that had regulated superheroes for so many years. Thus, the new version of *Cyborg 009* was a hybrid between episodic and serialized.

This was also the case for *Kidō Senshi Gundam* (*Mobile Suit Gundam*), an original creation by Tomino and Sunrise. Super robot series used to shine because of their dualism, but *Gundam* stood out with a realistic political, economic, and social context, in which viewers saw both sides of a war. In the era of space colonization, humanity was divided into two groups: Earthnoids and Spacenoids (settlers). Several political and military factions were taking shape, creating tensions that led to a long conflict. Hard themes like war, armament, nationalism, fascism, independence, and indoctrination made the series resolutely more mature. Robots, called "Mobile Suits," were moderately sized and mass-produced. From this point on, viewers no longer watched robot series but space operas with war machines! However, the story maintained a kinship with the super robot, in both its need for a teenage pilot and the need to revisit fatherhood and its legacy (the robot).

But in 1979, this unique series didn't capture audiences because people weren't used to a serialized format for this kind of show, especially as the story and its many characters required viewers to watch consistently to understand what was going on. The decision was made to shorten the series by rushing the ending. And even though the *Gundam* series could have stopped there, Bandai hit hard in 1980 with **Gunpla**, plastic models from the *Gundam* universe that encouraged sci-fi fans to take an interest in the series. That's why the rerelease was such a huge hit. Super robot aficionados almost forgot their whimsical giants in favor of these machines that obeyed the laws of physics and left the spotlight to the humans. Even though there were certain structural patterns in each episode—audiences expected their necessary dose of mecha—the protagonists were at the forefront of the series. Tomino didn't hesitate to traumatize more than one of them to help relationships evolve, whether friendly, familial, romantic, or contentious, and to kill them off regularly as the story developed.

The *Gundam* series was held even more sacred by fans as the VCR became more affordable, allowing them to record episodes and watch them again and again. The public became truly addicted, analyzing innovative scenes and learning about the creators. Tomino, manga artist Yoshikazu Yasuhiko, and animator Ichirō Itano became superstars of the **otaku** culture that was permeating Japanese society.

Studios took a massive interest in the resurgence that mixed robotics with space operas, producing a large number of so-called "real robot series," a term later used in the game *Super Robot Taisen* to distinguish between robots with superpowers (super robots) and the more realistic ones (real robots).

A RACE TO THE STARS

By the 1970s, science fiction was no longer just popular entertainment. In 1968, *2001: A Space Odyssey* shifted mindsets by awarding the genre, showing how well stories about robots and spaceships could appeal to a demanding audience. Stanley Kubrick had asked Tezuka to bring his entire team to help produce it because *Astro Boy* was such a groundbreaking series with original themes and visuals. In the end, the collaboration didn't happen because the *mangaka* was tied to producing his own manga and TV series. But such a craze illustrated how much Japanese science fiction was growing and gaining in identity, to the point of becoming exotic. The country now had its own codes and heroes. And while the Cold War was driven by a race for the stars, which would lead Russians to go to space, then Americans to set foot on the Moon, young people around the world were dreaming of becoming astronauts. Space travel became an interesting subject insofar as artists saw space as a perfect outlet for their imagination.

This was the case for *mangaka* Leiji Matsumoto, who created *Space Battleship Yamato* with Yoshinobu

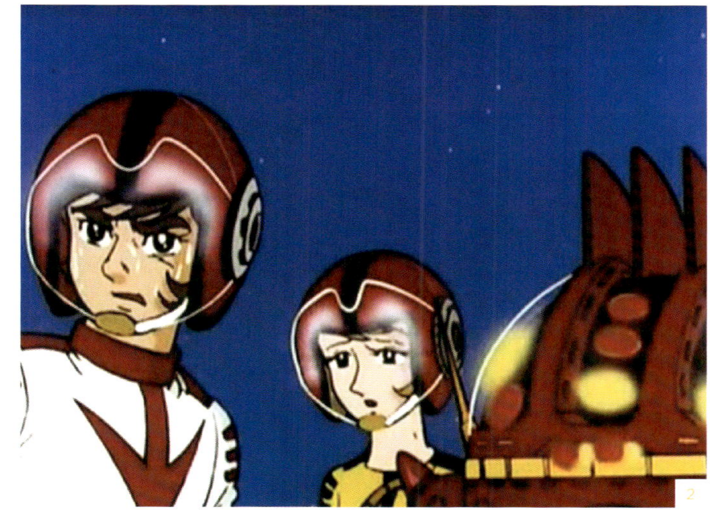

2

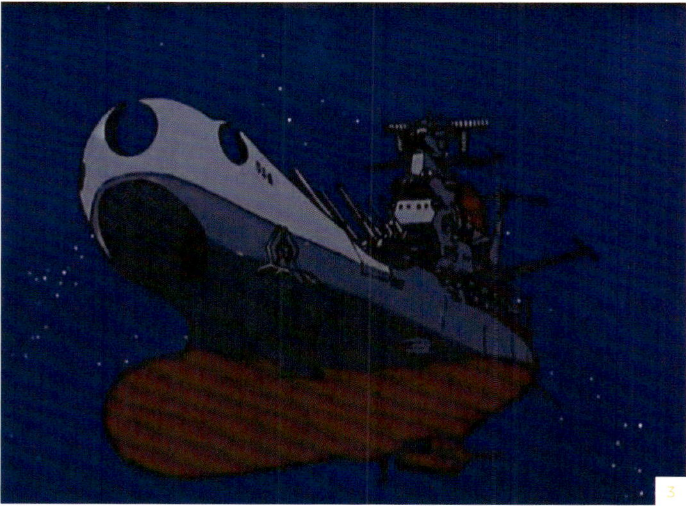

3

2 and 3
1974
Uchū Senkan Yamato (Space Battleship Yamato)

Nishizaki in 1974. In order to save Earth, heavily irradiated in the aftermath of an endless war against aliens, humans cross the universe aboard the *Yamato*, a World War II battleship transformed into a powerful spaceship. It was a considerable challenge because such an initiatory voyage required different environments, leading to distinct storylines and settings from one episode to the next. And although it replaced the giant robot in its glory, the *Yamato* was a ship, not a mechanical colossus with superpowers. The series was thus aimed at an older audience, fans of sci-fi works such as *Star Trek*, from which it took the concept of the galactic journey with an endearing crew. With this resurrection of the Japanese navy's famous warship, the anachronistic nationalism of the story was surprising. Leiji ("Warrior Zero") Matsumoto was the child of a World War II soldier, and his fascination for the war would forever be part of his work. The *Yamato* concept was reminiscent of the famous film *Kaitei Gunkan* (*Atragon*, 1963) by Ishirō Honda, in which politics and the military also played a large role.

To ensure that production ran smoothly, Toei appointed one of its renowned artists as codirector, Noboru Ishiguro, who would go on to find his true calling in space operas.

With its modern narrative and visuals, *Space Battleship Yamato* offered a new cinematic approach to space tales, helping Toei become the top studio in the anime boom of the 1970s. Several recap films were made and then a second season was produced in 1978. It was impossible for the Japanese to slip through Leiji Matsumoto's intergalactic web that year, with Toei producing three other series by the author. Matsumoto created an explosive space version of *Journey to the West* in *SF Saiyuki Starzinger* (*Force Five: Spaceketeers*). In *Ginga Tetsudō 999* (*Galaxy Express 999*), he depicted the galactic journey of a mysterious young woman and a young boy from the streets who dreams of mechanizing his body. Their journey fascinated TV audiences as the characters were tried and tested in tormented worlds, representing the evils of our society.

Most of all, these varied environments allowed Matsumoto to blend genres, a technique that was also one of the strengths of *Uchū Kaizoku Captain Harlock* (*Space Pirate Captain Harlock*). A clever fusion of science fiction and Western, *Space Pirate Captain Harlock* depicts ultra-stylized characters who seem to be connected to the *mangaka*'s other works, captivating viewers even more. The series, directed by Rintaro, introduced many additional characters and offered an ending, whereas the manga left readers wanting more (a recurring feature in Matsumoto's work).

Contrary to Go Nagai's manga adaptations, the series inspired by Matsumoto's work were not subdued versions of his manga but adaptations that explored his universe in greater depth. Melancholic and poetic, they reflect a pessimistic vision of a distant future, in which Earth regularly pays the price, as in *Shin Taketori Monogatari: Sennen Joō* (*Queen Millennia*, 1981) and *Waga Seishun no Arcadia: Mugen Kidō SSX* (*Arcadia of My Youth: Endless Orbit SSX*, 1982).

If Japanese television was so immersed in space in 1978, it was mainly because *Star Wars* (1977) further popularized galactic epics by mixing chivalry with politics. Toei forged ahead producing a new adaptation of the *Captain Future* novels, whose format of four episodes per story allowed for longer plotlines. TMS was also developing more extensive story arcs, as seen in its adaptation of Buichi Terasawa's *Space Adventure Cobra* manga (1982). Technical teams were creating less condensed scenarios in which heroes proudly crossed the galaxy with their sidekicks and indispensable ships.

Meanwhile, the Franco-Japanese coproduction *Uchū Densetsu Ulysses 31* (*Ulysses 31*, 1981) was part of this trend as a space version of the *Odyssey*. This series, much like Matsumoto's stories, reflects Joseph Campbell's concept of the monomyth, or the hero's journey, in which the protagonist must go on transformative adventure. This hero construction has been fully embraced by robot series since *Gundam*.

1 – **1978** *Uchū Kaizoku Captain Harlock (Space Pirate Captain Harlock)*

2 – **1982** *Space Adventure Cobra*

3 – **1981** *Uchū Densetsu Ulysses 31 (Ulysses 31)*

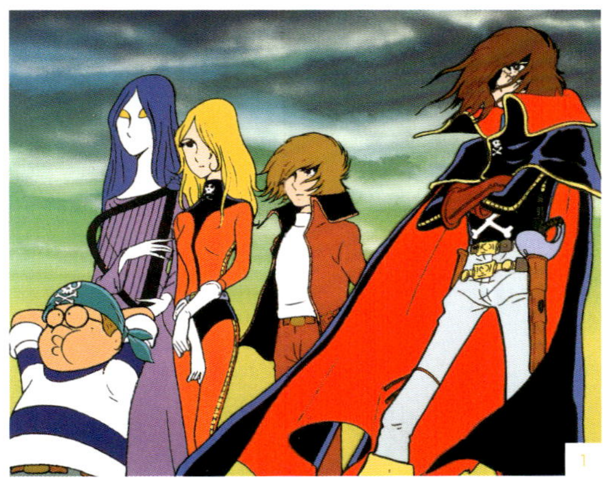

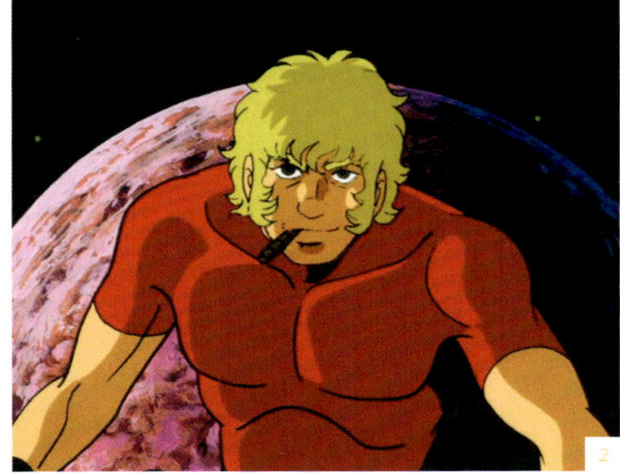

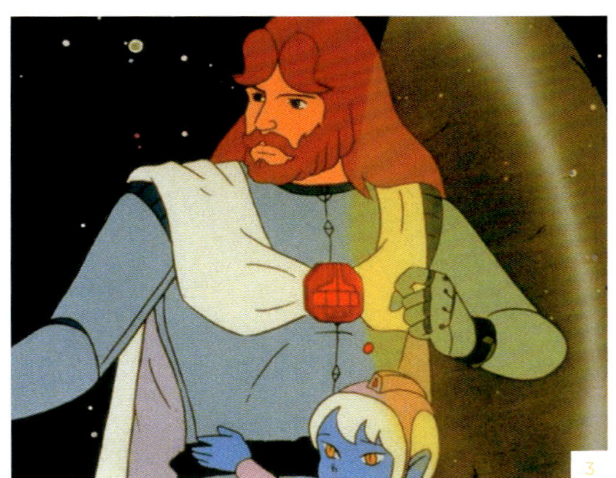

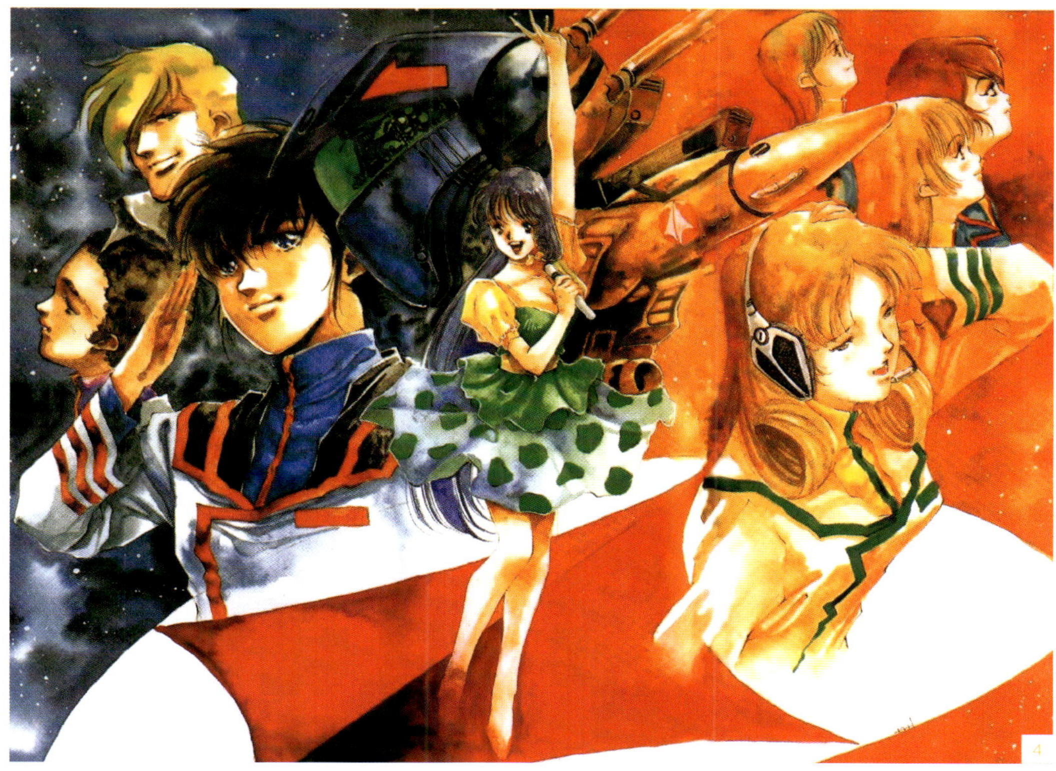

4

1978
Ginga Tetsudō 999 (Galaxy Express 999)

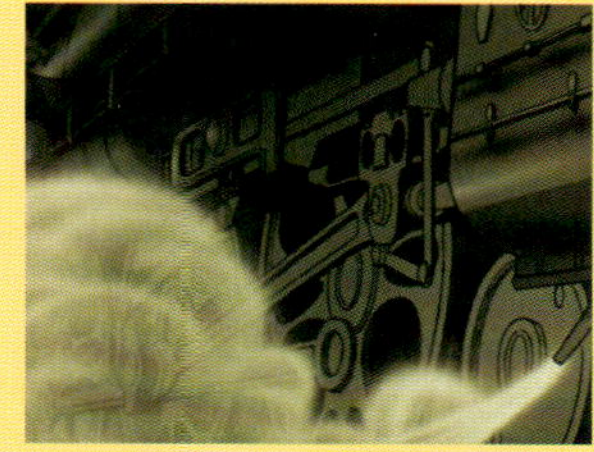

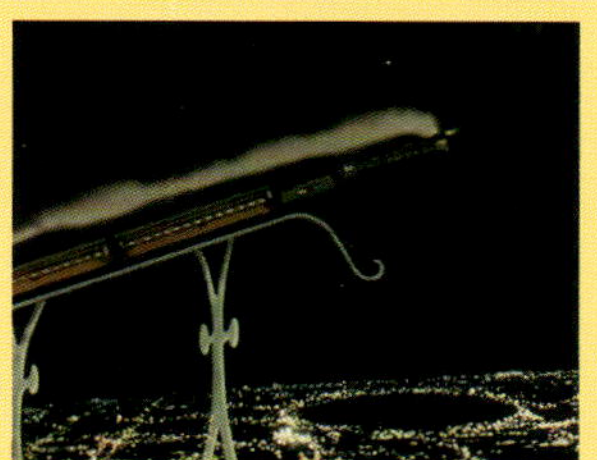

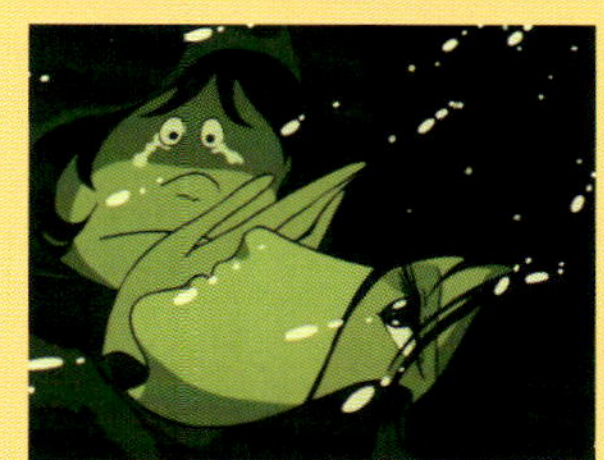

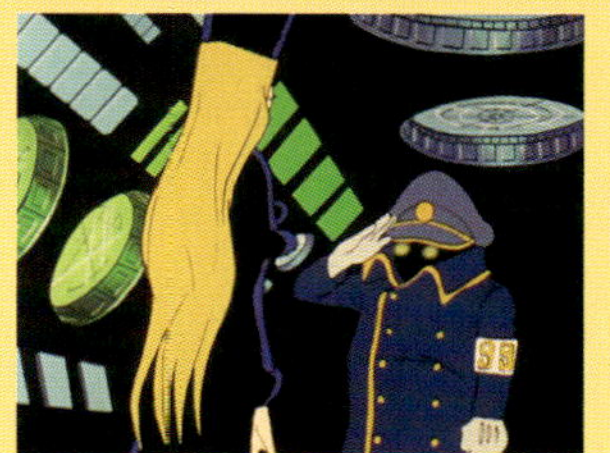

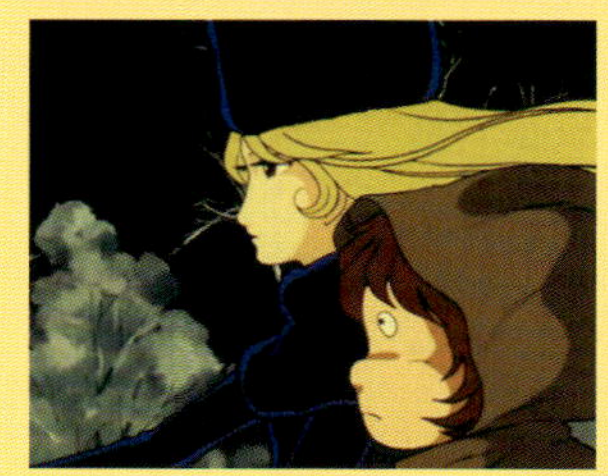

SPACE ROBOTS: SUNRISE WINS THE DAY

Although mecha was *Mobile Suit Gundam*'s main selling point, the biggest motivator for Yoshiyuki Tomino was directing a space series. The combination set a precedent, and Bandai's commercial success encouraged producers to send their new robots into space. Under the leadership of screenwriter Yū Yamamoto, Toei and Kokusai Eigasha studios produced a trilogy that caused a sensation: *J9 Series*, made up of *Ginga Senpu Braiger* (*Galaxy Cyclone Braiger*, 1981), *Ginga Reppu Baxinger* (*Galactic Gale Baxingar*, 1982), and *Ginga Shippu Sasuraiger* (*Galactic Whirlwind Sasuraiger*, 1983). Robots play only a minor role in these narratives, which take the three J9 teams on a wide variety of adventures. Criminals, industrialists, and corrupt politicians replaced aliens and mad scientists hungry for world domination.

Competition was fierce, forcing production companies to double down on their creative efforts to draw in both an ever-growing audience and financial sponsors who wanted to fill toy store shelves with merchandise. A collaboration between Studio Nue, Big West, and Tatsunoko Production made a breakthrough in 1982 by creating a worthy challenger—*Chōjikū Yōsai Macross* (*Super Dimension Fortress Macross*). Directed in 1982 by Noburo Ishiguro (*Space Battleship Yamato*), the series follows the space voyage of a rescued city traveling in a massive ship, whose goal is to return to Earth despite fierce attacks by an alien race. Young author and mecha designer Shōji Kawamori struck hard with machines that could be transformed into three combat positions, ranging from realistic fighter planes to giant robots. More upbeat than *Gundam*, *Macross* traded in the lyrical music of the space opera for songs by pop **idols** and brought a love triangle to the forefront of the story. The romantic recipe energized the story and left a lasting impression, creating a lucrative series.

Meanwhile, Sunrise reigned supreme over mecha series in the early 1980s. The studio was forcing political and martial themes into ever more ambitious narratives. Ryōsuke Takahashi caught viewers' attention with his more brutal and social approach to war in *Taiyō no Kiba Dougram* (*Fang of the Sun Dougram*, 1981). The director never glorified the

4
—
1982
Chōjikū Yōsai Macross (The Super Dimension Fortress Macross)

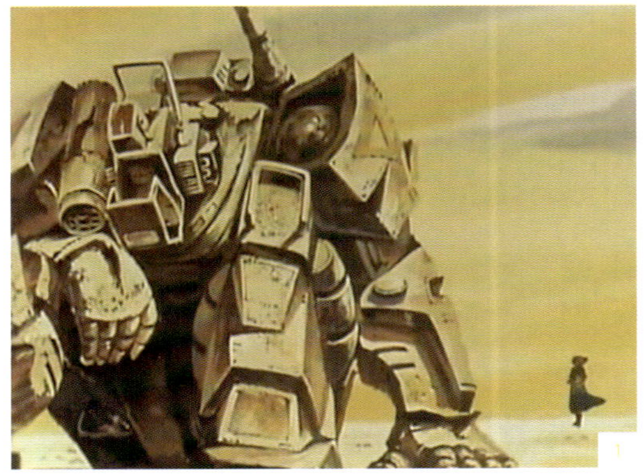

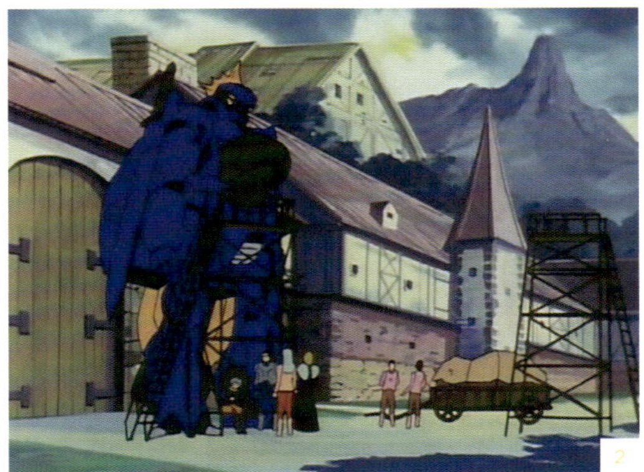

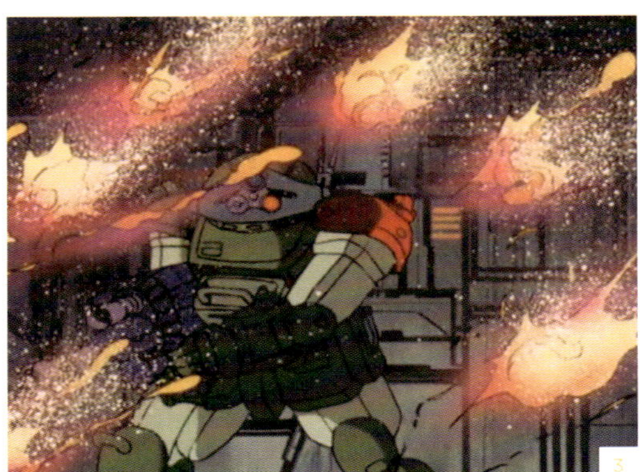

1
1981
Taiyō no Kiba Dougram (Fang of the Sun Dougram)

2
1983
Seisenshi Dunbine (Aura Battler Dunbine)

3
1983
Sōkō Kihei Votoms (Armored Trooper Votoms)

imposing robots, which were ultimately no more than murderous extensions of the human body. Resolutely focused on adult audiences, Takahashi did not feature any children as characters in *Sōkō Kihei Votoms* (*Armored Trooper Votoms*, 1983). With its taciturn hero, high visual quality, and confusing storyline, the series was both austere and fascinating, which would lead to many sequels. Sunrise gave its directors creative freedom to test and create concepts to remain a leader in the giant robot genre. Thus, Takahashi directed *Kikō Kai Galient* (*Panzer World Galient*), in which he placed his mecha in a heroic fantasy situation. He was following in the footsteps of the *Seisenshi Dunbine* (*Aura Battler Dunbine*) series, directed a year earlier by the master of the genre, Yoshiyuki Tomino.

Tomino's incredible production of original series, including *Gundam*, *Juusenki L-Gaim* (*Heavy Metal L-Gaim*, 1984), *Densetsu Kyojin Ideon* (*Space Runaway Ideon*, 1980), and *Sentō Mecha Xabungle* (*Combat Mecha Xabungle*, 1982), places the author-director in the pantheon of the era's most iconic artists. Sunrise commissioned him for a sequel to *Gundam*, still adored by fans. In 1985, *Kidō Senshi Zeta Gundam* (*Mobile Suit Zeta Gundam*) was the anticipated huge success, allowing the studio to produce another sequel, *Gundam ZZ* (1986), and then several canonical, original works, creating a franchise that would become Sunrise's identity.

The *Votoms*, *Macross*, and *Gundam* series would proudly span decades, responding to the fascination of a growing number of fans around the world and a toy market that would become increasingly more powerful.

Celluloid's return to cinema

THE RECAP MOVIE

The number of series produced each year continued to grow, as did the number of fans, who were becoming more obsessed with anime and science fiction. The commercial potential of these enthusiasts did not escape the attention of the companies creating magazines about these imaginary universes, feeding this new thirst for knowledge. This was how the magazines *Out* (1977), *Animage* (1978), *Animec* (1978), *The Anime* (1979), *My Anime* (1981), *B-Club* (1985), and *Newtype* (1985) became indispensable to the emerging otaku community. Analytical articles about the series; interviews with animators, authors, and voice actors; exclusive information about the shows; and prerelease content, artwork, and more were in every issue, drawing fans closer to the artists and their work. Yoshinobu Nishizaki, *Yamato* cocreator and producer, saw in this audience a massive opportunity to spread the word about *Yamato*'s first feature film, released in 1977. He recruited the fans of the 1974 series to indirectly promote the film through various media. First, he provided them with production documents that would be used in many issues of the sci-fi magazine *Out*. He also targeted traditional networks by encouraging his followers to ensure that the title was everywhere by broadcasting the theme song on the radio, publishing articles in the press, and so forth—work that Nishizaki rewarded with precious animation cels and merchandise. *Out* magazine quickly sold out, a phenomenon that would happen again every time it featured *Yamato*, to the point that it specialized in the franchise to prevent sales from falling again. The craze surrounding the title had become overwhelming, prompting Toei to release the film in its network of cinemas, despite the fact that a more discreet release had been planned. It was an immense success with the box office topping out at ¥900 million, a record for an anime film, which was surpassed by its sequel in 1978! Anime was once again attracting the general public, who preferred cinematic releases for Toho's monster movies and Hollywood blockbusters.

With each one going well over two hours, the two *Space Battleship Yamato* feature films weren't simply the twenty-minute adventures that Toei had been producing since the advent of *Mazinger Z* but a skillful recap of the series, allowing viewers to revisit the space epic on the big screen or discover it in a more condensed format. And it was a godsend for producers, who could breathe a lucrative second life into material that had already been used, like Toei did with *Force Five: Spaceketeers* (1978) and TMS with *Nobody's Boy: Remi* (1980).

Like a booster shot, these extremely profitable productions also prepared Japanese audiences for a second season when it wasn't produced as a continuation of the first. Feature films became promotional material reimbursed by ticket sales. With this in mind, Tatsunoko Production revived the *Gatchaman* series in a film version in 1978. The studio had been struggling since the death of its cofounder

1981
Kidō Senshi Gundam (Mobile Suit Gundam)

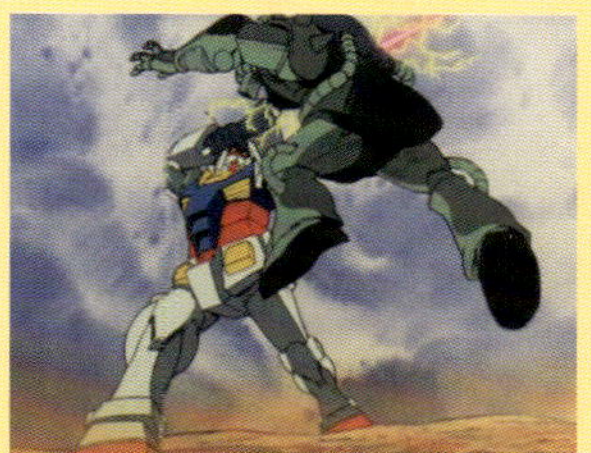

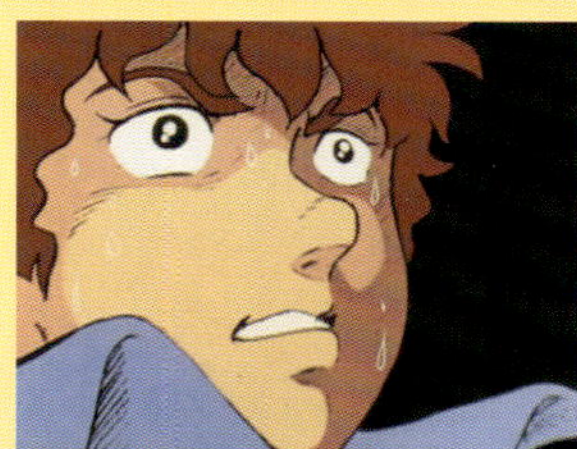

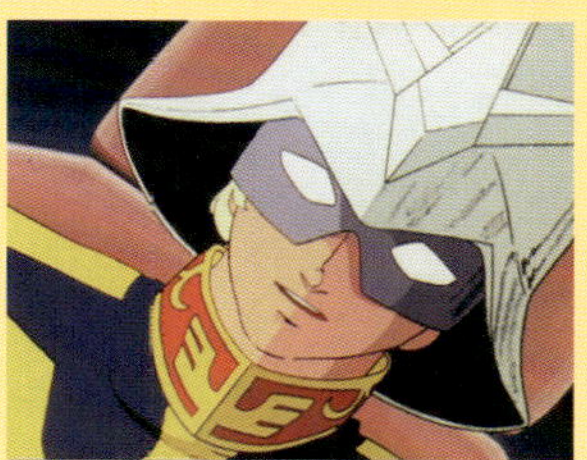

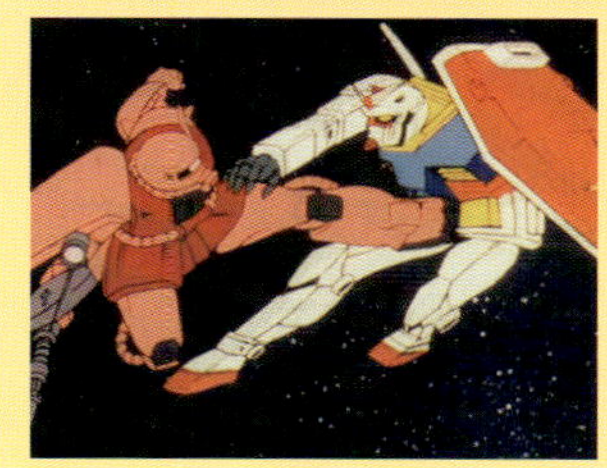

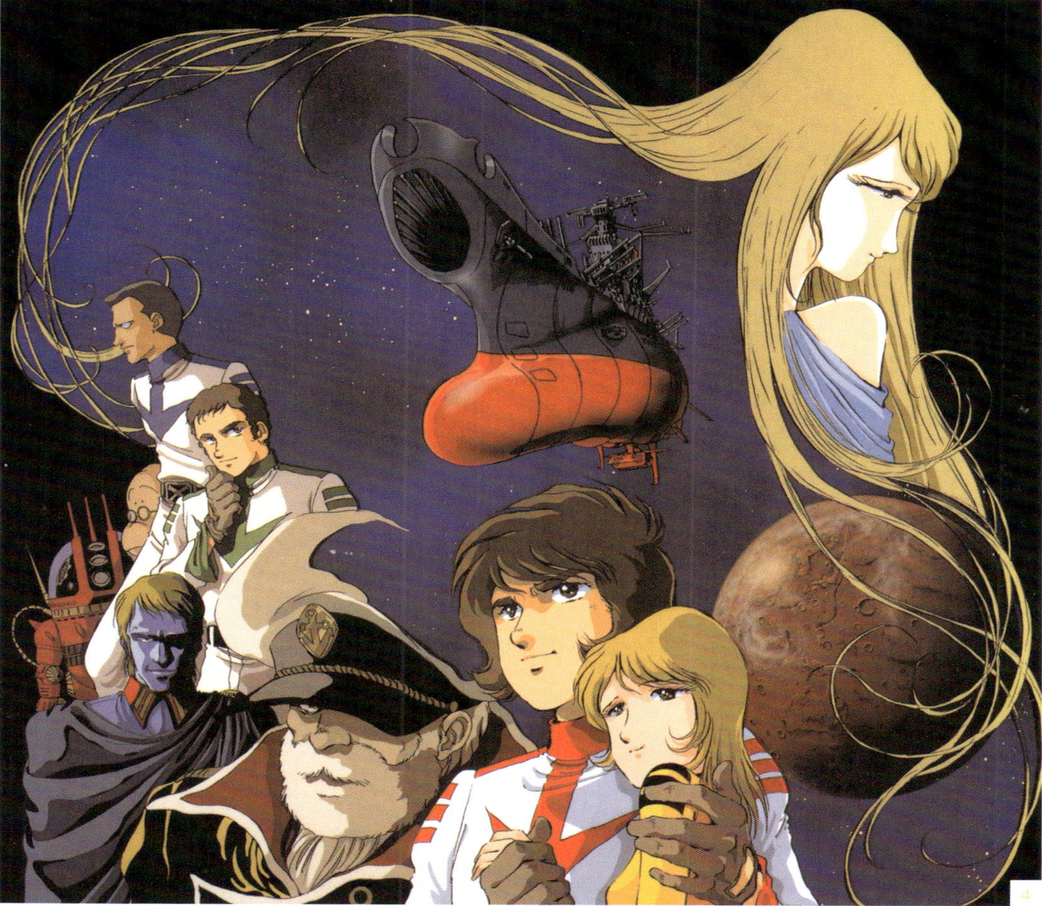

4
—
1977
Uchū Senkan Yamato (Space Battleship Yamato)

1: Taiyō no Kiba Dougram © *Sunrise.* **2:** Seisenshi Dunbine © *Sunrise.* **3:** Sōkō Kihei Votoms © *Sunrise.* **4:** Uchū Senkan Yamato *(1977 film) © September 1977 Voyager Entertainment.* **Panels:** Mobile Suit Gundam © *Yoshiyuki Tomino, Hajime Yatate, Sunrise, Sotsu Agency, Nagoya Broadcasting Network.*

1981
Densetsu Kyojin Ideon: Hatsudou Hen (The Ideon: Be Invoked)

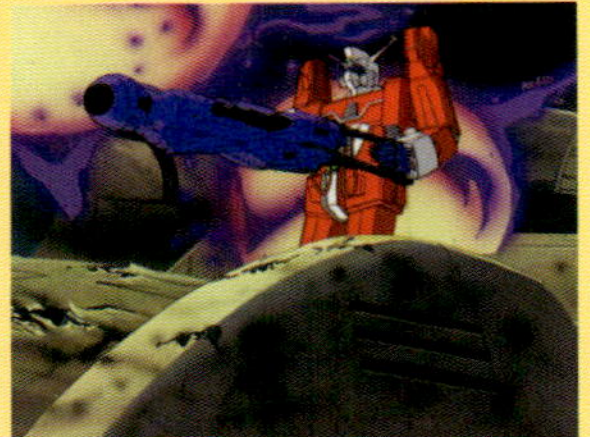

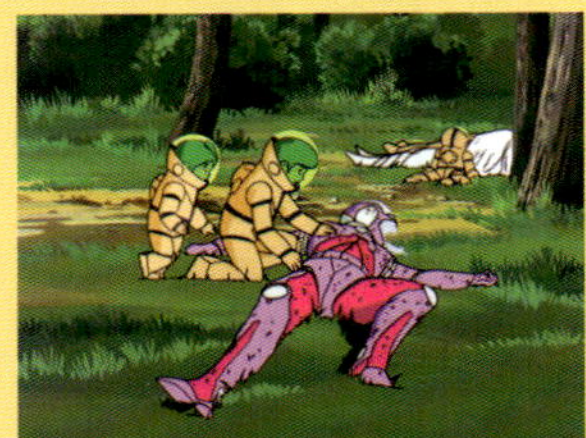

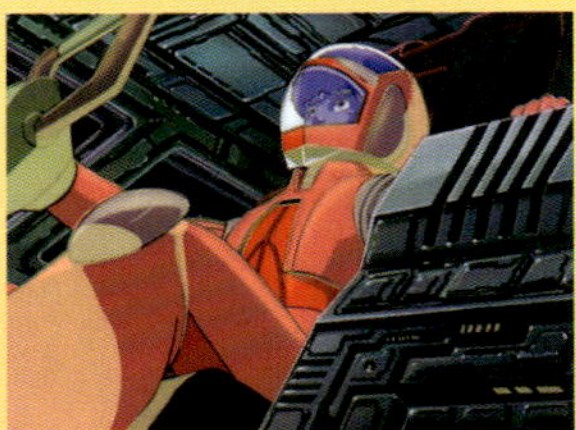

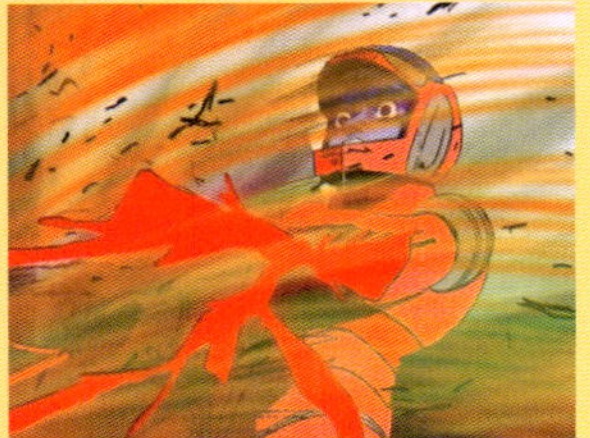

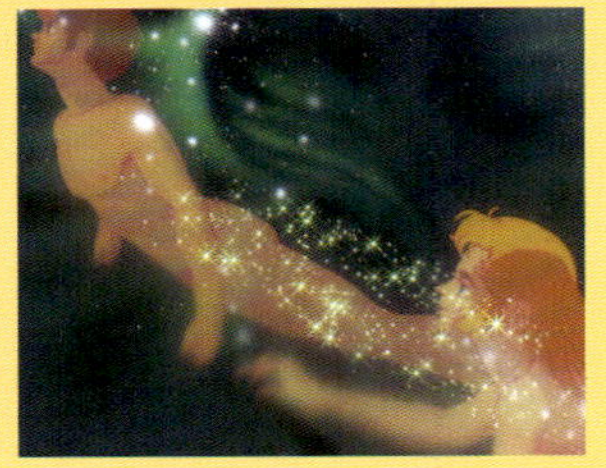

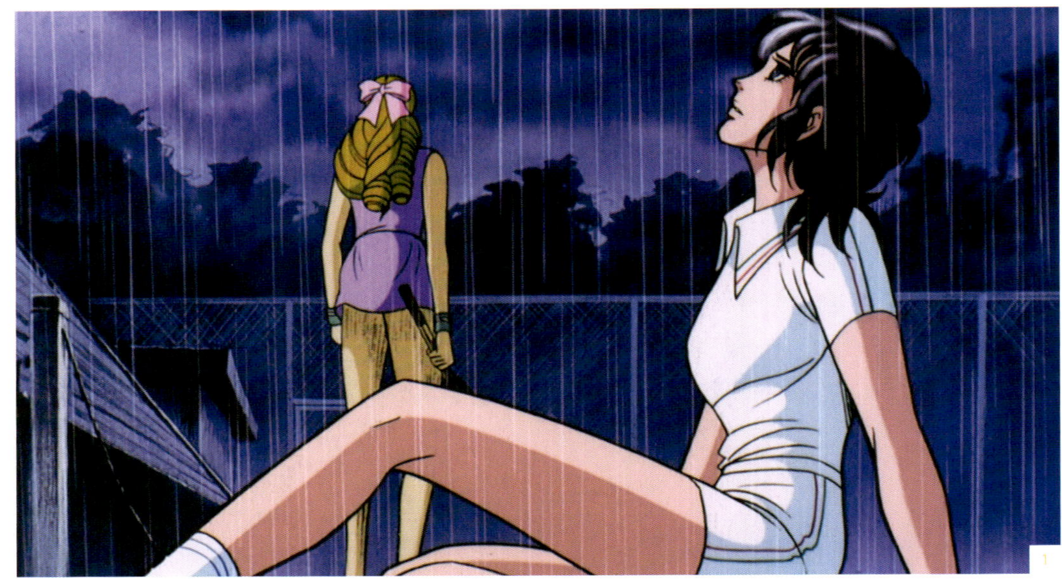

1

1979
Ace o Nerae! (Aim for the Ace!)

Tatsuo Yoshida the year before and took advantage of the film's success to renew its multicolored superheroes three months later on TV. TMS also used this strategy to produce the sequel to *Ashita no Joe*. The 1970 series was then condensed into two feature films ten years later. But, unlike *Gatchaman*, Osamu Dezaki's *Ashita no Joe* didn't have the repetitive structure that allowed films to omit certain passages without great consequence to the plot. By only hitting the plot highlights, the recap movies lost much of their intensity. Dezaki was offended at not having been forewarned about this, and the producer at TMS offered him the opportunity to direct the second season by way of apology. His annoyance was all the more understandable given that he had revamped his *Aim for the Ace!* series the year before, proposing a remake created especially for cinema, and not a montage of sequences from the series. This artistic choice allowed the director to impose his graphic codes on the big screen, such as natural lighting effects and stylized frame-within-a-frame techniques. With reworked images and animation, the film justified the ticket price to see the story from a new angle. The big-screen summary was also a way to limit the damage, offering a second chance for series that didn't find their audience when they were first broadcast. The *Uchū Senshi Baldios* (1981) film even revealed a new ending, whereas the series had ended early due to low ratings. Yoshiyuki Tomino compiled the forty-three episodes of *Gundam* into three films between 1981 and 1982, with new scenes and a much more generous finale than the series' last few episodes. Moreover, whereas Tomino followed the main events from the *Space Runaway Ideon* series in its first film, *Sesshoku Hen* (*A Contact*, 1981), he expanded on its resolution in the second, *Hatsudou Hen* (*Be Invoked*, 1982). He captivated fans with the film's violence and gore, showing many deaths, including beheaded children. By adding a philosophical message to this collection of beloved characters' corpses, Tomino tried to directly address fans who had sung his praises. Even though he freely adapted his own series, he confirmed that cinema was becoming a means for directors to express themselves in a new way, targeting a mature audience.

FREE ADAPTATION

Since Hollywood had freed itself from the Hays Code that had imposed rules of decency upon studios from 1934 to 1968, American cinema was developing genre films in a more spontaneous and assertive way. The new generation of directors, such as Arthur Penn, Sam Peckinpah, Brian de Palma, Martin Scorsese, and John Carpenter were no longer limited by a censorship that regulated the whole production and could now create violent, erotic, or satirical works. It was a more realistic approach than studio movies driven by the "star system." Throughout the 1970s, spectators around the world had become accustomed to seeing more ambiguous characters, even sympathizing with the criminals (*Bonnie and Clyde*, *The Godfather*), which had been unimaginable a few years earlier.

On the Japanese side, the golden age of the major studios was on the decline, giving way to a new wave of protest and exploitation films. Gangster (*yakuza eiga*), sword fight (*chanbara*), and erotic (*pinku eiga*) movies accustomed audiences to a certain level of unconventional violence and sexuality. Although crushed by recent American blockbusters, such as *Jaws*, *Close Encounters of the Third Kind*, and *Star Wars*, the marginal production of Japanese films retained a certain level of creative independence, and manga adaptations for adults that didn't have to be toned down became possible. Thus, a *Golgo 13* film was produced in 1972, and another in 1977. Kenji Misumi adapted *Lone Wolf and Cub* with *Baby Cart to Hades* (1972), in which he got rid of music during the fight scenes, a fascinating way to amplify the intensity of the blows while keeping the feel of the original medium. Director Toshiya Fujita glorified the vengeful woman in a macho society in *Lady Snowblood*. Filmmakers broke taboos and developed formal eccentricities.

This trend toward free expression reached the generation of directors who became the leading figures in animation studios in the late 1970s. Financing original work for cinema still wasn't possible because the budget for a feature film was far too large to ensure minimum economic security. However, artists began asserting themselves through free adaptations.

2
—
1978
Lupin III vs. Fukusei-ningen (Lupin III: The Secret of Mamo)

3
—
1979
Lupin III: Cagliostro no Shiro (The Castle of Cagliostro)

4
—
1979
Ginga Tetsudō 999 (Galaxy Express 999)

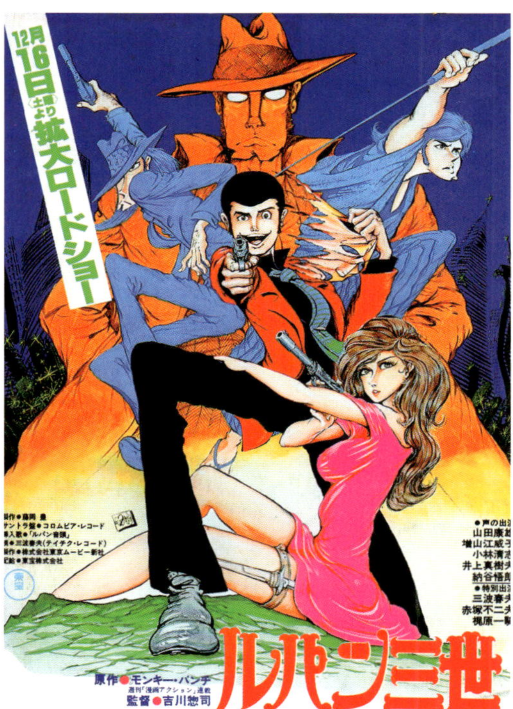

2

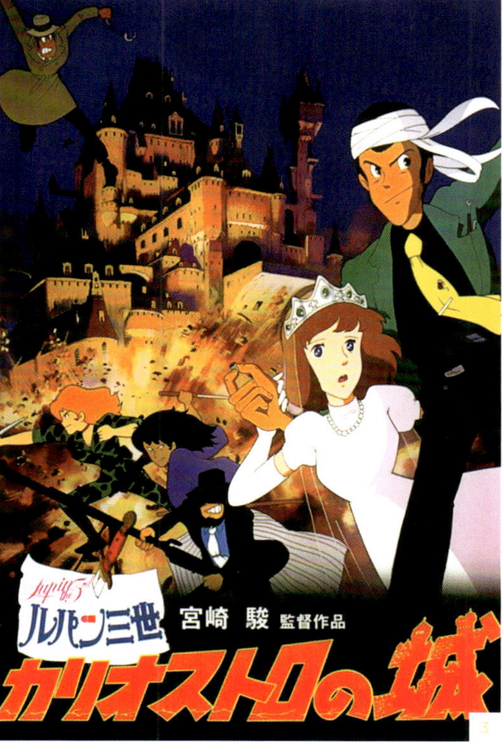

3

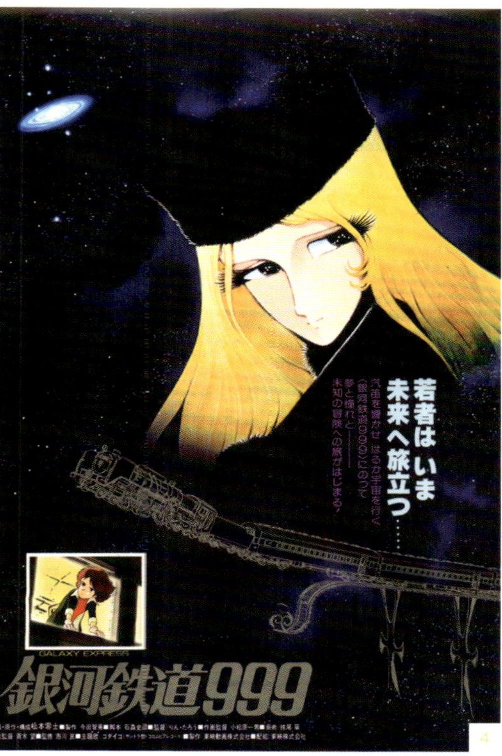

4

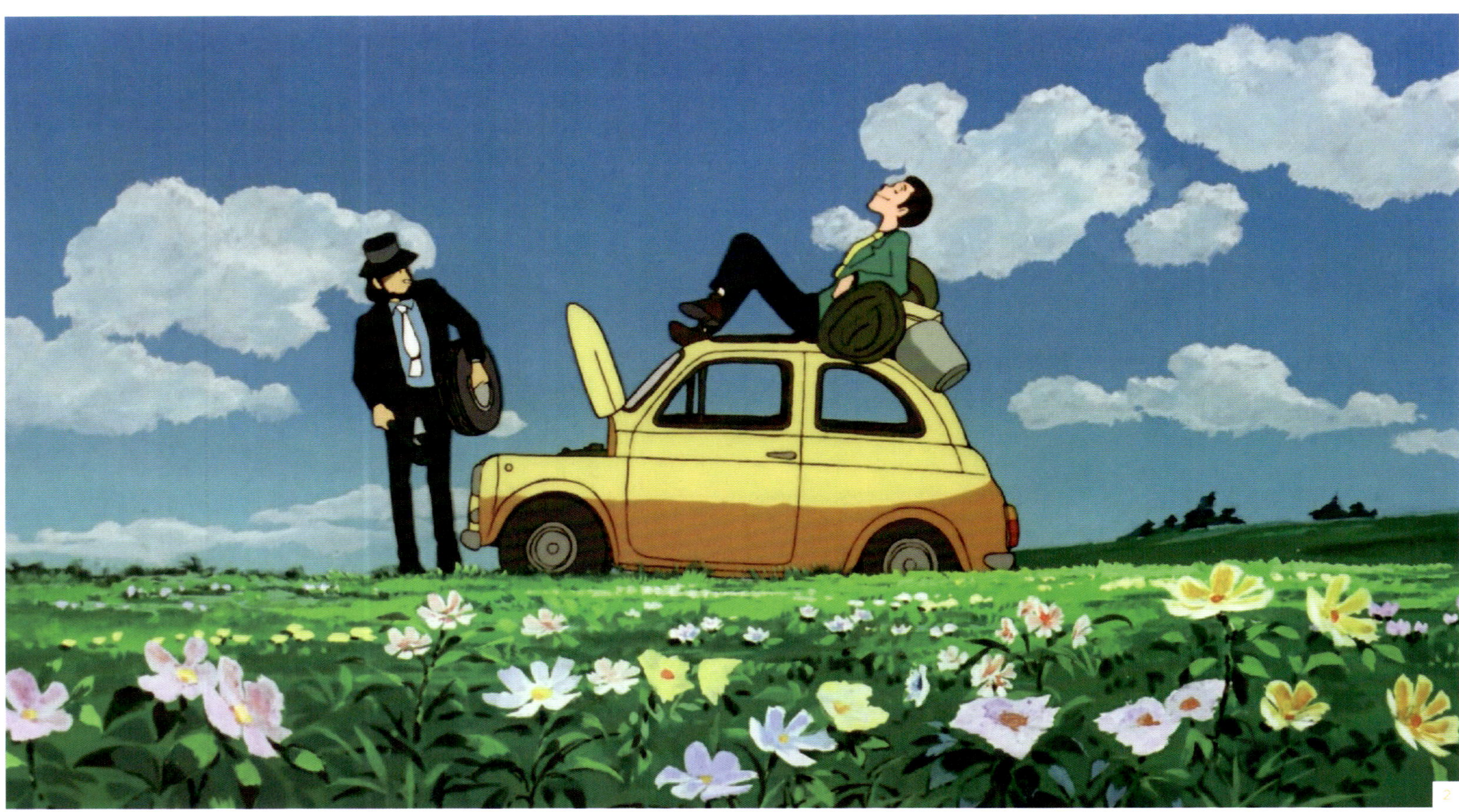

1

1979
Lupin III : Cagliostro no shiro (The Castle of Cagliostro)

Animator Yasuo Ōtsuka and screenwriter Sōji Yoshikawa were at the helm of the outlandish and provocative *Lupin III vs. Fukusei-ningen* (*Lupin III: The Secret of Mamo*, 1978). The film was a step above other media, with higher quality animation, more elaborate drawings, a different soundtrack, and the necessary freedom of tone for the film to be independent, especially as a stand-alone. Because the film had a less restrictive format than television, it could target an audience who could watch a longer, more complex, and sometimes erotic story—the movie ends with that naughty Lupin wantonly squeezing Fujiko's breast.

Filmmakers began to create their own vision of popular titles. Hayao Miyazaki, for example, took over Monkey Punch's project in 1979 with *Lupin III: Cagliostro no Shiro* (*The Castle of Cagliostro*), the franchise's second feature film. Rich in themes near to the young director's heart, the film was unusual for its time, and the artistic direction contrasted widely with the manga and the series without misrepresenting them. Even though it was not a resounding success, it gradually became a cult classic that went on to influence many a future animator. Miyazaki had been captivated by *The Tale of the White Serpent* and *La Bergère and le Ramoneur*, a French film that he had studied in such detail that his fascination shows through in *The Wonderful World of Puss 'n Boots* and *The Castle of Cagliostro*. And now it was his work captivating the new generation.

Rintaro also directed the *Galaxy Express 999* feature film in 1979. The former Mushi Production director now excelled at low-budget storytelling, with *Space Pirate Captain Harlock* as a good example of the tricks he used to compensate for the lack of movement. But he created a much more ambitious adaptation for his first feature film. With sophisticated staging that oscillated between brutal and poetic, he retold Leiji Matsumoto's story with a surprise ending, perfectly integrating the concept of *toki no wa* (time loop) and allowing the author's star characters from multiple works to cross paths. Rintaro also updated the drawings of the protagonists by asking artist Kazuo Komatsubara (*Getter Robo*, *Devilman*) to make them more graceful than in the manga or series.

The film's commercial success led him to direct the 1981 sequel, *Sayonara Ginga Tetsudō 999: Andromeda Shuchakueki* (*Adieu Galaxy Express 999*). Throughout the original story, he explored the theme of fatherhood in depth, which Matsumoto also held dear, and became more embittered toward government institutions. The two-part tale played on the enthusiasm for space stories, like most films of that time, while at the same time introducing a more ambiguous narrative style and using the staging codes of live-action films.

In 1980, Toei produced the film *Cyborg 009 Gekijō Ban: Chō Ginga Densetsu* (*Cyborg 009: Legend of the Super Galaxy*) and sent the team of scarf-clad heroes across the universe. This original story blends action, meditation, and philosophy to such an extent that the superhero story gives way to a more dreamlike adventure. The same year, the studio confirmed its expertise in space odysseys with *Terra e...* (*Toward the Terra*), an adaptation of Keiko Takemiya's manga that established itself as a humanist masterpiece, in which human evolution was not to be hindered by conservative ideologies.

There was no stopping Toei when it came to exploiting the stars! In 1982, the studio followed up the *Shin Taketori Monogatari: Sennen Joō* (*Queen Millennia*, 1981) series with a mesmerizing film remake: *Sennen Joō* (*Queen Millennia*). Toei and Leiji Matsumoto's collaboration continued to be as prolific as ever, as *Waga Seishun no Arcadia* (*Arcadia of My Youth*) brought the famous space pirate to the big screen with an original storyline. The film served as a prequel to the series *Waga Seishun no Arcadia: Mugen Kidō SSX* (*Arcadia of My Youth: Endless Orbit SSX*), which ended after just twenty-two episodes. Was Matsumoto's style becoming outdated at a time when mecha series were all the rage? After the release of *Yamato*'s fifth film the following year, the production of works inspired by Matsumoto came to an abrupt halt. It would be more than ten years before he reappeared in animation. And Toei, the queen of celluloid output, jumped on an entirely different trend in 1983: *shōnen nekketsu*.

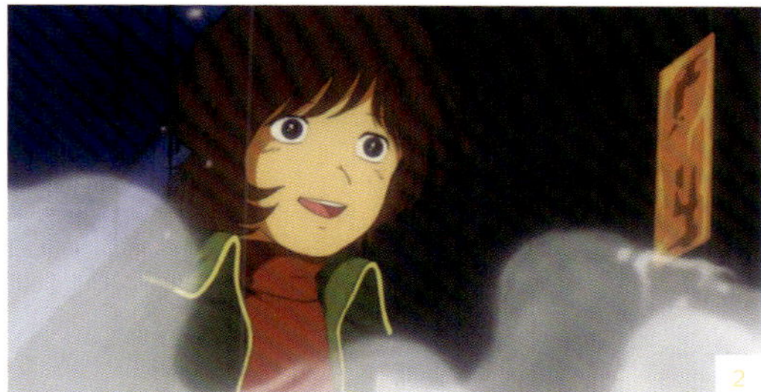

2

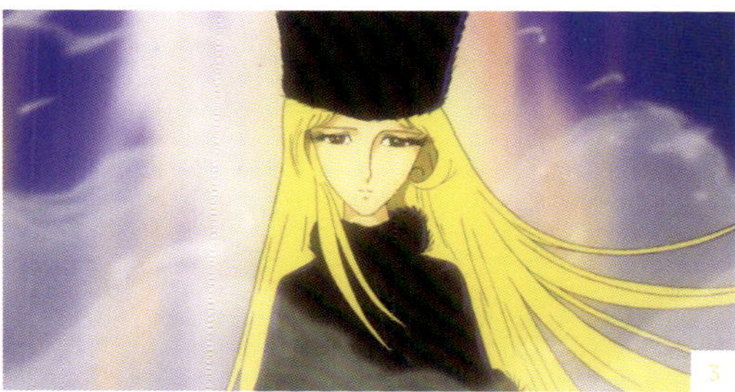

3

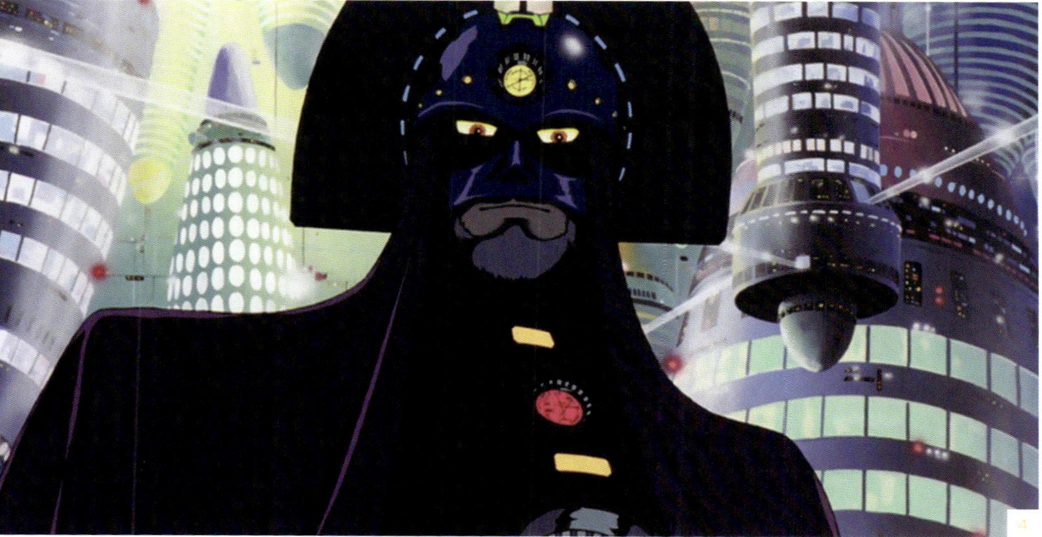

4

2 to 4

1981
Sayonara Ginga Tetsudō 999: Andromeda Shuchakueki (Adieu Galaxy Express 999)

TEZUKA'S RETURN

It was inevitably through science fiction that the "God of Manga," Osamu Tezuka, returned to his mistress, animation, in 1977. His new project was a big one—a color remake of *Astro Boy*. The TV series was coproduced by Madhouse and Toei, who brought in a wealth of experienced creative talent, including Rintaro, Osamu Dezaki, Akio Sugino, and Yūgo Serikawa. But Mushi Production's financial difficulties before it closed meant that Osamu Tezuka had lost the rights to the characters. In order not to jeopardize the project, he renamed the series *Jetter Mars* and slightly modified the designs. However, despite its good technical quality, *Jetter Mars* failed to win over the public, who kept comparing it to *Astro Boy*.

Tezuka's experience in animation wasn't all bad, and he used his Tezuka Production company as a base for a new animation team, made up of former Mushi Production employees and young artists. In 1978, he split the studio to take on two very special projects: Kon Ichikawa's live-action adaption of *Phoenix*, which contained animated sequences by Tezuka, and *Hyakumannen Chikyū no Tabi: Bander Book* (*One Million-Year Trip: Bandar Book*). The latter was commissioned by Nippon Television, which celebrated its twenty-fifth anniversary with a twenty-four-hour charity program. As a result, *One Million-Year Trip: Bandar Book* was Japan's first full-length animated TV movie. Its success led Tezuka to repeat the experience in subsequent years. In 1979, he continued to explore the realms of science fiction with *Kaitei Chōtokkyū Marine Express* (*Undersea Super Train: Marine Express*, 1979), in which he placed his iconic characters at the center of a closed-door investigation. He followed with *Fumoon* (1980), an adaptation of *The Next World*, one of his early manga, and *Time Slip Ichimannen Prime Rose* (1983), which was directed by Satoshi Dezaki, older brother of Osamu. These television movies retained Tezuka's high technical standards, as well as the absurdity of certain situations, lightening the gravity of the themes they addressed, such as environmental destruction and human greed.

With his sights set on international distribution, Tezuka embarked on a project on an entirely different scale—the feature film *Hi no Tori 2772: Ai no Cosmozone* (*Phoenix 2772*, 1980). Using his manga as the basis, he created an original sci-fi story in which a man and his robot nanny set out to find the immortal Phoenix. Tezuka wanted every stage in the creation of this film, which was particularly close to his heart, to be cutting edge, and he encouraged animators to use multiple techniques. Rotoscopy (for human and ship movements), Scanimation (to create relief from a flat image), and live action combined with animation were all processes requiring state-of-the-art technological equipment and a large team. Tezuka even reorganized

1983
Time Slip Ichimannen Prime Rose

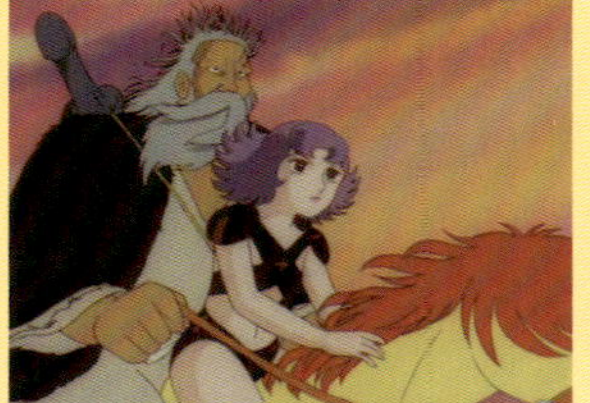

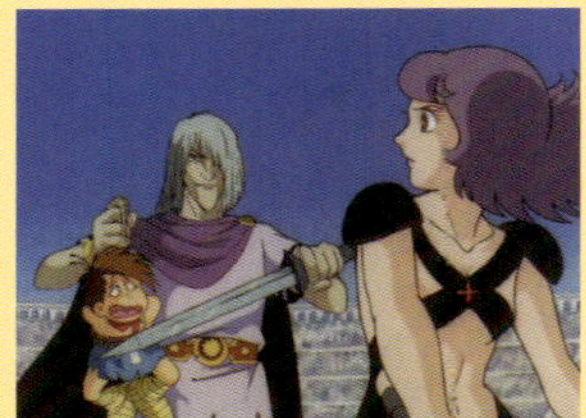

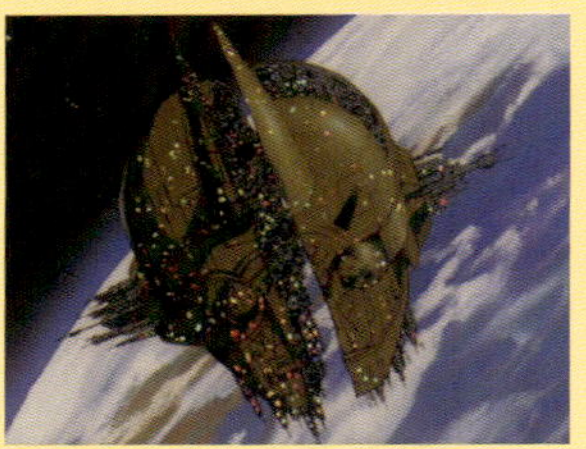

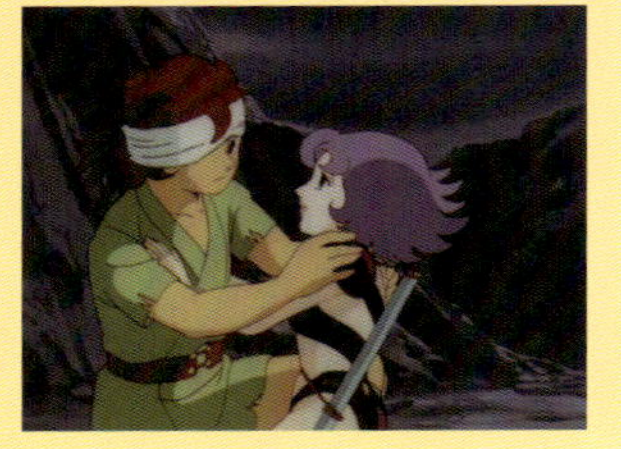

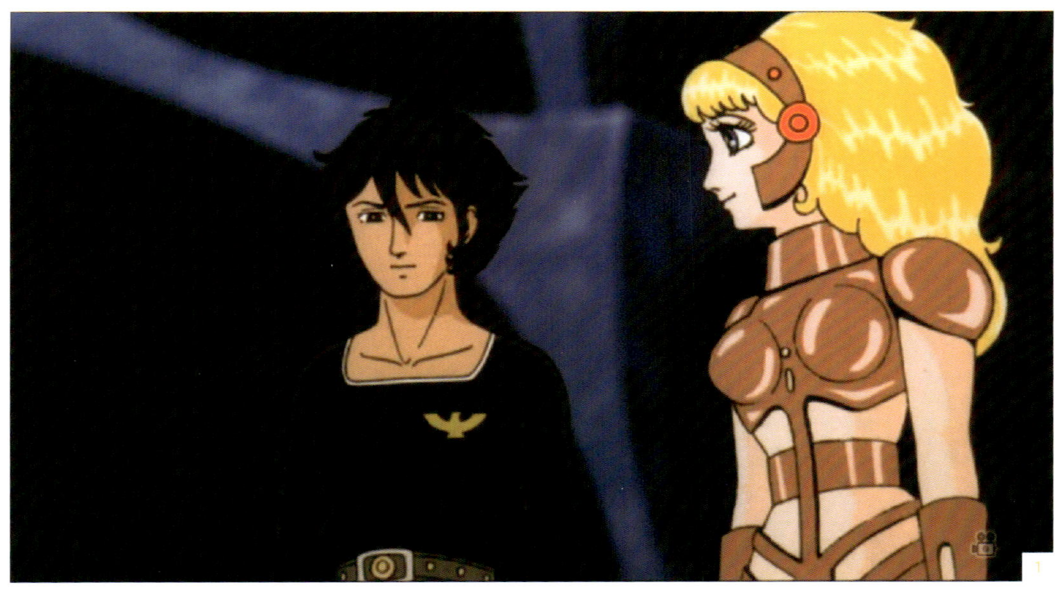

1
1980
Hi no Tori 2772: Ai no Cosmozone (Phoenix 2772)

working methods, assigning a specific character to each animator.

The film was impressive with its many environments, fluidity of movement, and freedom of camera action. For example, in order to animate a long take (fifty seconds) overlooking a futuristic city, the technology of the time obliged animator Junji Kobayashi to redraw the scenery shot by shot from a different perspective. Thanks to his admirable work, Tezuka called him back a few years later to animate *Jumping*, a short film shot in subjective perspective.

Phoenix 2772 was targeted at a wide audience, as the author-director-producer-screenwriter-storyboarder sought to bring international recognition to anime. In the end, the film was a commercial failure in Japan but met with some success in North America. In 1981, Tezuka Productions teamed up with Madhouse to make the feature film *Unico*. But the contagious purity of the little unicorn's feelings didn't appeal to adults looking for complexity or children who were more entertained by the extravagance of *Doraemon* on TV.

TALES FROM AROUND THE WORLD: CINEMA FOR CHILDREN

As the Toei studio shifted its focus to sci-fi movies, it gradually abandoned its adaptations of the great works of children's literature. The last feature films based on Andersen's fairy tales—*Andersen Dōwa: Ningyo Hime* (*Hans Christian Andersen's The Little Mermaid*), *Hakuchō no Ōji* (*The Wild Swans*, 1977), and *Oyayubi Hime* (*Thumbelina*, 1978)—were already a thing of the past, despite their more contemporary designs. In 1979, when *Galaxy Express 999* marked a turning point in the studio's cinematic creation, *Tatsu no ko Taro* (*Taro the Dragon Boy*) seemed to serve as a testament to an era of old-fashioned classicism. Yōichi Kotabe (who had

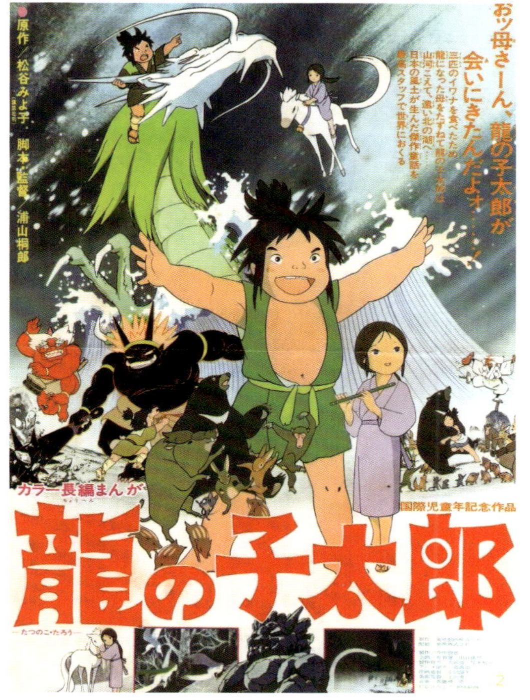

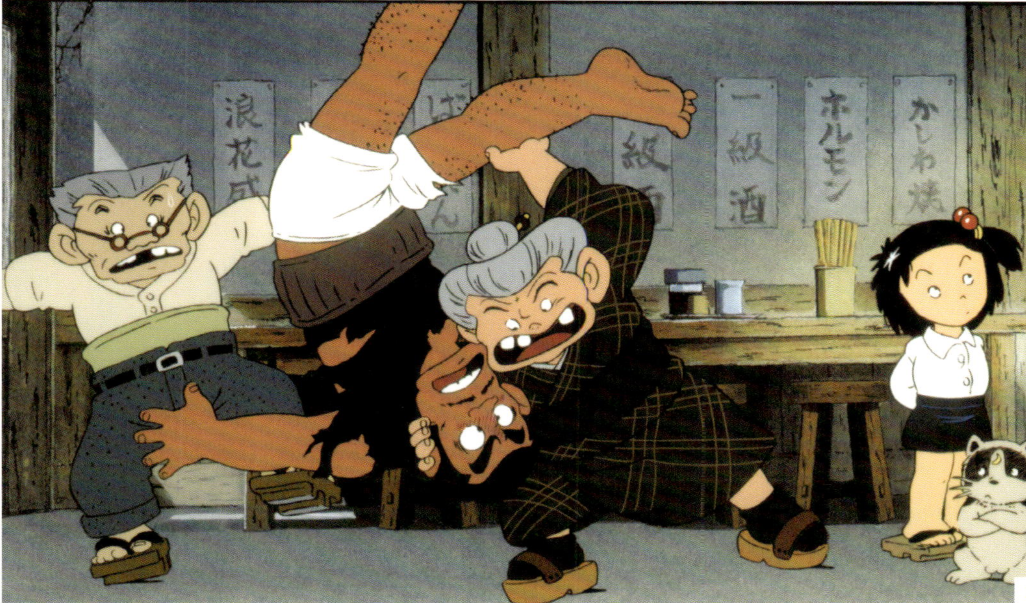

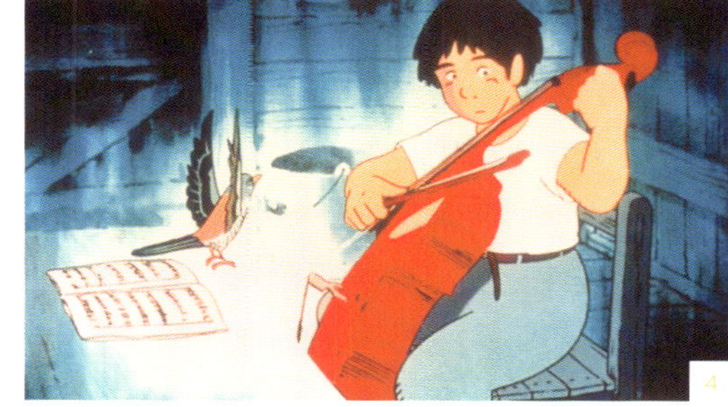

2
1979
Tatsu no Ko Taro (Taro the Dragon Boy)

3
1981
Jarinko Chie (Chie the Brat)

4
1981
Serohiki no Gōshu (Gauche the Cellist)

left the studio with Takahata and Miyazaki) worked on the film, an adaptation of a novel by Miyoko Matsutani, herself inspired by a Japanese legend. The woodblock sets, energetic, youthful heroes, and theatrical singing were reminiscent of Toei Dōga's lavish early feature films.

From 1980 onward, adaptations of literary works were displayed in a 4:3 aspect ratio, a format conducive to video that was gradually being introduced into homes. And so, *Mori wa Ikite iru* (*Twelve Months*, 1980), *Hakucho no Mizuumi* (*Swan Lake*, 1981), and *Aladdin to Mahou no Lamp* (*Aladdin and the Wonderful Lamp*, 1982) humbly continued the *Sekai Meisaku Dowa* (*World Fairy Tales Series*), begun in 1977 with *The Wild Swans*, without Toei's legendary cinemascope. The studio marched on with the series with the aim of preserving this part of its identity.

Other genres weren't completely eclipsed by science fiction, which had given animated cinema a new lease on life. At TMS (*Lupin III*), Kotabe joined Yasuo Ōtsuka to animate Isao Takahata's new film *Jarinko Chie* (*Chie the Brat*, 1981). In adapting Etsumi Haruki's satirical manga, the director departed from the folktales that had dominated children's cinematic entertainment. Instead of a tale of whimsical escapism, he told a realistic and humorous family satire, immersing himself in an underprivileged district of Osaka. The following year, he directed *Serohiki no Gōshu* (*Gauche the Cellist*), which won the Noburō Ōfuji Award. Adapted from a short story by Kenji Miyazawa, the film depicts the apprenticeship of a poor, awkward musician who is supported by the surrounding animals. The films were intended to be closer to their target audience—children—who were looking for realistic stories rather than tales and legends. Big-screen animation was fully recovered when the first three *Doraemon* films successively exceeded one billion yen at the box office. Japanese children could identify with the young heroes, and the robot cat from the future added a touch of sci-fi to spice up the daily lives of the protagonists from different classes

By the early 1980s, animation was no longer a separate genre in the Japanese audiovisual industry but a different technique used to tell a variety of stories. Because everyone had a television, cinema became exotic once again, and audiences of all ages grew accustomed to watching their favorite animated characters at twenty-four frames per second.

But even if directors had more freedom, they were still dependent on the original works they were adapting, as well as on contracts with distributors. A third medium naturally emerged in 1983, once again shaking up the world of animation in Japan . . .

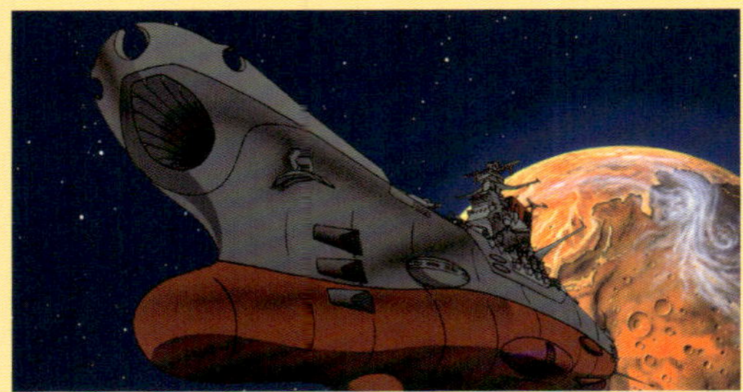

UCHŪ SENKAN YAMATO

Space Battleship Yamato

Year: 1974
Category: TV
Directors: Noboru Ishiguro and Leiji Matsumoto
Animation Studio: Office Academy

AT A GLANCE:
This pioneering space opera revealed more than just its author's patriotic subtext. It was a showcase of Leiji Matsumoto's poetry, which he has since developed in his personal productions.

YOU MAY ALSO LIKE . . .
Space Pirate Captain Harlock and *Galaxy Express 999*, major works by Leiji Matsumoto. *Captain Future*, a more grown-up space opera. *Macross*, the account of an interstellar human exodus.

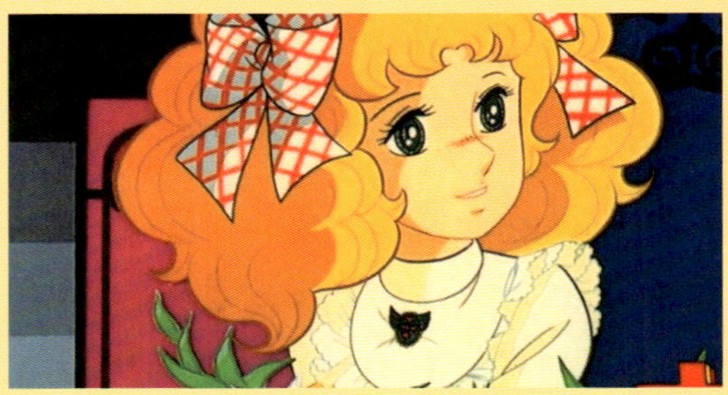

CANDY CANDY

Candy Candy

Year: 1976
Category: TV, film
Directors: Hiroshi Shidara and Tetsuo Imazawa
Animation Studio: Toei Dōga

AT A GLANCE:
This melodrama, featuring a heroine who is positive despite all odds, was the first series designed for girls by women, breaking new ground in a market that had been dominated by shows for boys.

YOU MAY ALSO LIKE . . .
Angie Girl, in which Sherlock Holmes's niece assists Scotland Yard. Charlotte and her family drama in Quebec in *Wakakusa no Charlotte* (*Honey Honey's Wonderful Adventures*), featuring a heroine who is being chased because of a ring her cat ate.

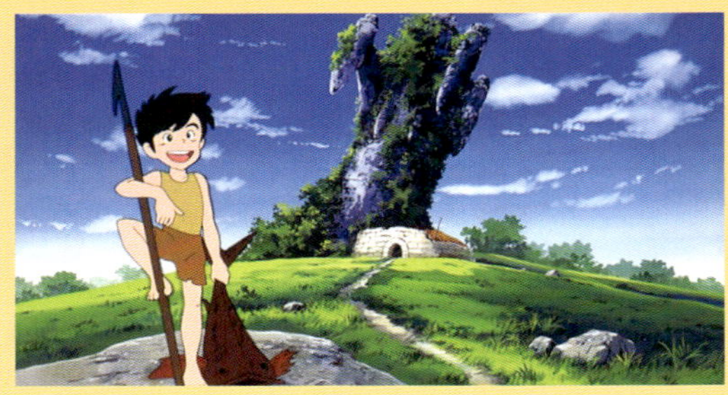

MIRAI SHŌNEN CONAN

Future Boy Conan

Year: 1978
Category: TV
Director: Hayao Miyazaki
Animation Studio: Nippon Animation

AT A GLANCE:
A scaled-down *Odyssey*, Hayao Miyazaki's first production encompasses the key elements of his future films and themes yet unseen in children's series.

YOU MAY ALSO LIKE . . .
Kum Kum, prehistoric adventures with an eco-friendly message. *Treasure Island* and its ten-year-old hero, swept away on an epic journey. Shipwrecked survival in *The Swiss Family Robinson: Flone of the Mysterious Island*.

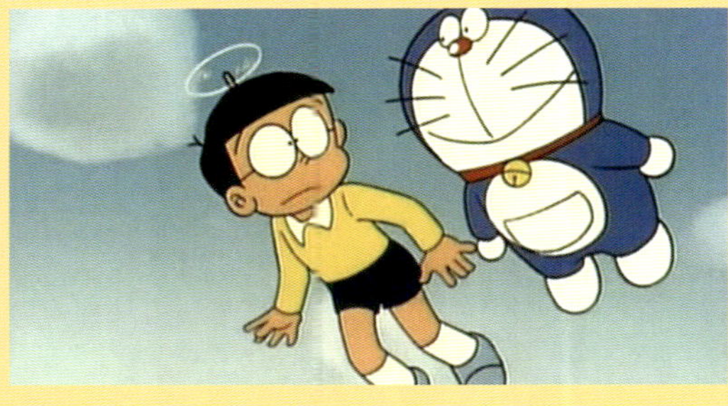

DORAEMON

Doraemon

Year: 1979
Category: TV, film
Director: Tsutomu Shibayama
Animation Studio: Shin-Ei

AT A GLANCE:
After a brief pause in 2005 for a reboot, the series is still as popular as ever forty years after its debut. The blue robotic cat from the future is a Japanese cultural icon.

YOU MAY ALSO LIKE . . .
Rascal the Raccoon, Nippon Animation's mascot, which inspired thousands of toys. *Ninja Hattori-kun*, ninja apprentices by the same creators.

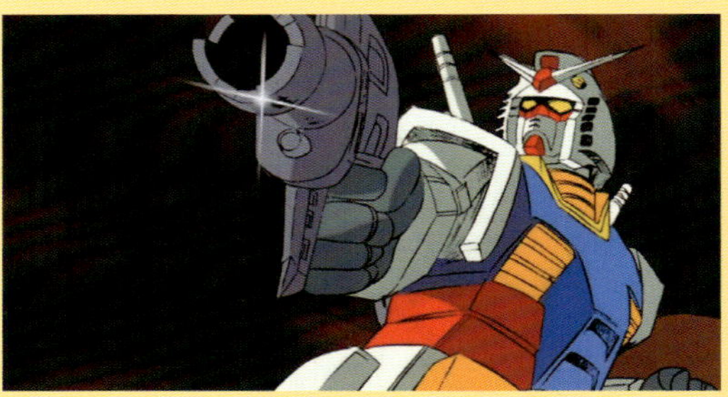

KIDŌ SENSHI GUNDAM

Mobile Suit Gundam

Year: 1979
Category: TV, film
Director: Yoshiyuki Tomino
Animation Studio: Sunrise

AT A GLANCE:
By reinventing the giant robot genre with believable machines, realistic worlds, and human and political conflicts, *Gundam* paved the way for mature, adult science fiction.

YOU MAY ALSO LIKE . . .
Legend of the Galactic Heroes, an interstellar tale of epic proportions. *Fang of the Sun Dougram*, planetary guerrilla warfare in giant robots against a galactic dictatorship.

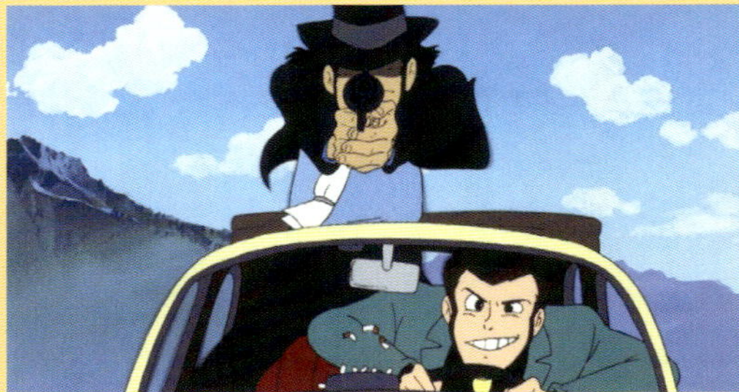

LUPIN III: CAGLIOSTRO NO SHIRO

Lupin III: The Castle of Cagliostro

Year: 1979
Category: Film
Director: Hayao Miyazaki **Animation Studio:** TMS

AT A GLANCE:
Miyazaki was still true to the spirit of the 1971 series but broke away from the original to establish his own style in his first feature film.

YOU MAY ALSO LIKE . . .
Lupin III Part II, an original series with a more adult tone. *City Hunter*, *Lupin III*'s bawdy, tough-as-nails spiritual successor.

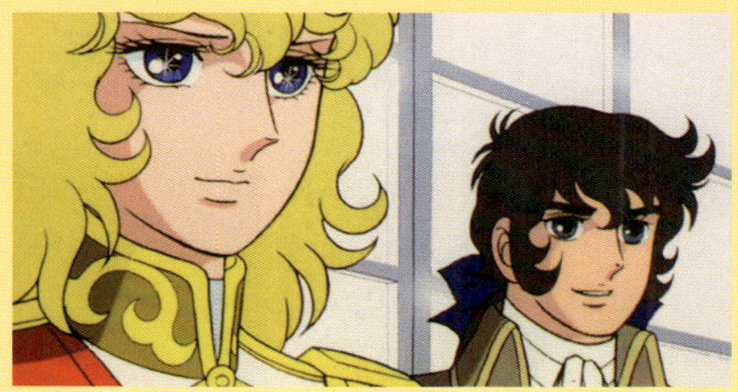

VERSAILLES NO BARA

The Rose of Versailles

Year: 1979
Category: TV, film
Directors: Tadao Nagahama and Osamu Dezaki
Animation Studio: TMS

AT A GLANCE:
Set against the backdrop of a fantasized French Revolution, the sexual equality advocated by the series was in tune with the times, making it a symbol of feminism still today in Japan.

YOU MAY ALSO LIKE . . .
The athletes' thwarted romances in *Aim for the Ace!* The ambiguous relationships between the members of the all-girls' high school in *Dear Brother.*

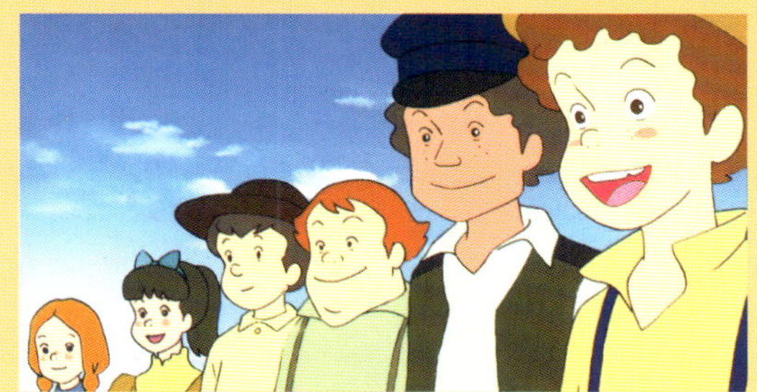

TOM SAWYER NO BŌKEN

The Adventures of Tom Sawyer

Year: 1980
Category: TV
Director: Hiroshi Saito
Animation Studio: Nippon Animation

AT A GLANCE:
One of the most famous titles in Nippon Animation's *World Masterpiece Theater* collection, which adapted Western literature classics from 1975 to 1997.

YOU MAY ALSO LIKE . . .
Other, more sentimental *WMT* series like *Princess Sarah* and *Pollyanna* have the same high-quality standards. *The Wonderful Adventures of Nils* and *Around the World with Willy Fog* share a taste for adventure.

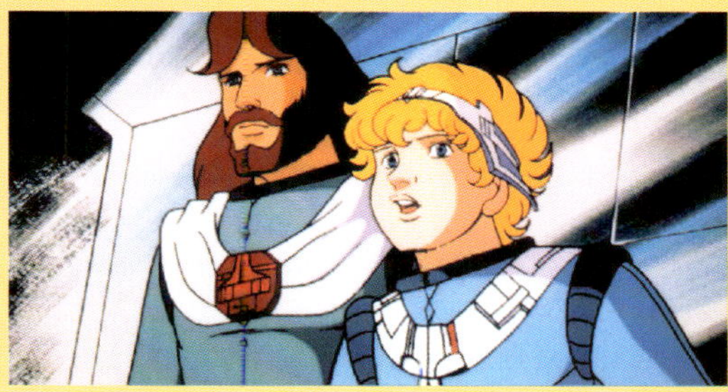

UCHŪ DENSETSU ULYSSES 31

Ulysses 31

Year: 1981
Category: TV
Directors: Bernard Deyriès and Tadao Nagahama
Animation Studios: DIC and TMS

AT A GLANCE:
This sci-fi retelling of Homer's *Odyssey* launched a wave of international collaborations made possible by the fax machine.

YOU MAY ALSO LIKE . . .
Once Upon a Time . . . Space, another Franco-Japanese sci-fi coproduction. *ThunderCats* and *Transformers*, Japanese productions for the United States.

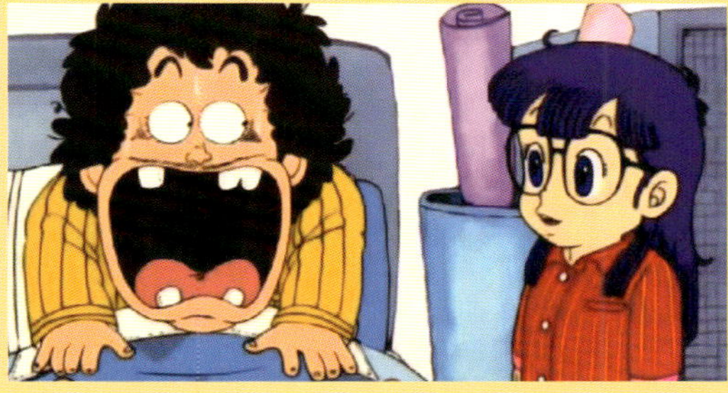

DR. SLUMP: ARALE-CHAN

Dr. Slump

Year: 1981
Category: TV, film
Director: Minoru Okazaki
Animation Studio: Toei Animation

AT A GLANCE:
Wacky, referential, and full of bathroom humor, the series established its original creator, Akira Toriyama, and paved the way for humor shared by children and parents alike.

YOU MAY ALSO LIKE . . .
The wild comedy in the Funny Face Club from *High School! Kimengumi. Kinnikuman*'s absurd wrestling matches. The whimsical giant pink chicken in *Gu Gu Ganmo.*

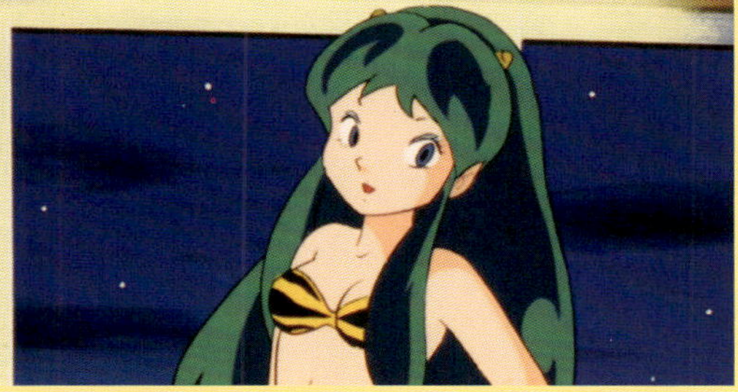

URUSEI YATSURA

Urusei Yatsura

Year: 1981
Category: TV, film
Directors: Mamoru Oshii and Kazuo Yamazaki
Animation Studios: Studio Pierrot and Studio Deen

AT A GLANCE:
Drawing on Japanese folklore and sci-fi, this woman-designed series for boys is particularly innovative due to integrating romantic comedy, a new genre for Japanese animation.

YOU MAY ALSO LIKE . . .
The bittersweet romance in *Maison Ikkoku* by the same author. The megalomaniac delusions of the monarch in *Patalliro!* The love triangle in *Wingman.*

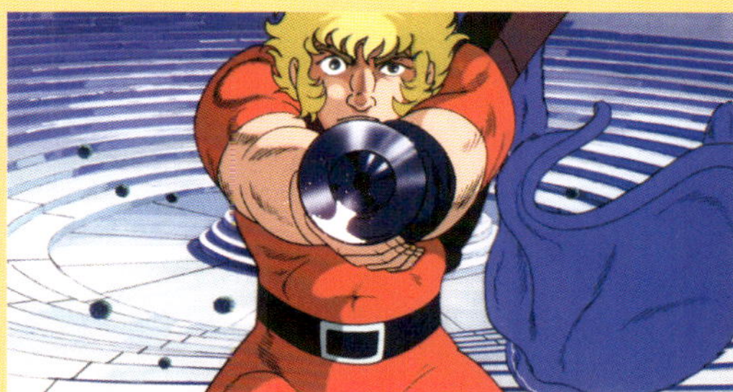

SPACE ADVENTURE COBRA

Space Adventure Cobra

Year: 1982
Category: TV, film
Directors: Osamu Dezaki and Yoshio Takeuchi
Animation Studio: TMS

AT A GLANCE:
With a hero inspired by France's Jean-Paul Belmondo, Cobra embraces his Western influences and is a breath of fresh air in space opera, making a fundamental genre in anime more accessible.

YOU MAY ALSO LIKE . . .
Cobra is the spiritual successor of the mischievous scoundrel of a hero in *Lupin III.* Rebels feared across the galaxy, the girls in *Dirty Pair* are the female counterpart, and *Trigun* the successor.

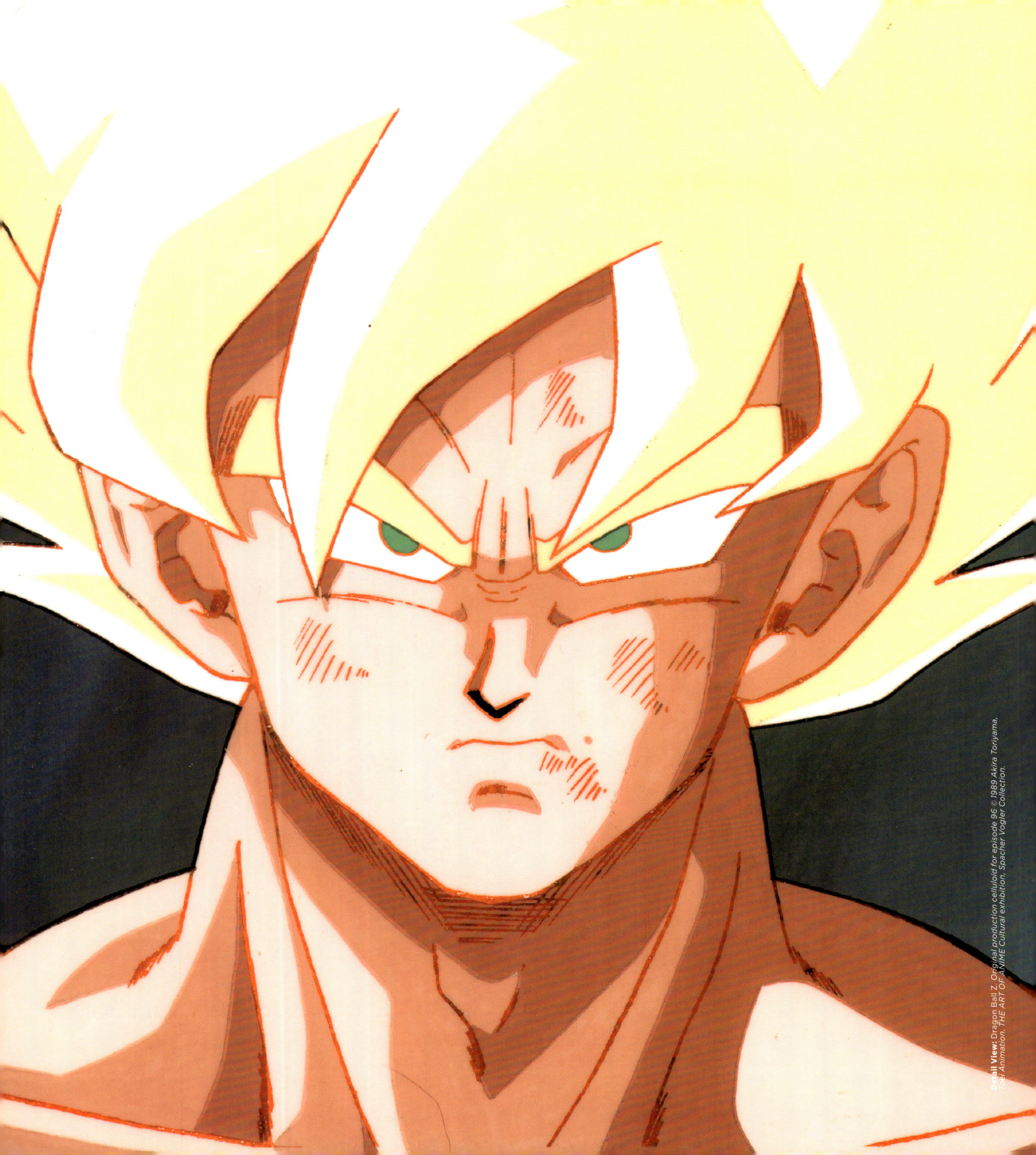

Detail View: Dragon Ball Z. *Original production celluloid for episode 96* © 1989 Akira Toriyama, Toei Animation. *THE ART OF ANIME Cultural exhibition, Spacher Vogler Collection.*

1983 TO 1995
THE THREE MEDIA

The adolescent crisis

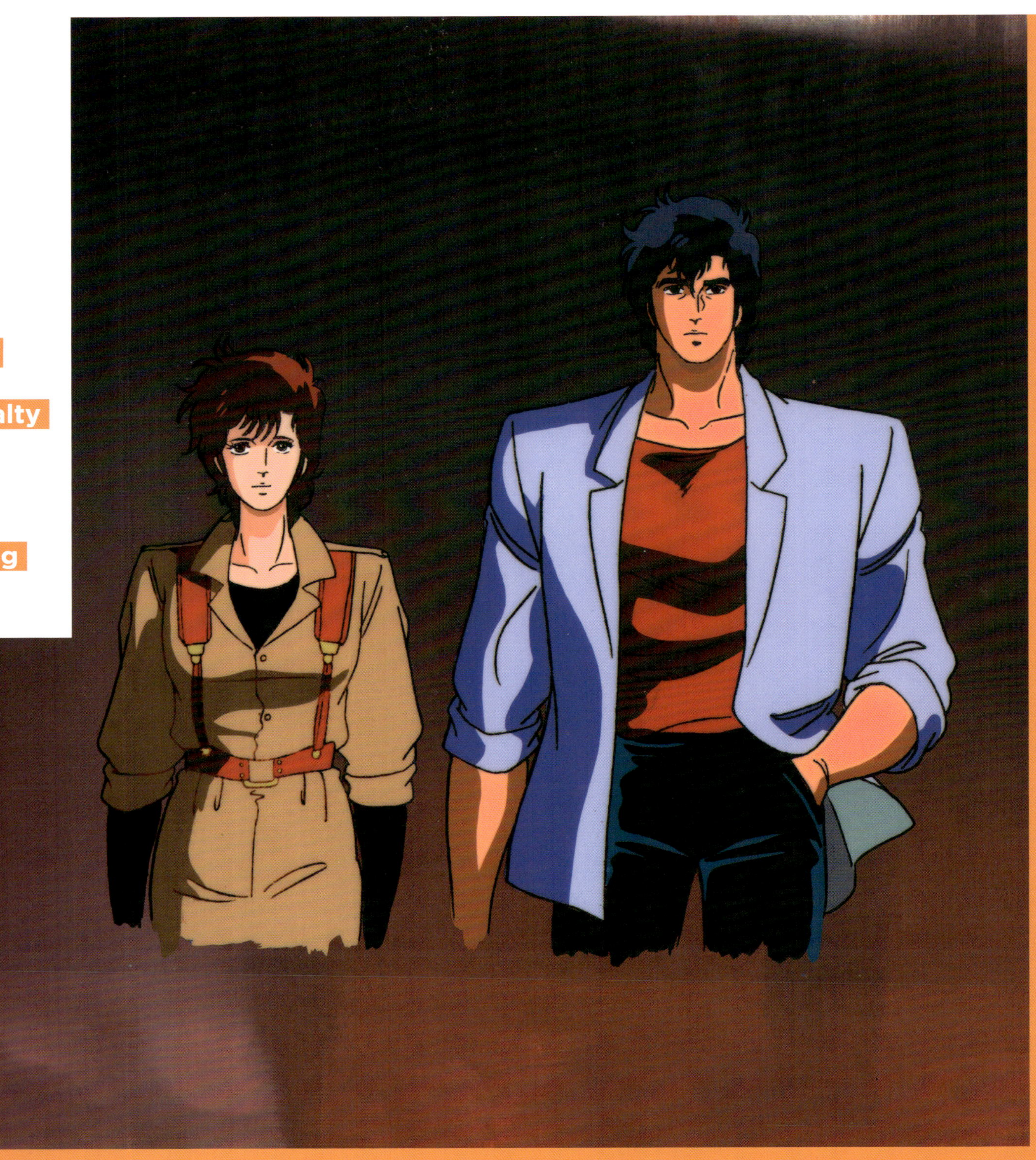

Detail view: City Hunter 2. *Original production celluloid for the opening credits © 1988 Tsukasa Hōjō, Sunrise. THE ART OF ANIME cultural exhibition, Spacher Vogler Collection.*

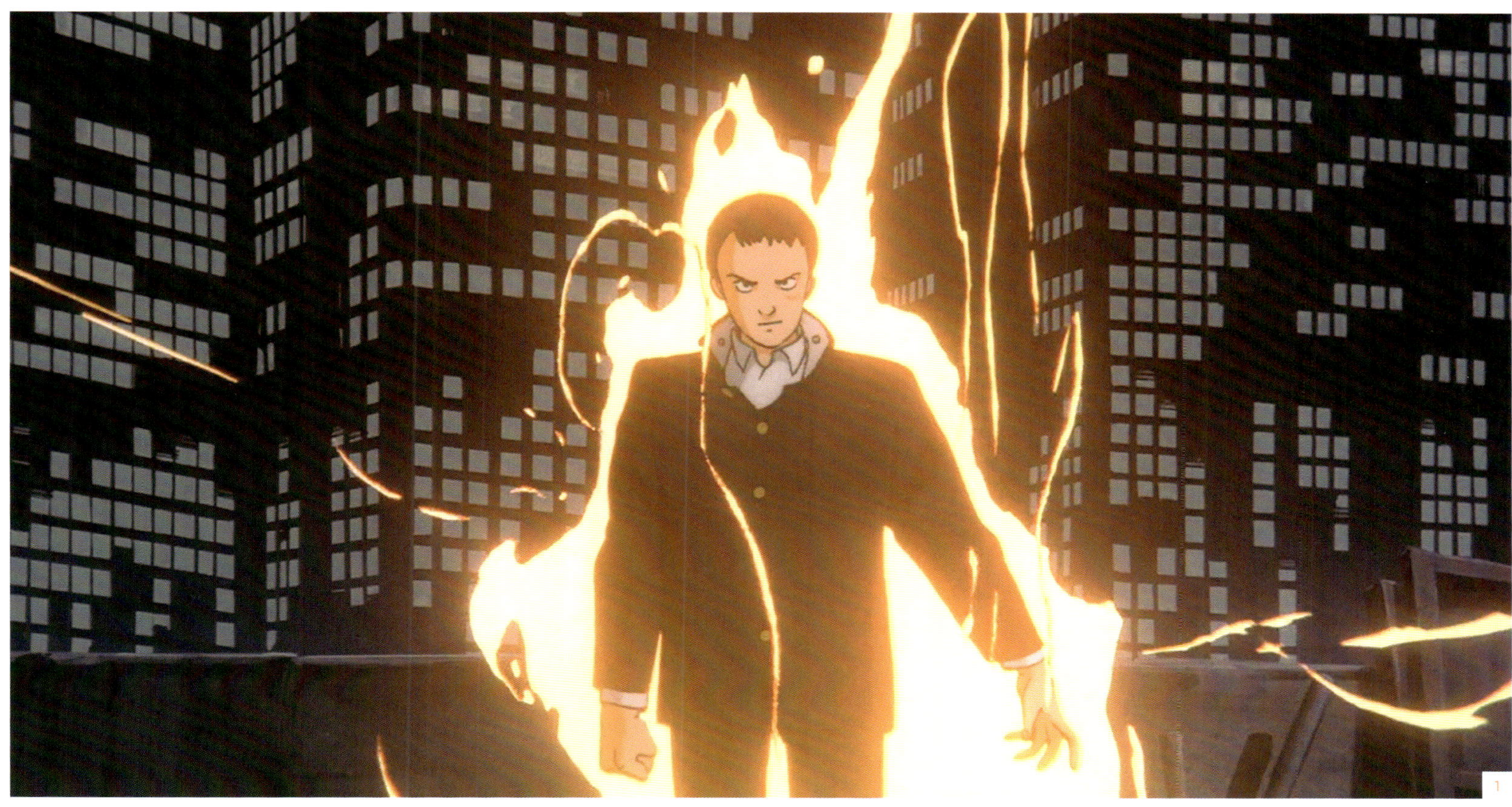

1
1983
Genma Taisen (Harmagedon)

1983
Genma Taisen (Harmagedon)

OAVs: A new market

1983: TENSION AND EXTERNALIZATION

At the dawn of the 1980s, Japan's animation industry had finally reached a certain equilibrium—genres were reaching a variety of audiences and large-scale television production was no longer eclipsing cinematic releases. Unfortunately, original creation for the cinema was still illusory, as films required substantial budgets, and financiers preferred to capitalize on popular projects that already existed. Despite this, directors and screenwriters were drawing in crowds thanks to their impressive adaptations. Feature films drew audiences by offering technical quality that was far superior to television series and emotional involvement that wouldn't be segmented to a weekly episode or chapter. But viewers who had adored the productions of the 1970s had grown up and were now looking for more mature subjects. Directors took advantage of the backlash against the "Glorious Thirty" post–World War II boom to hit where it hurt: fear of an uncertain future. With unemployment, oligarchy, the AIDS crisis, and the trauma of the atomic bomb, reality was catching up with the reverie of past decades, reinforced by impressive economic growth. Since *Mobile Suit Gundam 0079* and *Galaxy Express 999* (1979), productions for adults were increasingly flooding the market and reached a major turning point in 1983. That year, four cinematic successes of varying degrees of impact demonstrated that the new wave of auteur directors was no longer shying away from sensitive subjects.

For TMS, Osamu Dezaki adapted Takao Saito's manga *Golgo 13*, taking on powerful megalomaniacs. He perfected his style with the *Aim for the Ace!* (1979) and *Space Adventure Cobra* (1982), films featuring human drama. But for Dezaki, *Golgo 13: The Professional* was his aesthetic manifesto in which he deployed unprecedented violence to denounce the actions of

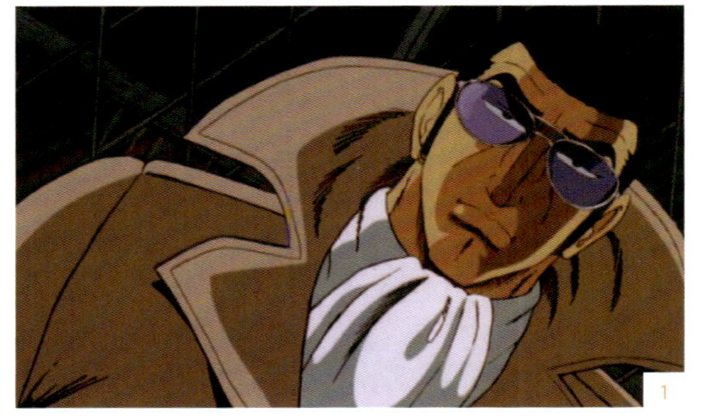
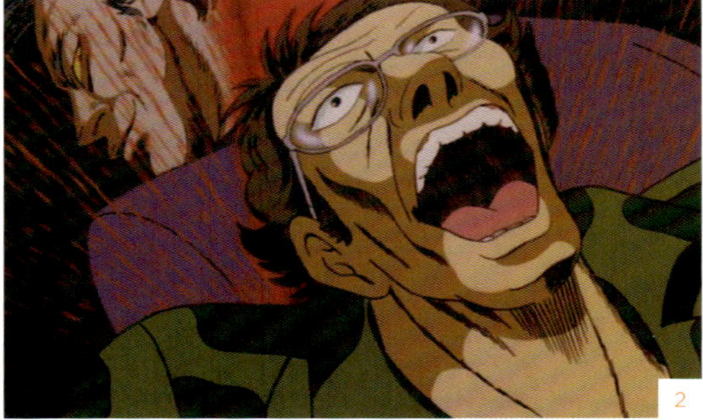
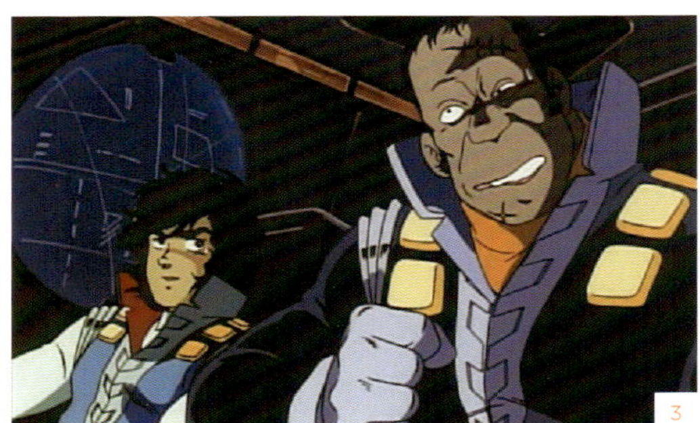

1 and 2
1983
Golgo 13
(Golgo 13: The Professional)

3
1983
Crusher Joe

major industrialists who were flaying society to the bone. Multinationals in collusion with the government became the new enemy to fear. Lighter but no less disturbing, Yoshikazu Yasuhiko's sci-fi film *Crusher Joe* won *Animage*'s Anime Grand Prix. Produced by Studio Nue and Sunrise, this cinematic adaptation of Haruka Takachiho's novels features action sequences as fast-paced as its young anti-conformist hero. Youth is narrow-minded and misunderstood, as demonstrated by Rintaro, who placed it at the center of a decisive war for humanity in *Genma Taisen* (*Harmagedon*), a nightmarish vision of the end of the world. If the film's economic impact was significant (it exceeded one billion yen at the box office, placing it ahead of the last *Yamato* film), so too was its artistic impact—never before had an animated work taken realistic imagery so far. To produce the 131 minutes of revolutionary animation, publisher Kadokawa relied on Madhouse, which was beginning to move away from subcontracting to focus on its own productions. Rintaro asked *mangaka* Katsuhiro Ōtomo to work on **character design**, the start of a long collaboration. Ōtomo's more brutal style went against the grain of the usual graceful or humorous strokes, especially for women, who until then had always been enhanced by delicate drawings. He freed himself from the imperious visuals of Tezuka, Ishinomori, Matsumoto, and Go Nagai. Takuo Noda (*Captain Future*) was the anime director, mentoring young talent who would go on to make their mark in subsequent years, including Yasuomi Umetsu, Takashi Nakamura, Kōji Morimoto, and Yoshinori Kanada. The film's success allowed Madhouse to establish its reputation on the silver screen. The studio struck gold twice that year by also coproducing the anime adaptation of the manga *Hadashi no Gen* (*Barefoot Gen*). Mori Masaki brought the horror of the nuclear bomb to cinemas as part of this drama. With frontal, documentary-like staging, the film was a descent into radioactive hell, leaving the viewer clinging to the slightest glimmer of hope. Gone were the uncluttered backgrounds of the 1970s! From now on, realistic themes were accompanied by extremely detailed visuals.

Television production also began to target an increasingly adult audience. Ryōsuke Takahashi concluded his long-running warrior series *Fang of the Sun Dougram* and continued with *Armored Trooper Votoms*, which didn't spare viewers either, with its fierce battles, oppressive atmosphere, and nihilistic characters. Even the colorful magical girl series *Magical Princess Minky Momo* tackled human disillusionment, leading to a highly ambiguous last episode.

Disenchanted fantasy accompanied by increasingly shocking imagery swept across all genres, heralding a trend toward alarmism. The year 1983 concluded with another opaque, tortured work: *Dallos*. This anime was distributed in a surprising way—it was only available on video—opening up a market that would revolutionize the Japanese animation industry while serving as a pressure relief valve at the same time.

FROM VIDEO TO OAV

Since the late 1970s, the video market had been revered by fans of anime (and audiovisual productions in general), who could record their television shows and buy or rent movies to watch in small groups. Older works became accessible without having to wait for a cinematic rerelease or television broadcast. With video, archiving became possible at low cost since one only needed a VCR connected to the TV set. The manufacturers' war raging between Sony (Betamax) and JVC (VHS) further fostered the cult following for this medium. Another format was added: LaserDisc (LD), an optical disc offering better picture and sound quality. But its much higher cost, large format, and inability to record prevented it from taking the lead over magnetic tape.

The video market made a major contribution to the growth of the anime fan community, which increasingly took part in public events, such as the Comic Market (Comiket), created in 1975. This quarterly event (which became semiannual in 1983) enabled visitors to buy amateur creations, known as *dōjin*, whether manga, picture books, music, or, later, video games. Comiket also became a meeting place for **cosplayers**—fans who dress as their favorite heroes with costumes and accessories they've created themselves.

Another major convention, the Nihon SF Taikai, had been an annual celebration of sci-fi since 1962. In 1981, the city of Osaka hosted the event, whose opening animation created entirely by amateurs was called *Daicon III*. The anime shows the journey of a little girl stalked by a robot, ending with a confrontation between several figures from pop culture. Thanks to video sales, a second film was made for the 1983 convention: *Daicon IV*. Now a teenager in a bunny suit, the heroine battles a horde of iconic characters. The *Daicon* films were highly enjoyable for sci-fi fans because they drew on an impressive number of references. Their creators, Hiroyuki Yamada, Hideaki Anno, and Takami Akai, went on to become otaku culture icons when they went professional and founded the Gainax studio.

The *Daicon* videos showed just how much fan communities claimed their cultural identity, and how crucial their thirst for knowledge in these imaginary realms was. The video market was perfectly suited to them because it made up for the frustration caused by the inaccessibility of animated works. Audiovisual consumption was completely redefined, and so was its production! This led to anime specially created to be sold directly on video, starting with the short *Dallos* series.

1981
Daicon III

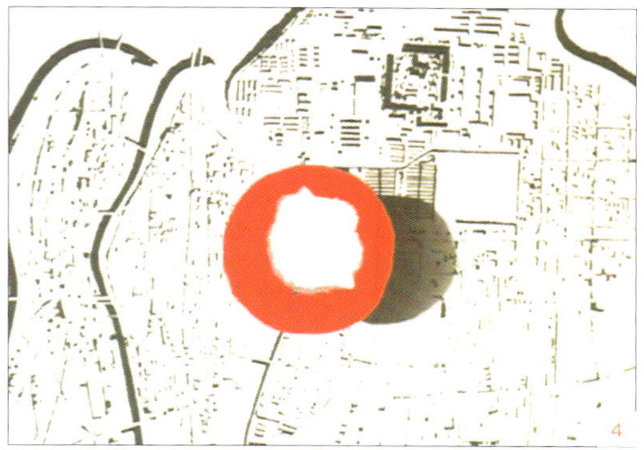

4

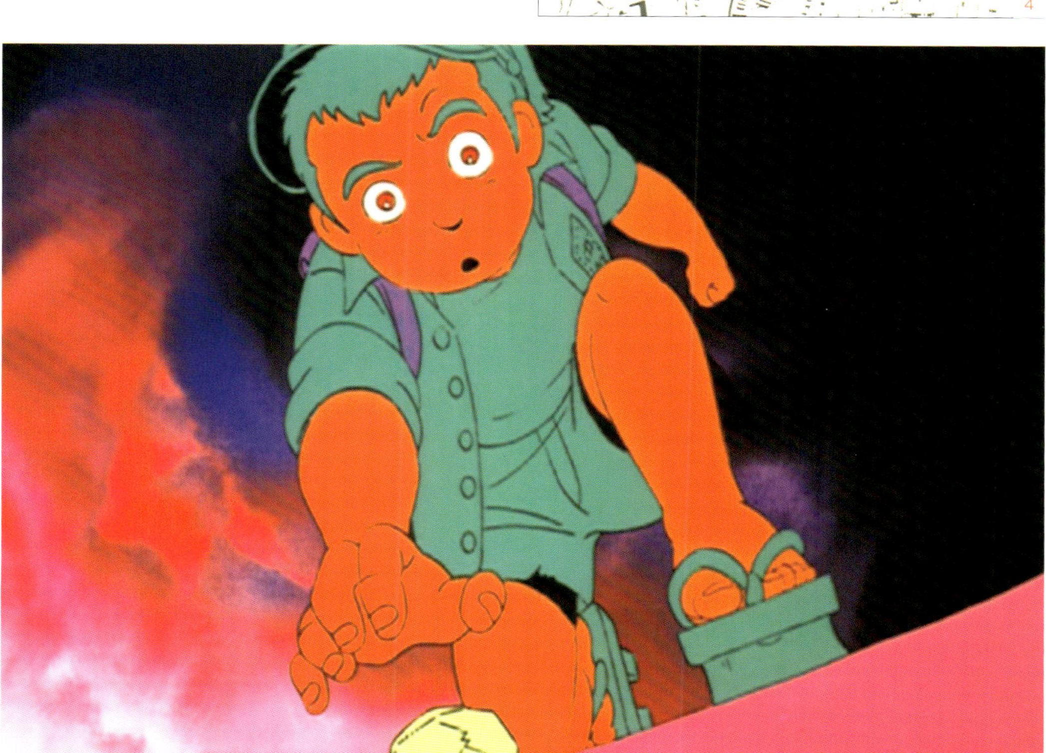

5

4 and 5
1983
Hadashi no Gen
(Barefoot Gen)

1983
Dallos

1
-
1984
Birth

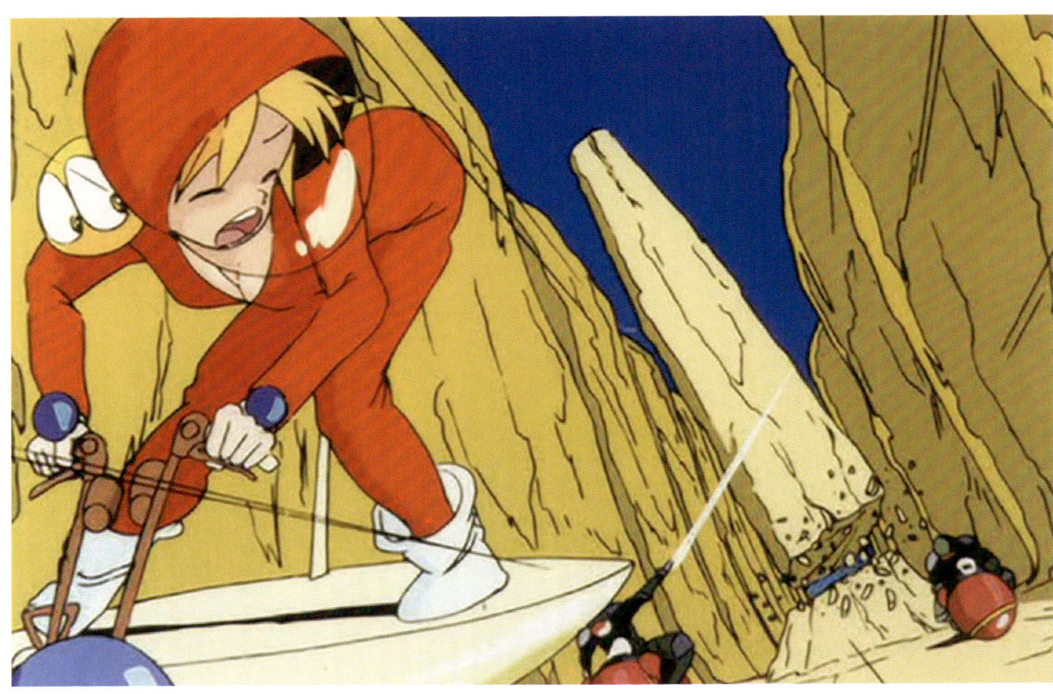

ALLOS: THE FIRST OAV

While working at Studio Pierrot, Mamoru Oshii trained in directing techniques for *The Wonderful Adventures of Nils* and *Urusei Yatsura* series, while dreaming of developing more complex and mature stories. Meanwhile, Studio Pierrot had responded to a request from Bandai to produce a fifty-two-episode sci-fi series. Oshii was approached by his mentor Hisayuki Toriumi (cocreator of the studio) to cowrite and direct the series. Unfortunately, Bandai was not convinced by their proposal and sensed it would be a commercial failure. The firm decided to cancel production of the series but still wanted to recoup development costs. As the animations were not worthy of a theatrical release, which proved to be more expensive, it was decided to reduce the story to four episodes and distribute them independently on video. The first episode of *Dallos* was released on VHS on December 21, 1983, marking the creation of the first animated work to be sold directly on video. A new market had just been born—**original animation video (OAV)**. The four thirty-minute episodes did not sell more than 20,000 copies, but they showed other studios the potential of such a market. Although the series was distributed on video by default, *Dallos* took advantage of the format to target a niche audience who could relate to its mystical and violent themes. This concept also encouraged the *otaku* community, who discovered productions created especially for them. As for directors and animators, they now had their own medium in which to express themselves.

The enormous commercial potential of the OAV market was quickly recognized by animation studios, who saw it as an opportunity to create ambitious productions without putting themselves at risk. Unencumbered by television censorship or the huge budgets required for film production, OAVs became an extremely free means of graphic and storytelling expression. Best of all, the video cassette sales proved highly profitable since the links in the distribution chain were reduced to the video editor, the transporter, and the store, resulting in an ever-faster return on investment, especially when the VHS only contained a single episode. The format varied from thirty to ninety minutes, with a predilection for productions of around fifty minutes. And because yesterday's teenagers were now adults with greater purchasing power, publishers and producers were playing the collector's card, a pathology of the enthusiast that was spreading like wildfire thanks to unparalleled word of mouth.

A NEW FORMAT ON THE RISE

Video productions required low budgets, but they were technically superior to TV series, allowing new studios to distinguish themselves in the field. Young studios such as A.P.P.P., Kaname Production, and AIC were thriving in this market, demonstrating the extent to which producers and directors wanted to break away from the traditional companies. These studios were more flexible and even allowed themselves to alternate between adaptations and original productions.

Machikado no Märchen (*Radio City Fantasy*) was released in July 1984. Produced by Kitty Films from an original screenplay by Takeshi Shudō, this fifty-five-minute mid-length film depicts an urban romance in which the pair of protagonists escape into their shared imaginary world. The viewer is immediately plunged into a surprising phantasmagoric dream world; it would have been impossible to develop such an auteur project in another medium! The director, Toshihiko Nishikubo, later experimented with other visual styles in OAV, such as the 1987 film *California Crisis: Tsuigeki no Hibana*, in which shadow outlines were added to visuals taken from American advertising posters.

Experimentation was at the very heart of OAV production, encouraging a return to technical and narrative challenges. In *Birth*, a feature film produced by Kaname Production and released in the same month as *Machikado no Märchen*, episode director Shinya Sadamitsu (*Zambot III*, *Gundam 0079*) featured a fast-paced original work whose story fits on a subway ticket—Aquanoid is a planet dominated by Inorganics who wish to destroy all traces of life. A group of humans discovers a magical sword that allows them to confront the exterminating race. The simplistic plot allowed the animation team to create innovative action sequences, particularly in the numerous chase scenes. Character designer and animation director Yoshinori Kanada (*Zambot III*, *Harmagedon*) imposed his refined graphic style, favoring movement via sequence shots (in which the sets are entirely redrawn frame by frame), perspective distortions, numerous stylized lighting effects, and constant gestures. The production was brought to life by an original soundtrack by Joe Hisaishi, who had just composed the music for the film *Kaze no Tani no Nausicaä* (*Nausicaä of the Valley of the Wind*). *Birth* infused the OAV market with a sensitive resonance—the viewer was buying not just a story but an experience that would demand to be lived over and over again, creating a craving for adrenaline that production companies would respond to in droves.

In January 1985, Studio Pierrot released the first full-length episode of *Area 88*, an adaptation of Kaoru Shintani's aviation manga. The martial story captivated fans with its realistic aircraft and the suspense that each high-risk mission entailed. Although the film was only a minor success as the market was slowly gaining a foothold, a commercial knockout arrived a few weeks later with two original feature films: *Genmu Senki Leda* (*Leda: The Fantastic Adventure of Yohko*) and *Megazone 23*.

Conceived by Kaname Production, *Leda* depicts a world steeped in fantasy and science fiction. Though the story is more complex than in *Birth*, the film retained its energetic quality, especially in the high-octane chase scenes. Audiences were now looking for novelty, even exclusivity, as confirmed by *Megazone 23*. To call it a success would be an understatement, as it quickly became a monument of pop culture that every fan needed to own. Stemming from the production of *Macross*, the technical team created a cyberpunk story in which a young man is hunted down by the police after finding a motorcycle that can be transformed into mecha. His escape leads him to discover that his reality is merely a manipulation of a supercomputer. With its demanding visuals and complex storyline, *Megazone 23* showed that OAV wasn't just a by-product of the audiovisual market but a medium that was

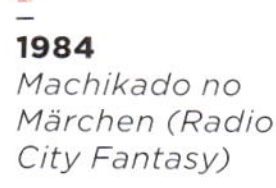
2
—
1984
Machikado no Märchen (Radio City Fantasy)

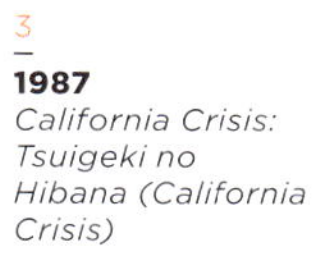
3
—
1987
California Crisis: Tsuigeki no Hibana (California Crisis)

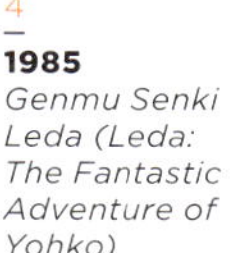
4
—
1985
Genmu Senki Leda (Leda: The Fantastic Adventure of Yohko)

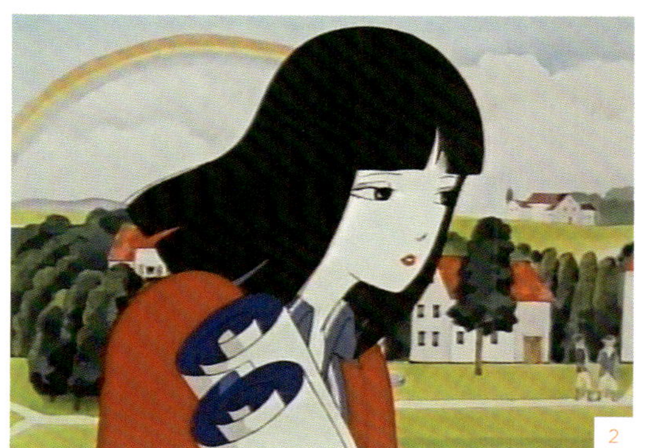
2

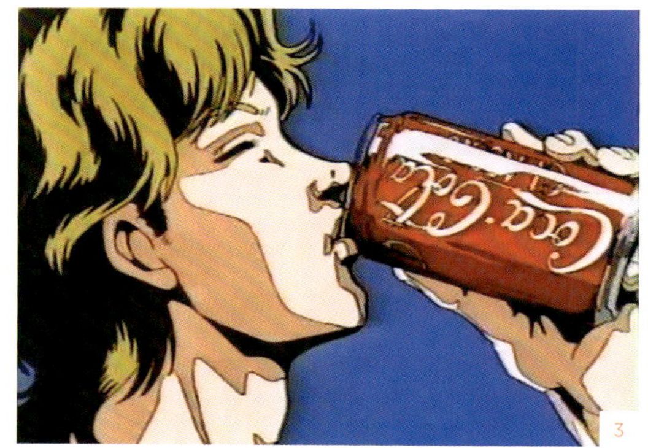

3

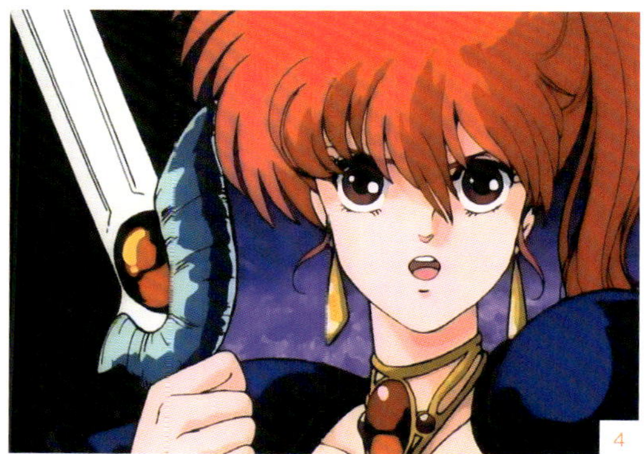
4

now competing on an equal footing with television and film!

The film's music was produced by Victor Music Industries (later Victor Entertainment media company), a subsidiary of JVC that was expanding into anime creation. From that point on, its presence in productions had a direct influence on video distribution. The scale was tipped in favor of VHS, already preferred by the general public for its affordable price and greater recording capacity than Betamax.

The significant increase in the number of titles and the first major successes boosted anime video sales, which went from 4.8 million copies sold in 1984 to 8.2 million in 1985, an increase of more than 70 percent in a year! And this was only the beginning of a thriving market that grew even stronger with a film grammar based on blending genres.

A PATCHWORK OF EXTREMES

Since *Astro Boy* in 1963, Japan's animation industry had diverged considerably from American economic and artistic models. But the generation of Japanese auteur directors in the 1980s drew their strength from reference, whether from the exploitation films of the previous decade or the American blockbusters that emerged from a subversive New Hollywood. *The Godfather* and *Taxi Driver* offered a more modern version of film noir, *Star Wars* democratized entertaining science fiction, *Alien* popularized horrific space opera, *Conan the Barbarian* established himself as a worthy representative of dark fantasy, and *Blade Runner* launched the cyberpunk movement. These films were distributed internationally, paving the way for complex themes and virulent imagery, which were later embraced by the OAV industry.

Science fiction had been on a pedestal to the point of shaping the vast majority of the OAV industry, but soon found itself overtaken by trendy genres like fantasy, horror, and even pornography. With no set format, productions included mid-length films, feature films, and short series. Not only that, but the technical constraints were less onerous, and there were plenty of fashionable themes to tackle! In the 1970s, directors had opened up to different genres, but now they no longer needed to make a choice

1985
Megazone 23

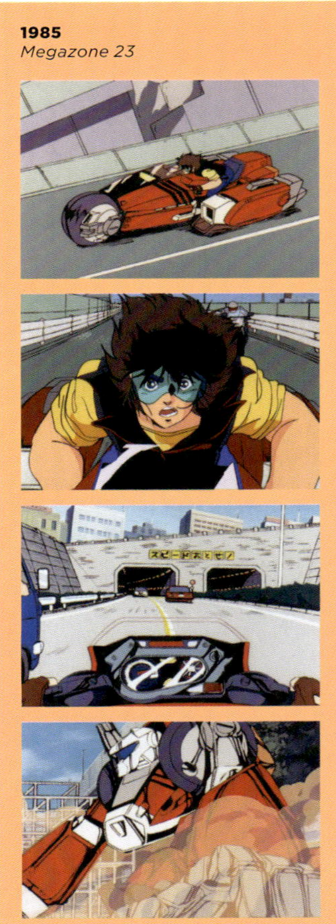

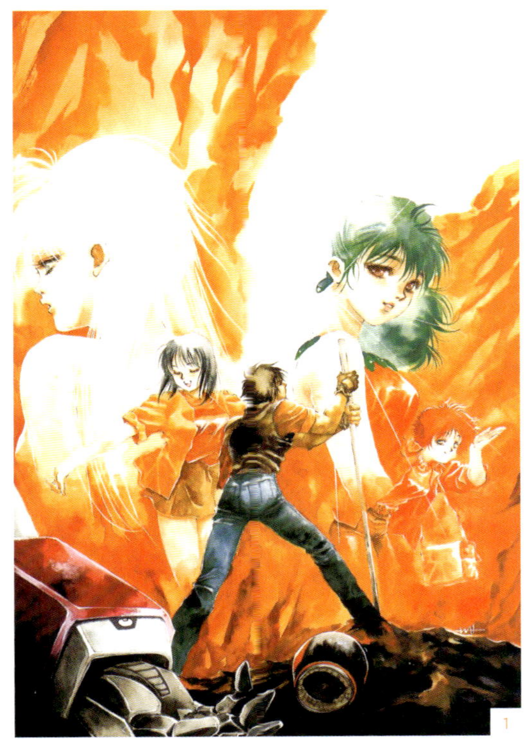

1

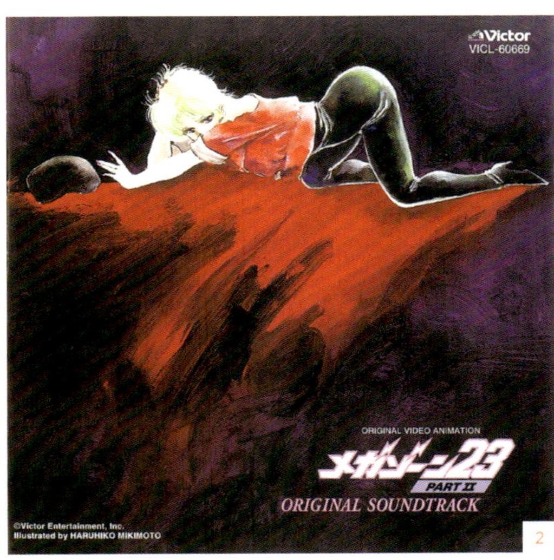

2

1 and 2
1985
Megazone 23

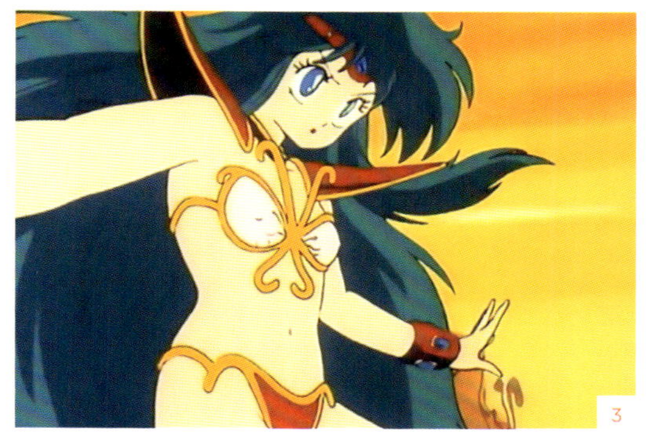

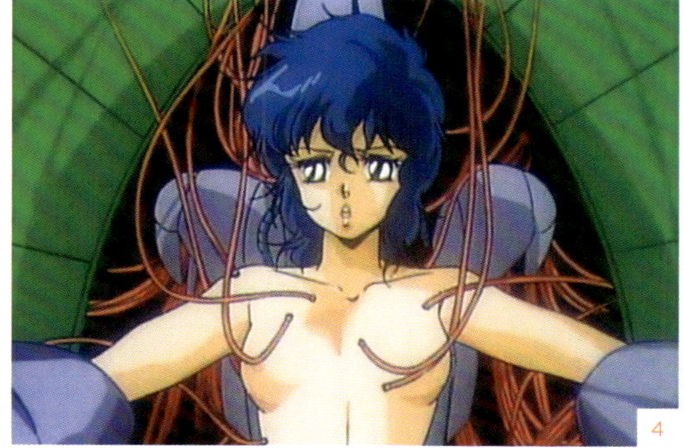

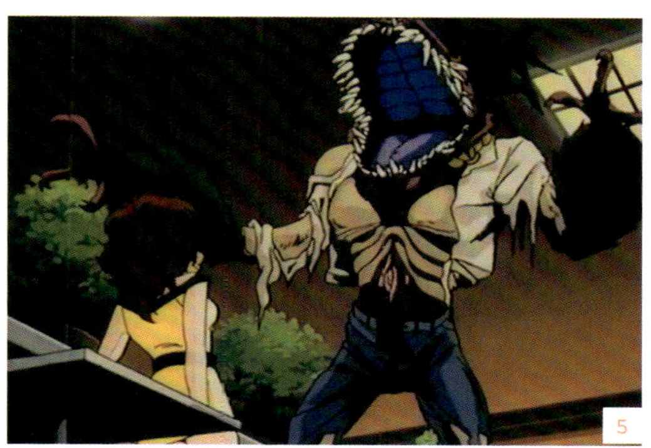

3
1985
Dream Hunter Rem

4
1985
Tatakae! Iczer-1 (Fight! Iczer One)

5
1986
Call Me Tonight

because combining genres was a perfect marketing strategy. What was exceptional in 1969 with *Cleopatra*, in which Tezuka and Yamamoto combined period films with eroticism, comedy, and science fiction, was now commonplace on video. Whereas film and TV series used to link certain genres with finesse, as in *Captain Harlock* and *Gundam*, the OAV was a no-holds-barred creative outlet, punctuated by scripted and stylistic one-upmanship. In 1985, Toshihiro Hirano adapted Rei Aran's ultraviolent manga *Iczer One* into three episodes combining science fiction, horror, and eroticism. With its fluid animation and complex visuals enhanced by the interplay between light and shadows, the OAV was technically impressive. *Fight! Iczer One* was followed by several sequels, including *Dream Hunter Rem* (1985), which revisited the magical girl concept with a young detective tasked with freeing people from the demons haunting their dreams. Pretty girls, robots, monsters, sex, and blood were what the majority of OAVs promised their audiences, who were now consuming adult anime in the utmost privacy.

With its intimate relationships between women (*yuri*) and accentuated body shapes, *Fight! Iczer One* showed that the OAV industry was clearly targeting a male audience. The emphasis on women was not intended to win over female viewers, who couldn't identify with action stories, but to satisfy a postpubescent audience by catering to their libidos. These **fan service** titles showcased the outrageous femininity of the heroines with sexy combat outfits that showed more skin than they protected. Thus Yoko (*Leda: The Fantastic Adventure of Yohko*, 1985), Fandora (*Yume Jigen Hunter Fandora*, 1985), Rem (*Dream Hunter Rem*), Maris (*Maris the Chojo*, 1986), and Princess Kahm (*Outlanders*, 1986) were warriors idolized by viewers, who now fell in love with the lead characters. Even the brand-new studio J.C. Staff took advantage of the niche with the zany *Elf 17*, featuring a powerful wrestling elf.

By following the opposite sex, the male viewer experienced their intimate moments, as in *Dream Hunter Rem* (1985), which took a gratuitous look at a teenage girl's first period; unhealthy scenarios began permeating OAV productions. *Call Me Tonight* (1986), for example, features the eccentric owner of a phone-sex company who decides to help a stranger unable to get an erection without turning into a monster. While directors weren't playing fast and loose with societal issues (here a sexual disorder), the accumulation of deviant themes meant that video production was increasingly made up of well-packaged B movies.

HENTAI: EXTREME SEXUALITY

When *Dallos* opened the door to the video market in December 1983, it was the pornography sector that was the most responsive. In February 1984, the first episode of *Lolita Anime* was released on VHS, becoming the first animated adult video (AV, not to be confused with OAV), better known in the West by the word *hentai* (perversion). Adapted from a manga by Fumio Nakajima and first published in the erotic magazine *Lemon People* founded in 1982, *Lolita Anime*'s very first episode skimmed over the romantic aspect to develop dramas centered on sadomasochism, in which stories of rape and bondage ended in tragic fates. The tone had been set, and animation would certainly not limit itself to the scenarios that live-action pornography could offer, instead going ever further in the imagery of desire and pleasure.

Not only did animation allow for visual freedom, but it also provided the opportunity to stage sexual escapades involving minors. At that time, Japan had no laws regulating child pornography, and when the state legislated a ban on its distribution in 1999, then on its possession in 2014, anime and manga were spared. The *hentai* market had plenty of time to develop more and more perverse stories involving teenage girls, or even younger girls. Thus emerged the viewer who loved eroticized little girls: the **lolicon**, short for Lolita complex. Lolicon is just one of the many AV subgenres, designed to meet every specific desire: hermaphrodites, catgirls, succubi, tentacled monsters, and more.

A few months after the release of *Lolita Anime*, *Cream Lemon* became the gold standard in the genre. The series, produced by Fairy Dust and animated by A.P.P.P., is a succession of thirty-eight independent episodes by various artists, like so many high-end short films. The films each have their own graphic style and develop varied stories, to the point that the pornographic aspect is sometimes secondary. As it was developed by the generation of fans whose strength was referencing other works, *Cream Lemon* regularly focused on parodic humor. Moreover, when Katsuhiko Nishijima directed a *yuri* (female-female romantic relationships) episode, its potential led the production team to develop it into a cinematic feature film, whose eroticism was toned down to "panty shots." And so, *Project A-Ko* was born, a pastiche referring to both *Captain Harlock* and *Hokuto no Ken* (*Fist of the North Star*).

Adult video production intensified rapidly, taking off in many different directions. Even the folkloric Princess Kaguya was given a pornographic retelling in 1987! The market became abundant, but low budgets and tight deadlines restricted animation, standardizing its low quality despite elaborate storylines (for pornography). The winning fantasy-erotica-gore formula reached a climax in 1987 with the terrifying *Chōjin Densetsu Urotsukidōji* series. The brainchild of *mangaka* Toshio Maeda, this OAV series depicts a story of bestial monsters and demons with superpowers, all addicted to the pleasures of the flesh, combining sex and evisceration. At the center of this sordid mess are humans whose fate is linked to the resurrection of a powerful entity capable of intertwining the worlds of all three races. The interplay of romance, gore, and rape launched the title into the pantheon of anime extremes. *Urotsukidōji* became the symbol of the controversy around violence and pornography in the Japanese animation market across all media. The controversy spread internationally, especially when films compiling (and heavily censoring) the series were released in the United States in 1989. Despite its limited target audience, *Urotsukidōji* boasts animation above the average OAV. The series popularized pornographic horror, which was found in a host of future productions, including *Demon Beast Invasion* (1990) and *La Blue Girl* (1992).

HORROR AND ULTRAVIOLENCE

In 1987, horror productions invaded video shelves. Thrills before morality was the name of the game! Viewers were subjected to an outburst of graphic rage, enhanced by increasingly grim, frightening designs. Hate, fear, and suffering became the obligatory passage for heroes who lost themselves in tormented worlds. In addition to shocking shots, staging focused on facial expressions reflecting

1
1984
Cream Lemon

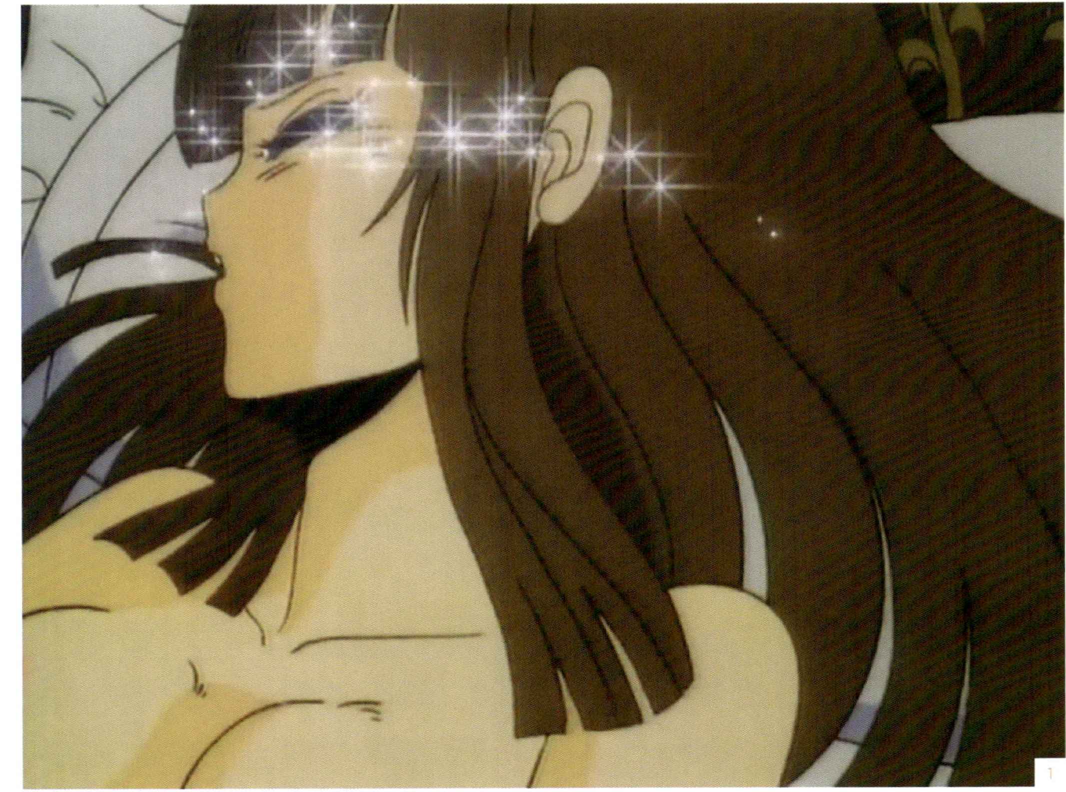

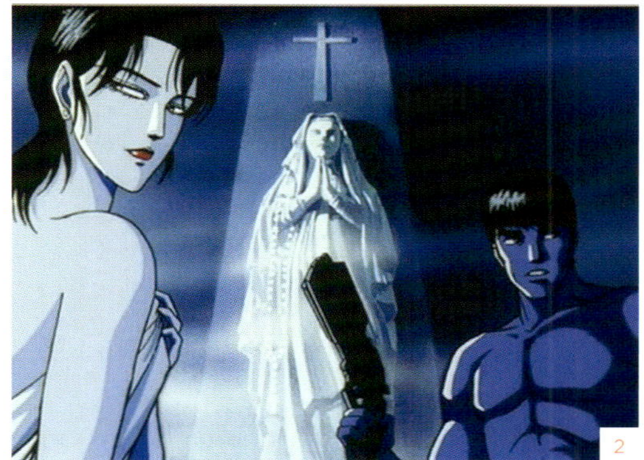

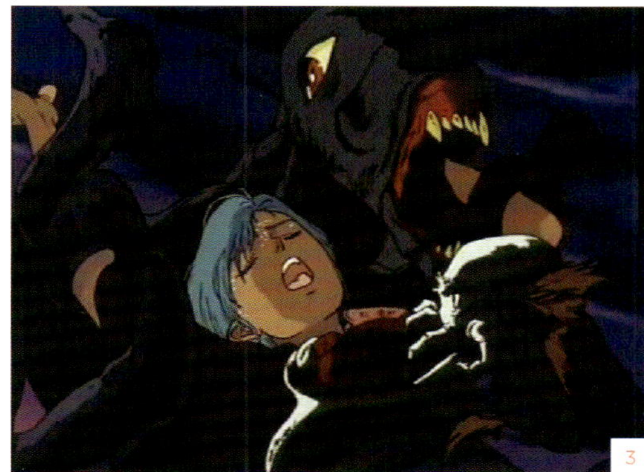

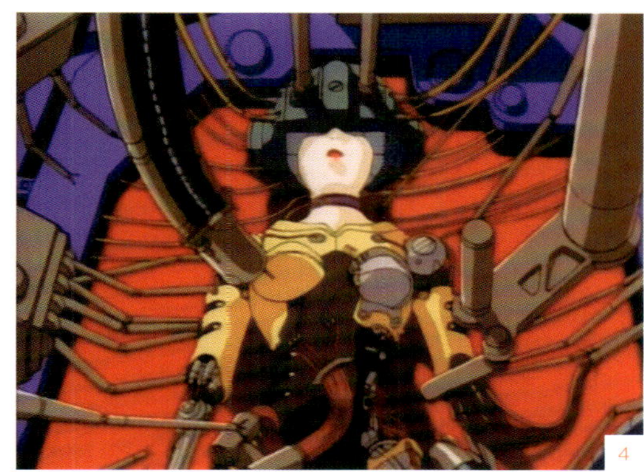

traumas and perversions. Highly inspired by Ridley Scott's *Alien* and John Carpenter's *The Thing*, the OAVs *Roots Search* (1986), *Hell Target* (1987), and *Lily C.A.T.* (1987) plunged viewers into space survival horrors where crew members battle alien monsters. Paranoia and claustrophobia were the order of the day in an anxiety-inducing setting. Yoshiaki Kawajiri established himself with *Yōjū Toshi* (*Wicked City*, 1987), a production intended for the video market that was only supposed to be half an hour long, but whose running time was extended to eighty minutes so it could be released in cinemas. Heavily inspired by author Hideyuki Kikuchi (*Wicked City*, *Demon City Shinjuku*, *Vampire Hunter D*), Kawajiri developed his ultraviolent, dark world by marrying film noir with fantasy while adding shocking rape scenes with tentacled monsters. He became one of the star directors of Madhouse studio, where in 1993 he directed his manifesto film, revered by an entire generation: *Ninja Scroll*.

The bold stories of the *mangaka* from the 1970s could finally be faithfully adapted into anime without watering them down. Author Go Nagai, who had taken over the exploitation rights to his titles through his production company, Dynamic Planning, was taking on the OAV market with his most radical works, such as *Violence Jack* and the apocalyptic *Devilman*, both of which were strewn with shredded bodies and pools of blood. Even if the violence was absurd, exaggerated, and far removed from realism, guilty pleasure still gripped viewers, who remained captivated by the extremely brutal style.

The violence was graphic but not necessarily gratuitous, as the evil depicted was far more vicious than when anime had been more simplistic. Physical pain became a reflection of psychological ailments, pushing the emotional impact to its peak. Alas, more and more productions were making ultraviolence their main attraction, which did not displease the American market, where sales of titles like *M.D. Geist* and *Guyver* were booming. The geysers of blood reached a pinnacle in 1994 with *Genocyber*, which went so far as to slaughter a group of children on screen! But that OAV series stood out the most for its fusions of flesh and metal, in line with the burgeoning cyberpunk movement.

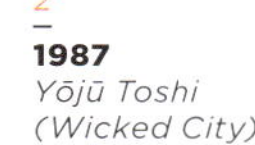

2
1987
Yōjū Toshi (Wicked City)

3
1988
Chōjin Densetsu Urotsukidōji

4
1994
Genocyber

1986
Roots Search

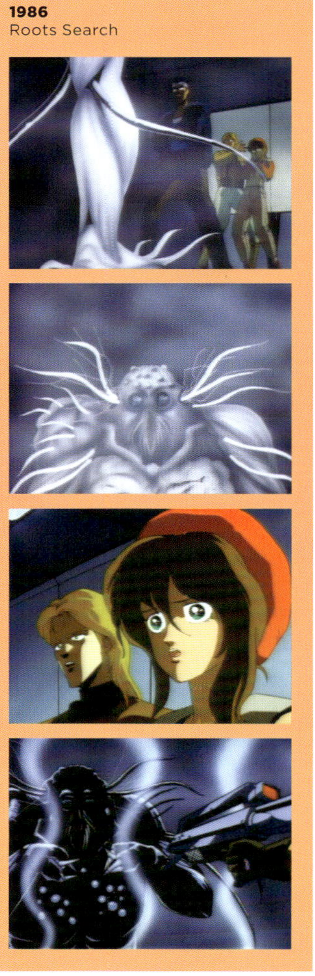

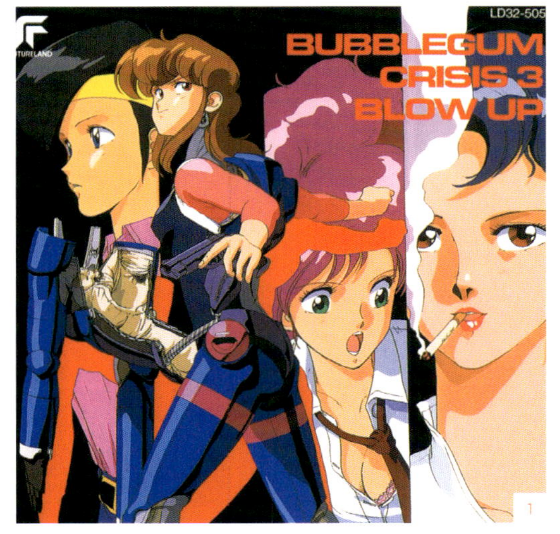

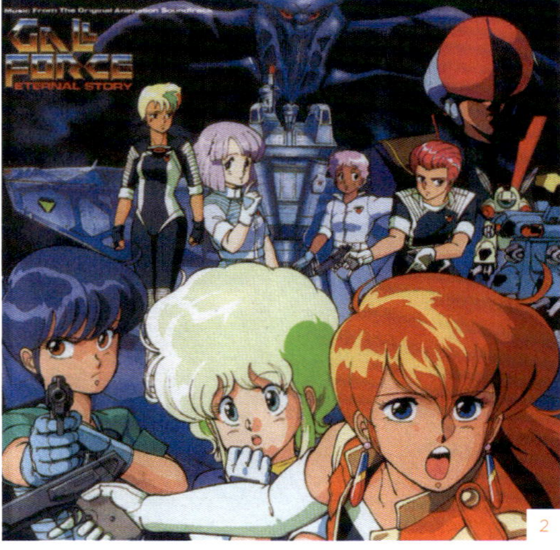

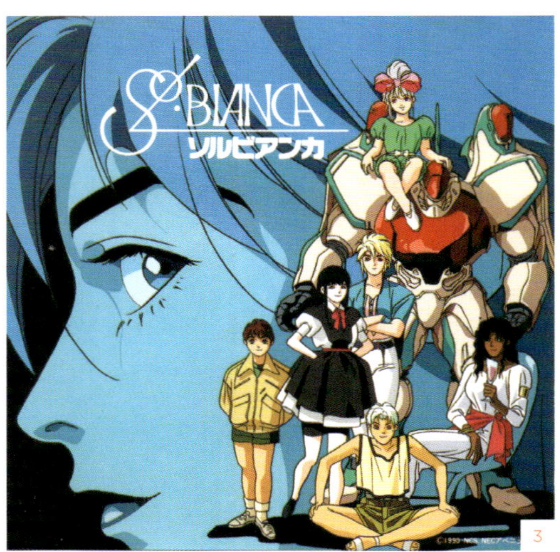

1
1987
Bubblegum Crisis

2
1986
Gall Force

3
1990
Sol Bianca

MEN AND MACHINES: CYBERPUNK AND MECHA

The cyberpunk wave that swept through American literature and cinema soon spread to the Land of the Rising Sun, where the themes of this nonconformist sci-fi movement were echoed: futuristic megacities governed by consortia, the race for technology, cybernetics, computer networks, and so on.

As the Japanese Economic Miracle drew to a close, the Japanese speculative bubble that emerged in 1986 propelled the country's economy. It was impossible not to see the parallels between the themes of cyberpunk and Japan's economic future, where the gap between the people and industrial powers was widening. The resulting storylines were still far too complex and serious for television, making OAV a perfect format because cyberpunk is a master of conceptual short stories. In the 1987 anthology *Robot Carnival*, A.P.P.P. animation studio portrayed a series of case studies focused on robotics, a central component of future society. The seven short films were directed by animators who had left their mark on various productions over the years. Katsuhiro Ōtomo orchestrated the opening and closing films, Kōji Morimoto (*Ashita no Joe 2*, *Cobra*) retold the story of the birth of Frankenstein's monster, and Hiroyuki Kitakubo (*Macross*) blew off steam with a giant robot battle in the middle of a medieval city. That same year, Kitakubo codirected *Black Magic M-66* with the author of the original manga, Masamune Shirow, who specialized in cyberpunk to such an extent that he became Japan's authority in the genre. Cashing in on the *Terminator* craze, their adaptation focused on a scenario in which a woman is stalked by a killer robot. Without any real technical feats, *Black Magic M-66* simply jumped on the trend, followed by *Appleseed* and *Dominion Tank Police* in 1988, other adaptations of Shirow's manga, showing that cyberpunk allowed for a real mash-up of popular themes. In the end, *Bubblegum Crisis* became the ambassador of the genre in 1987.

After an earthquake in the near future, Tokyo had to rebuild. The multinational GENOM Corporation took advantage of the situation to establish itself economically, bringing in its biomechanical beings to help with industrial development. The AD Police are tasked with intervening in cases where these "Boomers" get out of hand, and whereas the police have their limits, the Knight Sabers are happy to overstep them. Created by Toshimichi Suzuki (*Techno Police 21C*, *Call Me Tonight*), the OAV series was a resounding success, marking a high point in the collaboration between his studio Artmic and AIC (*Gall Force*).

The exoskeleton-wearing heroines in *Bubblegum Crisis* convey positive feminist values. They came from civilized society, had varied personalities and their own demons, and were participating in society and making progress where the macho system was more bogged down than ever. Women became fully emancipated as they fought the domineering male, like in the works of Masamune Shirow but without hypersexualized protagonists. Director Katsuhito Akiyama was no stranger to an all-woman team of protagonists, having orchestrated the *Gall Force* series whose first film was about a crew of women stuck in a ship in the middle of stellar warfare. The director centers the drama around the different relationships within the group, a formula he used again in 1990 for *Sol Bianca*, featuring an impressive group with a coherent, mature makeup.

Cyberpunk can be difficult to access and draws its strength from its tortured characters, which sometimes leads to extremely distressing stories about the relationship between man and machine. Such is the case in *AD Police*, the *Bubblegum Crisis* spin-off that retells the *Robocop* narrative in a much more sinister way. Cybernetics became an extension of the human body, introducing viewers to a graphic design focused on flesh and metal.

In parallel with cyberpunk, the video market fostered highly profitable mecha anime, boosting its giant machines with much more sophisticated visuals than in TV series. Shinji Aramaki's 1987 film *Metal Skin Panic MADOX-01* was particularly impressive with its rich mechanical details. And the short series *Dangaioh*, *Hades Project Zeorymer*, and later *Detonator Orgun*, all produced by the AIC-Artmic duo, breathed new life into the subgenre by exploring the psychology of the characters and modernizing mecha imagery with lanky styles, numerous metal reflections, and more. But it was Gainax that struck it big in 1988 with the VHS release of the first two episodes (out of six) of *Gunbuster*. Writer-director Hideaki Anno implemented a formula that would become the studio's hallmark: impressive original work with meta reflection on the anime industry and a healthy dose of fan service. *Gunbuster* reexamined space travel and its temporal consequences in a story with giant robots piloted by women. Women were now in the cockpit, as in *Patlabor* and *Dominion Tank Police*, whose heroines named their machines (respectively, Alphonse and Napoleon). The relationship between pilot and mecha became more passionate, shifting the balance of power between men and women.

TEMPERED URGES

By 1988, OAV production was completely scattered. Despite this, ongoing series such as *Patlabor*, *Crying Freeman*, *Gunbuster*, and *Vampire Princess Miyu* maintained high-quality graphics and storytelling. Was the OAV free-for-all finally slowing down to give way to artistic expression? *Crying Freeman*, for example, is a unique adaptation of the mafia manga by Ryoichi Ikegami and Kazuo Koike. Each episode was directed by a different team, breaking with graphic continuity to encourage the directors to make the work their own. With its contemplative style and long monologues, the *Patlabor* series went against the grain of fully supercharged productions. Director Mamoru Oshii knew that the OAV format was conducive to creative experimentation, which he highlighted in the second episode of *Twilight Q* with a considerably lower number of shots.

In late 1988, the first episode of the longest OAV series ever created was released: *Ginga Eiyū Densetsu* (*Legend of the Galactic Heroes*). This extraordinary space opera spans 110 episodes, a tour de force for a video production! Directed by the experienced Noboru Ishiguro, the series is based on the novels by Yoshiki Tanaka that had recently been adapted into a manga in 1986, as well as a pilot film. With high political-military stakes and mature visuals, *Legend of the Galactic Heroes* proved that the OAV market was growing in both wisdom and ambition.

4
1988
Ginga Eiyū Densetsu (Legend of the Galactic Heroes)

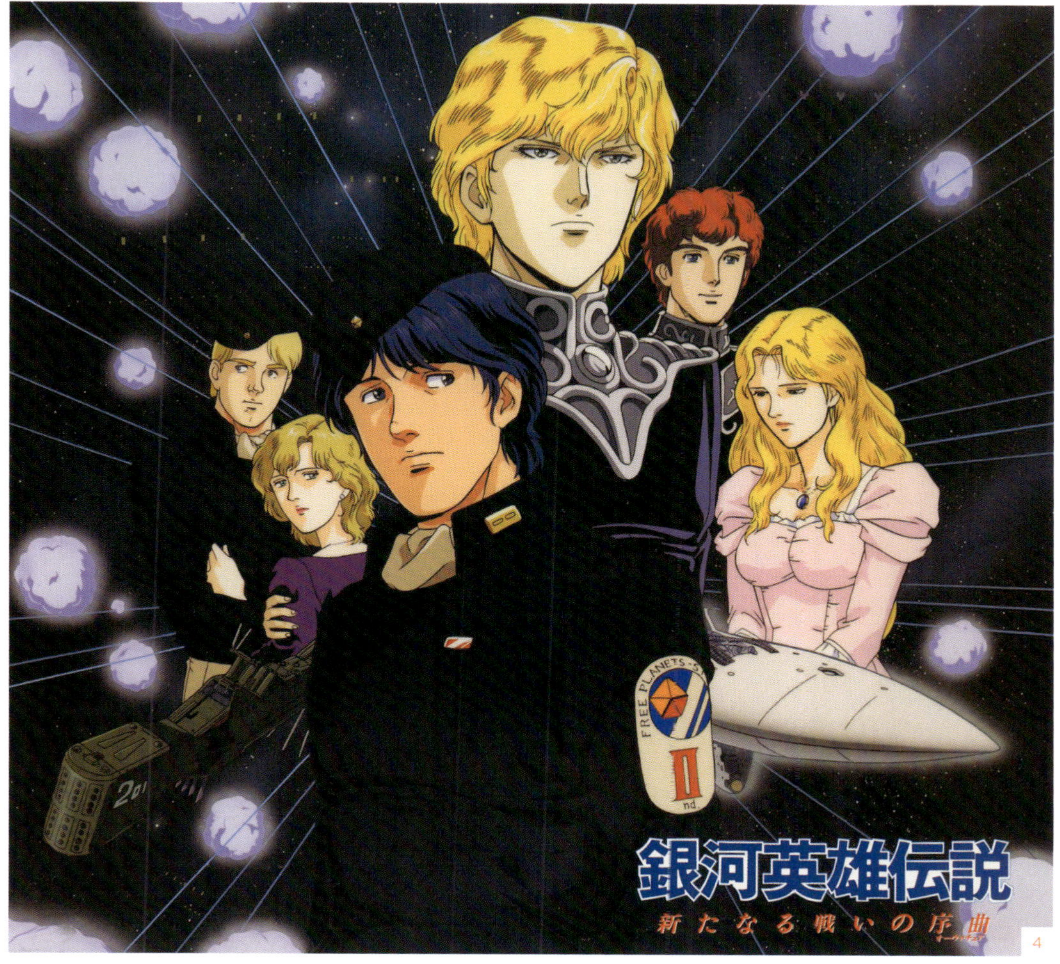

4

Television: Building viewer loyalty

THE LAND OF THE CATHODE-RAY TUBE

Television culture had never been stronger than in Japan, to the extent that in 1979, 60 percent of the population found it necessary to have a TV set at home, and 32 percent were convinced that it was absolutely essential. In 1981, a quarter of Japanese people had at least three TVs at home—enough to fully enjoy their favorite medium, now creating content for every member of the family!

This loyalty to the small screen was rewarded with sequels of iconic series, including *Ashita no Joe 2* (1980) and *Tiger Mask 2* (1981), as well as a third *Lupin III* (1984) and *GeGeGe no Kitarō* (1985) series. In 1980, the industry was even revitalized with remakes of the great classics *Astro Boy* and *Tetsujin 28*!

But nostalgia obviously wasn't enough to satisfy audiences, and new adaptations were broadcast in greater numbers each year, with a programming schedule that had proven its effectiveness. Nippon Animation, for example, maintained its annual adaptations of Western literary works such as *Shōkōjo Sara* (*Princess Sara*, 1985) and *Ai Shōjo Pollyanna Story* (*Pollyanna*), whose orphaned heroines were reminiscent of the earlier *Heidi, Girl of the Alps*. Even TMS jumped on board with *Meitantei Holmes* (*Sherlock Hound*, 1984), a humorous anthropomorphic version of Arthur Conan Doyle's work, with Miyazaki supervising the first six episodes.

But the real treasure trove was found in a production right at home: manga. Television channels could not afford to lag behind in this lively anime boom, especially since long-running manga were so successful that their numerous installments were selling tens of millions of copies. Adapting those manga was a given, and channels already had a pass to animate screens abroad.

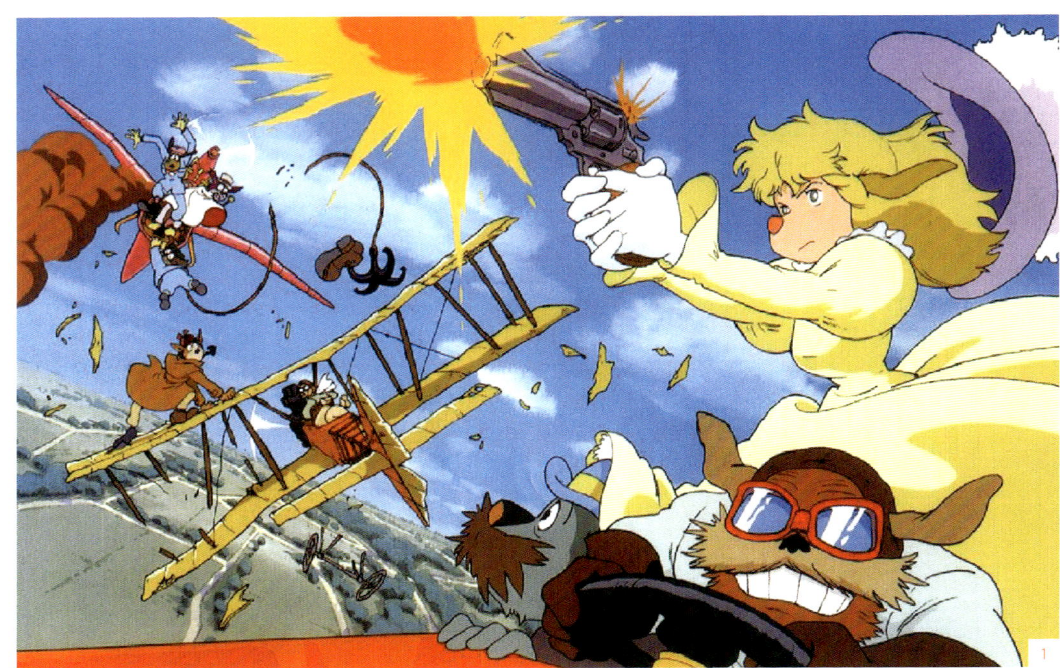

1
1984
Meitantei Holmes (Sherlock Hound)

STUDIO REORIENTATION

Anime was entering its golden age, and the abundant production of series for all audiences was forcing studios to break out of their chosen fields to meet the diversified demand. In 1981, Hiroshi Shidara, who had directed Toei's last two magical girl series, embraced the studio's new direction with *Hello! Sandybell*, casting aside magic wands (the genre had never really taken off with audiences) for romance with a Western flair, popularized by *Candy Candy* and *The Rose of Versailles*. Various other studios were also exploring this niche, such as TMS with *Lady Georgie* in 1983 and Tatsunoko Production with *Honō no Alpen Rose: Judy & Randy* (*Alpen Rose*, 1985). Shidara responded with *Lady Lady!!* in 1987.

Toei had put an end to the magical girls' run with *Mahō Shōjo Lalabel* (*Lalabel, the Magical Girl*) in 1980, but Ashi Productions reopened the door two years later with *Magical Princess Minky Momo*. The studio embraced the codes of the genre to better circumvent them, transforming the cute little princess Momo into a fully formed young woman to revive the Kingdom of Dreams, forgotten by humans. The shift from girl to woman and the disillusionment of humanity made the series more mature, to the point that the Popy toy company stopped merchandise production while it was broadcast. With little connection to the character, young female viewers weren't buying enough dolls. Rescued by an audience that turned out to be less young (and less female), the series took on a more spiritual resonance in its second half, when Momo gets hit by a truck . . . of toys! The series still ran for sixty-three episodes. Studio Pierrot immediately took up the innovative concept of adult transformation to specialize in the genre, notably with *Magical Angel Creamy Mami*, which replaced *Minky Momo* on Nippon TV, followed by *Mahō no Yōsei Perusha* (*Persia, the Magic Fairy*) and *Magic Star Magical Emi*.

Well-established studios were also forced out of their comfort zone of the dominant genre, science fiction, as numerous production companies took it by storm in 1983 and 1984. Ashi Productions released two giant robot series, *Tokusō Kihei Dorvack* (*Special Armored Battalion Dorvack*) and *Chōjū Kishin Dancouga* (*Dancouga: Super Beast Machine God*), while Kokusai Eigasha produced *Chō Kōsoku Galvion* and *Galactic Patrol Lensman*. TMS chose to bring in the experts: Studio Nue for *Chōjikū Seiki Orguss* (*Super Dimension Century Orguss*) and Dynamic Productions for *God Mazinger*. Sunrise, Toei Animation, and Tatsunoko Production were facing fierce competition. Whereas Toei almost abandoned science fiction to devote itself entirely to manga adaptations for teens, Tatsunoko shifted radically from superhero series to romances like *Alpen Rose* and *Hikari no Densetsu* (*Legend of Light*).

Sunrise countered with several titles like *Mobile Suit Zeta Gundam* and *Dirty Pair* in 1985 to remain the undisputed leader of the genre, but it couldn't ignore the *City Hunter* series in 1987. The studio hoped to achieve the same success as TMS with *Cat's Eye*, based on a work by the same author, Tsukasa Hōjō. Far removed from giant robots, Ryo Saeba, a perverse mercenary and sniper who brought justice to Tokyo's underworld, targeted mature audiences who were now entitled to their own long-running series. And at 140 episodes, it was the studio's longest. In the same year, the studio produced *Mister Ajikko*, a culinary show that kept viewers drooling over 99 episodes. Both titles were products of an industry that stretched the same concept further and further, like protecting a new young woman in every episode of *City Hunter* or creating a new dish for *Mister Ajikko*.

A HIGHLY ANIMATED DAY-TO-DAY

By the early 1980s, Japanese households had become accustomed to their regularly scheduled shows. Eiken studio's unrivaled *Sazae-san* never ceased to amuse the household with its own comic reflection. The prime minister's office even took advantage of the studio's expertise to sponsor the series *Hoka Hoka Kazoku* (*The Affectuous Family**) which, over the course of its 1,428 episodes produced between 1976 and 1982, relayed a few rules for life in society.

With their eccentric good humor, the popular series *Urusei Yatsura* and *Dr. Slump* were shining stars of Fuji TV from 1981 to 1986. The channel didn't skimp on wacky humor, especially in the 86 episodes of the hilarious, **super-deformed** (**SD**) characters with small bodies and huge heads in *High School! Kimengumi*.

Now there wasn't a day that went by without a show for preschoolers. Kids could sleep soundly

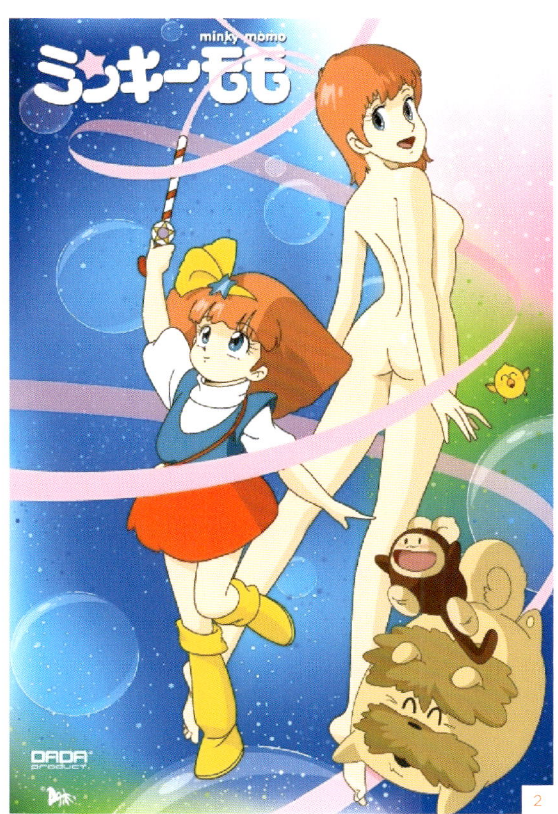

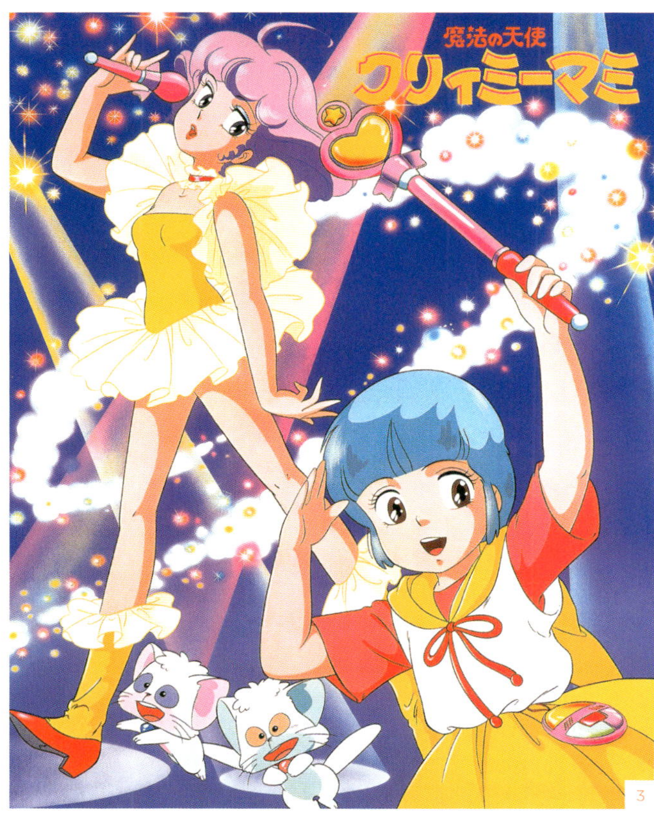

2
1982
Mahō no Princess Minky Momo (Magical Princess Minky Momo)

3
1983
Mahō no Tenshi Creamy Mami (Magical Angel Creamy Mami)

knowing they would see their favorite shows the next day. *Nippon Mukashi Banashi* (*Folktales from Japan**) from Group TAC had been educating children in tales and legends since 1975 and would only bow out in 1994 after 1,488 episodes. As for the famous *Doraemon*, his second series began in 1979 and didn't stop until 2005, resuming the same year after only a brief pause! Even the car Boumbo (*Bumpety Boo*, 1985) taught children about road safety over 130 episodes. And how could anyone pass up the sweetness of the 102 episodes that made up the two-part *Maple Town Monogatari* (*Maple Town*) series?

Formulaic TV shows were still very popular, and they had changed and varied their genres since the early Toei series based on the valiant hero confronting the villain of the week. Slice-of-life shows now allowed the Japanese to feel closer to the protagonists, who were growing more numerous on screen to reduce repetition.

Aishite Night (*Love Me, My Knight*) hit it big in 1982, whose young heroine was in love with sensitive rock stars, as did *Kimagure Orange Road*, which charmed viewers with a love triangle against a backdrop of the paranormal. The romantic red thread was enhanced in each episode by a different problem, in tune with the torments of teenage life. These modern series even feature single-parent families, like in *Ohayō! Spank* and *Ranma ½*, where the mother figure is also absent. At a time when divorce was on the rise in Japan, children from broken families could more easily identify with it. Rumiko Takahashi's works popularized long-running, epic romances: *Urusei Yatsura* (195 episodes) and *Ranma ½* (161 episodes) brought science fiction and martial arts, respectively, into frenzied quests for love. The more mature *Maison Ikkoku* (1986) depicts adult roommates faced with societal problems, such as alcoholism, bereavement, and unemployment. No extraterrestrials or special powers were on the agenda in this very realistic, sentimental 96-episode series.

Realism was the specialty of author Mitsuru Adachi, who was a fixture in families' daily lives with his series *Miyuki* (1983), *Touch* (1985), and *Hiatari Ryōkō!* (1987). The pace of the episodes was no longer constrained by a forced dynamic, and viewers felt the ambient melancholy, generating a poetry unique to contemporary anime. Adachi's style was all the more appreciated in Japan for mixing baseball with romance. And sports competitions are a perfect setting for multiple episodes!

VYING FOR FIRST

In Japan, sports broadcasts accounted for a large share of the viewing audience, reflecting a culture of physical activity taught in school curricula from an early age. Since *Star of the Giants* in 1968, sports had naturally played a key role in animation. Baseball reigned supreme, especially with the immense success of Nippon Animation's *Dokaben* (1976), with a total of 163 episodes on Fuji TV. No need for an "eat healthy, be active" slogan with TV shows that were perfect recruiters for sports teams. Nippon Television responded with director Satoshi Dezaki's made-for-TV movie *Captain*, released in cinemas and then as a TV series in 1983. But it was the captain of different sport who won big that year.

Tsuchida Production, a subcontractor on the *Dokaben* series, ran with the ball by adapting Yōichi Takahashi's recent manga *Captain Tsubasa*. The author was part of the new wave of *mangaka*, along with Rumiko Takahashi, Mitsuru Adachi, and Akira Toriyama, who were making a name for themselves with atypical character designs. A new generation of viewers was identifying with these highly distinctive characters.

1
1989
Ranma ½

2
1986
Maison Ikkoku

3
1986
Hikari no Densetsu (Legend of Light)

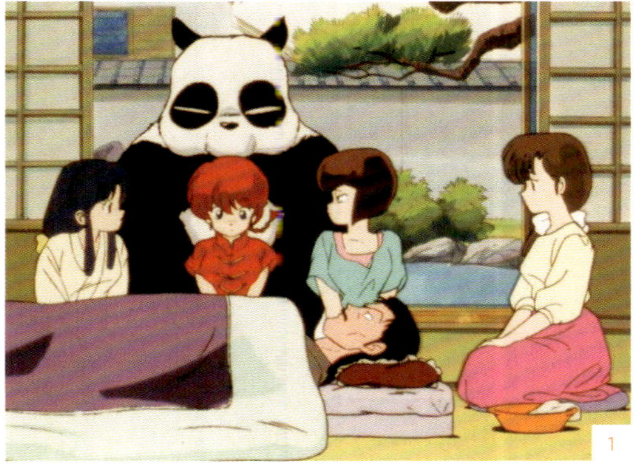
1

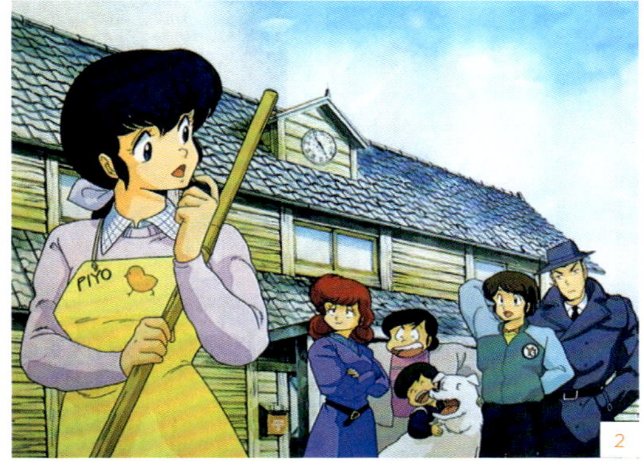

2

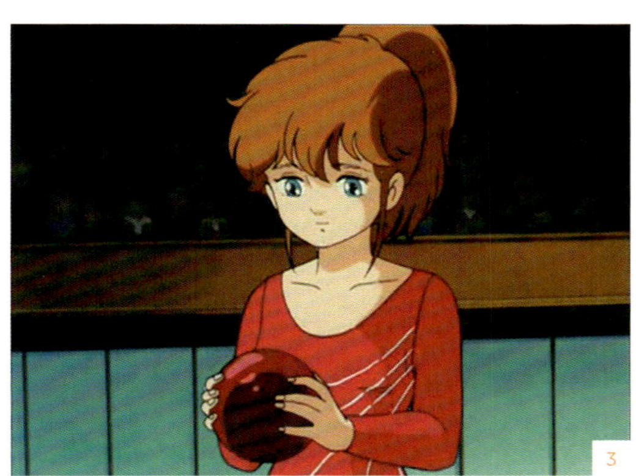
3

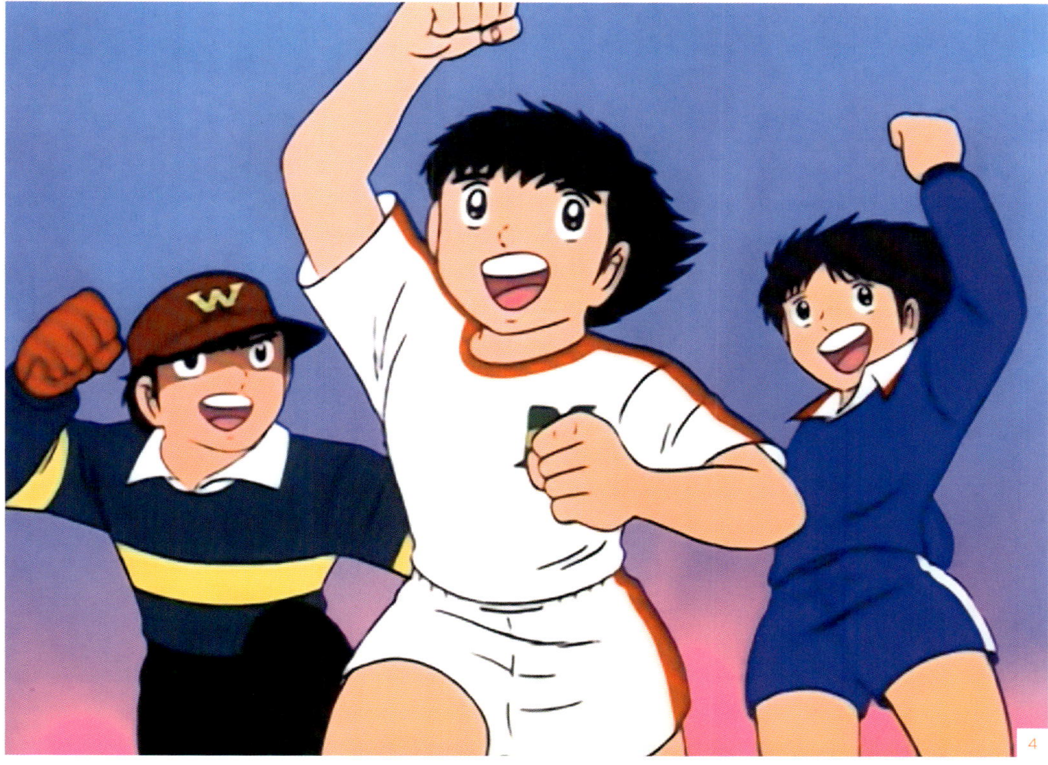

4
1983
Captain Tsubasa

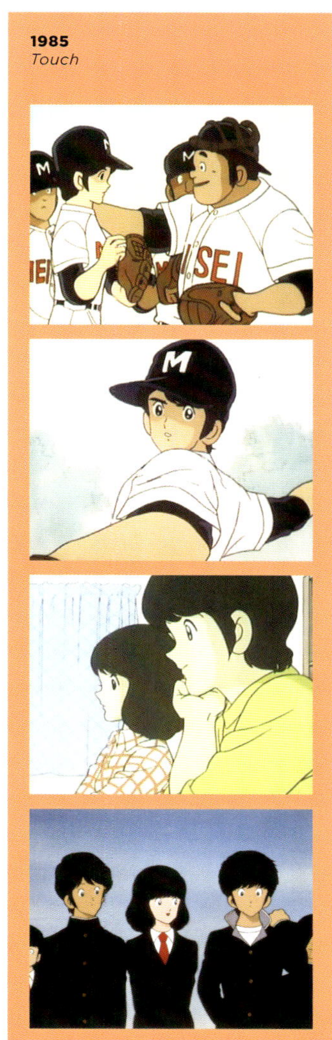

1985
Touch

When young Tsubasa Oozora joins his school's soccer team, his talent sets him apart from the others, leading him to a professional career. Viewers watch his soccer games, punctuated by training sessions and a few phases of everyday life. Drawing on his experience as an episode director on *Dokaben*, Hiroyoshi Mitsunobu stretched the manga's narrative over 128 episodes. Audiences watched the increasingly dramatic scenes as strikers shot the ball in pairs, the ball tore through the net at high speed, and so on. Viewers had no choice but to tune in each week to watch games that spanned several episodes. Television channels and studios were quick to seize on this highly profitable, addictive formula. Beginning in 1984, Mitsunobu and Tsuchida Production applied their know-how in the golf series *Ashita Tenki ni Nāre* (*A Great Super Shot Boy*), commissioned by Fuji TV to target white-collar businessmen, a demographic known as **salarymen**. TV Asahi responded immediately with *Pro Golfer Saru*, a series produced by Shin-Ei Animation, based on an idea by the author of *Doraemon*, that lasted 147 episodes!

Female viewers also got their adrenaline fix with the romantic volleyball series *Attacker You!* (1984) from the studio Knack (*Astroganger*). Like *Captain Tsubasa*, *Attacker You!* extended the game highlights through long glances and flashbacks. The animation allowed for mid-action introspection and a better understanding of the various techniques. This style created excitement in every discipline it touched, as directors did with gymnastics in *Legend of Light* (1986). Fusing baseball, the king of sports, with bittersweet romantic comedy, *Touch* reached a whopping 32.9 percent viewership on Fuji TV following a twist that brought tears to the eyes of the whole country. Viewers were anticipating a classic love triangle between Minami and the twins Tatsuya and Kazuya. While she had a crush on Tatsuya, a lazy crybaby, everyone could already see Minami married to Kazuya, the captain of the baseball team who would lead the team to the high school championship finals . . . if he hadn't been hit by a truck. In sports and in love, would Tatsuya emerge from his late brother's shadow? The answer would come in the 101st episode of the series adapted from Adachi's best-selling manga, which sold more than 100 million copies.

Viewers were now accustomed to watching every episode to keep up with their series, no longer watching out of habit, but out of addiction. From then on, long-running series weren't confined to sports shows; the lion's share were now *shōnen nekketsu* (hot-blooded young boy), whose theme of surpassing one's own limits was the pride of the manga industry.

DRAGON BALL, OR AN OVERFLOW OF CELLULOID

Martial arts series were making a comeback, with *Ashita no Joe 2*, *Genki*, and even *Tiger Mask 2*, and they quickly took on a comedic twist with the adaptation of the manga *Kinnikuman*. The alien wrestler, known for his unattractive face, simple-mindedness, and great cowardice, became endearing when promoting good human values. The zany, parodic superhero series hooked viewers right away, who were by then already accustomed to the bombastic *Dr. Slump*. Logically, Toei continued drawing on publisher Shueisha's catalog to guide its new productions. It's no coincidence, then, that the studio adapted Tetsuo Hara and Buronson's manga *Hokuto no Ken* (*Fist of the North Star*) to great fanfare the following year. It had been number one at the time in the publisher's flagship magazine, *Weekly Shōnen Jump*. The series depicts an apocalyptic world inspired by *Mad Max*, where people live in terror of the law of the strongest, established by self-proclaimed dictators. Scarred across the chest, Kenshiro emerges as a messianic hero, freeing cities from tyrannical yokes with his extremely brutal, legendary martial arts. With bodies exploding all over the place, *Fist of the North Star* gradually got viewers used to extreme, unabashed violence exaggerated to the extent of surrealism, which allowed the series to be shown at 5 p.m. The anime is graphically ambitious for a weekly show, and Masami Suda's character design even grew in detail over the course of its 152 episodes.

No longer outsourcing only to Korea, but also to the Philippines, the Toei steamroller was setting an animation standard that many production companies would have to follow to stay in the race. And while the studio adapted short manga in the 1970s by reducing them down to repetitive formulas, the current trend was religious fidelity to long-running manga series. But how could they do this when weekly production was catching up to the pace of publication? Toei resorted to using filler episodes, bolstering the story until the manga had progressed far enough to relaunch the main plot, which could not be altered. *Fist of the North Star* put a new face on action series, which would be perfected with one of the anime industry's most striking titles: *Dragon Ball*! The manga's huge success in *Weekly Shōnen Jump* (toppling *Fist of the North Star* from first place) and the fact that it was by Akira Toriyama (*Dr. Slump*) left no room for doubt about its TV potential. In its opening chapters, *Dragon Ball* follows the adventures of a young boy, Son Goku, with a monkey tail and Herculean strength, and a manipulative teenager, Bulma, on their quest for seven crystal balls that, once reunited, would conjure a Dragon capable of granting their greatest wish. Inspired by the *Saiyuki* legend, the story moves quickly through cyclic arcs of adventure, training, and tournaments.

Less radical than *Fist of the North Star* and less wacky than *Kinnikuman*, *Dragon Ball* stands out as a model of balance designed to appeal to a wider audience. What's more, with his optimistic naivete and gradual strength illustrated in his developing powers and appearance, Son Goku represented a new genre of heroes that would serve as the basis for any *shōnen* title about surpassing one's limits. Toei put Minoru Okazaki and Daisuke Nishio in charge of the series, two veterans in the field who were familiar with Toriyama's style from *Dr. Slump*, one of the studio's greatest successes.

Everything about the anime, which debuted in 1986, became iconic—the sound effects, *seiyū* Masako Nozawa's voice, Shunsuke Kikuchi's music, and so on. On playgrounds, Kenshiro's catchphrase, "You are already dead," gave way to Son Goku's cry of

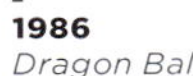

1

1986
Dragon Ball

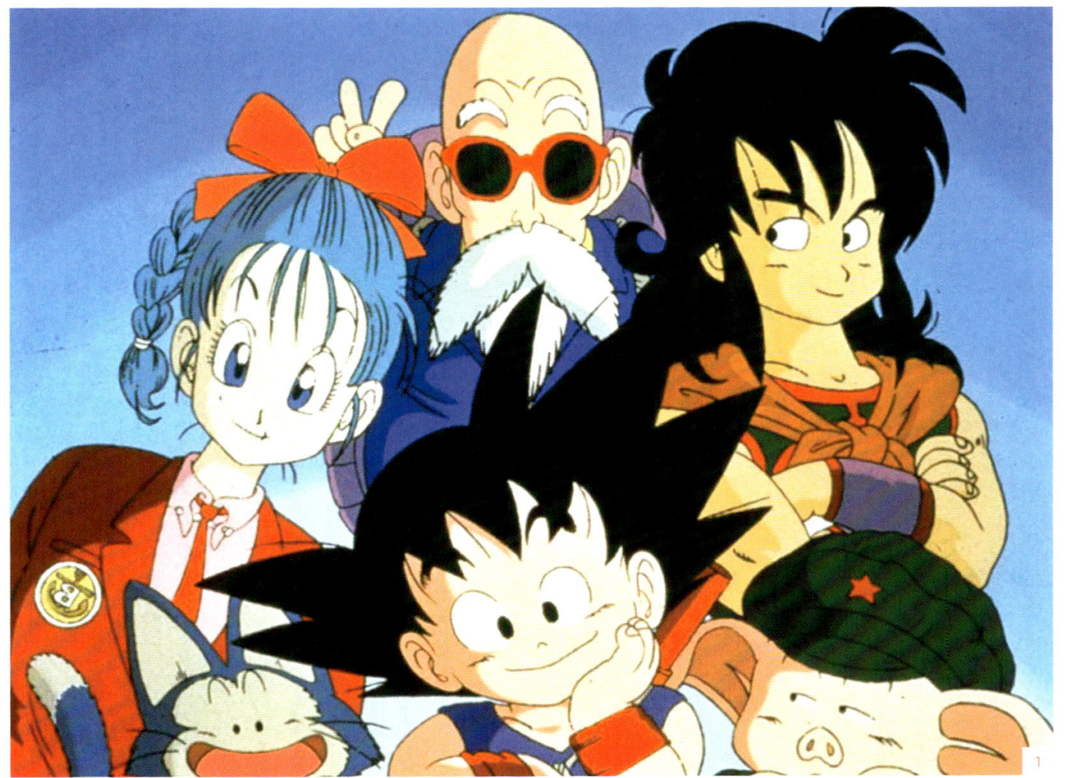

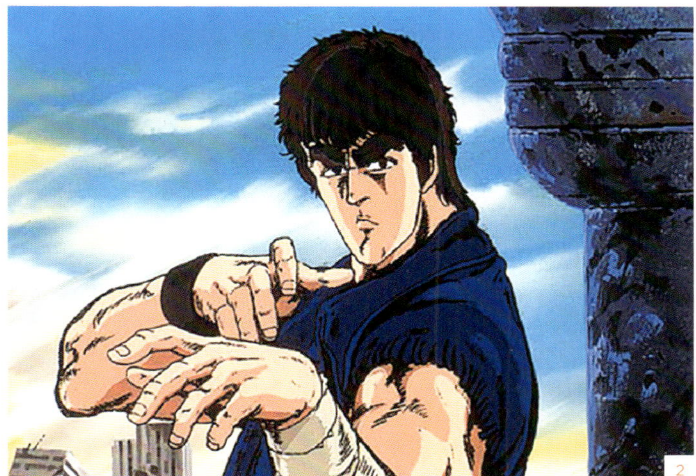

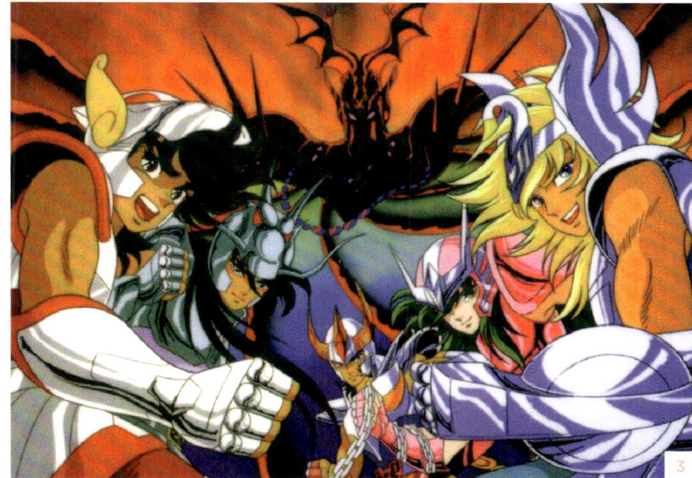

2
1984
Hokuto no Ken (Fist of the North Star)

3
1986
Saint Seiya

"Kamehameha" when he delivered his signature blow. And because the manga had already been published for two years, only 23 out of 153 episodes are fillers, allowing the story to maintain its dynamism. The Shueisha-Toei-Fuji TV partnership was at its peak, especially when *Dragon Ball* made its way to Europe in 1988. In order to mark the evolution of Son Goku, who now had a son, Toei produced *Dragon Ball Z* in 1989, a sequel that is simply the continuation of the manga, as with *Fist of the North Star 2*. The series was more mature with more angular designs (the 1990s syndrome), appealing to teenagers who saw these increasingly potent superpowers as a real outlet. But this time, the anime had caught up with the manga completely, and Daisuke Nishio decided to mix hard-hitting episodes with fillers to keep both the fast pace of the story and the viewer's attention.

A few months after *Dragon Ball* was launched on Fuji TV, TV Asahi broadcasted *Saint Seiya*, another Toei hit production, strengthening the company's position as a leader in youth programming. Drawing its inspiration from Greek mythology and stories of colorful superheroes, the adaptation of Masami Kurumada's manga saw many knights in sacred armor battle their way across 110 episodes. With its tortured heroes and sacrifices, the tone in *Saint Seiya*, enhanced by Seiji Yokoyama's epic and nostalgic musical scores, reached beyond middle school students to their older sisters. Shingo Araki's and Michi Himeno's artistic androgyny of some of the knights also contributed to the series' female **fandom**.

Fist of the North Star, *Dragon Ball*, and *Saint Seiya* became the geese that laid the golden eggs. Thanks to these "Big 3," Shueisha sold countless books, Toei redefined its image as the three series became international hits, and Bandai used its popular *B-Club* magazine to promote the iconic characters and their worlds. Seiya, Kenshiro, and Son Goku were now alongside the robots on toy store shelves. It was such a well-oiled machine that Bandai went as far as asking for additional knights to be incorporated into the series to expand its product range. No problem—in addition to gold, silver, and bronze armor, they would now sell steel armor as well, which would become very rare!

CULTURE SHOCK

With the flood of anime hitting TV airwaves, studios and toy manufacturers were gradually capitalizing on an international market, with growing demand in America, Europe, and North Africa. The exoticism of these series and their relatively low broadcasting costs made them very attractive. But it was precisely this exoticism that created a number of cultural concerns, whether in the simple fact that the names prevented young audiences from identifying with them, or the fact that in the West, cartoons were aimed mainly at children. This preconception was challenged by the violence and eroticism, which led to significant censorship: in France, the numerous sexual allusions and sadistic moments in *Dragon Ball* were cut out, and the ubiquitous bottles of alcohol in *Maison Ikkoku* became lemonade. On the other side of the Atlantic, the number of episodes in a Japanese series was incompatible with American programming. When local company World Events Productions acquired the rights to Toei's *Hyaku Jūō Golion* (*Beast King GoLion*, 1981) and *Kikō Kantai Dairugger XV* (*Armored Fleet Dairugger XV*, 1982) at fifty-two episodes each,

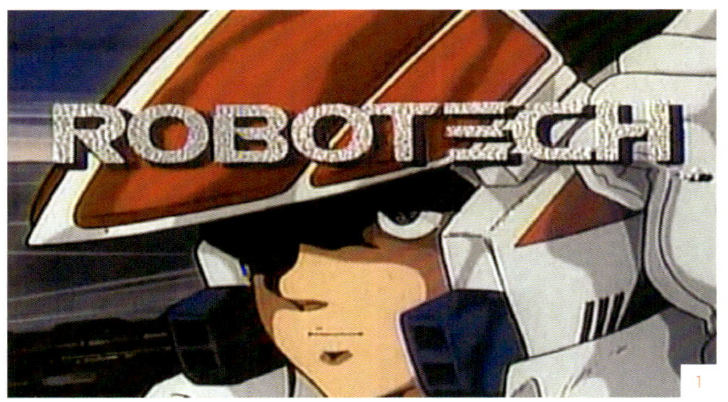

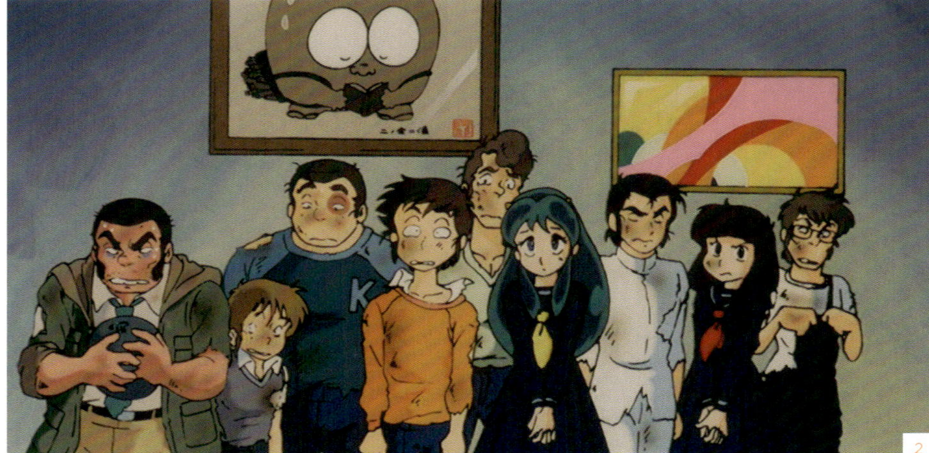

1
1985
Robotech

2
1984
Urusei Yatsura 2: Beautiful Dreamer

it decided to combine them to create *Voltron* (1984). But because there weren't enough episodes, the company asked the animation studio to design the last twenty, exclusive to this version. Although it could not compete with *Transformers*, the series became a cult classic in the West, as did the remakes of *Macross*, *Southern Cross*, and *Mospeada* by Harmony Gold, which came together to create the *Robotech* series in 1985. With its Americanized names and new soundtrack, Harmony Gold transformed the series in depth to suit the audience. The company even commissioned a sequel from Tatsunoko Production, *Robotech II: The Sentinels*, and took advantage of acquiring the rights to *Megazone 23* by creating *Robotech: The Movie*.

By the end of the 1980s, Japanese animation was well established in foreign television programming, and publishers such as Dark Horse Comics were turning their attention to Japanese production. The publisher Shogakukan (creator of Shueisha) even created an American company, Viz Media, to distribute manga and anime. Aficionados of "manga culture" could now be found across the globe.

Film: Strong franchises

FROM SMALL SCREEN TO BIG SCREEN

Television alone could not contain the enthusiasm being generated for anime series; viewers simply couldn't get enough of their colorful heroes. So, the industry gave audiences the chance to follow their favorites on the big screen in new, exciting standalone adventures! Doraemon's gadgets, *Kinnikuman*'s oiled-up muscles, *Urusei Yatsura*'s eccentric alien Lum, Tsubasa's legwork, *Lupin III*'s sly tricks, Son Goku's cries of "Kamehameha," and the kidnappings of Princess Athena now came to life annually in highly profitable films. Doraemon even became king of the box office, with his feature films racking up billions of yen in revenue! But these films weren't just extras to use up household entertainment budgets; their original stories offered far more freedom to directors and animators, usually limited by the TV format.

After directing the first film in the *Urusei Yatsura* series, *Only You* (1983), Mamoru Oshii was naturally called in for the second by Studio Pierrot, who gave him full control over the writing and directing. He was inspired by the tale *Urashima Tarō* to create *Urusei Yatsura 2: Beautiful Dreamer* (1984), a sophisticated story in which the protagonists are locked in a time loop. Oshii adapted the manga with a complex script and dramatic staging, which, despite good press, displeased author Rumiko Takahashi. Like Hayao Miyazaki's *Lupin III: The Castle of Cagliostro*, Mamoru Oshii produced a film all his own, if not an entirely original creation. Other directors would repeat this exercise in appropriation, such as Tomomi Mochizuki. In 1988, he directed films to complement the *Kimagure Orange Road* and *Maison Ikkoku* series, adding a more mature, dramatic dimension. This model had been gaining momentum since the original sequel *Adieu Galaxy Express 999* gloatingly surpassed the symbolic billion-yen box office milestone in 1981, paving the way for the production of major sci-fi films. When Shōji Kawamori and Noburo Ishiguro directed *Chōjikū Yōsai Macross: Ai Oboete Imasu Ka* (*Macross: Do You Remember Love?*) in 1984, capitalizing on the triumph of the series that generated numerous spin-offs, the substantial ¥400-million budget enabled them to create a technically vertiginous blockbuster. This alternative version of the original story grossed up to ¥700 million. Sunrise responded in 1988 with *Kidō Senshi Gundam: Gyakushū no Char* (*Mobile Suit Gundam: Char's Counterattack*), in which Yoshiyuki Tomino offered a lavish conclusion to his three successful series, bringing in over ¥600 million.

Although these large-scale productions were highly profitable, they fell far short of the billion-yen *Harmagedon* (1983), Rintaro's film that hadn't had the benefit of TV promotion to fill theaters. Could this be the dawn of a new business model? Yes—especially given that in the same year, the hits *Crusher Joe*, *Barefoot Gen*, and *Golgo 13* all came directly from manga or novels! And in 1984, a sci-fi feature with a budget far below that of *Macross: Do You Remember Love?* achieved the same results at the box office despite having no television predecessor. With *Nausicaä of the Valley of the Wind*, Hayao Miyazaki proved that TV broadcast was no longer a prerequisite for commercial success.

STUDIO GHIBLI: A SUCCESSFUL DUAL PATH

When publishing giant Tokuma approached Hayao Miyazaki about writing a sci-fi manga for its *Animage* magazine, the director accepted on the condition that he retain control of his work. He began publishing *Kaze no Tani no Nausicaä* (*Nausicaä of the Valley of the Wind*) in 1982 and took the liberty of pausing it when he became involved in preproduction on the *Sherlock Hound* series. Despite the break, the manga's popularity prompted Tokuma to consider an animated adaptation. Producer Yasuyoshi Tokuma joined forces with a major advertising agency, Hakuhodo, to produce a cinematic feature. Miyazaki chose his colleague Isao Takahata (*The Great Adventure of Horus, Prince of the Sun*; *Heidi, Girl of the Alps*) to produce the animation, which was taken on by Topcraft studio. The film depicts the adventures of a young princess battling an invading army in her Valley of the Wind, a rare peaceful haven in a postapocalyptic world where nature, now hostile to humans, has taken over. With

1988
Kidō Senshi Gundam: Gyakushū no Char (Mobile Suit Gundam: Char's Counterattack)

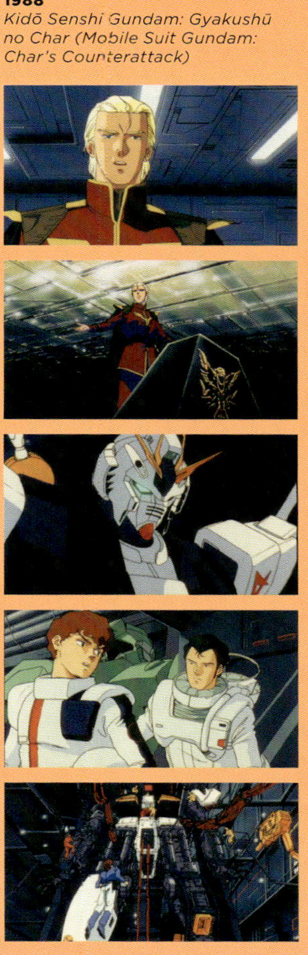

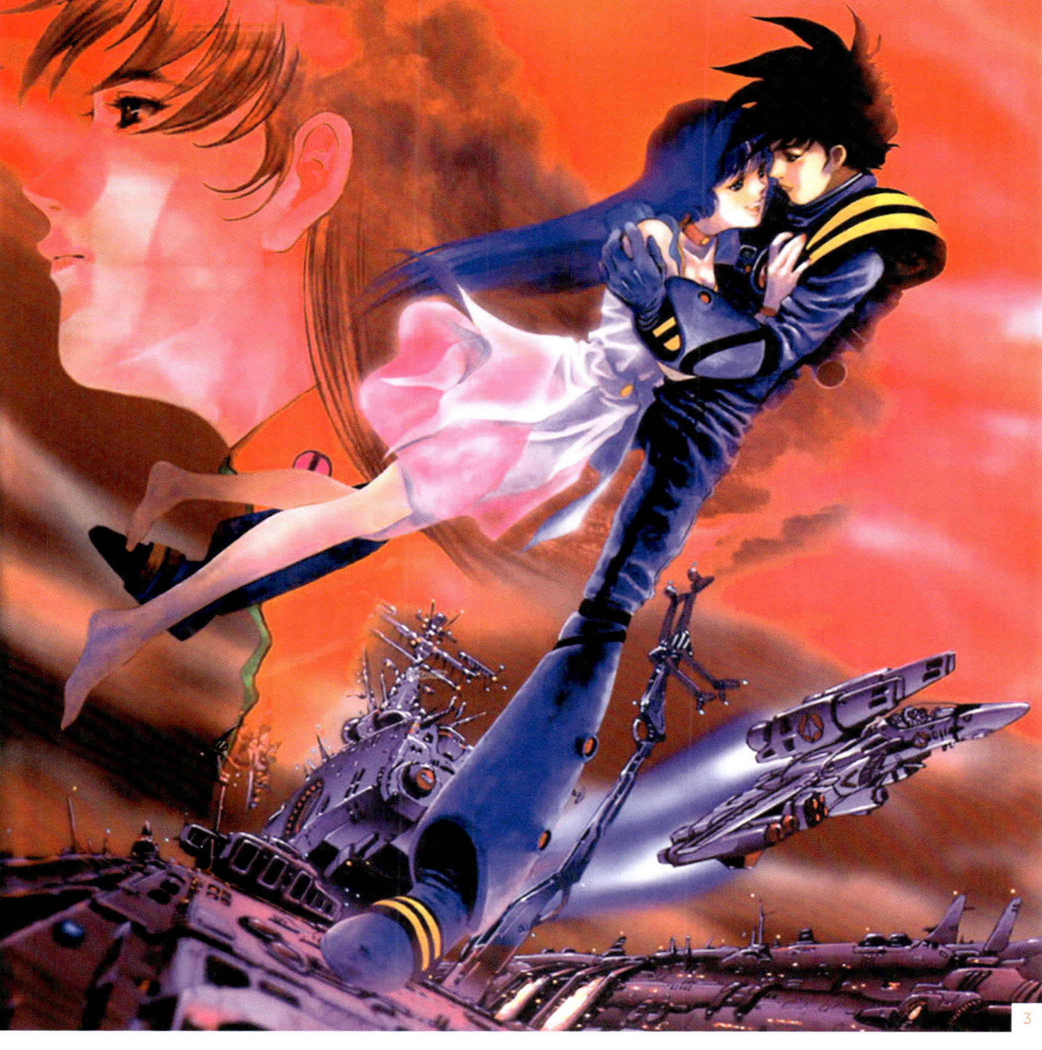

3

1984
Chōjikū Yōsai Macross: Ai Oboete Imasu Ka (Macross: Do You Remember Love?)

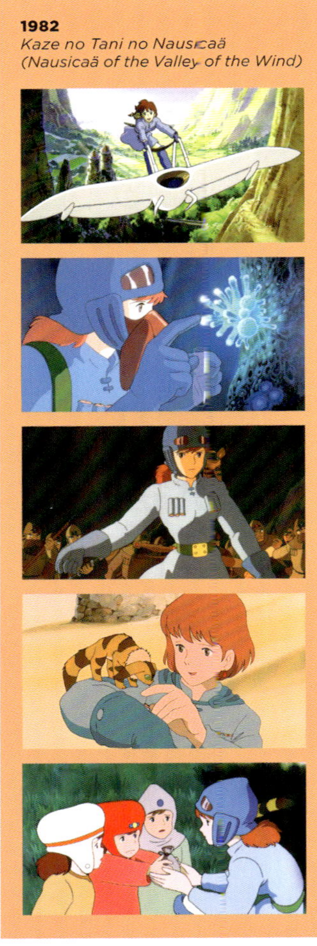

1982
Kaze no Tani no Nausicaä (Nausicaä of the Valley of the Wind)

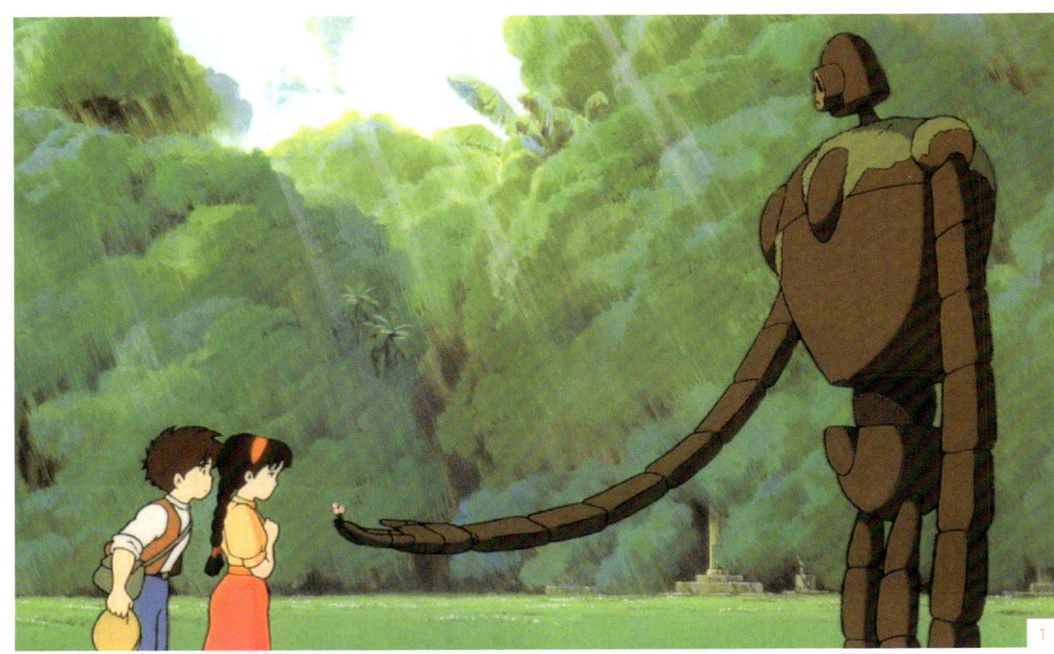

1
1986
Tenkū no Shiro Laputa (Castle in the Sky)

its young strong heroine, ecological resonance, and meticulous animation, the film attracted 915,000 viewers during its fifty-two-day run. This success led the Tokuma Shoten Publishing Company, Miyazaki, and Takahata to create Studio Ghibli in 1985. This new company's purpose? To create feature films that were more artistic than commercial.

The young studio took on a large part of the *Nausicaä* team to work on the production of *Tenkū no Shiro Laputa* (*Castle in the Sky*), released in 1986. Whereas *Nausicaä* was a free adaptation of his own manga, this time Miyazaki created an original film with strong thematic ties to *Future Boy Conan*, asserting an idiosyncratic style that would set the studio's work apart from other Japanese productions. Following the film's moderate success, Studio Ghibli needed to produce another immediately. In the end, the studio released a double bill on April 16, 1988, featuring Miyazaki's *Tonari no Totoro* (*My Neighbor Totoro*) and Isao Takahata's *Hotaru no Haka* (*Grave of the Fireflies*). It was a unique choice of showings given the differences between the two films, as the first is a hymn to the innocence of childhood, whereas the second is a macabre look at youth during the war. The two works clearly identify the filmmaking of each director: Miyazaki was the dreamer who escaped in soaring adventures, and Takahata the realist who adapted more social works. But the studio shared a few similarities between directors, including character designs, delicate animation (a Toei legacy), and the importance of family ties. The films were not as successful as they had hoped, but the studio turned the economic tide with sales of plush toys featuring the fantastic characters from Miyazaki's film. Totoro became the mascot who introduced Studio Ghibli in the opening credits of *Majo no Takkyūbin* (*Kiki's Delivery Service*), Hayao Miyazaki's new feature film, released on July 29, 1989. This adaptation of a children's book by Eiko Kadono was a huge success, grossing over ¥2 billion, neck-and-neck with the ninth *Doraemon* movie.

A PLACE FOR FILMMAKERS

The creation of Studio Ghibli was perfectly in line with the logic of the times, when animation companies needed to rely on experienced directors to make increasingly expensive productions. These leaders surrounded themselves with a consistent team, giving each production company a distinct graphic identity. United around Madhouse's historic founders, the Project Team Argos collective shaped the studio's new direction. Rintaro orchestrated major studio projects such as *Harmagedon*, *Kamui no Ken* (*The Dagger of Kamui*, 1985), and the *Hi no Tori* trilogy (*Phoenix*, 1986 to 1987), backed by producer Masao Maruyama and art director Takamura Mukuo (the *Galaxy Express 999* films). With their realistic designs and complex storylines, Madhouse's films were aimed at adult audiences, like *Toki no Tabibito: Time Stranger* (1986), in which Mori Masaki takes a dark look at patriotic blindness during World War II and the internal wars of the Sengoku era at the same time as revisiting the trauma of the bomb and the misery hidden by an elitist society.

While Madhouse created hard-hitting productions, Group TAC focused more on poetry. Gisaburō Sugii (who earned his stripes at Mushi Production like Rintaro, Maruyama, and Tomino) developed his studio by adapting popular works by Mitsuru Adachi, including the two *Nine* feature films in 1983, and the *Touch* series recap movies. These assured successes enabled him to tackle more intimate projects, such as his adaptation of a major work of Japanese literature, *The Tale of Genji*, as well as one of a contemporary novel, *Ginga Tetsudō no Yoru* (*Night on the Galactic Railroad*) by Kenji Miyazawa. Alongside OAVs, cinema became a field of experimentation for directors, who take advantage of the opportunity to develop their art in personal productions. From then on, the director's name took precedence over that of the studio.

Ever since the egocentric pirouette that was *Urusei Yatsura 2: Beautiful Dreamer*, Mamoru Oshii had been eager to break away from the concept of adaptation. In 1985, the filmmaker created *Tenshi no Tamago* (*Angel's Egg*) in collaboration with illustrator Yoshitaka Amano (*Gatchaman*, *Vampire Hunter D*). Animated by Studio Deen and produced by Tokuma Shoten, the OAV is a contemplative, almost silent art film with biblical allusions. In other words, its success was cut short, and all the more so because the feature was only allowed a limited theatrical release. But, like *Nausicaä* for Miyazaki and *Harmagedon* for Rintaro, this film became a cornerstone of Oshii's filmmaking identity, which trends toward the esoteric. Whereas the commercial failure of *Angel's Egg* had been relatively anticipated, the lack of success of *Odin: Koshi Hansen, Starlight* (*Odin: Starlight Mutiny*) was symbolic of a changing wind. This Toei production also had an original story and was intended to be a follow-up to the *Space Battleship Yamato* franchise that had ended two years earlier. And it was *Yamato*'s author, Yoshinobu Nishizaki, who created the space opera plot, intending it to be a trilogy. Admittedly, the film reveals its many production issues, which led to several hands directing it, including Eiichi Yamamoto (*Belladonna of Sadness*). But its box office fiasco emphasized that film production was on very thin ice. Toei would recover by falling back on its TV licenses, a tactic that proved far more complicated for other studios.

THE COLLAPSE OF BLOCKBUSTERS

The team that had made the *Daicon* opening animations as amateurs had turned pro, working on the *Macross* and *Nausicaä* films, and they created the Gainax production company in 1984. To get started, the young firm produced a dynamic four-minute pilot called *Royal Space Force*. This story about military astronauts immediately appealed to Bandai, which

2
1988
Tonari no Totoro (My Neighbor Totoro)

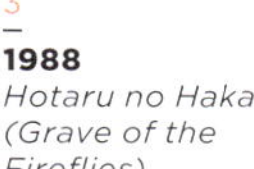

3
1988
Hotaru no Haka (Grave of the Fireflies)

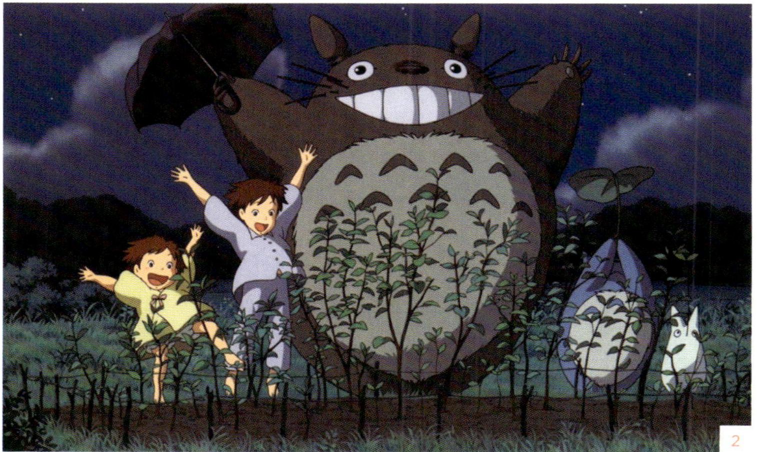

2

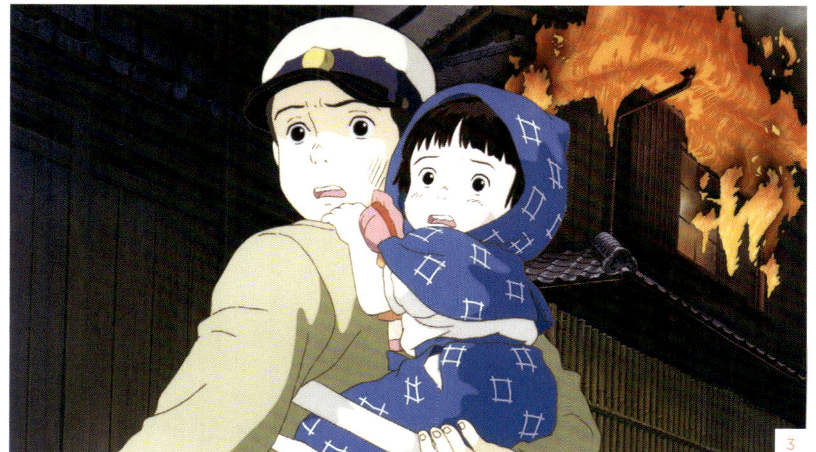

3

1985
Tenshi no Tamago
(Angel's Egg)

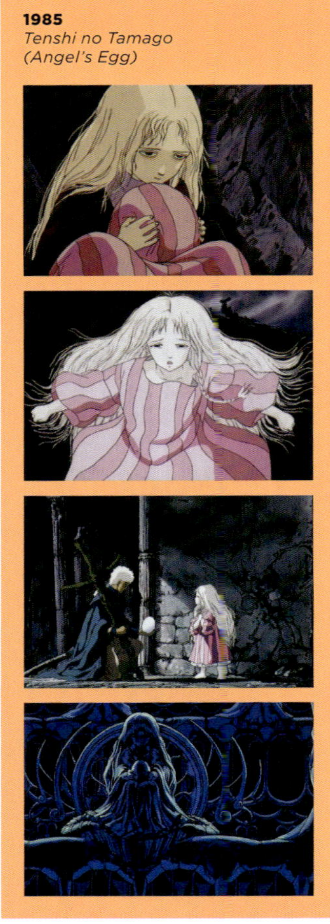

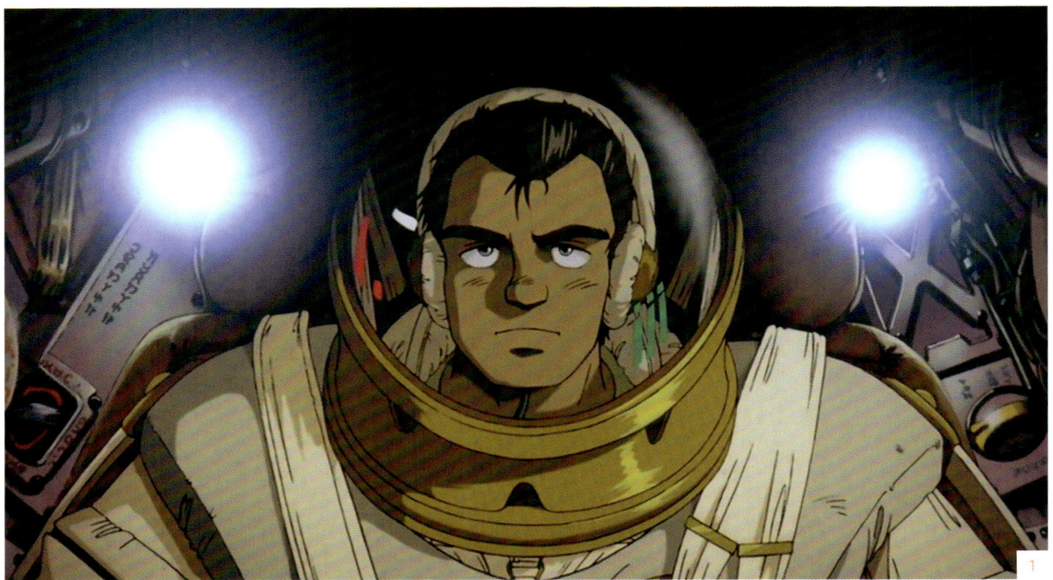

1

1987
Oneamisu no Tsubasa (Royal Space Force: The Wings of Honnêamise)

opened an animated film production department. With the success of *Adieu Galaxy Express 999*, *Crusher Joe*, *Harmagedon*, and *Nausicaä*, the general sci-fi craze prompted many investors to participate in the production of what could well be a new franchise on par with *Yamato* and *Gundam*! A production committee was set up composed of the various financial players, including an airline company that required the word *tsubasa* (wings) in the title. The film benefited from a record-breaking budget of ¥800 million, which led the technical team to go international. Art nouveau is central to the architectural design in the imaginary neo-futuristic world of *Oneamisu no Tsubasa* (*Royal Space Force: The Wings of Honnêamise*), which follows the journey of a pilot assigned to a unit in charge of the first space flights. In 1986, when almost the entire film had been shot, the production committee, including Bandai, panicked when they saw that the imagery was reminiscent of a drama more akin to *The Right Stuff* than *Star Wars*, with a pervasive religious dimension. How could such a film make a profit of ¥800 million when last year's sci-fi project *Odin* had ended in failure? All the indications were that this team, who had packed its *Daicon* animations with iconic characters, would have made a more commercial zeitgeist like the parody *Project A-Ko*, which hit it big in 1986. Worse still, the film had no real spin-off potential! Producers made several attempts at transformation, like shortening its running time to increase the number of showings, and promotional trickery—Toho commissioned cartoonist Yoshiyuki Sadamoto to create a visual in which a giant insect attacks the city, whereas the beast is a simple toy in the film. In the end, Hiroyuki Yamaga's film was released in 1987 and barely broke ¥300 million in box office sales.

In the wake of this fiasco, Gainax relaunched lofty projects with fan service as their trademark. Hideaki Anno, an animator specializing in mecha and explosions, directed the highly successful *Gunbuster* OAV at the end of the year, followed by the series that would definitively restore the studio's financial fortunes—*Nadia: The Secret of Blue Water* (1990). As for Yamaga, he was content to stay in the shadows of production for a very long time. In parallel with the production of *The Wings of Honnêamise*, Bandai also cofinanced a project that promised to be the blockbuster of the decade: *Akira*. Following in the footsteps of Hayao Miyazaki on *Nausicaä of the Valley of the Wind* and Yoshikazu Yasuhiko on *Arion*, *mangaka* Katsuhiro Ōtomo directed a free adaptation of his cyberpunk manga that plunges viewers into the Neo-Tokyo of 2019, plagued by gangs of junkies battling it out on motorcycles. One of these young delinquents is captured by the army and used as a weapon of psychic warfare in an experiment closely linked to the explosion that had devastated the Japanese capital in 1982.

Ōtomo had already distinguished himself in animation on productions such as *Harmagedon* and the *Robot Carnival* and *Neo Tokyo* anthologies, in which he directed short films about robotics. But with the feature film *Akira*, his great ambition led him to design a blockbuster with a record-breaking budget of ¥1.1 billion! That amount of money can be seen in every shot of the techno-organic anime for adults. Ōtomo even shot with 70 mm film to increase the image size and detail. With dazzling lighting effects, constant movement, many layers of celluloid, and preproduction dubbing to synchronize lip movements and voice, the film's technical level was only rivaled by its thematic density. Contentious, violent, and boisterous, *Akira* is a countercultural manifesto, an opulent representative of cyberpunk, a movement that was reaching its pinnacle in the OAV industry. The production committee, which had raised such a large budget, had every reason to believe that it would be a great success. But they lost the bet! The film was released on August 18, 1988, and barely managed to pull in ¥700 million at the box office.

The two successive failures of *The Wings of Honnêamise* and *Akira* severely curbed blockbuster momentum. Ōtomo would continue to supervise and direct films but would have to wait more than fifteen years to make a comeback with such a large-scale project.

As with *The Wings of Honnêamise*, *Akira* quickly became a cult classic on video, a medium that played a large role in emptying out movie theaters. But the repeated failure of such high-end sci-fi films heralded several serious events that would greatly weaken the Japanese animation market in the late 1980s.

2 to 4
1988
Akira

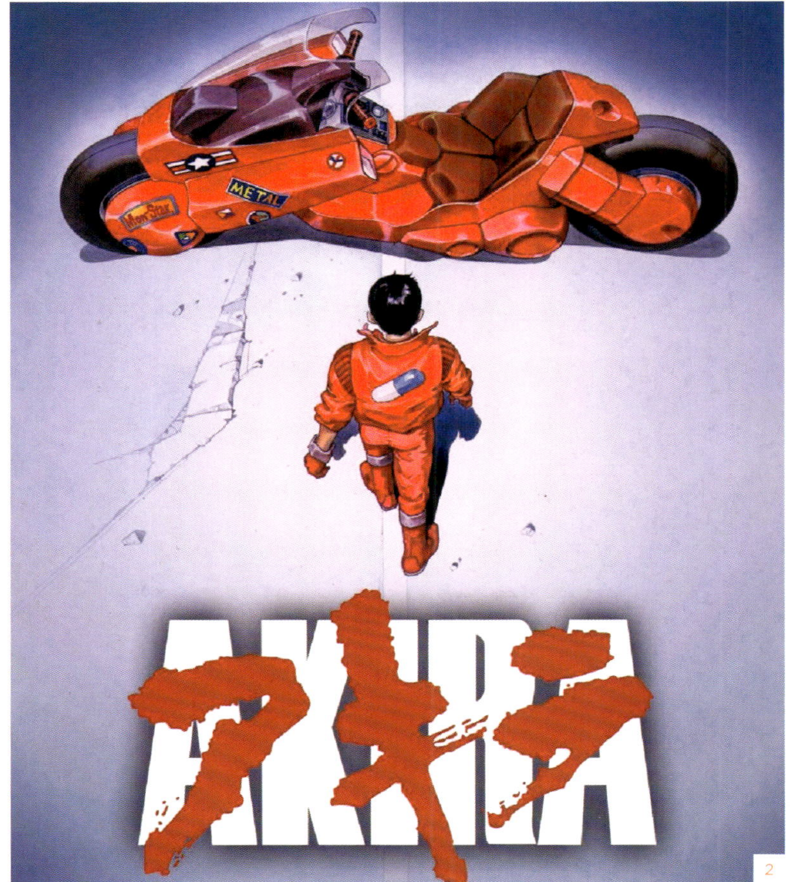

2

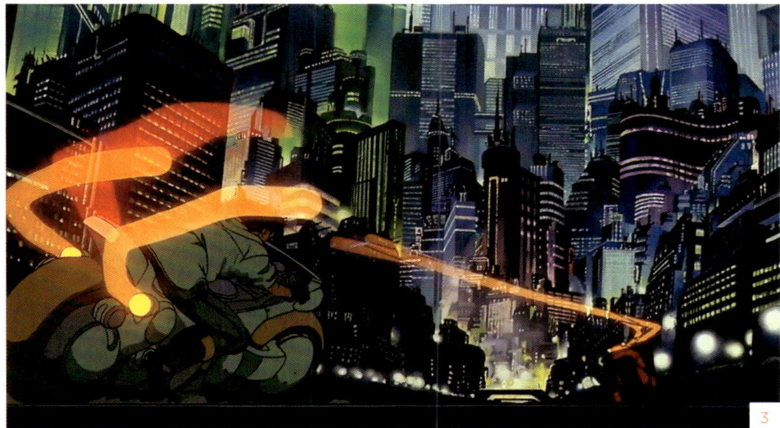
3

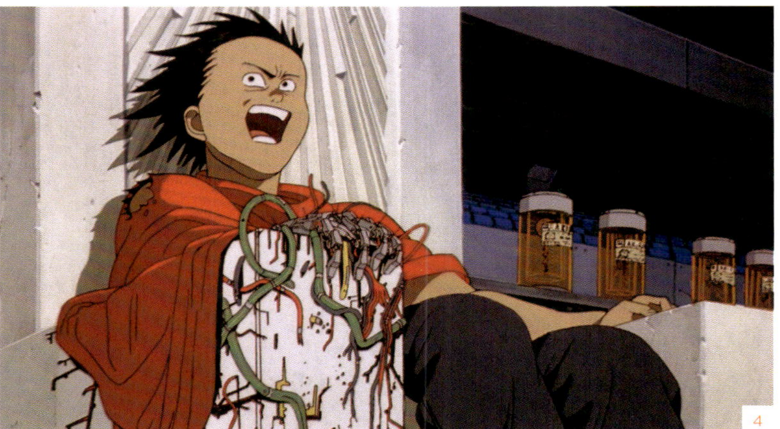
4

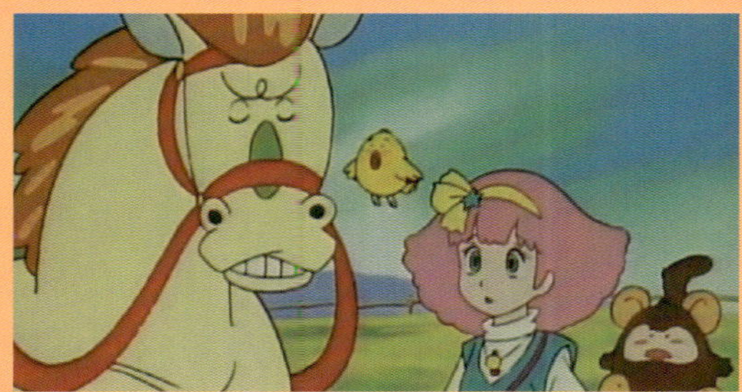

MAHŌ NO PRINCESS MINKY MOMO

Magical Princess Minky Momo
Year: 1982
Category: TV
Director: Kunihiko Yuyama
Animation Studio: Ashi Production

AT A GLANCE:
A graphic and thematic modernization of the magical girl, the series revisits the concept of Sally's two worlds, adding adult transformation and more mature, ambiguous plotlines.

YOU MAY ALSO LIKE . . .
Series inspired by Studio Pierrot's *Magical Princess Minky Momo*, which had taken the genre by storm with *Magical Angel Creamy Mami*; *Persia, the Magic Fairy*; and *Magic Star Magical Emi*.

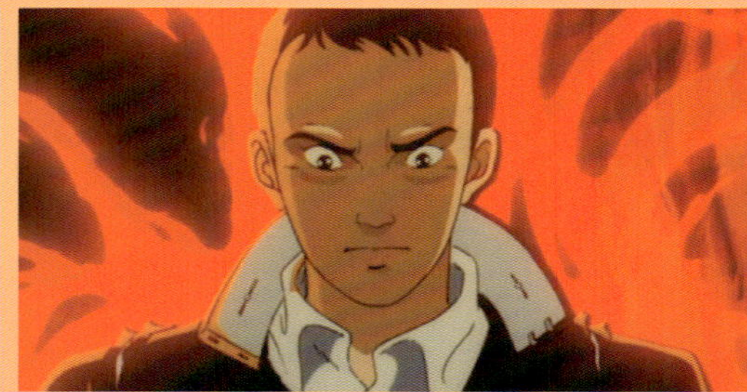

GENMA TAISEN

Harmagedon
Year: 1983
Category: Film
Director: Rintaro
Animation Studio: Madhouse

AT A GLANCE:
A free adaptation of Shotaro Ishinomori's manga, marking the beginning of the collaboration between Katsuhiro Ōtomo and Rintaro, whose imagery is as realistic as it is virulent.

YOU MAY ALSO LIKE . . .
The adapted original works *Crusher Joe*, *The Dagger of Kamui*, and *Golgo 13*, the latter of which even experiments with the first 3D scenes in an animated film.

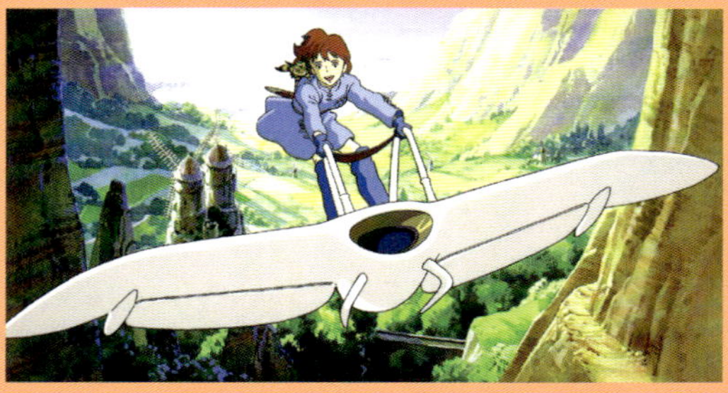

KAZE NO TANI NO NAUSICAÄ

Nausicaä of the Valley of the Wind
Year: 1984
Category: Film
Director: Hayao Miyazaki
Animation Studio: Tokyo Movie Shinsha

AT A GLANCE:
Hayao Miyazaki's first feature film, with its daring heroine, fantastic world, and spellbinding music, was a great success and led to the creation of Studio Ghibli.

YOU MAY ALSO LIKE . . .
Miyazaki's *Castle in the Sky*, filled with fantasy and atypical aircraft. *Arion* by Yoshikazu Yasuhiko, who adapted his own manga inspired by Greek mythology.

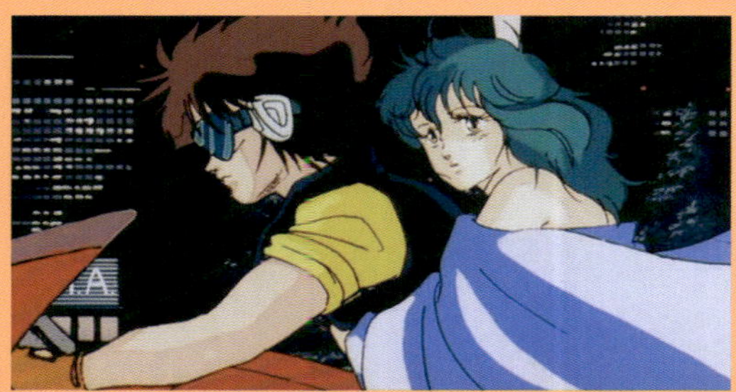

MEGAZONE 23

Megazone 23
Year: 1985
Category: OAV
Director: Noboru Ishiguro
Animation Studios: AIC, Artmic, and Youmex

AT A GLANCE:
The first OAV to achieve commercial and critical success. This complex story brought cyberpunk to anime and was a major influence on the *Matrix* movies.

YOU MAY ALSO LIKE . . .
Super Dimension Fortress Macross and *Super Dimension Cavalry Southern Cross*, the graphic roots of *Megazone 23. Birth*, which introduced the sensory element of OAVs. *Running Man* in *Neo Tokyo*, *Dead Heat*, and *Download: Devil's Circuit* for their turbocharged vehicles.

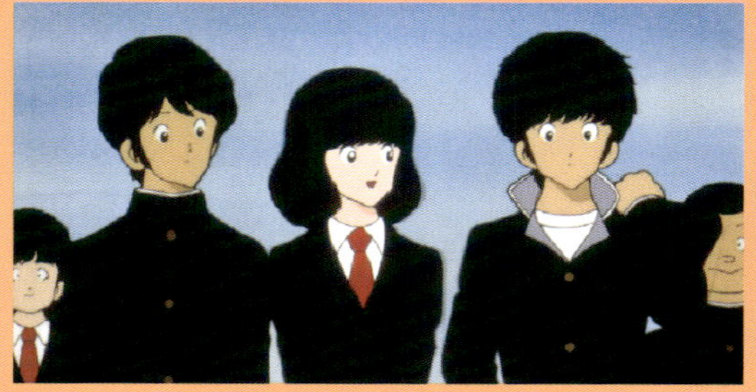

TOUCH

Touch
Year: 1985
Category: TV, film
Directors: Gisaburō Sugii and Hiroko Tokita
Animation Studios: Group TAC and Studio Gallop

AT A GLANCE:
The crowning achievement of the collaboration between the TAC studio and *mangaka* Mitsuru Adachi, this series was a huge success, combining sports with romance, drama, and humor.

YOU MAY ALSO LIKE . . .
The author's passion for baseball in the *Nine* films, the *Slow Step* OAVs, the *H2* series, and especially *A New Life*, whose story structure and designs are very similar to *Touch*.

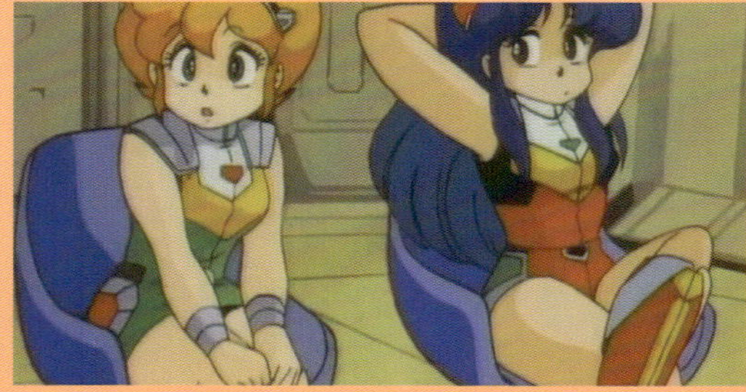

CREAM LEMON

Cream Lemon
Year: 1984
Category: OAV
Director: Multiple
Animation Studio: Fairy Dust

AT A GLANCE:
A trailblazer of animated *hentai*, this OAV series gave many artists the chance to train on a variety of short films. It quickly gained a cult following among *otaku*.

YOU MAY ALSO LIKE . . .
Lolita Anime, the first *hentai*. *Urotsukidōji*, an apocalyptic erotic horror; tentacle erotica *La Blue Girl*; and the occult *Bible Black*. *Project A-Ko*, a comedy for all ages inspired by *Cream Lemon*.

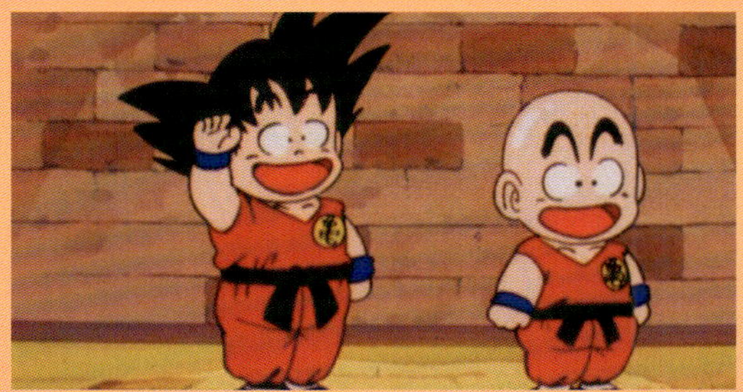

DRAGON BALL

Dragon Ball
Year: 1987
Category: TV, film
Directors: Daisuke Nishio and Minoru Okazaki
Animation Studio: Toei Dōga

AT A GLANCE:
A cultural phenomenon, this retelling of *Saiyuki* redefined the technical standards of weekly series and reshaped *shōnen nekketsu*, which now featured fantasy and leveling up!

YOU MAY ALSO LIKE . . .
The ultraviolent postapocalyptic epic *Fist of the North Star.* The evolutionary journey in *Saint Seiya: Knights of the Zodiac*, inspired by Greek mythology. The spiritual adventures of the hoodlums in *Yu Yu Hakusho.*

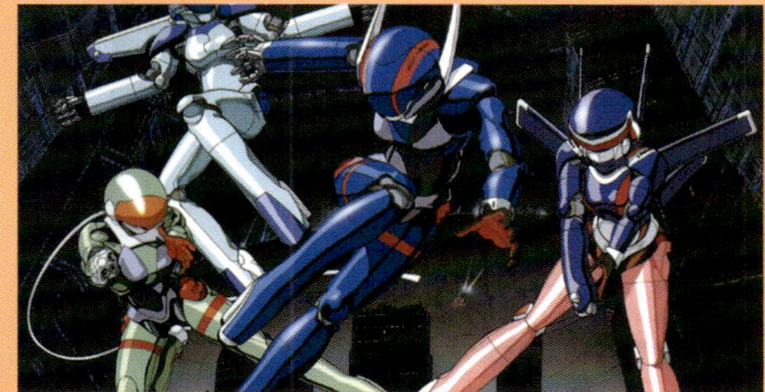

BUBBLEGUM CRISIS

Bubblegum Crisis
Year: 1987
Category: OAV
Directors: Katsuhito Akiyama, Masami Ōbari, and Hiroaki Gōda
Animation Studios: AIC, Artmic, and Youmex

AT A GLANCE:
Blowouts, neon lights, leather, and cybernetics are all part of the program in this 1980s Japanese cyberpunk, which drew on the genre's own themes while undermining age-old machismo.

YOU MAY ALSO LIKE . . .
AD Police Files, a violent and disturbing spin-off. *Armitage III*, an eccentric series inspired by the work of Isaac Asimov and William Gibson. *Angel Cop* with its chilling setting.

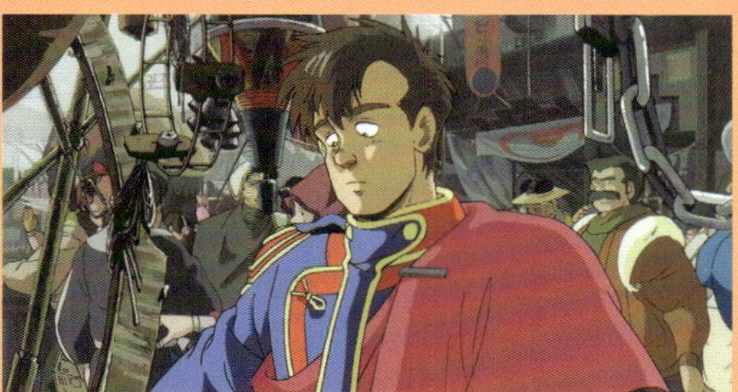

ONEAMISU NO TSUBASA

Royal Space Force: The Wings of Honnêamise
Year: 1987
Category: Film
Director: Hiroyuki Yamaga
Animation Studio: Gainax

AT A GLANCE:
Despite its record budget granted by a production committee, Gainax's first feature was an auteur film. Its commercial failure prompted the studio to turn to fan service.

YOU MAY ALSO LIKE . . .
The realism of the conquest for the stars in *Moonlight Mile* and *Space Brothers.* The satire of our waste management in *Planetes.* The ambitious mecha series *Gunbuster*, Gainax's comeback.

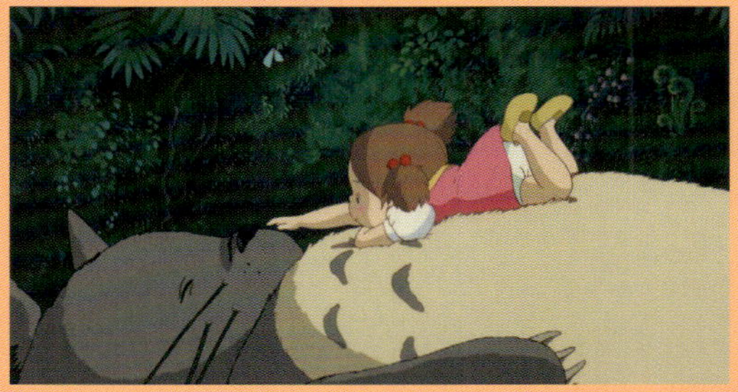

TONARI NO TOTORO

My Neighbor Totoro
Year: 1988
Category: Film
Director: Hayao Miyazaki
Animation Studio: Studio Ghibli

AT A GLANCE:
This film is an ode to family and childhood. Totoro, a large, fantastic creature, saved Studio Ghibli from bankruptcy with merchandise sales and became the company's mascot.

YOU MAY ALSO LIKE . . .
Unico, spreading happiness Tezuka-style. *Kiki's Delivery Service*, an enchanting journey of initiation. *Catnapped!*, an off-the-wall quest overflowing with imagination. *Little Nemo: Adventures in Slumberland*, a universal dream journey.

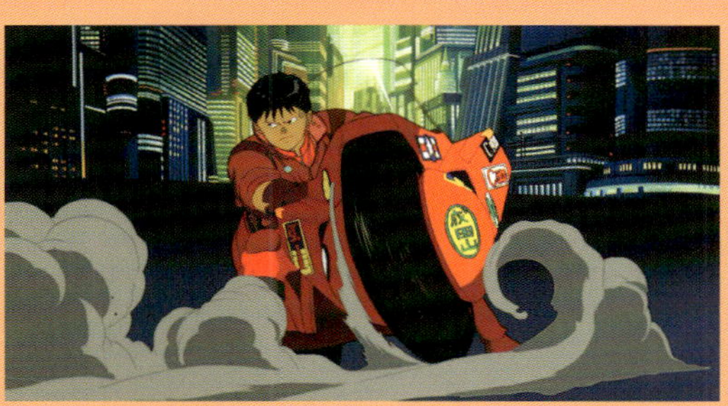

AKIRA

Akira
Year: 1988
Category: Film
Director: Katsuhiro Ōtomo
Animation Studio: Tokyo Movie Shinsha

AT A GLANCE:
This compendium of 1980s subculture set a new budgetary record. Ōtomo's high-end film was as instructive for new animators as it was for anime fans.

YOU MAY ALSO LIKE . . .
The young biker resistance fighters in *Venus Wars.* The psychological showdowns in *Ai City* and *Spriggan.* The anticipation in Ōtomo's anthologies: *Robot Carnival*, *Neo Tokyo*, and *Memories.*

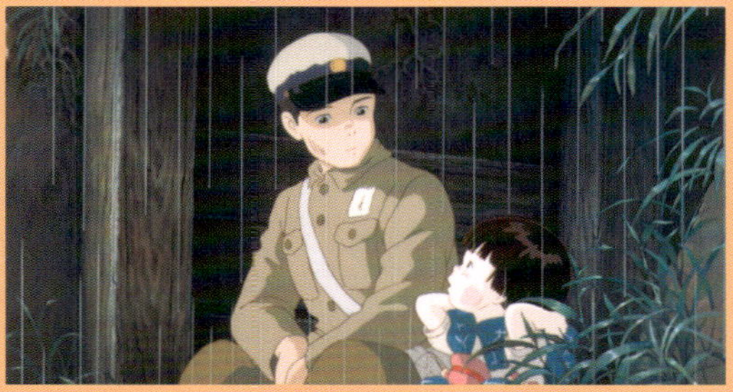

HOTARU NO HAKA

Grave of the Fireflies
Year: 1988
Category: Film
Director: Isao Takahata **Animation Studio:** Studio Ghibli

AT A GLANCE:
A chaotic vision of childhood during World War II. Committed to realism, Takahata leaves no details out to force immersion in this deeply moving tragedy.

YOU MAY ALSO LIKE . . .
Barefoot Gen, the apocalyptic journey of children who suffer the full force of the atomic bomb. *In This Corner of the World*, a poignant portrait of a young woman during the war.

Channeled energy

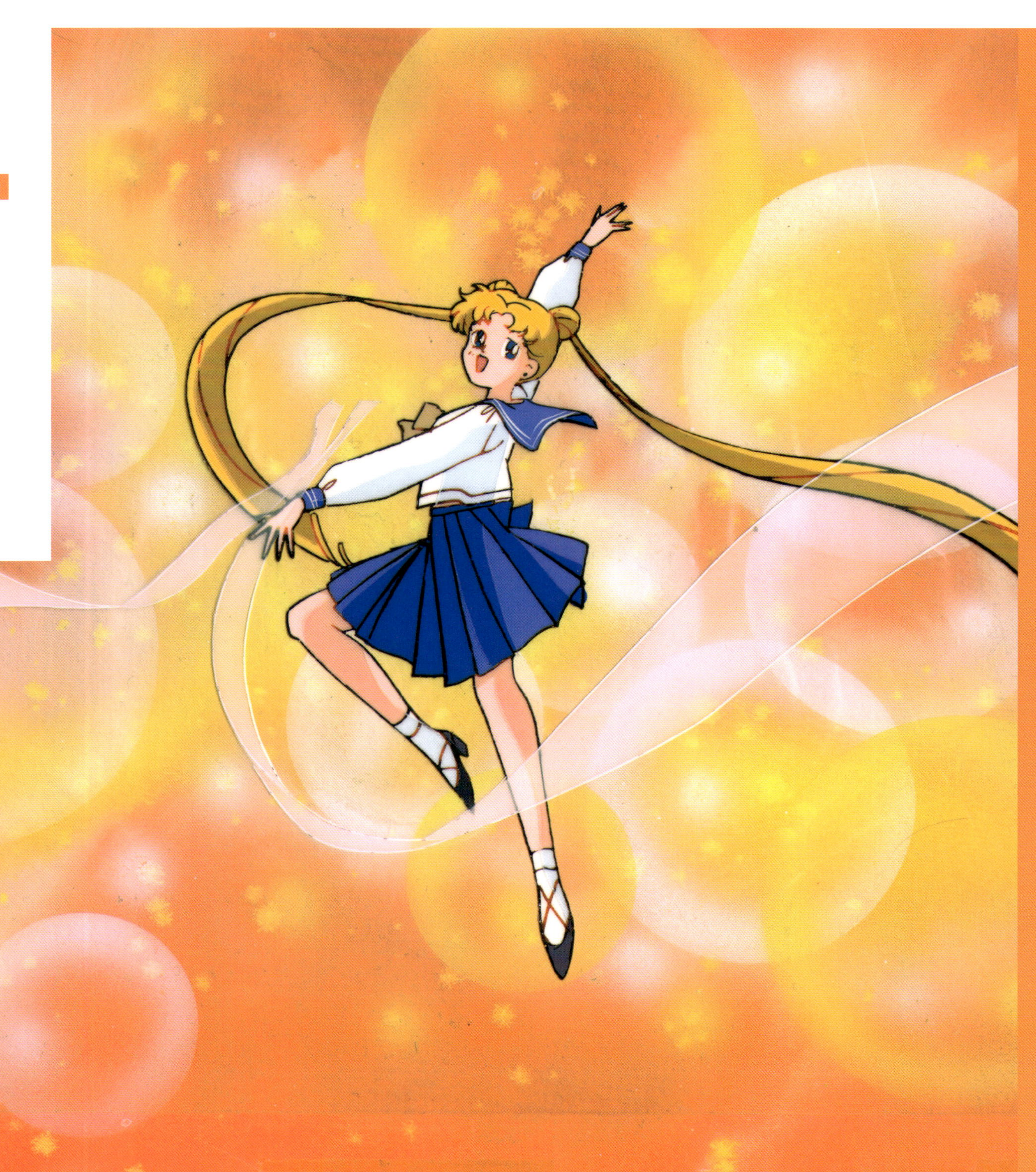

Detail view: *Sailor Moon*. Original production celluloid for the opening credits © 1993 Naoko Takeuchi, Toei Animation. THE ART OF ANIME cultural exhibition, Spacher Vogler Collection.

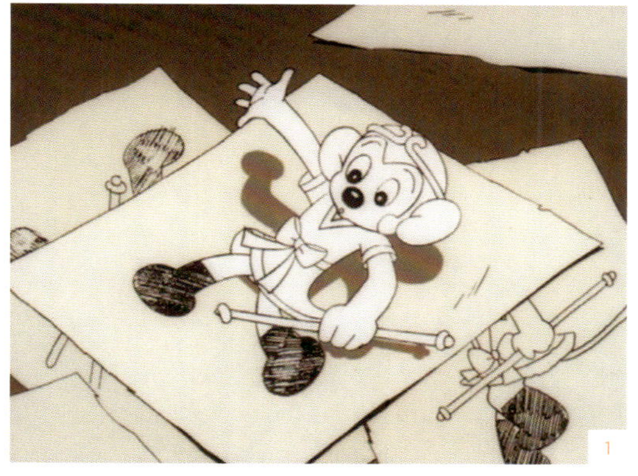

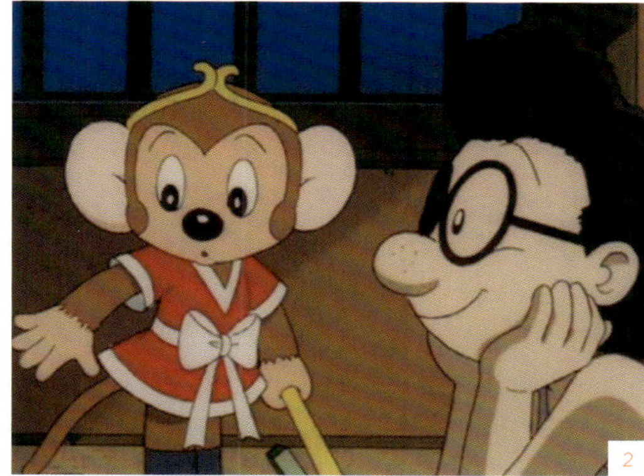

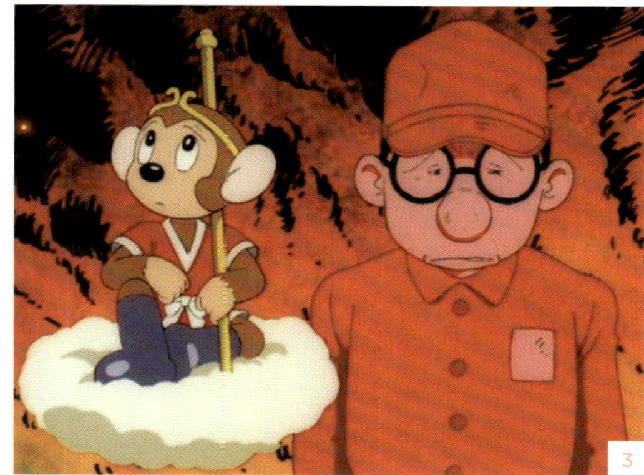

1 to 3
1989
Boku wa Son Goku (I am Son Goku)*

Artist emancipation

THE END OF AN ERA

The year 1989 was pivotal in the history of Japan and its animation in more ways than one, with two nationally significant deaths just a few weeks apart. The whole country went into a state of turmoil on January 7 after the death of Emperor Hirohito. His son Akihito's succession to the throne marked the end of the Shōwa era and the beginning of the Heisei era, which would end in his death (or abdication). Official documents needed to be updated to this new dating system in all administrations and companies!

The entire foreign diplomatic corps, from François Mitterrand to the newly elected George Bush, attended Hirohito's funeral and paid their respects on February 24 and 25, more out of respect for the new economic partner Japan had become than for the former adversary of the Second World War. Usually fascinated by the arrival of the world's elite (as seen by the 1964 Tokyo Olympics and the 1970 Osaka World Expo), the Japanese were not so enthusiastic about the event, stricken to the core by another bereavement.

In a hospital room, where he was still overseeing his final projects, Osamu Tezuka died of stomach cancer on February 9, at sixty years old. His last words were to the nurse who had confiscated his drawing equipment to force him to rest: "I'm begging you, let me work!" Unlike that of their political leader, the death of the "God of Manga" intimately affected every Japanese person, regardless of age, sex, or social standing. TV channels replayed reports and animated archives, bookstore sales exploded, and his funeral took on such proportions that it overshadowed Hirohito's in the memories of many.

Tributes poured in from all over the country, especially from his followers. In an agreement with the employees of Tezuka Productions, Rintaro transformed the script of *Boku wa Son Goku* (*I am Son Goku**), the master's unfinished animated project, to combine the futuristic adaptation of *Journey to the West* with an idealized biography of the "God of Manga." Everyone knew that Tezuka's passing, "the death of the father," marked a definitive turning of the page in animation history. The stage was now free for new artists to develop their own style, their own personal vision of animation, without being overshadowed by the pioneer. Especially since audiences were receptive to more artistic and less sensationalist works than the productions that had been proliferating in the OAV market.

A few months later, a tragic event would force a reappraisal of this booming market. On July 23, 1989, police raided the home of Tsutomu Miyazaki, a twenty-six-year-old man arrested for molesting a young girl. The agents discovered that they had their hands on a serial killer who, over the course of a year, had killed four little girls aged four to seven, before desecrating their corpses. His apartment was overflowing with books and videos of child pornography, slasher movies, and erotic horror OAVs.

It was that last point that caught the attention of the Japanese media, who dubbed him "the otaku killer." That was all it took to stigmatize all die-hard anime fans as potential psychopaths. Production companies were facing a firestorm and reacted by considerably reducing the supply of "deviant" titles, without abandoning the adult content that was their strength. In 1992, *La Blue Girl* would be the last great representative of tentacle erotica, diluted with a great deal of humor.

FROM ADULT TO MATURE AUDIENCES

Because lewdness alone was no longer selling and lent itself to attacks by the general public, adult-only OAVs now featured extensive storylines. Satoshi Urushihara, nicknamed the "Master of Breasts" by otaku, became an expert in the field, embellishing fantasies like *Kyokkoku no Tsubasa Valkisas* (*Legend of Lemnear*, 1989) and sci-fi films like *Plastic Little* (1994) with "boob shots." *Golden Boy* (1995), adapted from a manga by Tatsuya Egawa, was a model of this new direction, humorously mixing sociological reflection with explicit eroticism.

But another genre took advantage of this opportunity to make its voice heard. In just a few years, an adult audience had discovered the video market. An audience old enough to hear stories that

1 to 3: Boku wa Son Goku © Tezuka Productions, Artvivor.

were clearly not for children, without clamoring for violence or exaggerated sexuality. It was the perfect opportunity to adapt manga that, though unable to attract a large enough audience for a TV broadcast, could be profitable if created for video sales alone.

The steampunk backgrounds in the 1992 animated episode of *Spirit of Wonder*, for example, feature the same avalanche of details as in Kenji Tsuruta's original manga, a technical feat unimaginable for a TV series. In any case, the absurd yet poetic plot about the pretty Miss China following her deadbeat tenants on their journey to the moon would never have suited sponsors. Neither would the extreme violence in *Gunnm* (*Battle Angel*, 1993), based on Yukito Kishiro's cyberpunk manga, even though it only plays a small role compared to the emotions packed into this futuristic love tragedy.

Boku no Chikyū wo Mamotte (*Please Save My Earth*) is a unique film that is representative of this new genre. Young Alice Sakaguchi meets up with other teenagers who all have recurring dreams in which they are reincarnations of extraterrestrial scientists who died on the moon. The loves and betrayals experienced by their past selves would turn their relationships upside down. Saki Hiwatari's manga was more complex than it seemed and appealed mainly to young working women, so it was logically divided into six OAVs between 1993 and 1994, which the **office ladies** could watch when they chose to. The gentle score by debutante composer Yoko Kanno played a major role in the anime's success.

In 1995, *Gunsmith Cats* synthesized all these new trends. Two pretty bounty hunters track down Chicago thugs in a *Bullitt*-like adventure, with firearms and street cars depicted with painstaking care that delighted fans of the genre for three episodes. *Gunsmith Cats* was competing on an equal ground with American action blockbusters in video stores with the general public and enshrined the author of the original manga, Kenichi Sonoda, in the hearts of otaku, eight years after he had created the *Bubblegum Crisis* characters.

Nevertheless, it was increasingly difficult for new talent to make a name for themselves on a medium that was now popular and overrun by big names selling hundreds of thousands of VHS tapes. The video market was following in the footsteps of the cinema market, which had been swallowed up by Toei thanks to its major titles, and the Manga Matsuri festival. Still, new franchises, this time for the whole family, rose to the challenge and carved out a place on screens big and small.

CHILDREN'S IDOLS

At the very end of the 1980s, animation for the general public was hard to find on television. The *World Masterpiece Theater* was languishing, *Doraemon* had become a familiar figure, and children were clamoring for something new. With at least three remakes (*Kimba the White Lion*, *Hutch the Honeybee*, and *Sally the Witch*), 1989 exemplified this scarcity. Three pint-size new heroes arrived on scene to meet the demand for children's TV, each in their own distinct way.

Beginning in 1990, the series *Chibi Maruko-chan* brought together children and parents who already loved Momoko Sakura's autobiographical manga, published between 1986 and 1992, which remains a bestseller in Japan today. The artist drew on her memories to tell stories from her own life as Maruko, a nine-year-old girl living in Japan in the late 1970s. In addition to the popular references rooted in the era, nostalgia was reinforced in the show with a

1993
Boku no Chikyū wo Mamotte (Please Save My Earth)

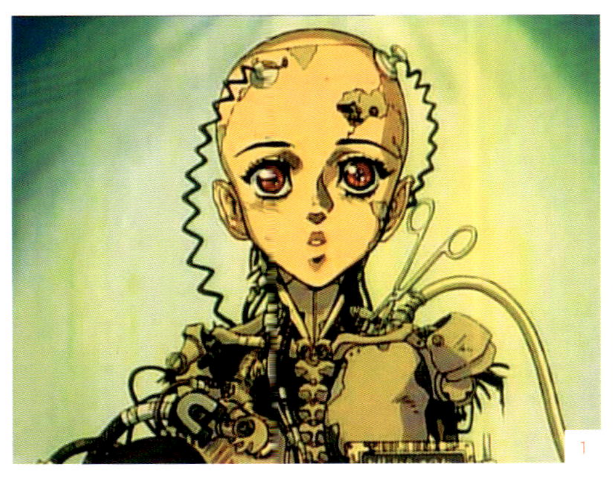

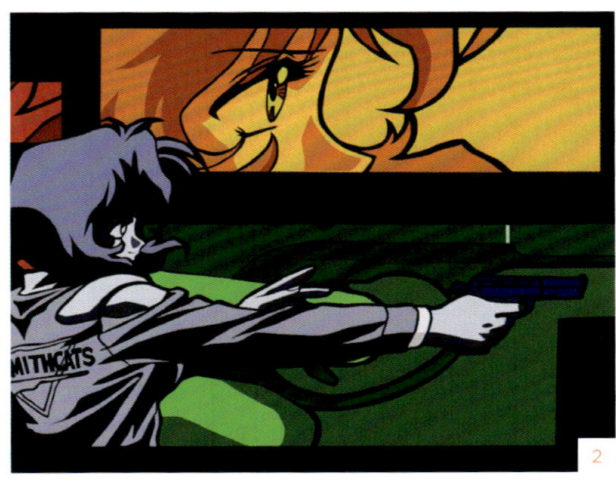

1
1993
Gunnm (Battle Angel)

2
1995
Gunsmith Cats

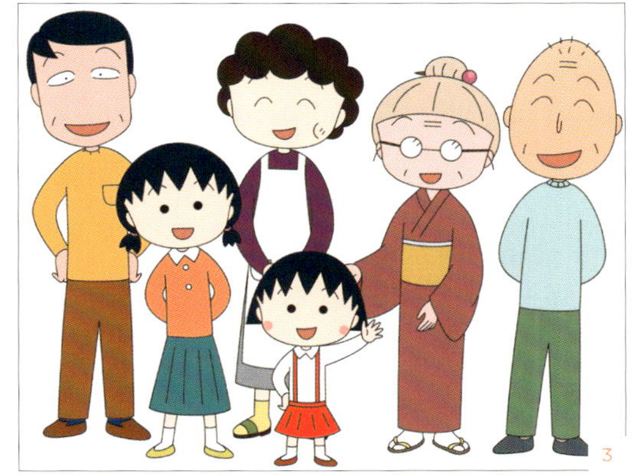

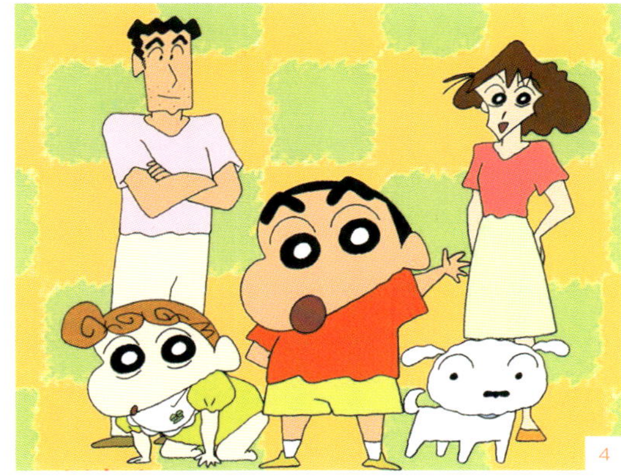

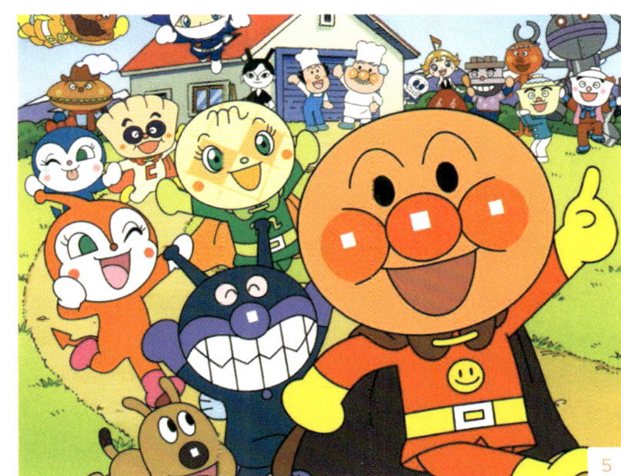

3
1990
Chibi Maruko-chan

4
1992
Crayon Shin-shan

5
1988
Sore Ike! Anpanman (Let's Go! Anpanman)

deliberately childlike, naive style that is reminiscent of having discovered the beloved manga in an old trunk in the attic.

The simplicity of the drawings was a godsend for the Nippon Animation team, who produced 142 episodes and two feature films under the direction of Jun Takagi until 1992, the year the manga came to an end. But "Little Maruko" remained popular! The team reunited with the *mangaka*, who wrote the original scripts for a new series launched with great fanfare on January 8, 1995. The new version of *Chibi Maruko-chan* had over 1,400 episodes by the end of 2024 and continues to this day. A team of scriptwriters took over after the 220th episode, but until her death, Momoko Sakura continued to supervise every episode and feature film in a franchise that has been a household name for generations in Japan.

Crayon Shin-chan's eponymous hero is even younger. At five years old, Shin-chan has a knack for misinterpreting Japanese idioms and expressions, with comical confusion leading to mischievous adventures. *Mangaka* Yoshito Usui also opted for a graphic style similar to children's drawings, speaking to every generation—everyone in Japan knows Shin-chan's "elephant dance," in which he swings his genitals to imitate an elephant's trunk.

Although the manga came to an end in 2010 shortly after the author's death, the 1992 animated series has survived, still on the air with more than 1,200 episodes. When Mitsuru Hongō left the company in 1996, Shin-Ei called on Keiichi Hara, who had made a name for himself ten years earlier on their other hit show, *Doraemon*, to take over as director. Thanks to *Crayon Shin-chan*, he was able to make the contacts he needed to produce his own film *Kappa no Kū to Natsuyasumi* (*Summer Days with Coo*) in 2007.

And although less well-known internationally than his other two titles, *Nintama Rantarō* (*Ninjaboy Rantaro*) remains an undisputed classic in Japan. Absurd and anachronistic, it's been one gag after another in a ninja school unlike any other since 1995, the year the flagship series was launched by Ajia-do, a company founded in 1978 by former members of A Production such as Osamu Kobayashi (*Kimagure Orange Road*) and Tsutomu Shibayama. The latter, who had been in charge of the long-running *Doraemon* for Shin-Ei since 1984, was also directing *Nintama Rantarō*, still broadcast on NHK with over 2,500 episodes to its credit.

Just like the musketeers, the three new children's heroes were actually four! And, like d'Artagnan, *Anpanman* took all the credit. Takashi Yanase had been publishing this series of stories for children since 1973, featuring food-related characters, recalling his years of famine during the war: children at the time dreamed of nothing more than eating an *anpan*, a sweet roll filled with red bean paste. The hero, Anpanman, can rip off pieces of his head to feed his friends. But don't worry—Jam, the pastry chef, always cooks him up a new one.

This cartoon stood out from the other three on many levels. The first was its false start, with a single pilot episode broadcast on NHK in March 1979. Nine years later, in 1988, the hunger-stopping hero appeared on screens in the midst of the children's programming shortage, well ahead of its rivals. But first and foremost, *Anpanman* was the first series aimed at children under five years old! The TMS production is still on the air today, with more than 1,600 episodes. It even set a Guinness World Record as the animated series with the highest number of characters (1,768)—so many *kawaii* (cute) icons endlessly featured on cakes, cookies, and candy wrappers.

ARTISTS IN THEIR OWN RIGHT

In 1985, after sending in her nursing school application, an eighteen-year-old Japanese woman stopped at a bookstore, where she came across an advertisement for voice-acting auditions. She got the job and recorded the voices of secondary characters in *Maison Ikkoku* in 1986, the first series to include her name, Megumi Hayashibara, in its credits. Three years later, in 1989, the actress took part in six series, including three in which she played the lead role: the valiant duck hero in *Alfred J. Kwak*, the heroine in *Chimpui*, with her two cute aliens, and the female version of the *Ranma ½* hero, who changes sex on contact with hot or cold water.

Her female Ranma role earned acclaim from otaku and the general public alike. Megumi Hayashibara's fan club continued to grow in the 1990s; she was a true voice-acting queen, and her mere presence in the cast guaranteed thousands of loyal viewers! The voice actress became the symbol of a new era in animation, a quarter of a century after *Astro Boy*. Flooded with information thanks to industry press, fans understood everything about the anime production process, where each essential role now had its own stars and master artists. Of course, the name of the director was still paramount—a stylistic gulf separated Hayao Miyazaki from Katsuhiro Ōtomo. But fans also focused on the designers of characters, vehicles and robots (mecha designer), and backgrounds, as well as animation directors, scriptwriters, composers, voice actors, and more.

Production was constantly on the rise. In addition to adaptations of long-running manga, such as *Dragon Ball*, which became *Dragon Ball Z* in 1989, new material was also being released. There were plenty of places in the sun, but only the best in their respective fields could claim them. A healthy spirit of competition blew through production, driven by the ambitions of the most talented. Hironobu Kageyama, singer of the *Dragon Ball* songs, joined veterans Ichirou Mizuki and Mitsuko Horie in the pantheon of original theme vocalists, earning the nickname "Prince of the *Anison* World." In the crowded field of anime adaptations, productions needed to be original to stand out. Such was the case for Hideaki Anno, the talented animator to whom Hayao Miyazaki entrusted the most complicated scenes of *Nausicaä of the Valley of the Wind*. This Gainax cofounder adapted Jules Verne's *20,000 Leagues Under the Sea* for the studio's first series in 1990, stunning Japanese viewers with *Fushigi no Umi no Nadia* (*Nadia: The Secret of Blue Water*). Beginning with circus acrobat Nadia being stalked by pathetic thieves, the series takes a desperate turn portraying the struggle of a group of rebels against the Neo-Atlanteans,

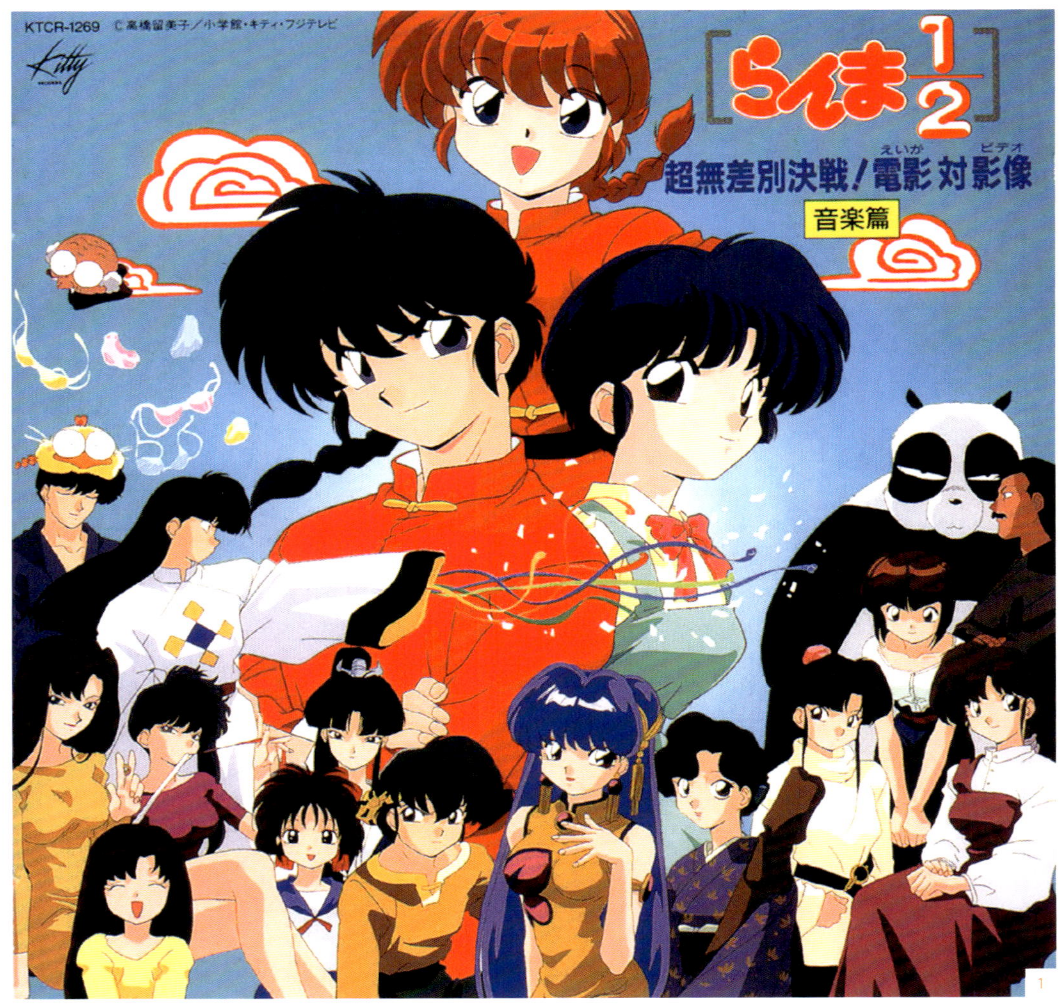

1
1989
Ranma ½

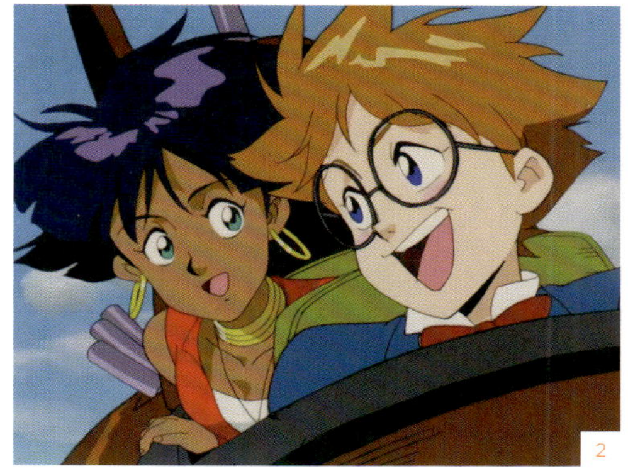

2

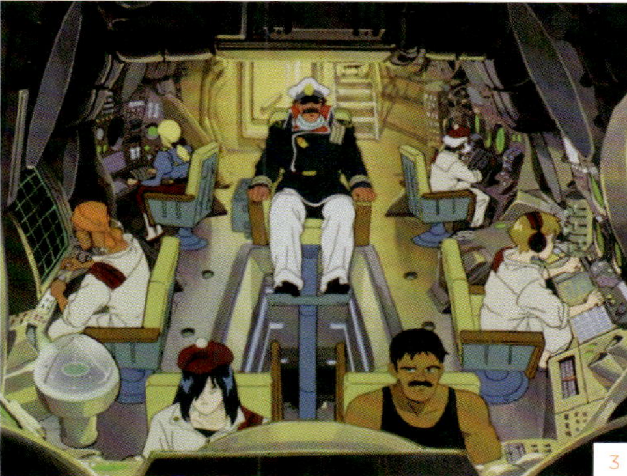

3

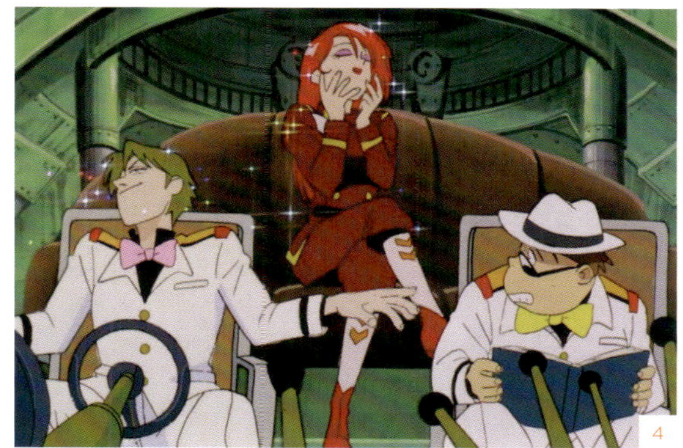

4

who are determined to dominate the Earth in 1889. As *Nadia* found its audience, it became part of the ongoing trend of launching celebrities. Anno wasn't the only one to gain recognition: composer Shirō Sagisu and character designer Yoshiyuki Sadamoto instantly became key figures in the industry.

MADE IN JAPAN

The animation industry had much to be proud of in the early 1990s. Its consumerist **fan base** was constantly growing, it spawned numerous parallel industries (soundtracks, specialized press, merchandising, and more), and it financially rewarded the best artists in each of its fields. However, it had not yet managed to free itself from a final constraint left behind by Osamu Tezuka during the production of *Astro Boy*. Already imbued with international ambitions, he made sure that his work was "non-localizable," giving his futuristic city an imagery common to children in any country.

This lack of reference to Japan was one of the factors that justified its cross-border success in the 1980s. Just ask little French, Italian, or Spanish children on their school playgrounds—between the Grendizer pilot working on a ranch and the little orphan Candy White, there was everything to suggest that their favorite series took place in the United States! Drawing on Western literature, Nippon Animation's *World Masterpiece Theater* played on familiar ground, and it's hard to imagine anything more universal than space opera with its interplanetary dimension. Japanese animation, recognized for its technical quality with many requests for collaboration, finally embraced its origins by shifting gears in the 1990s.

Beyond the obvious, such as *City Hunter*'s setting in Shinjuku City, the central district of the Japanese capital, and *Akira*'s Neo-Tokyo, romantic comedies like *Kimagure Orange Road* and *Maison Ikkoku* describe the Japanese habits and customs of their time, in their fictional or anonymous cities. Now international audiences were ready to follow the adventures of Japanese heroes in Japan, accustomed to conventions such as the school uniform worn by male (*Yu Yu Hakusho*) or female (*Sailor Moon*) main characters in 1992.

Despite the ubiquitous Greek mythology, viewers all knew that *Saint Seiya* was a Japanese cartoon. But they were unaware of its origin as a manga, as evidenced by the surreal telephone interview in 1990 between the show host and Masami Kurumada, the creator of the original *Saint Seiya* comic book. The 1993 publication of the French version of the *Dragon Ball* manga by the Glénat publishing house, and the emergence in 1991 of Manga Entertainment, a company located in the United Kingdom, which distributed subtitled anime on VHS, led to confusion about the distinction between anime and manga. The cartoons that were so beloved by teenagers were mistakenly called "manga," which refers only to comic books and not animated productions.

Like electronics, Japan had become the undisputed leader in animated entertainment in the eyes of the world. Entertainment, but not art. Here again, France is particularly representative of this

2 to 4

1990
Fushigi no Umi no Nadia (Nadia: The Secret of Blue Water)

1987
City Hunter

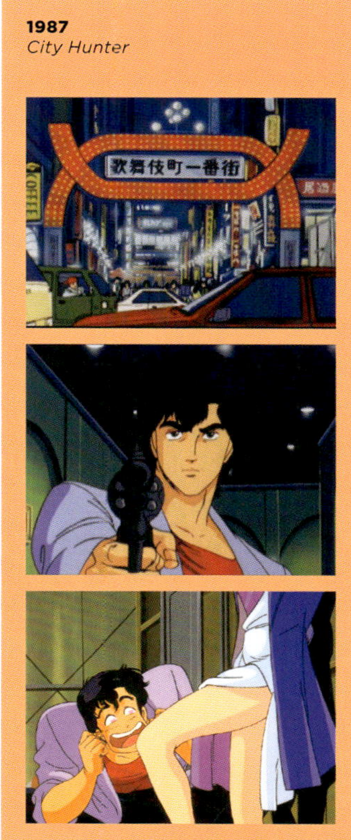

1: Ranma ½ © *1989 Rumiko Takahashi, Shogakukan, Kitty Film, Fuji TV.* **2 to 4:** Nadia: The Secret of Blue Water © *NHK, NEP © 1989 NHK, Sogo Vision, Toho.* **Panels:** City Hunter © *Tsukasa Hōjō, NSP, YTV, Sunrise.*

worldwide opinion: in 1995, Hayao Miyazaki's *Kurenai no Buta* (*Porco Rosso*), despite the prestigious voice acting of Jean Reno and Jean-Luc Reichmann, sold 150,000 tickets, three times fewer than the French release *Dragon Ball Z: Broly—The Legendary Super Saiyan*, a combination of two mid-length films that brought in half a million viewers!

Economic change

MEDIA MIX 2.0

The year 1989 was also an economic turning point. On December 29, the Nikkei index hit an all-time high after five years of unparalleled real estate speculation—commercial and private land values had quintupled and doubled, respectively, since 1985! The violence of the crash was proportional: between December 1989 and December 1991, share prices plummeted by 40 percent, followed by land prices, which fell by 30 percent in the six major cities between 1991 and 1993. In four years, ¥1,500,000 billion (three times Japan's GDP) had evaporated.

Annual economic growth, once above 4 percent, would not exceed 0.8 percent from 1992 to 2002. Japan, which had just reached record unemployment in 1987 at 2.8 percent, now faced deflation. The first victims in the animation industry were studios that had emerged with the OAV market, and more specifically in the erotica realm, such as Unicorn, Youmex, and Kaname. Japanese employees had less money to spend on entertainment, and many micro-businesses, the opportunistic start-ups of the time, had to file for bankruptcy. The financial crisis, coupled with the consequences of the Tsutomu Miyazaki "otaku killer" affair, indirectly led to a profound transformation of OAVs for adults in the 1990s.

Nevertheless, the real upheaval caused by Japan's entering its "lost decades" was happening in the marketing offices of the largest studios. Until now, the rights to a popular title were confined to the manga or its animated TV or film adaptation, whose soundtrack could also be sold. With the advent of VHS and video games, new partnerships were created, cross-media bridges that offset production costs and generated additional sources of revenue. One such example is the sports series *Yawara!*, based on Naoki Urasawa's best-selling manga beginning in October 1989. The progress of a young judoka aiming for the Barcelona Olympics is punctuated at the end of each of its 124 episodes by a countdown to the date of the actual event to reflect current affairs. The title also has live-action and animated film adaptations, OAVs, and a video game.

This marketing strategy, quickly dubbed "media mix," would have rapid short-term consequences in the animation industry, but not only economically. Studios, influenced by video games, were preparing to explore a new artistic genre that is now vital to the industry. The innovative concept also lent itself perfectly to the young stars in animation, who could find cofinancing and develop their creations across several media, thus reaching many audiences.

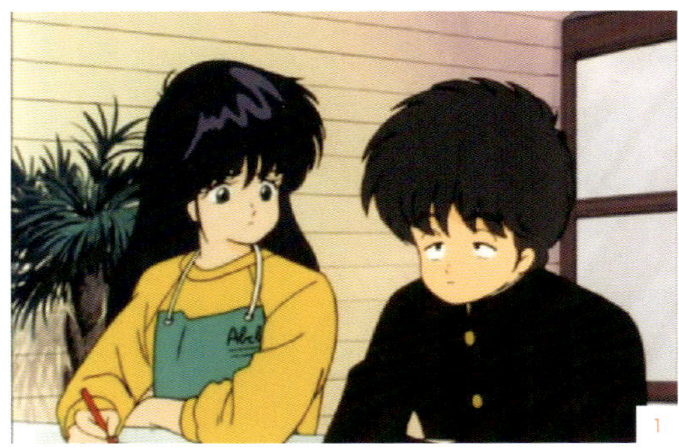
1

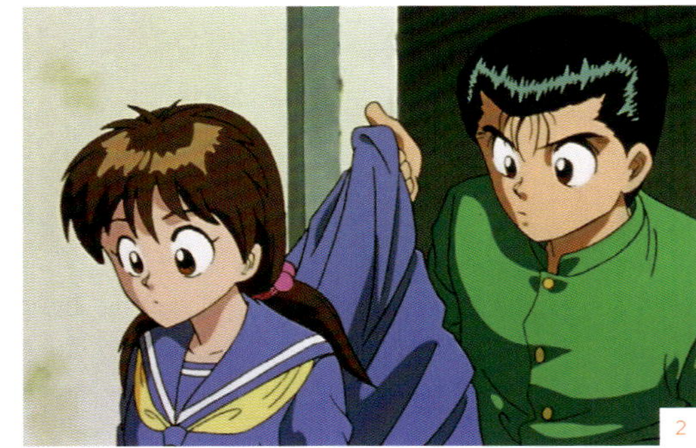
2

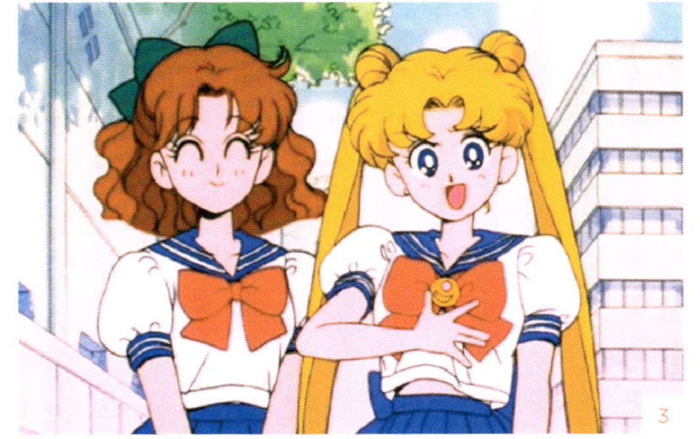
3

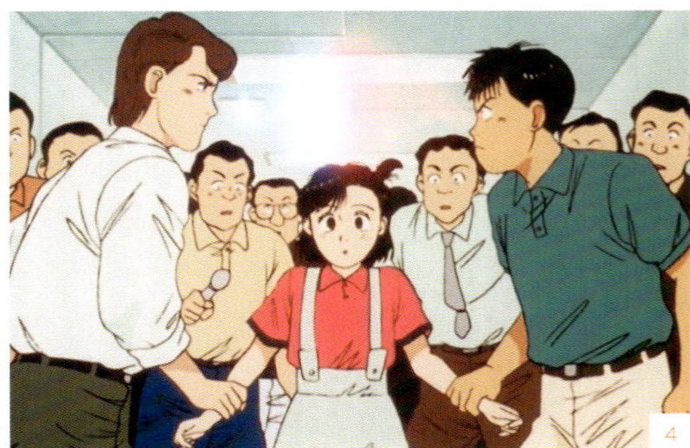
4

1
1987
Kimagure Orange Road

2
1992
Yu Yu Hakusho

3
1992
Bishōjo Senshi Sailor Moon (Sailor Moon)

4
1989
Yawara!

5
1993
Dragon Ball Z (Dragon Ball Z: Broly—The Legendary Super Saiyan)

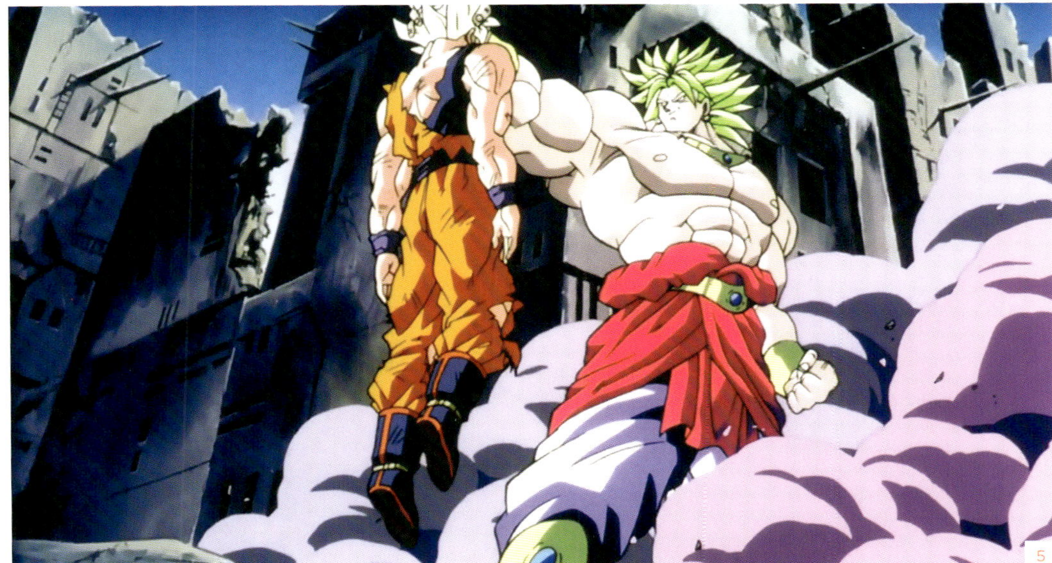

5

HOME ENTERTAINMENT TECHNOLOGY

The overexploitation by major studios of their biggest franchises was just the tip of the iceberg. In 1989, Sunrise chose to release a feature-length *City Hunter* film to tide over viewers between the end of the second season (April 1988 to July 1989) and the beginning of the third season (October 1989 to January 1990). However, more than a year separated the second season from the final season (April to October 1991)! The studio strategically adopted the VHS format and simultaneously released two different titles on August 25, 1990: *Hyakuman Doru no Inbou* (*City Hunter: Million Dollar Conspiracy*), in which Ryo Saeba is pursued by a hit man, and *Bay City Wars*, in which he is defusing a hostage situation and a nuclear threat in South America. The two OAVs directed by Kenji Kodama have a distinct appeal for die-hard fans because the director, who had been in charge of the franchise since the beginning, had to give up his position for the last TV season to take on *Reporter Blues*, a coproduction between TMS and the Italian channel RAI.

For its part, Kitty Films chose to revitalize its main franchises, most of which were based on titles by Rumiko Takahashi. The shows may have ended, but each of the *mangaka*'s stories was so rich that it was easy to create more original stories and capitalize on the additional sources of income a little longer. A pioneer in this approach, *Urusei Yatsura* began releasing an annual OAV in 1985, shortly before the end of the TV series in 1986. The pace climbed to two OAVs in 1988, four in 1989, and ended with a total of eleven VHS specials in 1991. Similarly, *Maison Ikkoku* revisited its heroes' journeys with three OAVs between the end of the series in 1988 and 1992.

But the undisputed champion is still *Ranma ½*. The 161-episode series, which ended in 1992, only covered half of the madcap manga about a group of cursed martial artists who transform into animals on contact with water. Kitty Films continued the successful anime adaptation with a series of eleven OAVs between 1993 and 1996, much to the delight of fans who were ready to reach into their wallets to ease their frustration, evidenced by the theatrical success of the three feature films released between 1991 and 1994.

Its success was all the greater given Toei's outrageous domination of the cinema market, where it had released its biggest TV hits successively: four *Saint Seiya* films between 1987 and 1989, three *Sailor Moon* films from 1993 to 1995, four *Slam Dunk* films between 1994 and 1995, and, obviously, *Dragon Ball*, and, more particularly, *Dragon Ball Z*, got top billing! From 1989 to 1996, *Dragon Ball Z* had fourteen mid- or feature-length films released in Japanese theaters, compared to just three for *Dragon Ball*. Cleverly, Toei took advantage of Akira Toriyama's popularity to release two new *Dr. Slump* films in 1993 and two in 1994.

This hyperproductivity can be easily explained—broadcast in some forty countries, the series now had more fans outside Japan than in it. Each new *Dragon Ball Z* movie was guaranteed to sell millions of dubbed or subtitled VHS copies across the world and bring a few more yen into Toei's coffers. The worldwide surge was accompanied by a wave of combat video games for the growing home console market, demonstrating the effectiveness of media mix.

In spite of itself, the *Macross* series epitomized the importance of foreign markets with the standardization of VHS. In 1987, after the production of the OAV commemorating the fifth anniversary of the series, Studio Nue, led by Shōji Kawamori, abandoned any notion of a new animated version. The main sponsor, Big West, then decided to go it alone, producing a series of six OAVs in 1992, *Macross II*, with only three team members from the original series. It didn't matter because Japanese fans weren't the target—Big West was interested in the American market!

In 1985, the United States was hit hard by the *Robotech* series, a remix by local publisher Harmony Gold between *Macross* and two Tatsunoko series, *Chōjikū Kidan Southern Cross* and *Kikō Sōseiki MOSPEADA*. The three titles all have space opera and mecha, but their plots have absolutely nothing in common. Since then, young Americans had been desperate for a sequel, and *Macross II* met all their expectations in 1992. Even though the VHS trilogy sold millions of copies in the United States, the liberties taken with the original concept caused a lot of grumbling in Japan. Starting with the members of Studio Nue, who were forced to take matters into their own hands with the *Macross Plus* OAV series in 1994. The resurrection of the classic franchise also became a video game, with four titles between 1997 and 2001.

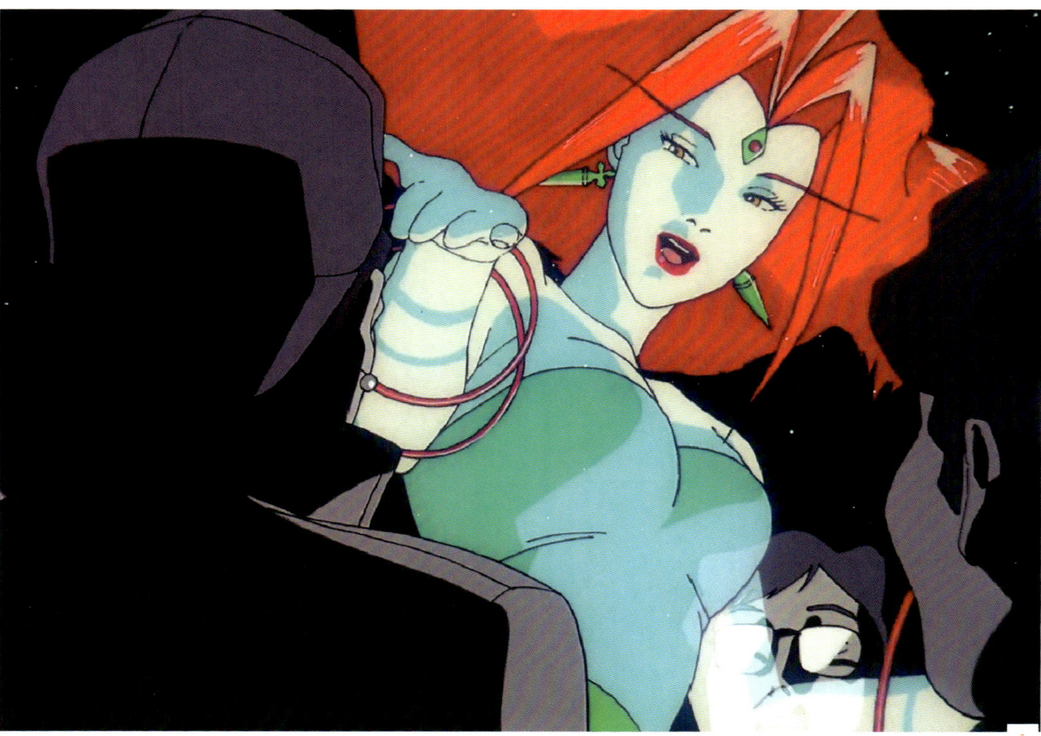

1
1994
Macross Plus

NEW ON-SCREEN DELIGHTS

With the appearance in 1983 of the Nintendo Entertainment System which sold almost 20 million units in Japan, and its new icon Mario, one might logically have feared competition between video games and animation. After all, any time spent playing meant fewer viewers for TV broadcasts. However, the medium quickly became a privileged partner for successful franchises, especially as the range of consoles broadened with the arrival of 16-bit machines, like the Super Nintendo in 1990 (17 million consoles sold in Japan) and the Sega Mega Drive in 1988 (4.3 million sold). The relationship between anime and video games was far from one-sided, and it wasn't long before the most popular games were adapted into TV series. And, at the beginning of the 1990s, role-playing games were dominating the market.

Role-playing games, or **RPGs**, began in the United States in 1974 with *Dungeons and Dragons*, and the new hobby quickly caught on in the West. Teens everywhere gathered in bedrooms, garages, and living rooms to spend nights immersed in fantastic adventures. Playing as an elf archer, a human magician, or a dwarf warrior, they used dice to confront the obstacles placed in their path by the Dungeon Master (or game master outside of *D&D*), who adapted the story to the players' input. It wasn't until 1985 that a clumsy translation reached Japan, with the game's coinage going from "platinum pieces" to "plutonium pieces." Interestingly, the American series adapted from *Dungeons and Dragons* (1983 to 1985) and broadcast in France as *Le Sourire du dragon*, was animated by Toei, at a time when Japan was still completely unaware of this form of entertainment.

The popularity of this fantasy world inspired by J.R.R. Tolkien's *Lord of the Rings* was unparalleled in Japan. Nevertheless, whereas Western teenagers preferred RPGs, embodying their characters like an actor (with varying degrees of seriousness), Japanese teens were captivated by **game systems**, precise game mechanics. What equipment should a player choose, and which skill should they increase to maximize the odds in favor of a roll of the dice? With the development of new technologies, these principles quickly found their way into video games. Even today, while RPGs on consoles and PCs are commonplace, a distinction is made for those that originated in Japan, JRPGs, which retain this inordinate affection for class and skill systems pushed to the extreme and turn-based combat phases.

Two iconic representatives of the genre came out in 1986: *The Legend of Zelda*, and most notably *Dragon Quest*, whose characters were drawn by Akira Toriyama. The game was so popular that when *Dragon Quest III* was launched on February 10, 1988, school absenteeism reached record levels—even the most serious students would rather skip class than risk the game selling out! To avoid this happening again, the publisher now systematically chooses a public holiday to launch a new game.

Dragon Quest's phenomenal success and Toriyama's popularity, which had been soaring since *Dragon Ball*, were compelling arguments for an anime adaptation, to be created by Studio Pierrot and Studio Comet. Studio Comet was created from the ashes of Tsuchida Production, a company launched in 1976 and forced into bankruptcy ten years later as the first victim of the oncoming economic crisis, despite its acclaimed work on *Captain Tsubasa*. The new studio had everything to gain from the project. Whereas

Mario was the first video game to be made into a feature-length cartoon in 1986, *Dragon Quest* gave rise three years later to the first animated series from this new market, *Dragon Quest: Yūsha Abel Densetsu* (*Dragon Quest: Legend of the Hero Abel*), a forty-two-episode coproduction between Pierrot and Comet, directed mainly by Rintaro.

Two years later, in 1991, Toei produced *Dragon Quest: Dai no Daibōken* (*Dragon Quest: The Adventures of Dai*), an adaptation of a manga based on a game released in 1989. Media mix was more effective than ever! However, animation studios soon abandoned RPGs, despite their growing popularity in Japan; in addition to *Dragon Quest* and *Zelda*, the *Final Fantasy* and *Phantasy Star* games debuted in 1987. Instead of focusing on the domestic market, they opted to tap into a new social phenomenon that was a mainstay in arcades worldwide—combat games!

The game company SNK opened the floodgates with two TV movies and a feature film based on *Fatal Fury* between 1993 and 1995. But the apotheosis was Capcom's *Street Fighter II*, whose various console versions had sold more than fourteen million copies worldwide. After a feature film in 1994, Gisaburō Sugii (best known for his Mitsuru Adachi adaptations) directed a series for Group TAC, *Street Fighter II V*. The twenty-nine episodes were broadcast in 1995, the same year as the American film starring Jean-Claude Van Damme and Kylie Minogue dressed as the game's heroes. The film was a flop and showed that even though the West had now incorporated Japanese digital entertainment into its daily life, its show business tycoons had failed to understand the real reasons behind its success.

A TOUCH OF FANTASY

The arrival of *Dungeons and Dragons* in Japan spawned the success of JRPGs, including *Dragon Quest*, which opened the door to Western heroic fantasy in anime. And the American RPG rolled out the red carpet for this new genre. The committee of enthusiasts responsible for localizing the *Dungeons and Dragons* rule book into Japanese became a professional company in 1986 under the name SNE, short for Syntax Error—a funny way of apologizing for their typos. Young role players embodied the archetypal teams in game master Ryo Mizuno's campaign: Parn the Paladin, Ghim the dwarf, Etoh the priest, and

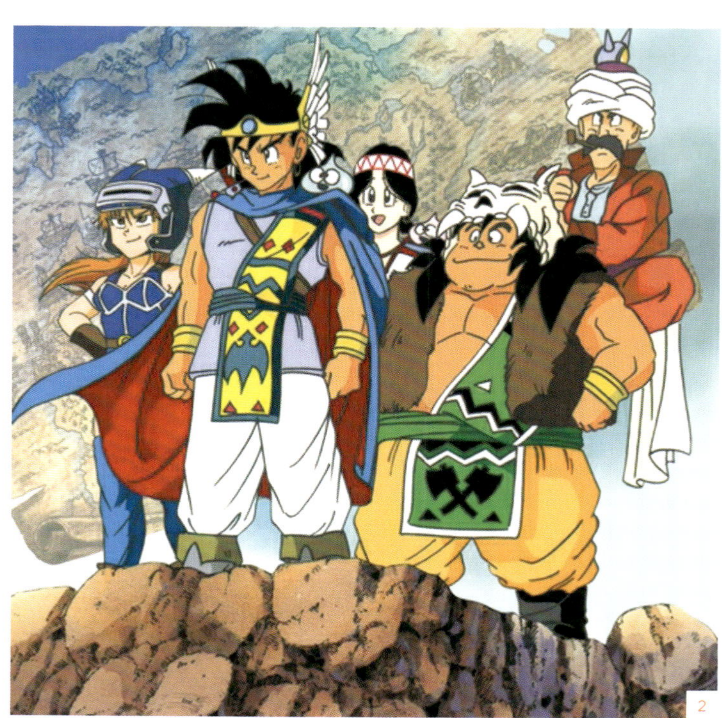

2

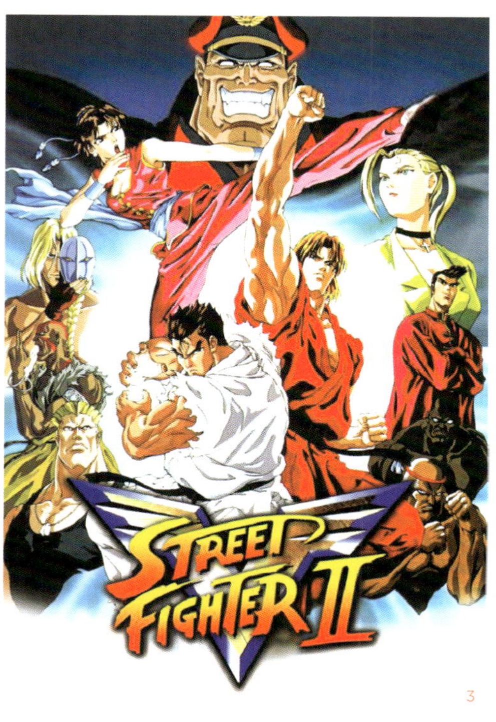

3

2
—
1989
Dragon Quest: Yūsha Abel Densetsu (Dragon Quest: Legend of the Hero Abel)

3
—
1994
Street Fighter II

Slayn the sorcerer. Because only men were around the game table, sci-fi writer Hiroshi Yamamoto took the gamble of adding a touch of femininity to the group by bringing to life a character of the opposite gender, the dazzling elf Deedlit.

Session after session, the *Lodoss* universe in which these characters evolved was taking shape as geography was established, and ancestral myths were evoked. As their quest grew in scope, Ryo Mizuno carefully transcribed the team's rise to power, eventually publishing these "replays" in the computer magazine *Comptiq*. An entire niche audience quickly fell in love with these adventures, which were certainly scripted, but still random chance—what would they do when rolls of the dice led to successive critical failures?

The episodic replays were compiled into a series of novels published between 1988 and 1993, and the nine volumes of *Lodoss tō Senki* (*Record of Lodoss War*) have now sold more than ten million copies. It was thirty-year-old designer Yutaka Izubuchi who took on the onerous task of illustrating them, giving an appearance to the heroes who had achieved iconic status. In 1989, SNE came full circle with *Sword World RPG*, a role-playing game with its own specific system, so that the Japanese could create their own adventures in its deep, coherent universe. Although distinct, the circles of RPG, anime, and computer fans overlapped quite a bit, and the world of fantasy was gathering steam. Even though Go Nagai's 1985 release *Mujigen Hunter Fandora* was a nod to H.P. Lovecraft's demon Yog-Sothoth, it was still mostly science fiction, with evil threatening the entire galaxy. By contrast, screenwriter Keisuke Fujikawa, who had built his reputation working on the scripts for *Space Battleship Yamato* and *Cat's Eye*, tackled the genre head-on with his novel *Windaria*, which he oversaw adapted into a feature film in 1986. A reinterpretation of *Romeo and Juliet* set against the backdrop of a medieval civil war, the melancholy of *Douwa Meita Senshi Windaria* (*Windaria*) is enhanced by the graphic style of *shōjo* illustrator Mutsumi Inomata and the elegant direction of Kunihiko Yuyama, a future pillar of the *Pokémon* franchise. On the same day as its theatrical release, July 19, 1986, fantasy also made its way into the OAV market with *Amon Saga*, based off the manga illustrated by Yoshitaka Amano.

Four years later, Madhouse turned to VHS for its anime adaptation of *Record of Lodoss War*, calling on a young but already experienced team. They started with director Akinori Nagaoka, who, at thirty-six years old, had created some of the biggest hits of the past decade, including *Dr. Slump*, the third *Touch* film, and *Anpanman*. The twenty-eight-year-old character designer Nobuteru Yūki, who became well-known for *The Five Star Stories* in 1989, refined Yutaka Izubuchi's characters while preserving their extreme detail. It was quite the feat for the animation team because tracking and zoom shots of warriors in elaborate armor and gigantic dragons on inanimate cels were a dime a dozen. To make up for this, Madhouse executives applied the lessons of limited animation they learned from Tezuka and prioritized storyboards, which were assigned to Rintaro. Just like the oral legends at the root of fantasy, storytelling was paramount.

Published between June 1990 and December 1991, the thirteen episodes of *Record of Lodoss War* became a large-scale phenomenon. Thousands of RPG players around the world discovered anime through the series, and game masters pounced on CDs of the soundtrack, composed by Mitsuo Hagita; a bridge was created between the two fan communities, both widespread and stigmatized. The series put fantasy on the map in Japan ten years before the first *Lord of the Rings* film. Finally, its very genesis is remarkable—with a lot of imagination and a few connections, a small creative circle was able to transform its creation into an anime!

FORTUNE FAVORS THE BOLD

The five members of the Headgear artist collective had plenty of imagination and more than a few connections, given that they were all already in the graphic entertainment industry—most of them met on *Urusei Yatsura*. Well aware of the possibilities offered by media mix, the five artists pooled their talents to create a cross-disciplinary production. It was no longer a question of creating a manga, which would become a series, then a film and/or OAV

1
1986
Douwa Meita Senshi Windaria (Windaria)

2 and 3
1991
Lodoss tō Senki (Record of Lodoss War)

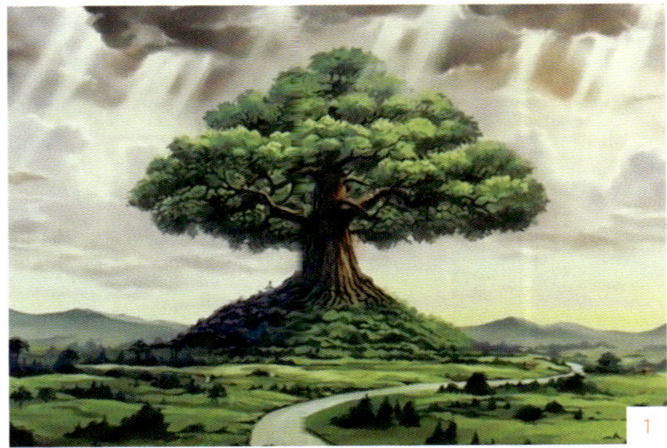
1

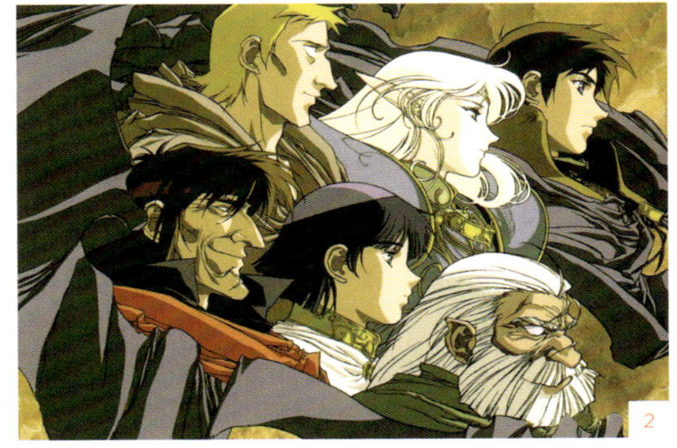
2

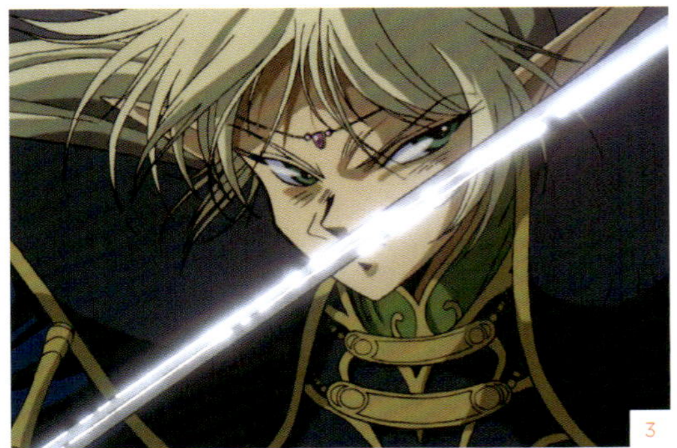
3

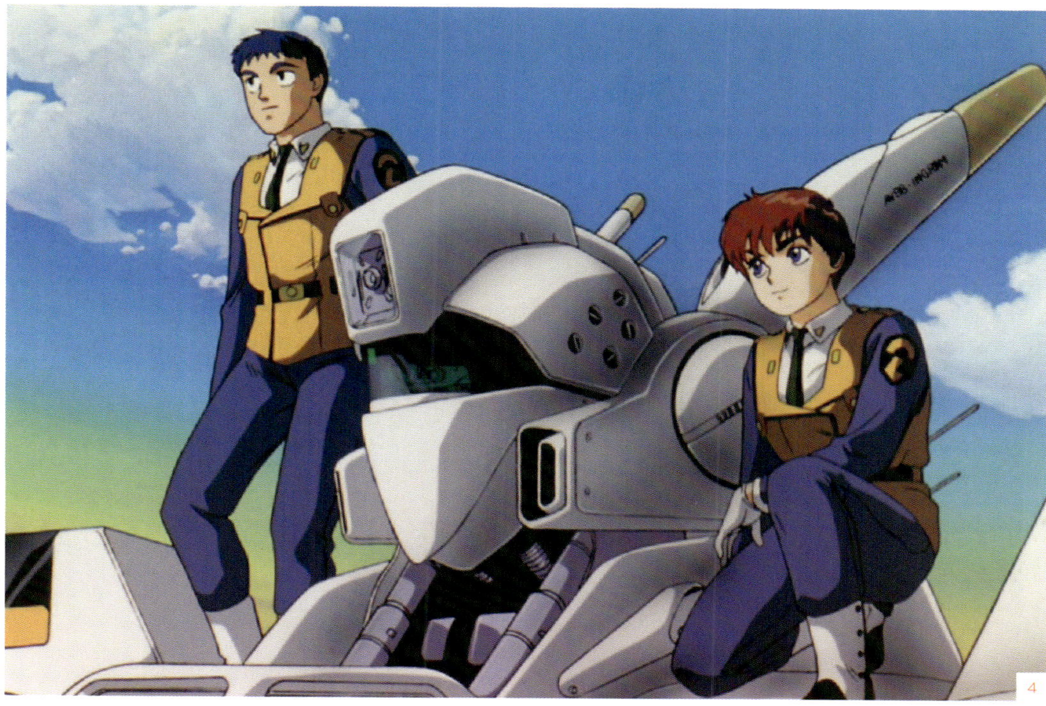

and a video game, but of tackling all these media simultaneously with a project planned out in advance. It was up to screenwriter Kazunori Itō (*Magical Angel Creamy Mami*, *Urusei Yatsura*, *Maison Ikkoku*) to develop a coherent universe that could be approached from a different angle for each medium.

He chose Tokyo, a location familiar to the Japanese, in the near future (1998, less than ten years later) as the setting for his story and incorporated futuristic elements such as gigantic humanoid construction robots, the Labors, machines of such power that they would wreak havoc in the wrong hands. A special police force was equipped with robots for emergency intervention and tasked with protecting the capital. *Kidō Keisatsu Patlabor* (*Patlabor*) used this as the basis for a TV series focused on the daily life of Special Vehicle Section 2 (including robot maintenance and training) between missions, a film with a thriller feel, and OAVs that tell the origin story of the special police force, a VHS prequel that was a must for fans but unnecessary for the general public.

Masami Yūki worked from an alternative timeline for the manga version and created an independent work to reach a different audience from the anime fans. The manga is a counterespionage adventure featuring the internal struggle between SV2 and a suspicious brigade. Nevertheless, it adapted easily to the style of characters created by character designer Akemi Takada (*Magical Angel Creamy Mami*, *Urusei Yatsura*) and the mecha designs of Yutaka Izubuchi, one of the contributors to the success of *Lodoss*. This duo single-handedly managed the art direction of the entire franchise. The last member of Headgear, director Mamoru Oshii (*Urusei Yatsura*, *Dallos*), simultaneously directed the series of seven OAVs and the feature film! However, it was impossible for him to add the TV series to his busy schedule, and the series was taken on by Naoyuki Yoshinaga, who had proven his skills on *Maison Ikkoku* and episodes of *Urusei Yatsura*.

The collective worked with contagious passion. In addition to Yoshinaga, many artists who had collaborated with Headgear members in the past were eager to contribute to the *Patlabor* venture, including composer Kenji Kawai, who further solidified his friendship with Oshii. But it was the production companies who were most excited about the *Patlabor* gold mine. Sunrise was happy to accept the forty-seven-episode TV series and the seven

4
—
1989
Kidō Keisatsu Patlabor (Patlabor)

1989
Kidō Keisatsu Patlabor (Patlabor)

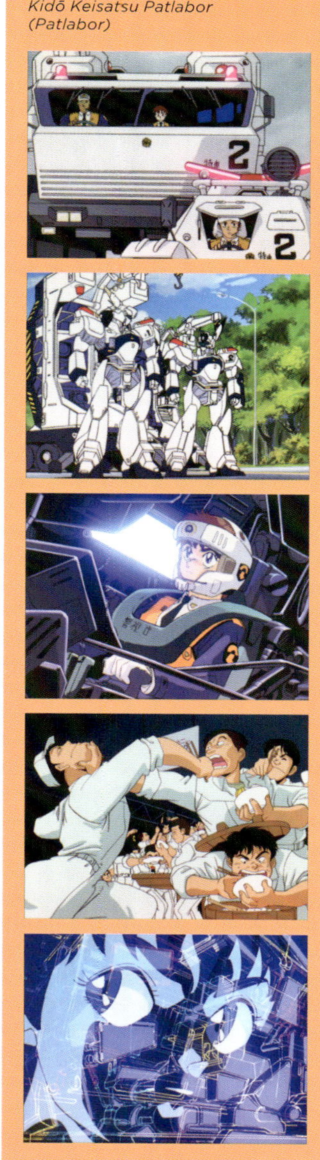

OAVs from their offshoot, Studio Deen. The latter, however, could not bear the additional burden of the feature film alone, and sought the support of another satellite office, I.G Tatsunoko. The young company, on the verge of separating from its parent company in December 1988, could not have dreamed of a better project to gain its independence. The *Patlabor* phenomenon took off in 1988, the year Masami Yūki's manga was published (which ended with its twenty-second volume in 1994) and the first OAV was directed by Oshii. On January 24, its mecha were brought to life in the first video game adaptation. The final VHS was released on June 25, 1989, a few days before the feature film on July 15, setting the stage for the TV series to be broadcast starting October 11. It took *Patlabor* eighteen months to become an iconic franchise, still popular today. Beyond that, it become a textbook case—from the 1990s onward, its biggest hits were produced with a well-anticipated multimedia strategy.

Entering a new world

METAMORPHOSIS IN PROGRESS

This change, which encouraged horizontal collaboration between several media from the outset, came at just the right time. The classic vertical model of drawing source material from a long-running manga to produce a hundred episodes would soon be obsolete, but no one had realized it yet. The comic book market was about to enter a crisis from which it is still struggling to recover. *Shōnen Jump*, the undisputed market leader and official supplier of long-running series, was about to suffer its first setback in its history.

In 1990, two new manga boosted sales of Shueisha's weekly magazine: *Yu Yu Hakusho* and *Slam Dunk*. The first title is rooted in the supernatural, in which delinquent teen Yusuke dies protecting a child, but fate brings him back. The divine authorities decide to resurrect him on the condition that he become their underworld investigator in the world of the living. The second show is dedicated entirely to the glory of basketball, at the height of the Michael Jordan era. Created by Yoshihiro Togashi and Takehiko Inoue, respectively, the two titles, along with *Dragon Ball*, made up *Shōnen Jump*'s new "Big 3."

Thanks to Son Goku's adventures, the weekly magazine's sales had risen from 4 million (1984) to 5 million (1990). The first issue in 1995 exceeded 6.5 million copies! But the Big 3 bowed out for good within two years of each other: *Yu Yu Hakusho* came to an end first in July 1994, followed by *Dragon Ball* in May 1995, and *Slam Dunk* in June 1996. Sales plummeted, slamming the brakes on new series—shows with more than 100 episodes became as rare as they were exceptional. In this sense also, *Yu Yu Hakusho* (Studio Pierrot, 1992 to 1995, 112 episodes) and *Slam Dunk* (Toei, 1993 to 1996, 101 episodes) exemplified the swan song of a golden age.

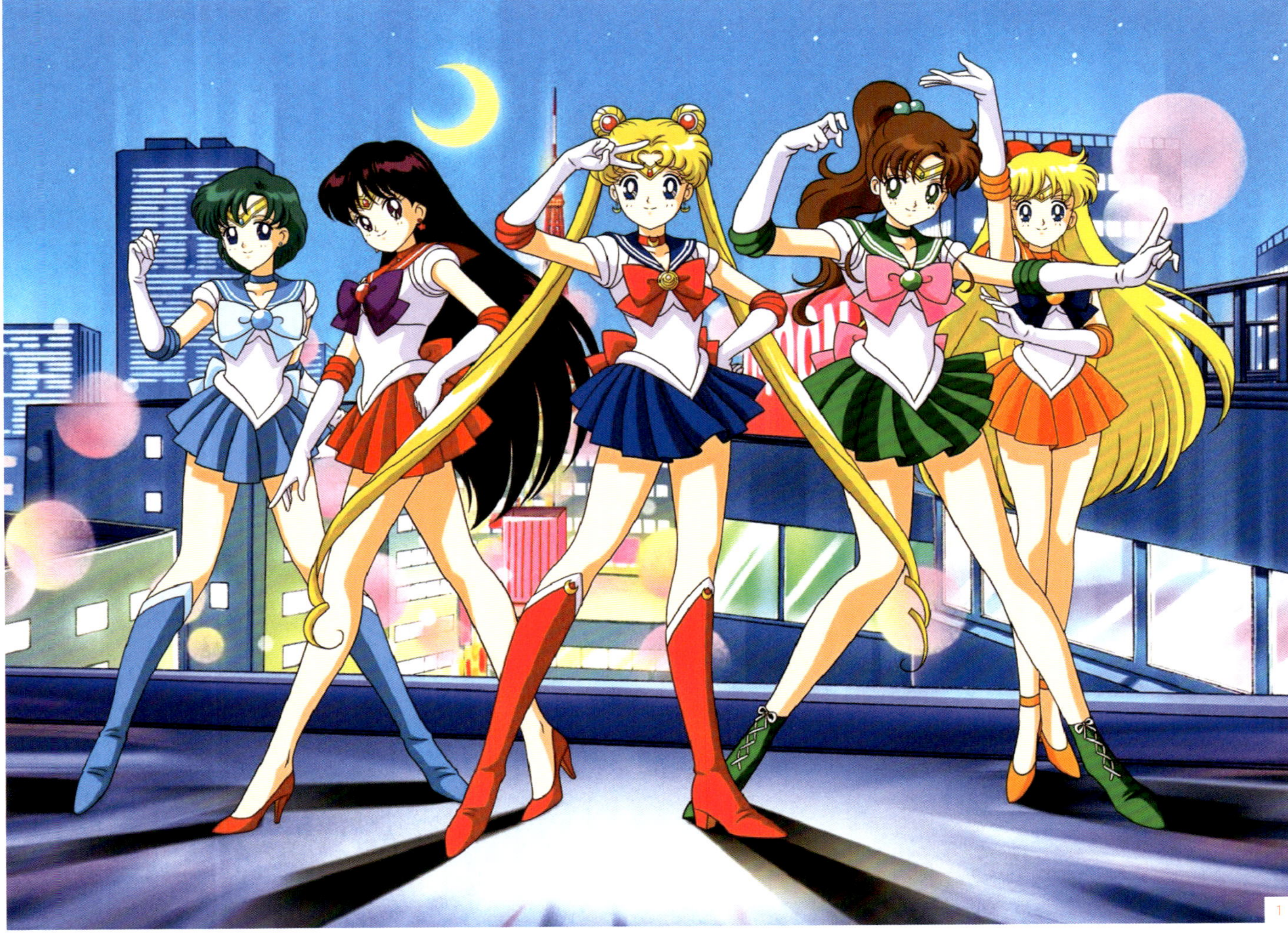

1
1992
Bishōjo Senshi Sailor Moon (Sailor Moon)

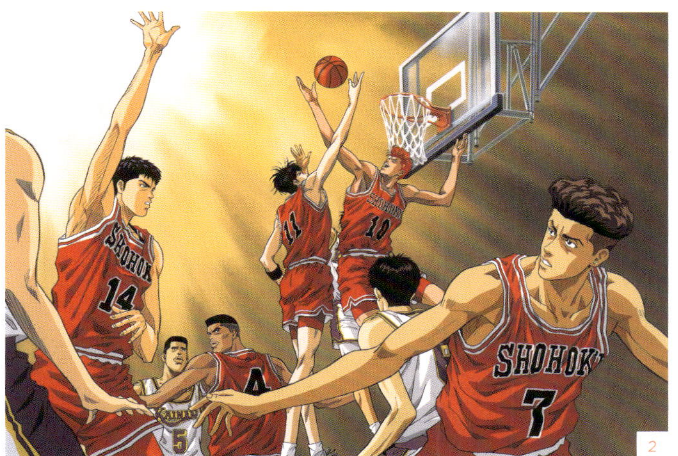

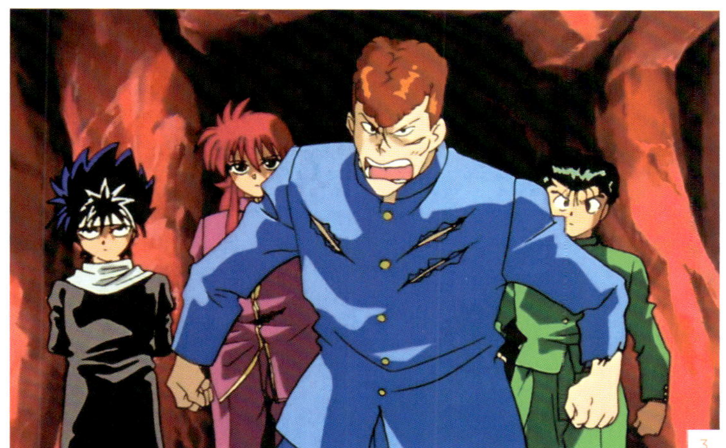

2
1993
Slam Dunk

3
1992
Yu Yu Hakusho

Sailor Moon managed to bridge the gap between the innovative new production method centered around a multimedia strategy, and the former, soon-to-be obsolete method. On discovering her manga *Codename: Sailor V*, Toei contacted manga artist Naoko Takeuchi. Her concept of a heroine dressed in *sailor fuku* (a girls' school uniform inspired by sailors) was brilliant, and they wanted to capitalize on it! The teams from Kodansha's monthly *Nakayoshi* magazine and Toei Animation worked together with the *mangaka* to produce the first chapter and the first episode within weeks of each other in early 1992, marking the start of a social phenomenon.

It wasn't the first time that such synchronization between media had been organized, and this was even one of the constraints imposed on Go Nagai during the creation of *Mazinger Z* twenty years earlier. But this time, the media-mix strategy went much further. Throughout its 200-episode run until February 1997, the franchise consistently released new films and video games annually. Additionally, the merchandising strategy was the result of thorough and deliberate planning. Toy sales had previously shown a stark difference between the coveted heroes and their "enemy of the week" opponents who never left store shelves. By drawing inspiration from the *super sentai* teams, producers added astral warriors around the heroine and increased their sources of revenue tenfold—a true fan wanted the complete collection!

The adventures of Usagi, a schoolgirl who inherited the powers of lunar warrior *Sailor Moon* to protect Earth alongside her friends, represent this evolution. Combining themes for girls (magical girls) and boys (*sentai*), *Sailor Moon* used adaptation "the old way" and media-mix strategy together to create a completely Japanese product with significant international impact. It was broadcast on the French show *Club Dorothée* in 1993, less than two years after its release in Japan, and became a hit two years later in Germany, one of the few European countries to have rejected *Goldorak* due to its violence in the early 1980s.

Even after reunification, Germany still preferred familiar titles like *World Masterpiece Theater*, with its anthropomorphic animals and sentimental comedies. The television channel RTL2 was launched on March 6, 1993, for a teenage audience in an effort to catch up. Two years later, titles such as *The Rose of Versailles* (1972) and *Captain Tsubasa* (1983) also made it to Germany. Much more recently, *Sailor Moon* won over the public (10 percent of the country tuned in), sparking a social phenomenon on par with *Dragon Ball* and the as yet unreleased *Saint Seiya*. Two markets began to emerge in Europe: one for boys (France, Italy, Spain) and one for girls (Germany, Austria).

IT'S A SMALL WORLD AFTER ALL

Sailor Moon was having the same effect around the globe. Finally, little girls could see themselves in the role of a strong, determined heroine. Historically, female characters had been typically relegated to supporting roles in action series primarily targeting male audiences. In elementary and middle schools, while the boys were debating whether *Dragon Ball*, *Saint Seiya*, or another series was the best, girls were rallying around *Sailor Moon*. The emergence of this committed, supportive female fandom cemented the global trend for good. It diversified the airwaves beyond the family and boys' cartoons abounding on TV and the shows for older teenagers on the VHS market, which had been established just about everywhere (AnimEigo in the United States in 1988, Manga Entertainment in the UK in 1991, Yamato Video in Italy in 1991, Kazé in France in 1994, and so on).

In the 1980s, *Goldorak* and *Captain Harlock* merchandise in Europe was often produced in-house, and Japanese rights holders didn't make a cent on those coloring books and other collectibles. The anime industry also took advantage of the video game boom to control its brand licenses, which had become global in scope. This involved supplying posters, T-shirts, and figurines to Western countries, and keeping an eye on continental Asia (and particularly

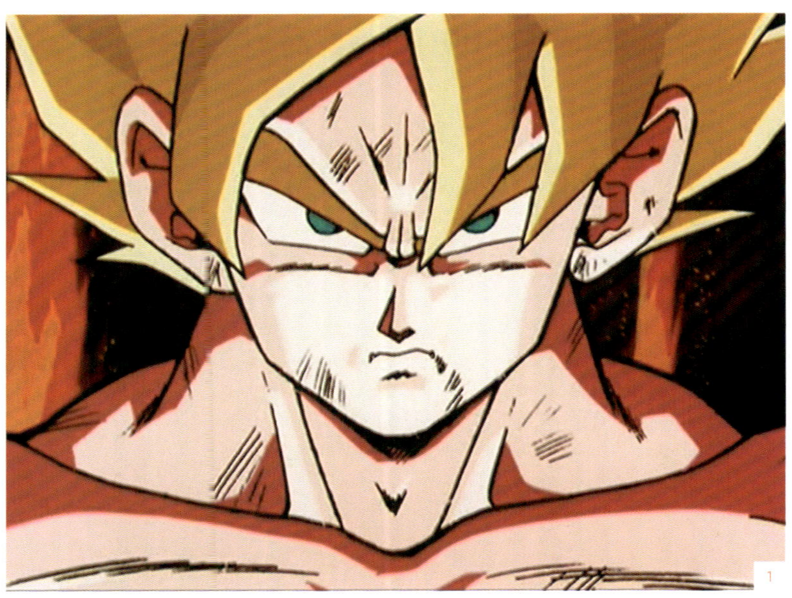

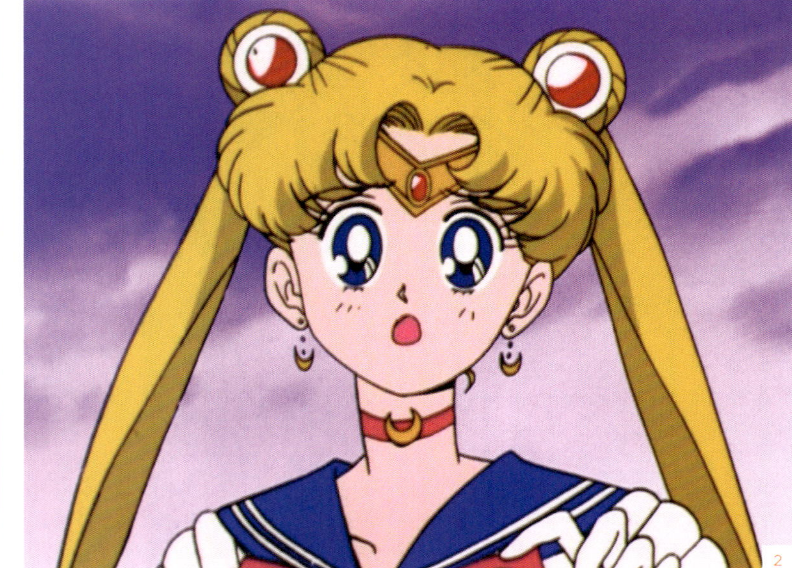

1
1989
Dragon Ball Z

2
1992
Bishōjo Senshi Sailor Moon (Sailor Moon)

Hong Kong), where a lucrative counterfeit market was developing.

Fans could go to specialty stores, where anime sections were taking over spaces previously reserved for comic books and video games, and also fan conventions, which were making a timid appearance in the United States. Texas was first with YamatoCon in 1983, then A-Kon in 1990, now two among many. AnimeCon broke through a symbolic barrier in 1991: thanks to the official support of American and Japanese rights holders—a first in the history of these festivals backed by passionate fans—the California convention drew in over 1,000 participants! The following year, Anime Expo took shape in the same state and moved to Los Angeles in 2007 to become the top anime convention in the country.

It took a while for the wave to cross the Atlantic Ocean, but it finally hit British shores on February 19, 1994, at AUKCon. The London convention sought to go beyond mere entertainment, with stores, screenings, karaoke, and sessions put on by anime expert Helen McCarthy. The following year, a thousand Spanish-speakers gathered at Barcelona's first Salón del Manga, which today draws in over 150 times as many. The convention trend would spread all the way across Europe by the end of the millennium.

Fans could bond even further over specialized press when it arrived on scene; in this pre-internet era, sources of information were both precious and rare. It would be impossible not to mention *Dorothée Magazine* launched at the start of the 1989 school year in France with a print run of 150,000 copies. The weekly magazine sold mainly for the detailed fact sheets on series featured by *Club Dorothée* and for its posters. In addition to official sales and merchandise, enthusiasts gathered to create fan publications (fanzines) with in-depth content, including reports on major works and artists, exclusive information from Japan, reviews, and more.

A pioneer in manga and anime press, *Protoculture Addicts*, whose title refers directly to *Macross*, took advantage of its Canadian publisher Claude J. Pelletier's proximity to the United States to cover works available on the American market as well as the French-speaking market in 1987. The United States would have to wait until 1992 for *Animerica*, published by Viz Media, the American branch of Shueisha. And in Europe, specialized press had exploded! *Anime UK* and *AnimeLand* debuted in the UK and France, respectively, in 1991, *AnimaniA* in Germany in 1994, and in 1995, the highly specific *Lodoss Magazine* joined *Mangazine*, created six years earlier, on Italian newsstands. Far from being limited to popular series, these cutting-edge magazines, which had become increasingly professional over time, presented previously unpublished masterpieces, including Studio Ghibli films, which, apart from *Porco Rosso* in France in 1995, had never left Japan.

NEW MEDIA, NEW TALENT: THE GHIBLI EVOLUTION

The studio founded by Hayao Miyazaki and Isao Takahata became the benchmark in Japan following the success of *Kiki's Delivery Service*. Through the streets of every town, kindergarten students sang the chorus of *My Neighbor Totoro*, a custom that continues to this day. Under Toshio Suzuki's leadership, Ghibli stood out in the animation industry for its economic system, in which profits from feature films were automatically reinvested in the production of subsequent films to pay the permanent animator and designer salaries, whereas all other studios employed freelancers.

This fundamental difference didn't prevent Studio Ghibli from adapting to the new trends emerging from the bustling animation industry. Released in 1991, *Omohide Poro Poro* (*Only Yesterday*), a twenty-seven-year-old Tokyoite's return to her roots over the course of a summer, was a hit at the box office. But Takahata's requirement of hyperrealistic facial animation, particularly for mouths, exhausted the entire team during production. Miyazaki and Suzuki then turned their attention to a partnership with Japan Airlines, which was seeking exclusive programming for salarymen on domestic flights. Unable to rein in his ambitions, the director turned the initial project into a feature film, *Kurenai no Buta* (*Porco Rosso*), the following year.

But the idea of films venturing beyond cinema walls had now been established. In 1993, NTV, a sponsor since Studio Ghibli's launch, aired *Umi ga Kikoeru* (*Ocean Waves*), a TV movie by Tomomi Mochizuki. The animator-director had been recruited for his television experience in both TV series (*Legend of Light*, *Ranma ½*) and OAVs (*Twilight Q*, *Koko wa Greenwood* [*Here is Greenwood*]). Even Miyazaki tried his hand at something new—music videos! His six-minute, forty-second silent short *On Your Mark*, illustrating the eponymous song by the duo Chage

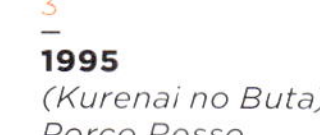

3
1995
(Kurenai no Buta)
Porco Rosso

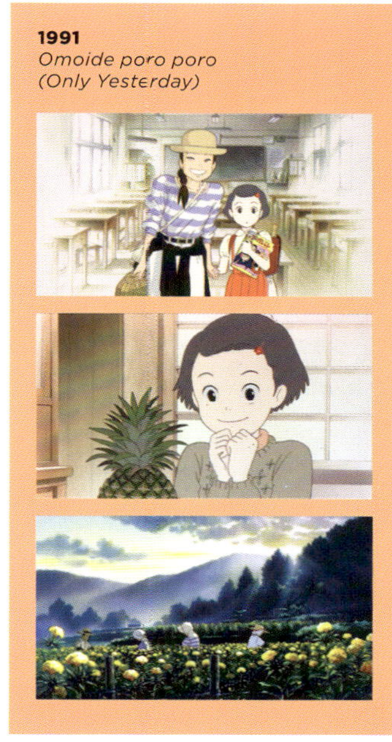

1991
Omoide poro poro
(Only Yesterday)

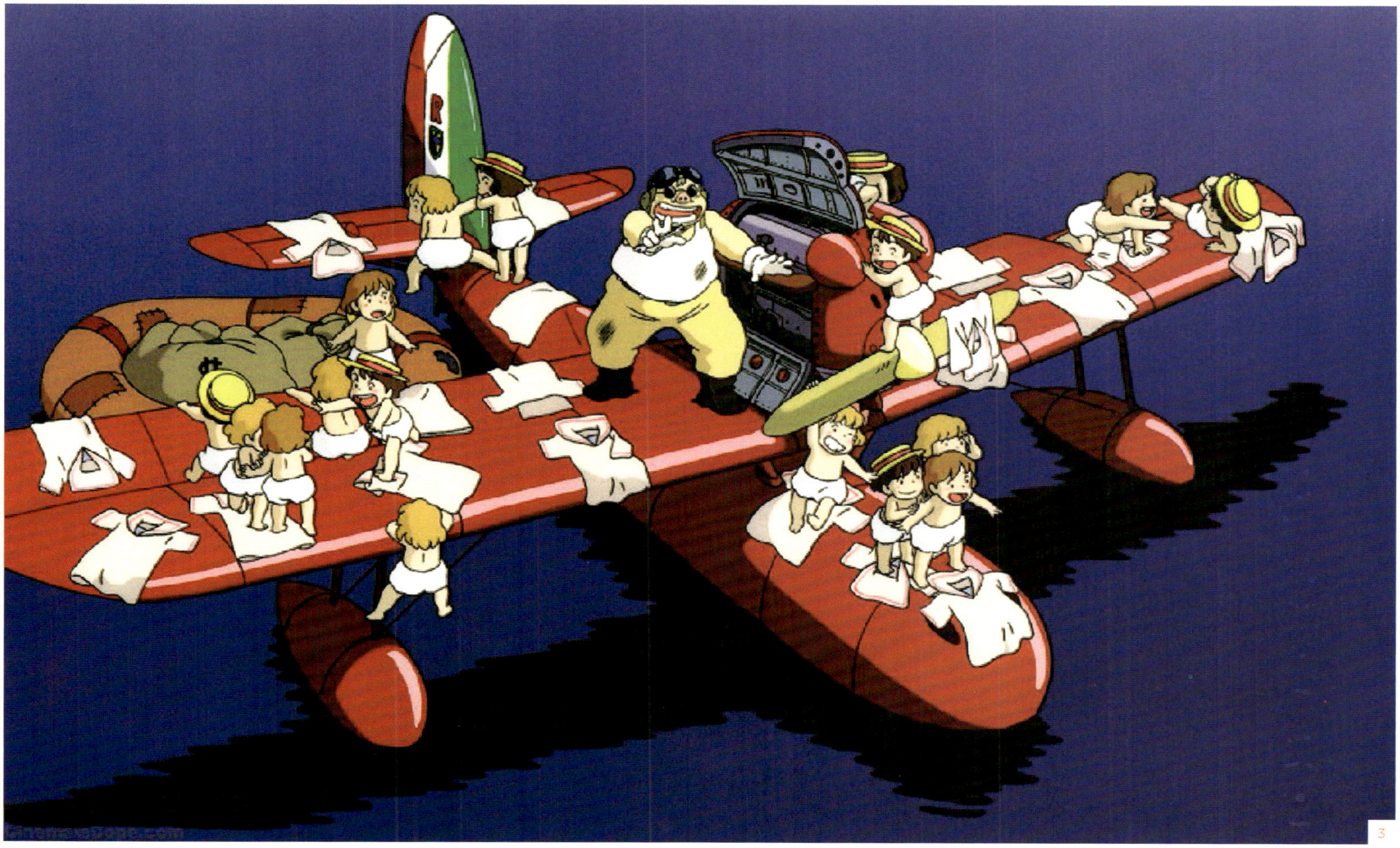

3

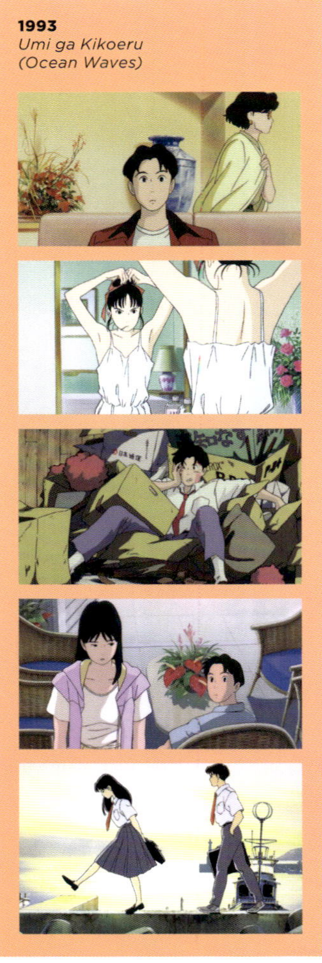

1993
Umi ga Kikoeru (Ocean Waves)

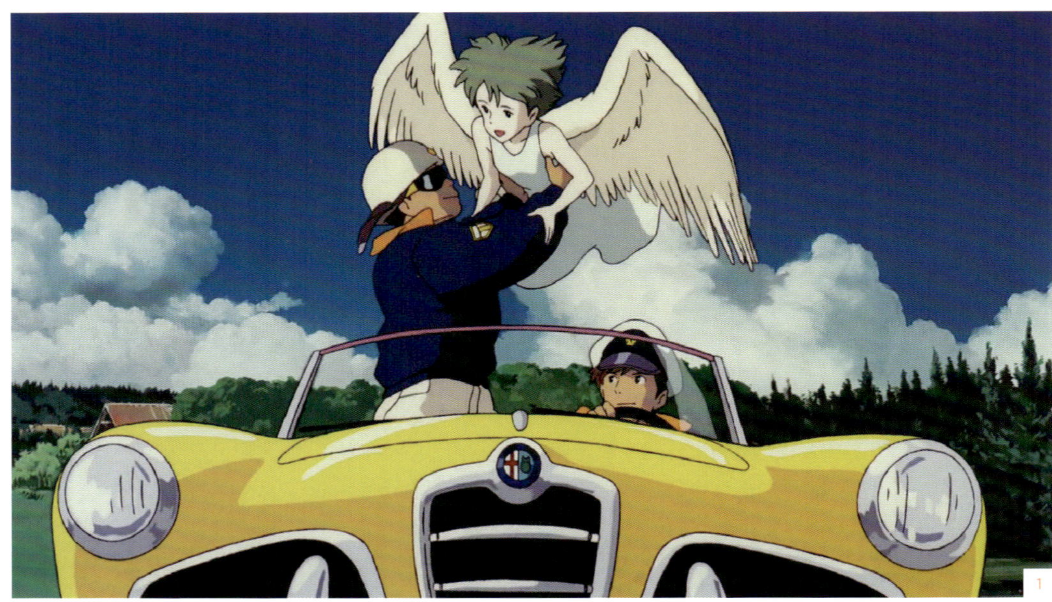

1
1995
On Your Mark

and Aska, was mainly used as advertising for *Mimi o Sumaseba* (*Whisper of the Heart*) in 1995.

That feature film was the first Ghibli production not directed by Miyazaki or Takahata. Since *Lupin III*, the talented animator Yoshifumi Kondō had steadily earned the esteem of directors, who assigned him key roles in their recent productions *Grave of the Fireflies* and *Kiki's Delivery Service*, such as character designer, animation director, and storyboard artist. Although he was widely considered Miyazaki's successor, his name didn't have the same popularity attached. A music video by the master in the preview attracted as many viewers as the plot of the slice-of-life film about a teenager awakening to music and love.

These attempts were all short-lived (Ghibli would quickly refocus on feature films, and Yoshifumi Kondō would die of exhaustion in 1997), unlike the studio's latest evolution. Miyazaki, a purist and staunch defender of traditional animation, stormed on but to no avail, as Takahata, always striving to push the limits of the medium, incorporated 3D animation in *Pom Poko*, released in 1994. This decision marked a turning point for Ghibli, which gradually introduced computer technology into its production without ever lowering its standards—*Porco Rosso* was the last Ghibli production to be 100 percent handmade.

EROTIC ELECTRONICS

The 1980s saw the emergence of computers, and the 1990s saw them become widespread as manufacturing costs fell. Now accessible, PCs (or *persocons*, the Japanese abbreviation for personal computers) were invading homes and businesses. Animation was no exception, and entirely handcrafted productions were in their last hours. The video game industry would prove to be a valuable ally in the deep shift in the production process, further multiplying bridges between the two media. Toei is the perfect example of this rapid and far-reaching change. In December 1991, the company produced its own CATAS (Computer Aided TOEI Animation System) software, designed to digitize production. A few months later, the team of animators working on a video game adaptation of *Fist of the North Star* integrated it into a complete suite of tools, the Revolutionary Engineering Tool Animation System. And RETAS was revolutionary in more ways than one! First incorporated into TV productions as early as 1993, the software suite cut colorization costs by 20 percent. Different shots, including zoom shots and parallax effects, no longer required an imposing multiplane camera but just a few clicks of the mouse. The company did not begin its conversion to fully digital until 1997 with the remake of *Dr. Slump*, the first series to no longer use cel animation.

As processors continued to become more powerful, video games increasingly contained digitally animated sequences requiring the skills of a storyboard artist. The growing fluidity between media became more pronounced, and studios emerged specializing in computerized animation, subcontracting with both television and film productions, as well as video games. Oriental Light and Magic paved the way in 1990, followed by Gonzo in 1992, and Production I.G the following year. Now freed from its parent studio Tatsunoko, Production

2 to 5
1995
Mimi o Sumaseba (Whisper of the Heart)

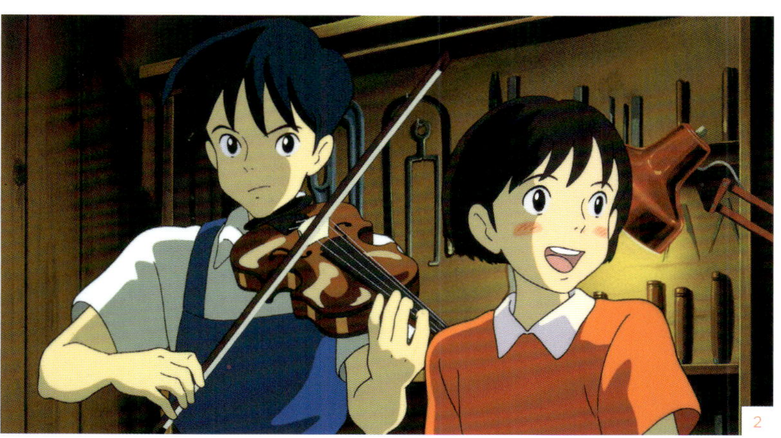
2

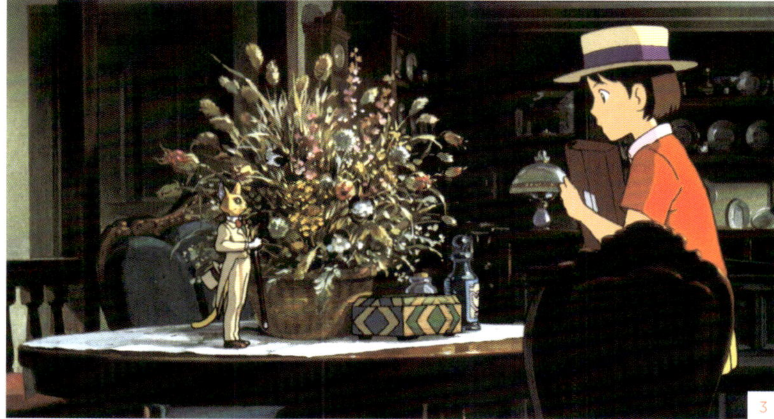
3

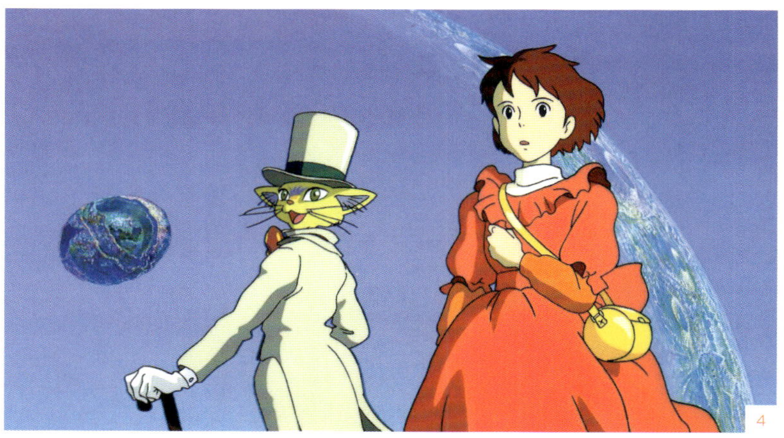
4

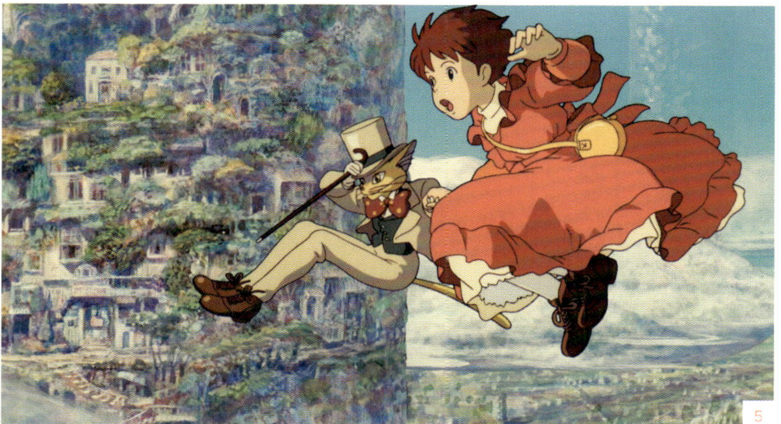
5

I.G created a sister company in 1995, Xebec, to focus on TV series, while Production I.G concentrated on feature films. Satelight, soon to be associated with the *Macross* franchise, appeared that same year in a totally different sector: **pachinko** games! The Japanese spent hours unwinding with these vertical pinball machines, which now had screens with video-animated bonus levels, opening up a whole new market.

The steady expansion of PCs was generating the same opportunistic wave as the popularization of VCRs ten years earlier. **Visual novels**, interactive stories with a simple series of choices along the lines of a Choose Your Own Adventure book, didn't require a state-of-the-art PC to work. Settings, character illustrations, and blocks of text were all players needed to get lost in a story where the aim was often to seduce the heroines. The market for erotic games, known in Japanese as *eroge* (a contraction of "erotic game"), grew at the same rate as PC sales and needed designers to create the pretty heroines for players to choose. It was a lucrative business for many animators, who worked under pseudonyms.

This new trend, which surrounded the hero with potential girlfriends, was hitting the anime market in spades. A far cry from the love triangles in *Urusei Yatsura* and *Kimagure Orange Road*, the hero's female sidekicks could now be counted on two hands, each one conforming to a different physical or behavioral stereotype. The OAV series *Tenchi Muyo!*, produced by AIC in 1992, laid the foundation for **harem anime**. When Tenchi frees the curvy and demonic Ryoko from a sealed 700-year-old cave, she turns out to be a space smuggler. She is soon joined by the temperamental alien princess Ayeka and her wise, disciplined younger sister Sasami, the naive policewoman Mihoshi, and the motherly scientist Washu. In short, enough clichés to make the hero's head spin! This overabundance of female characters

1998
Top o Nereae! (Gunbuster)

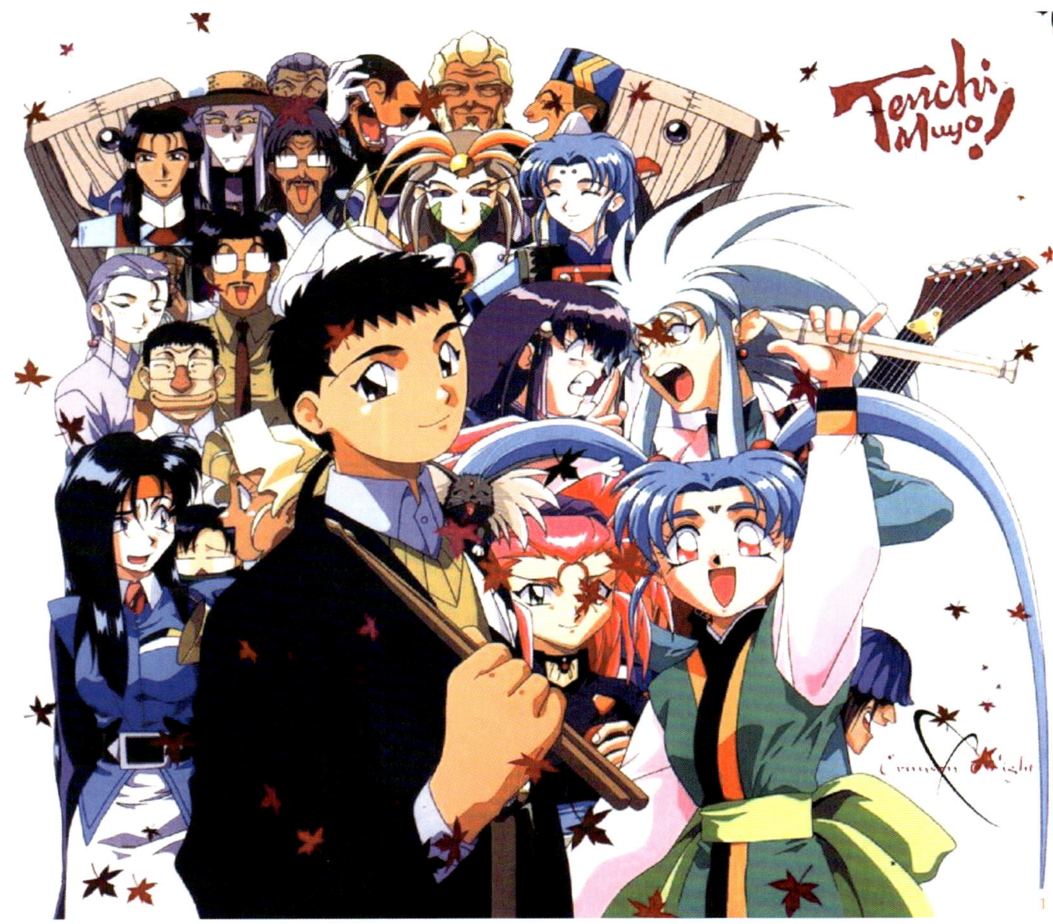

1
1992
Tenchi Muyo!

was accompanied by assertive hypersexualization: by appealing to their more basic instincts and using offbeat humor, producers hoped to attract otaku. Even under the guise of comedy, the displays of gratuitous fan service shots became increasingly outrageous. In 1988, *Gunbuster* became known for the "Gainax Bounce," gravity-defying breast animation that became a studio signature.

This trend was particularly noticeable in Tokyo's Akihabara district. Whereas the town had been known for selling household appliances after the war, earning it the nickname "Electric Town," in the 1980s it turned to computers, video games, and by extension, cartoons. The shelves of specialty shops were now lined with giant model robots alongside curvaceous girl figurines and life-size posters of *eroge* heroines, all sold in abundance. Akihabara became the heart of otaku culture, which went into tachycardia in 1995 under the impact of two fundamental productions, crystallizing the many market changes over the past dozen years. The first title exploded the industry's cozy cocoon from within, whereas the second propelled it into the connected future foreshadowed by the internet.

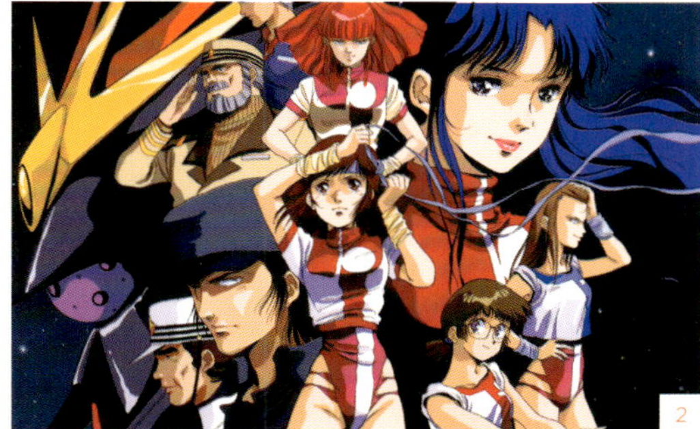

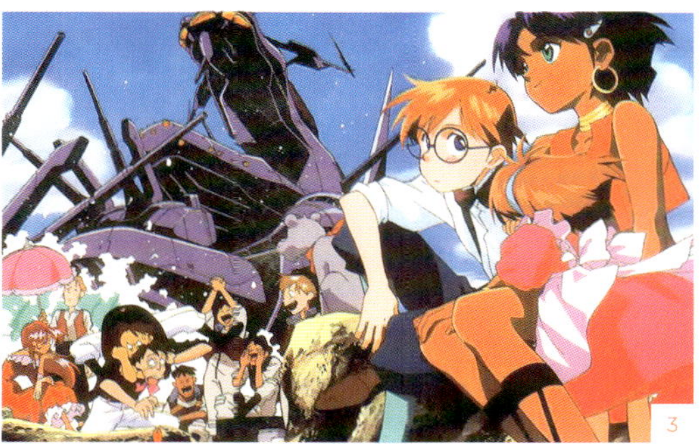

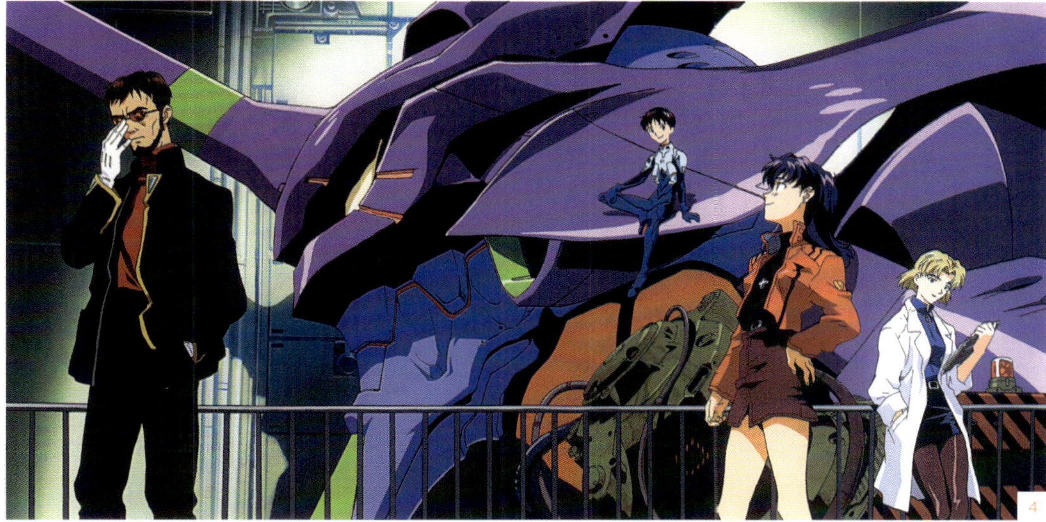

2
1998
Top o Nerae! (Gunbuster)

3
1991
Fushigi no Umi no Nadia (Nadia: The Secret of Blue Water)

4
1995
Shin Seiki Evangelion (Neon Genesis Evangelion)

EVANGELION: HIDEAKI ANNO'S APOCALYPTIC TALE

After the last episode of *Nadia: The Secret of Blue Water* aired in 1991, Hideaki Anno entered a deep depression. A pure product of otaku culture, he questioned the show's tendency to cater to the viewer (consumer) above all else in order to keep them in the comfort of a fictional universe for as long as possible. As the director explained to producer Toshimichi Ōtsuki one drunken evening in 1993, he wanted to create a more psychological, more mature work. Seeing the artist's despair, the head of King Records guaranteed him a time slot for a carte blanche series produced by Gainax. Anno then began work on *Shin Seiki Evangelion* (*Neon Genesis Evangelion*), whose nihilistic tone reflected his state of mind.

The show's premise is that in the year 2000, a cataclysm decimated the Earth, killing two billion people and causing global water levels to rise. Fifteen years later, gigantic extraterrestrial creatures seek to invade the planet. More specifically, the rebuilt underground city of Tokyo-3, home to the headquarters of NERV, the organization responsible for fighting off these "Angels." Under the direction of Gendo Ikari, advanced EVA fighting machines have been designed in the utmost secrecy since the devastating "Second Impact." And, to pilot the first model to go into real combat, the Machiavellian director decided to recruit his own son, Shinji . . .

The series got off to a rocky start. Broadcast on TV Tokyo every Wednesday at 7:30 p.m. starting October 4, 1995, it didn't have enough viewership. However, the late-night rerun on Fridays around midnight won over more and more fans. Word of mouth was spreading among otaku: you need to watch *Evangelion*, it's bringing back **robot anime**! The pilot, telepathically linked to his machine, physically feels the pain of every wound. But beyond that, the EVAs' very nature is unclear—are the colossal living creatures protected or constrained by their robotic armor? What is their relationship with the Angels they inevitably attract? The threat of giant aliens is never clearly addressed, apart from the mention of a "Third Impact," and is revealed over the course of an intentionally cryptic storyline.

In essence, *Evangelion* reflects Anno's depression through his hero, Shinji, forced to face adversaries in spite of himself. Far from the valiant heroes of the 1980s, he takes refuge in escape or isolation, even if it means endangering his friends and humanity. For the first time, this anime demonstrates the consequences of each battle between giants on a human scale; the planet may be saved in the end, but thousands of civilians perished or suffered fatal wounds in the collapsed buildings. In terms of form, otaku shines through, with extreme mecha designs, a gallery of fantastical female characters (icy Rei, stuck-up Asuka, and extroverted Misato, to name a few), and above all, constant references to the Old Testament that give an esoteric coherence to the whole, reinforced by graphic symbolism throughout.

Like his mentors Miyazaki and Takahata on *Heidi, Girl of the Alps* twenty years earlier, Hideaki Anno's production of *Evangelion* forged ahead without a safety net. Struggling with deadlines, the Gainax team began piling up cels beyond the budget and had to deal with incessant revisions to the script. The director, who had planned to end his series with the extinction of humanity, censored himself for fear that the show's nihilistic tone would undermine its success. The Japanese public was struggling to recover from two recent traumas, the Kobe earthquake on January 17, 1995, (6,437 dead; 43,792 wounded) and the Tokyo

1 to 4
1995
Shin Seiki Evangelion (Neon Genesis Evangelion)

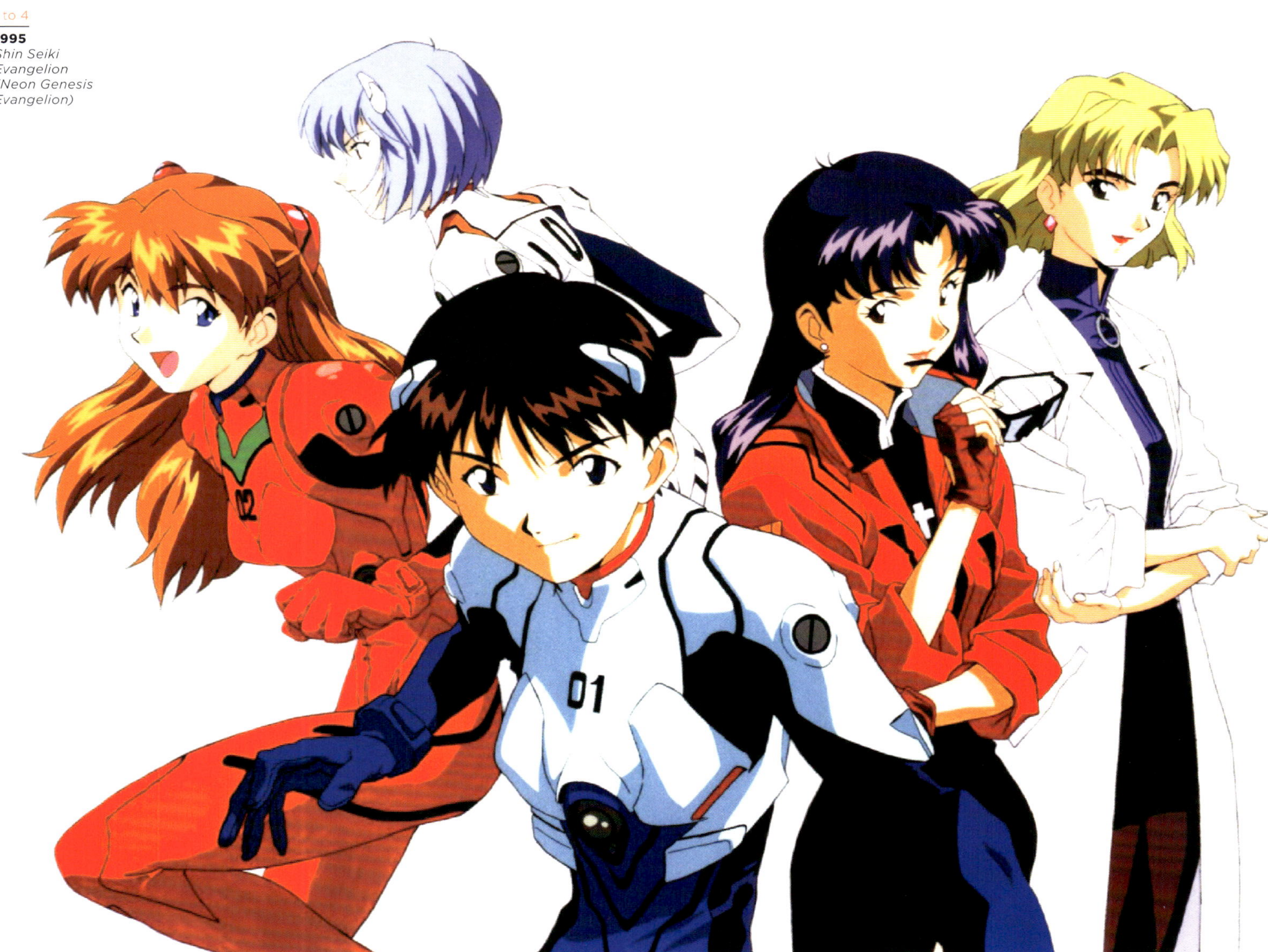

1

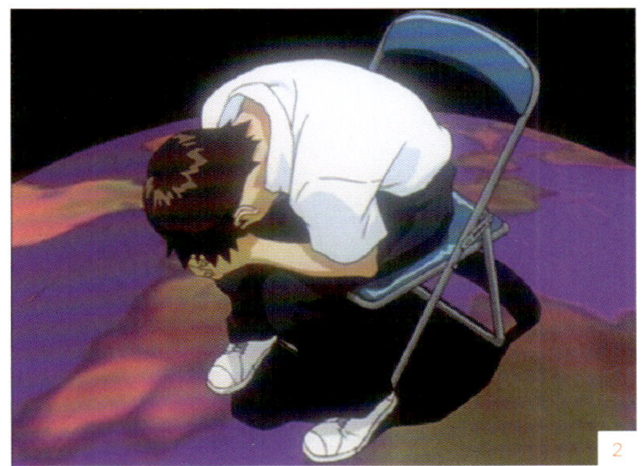

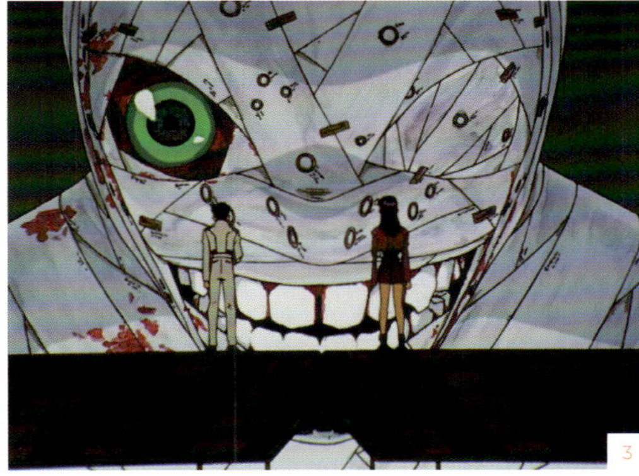

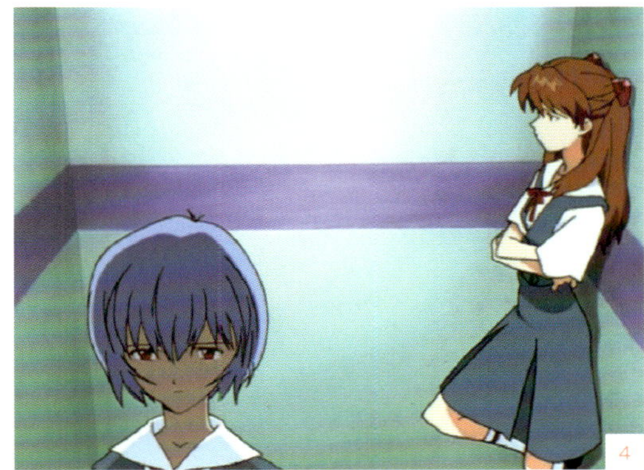

subway sarin attack on March 20, 1995 (12 dead; 50 seriously injured; 5,000 minorly wounded), which *Evangelion* indirectly mirrored.

From episode 16 onward, the series moved away from its main plot and went where no TV production had dared go before. Episodes 18 and 19 were out of control, with the EVA-01 tearing through its opponents (including another robot piloted by a human) like a wild beast in sequences of graphic violence never before seen on the small screen. In episode 20, although out of frame, an explicit sex scene aired nationwide. It was no longer a question of stimulating audiences like Go Nagai but of developing characters' psychology in a quasi-Freudian way. And shredding the typical narrative codes—when episode 21 played with temporality so that the viewer deduces the crucial twist without ever seeing it, the next episode features a still, silent shot lasting 53 seconds (4 percent of the episode) of two motionless characters in an elevator. It was also about transforming the calamitous constraints of the end of production into an artistic process.

Gainax came close to its breaking point as the final episodes approached, running out of time, money, and energy. Anno personally handled the scripts for the last two episodes, directed by his longtime partner and right-hand man, Kazuya Tsurumaki. Blending abstract animation, still shots, and other experiments, episodes 25 and 26 conclude Shinji's introspective journey as he finally decides to leave his protective, comfortable bubble to face the challenges of real life. It's a thinly disguised message to otaku, who are encouraged to abandon the virtual shelter of their fictional worlds and live life to the fullest.

This unprecedented ending provoked an outcry among fans, who could not accept that this life lesson should take precedence over an entire imaginary mythology that they had dissected in minute detail. Anonymous death threats piled up in Anno's mailbox, and he immediately fell back into depression for six months, before tackling two feature films that would definitively complete the plot of the series. By the time they were released in 1997, the franchise had grossed more than ¥30 billion ($260 million) between VHS sales and merchandising. But more than that, it has become a social phenomenon in Japan, forever transforming its animation industry.

1995
Shin Seiki Evangelion
(Neon Genesis Evangelion)

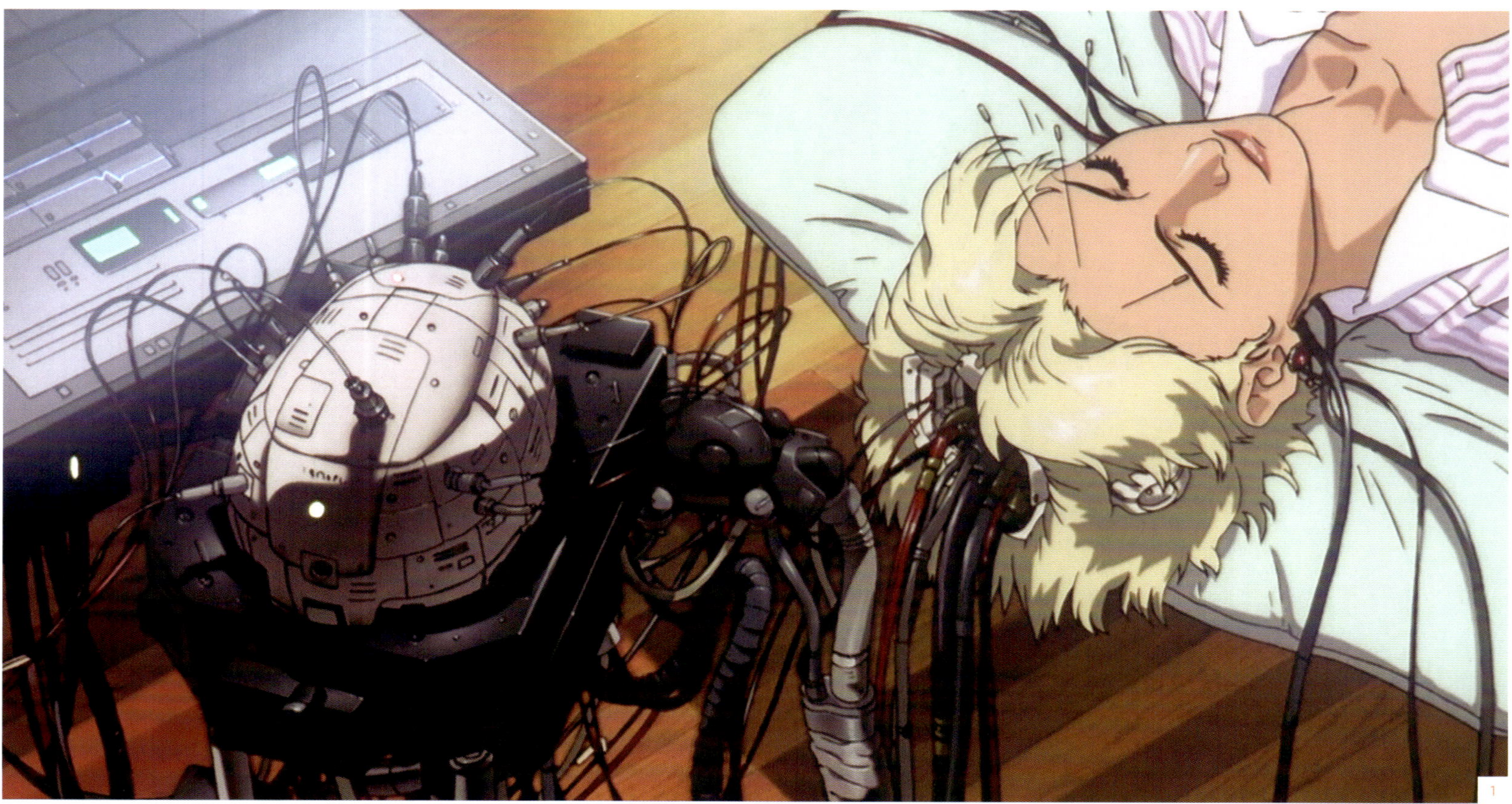

1

1 to 3

1995
Kōkaku Kidōtai (Ghost in the Shell)

GHOST IN THE SHELL: ENTERING THE FUTURE

In the early 1980s, an office worker drew panels of his amateur comic strip every night. *Black Magic* appeared in the pages of the fanzine *Atlas* and caught the eye of the head of Seishinsha publishing company, who professionally launched Masamune Shirow (a pseudonym so as not to be recognized by his superiors) with *Appleseed* in 1985. Four years later, *Kōkaku Kidōtai* (*Ghost in the Shell*) was a manga that differed from the usual output by including explanatory notes and focusing on various technological advances. With electronics, quantum mechanics, weaponry, nanotechnologies, and computer networks, the fusion of the human body with cybernetic implants is central to the story. Is there still a soul when the body is no more than a high-tech shell? The question haunts Major Motoko Kusanagi, leader of Public Security Section 9, a government brigade tracking the cyberterrorist "Puppet Master" in New Port City, the new cyberpunk capital of Japan in 2029. The existential question was a godsend for Mamoru Oshii, who had already turned the humorous *Urusei Yatsura* series into the otherworldly film *Beautiful Dreamer*, the second in the series.

After the 1993 feature *Patlabor 2*, a politically themed film that was a veiled reflection on Japan's faltering position on the world stage, the director began production of *Ghost in the Shell*, a film synthesizing the past decade. The project broke new ground right from the outset when the British company Manga Entertainment took on 30 percent of the budget—an unprecedented international coproduction! From a technical point of view, the leap forward was even greater.

The possibilities provided by computer and digital tools were maximized on *Ghost in the Shell*. Characters and backgrounds were scanned separately before being integrated using appropriate software, and this new stage, compositing, would soon be indispensable in every production. Each frame of the film was digital, allowing Oshii to experiment with nonlinear editing on an AVID system, which was all the rage in Hollywood. This evolution is reminiscent of the transition from cassette to CD—you no longer needed to scroll through the entire film to get to a specific scene; now you could get there instantly. The iconic opening scene, in which Motoko Kusanagi free-falls from the top of a building and literally blends into the background using an optical camouflage suit, was a technical masterpiece. The film sent a shock wave through the anime industry, which was finally discovering the potential of computer technology. Its lag in the field was glaringly obvious, especially as the day after the release of *Ghost in the Shell* in Japan on November 18, 1995, Pixar Animation Studios released *Toy Story*, the first entirely computer-animated feature film in history.

Buoyed by Kenji Kawai's atmospheric score, the cybernetically modified heroine's introspections echoed the ultramodern loneliness of the Japanese in a country in crisis, and yet *Ghost in the Shell* was only moderately successful at the box office. It was saved by its international success, opening in the United Kingdom a few days after its Japanese release (December 8, 1995) and a year later in France (January 29, 1997). The rest of the world would be content with the VHS released by Manga Video, which sold more than a million copies, and festivals where *Ghost in the Shell* was screened. The film brought critics to their knees, stunned by this mature work light-years beyond disparaged titles like *Dragon Ball*. Oshii's feature film ushered in a new era for Japanese animated cinema, now fully appreciated on the international stage. He was a trailblazer once again, setting the standard for alternatives to Studio Ghibli's productions, which were becoming the new norm.

A harbinger of the digital technologies still in use twenty years later, *Ghost in the Shell* also foretold of the upheaval whose beginnings were already being felt. This global revolution, which would change consumer habits forever, would accelerate the phenomena that began in the first half of the 1990s at the turn of the new millennium. The closing line of the film sums up this shift: "The net is vast and infinite."

1995
Kōkaku Kidōtai
(Ghost in the Shell)

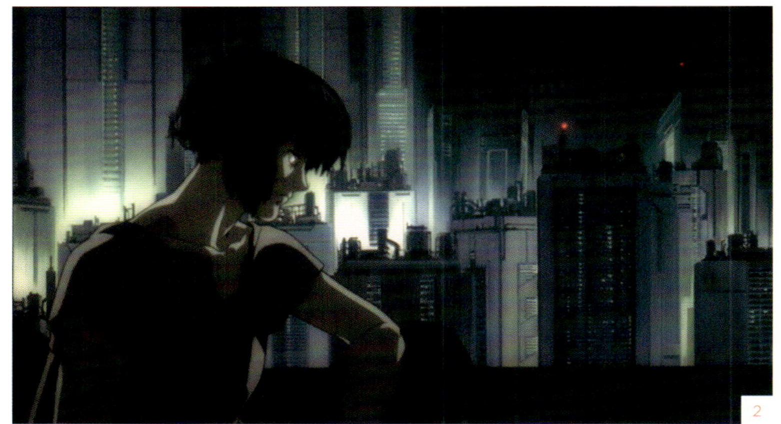
2

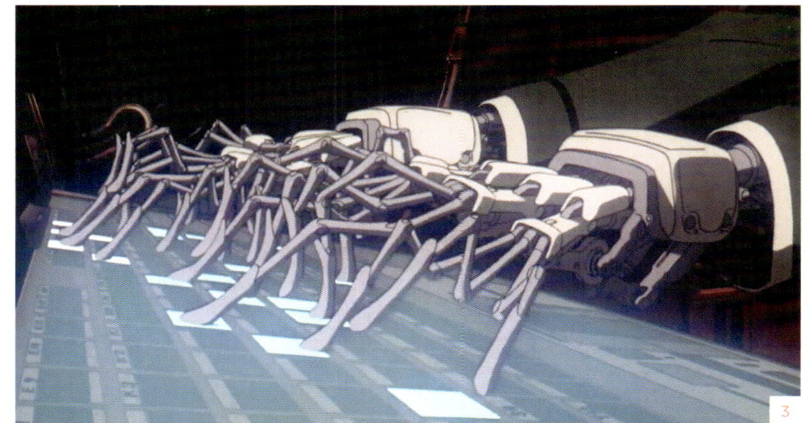
3

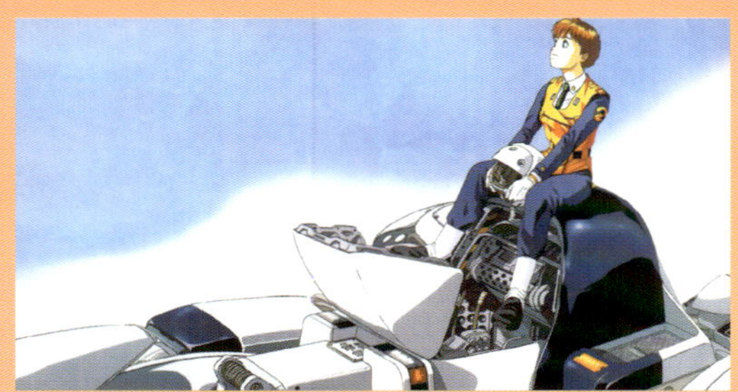

KIDŌ KEISATSU

Patlabor
Year: 1988
Category: TV, OAV, film
Directors: Mamoru Oshii (film and OAV) and Naoyuki Ishinaga (TV)
Animation Studio: Studio Deen

AT A GLANCE:
The brainchild of a team of fans, this series was designed to be run simultaneously over several different media, taking full advantage of their specificities. It was the dawn of media mix.

YOU MAY ALSO LIKE . . .
Dominion Tank Police, in which mecha are an integral part of everyday life. *Roujin Z*, an ironic fable about robotic hospital beds and geriatric patients. *Jin-Roh* if you prefer films with a darker tone.

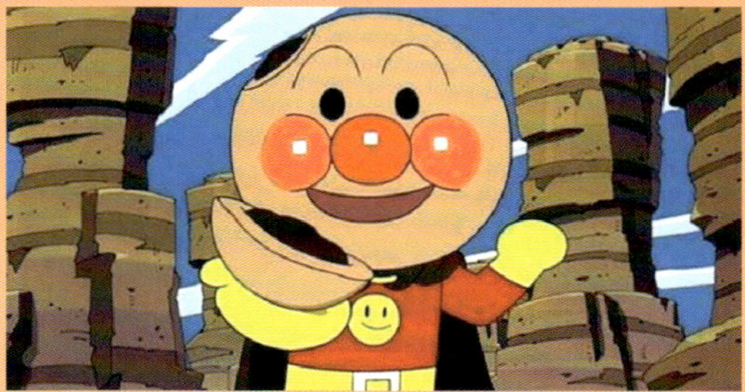

SORE IKE! ANPANMAN

Let's Go! Anpanman
Year: 1988
Category: TV, film
Director: Akinori Nagaoka **Animation Studio:** TMS

AT A GLANCE:
Japanese animation had long been aimed at children, and *Anpanman* targeted preschoolers for the first time, now an essential part of the viewership.

YOU MAY ALSO LIKE . . .
The adorable *Moomin* from Finnish children's literature. The great adventures of *Hamtaro*'s hamsters. *Pom Poko* and its magical forest creatures.

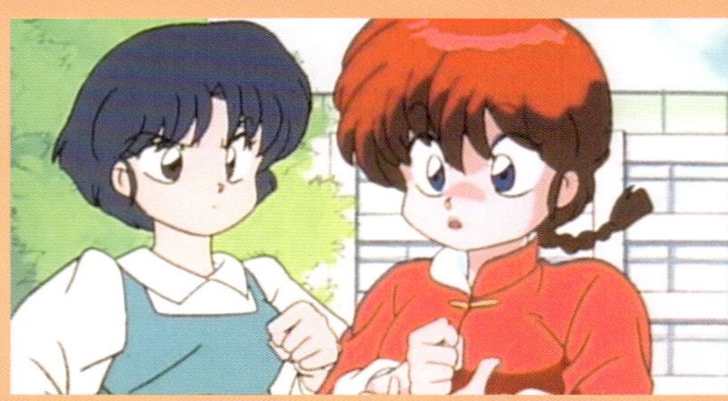

RANMA ½

Ranma ½
Year: 1989
Category: TV, OAV, film
Directors: Tomomi Mochizuki, Tsutomu Shibayama, Kōji Sawai, and Junji Nishimura
Animation Studios: Kitty Films and Studio Deen

AT A GLANCE:
The creator of *Urusei Yatsura* combined comedy, martial arts, romance, adventure, and a slice-of-life story into one! From this point on, it was difficult to limit stories to just one genre.

YOU MAY ALSO LIKE . . .
Fruits Basket, whose heroes also transform into animals. *Inuyasha*, a series for boys led by a heroine protagonist, another creation by Rumiko Takahashi.

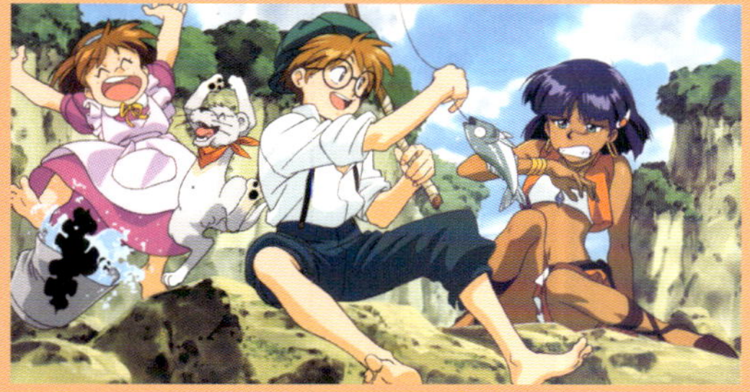

FUSHIGI NO UMI NO NADIA

Nadia: The Secret of Blue Water
Year: 1990
Category: TV
Directors: Hideaki Anno and Shinji Higuchi
Animation Studio: Gainax

AT A GLANCE:
With the support of Miyazaki, who contributed to the script, the members of Gainax, who started out as amateurs in a garage, made a name for themselves with this series.

YOU MAY ALSO LIKE . . .
The Mysterious Cities of Gold, where science fiction meets mythology. *Now and Then, Here and There* for its uncompromising plot development.

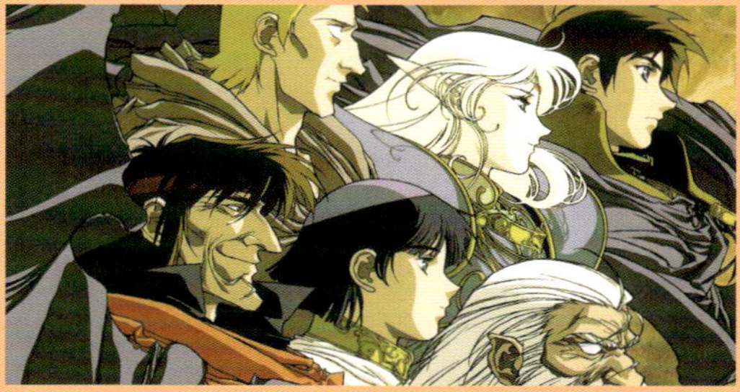

LODOSS TŌ SENKI

Record of Lodoss War
Year: 1990
Category: OAV
Director: Akinori Nagaoka
Animation Studio: Madhouse

AT A GLANCE:
After hitting video games, the wave of fantasy reached the shores of anime. This pioneering OAV series paved the way for a genre that is now an industry star.

YOU MAY ALSO LIKE . . .
Slayers, a combination of medieval fantasy, action, and comedy available across all media. *The Heroic Legend of Arslan*, another epic and mythical OAV. *Berserk*, which plunges viewers into a dark fantasy to la *Conan the Barbarian.*

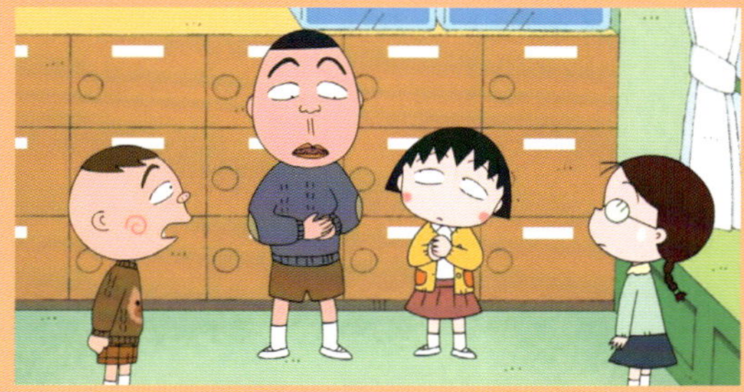

CHIBI MARUKO-CHAN

Chibi Maruko-chan
Year: 1990
Category: TV, film
Directors: Yumiko Suda and Tsutomu Shibayama
Animation Studio: Nippon Animation

AT A GLANCE:
A naive retelling of the 1970s through the eyes of children, the series strengthens the bonds between family members.

YOU MAY ALSO LIKE . . .
Crayon Shin-chan, the story of a mischievous little rascal. *Chie the Brat*, a *War of the Buttons* in the streets of Osaka.

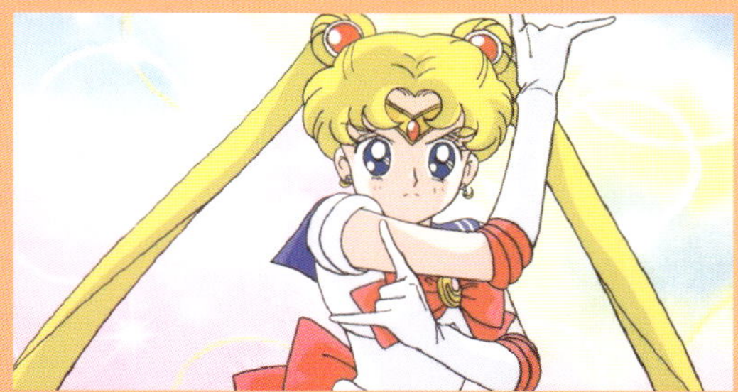

BISHŌJO SENSHI SAILOR MOON

Sailor Moon

Year: 1992
Category: TV, film
Directors: Junichi Satō, Kunihiko Ikuhara, and Takuya Igarashi
Animation Studio: Toei Animation

AT A GLANCE:
For the first time, it's a woman battling the threats against humanity! *Sailor Moon* paved the way for fighting heroines, who no longer needed to envy male heroes.

YOU MAY ALSO LIKE . . .
Wedding Peach, which swaps school uniforms for wedding dresses. The ambiguous relationships throughout *Revolutionary Girl Utena*.

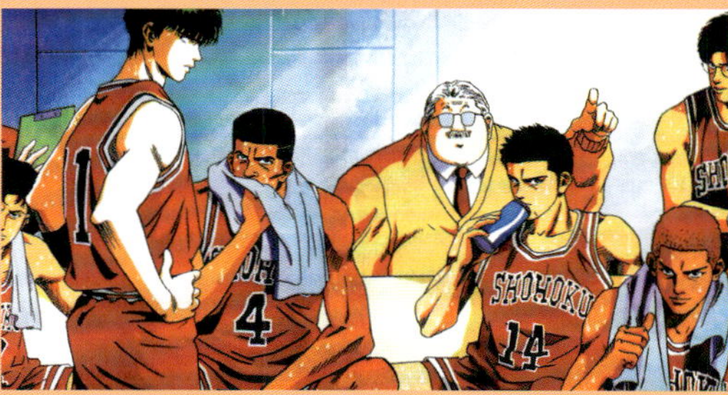

SLAM DUNK

Slam Dunk

Year: 1993
Category: TV, film
Director: Nobutaka Nishizawa
Animation Studio: Toei Animation

AT A GLANCE:
This series is a classic sports anime but also takes time off the court to develop the heroes' personalities. Athletes are finally shown as regular people!

YOU MAY ALSO LIKE . . .
The superhuman performance of the soccer players in *Captain Tsubasa*. The hero's challenge in *Kuroko's Basketball*.

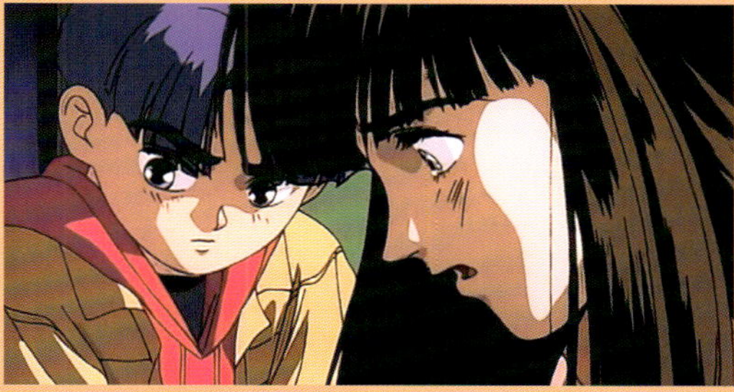

BOKU NO CHIKYŪ WO MAMOTTE

Please Save My Earth

Year: 1993
Category: OAV
Director: Kazuo Yamazaki
Animation Studio: Production I.G

AT A GLANCE:
This story is aimed at young female twenty-somethings. The OAV introduces composer Yoko Kanno, foreshadowing the musical trend of the coming century.

YOU MAY ALSO LIKE . . .
Love thwarted by destiny against an apocalyptic backdrop in *X*. The future of a parallel world in the hands of schoolgirls who teleported there in *Fushigi Yuugi*.

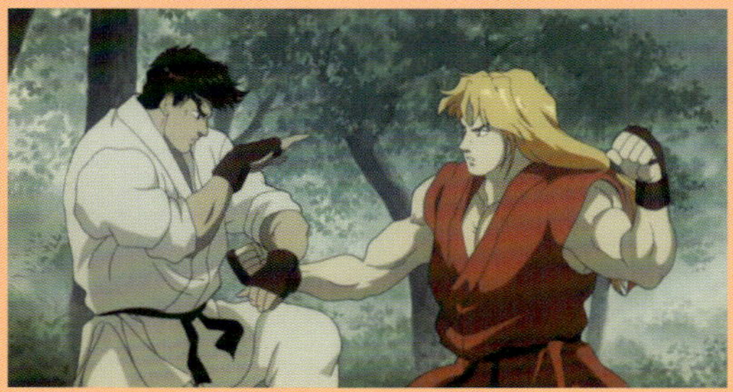

STREET FIGHTER II V

Street Fighter II V

Year: 1994
Category: Film
Director: Gisaburō Sugii
Animation Studio: Group TAC

AT A GLANCE:
The links between anime and video games, an emerging medium, are instantaneous, and the media-mix strategy expands to conquer the world with the most popular titles.

YOU MAY ALSO LIKE . . .
Virtua Fighter and *King of Fighters*, also adapted from combat games. *Dragon Quest: The Adventures of Dai*, based on the best-selling *Dragon Quest* RPG. The *Final Fantasy* OAV, an original adventure from the famous franchise.

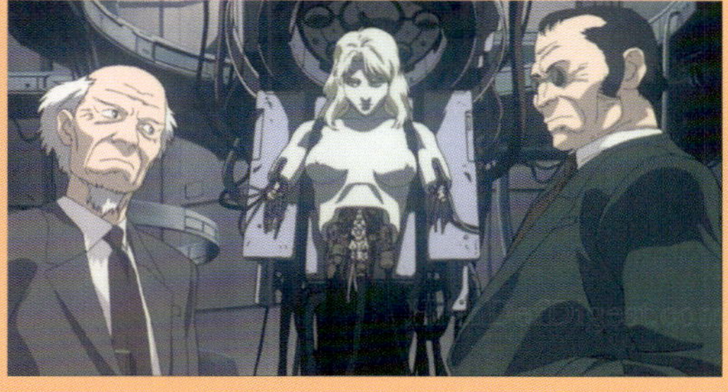

KŌKAKU KIDŌTAI

Ghost in the Shell

Year: 1995
Category: Film
Director: Mamoru Oshii
Animation Studio: Production I.G

AT A GLANCE:
Anime goes international! Thanks to foreign investors, animators adopted the computer and digital tools already popular in the West for this film.

YOU MAY ALSO LIKE . . .
Serial Experiments Lain and its anticipatory questioning of the impact of the internet. *The Animatrix*, a US-Japan cultural bridge built on cyberpunk.

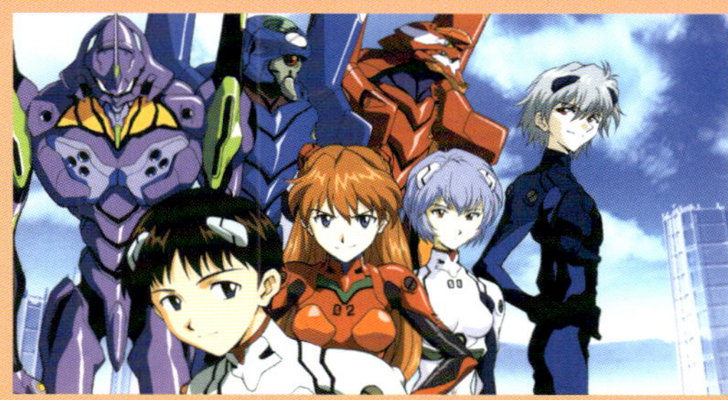

SHIN SEIKI EVANGELION

Neon Genesis Evangelion

Year: 1995
Category: TV
Director: Hideaki Anno
Animation Studio: Gainax

AT A GLANCE:
Combining psychoanalysis and giant robots, the series that shook up actors and anime fans alike is still a lasting social phenomenon thirty years later.

YOU MAY ALSO LIKE . . .
Space Runaway Ideon and *Hades Project Zeorymer*, the referential basis of *Evangelion*. *RahXephon*, an introspective quest amid an alien invasion. *Bokurano*, in which children must pilot a giant robot.

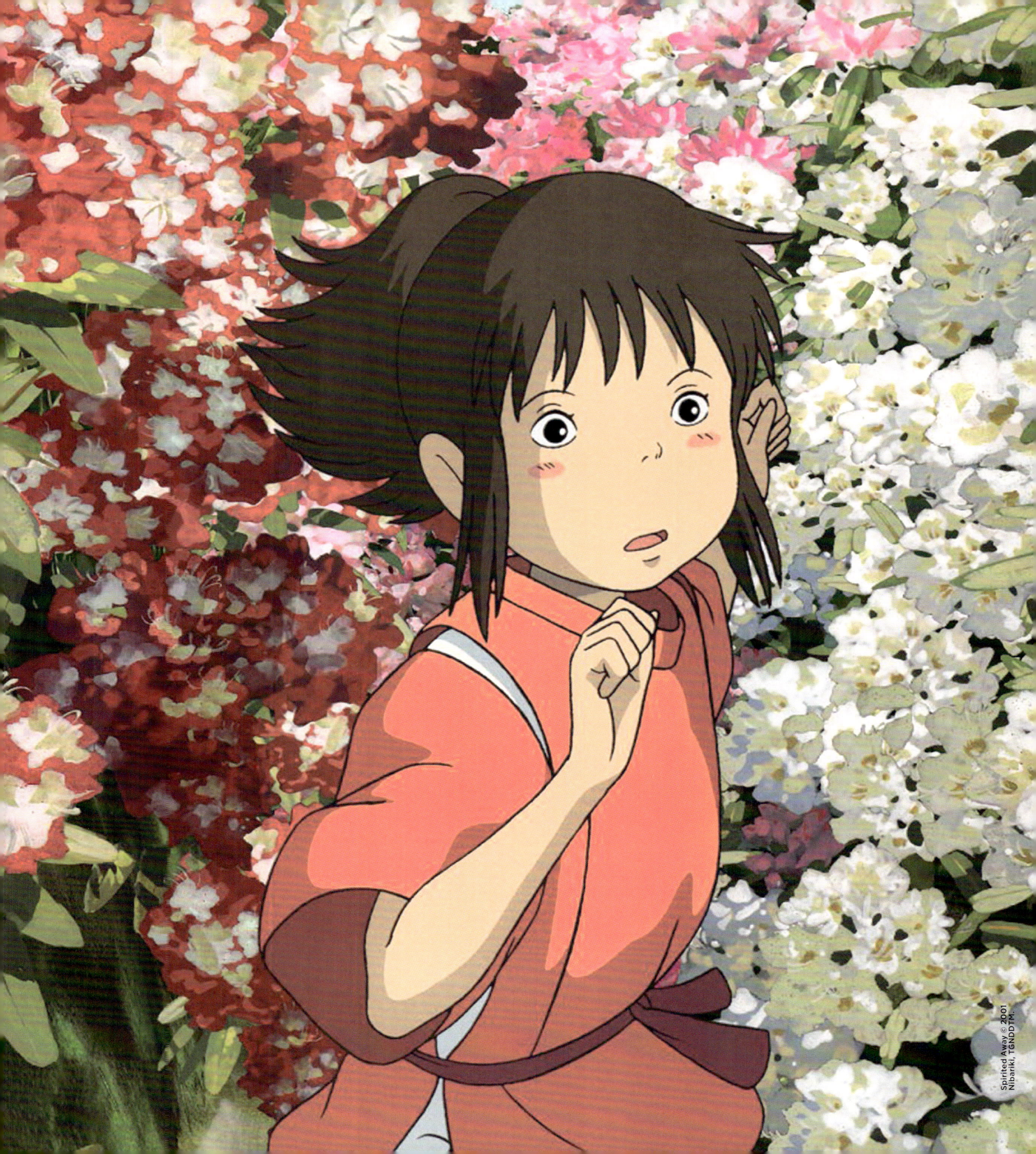

1996 TO 2017

THE DIGITAL ERA

Delusions of grandeur

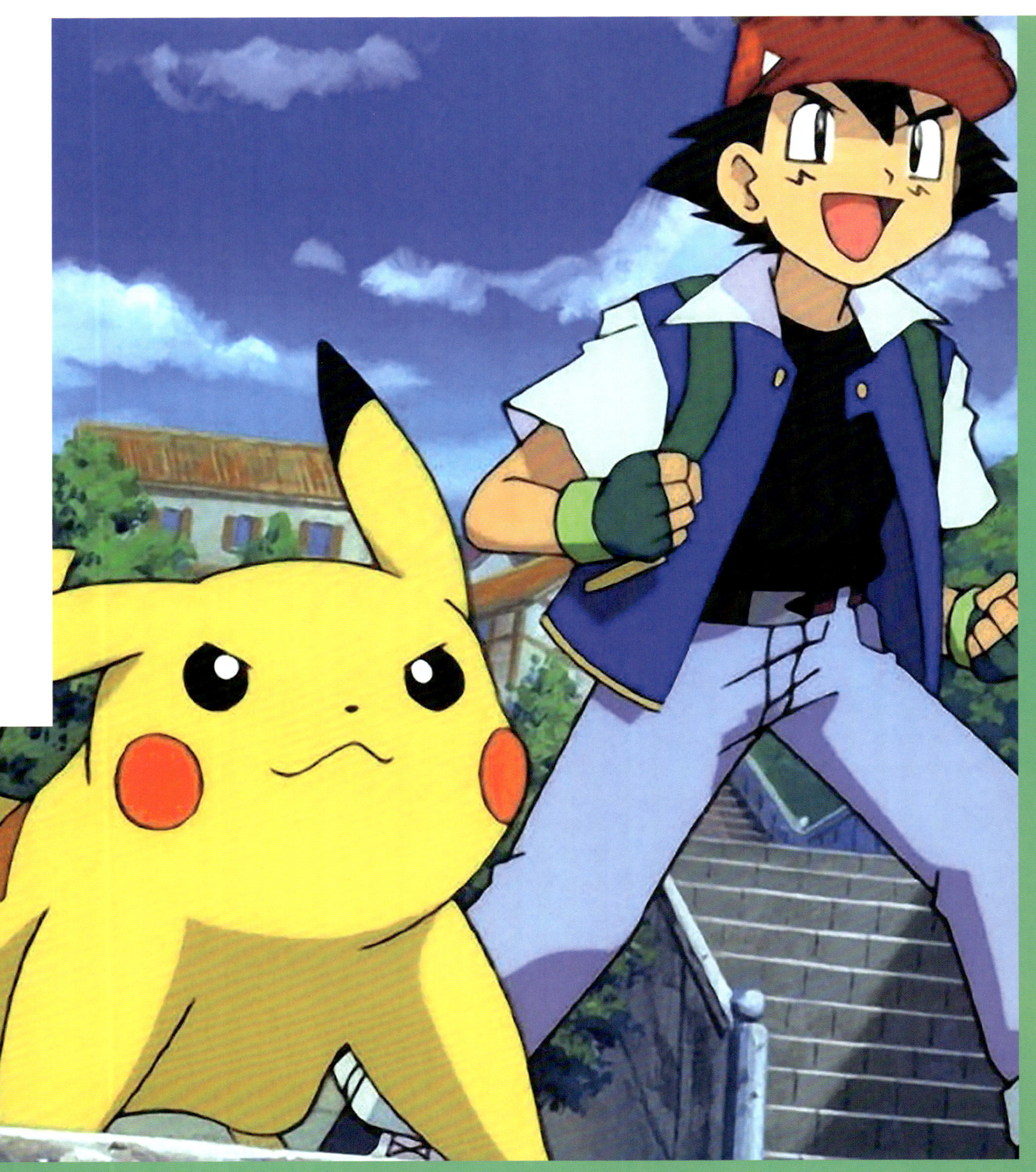

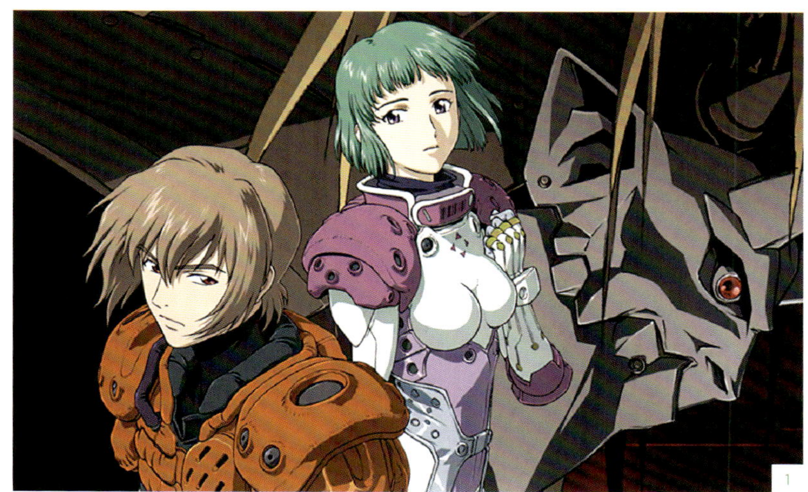

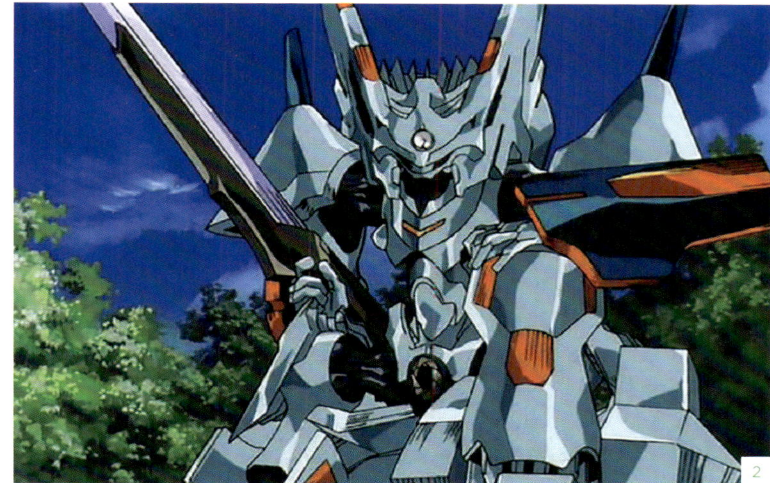

1
1998
Gasaraki

2
1998
Brain Powerd

2002
RahXephon

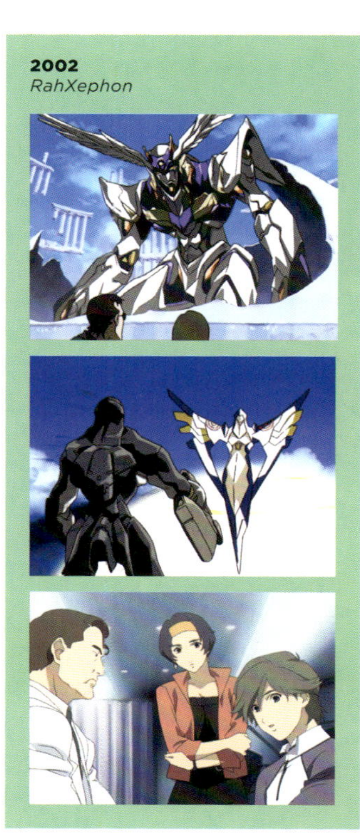

Artistic freedom

THE ERA OF ORIGINAL CREATION

Like *Space Battleship Yamato* and *Mobile Suit Gundam* in the late 1970s, *Neon Genesis Evangelion* became a pivotal work in the anime industry. With its pervasive references to audiovisual culture and emphasis on mysticism and the psyche of its heroes, the series became sacred to otaku and was embraced by a wider audience, who saw it as a gateway to anime. From then on, mecha studios followed the *Evangelion* phenomenon, which never ceased to fascinate viewers and creators alike, starting with its labyrinthine storyline punctuated by religious symbolism and tortured relationships.

The similarities between *Evangelion* and the 2002 series *RahXephon* are clear, although the newer series boasts superior technical quality and cleverly trades Hebraic references for Mayan legends. Sunrise also followed the trend, as the mecha expert's *Gundam* series was no longer as successful as it once was, despite having reinvented itself with each new production. Even the studio's longtime directors, Ryōsuke Takahashi and Yoshiyuki Tomino, were working on the mysterious *Gasaraki* and *Brain Powerd* series, respectively.

By revisiting creationism, evolution, mythology, and existentialism, new productions demonstrated that investors were no longer shy about capitalizing on original, complex works, even those meant for television broadcast. In addition, standardizing short seasons into thirteen and twenty-six episodes was highly profitable—it greatly limited financial risk, while encouraging a second lease on life on video, an ever-booming market. Fans were now buying entire series on a few VHS tapes. The concept of "the entire collection" went hand in hand with new production habits, where scheduling encouraged increasing the power of chief directors, who oversaw their entire series with teams of directors and scriptwriters. As

2003
Texhnolyze

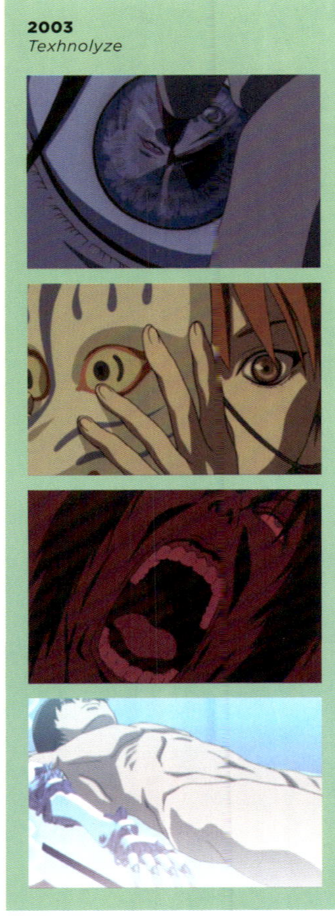

a result, a large proportion of TV production was moving away from shows designed to be stretched as far as possible and toward an artistic freedom that had previously been largely confined to OAVs and film.

Shinichirō Watanabe's *Cowboy Bebop* (1998) is a perfect example of the wave of original series now flooding the market. To finance the space opera project, Bandai had a single requirement—an omnipresent spaceship—in order to sell toys. From then on, Watanabe was given carte blanche to produce his series depicting the adventures of the Bebop spaceship's ragtag crew, made up of temperamental bounty hunters. *Cowboy Bebop* is a cultural landmark that draws its essence from cinematic and musical references. Westerns, comedies, and film noir give each episode its own identity, backed by a diverse soundtrack ranging from jazz to heavy metal by composer Yoko Kanno (*Please Save My Earth*). *Cowboy Bebop*'s animation is far superior to the usual standards, and its cast includes some of the most famous *seiyū* of the time, such as Koichi Yamadera (the voice actor for many American actors, including Brad Pitt and Jim Carrey) and Megumi Hayashibara. It was a hit with audiences and critics alike! The show quickly became an international sensation, contributing to the new image of mature, sophisticated anime. Many ambitious series followed, with conceptual storylines and distinct graphic worlds, including *Argento Soma* (2000), *Heat Guy J* (2002), *Serial Experiments Lain* (2003), and *Witch Hunter Robin* (2002). Artistic integrity began to take precedence over the commercial aspect, as illustrated by the newly established Manglobe studio with *Samurai Champloo* (2004), Watanabe's latest series blending *chanbara* (sword fight films) and hip-hop.

Since the release of *Evangelion*, anime had been delving further and further into complex subjects, such as the intricacies of quantum physics in *Noein* (2005). With the surge of original titles, the animation market had established itself as a mature player in audiovisual entertainment, and television now supported auteur-style films, which straddled the line between meta-artistic and experimental. Two such examples are Ryūtarō Nakamura's cyberpunk series *Serial Experiments Lain*, depicting a teenager's hypnotic and disturbing plunge into the anguishing virtual realm of the Wired, and *Texhnolyze*, in which Madhouse developed a tortured story of homosexuality, sadomasochism, pedophilia, and visceral violence.

UPDATING NOSTALGIC CHARACTERS

Although mainly broadcast at night, the presence of these original series on the airwaves proved that consumer habits had definitely changed. High-tech themes, which were only found in OAVs or films just a decade earlier, were now becoming commonplace in TV production, to the extent that old series were being revived and transformed. The AIC animation studio took advantage of the rise in cyberpunk and heroic fantasy to update *Lodoss* and *Bubblegum Crisis* in mainstream series.

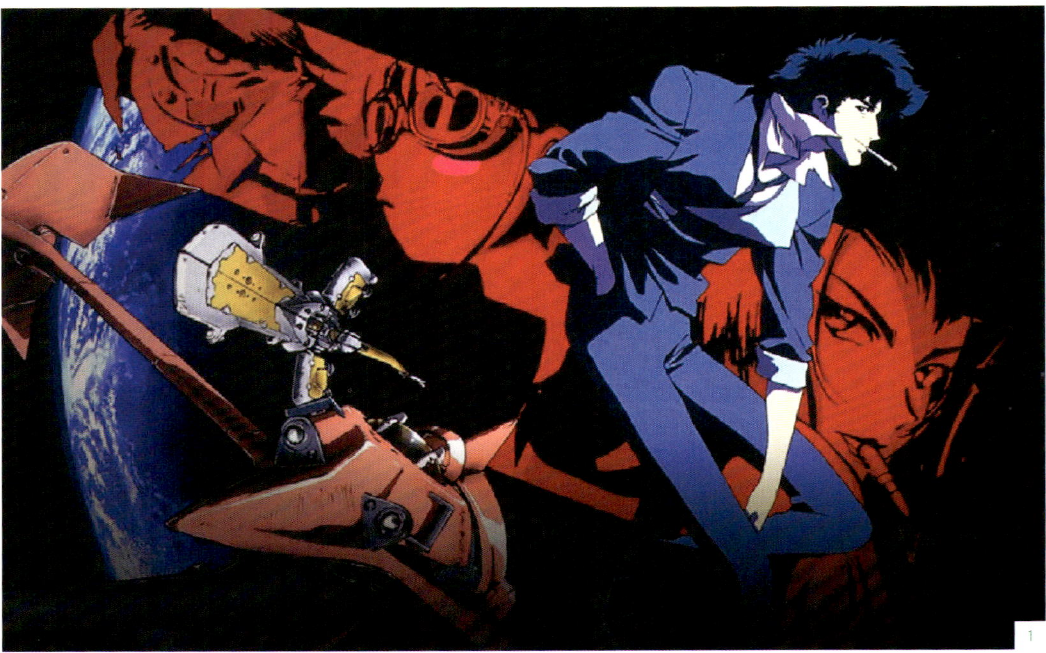

1
1998
Cowboy Bebop

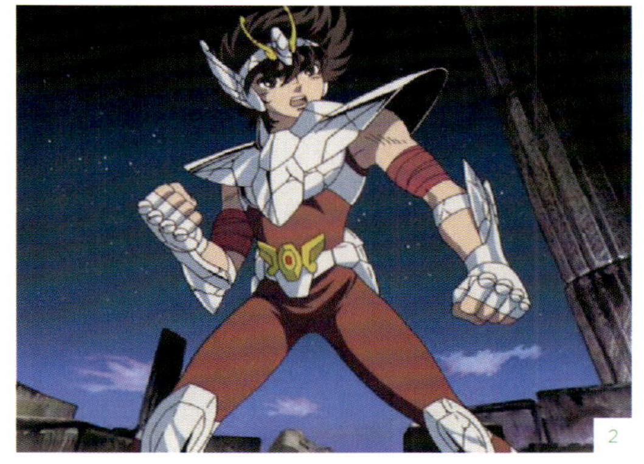

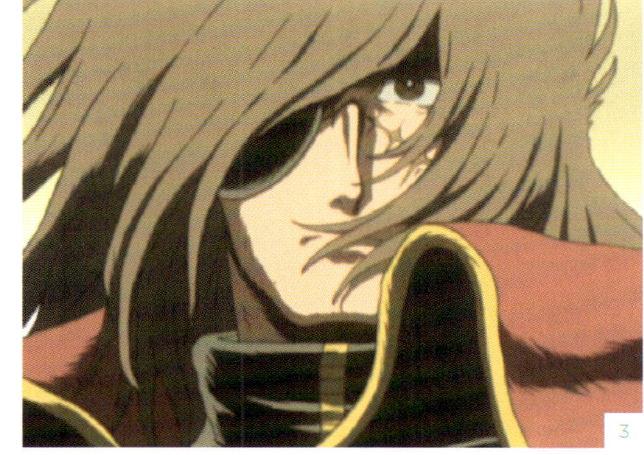

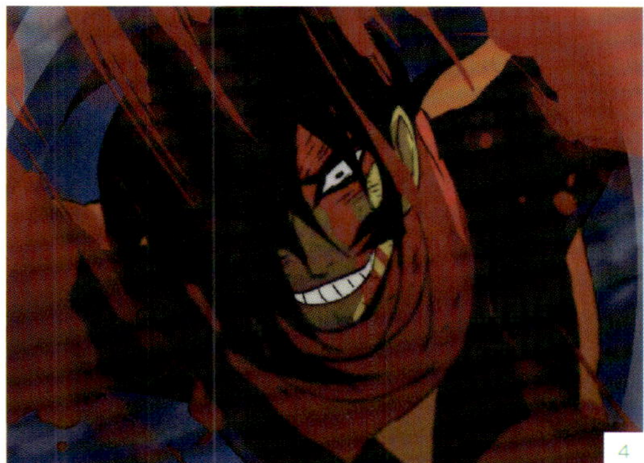

2
2002
Saint Seiya: Meiō ādesu Jyūnikyū Hen (Saint Seiya: The Hades Chapter)

3
2004
Space Pirate Captain Herlock: Endless Odyssey

4
2004
New Getter Robo

Studios were realizing that nostalgia was a financial opportunity not to be underestimated. As a result, internationally renowned *mangaka* were making a comeback. Between 1996 and 2004, no fewer than thirteen adaptations of Leiji Matsumoto's work were produced as series, OAVs, or films. The "Leijiverse" was back in vogue, thanks to popular figures such as Maetel, Queen Emeraldas, and especially Captain Harlock. Moreover, when Madhouse produced *Space Pirate Captain Herlock: The Endless Odyssey* (2002) as a tribute to the original 1978 anime, Rintaro returned to directing, catering to a growing fandom. Go Nagai was also making a big comeback, since his company, Dynamic Planning, had teamed up with Bandai to produce series that were more in keeping with his creations. The *Mazinkaiser* OAVs (2001) and the *New Getter Robo* series (in collaboration with author Ken Ishikawa) emerged as highly energetic apocalyptic reboots, whose relentless heroes revel in the violence they engender. *Devilman Lady* (1998) brought back the gigantic scale of the 1973 series, but more than anything, it reintroduced the tortured setting of the first manga that had previously been toned down.

Like Go Nagai, Tetsuo Hara reclaimed the broadcasting rights to his work and created the studio North Star Pictures in 2004. *Fist of the North Star* returned to cinemas in 2006, followed by several movies, OAVs, and series. As for Toei Animation, it revitalized the *Saint Seiya* franchise in 2002 by adapting the final part of Masami Kurumada's manga into an OAV. And now that the children of yesteryear had grown up, Bandai created a targeted toy collection just for them: Myth Cloth. It was a complete success! The resounding return of old favorites wasn't intended only to strike a chord with nostalgic fans but also to reach out to younger audiences so that they could make the popular icons their own. There's no way any generation could miss *Astro Boy*, *Cyborg 009*, and *Tetsujin 28*, which regularly return with new, more modern series!

INVISIBLE BARRIERS

In the throes of change since the *Evangelion* shock, the Japanese audiovisual landscape also had to grapple with the legacy of *Sailor Moon*. Female audiences were no longer satisfied with the perfect heroines of the past and were demanding deeper storylines. The heroines in *Ojamajo Doremi* (*Magical DoReMi*, 1999) faced moral dilemmas (Should they keep their powers for the common good or sacrifice them to save their friend?), reinvigorating the magical girls genre for 200 episodes. In 2000, *Kodomo no Omocha* (*Kodocha*) tackled both the cruelty of show business and child abandonment with a rawness that contrasted with the sentimentality in *Love Me, My Knight*.

As teenage girls demanded series in touch with their generation, studios responded by taking fantasy by storm. The first attempt was the hit series *Fushigi Yuugi* in 1995, which teleported two schoolgirls into a world reminiscent of feudal China over fifty-two episodes, then extended by two OAV series. In 1996, Sunrise followed suit with Shōji Kawamori's original series *Tenkū no Escaflowne* (*The Vision of Escaflowne*), depicting the adventures of Hitomi, a high school girl thrown into a medieval world at war, where knights battle with the help of giant robots. Although *Escaflowne* is *shōjo*, Kawamori used the *Macross* formula (love triangles, war, mecha, and more), which in no way bothered viewers who identified with the heroine. Like *Fushigi Yuugi*'s Miaka, and later Yoko in *Jūni Kokuki* (*The Twelve Kingdoms*, 2002), Hitomi is tormented by real-life worries, and the journey into a fantasy world becomes an escape from social pressure.

1998
Kareshi Kanojo no Jijō
(His and Her Circumstances)

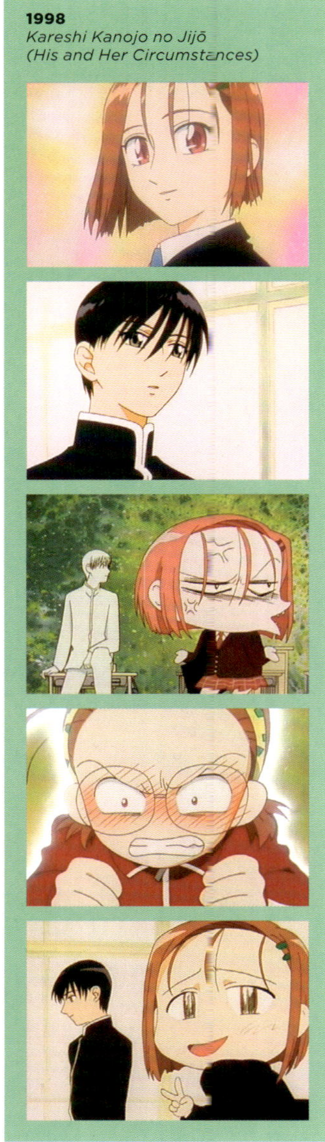

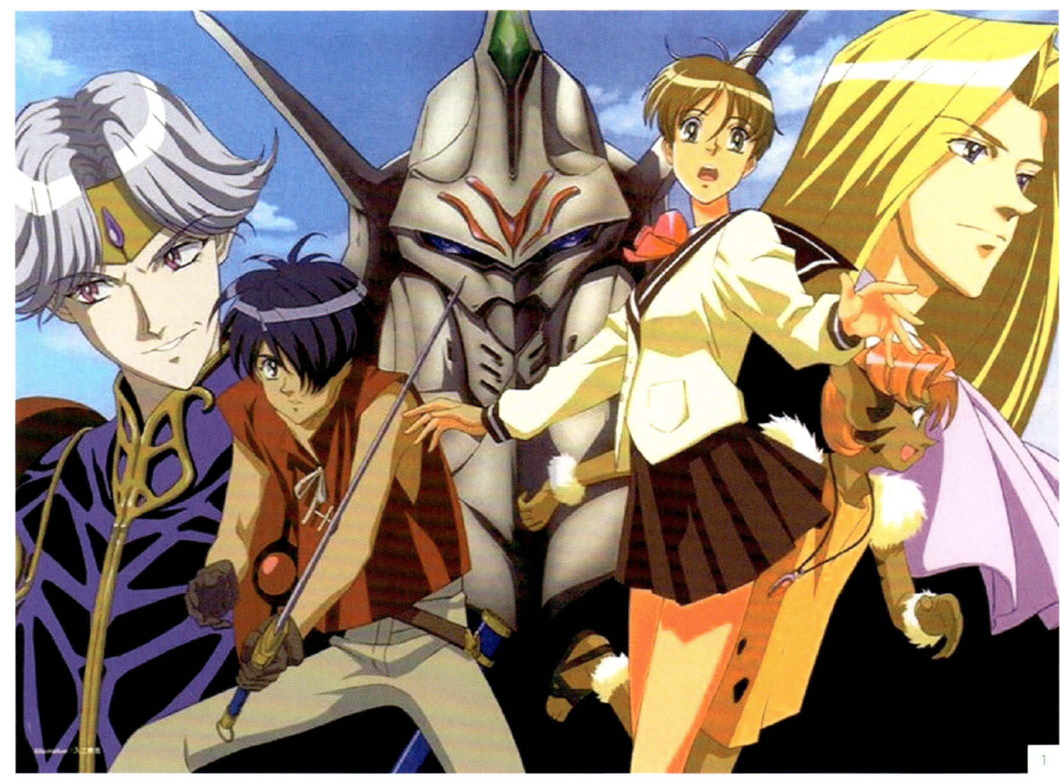

1
1996
Tenkū no Escaflowne (The Vision of Escaflowne)

At the request of composer Yoko Kanno, Hitomi's voice actor also sang the *Escaflowne* theme song. Maaya Sakamoto, a young high school student, thus embarked on her dual career path and would represent the impact of the female audience that emerged at the end of the century in the decades to come. Sakamoto couldn't have asked for a better mentor! Like Kenji Kawai (*Ghost in the Shell*) and Shirō Sagisu (*Evangelion*), Kanno became such a star that studios could use her name to finance their work. Victor Entertainment was rubbing its hands with glee over the huge success of the soundtracks for *Macross Plus*, *Cowboy Bebop*, and *Turn A Gundam*.

Just as the creator of *Macross* had done, *Evangelion*'s creator broke free of the limits defining *shōjo* and *shōnen* with the 1998 production of *Kareshi Kanojo no Jijō* (*His and Her Circumstances*), an over-the-top romantic comedy that allowed Hideaki Anno to play on the historical specificities of the medium with cartoon-style jokes and explanations. The two types of media became more fluid as women created manga for boys, such as *Fullmetal Alchemist* by Hiromu Arakawa. The Bones studio took some liberties with the manga but was quickly redeemed by its 2003 animated adaptation, which departed from the original plot with an alternative ending. The Elric brothers, battling to find their bodies using alchemy, now brought boys and girls together at the same time for the same show.

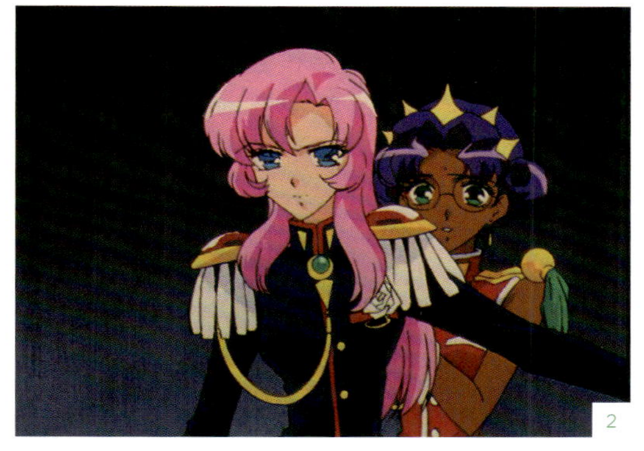

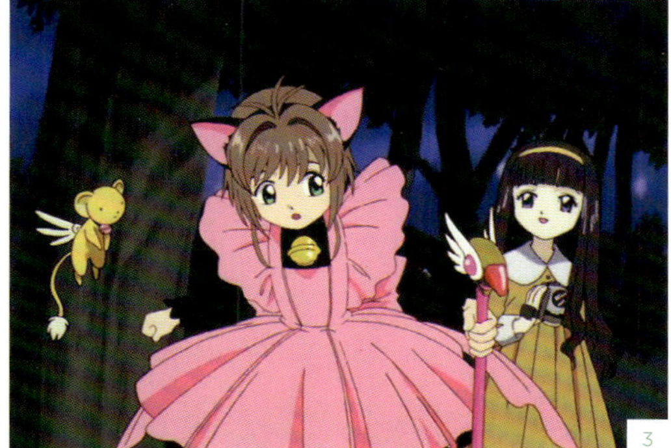

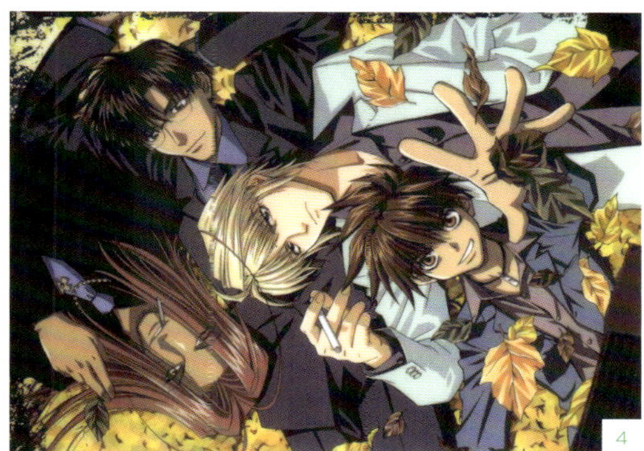

2
1997
Shōjo Kakumei Utena *(Revolutionary Girl Utena)*

3
1998
Cardcaptor Sakura

4
2000
Saiyuki

OTOME ROAD OTAKU

By popularizing the sexual ambiguity that had previously been confined to a small circle of fans, *Sailor Moon* ushered in a profound transformation in the female anime market. The series was a natural fit for the *shōnen-ai* that emerged in the 1980s, featuring topics like lesbian romance and cross-dressing. When the genre became more explicit, it was designated as *yaoi* and depicted romantic and erotic relationships between its male characters. In Comiket's self-published *dōjinshi* material, the confrontations between *Saint Seiya*'s androgynous characters became intimate, instead of portraying the violence of the original series.

The director of *Sailor Moon*, Kunihiko Ikuhara, left Toei Animation for J.C. Staff, where he could push these ambiguous relationships even further in his next series, *Shōjo Kakumei Utena* (*Revolutionary Girl Utena*). Based on the manga by Chiho Saito, the anime tells the story of Utena, a high school girl dressed as a boy and dreaming of becoming a prince, who takes on the school's Student Council in a duel. What's at stake? Anthy, a classmate who would give the winner the "power to revolutionize the world."

Like *Princess Knight* and *The Rose of Versailles* series, *Revolutionary Girl Utena* embraced cross-dressing to challenge machismo and homophobia. The series oscillates between comedy and drama while developing undefined relationships between heroines, echoing Osamu Dezaki's adaptation of Riyoko Ikeda's manga *Oniisama e...* (*Dear Brother*, 1991). The elite, whether they be academic or social, led to the creation of unhealthy powers of influence. A shock of script and style, the series was a resounding success with teenage girls, who in turn formed an otaku culture designed for them. For merchandise and the psychedelic-symphonic soundtrack (spanning at least seven CDs) these new fans could head to the growing number of specialty shops in Ikebukuro. The trend continued throughout the decade before finally taking root—in 2004, the area became known as Otome Road, the female equivalent of Akihabara. Female otaku even chose a self-deprecating nickname for themselves, *fujoshi*, literally "rotten girls," a play on words implying that a woman is unfit for marriage.

Cardcaptor Sakura, adapted from a manga by the CLAMP artist collective, barely conceals the subtext in the relationships between its characters, whose love ignores differences in age and gender. This type of storyline had never been featured in a show for girls! When she opened a book in her father's library, Sakura accidentally released magical cards whose power could prove dangerous for all humanity. Their guardian (a cute, winged stuffed animal) entrusts Sakura with the task of recovering them, gathering their powers, and putting them to good use. This magical girl's story had all the popular ingredients: collecting items, weekly battles, evolving powers, an eccentric mascot, romance, theme songs by Yoko Kanno and Maaya Sakamoto, and a pinch of *yaoi*! Adored by *fujoshi*, CLAMP gradually imposed its lanky figures, redefining graphic conventions for heroes, who became slender and delicate. Virility was no longer expressed with a huge, muscled physique. Times had changed, and girls were now exploring themes that were previously reserved for boys. With *Saiyuki*, they began following the warriors from *Journey to the West* (the origin of *Dragon Ball*), who became oddly charming in artist Kazuya Minekura's style. Several animated adaptations (three TV series, three OAV series) were huge hits from 1999 onward, and the hairless torsos of the stylized heroes were on display in specialty shops. They were also featured in many female *dōjinshi*, as were the five pilots from *Gundam Wing* in 1995.

NEW FILMMAKERS

In the early 1990s, the film industry was slowly recovering from the failures of *Royal Space Force: The Wings of Honnéamise* and *Akira*. Production was less prolific, and despite a few ambitious attempts, major domestic successes were limited to the umpteenth *Doraemon* or *Dragon Ball Z* films. Only Studio Ghibli films like *Only Yesterday*, *Porco Rosso*, and *Pom Poko* comfortably dethroned them.

The successes of Miyazaki and Takahata's films, as well as the international craze for anime, logically encouraged financiers and animation studios to continue supporting filmmakers in their artistic endeavors. The result was the emergence of many first-time directors, most of whom came to prominence through two influential figures: Katsuhiro Ōtomo and Mamoru Oshii.

Ōtomo mentored many of the animators who worked on *Akira*, giving them the opportunity to direct on his ambitious projects. Two such directors took part in the *Robot Carnival* anthology: Takashi Nakamura and Kōji Morimoto. Nakamura preserved *Akira*'s obsession with constant movement in his feature films, both zany (*Catnapped!*, 1995) and melancholic (*A Tree of Palme*, 2002), whereas Morimoto made experimentation the guiding principle of the production company he cocreated, Studio 4°C. Here, he worked on *Magnetic Rose*, a short in the *Memories* anthology (1995), and Hirotsugu Kawasaki directed the action film *Spriggan* (1998), both overseen by Ōtomo.

Unlike the others, Satoshi Kon did not work on the *Akira* film, but on the manga. Ōtomo's former assistant became a *mangaka* and then a filmmaker at Madhouse, where he was given a trial run in 1997 on the TV movie *Perfect Blue*. Narrating the harrowing conversion of a pop idol into a TV actress, Kon crafted a tortured screenplay with meticulous direction. Released in theaters in the end, the horrific psychological thriller debuted a filmmaker who plays as much with the psyche of his characters as with social conventions.

Faithful to Madhouse, Kon continued to make personal films. In 2001, he paid homage to cinema with *Millennium Actress*, in which the viewer is plunged into the memories of a retired actress. Two years later, he tackled marginality and exclusion in *Tokyo Godfathers*, a tragicomedy in which a group of unhoused people find an abandoned baby on Christmas Eve. Then, in 2006, he adapted Yasutaka Tsutsui's novel *Paprika*, whose concept of exploring dreams for curative purposes led him to play with perceptions of reality.

His characters are exceptional for their psychological depth, to the extent that the theme of "The Double" (schizophrenia, identity crisis, and more) recurs in every one of his productions. With his style that is sometimes lyrical, sometimes realistic, Kon quickly became an international anime star, winning acclaim and many awards.

Another leading figure, Mamoru Oshii, became the star of Production I.G, where he oversaw major film productions. In 1999, he wrote the screenplay for the anime adaptation of his manga *Kerberos Panzer Cop*, which was directed by Hiroyuki Okiura, an animator who brought his penchant for realistic graphics to the

1
1995
Memories

2
1999
Jin-Roh (Jin-Roh: The Wolf Brigade)

3
2002
Millennium Actress

1997
Perfect Blue

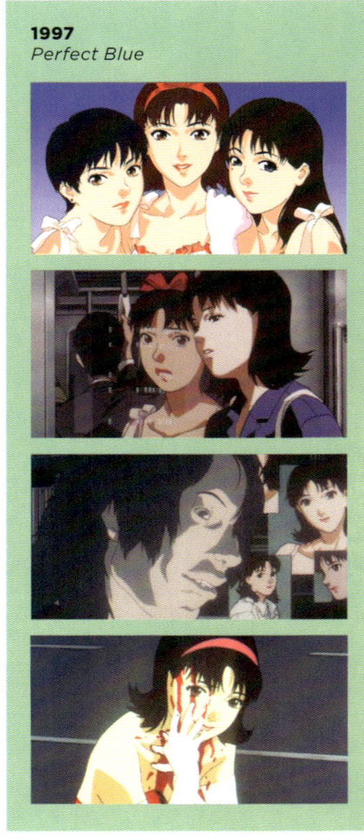

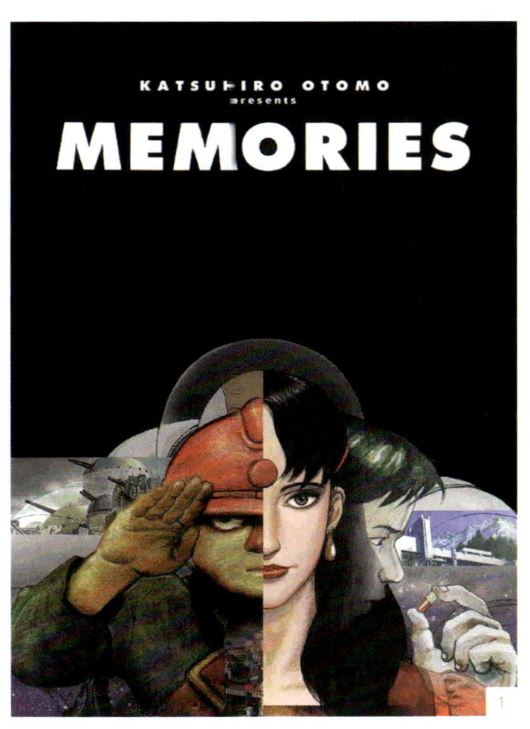

1

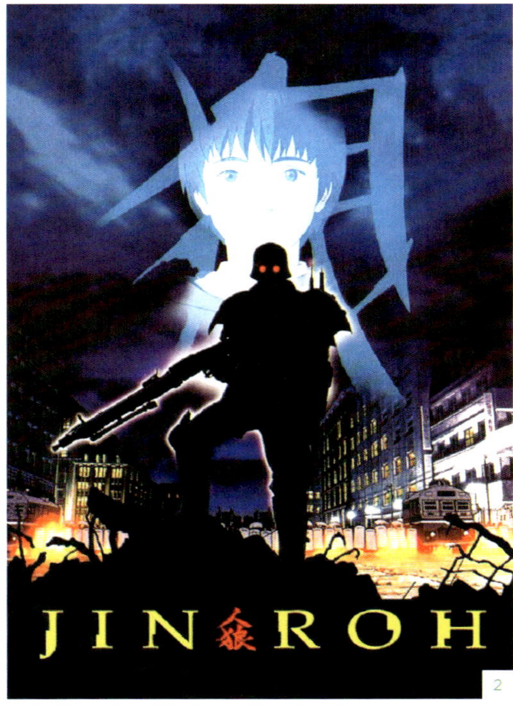

2

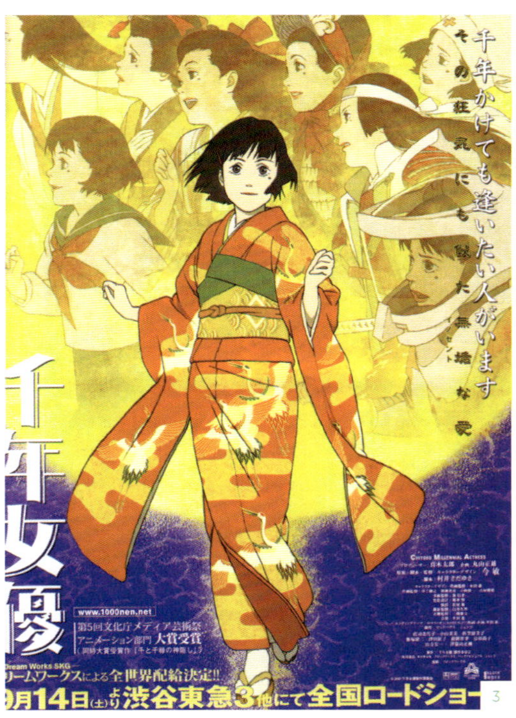

3

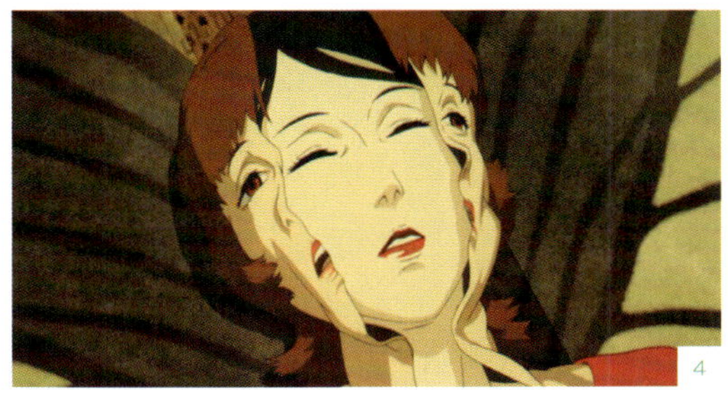

4
2006
Paprika

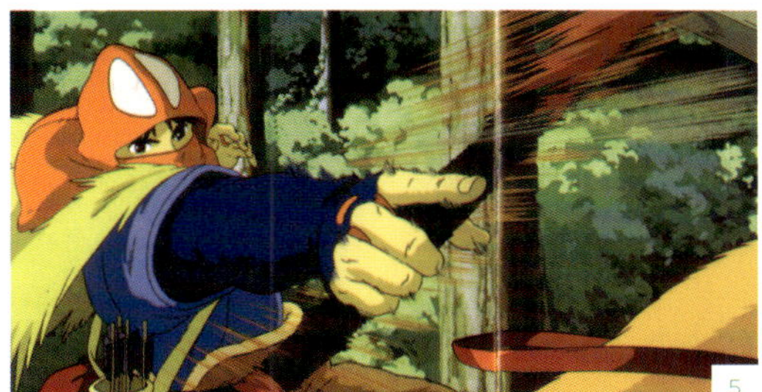

5
1997
Mononoke Hime (Princess Mononoke)

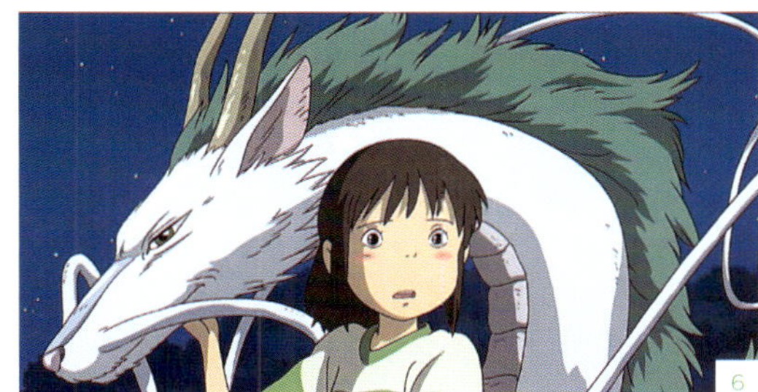

6
2002
Sen to Chihiro no Kamikakushi (Spirited Away)

table. *Jin-Roh* (*Jin-Roh: The Wolf Brigade*, 1999) won a string of awards at foreign festivals and reinforced the studio's philosophy among fans. Hiroyuki Kitakubo was recruited by Ōtomo in 1991 to direct his satirical scenario on the aging population, *Roujin Z*, and then took on Oshii's *Blood: The Last Vampire* in 2000, an impressive mid-length fantasy with sophisticated digital imagery and a morbid tone. With a creative master on board, Oshii himself orchestrated a parody of the *Patlabor* films in 2002, *MiniPato*, by his protégé Kenji Kamiyama. Meanwhile, in 2001, he directed *Avalon*, his fourth live-action feature, demonstrating his interest in live-action films. Like Hideaki Anno and Katsuhiro Ōtomo, Oshii didn't limit himself to cel animation to expand his universe.

THE RISE OF THE GREATS

Studio Ghibli, led by Toshio Suzuki, had grown used to dominating the animation market in Japan, but when Miyazaki's new film was released in 1997, they didn't expect it to shatter so many records. Over 13 million viewers went to see *Mononoke Hime* (*Princess Mononoke*), grossing a whopping ¥17.76 billion, whereas *Kiki's Delivery Service* had proudly brought in ¥2 billion in 1989. The movie's great success was all the more surprising as the fantasy tale is both obscure and very violent, a far cry from the director's usual family films.

In 2002, Miyazaki struck a decisive blow to the Japanese film world with *Sen to Chihiro no Kamikakushi* (*Spirited Away*), which became the biggest Japanese box office hit of all time, drawing in over 23 million viewers and grossing nearly ¥30 billion! This original film tells the story of a young girl who, in order to save her parents, must work in a bathhouse for spirits and magical creatures. Chihiro is a ten-year-old girl with an unremarkable appearance and lots of tenacity who resonates with Japanese families. The filmmaker's next project was more distinctive, as he took over direction for *Hauru no Ugoku Shiro* (*Howl's Moving Castle*). The adaptation of the eponymous novel by Diana Wynne Jones had originally been assigned to a promising director, Mamoru Hosoda. However, following significant delays, Hosoda left the production and Miyazaki decided to start from scratch, much to the chagrin of the animators who had already made significant progress on their work. The film's release did not get the same intense promotion as *Spirited Away* because Miyazaki wanted moviegoers to be surprised. At any rate, the star Takuya Kimura as the voice of the hero was enough to attract viewers! In the end, the film far surpassed *Princess Mononoke* by a wide margin, taking in over ¥18 billion.

These staggering figures prompted other studios to capitalize on the influx of moviegoers to jump back on board the blockbuster trend. It was a golden opportunity for experienced directors to achieve some level of acclaim. At Madhouse, Yoshiaki Kawajiri set the standard for horror movies with *Ninja Scroll* in 1993. After *Wicked City* and *Demon City*, he developed a third feature based on a novel by Hideyuki Kikuchi, *Vampire Hunter D: Bloodlust* (2000). Leveraging the filmmaker's international reputation, Madhouse chose to coproduce the film with an American company, who would be responsible for postproduction. The result was Kawajiri's blend of graphic and thematic obsessions in a high-end adventure, which, in the end, was released first in the United States in its original language—English.

Rintaro had also been busy at Madhouse developing his biggest project to date: *Metropolis* (2001), an adaptation of a manga by his mentor Osamu Tezuka, scripted by his colleague and friend Katsuhiro Ōtomo. The film was close to the heart of Rintaro and producer Masao Maruyama, both of whom had trained at Mushi Production and built strong partnerships with Tezuka Productions. The feature film had a comfortable budget (¥1 billion), giving Rintaro the opportunity to link his mentor's well-known drawings to an impressive 3D production.

For his part, Oshii produced another major cyberpunk project: *Ghost in the Shell 2: Innocence*, with a considerable budget of ¥2 billion. Despite the financial stakes involved and the fact that Production I.G was counting on foreign sales, Oshii made no attempt to appeal to the general public, instead making Masamune Shirow's work his own by developing an airtight plot.

The same year, Ōtomo made his big return to directing with *Steamboy*, an action film he had been working on for 10 years. It became the most expensive project in the history of anime with budget of ¥2.4 billion (about $20 million), just exceeding that of *Princess Mononoke* (¥2.35 billion). Unfortunately for Ōtomo, his steampunk family drama ended in box office failure, with ticket sales not covering even half of the initial outlay.

Although none of these luxurious productions succeeded in generating commercial success, their large budgets made it possible to better integrate 2D with 3D imaging. This graphic maneuver fit perfectly with the common theme of the man-machine relationship. *Metropolis*, *Innocence*, and *Steamboy* were all part of the advent of the digital era.

The death of Tadahito Mochinaga in 1999, a symbol of this technological turning point, left the animation world in mourning. The master of stop-motion had brought the multiplane camera to Japanese animation in 1940, spanned generations of directors, and linked his country's industry to China and the United States while preserving an art form with direct ties to Kabuki theater. That left his pupil, Tadahito Mochinaga, already well known to the Japanese thanks to his many independent short films broadcast several times on the public channel NHK. In 2003, he directed a segment in the anthology *Fuyu no Hi* (*Winter Days*), as did Isao Takahata. Three years later, he directed *Shisha no Sho* (*The Book of the Dead*), his final film, in which he explored the integration of Buddhism in Japan, while making the most of a career devoted to breathing life into puppets.

The digital revolution

WHEN THE SCANNER REPLACED FILM

The end of the twentieth century is marked by a major turning point in digital technology. The use of computer tools was revolutionizing the world and significantly impacting the audiovisual industry, which was redefining its production techniques entirely. As for animation, the long and glorious era of cel animation was coming to an end, to be replaced by various digital processes. A hybrid technique made it possible for drawings to be scanned, then cleaned, colorized, and assembled using dedicated software. The fully digital technique did away with pencil and paper, allowing designers to work directly in animation software. The stylus and graphics tablet became the new tools for animators.

Digital animation proved faster and simpler, and it facilitated superimposing many images without affecting the lower layers, unlike celluloid. With cel animation, it was sometimes necessary to animate several elements on the same sheet to avoid losing the sharpness of the backgrounds. Digitizing animation now made it possible to create more optimal gateways to combine various special effects or computer graphics. As a result, the organic grain of celluloid gradually gave way to sharper imaging. In 1996 and 1997, the new *GeGeGe no Kitarō* and *Dr. Slump* series ushered in the new era of fully computerized TV series. In 1999, *Jin-Roh: The Wolf Brigade* became the last fully hand-drawn film, the final production made without computer support.

As techniques went digital, so did the means of distribution; DVDs arrived on Japanese soil in 1996. Although expensive, this new video medium quickly became widely available, especially since the PlayStation 2 was equipped with a DVD player in 2000. That same year, over 60 million discs were sold in Japan.

The DVD immediately supplanted VHS and LaserDisc, exploding the video market thanks to its unprecedented interactivity. Users now had the ability to change audio tracks and subtitles, or watch bonus material, whether entertaining, educational, or commercial.

At the same time, the internet made a dramatic entrance on scene in Japan, and the percentage of households with internet access rose from 10 percent in 1997 to 50 percent in 2002. Just like the advent

1
2004
Steamboy

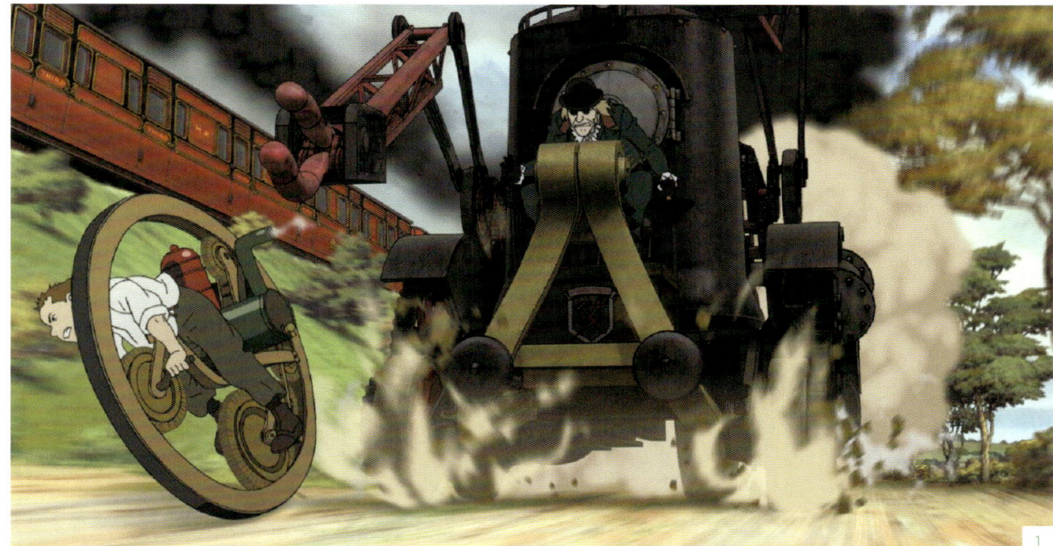

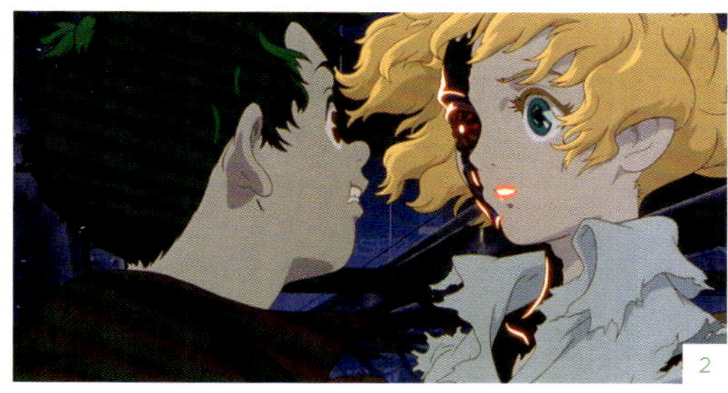

2

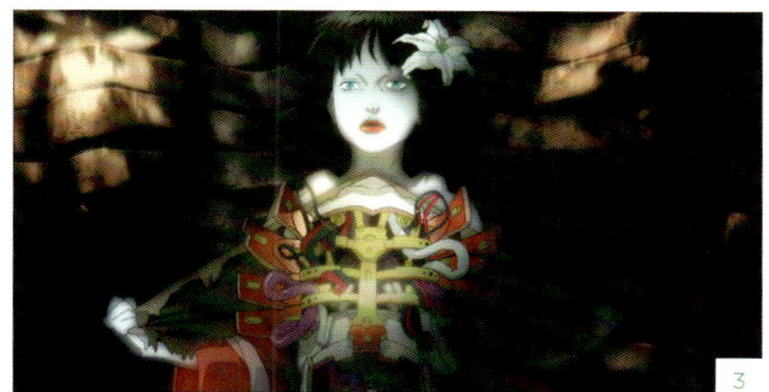

3

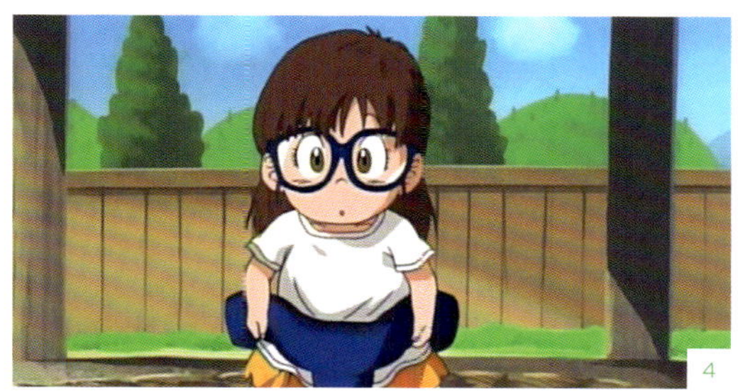

4

of video and specialty magazines at the end of the 1970s, DVD and the internet had a major influence on anime consumption. People could learn about anime on a variety of websites and order it in just a few clicks! Whereas Japan had previously shared the analog NTSC system with North America, the shift to DVD meant they were separated by the DVD encoding system, which splits up geographical zones to control marketing. Now it was European fans who could import anime without worrying about having a multizone player.

But unlike analog, the digital signal is easily duplicable with no loss of quality and can be shared on a large scale thanks to the "vast and infinite" network. Enthusiastic anime fans banded together to subtitle and share media that were not licensed in their country. Their ethical approach counterbalanced the illegality of the practice, but other sites were not bothered by such scruples and also offered the most popular titles—more visits meant more advertising revenue! **Fansub** (fan subtitles) took off, spreading anime across the internet and alleviating many fans' frustration while developing anime culture.

GRAPHIC DIVERSITY

In 1995, graphic cards became widely available, and 3D animation was poised to bring about a renaissance. Pixar demonstrated the changing tide that year when it released *Toy Story*, the first feature film to be produced using entirely **computer-generated imagery** (**CGI**). John Lasseter's film established a new cinematic approach that would gradually dominate production in the United States. On the Japanese side, traditional animation was so firmly rooted that it considerably delayed, if not canceled, this development. A marriage between the two techniques was born, one that would permeate all future productions.

Also in 1995, *Ghost in the Shell* was the first Japanese animated film to incorporate computer technology to a significant extent, enabling Mamoru Oshii to immerse himself more fully in the cybernetic network. The appeal of CGI was in its ability to create visuals that would be impossible or too costly to produce by hand, leading an idea to be simplified or abandoned. Even Hayao Miyazaki, a fervent defender of traditional animation, was convinced by his animators to use 3D to enhance the parasites swarming on infected animals and create organic morphing effects in *Princess Mononoke*.

Ironically, to produce the simplistic-looking visuals in *Hōhokekyo Tonari no Yamada-kun* (*My Neighbors the Yamadas*), Isao Takahata's film released in 1999, Studio Ghibli had to computerize its entire operation. Takahata and producer Toshio Suzuki wanted to keep *mangaka* Hisaichi Ishii's watercolor style, which posed a new digital challenge for the animators, who had to redraw all the lines transparently to define the colorized zones. The studio invested considerably in computer technology, which would have a major impact on future productions. Whereas *Princess Mononoke* used 3D effects on about 50 shots, *Spirited Away* used them on 100 (around 8 percent of the film),

2
2001
Metropolis

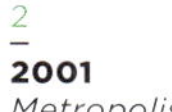

3
2004
Innocence (Ghost in the Shell 2 : innocence)

4
1997
Dr Slump: Arale-chan (Dr. Slump)

2001
Hōhokekyo Tonari no Yamada-kun (My Neighbors the Yamadas)

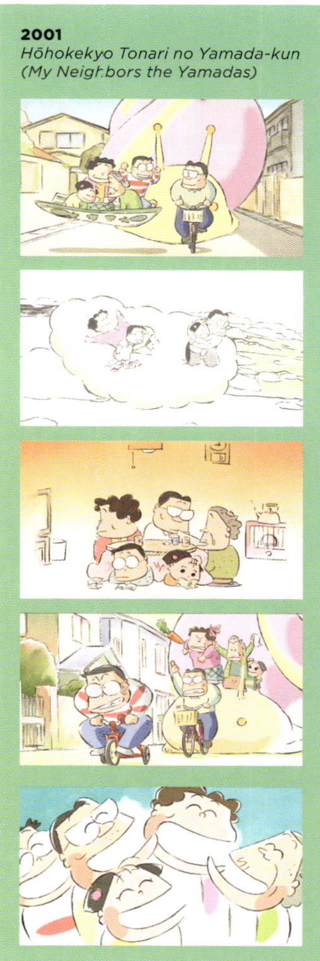

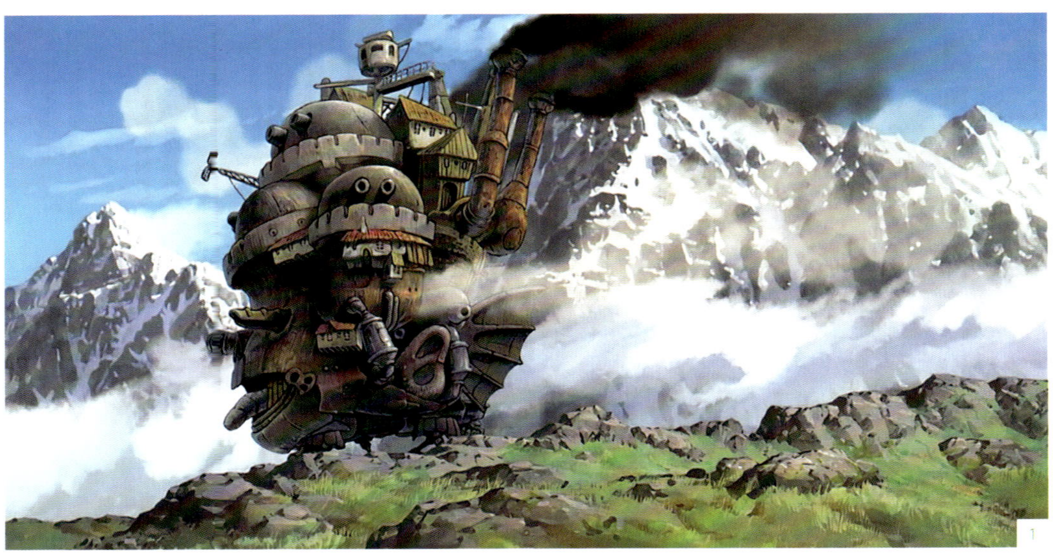

1
2004
Hauru no Ugoku Shiro (Howl's Moving Castle)

and *Howl's Moving Castle* on 200 (around 15 percent of the film). The traveling steampunk castle in that last film was animated using Softimage software to link several superimposed images in motion, evolving the Harmony technique used to move the Ohmu in *Nausicaä of the Valley of the Wind.*

In the 2004 film *Ghost in the Shell 2: Innocence*, only the characters were traditionally animated, whereas backgrounds and vehicles were designed in 3D by Polygon Pictures, the same studio that worked on Mamoru Oshii's *The Sky Crawlers.* Filmmakers could now enhance their shots with textures and other more realistic details and were freer to move their frames around, whereas the multiplane camera had previously limited them. *Steamboy* is a perfect example of this graphic freedom. In 1994, following the production of *Cannon Fodder* (a short film shot in long-take style in the *Memories* anthology), Katsuhiro Ōtomo realized that 3D could overcome the limits of traditional animation and live-action cinema. With this in mind, he embarked on the long and costly production of *Steamboy*, which included many tracking and aerial shots. Movements became extremely fluid using digital production; gone were the shaking cameras. CGI also made it possible to include smoke throughout, as intangible bodies were a major hassle to create using traditional animation. Unlike Oshii, who sought photorealism, Ōtomo focused on **toon shading**, also known as cel shading, which resembles traditional 2D animation by accentuating contours and simplifying colorimetry. Although each production used its own process for graphic uniqueness and stylistic choice, toon shading holds a prominent place in Japan's anime industry. First used in *The Lion King* in 1994, then in *Princess Mononoke*, the technique was reused by Makoto Endō in 2001 on the period film *Kai Doh Maru*, then in 2002 on the series *Ghost in the Shell: Stand Alone Complex*. The 3D animation team became indispensable in this new production system, and the 3D director played a vital role.

ROOM FOR NEW STUDIOS

Mainly used for backgrounds, mecha, and special effects, CGI had taken Japanese productions by storm. It became synonymous with visual ambition because the technology was still new and exotic in the late 1990s. Whereas computer graphics were used sparingly by established animation studios, new companies such as Satelight made digital tools the cornerstone of their productions.

Shōji Kawamori began his long collaboration with Satelight by creating *Chikyū Shōjo Arujuna* (*Earth Maiden Arjuna*, 2001), the company's first TV series. To produce this ecological fable punctuated by science fiction and mysticism, Kawamori ruled out celluloid because the medium proved highly polluting. He embraced 3D imagery, giving him the freedom to move his digital camera around. With *Earth Maiden Arjuna*, the author-director-mecha designer reconfigured his style, which he later refined on *Macross Zero* (2002) and *Macross Frontier* (2008), where the famous Valkyries now came to life in CGI.

The Gonzo studio also embraced the eco-friendly trend when expanding into the animation market. With the *Blue Submarine No. 6* (1998) OAVs, director Mahiro Maeda pitted humans against hybrid monsters in a postapocalyptic aquatic world. He used 3D CGI to create the omnipresent water and numerous marine vehicles. With its ambitious 2D-3D integration, *Blue Submarine No. 6* served as the studio's calling card, and Gonzo launched into TV production in 2000 with the *Gate Keepers* and *Vandread* series. The studio then stepped up its game substantially, producing four to five series a year, and showcasing its CGI know-how across its range of productions, which alternated between adaptations (*Full Metal Panic!*, *Gantz*) and original works (*Last Exile*, *Kiddy Grade*).

A retro-futuristic retelling of Alexandre Dumas' novel, Mahiro Maeda's *Gankutsuou: The Count of Monte Cristo* (2004) experimented with colorizing fabrics with textured patterns, offering a visual profusion akin to the works of painter Gustav Klimt. Unique in its genre, the series would never have been able to develop such an artistic direction without using computer tools.

TOWARD A 3D VISION

The United States asserted its technical superiority in the field of 3D CGI with *Toy Story*. The delay for Japan was significant, as it had been in the 1950s when animators struggled to respond to *Snow White*, a film that was already twenty years old! However, the first series to be produced entirely in 3D, *Bit the Cupid* (1995), was made in Japan. The fondness for 2D didn't rule out interest in this new animation, even if the budgets were far lower than Uncle Sam's productions.

This time though, Japan didn't get carried away by mimicry and retained its own graphic and thematic identity. When Pixar and DreamWorks produced the family films *A Bug's Life* and *Antz*, respectively, in 1998, Gaga Communications (*Tenchi Muyo in Love*) was

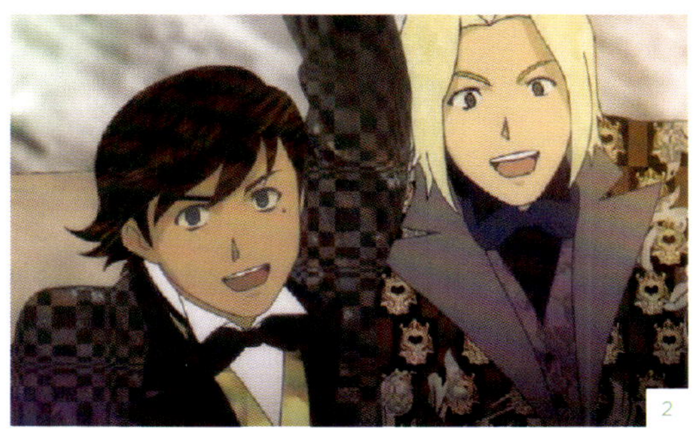

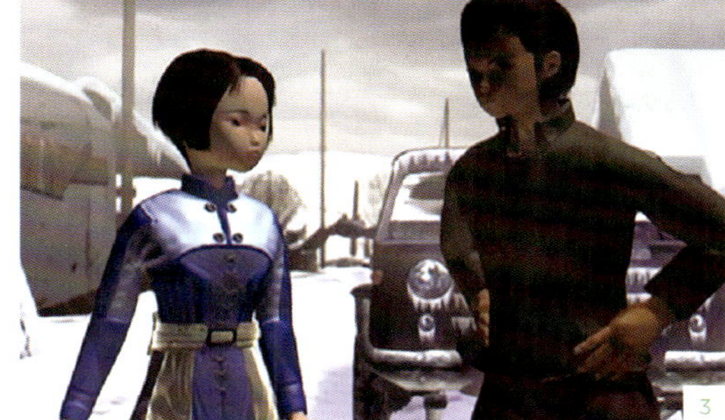

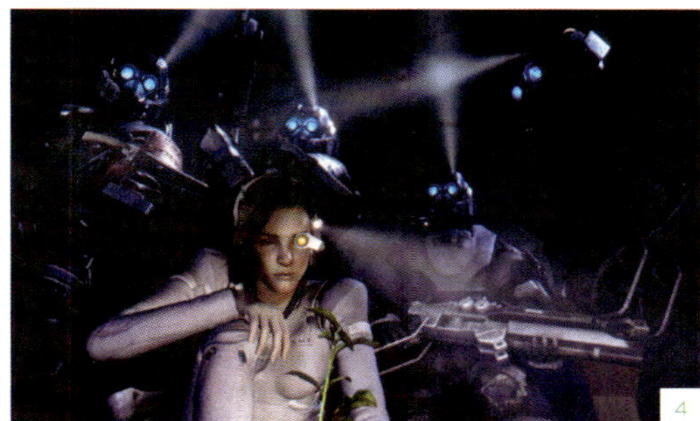

2
2004
Gankutsuou (Gankutsuou: The Count of Monte Cristo)

3
1999
A.LI.CE

4
2001
Final Fantasy: The Spirits Within

tackling science fiction with *A.LI.CE*, the first Japanese feature made entirely in 3D CGI. Versatile director Kenichi Maejima created an impressive film, but the graphics paled in comparison with the American giants, who had yet to venture into the realm of human main characters. Maejima's animation took on a puppet-like effect with rigid joints and movements that the Japanese would find hard to shake off. In the end, the film didn't even reach the West.

Japan's technical delay can be explained by a lack of funding, which affected all studios that were struggling to invest in both computer equipment and training for their many animators. Video game companies, which were more accustomed to 3D-modeled environments, had been investing in animation for some years by this point and were gradually expanding into feature film production. When *Final Fantasy VII* was released on PlayStation in 1997, Square exploited the power of the 32-bit console to develop a futuristic universe showcased in 3D animation sequences. It was the perfect marketing pitch! *Final Fantasy VIII* and *IX* even announced an hour of cut scenes, revealing true cinematic abilities.

After becoming president of Square USA, *Final Fantasy* creator, director, and producer, Hironobu Sakaguchi, took advantage of his franchise's recent successes to team up with Columbia Pictures to produce an animated film. In 2001, he directed *Final Fantasy: The Spirits Within*, which aimed to revolutionize 3D cinema with photorealistic human characters. The budget was colossal at $137 million (about ¥15 billion), as was its failure—it brought in only $85 million worldwide. By comparison, *Toy Story 2* (1999) and *Monsters, Inc.* (2001) had budgets of $90 million and $115 million, respectively, and grossed close to $500 million! Was it not family-friendly enough for an animated film of this magnitude? Too far removed from the video games? Too "American"? *Final Fantasy: The Spirits Within* was a hybrid production that minimized its loss through DVD sales. And although Sakaguchi immediately left Square to start a freelance career, the Japanese company didn't give up. It produced *Final Fantasy VII: Advent Children* in 2005, an OAV that follows the story of the 1997 video game. Although the primary target was a limited audience (gamers), the feature film was distributed by Sony Pictures, allowing it to capitalize on its universal media disc (UMD), a video format designed for the PlayStation Portable console. It was a resounding success, proving that the otaku target had become large enough to make major productions profitable.

Final Fantasy: The Spirits Within exemplifies another major turning point in animated cinema by popularizing motion capture, a technique that digitizes the movements of real people using sensors and a network of cameras. In 2004, the Digital Frontier computer graphics studio also jumped into the film industry, using this technique on *Appleseed*, the first film to be produced entirely in toon shading. It was another graphic shock, demonstrating the Japanese experimental approach to 3D. The adaptation of Masamune Shirow's manga was directed by mecha designer Shinji Aramaki, who embraced the new cyberpunk craze and used it to make a mainstream action film. Aramaki's success enabled him to specialize in 3D CGI films (*Appleseed Ex Machina*, *Starship Troopers: Invasion*), as did producer Fumihiko Sori, who made a name for himself as a director with another cyberpunk action film, *Vexille*, in 2006. As for Digital Frontier, the company went on to adapt other gaming franchises, such as *Resident Evil*, *Tekken*, and more *Final Fantasy*. Video games occupy a decisive place in anime, becoming a central medium for the development of cross-media entertainment.

Media mix at its peak

PRODUCTION COMMITTEES: THE NEW NORM

The runaway success of *Neon Genesis Evangelion* not only undermined the foundations of otaku culture, forcing studios to rethink their scripting requirements, but also called into question an industry whose production process was reaching saturation point with an overabundance of series. Where the production committees for *Royal Space Force: The Wings of Honnêamise* and *Akira* had failed, Gainax's Project EVA hit the jackpot! Under the banner of the main investors, these ephemeral structures were gradually taking over the industry.

The principle was based on the anime design chain, which includes script creation or adaptation of an original work, animation production, voice-over, music production, promotion, video editing, merchandising, video game design, and more. Companies specialized in each of these separate fields came together to form a production committee. Their numbers ranged from two to ten, each contributing a more or less substantial sum depending on its involvement. As a general rule, the video publisher held the majority, with its market generating the main source of income.

Unsuited for self-sufficient artistic manifestos, these structures found their scope in projects that could be developed across every medium of expression. The *Slayers* series is the perfect example of this shift, accumulating three television seasons, two OAV trilogies, and four theatrical features between 1995 and 1998. Part of the great fantasy trend that emerged at the beginning of the decade, *Slayers* parodied its codes and conventions with boundless humor. In this franchise, the corrupt, proud, and gluttonous witch Lina Inverse is feared the world over, guaranteeing disaster wherever she goes, especially when someone makes an inappropriate comment about her tiny breasts. Each medium offers its own specificities—Lina's shrill rival, Naga the Serpent, is absent from the TV series and appears only in films and OAVs. Production committees varied from one medium to another, even within the same format. Although the two OAV series shared the same soundtrack, they had different opening themes and production committees!

Despite these differences, the *Slayers* universe maintained a coherence between each medium, both graphically and vocally. The prolific Megumi Hayashibara not only voiced Lina Inverse, but she also sang all the theme songs of the series! It was

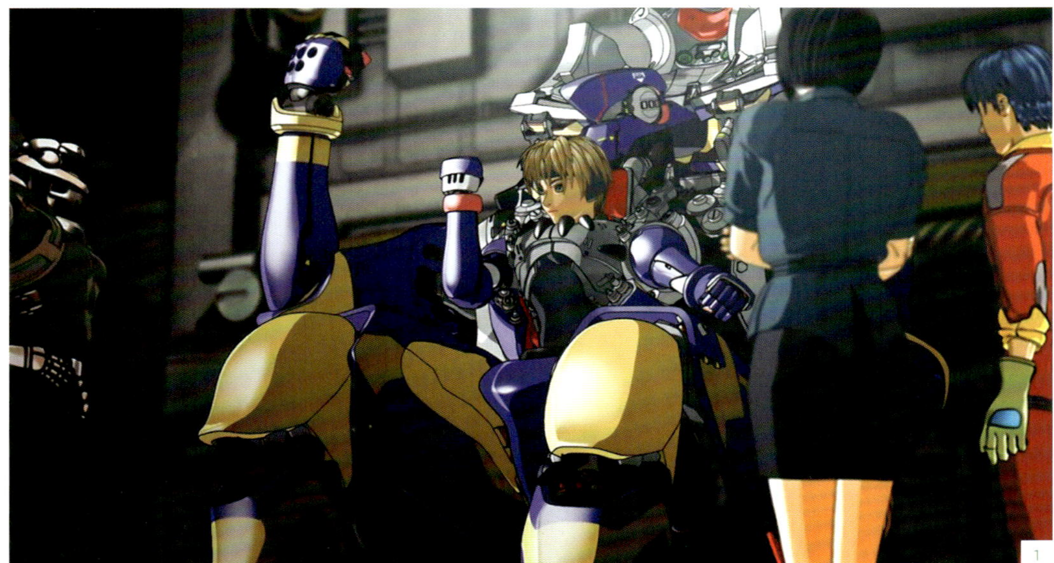

1

2004
Appleseed

a justified initiative by the production committee because mini CD singles had been growing in popularity since the late 1980s. With a diameter of 8 cm, the compact disc sold for ¥1,000 and was the new medium for radio hits and anime theme songs alike. The line between the two genres was gradually blurring, once again under the impetus of production companies seeking to reform *anison*'s economic system.

THANK YOU FOR THE MUSIC

This new marketing trend had its roots in an artistic approach that began in the mid-1980s. When Toei was looking for an introductory theme song for its *Fist of the North Star* series, hard rock was the logical choice to accompany this world of savagery, leather, and mechanics. The band Crystal King, made famous by its hit song "Daitokai" (1.5 million copies sold), composed and performed "Ai wo Torimodose!!" ("Take Back the Love!!"*), a deluge of saturated guitar tones and high-pitched vocals forever linked to the Hokuto warrior.

The studio applied the same formula to *Saint Seiya* but this time asked MAKE-UP to compose the theme music. The band's fourth single, "Pegasus Fantasy," became their biggest hit, buoyed by *Seiya*-mania. Transposed for a symphony orchestra or simply melodized under the baton of composer Seiji Yokoyama, the music for the opening credits even made it onto the soundtrack, further strengthening the links between Japanese pop music and anime.

City Hunter and *Maison Ikkoku* offered an alternative. The former drew on trending pop music in Shinjuku, where the story is set, and the latter used titles already familiar to the general public, with lyrics to match its bittersweet romance. For one episode (episode 24), it even features two songs by Irish singer Gilbert O'Sullivan!

Over the course of the 1990s, the trend coexisted well with *anison*, but little by little, credits explicitly quoting the series title or the hero's name disappeared in favor of *tie-ups*, a term used in Japanese stemming from the English "tie-in." These were preexisting songs associated with the series. In 1979, *Gundam* opened with a thundering chorus of "Moeagare,

Gundam!" ("Fire up, Gundam!"); a quarter century later, the duo Two-Mix's electro-techno pop music kicked off the episodes of *Gundam Wing* (1995). This marketing synergy was a win-win. For the musical artist, it meant guaranteed weekly exposure and the assurance that fans would buy their single. For anime, the benefits took different forms, depending on the production.

Long-running series were rarer but hadn't disappeared entirely—by regularly changing up their opening and closing credit sequences, they stayed relevant five, ten, even fifteen years after their debut. Just compare *Dragon Ball Z* with two of its spiritual successors, *One Piece* and *Naruto*, to see how quickly these tie-ups became crucial to the market. *Dragon Ball Z* came out in 1989, but it wasn't until its 200th episode that it got a new opening sequence, and that was the only change in the series. By its 200th episode, *One Piece* (1999) already had four opening sequences and thirteen closing credit sequences, while *Naruto* (2002) had eight and fourteen, respectively!

For more modest series, new credit sequences had double the bang for their buck. Not only did production committee members in charge of the music provide the committee with a ready-made song free of charge, but they were also responsible for promoting it! Cost-saving measures were essential for these projects, as they needed to update their now obsolete production processes to withstand the decline in the OAV market.

IN THE LIGHT OF THE MOON . . . AND THE SATELLITES

Since the start of the decade, voice actors had been hosting late-night radio shows that appealed to otaku audiences and reached unexpected listeners at such hours. *Evangelion* became successful through its midnight reruns, and producers caught on to an unexpected source of revenue—all the more so because nighttime slots were less expensive on the channels' fee schedules. This *shin'ya* (late-night) **anime**, broadcast between 11 p.m. and 4 a.m., came at just the right time for the OAV industry, which was struggling as the twenty-first century loomed closer.

The direct-to-video market was caught between a rock and a hard place. On one hand, the economic slump was putting a strain on otaku finances; on the other hand, DVDs, which were gradually overtaking VHS, were driving up prices! When Gainax chose the waning OAV as the medium for its eccentric *FLCL* series in 2000, it was to economically prolong director Kazuya Tsurumaki's artistic venture of not respecting any established rules.

In 1996, the production committee for *Elf wo Karu Mono-tachi* (*Those Who Hunt Elves*) decided to broadcast the twelve episodes originally planned for video release on television. The series contained a patchwork of their favorite themes, with a team of interdimensional travelers who must recover the tattoos of five beautiful elves in order to return to Tokyo. It broke the fourth wall and delighted otaku, who gave it the same word-of-mouth praise as *Evangelion*. Video sales exceeded the expectations of the production committee, who used the same formula in 1997 for the sequel. The only difference was that the show was no longer alone in its nighttime slot—TV Tokyo now aired ten *shin'ya* anime throughout the year!

The trend was further cemented when Nippon TV broadcast the *Berserk* anime during a late-night slot. Even when toned down, Kentaro Miura's dark fantasy manga, featuring torture, rape, bloody carnage during a demonic sabbath, and more, was too sinister to be shown during prime time. Fuji TV, which had abandoned the slot in 1992, returned to the fold in 1998, a pivotal year in the expansion of nighttime shows. This growth was brought on by two factors: the appearance of satellite channels and the development of local stations, particularly in the Kansai region, which slashed rates to fill their schedules.

Three trends stand out in this motley assortment of productions. First, there were series similar to *Berserk*—ultraviolent cathartic outlets that could only be broadcast once children were asleep—like *Blue Gender* (1999 with its insectoid monsters and *Hellsing* (2001) with its Nazi vampires. Other production committees chose to adapt to television audiences at these off-peak hours, most of whom were office workers in their thirties returning home from work. Productions emerged focusing on more human elements, akin to dramas, but free from the budgetary constraints of live action.

In 1998, female audiences began to play a major role in the broadcasting shift. This was exemplified by the thirty-nine-episode journey around the world of *Master Keaton*'s heroic insurance investigator and the thirteen-episode adaptation of the beginning of the postapocalyptic *shōjo* series *Basara*. The third target

2
1995
Slayers

3
1989
Dragon Ball Z

4
1999
One Piece

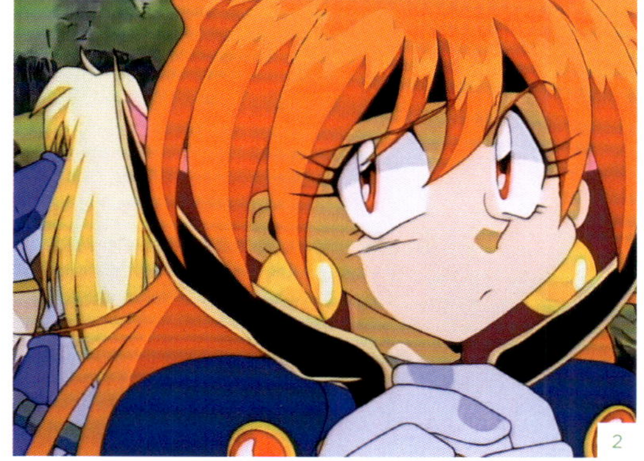

2

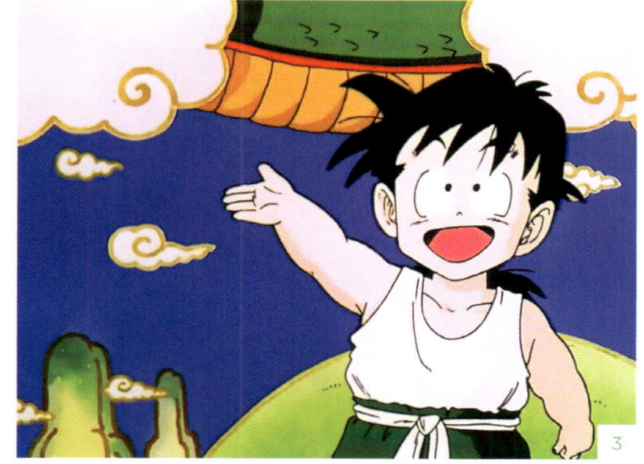

3

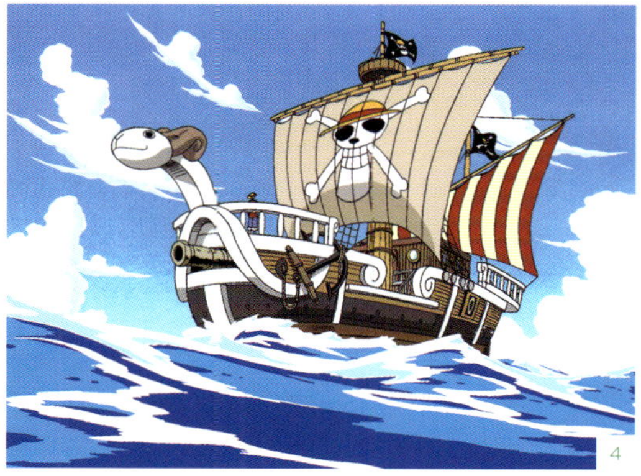

4

audience, inherited directly from OAVs, remained the otaku fringe community. Diversity was again the order of the day. The media mix *.hack* franchise chose to focus on the burgeoning world of MMORPGs, massively multiplayer online role-playing games. These games brought together thousands of players on the internet and capitalized on the impact of *Evangelion* both in form (same character designer, Yoshiyuki Sadamoto) and content (the tormented psychology of hero Tsukasa, prisoner of the game) with the *.hack//SIGN* series in 2002. Most companies, weakened by the financial crisis, preferred to bet on titles catering the ever-growing otaku demand for harem anime, whether adapted from video games (*To Heart*, 1999) or manga (*Happy Lesson*, 2002). This went beyond the nighttime slots, led by *Love Hina* (2000), the story of a down-on-his-luck student and his female dormitory tenants who are as charming as they are stereotypical.

Experimentation on satellite channels went even further, starting with the pioneering channel WOWOW, launched on April 1, 1991. Out of a concern for high standards (they needed to satisfy subscribers!), the channel became involved on the production committees of some of the series it broadcast and became a haven for alternative projects that were too anti-conformist (or too high-quality) for daytime—or nighttime—airwaves. Without WOWOW, there would be no *X* (2001), a battle for the fate of the world between friends destined to become rivals, based on CLAMP's apocalyptic *shōjo* manga. Nor would there be *Mōsō Dairinin* (*Paranoia Agent*, 2004), a legendary psychological thriller and masterpiece of direction by Satoshi Kon, his only TV production.

In 1999, *Ima, Soko ni Iru Boku* (*Now and Then, Here and There*), one of WOWOW's major hits, succeeded in combining the market's three main themes. The first episode is rich in reassuring clichés for otaku audiences, starting with Lala-Ru, a young girl with a strange blue pendant from a parallel dimension. But once the hero follows her to her home world, the mood changes radically—children are exploited there from an early age for military purposes! The main characters may be minors, but that doesn't save them from being raped or shot in the heart. The violence in *Now and Then, Here and There* is less graphic but more traumatic than other anime series, prompting the plugged-in audience of occasional anime consumers to reflect on the human condition and the plight of children. Only satellite channels and late-night programming could allow themselves the audacity of shocking viewers and making them question contemporary social issues, like in the foreboding *Serial Experiments Lain*, which examined the possible consequences of the nascent World Wide Web back in 1998. The primary purpose of animation remained the same into the new century: to entertain!

HEROES OF THE NEW MILLENNIUM

Shōnen Jump sales had fallen dramatically since the end of *Dragon Ball*. Son Goku brought Toei far too much money to retire him! An original creation, distinct from the manga, was broadcast starting in 1996, in which the hero was turned into a child. Scorned by fans, the opportunistic *Dragon Ball GT* drew the curtain after 64 episodes in 1997. *Shōnen Jump* suddenly stabilized the same year with the arrival of a new series that would accomplish the unimaginable—it surpassed *Dragon Ball* and became the best-selling manga of all time. After eating a Devil Fruit, the comic hero's body in *One Piece* became like rubber but sinks like a stone in water. He's not worried; in fact, Luffy is determined to become king of the pirates and takes on board his ship a crew of oddballs who are as whimsical as they are skilled at combat. Two years later, a foolhardy and arrogant young ninja, *Naruto*, proclaimed his goal loud and clear: to become the greatest clan leader ever known!

Where Eiichiro Oda's *One Piece* opted for humor and adventure (like *Dragon Ball*), Masashi Kishimoto's *Naruto* preferred action and virile oaths (like *Dragon Ball Z*). Even though they diverge in form, the two

1
1997
Berserk

2
1998
Master Keaton

3
2000
Love Hina

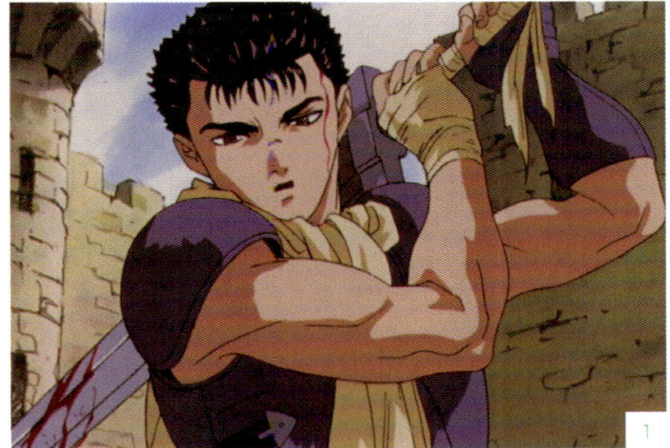
1

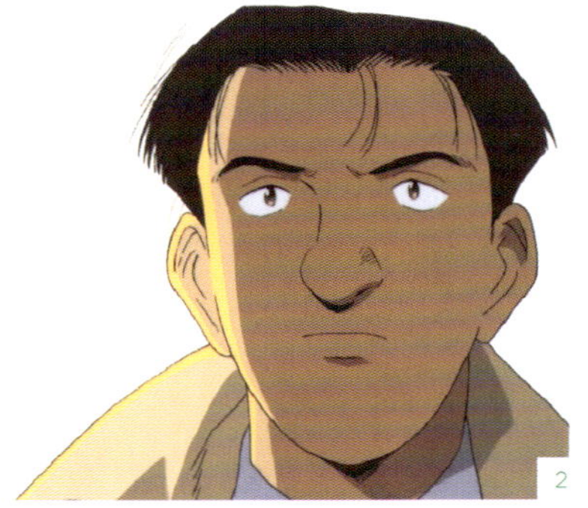
2

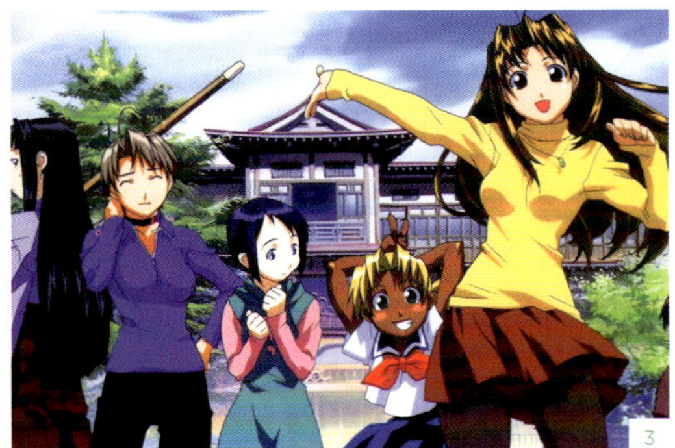
3

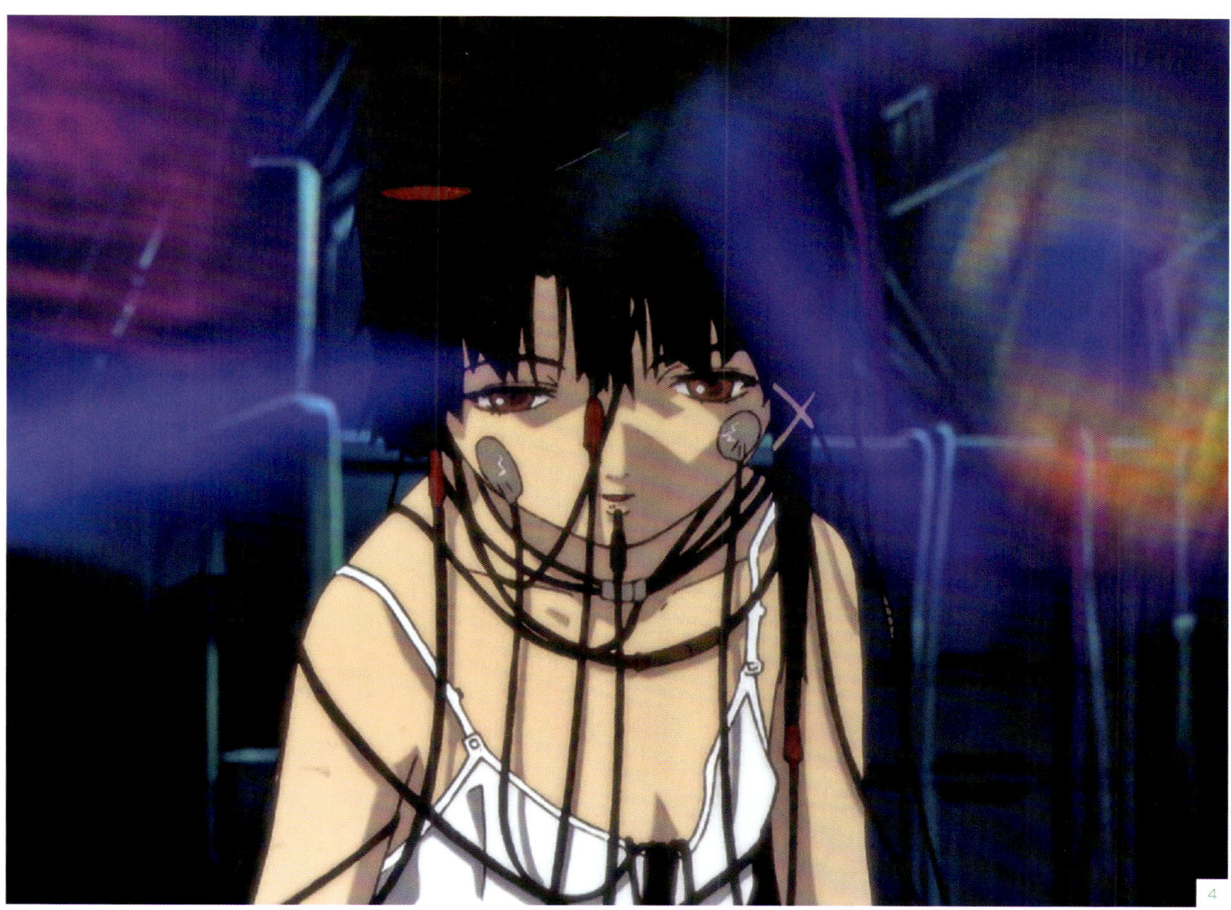

4 — 1998 *Serial Experiments Lain*

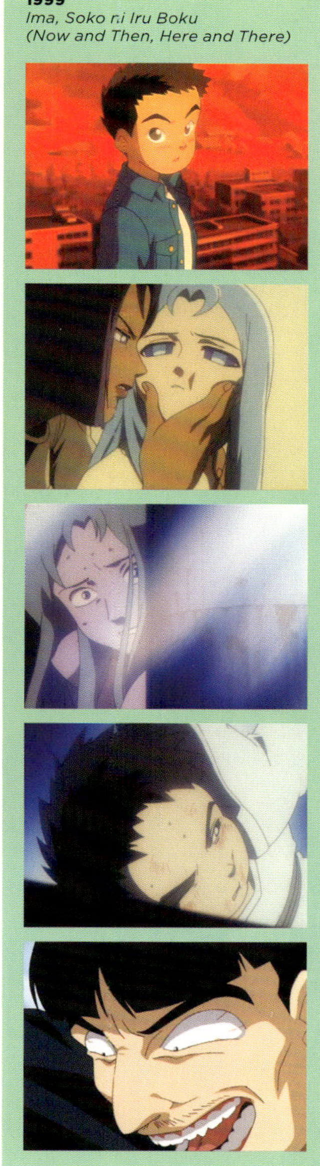

1999
Ima, Soko ni Iru Boku (Now and Then, Here and There)

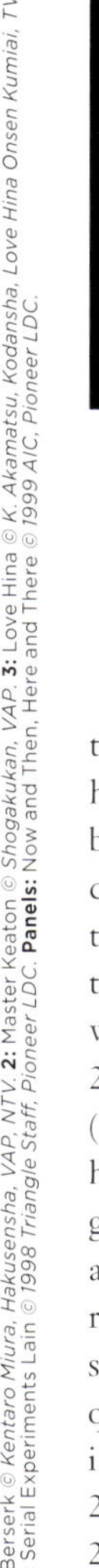

titles drew on the same roots and both feature heroes whose boundless ambition is matched only by a welcomed enthusiasm during this inextricable crisis. This ambition can be seen in the length of the series: *One Piece* (Toei, 1999), still going strong today, exceeded 1,000 episodes in November 2021, whereas *Naruto* (Pierrot, 2002), which ended in March 2017, totaled 720 episodes over two separate seasons (220 for *Naruto*, 500 for *Naruto Shippuden*). Although hugely successful, retellings of the skilled swordsman genre—as fantasy in *Bleach* (Pierrot, 2004 to 2012) and parody in *Gintama* (Sunrise, 2006 to 2018), neither reaching 400 episodes—didn't achieve the same status as social phenomena. Nevertheless, the anime quartet restarted the flow of *Shōnen Jump* adaptations, including the sports series *Prince of Tennis* (Trans Arts, 2001 to 2005, 178 episodes) and *Eyeshield 21* (Gallop, 2005 to 2008, 145 episodes).

In this surge of physical action, one great mind stands out: Shinichi Kudo, a genius high school detective who gets too close to the affairs of a mysterious mafia, was poisoned, and woke up . . . as a child! Born from the imagination of Gosho Aoyama in *Shōnen Magazine* in 1994, Detective Conan's childhood investigations came to life in *Case Closed* by TMS in 1996, bolstered by theme music by B'z, a rock duo with over 80 million records sold and a big fan of these Agatha Christie–style mysteries. The series surpassed 1,100 episodes in 2023 and is still ongoing.

As for the girls, they had been sharing in the adventures of the *Futari wa Pretty Cure* (*Pretty Cure*) heroines, magical girls of the twenty-first century. To make the most of its success, Toei developed the initial concept in several separate series (*Smile Precure!*, *Yes! Precure 5*, and more), whose heroines were brought together on the big screen in a gigantic annual crossover. This *sentai*-inspired formula enabled the franchise to create nearly 1,000 episodes by 2024.

All these new franchises were fully exploiting the possibilities offered by media mix to maintain their supremacy, from video games to annual feature films, and were planning international strategies along the lines of *Dragon Ball Z*. They all achieved success outside Japan but remained in the shadow of a global phenomenon of unprecedented magnitude, identifiable in any country in the northern hemisphere by a simple onomatopoeia: "Pika Pika."

FROM ANIME TO TRADING CARDS

The core of *Pokémon*'s success lies in the first product of its media-mix plan, the initial video game. The game is based on the "rock paper scissors" principle—a Fire-type Pokémon beats a Plant-type Pokémon, which beats a Water-type Pokémon, which beats a Fire-type Pokémon, and so on. After choosing a starting Pokémon, the player alternates between exploration phases to capture other creatures of various types (Poison, Flight, Insect, etc.) and duels between trainers. It's all about using strategy to choose the Pokémon most likely to beat your opponent's. Encouraging collaboration (two players could exchange Pokémon by connecting their Game Boys with a cable), Satoshi Tajiri's game contained remarkable game mechanics that won over the adults who played it when it was released in 1996. Children instantly fell in love with the *kawaii* design of all the pocket monsters who only know how to repeat their own name, with the word *Pokémon* itself being a contraction of "pocket monsters." With ten million copies sold in Japan, ten million in the United States (released in 1998), twenty million in Europe (released in 1999), the media-dubbed Pokémania was almost instantaneous across the globe, whereas in the past, several years had separated the success of behemoths like *Dragon Ball* from one continent to the next.

On the heels of the video game were a trading card game and an animated series, which followed the adventures of Sacha the trainer and his faithful electric Pokémon, Pikachu. The media-mix plan was in every detail—a battle in an episode of the show could provide a player, who had been stuck for months, with the strategy to finally capture a resistant Pokémon or beat his friends at cards during the next recess. The series, which celebrated its thousandth episode at the start of 2018, didn't rely solely on the popularity of the video game. Oriental Lights and Magic (OLM), an all-digital studio, called in Yōichi Kotabe, trained at the same school as Miyazaki, to achieve the best possible animation of the 151 *Pokémon* creatures for TV and film productions. Twenty years after *Heidi, Girl of the Alps*, the artist was involved in a second milestone in anime's history. Directed by Kunihiko Yuyama (*Magical Princess Minky Momo*), the series also owes part of its success to the performance of voice actors like Ikue Ōtani who, using only the syllables Pi, Ka, and Chu, conveys varied emotions and has become probably one of the most recognized voices in the world. All the more so as she also voiced

1
–
1999
One Piece

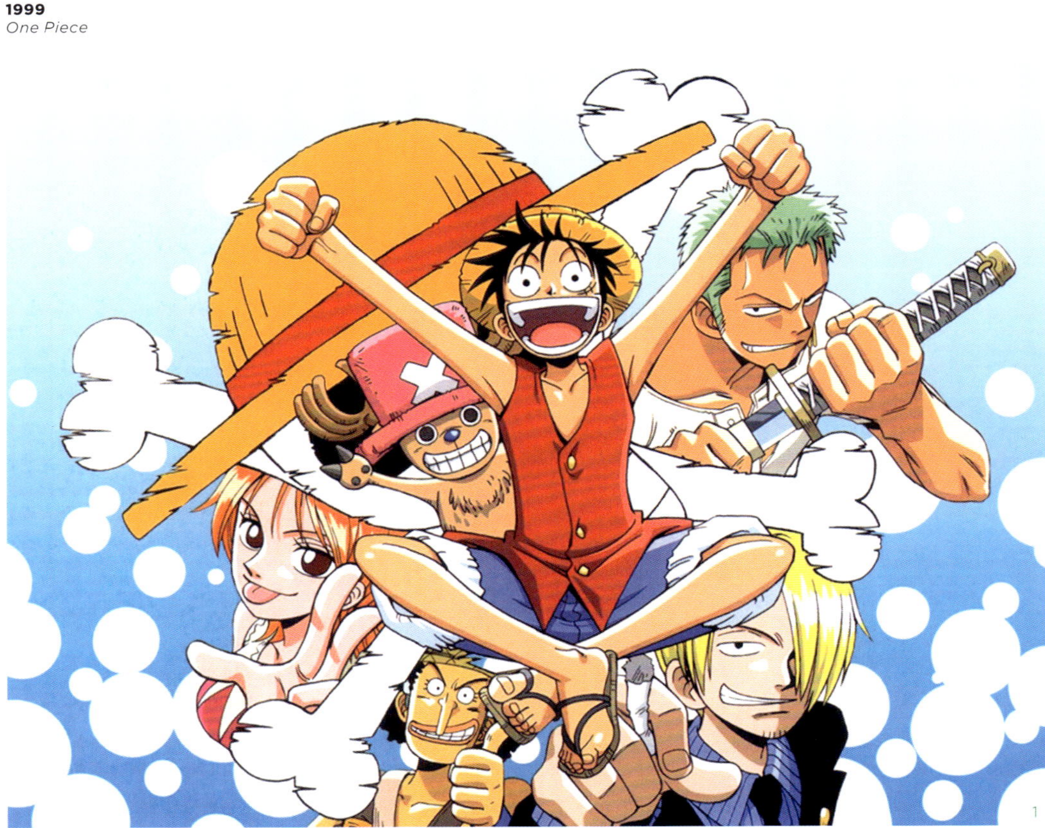

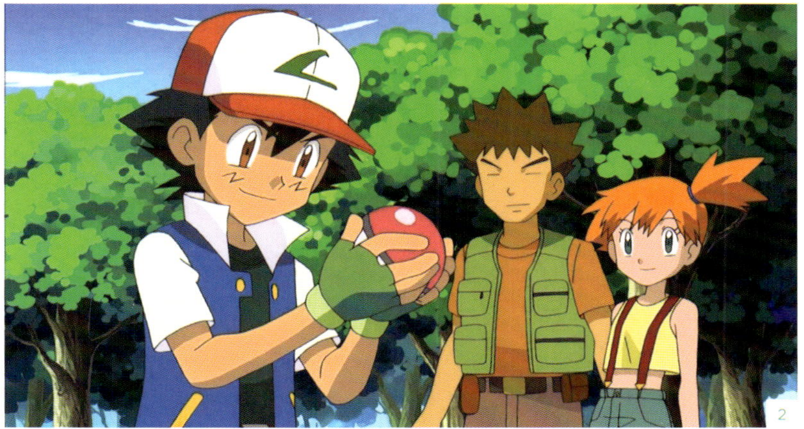

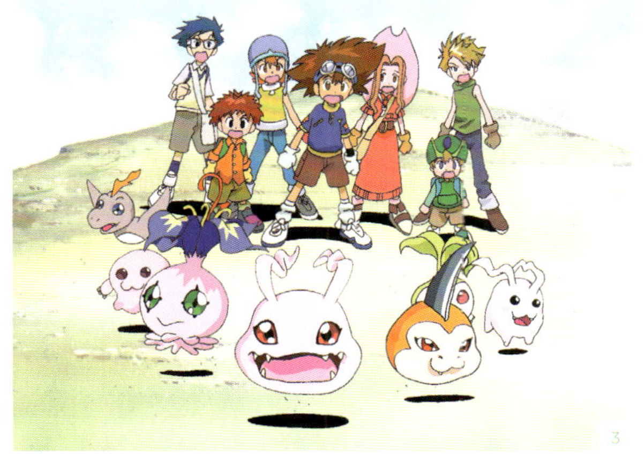

2
1997
Pokémon

3
1999
Digimon

the cute mascot Tony Tony Chopper in *One Piece*. The franchise was constantly revitalized, with a new *Pokémon* movie released in cinemas every year between 1998 and 2020.

Despite many similarities, Bandai's *Digimon* franchise succeeded in introducing its own original universe in which computers rule—the digital monsters were primarily designed to sell virtual pets, like Tamagotchi. And, unlike Pikachu and friends, they were endowed with speech in the series produced by Toei from 1999 onward. It ran for four uninterrupted seasons and then took several breaks, only to return again in 2006, 2010, and 2015. After an unsuccessful start in 1998, the anime adaptation of *Yu-Gi-Oh!* (Studio Gallop, 2000), Kazuya Takahashi's manga in *Shōnen Jump*, became inseparable from the spin-off card game that was all the rage with kids. Despite their remarkable success (over 500 episodes for *Digimon* and over 700 for *Yu-Gi-Oh!* and its spin-offs), neither franchise reached the same heights as Nintendo, who had the *Mazinger-Goldorak* generation, then the *Dragon Ball* generation, and now the *Pokémon* generation!

Worldwide acclaim

FOR DELIVERY OR TAKEOUT

The universal craze for *Pokémon* is a reminder of the extent to which Japanese animation has conquered the global market, but its modes of expansion vary considerably from country to country. The year 1997 marks very different turning points in anime's history in France and the USA. On the American side, the Cartoon Network children's channel launched a daily late-afternoon slot, targeting its oldest audience of eleven- to fifteen-year-olds. The following season, in 1998, Toonami (a contraction of cartoon and tsunami) gained its footing with its robot mascot TOM (Toonami Operations Module), and its nighttime slot, which opened the door to more violent titles—a mirror image of the booming *shin'ya* anime.

After grabbing kids' attention with three hit franchises in 1998 (*Dragon Ball Z*, *Sailor Moon*, and *Robotech*), Toonami had been churning out previously unseen classics, as well as "novelties" broadcast a few years earlier in Japan. American children didn't discover *Dragon Ball* until 2001, long after its sequel *Dragon Ball Z*! The time slot, which was one hour at its launch, reached four and a half hours between 2004 and 2007, reflecting American audiences' appetite for Japanese productions. However, Toonami was canceled in 2008 after its tenth season due to low ratings.

In France, 1997 signaled the end of *Club Dorothée*, which disappeared after ten years of hegemony in TF1 programming. This was cause for rejoicing for many parental committees worried about the exaggerated violence of the "mangas" being broadcast, confusing comic books with cartoons. The omertà against anime was immediately felt on the airwaves, where children's programming was being increasingly neglected—the last iconic show, *Les Minikeums*, went off the air in 2002. Salvation came from satellite TV, where new channels were springing up to meet teenage demand, featuring young program directors steeped in Japanese pop culture. A pioneer in this respect, the channel Game One emerged in 1998 as part of the Canal+ group. Although it focused on video games, it also took an interest in animation, especially with nights devoted to *Nadia: The Secret of Blue Water*. Created in 1996 by AB Groupe, the producer of *Club Dorothée*, the Mangas channel reran the big hits (*Dragon Ball*, *Saint Seiya*, and more *Captain Tsubasa*) once the show had ended on TF1.

However, due to budgetary constraints and coverage, satellite dishes were still rare in France. Anime consumers were turning to the video market, which brought together OAVs and compilations of episodes from recent series; the French discovered *Evangelion* in 1997 through the media publisher Dybex. The market had exploded with the switch to digital—the first wave of consumers bought every

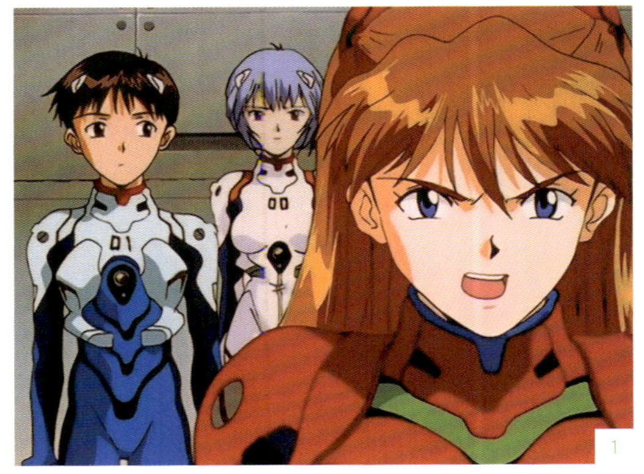

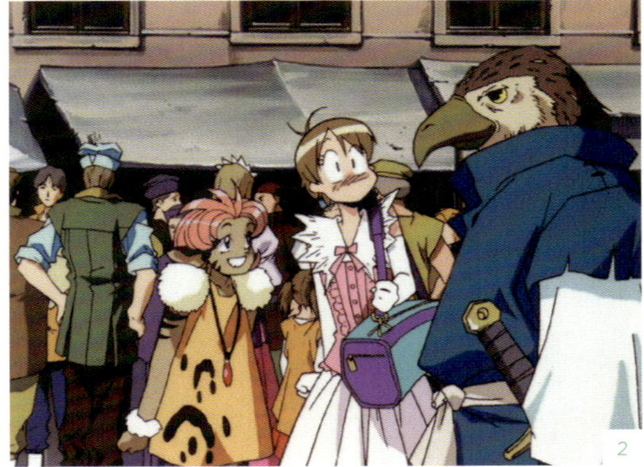

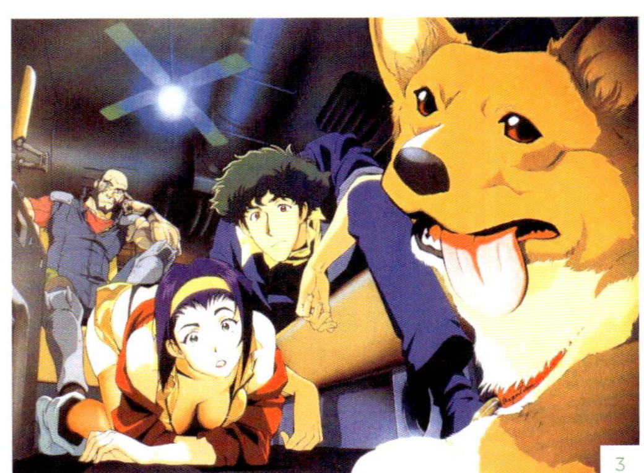

1
1995
Shin Seiki Evangelion (Neon Genesis Evangelion)

2
1996
Tenkū no Escaflowne (The Vision of Escaflowne)

3
1998
Cowboy Bebop

VHS when it was released, and then a second wave invested in the complete boxed sets. The cycle started all over for DVDs, which relied on back catalogs for previously released media and constant new releases. Better still, thanks to the possibilities offered by digital technology, each title was available in three modes: dubbed, subtitled, or both.

Déclic Images was another company that played on nostalgia, rereleasing titles from the 1970s and 1980s, flooding the market and growing by leaps and bounds. Founded in 1999, it reported sales in excess of $5.6 million in 2005. That same year, the company released *Goldorak* boxed sets without holding the rights to the series, triggering legal proceedings, which Toei won in 2009, resulting in a penalty of $5.4 million. From then on, Japanese studios kept a close eye on their anime gold mines.

Television channels were in a lull and took advantage of satellite and DVD platforms as a sounding board. Thanks to their success on Cartoon Network and Fun TV, respectively, *Cardcaptor Sakura* and *Gundam Wing* were broadcast on France's M6 in 2001 and 2002. They used a different approach to capture teenage audiences on Canal+. After two feeble attempts—*Escaflowne* and *Cowboy Bebop* broadcast free-to-air (FTA) in 1999 and 2000—the channel took the gamble of creating a time slot for anime programming. It was cleverly named *La Kaz*, a term that means both "time slot" and "comic book panel" in French. From September 2004 to June 2005, the best-selling titles on DVD were broadcast FTA daily in the late afternoon, just in time for middle and high schoolers to get home from school. For many teenagers who had grown up without Japanese cartoons on TV, the rebellious teacher in *GTO* (1999) and the alchemist brothers seeking redemption in *Fullmetal Alchemist* (2003) became instant icons, and the gateway to a culture that went beyond the original circle of initiates.

ANIME CONVENTIONS

The expansion of the fan base over the past decade could now be gauged by attendance at anime conventions. Between 1995 and 2005, Anime Expo went from 2,138 to 33,000 visitors, and the Salón del Manga de Barcelona rocketed from 1,000 to 63,000. And these were just the most popular festivals! Conventions were swarming across the United States and Europe, with three new ones cropping up in Europe in 1999: AnimagiC in Germany, AnimeCon in Finland, and Japan Expo in France. Caught up in their own success, the early amateur conventions quickly became more professional by learning as they went—they needed to rent larger and larger spaces, deal with more exhibitors every year, and diversify their activities! Traditional Japanese culture was gradually finding its place at conventions. Visitors could imagine themselves in the shoes of the heroes of *Hikaru no Go* (2001) as they learned the rules of the age-old game of Go or attend lectures on the Meiji restoration, the backdrop to the red-headed samurai's redemption in *Rurouni Kenshin* (1996), or the oriental zodiac essential to the fantasy rom-com *Fruits Basket* (2001). They could even give their all by learning a martial art.

The budgets were also increasing, allowing conventions to host Japanese artists! In 1996, Anime Expo welcomed Leiji Matsumoto, Hideaki Anno, Mamoru Oshii, and Yoshiaki Kawajiri, among others. They recounted their adventures to their colleagues when they returned home, determined to respond positively to any future invitations. Backed by the Japanese industry, emulation continued to grow. In 2002, the German convention welcomed Shinichirō Watanabe and Yoko Kanno to present the world premiere of *Cowboy Bebop: Knockin' on Heaven's Door*. With all these attractions, convention growth was staggering. In 2003, a huge line took up the forecourt of La Défense—the 160,000 square feet (15,000 square feet) of the Center of New Industries and Technologies convention center weren't enough to accommodate the 41,000 fans wishing to attend the Japan Expo in Paris. The show took a break in 2005, only to return in 2006, ushering in a new era for these festivals.

The more discreet biannual event *Nouvelles Images du Japon* (New Images of Japan) focused on the artistic side of Japanese animation. In addition to retrospectives of seminal works (*Tale of the White Serpent*, *Puss 'n Boots*, and so forth) and independent productions by up-and-coming filmmakers destined for greatness, the Parisian event offered a unique opportunity for interaction with the artists! The general public could ask any and all questions to the directors who came to present their films, including Satoshi Kon, Isao Takahata, and Sunao Katabuchi. Behind the scenes, hand-picked student animators benefited from the experience of Yasuo Ōtsuka (in 2001) and Yōichi Kotabe (in 2003) in brand-new master classes. The aim of the animation greats was simple: to pass on the Japanese know-how accumulated over almost a century to younger generations. In the very short term, the results were displayed to attendees, who were asked to spot any errors between the master teachers' original drawings and those completed by the students. In the long term, it paved the way to the Japanese industry for young French artists, who were preparing to head to Tokyo.

More intimate than conventions featuring commercial works, *Nouvelles Images du Japon* was overwhelmed by the crowd of visitors in 2001. The founders of Studio Ghibli, Isao Takahata and Hayao

2003
Hagane no Renkinjutsushi (Fullmetal Alchemist)

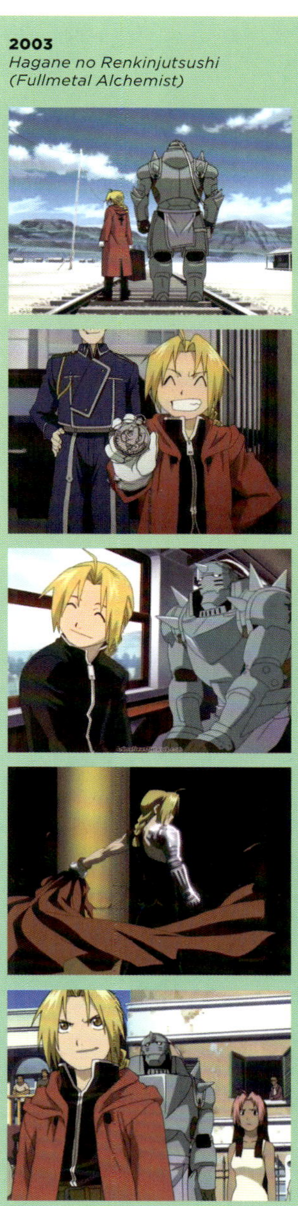

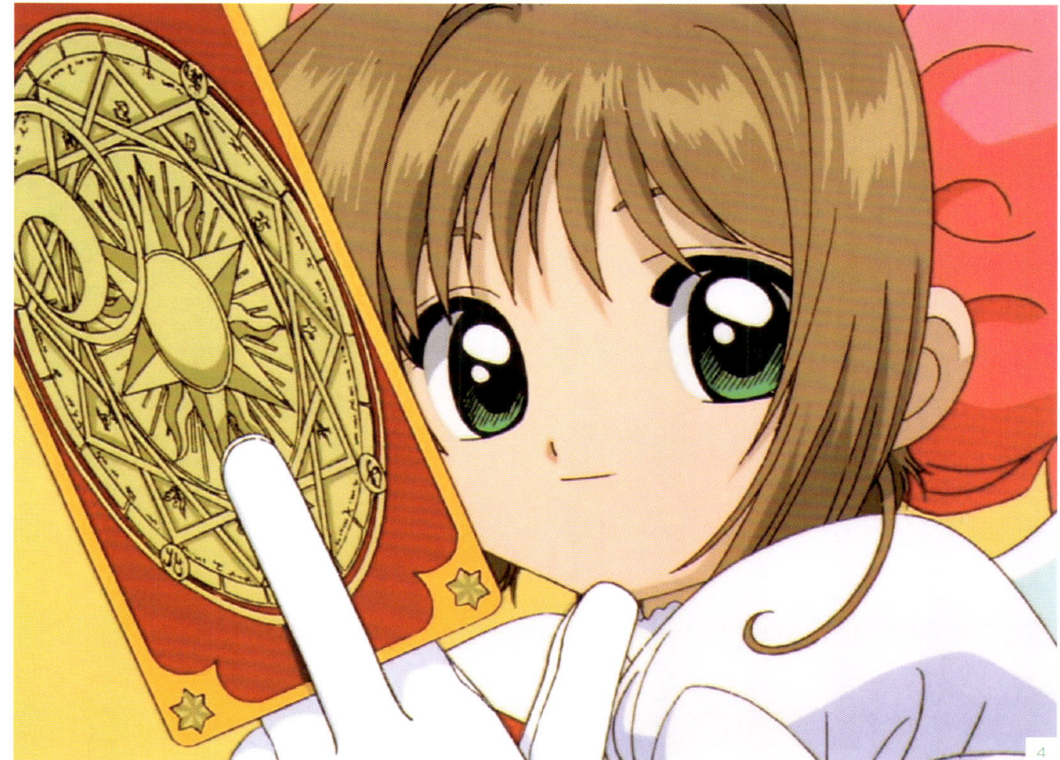

4
—
1998
Cardcaptor Sakura

2001
Hikaru no go

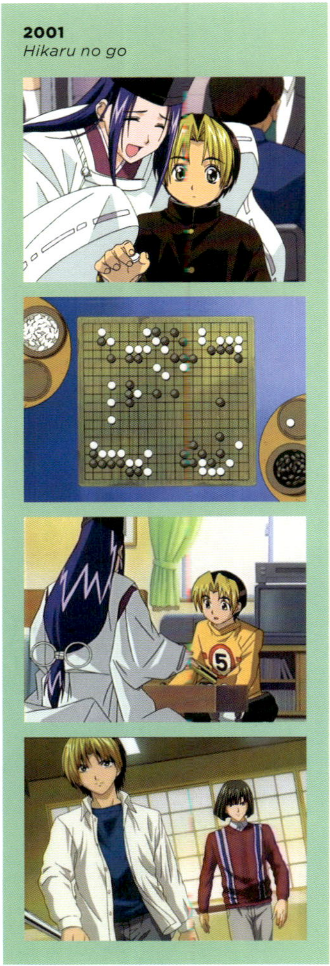

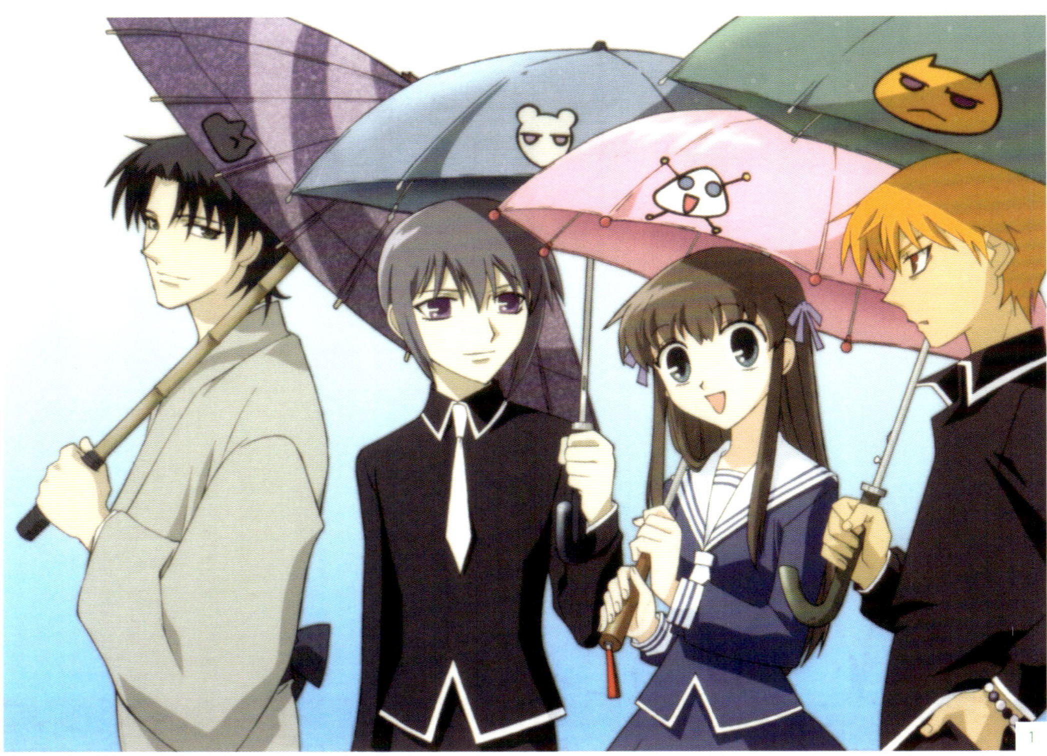

1
2001
Fruits Basket

Miyazaki, had made the trip to present their works, notably *Spirited Away*, for which tickets to the premiere were being sold on a spontaneous black market. Still unknown to the general public six years earlier, Miyazaki's name had been gaining international acclaim since the success of *Princess Mononoke*. Around the hard and fast otaku core from the early days, bolstered by a new generation of fans who had been bottle-fed on TV productions over the last decade, a much wider audience was gradually gathering, curious to find out more about this Japanese pop culture that was taking the world by storm. And especially in Hollywood.

THE RISING SUN IN DARK THEATERS

Disney executives had been eyeing Studio Ghibli for years. They finally reached an agreement in 1996, when Disney guaranteed that their subsidiary, Buena Vista, would not make any alterations to Ghibli films for distribution outside Asia. Disney, which had never before invested in a foreign production, would finance 10 percent of the budgets for Takahata's *My Neighbors the Yamadas* and *Spirited Away*!

But first, *Princess Mononoke* had to be distributed in the United States. Miyazaki's 1995 film, Japan's biggest box office success (to be topped a few months later by *Titanic*), dampened Disney's spirits with its Dantean battles, in-depth storyline, and lengthy running time at two hours and fifteen minutes. Furthermore, the "princess" in the story, San, a young girl raised among wolves fighting savagely against the humans invading and destroying the forest, was a far cry from Cinderella or Pocahontas. Its independent subsidiary, Miramax, was in charge of a carefully crafted American release—writer Neil Gaiman was in charge of the adaptation, and the voice cast includes stars such as Claire Danes, Gillian Anderson, and Billy Bob Thornton.

An ecological fable set in a mystical feudal Japan that oscillates between fury and poetry, *Princess Mononoke* flopped in US theaters but made up for it with video sales. In France, on the other hand,

Miyazaki's films were a hit, shattering preconceived notions of "japonaiserie" with 700,000 viewers. *My Neighbor Totoro* was released in cinemas in 1999, and the older films were released on DVD. Audiences were eager to catch up with the Ghibli leader's filmography, especially because he had announced his intention to retire after *Princess Mononoke*. During production of that film, the death of his friend, animation director Yoshifumi Kondō, prompted him to tackle a "final" film in the end.

A baroque, fantasy-filled odyssey, *Spirited Away* is a superlative film. The biggest hit of all time in Japan with twenty-three million viewers (one in five Japanese!), the film won the Golden Bear at the Berlin Film Festival and the Oscar for Best Animated Feature! Anime had finally earned its legitimacy in the eyes of the world by being recognized by professionals. Mamoru Oshii, who had paved the way, solidified anime's standing in 2004, when *Ghost in the Shell 2: Innocence* was competing for the Palme d'Or at the Cannes Film Festival.

This recognition was reflected in Hollywood blockbusters. Miramax, which had carefully nurtured *Princess Mononoke*, produced the breakthrough film of the end of the millennium in 1999: *The Matrix*. The dystopian cyberpunk future gets its graphic inspirations from anime, including mecha design, martial arts, a flood of shell casings, human-machine fusion, and more. In 2003, the project became a trilogy and was accompanied by a DVD bonus, *The Animatrix*, with eight short films delving deeper into the world of *The Matrix*. They were directed at Madhouse and Studio 4°C by Mahiro Maeda, Shinichirō Watanabe, Yoshiaki Kawajiri, Takeshi Koike, and Kōji Morimoto, and produced by American Michael Arias, who had won the confidence of the Japanese industry. Studio 4°C even commissioned him to direct *Tekkonkinkreet* in 2006, about the misadventures of street orphans confronting the mafia in a steampunk megalopolis.

Contemporary Western artists were now expressing their love for Japanese animation. In 2003, an entire chapter of Quentin Tarantino's *Kill Bill* was animated by Production I.G, using an unprecedented shaky-contour graphic style. In the same year, the electronic duo Daft Punk released a ninety-minute anime video, *Interstella 5555*, supervised and directed by Leiji Matsumoto, which used their entire *Discovery* album as its soundtrack. Shortly afterward, a test montage of a project seeking financing based on an amateur manga fell into the hands of Samuel L. Jackson, and the actor enthusiastically invested his money, his time, and himself (he voiced the main character) on *Afro Samurai*, produced by Gonzo for the international market in 2007.

This sudden international legitimacy was not without consequences for the anime industry. Strength was in numbers as the Association of Japanese Animations (AJA) was born in 2002, representing the majority of studios and working in close collaboration with public and private authorities at both the national and local level. Right from the start, the AJA scored a major coup with the first edition of the Tokyo International Anime Fair (TAF) in February 2002. Like Comiket, the TAF took place at Tokyo Big Sight, but the event was only open to the public on weekends. Behind the profusion of promotional stands showcasing upcoming new releases, behind the scenes, professionals from all over the world came to sign contracts with Japanese studios. Those studios did their utmost to facilitate international collaborations, as evidenced by Toei Animation, whose professionals had been using this company name unofficially in English-language exchanges, and it became the new official name of Toei Dōga in 1998.

Anime was proving to be an export product whose international profits were no longer negligible in the eyes of the government—although it barely reached 10 percent of the industry's total revenue in 1995, it reached almost half in 2002, thanks to the *Pokémon* wave! Taken as seriously as the IT or automotive industries, this soft power, known as "Cool Japan," encompasses manga and cartoons (both on television and in cinemas), Japanese pop culture (which Westerners discovered through tie-ups), and fashion (which they discovered in media content). Even the American phenomenon, *Power Rangers*, appearing in 1993 and based primarily on Japanese *sentai* series, was remastered by Saban Entertainment with dialogue scenes featuring local actors. Tarō

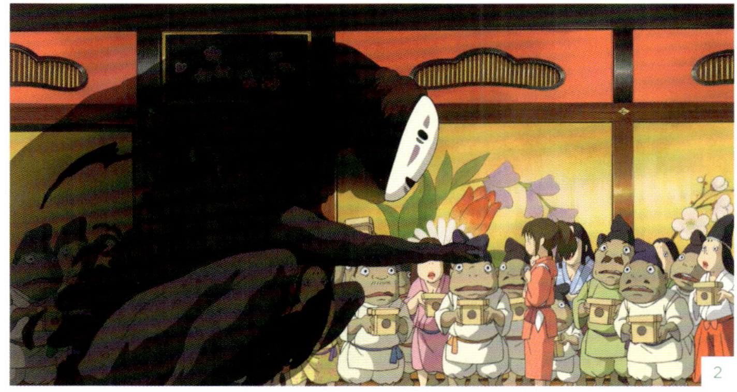

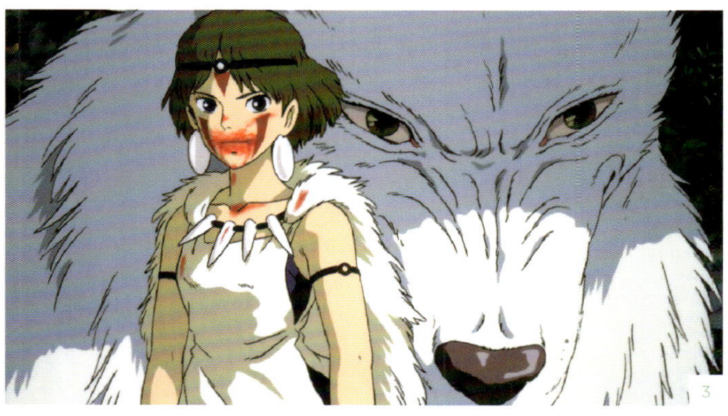

2
2002
Sen to Chihiro no Kamikakushi (Spirited Away)

3
1997
Mononoke Hime (Princesse Mononoke)

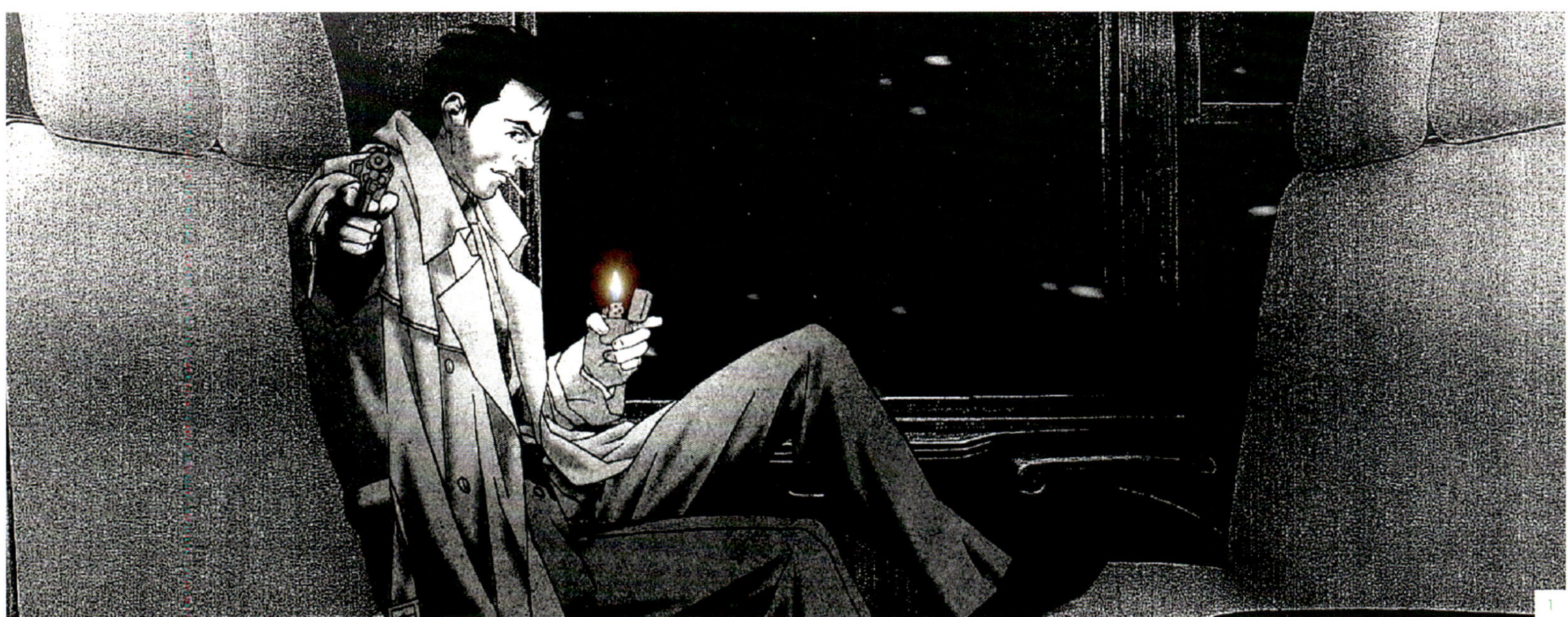

1
2003
The Animatrix: A Detective Story

Asō's appointment as the Minister of Foreign Affairs further amplified the movement, as he was a politician with a passion for manga. Could Cool Japan pull the country out of recession?

EYES BIGGER THAN THEIR BELLIES?

Over the past ten years, computer technology had radically facilitated the production of a series, and the number of television series continued to grow. The indestructible *Sazae-san* and *Doraemon* were rubbing shoulders with new titles destined to transcend the decades, *One Piece* and *Case Closed*, which filled the daytime slots for youth and general audiences. In the evening, more mature shows targeted a wide variety of viewers, from hardcore otaku to late-night salarymen, including everything from commercial productions with predictable marketing synergies to creations too atypical for prime-time broadcasting.

The international response to these titles, ranging from food to television specials, was driven by the retroactive critical and public acclaim for the works of Hayao Miyazaki, Isao Takahata, and Katsuhiro Ōtomo, who were now considered the equals of live-action directors. Mamoru Oshii, who navigated between the two media, released *Avalon* (2001), a questioning of network gamers' investment in their virtual universe, between his two *Ghost in the Shell* films. And Satoshi Kon's *Millennium Actress* (2001) spans the history of the Japanese seventh art in a thinly veiled tribute to the great actress Setsuko Hara.

Under the influence of *Neon Genesis Evangelion* and *Ghost in the Shell* in 1995, the anime industry completed the transformation it had begun in the early 1980s with the emergence of VCRs in less than a decade. There seemed to be only one way for the market to move forward—keep growing! Whether it was the annual number of TV productions or the budgets for feature films, the figures kept climbing. The industry was charging ahead, too fast to avoid the two obstacles that were in its path ahead.

It could have anticipated the first, which follows from common sense and the elementary laws of physics: infinite growth isn't possible with limited resources. Television channels were saturated day and night and had no more slots to sell for projects whose total volume, beyond the scope of the Japanese workforce alone, was outsourced to continental Asia. The second, on the other hand, took the industry by surprise. In February 2005, YouTube revolutionized the internet. People could now access videos on demand without needing to download them first. It was a godsend for the fansub scene! Their productions, which they had controlled with almost maniacal care, began to escape the grasp of Japanese studios. They had missed the internet boat, unlike their core target audience.

2 and 3

1996
Meitantei Conan (Case Closed)

4

1999
One Piece

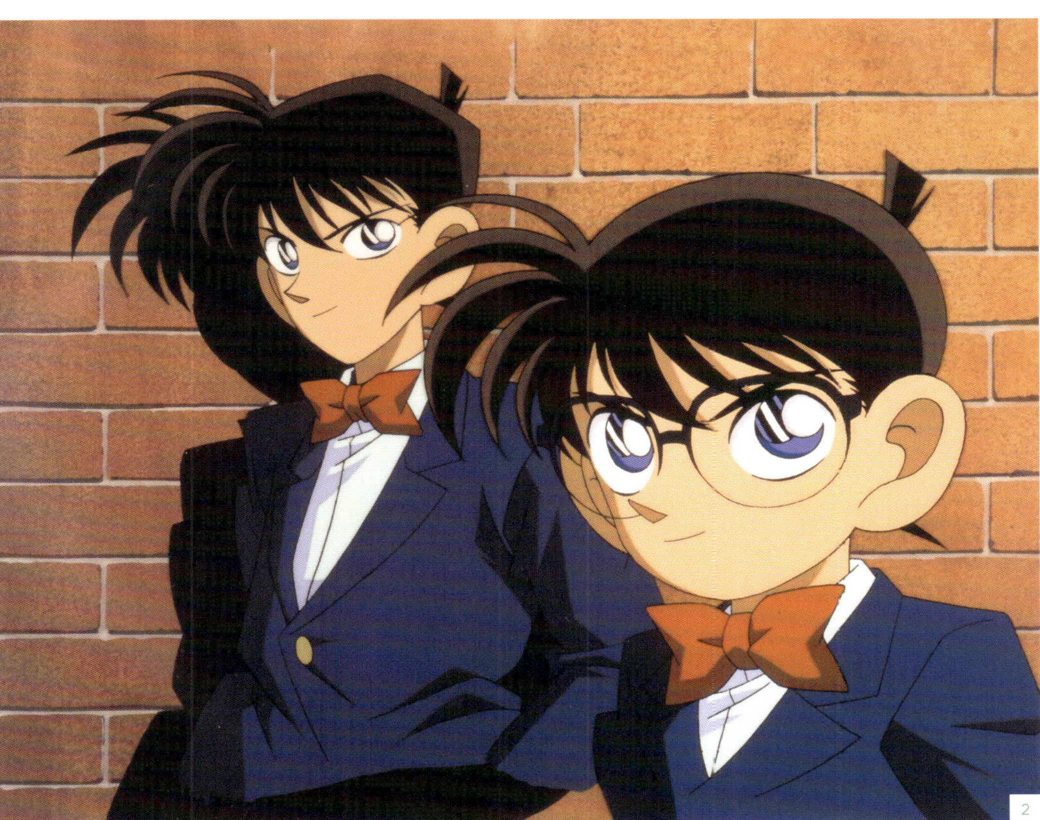
2

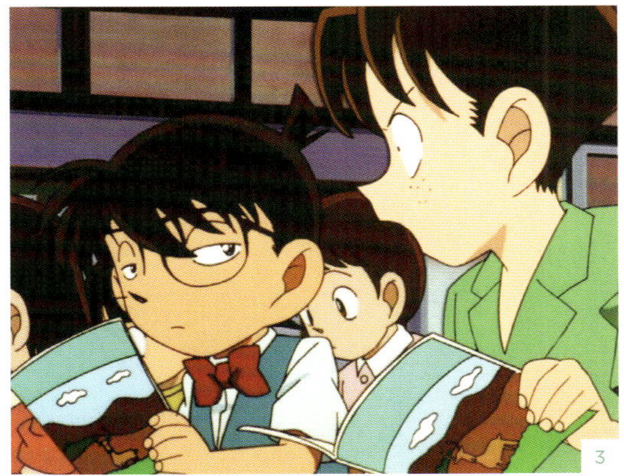
3

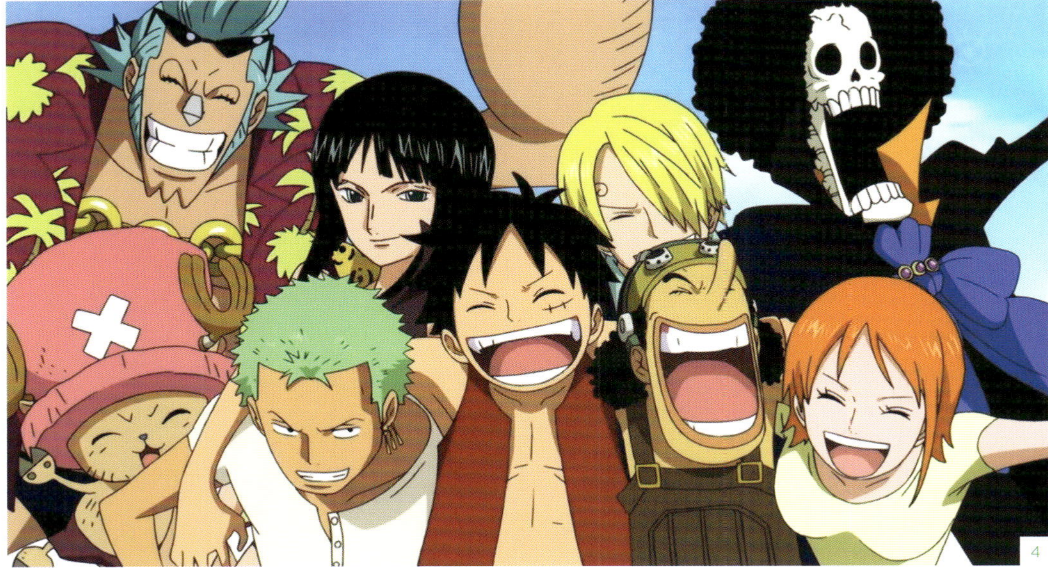
4

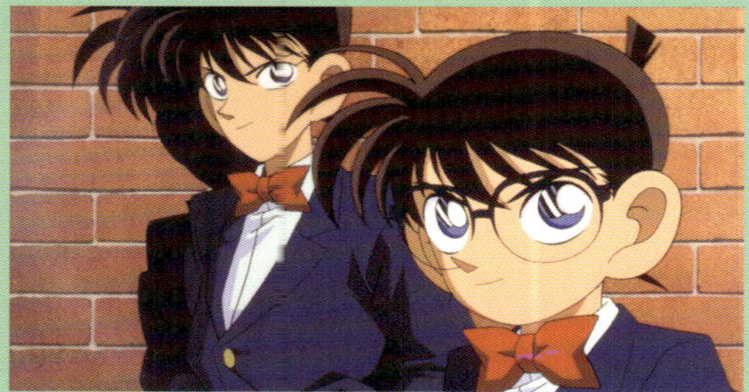

MEITANTEI CONAN

Case Closed

Year: 1996
Category: TV, film
Directors: Kenji Kodama and Yasuichiro Yamamoto
Animation Studio: Tokyo Movie Shinsha

AT A GLANCE:
The detective in a child's body becomes the new police idol whose investigations provide commercial comfort to the TMS, with over 1,100 episodes by 2023.

YOU MAY ALSO LIKE . . .
Toei's response a year later, with the adaptation of the manga *The Kindaichi Case Files*. The crime-solving students in *Detective School Q*.

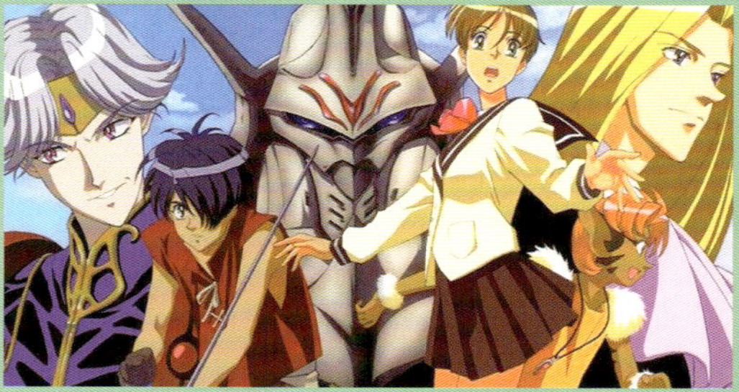

TENKŪ NO ESCAFLOWNE

The Vision of Escaflowne

Year: 1996
Category: TV
Director: Shōji Kawamori
Animation Studio: Sunrise

AT A GLANCE:
A daring *shōjo* series combining fantasy, mecha, and romance, with a sophisticated post-*Evangelion* plot. It's a combination that appeals to both girls and boys alike.

YOU MAY ALSO LIKE . . .
Fushigi Yuugi and *The Twelve Kingdoms*, in which heroines are transported to fantastic worlds. *Macross*, the original Shōji Kawamori template. *Aura Battler Dunbine* and *Panzer World Galient*, for more mecha-fantasy mash-ups.

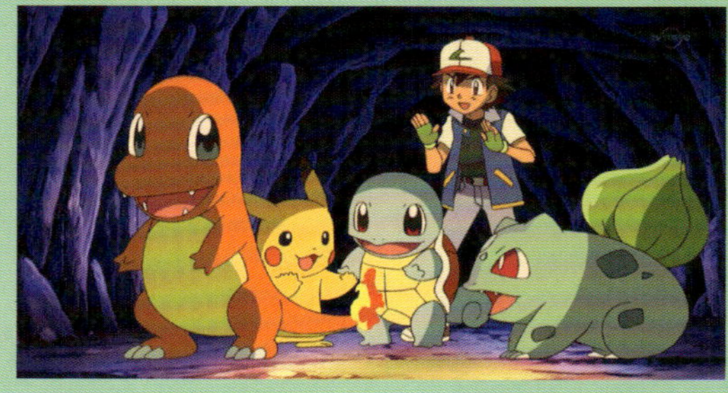

POKÉMON

Pokémon

Year: 1997
Category: TV, film
Director: Kunihiko Yuyama
Animation Studio: Oriental Light and Magic

AT A GLANCE:
The video game franchise based on monster-fighting collectibles deploys a meticulous media-mix strategy, with television series and annual films enhancing the worldwide phenomenon.

YOU MAY ALSO LIKE . . .
Digimon, Toei's response with a more mature concept. *Yu-Gi-Oh!*, a cross between the collectible card games *Magic: The Gathering* and *Pokémon*. *Yō-kai Watch*, another media-mix project whose anime is overseen by OLM.

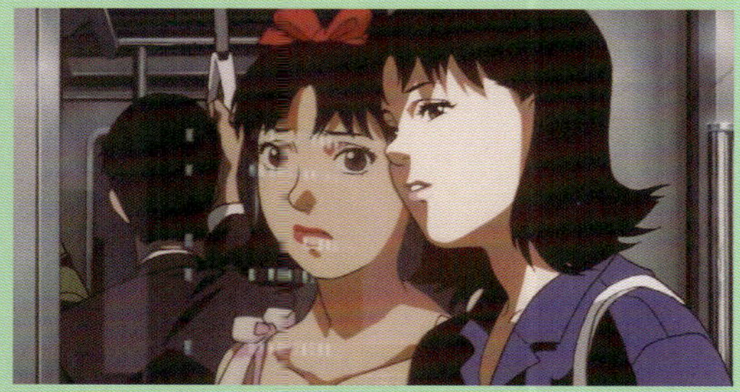

PERFECT BLUE

Perfect Blue

Year: 1997
Category: Film
Director: Satoshi Kon
Animation Studio: Madhouse

AT A GLANCE:
This horrific Hitchcock-style thriller marks the debut of director Satoshi Kon, whose mix of realistic and lyrical cinema focuses on the psychological construction of his characters.

YOU MAY ALSO LIKE . . .
Millennium Actress, Kon's ode to cinema. *Tokyo Godfathers*, his Christmas story of the down and out. *The Paranoia Agent* series, his caustic vision of social pressure in Japan.

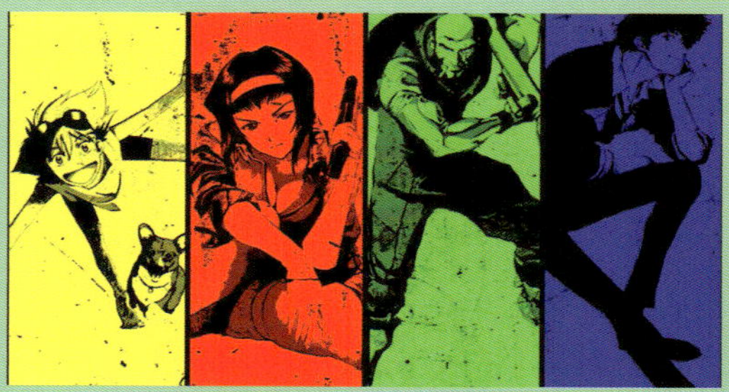

COWBOY BEBOP

Cowboy Bebop

Year: 1998
Category: TV
Director: Shinichirō Watanabe
Animation Studio: Sunrise

AT A GLANCE:
An homage to artistic creativity, *Cowboy Bebop* stands out for its explosive blend of genres, meticulous direction, and eclectic soundtrack.

YOU MAY ALSO LIKE . . .
The stellar adventures of the groundbreaking film *Crusher Joe* and the *Outlaw Star* series, produced in parallel by Sunrise. *Trigun*, Madhouse's response, and Satelight's *Heat Guy J*.

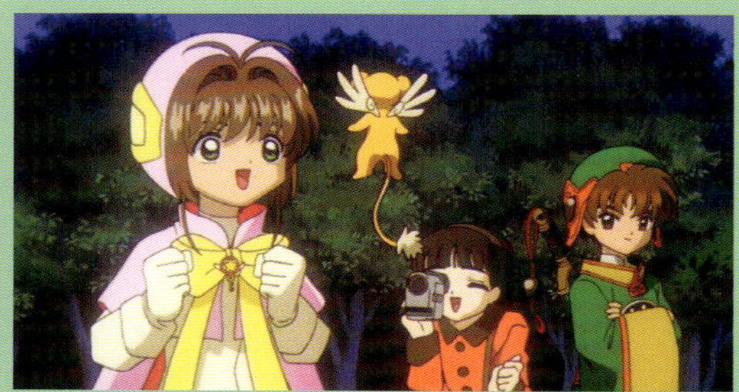

CARDCAPTOR SAKURA

Cardcaptor Sakura

Year: 1998
Category: TV
Director: Morio Asaka
Animation Studio: Madhouse

AT A GLANCE:
CLAMP revolutionizes the world of magical girls: the heroine, whose powers increase as she captures magical cards, must confront moral dilemmas to achieve her often challenged goal.

YOU MAY ALSO LIKE . . .
Magical DoReMi, a magical girl as cute as she is powerful. *Puella Magi Madoka Magica*, for its genre-bending and complex narrative. *Mirmo!*, a romantic comedy featuring a *kawaii* fairy-heroine duo.

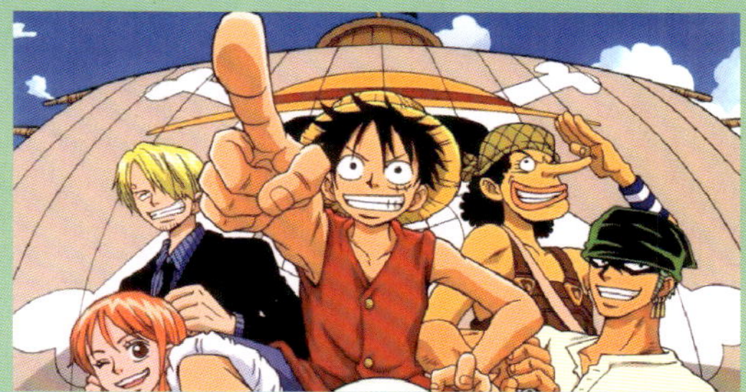

ONE PIECE

One Piece
Year: 1999
Category: TV, film
Director: Kōnosuke Uda
Animation Studio: Toei Animation

AT A GLANCE:
The world's best-selling manga boasts the longest animated version in the history of *shōnen nekketsu*. With his good humor and insatiable appetite, Luffy is a worthy successor to Son Goku.

YOU MAY ALSO LIKE . . .
The powerful ninja *Naruto*, the pirate show's biggest competition, or Ichigo, the hunter of wandering souls in *Bleach*. The unbridled humor in *Gintama*. Gourmet Hunter *Toriko*'s mouthwatering quests.

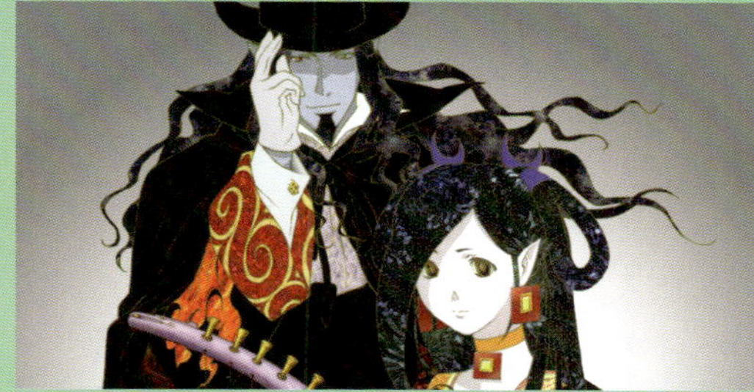

GANKUTSUOU

Gankutsuou: The Count of Monte Cristo
Year: 2004
Category: TV
Director: Mahiro Maeda
Animation Studio: Gonzo

AT A GLANCE:
This adaptation of Alexandre Dumas' novel stands out for its retro-futuristic style and graphic experimentation, where digital layering was used to eliminate internal lines, creating a minimalist look.

YOU MAY ALSO LIKE . . .
The 2D-3D combination in innovative projects, such as *Blue Submarine No. 6*, eco-friendly *Earth Maiden Arjuna*, the romantic horror *Le Portrait de Petite Cosette* OAVs, and the stunning *Last Exile* series.

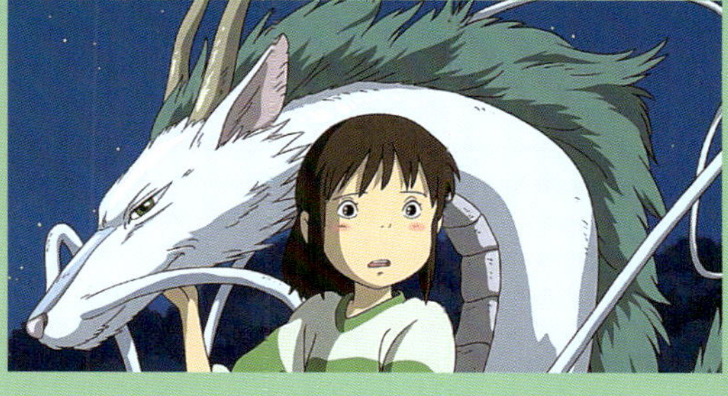

SEN TO CHIHIRO NO KAMIKAKUSHI

Spirited Away
Year: 2001
Category: Film
Director: Hayao Miyazaki
Animation Studio: Studio Ghibli

AT A GLANCE:
A commercial triumph for Ghibli, which now dominates the Japanese box office in all categories. This film won the Oscar and the Golden Bear, and the whole world was moved by the heroine's tenacity.

YOU MAY ALSO LIKE . . .
Princess Mononoke and *Howl's Moving Castle*, which introduce and conclude a mature arc in the director's filmography. The status of women in *The Tale of Princess Kaguya*.

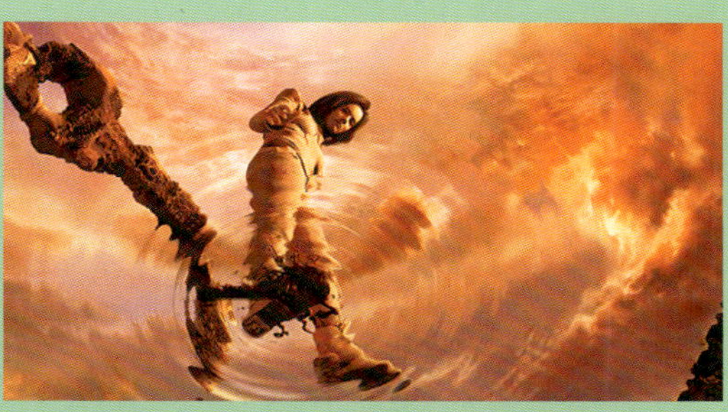

FINAL FANTASY: THE SPIRITS WITHIN

Final Fantasy: The Spirits Within
Year: 2001
Category: Film
Directors: Hironobu Sakaguchi and Motonori Sakakibara
Animation Studio: Square USA

AT A GLANCE:
This colossally budgeted American-Japanese coproduction experiments with photorealism and is the result of a cinematic ambition already evident in the franchise's previous video games.

YOU MAY ALSO LIKE . . .
Final Fantasy and *Resident Evil*, extensions of the video games. *Appleseed Alpha* and *Arcadia of My Youth: Endless Orbit SSX* for their photorealism.

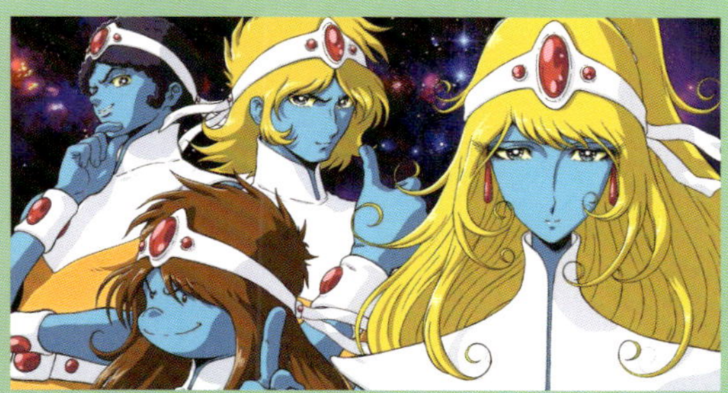

INTERSTELLA 5555

Interstella 5555: The 5tory of the 5ecret 5tar 5ystem
Year: 2003
Category: Film
Director: Kazuhisa Takenouchi
Animation Studio: Toei Animation

AT A GLANCE:
The album *Discovery* by the French duo Daft Punk is brought to life by Toei Animation, based on the graphic universe of *Captain Harlock*'s creator—the globalization of anime in all its splendor.

YOU MAY ALSO LIKE . . .
The *Animatrix*, *Halo Legends*, *Dante Inferno*, and *Gotham Knight* anthologies, coproductions that complement American video game franchises. Studio 4°C's music videos and Studio Ghibli's *On Your Mark*.

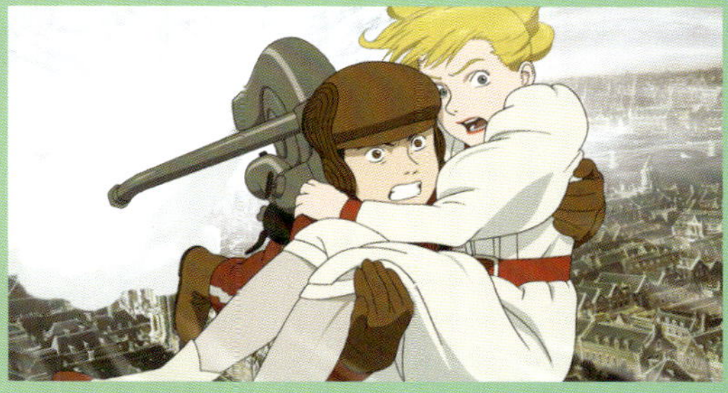

STEAMBOY

Steamboy
Year: 2004
Category: Film
Director: Katsuhiro Ōtomo **Animation Studio:** Sunrise

AT A GLANCE:
It took ten years to create this 100 percent digital feature, making it the most expensive anime film in history.

YOU MAY ALSO LIKE . . .
Metropolis and *Ghost in the Shell 2: Innocence*, two other lavish films that use computer graphic to explore the relationship between man and machine.

A Sisyphean task

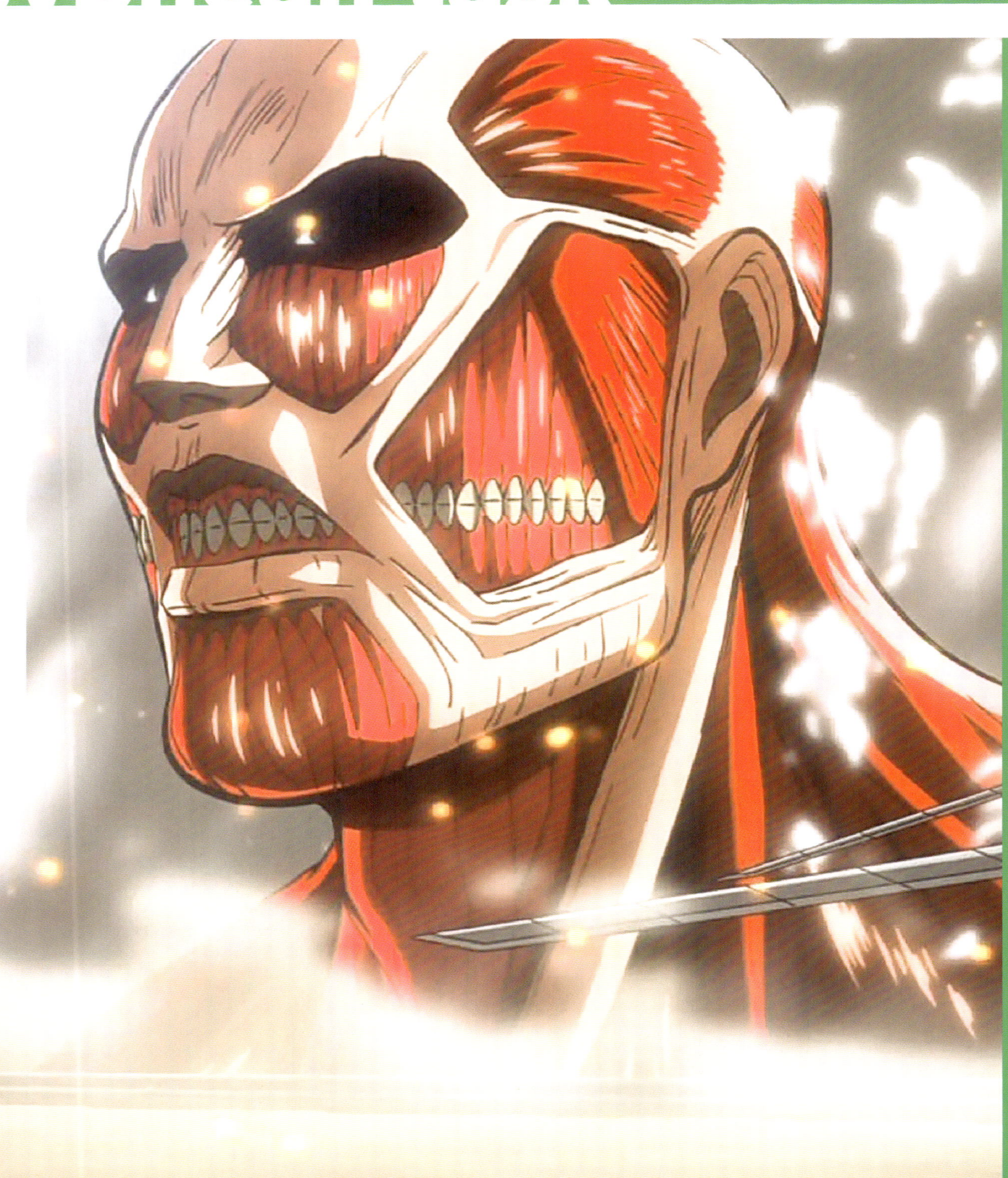

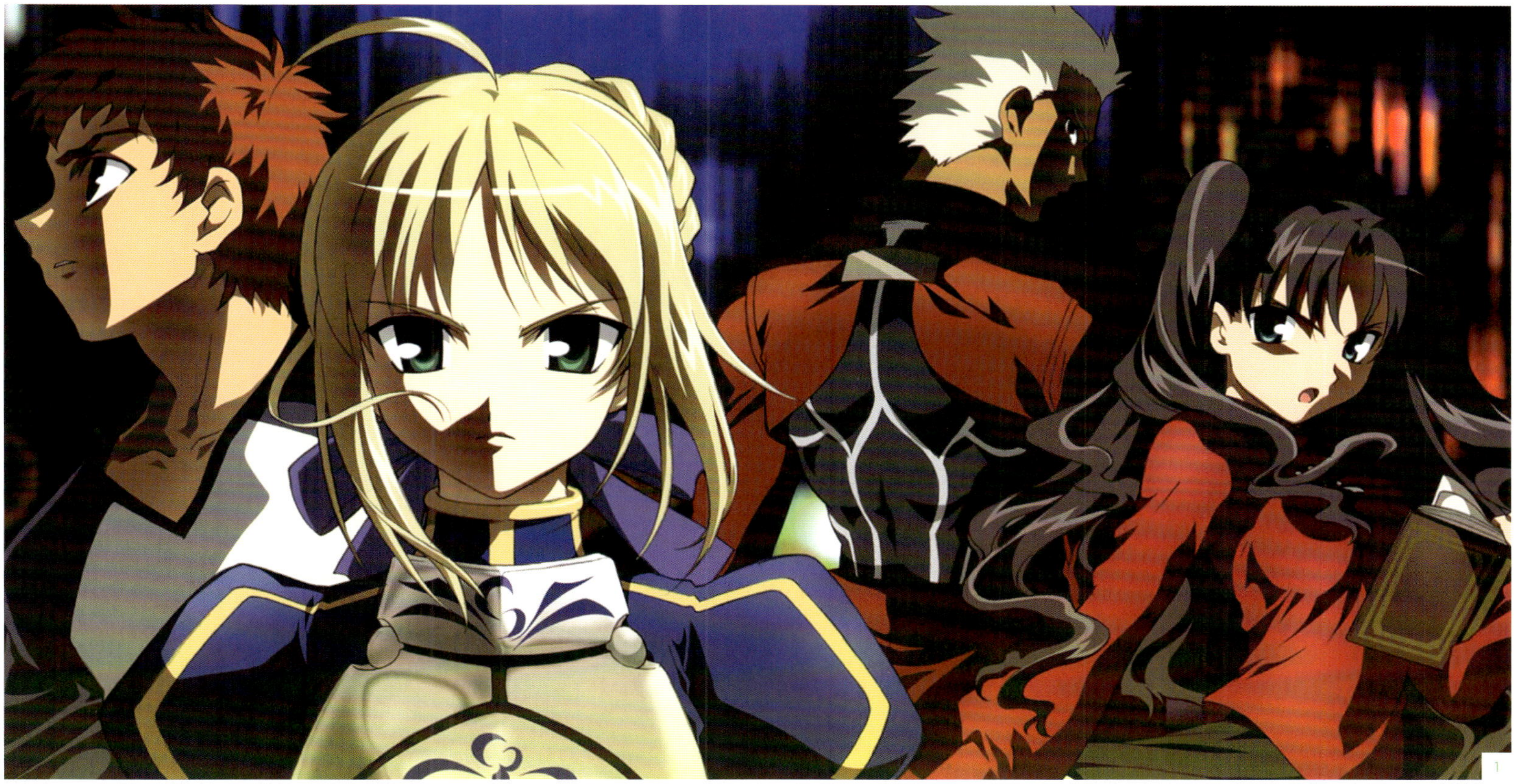

1
2006
Fate/Stay Night

Otaku, the hero of modern-day tales

THE OTAKU KING

Fan communities were multiplying across websites and discussion forums across the internet, where they had an unprecedented opportunity to express their opinions and desires. The digital landscape had become the ideal terrain for instant market research as fans could be quickly surveyed. Manga publishers even went so far as to supplement some volumes with OAVs specially designed to gauge the potential for a future series. Otaku needed to be given what they wanted, and the industry was perfectly content with that because it ensured that viewers would be there when the series was broadcast.

But by focusing on this target audience, television production became compartmentalized by cultivating recurring storylines, particularly in romantic comedies where the fetishization of women took on an exaggerated scope. Stereotypes became automatic, like the naughty girl who turned out to be lovable, girls wearing glasses, catgirls, shy girls, and so on. But how could otaku, whose social skills weren't their strong suit, identify with a character who rubs shoulders with so many beautiful young women? The solution was domestic service. The ordinary protagonist's daily life is turned upside down when a sweet, helpful young lady appears who supports and bonds with him. Sometimes a goddess (*Oh My Goddess!*), sometimes an android (*Chobits*, *Mahoromatic*), sometimes even a human (*Ai Yori Aoshi*), she responded to a growing interest in the maid persona, which spread all the way to Akihabara. **Maid cafés** sprang up, and young women and teenagers in maid outfits took to the sidewalks to advertise them. Over on Otome Road, it was the butlers taking care of customers, recalling the hero's elegance in *Black Butler* (A-1 Pictures, 2009). To both spice things up and capitalize on character clichés, protagonists were surrounded by a host of figures of the opposite sex,

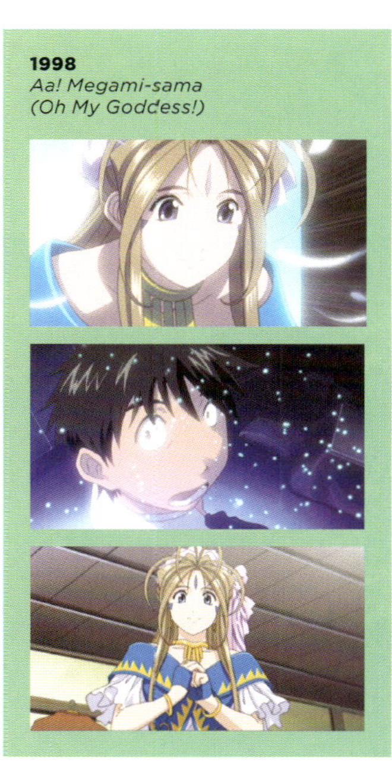

1998
Aa! Megami-sama (Oh My Goddess!)

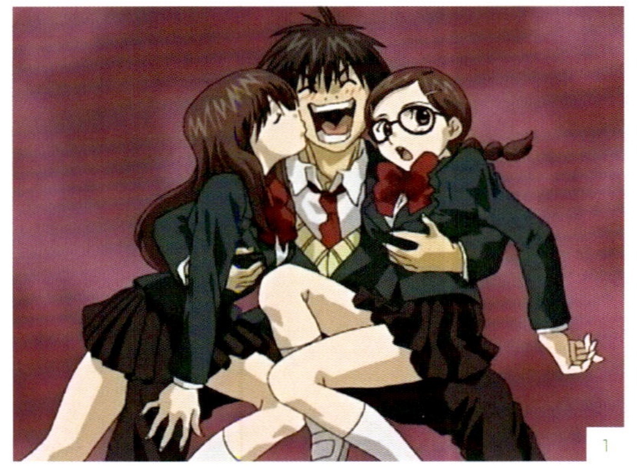

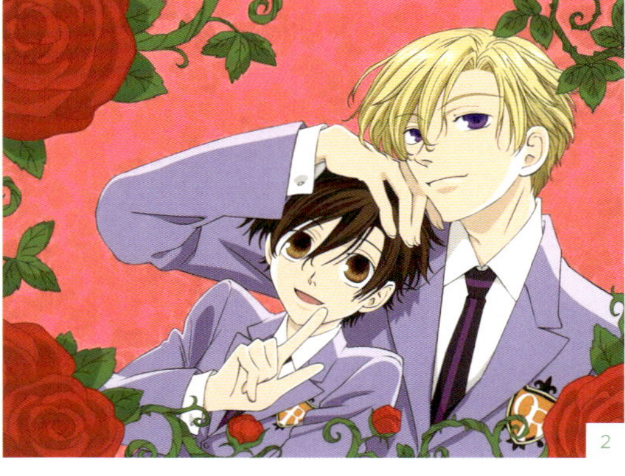

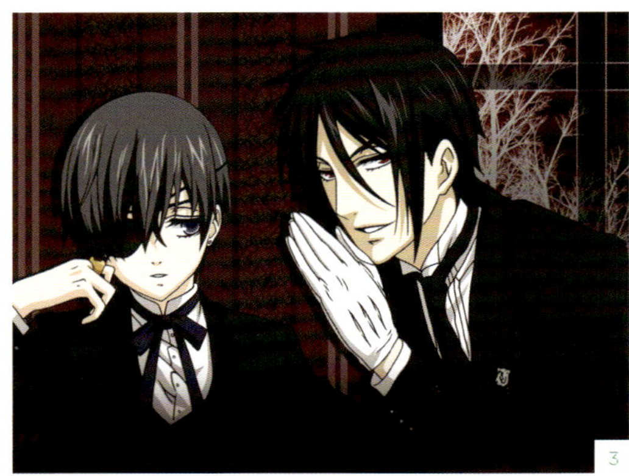

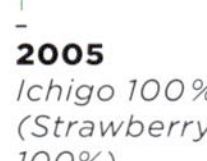

1
2005
Ichigo 100% (Strawberry 100%)

2
2006
Ōran Kōkō Hosuto Bu (Ouran High School Host Club)

3
2008
Kuroshitsuji (Black Butler)

a harem formula perfectly delivered in the risqué *shōnen Strawberry 100%* (2005) and in *Ouran High School Host Club*, which delighted female viewers with its handsome hosts.

The entertainment industry was increasingly drawing on otaku fantasies for new material. As a further extension of the harem trend, flirtatious video games became an important part of the otaku community, especially after the Key company created an elaborate scenario for *Kanon*, its flagship title, in 1998, making it one of the most popular developers in the field. These interactive video games quickly flooded the animation market, for which the sexual aspect of *eroge* games was often overshadowed. The trend was catching on, and a number of successful games were getting a new lease of life, such as *Kimi ga Nosomu Eien* (*Rumbling Hearts*, 2003), which played the dramatic romance card, in which a high school girl plunges into a coma after an accident, leading to her boyfriend's long depression. The series begins with romantic clichés and eventually turns to adult themes with a healthy dose of sentimentality.

In 2006, *Fate/Stay Night*, a sacrosanct favorite of text adventure fans who enjoyed visual novels, *eroge*, and the like, was adapted by Studio Deen. The best-selling erotic game of 2004 captivated players, not for its rare naughty moments, but for its fantastic story depicting the Holy Grail War, in which magicians clash by summoning servant warriors. The TV series was so successful that *Newtype* magazine ranked it as the ninth best anime of all time. Anime fans had come to admire the game developer Type-Moon, and *Fate/Stay Night* became one of the longest-running visual novels, still running in 2024 after several series and films.

Works by the Key studio were particularly popular. While Toei Animation produced the mystical drama *Air* (2005) and the romance *Clannad* (2007), both feature films directed by veteran director Osamu Dezaki, Kyoto Animation gained momentum with its own productions, releasing a new adaptation of *Kanon* in 2007. Faithful to the original works and driven by great technical ambition, Kyoto Animation was building its reputation with its fans, who were constantly switching between different media.

A LITTLE PURITY IN A FAN SERVICE WORLD

In 2006, viewers were introduced to Haruhi, a high school girl captivated by the paranormal, unlike Kyon, her down-to-earth classmate. In spite of himself, Kyon is drawn into the club Haruhi has set up to study supernatural phenomena: the SOS Brigade. They are soon joined by three other high school students whose hidden motives are directly linked to the eccentric club president. With Chiba TV just switching over to digital signals, the fourteen episodes of Kyoto Animation's *Suzumiya Haruhi no Yūutsu* (*The Melancholy of Haruhi Suzumiya*) seemed to be broadcast out of order. This was neither a bug nor a programming flaw but a choice made by the authors, fascinating viewers who had to put the pieces back together to understand the chronology of the story. It was impossible to be indifferent to Haruhi and her fantasies, especially as the story became more convoluted than a simple school comedy, with science fiction gradually invading the narrative.

The show won the Animation Kobe Award for a TV Feature in 2006 and the Best TV Anime Series at the Tokyo Anime Awards, and it was also hailed as a cultural phenomenon by fans the world over. Haruhi was so popular that the name "SOS Brigade" has been used by a number of clubs, associations, and blogs, and the dance in the closing credits, *Hare Hare Yukai*, has been meticulously reproduced in numerous flashmobs and other videos posted online. In 2011, after a second season and a film (at two hours and forty minutes long!), the first volume of *The Melancholy of Haruhi Suzumiya* became the first Japanese **light novel** to sell over a million copies. Otaku had their newest icon! However, Haruhi's sex appeal was not exploited, and paradoxically, this mesmerized fans.

The following year, Kyoto Animation brought together various female clichés in its adaptation of the *Lucky Star* manga, which follows the daily lives of a group of four high school girls led by Konata, an anime and video game aficionada. With no male protagonist to identify with, the viewer is directly connected to a group of girls and their lives. It was no longer a question of satisfying the libido of certain otaku, but rather their sentimental emptiness, which is the role of *moe* characters, often infantilized and akin to pure, comforting little sisters. Although the perspective is different from a hormone-driven harem story, the line between the two genres gets blurred, as in the incestuous *Koi Kaze* (*Love Wind*,* 2004) and the comical *Ore no Imōto ga Konna ni Kawaii Wake ga Nai* (*Oreimo*, 2010), whose little sister turns out to be an *eroge* addict!

In 2008, Kyoto Animation crystallized the concept of *moe* anime with its adaptation of the *K-On!* comic strip, in which five high school girls form a rock band. Music and sweetness are the order of the day in this technically sophisticated series. It was a resounding success, leading to a sequel and a film, and eventually generating over $217 million in profits from merchandise alone. Every fan could have a figurine of his or her favorite character, and why not have the whole group in different outfits?

In February 2011, the *K-On!* franchise became the first to sell over 500,000 Blu-rays and DVDs, a feat that reinforced Kyoto Animation's artistic direction and confirmed market trends in the genre. *Moe* anime, which began as a simple fan affinity for its characters, cemented itself as one of the many subgenres of Japanese animation.

THE SONG OF THE FANS

Moe anime also reflected a musical trend popularized at the turn of the century by the Morning Musume, a girl group who brought cheer and comfort to a country in crisis. Following in the footsteps of the all-female bands of the 1970s, these groups have seen their membership vary over time to maintain a young average age. This is because idols are recruited and trained from adolescence to meet specific criteria, such as remaining devoted to their fans by staying away from romantic or sexual relationships.

In 2005, AKB48 turned the industry on its head, directly targeting the hearts (and wallets) of otaku. AKB as in Akihabara, where girls were performing on stage, and "48" as in the number of members in the group—the choice of possible fantasies was worthy of a dating video game! The support of otaku audiences reached unprecedented levels: in 2015, AKB48 sold more than thirty-six million copies of their single "Kuchibiru ni Be My Baby." From this point on, maids and pop idols became an entertainment mainstay for

2008
K-ON!

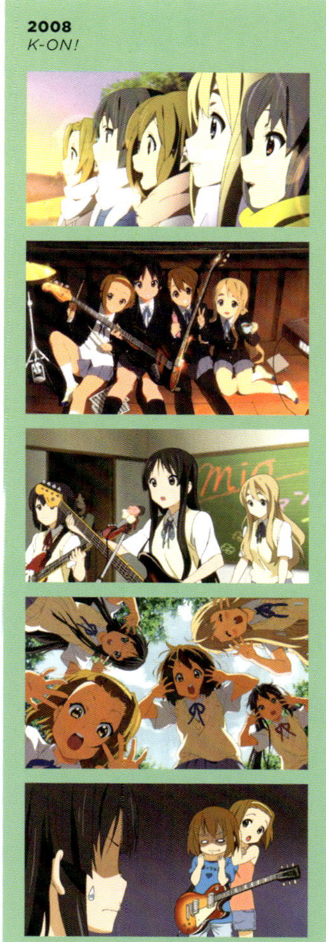

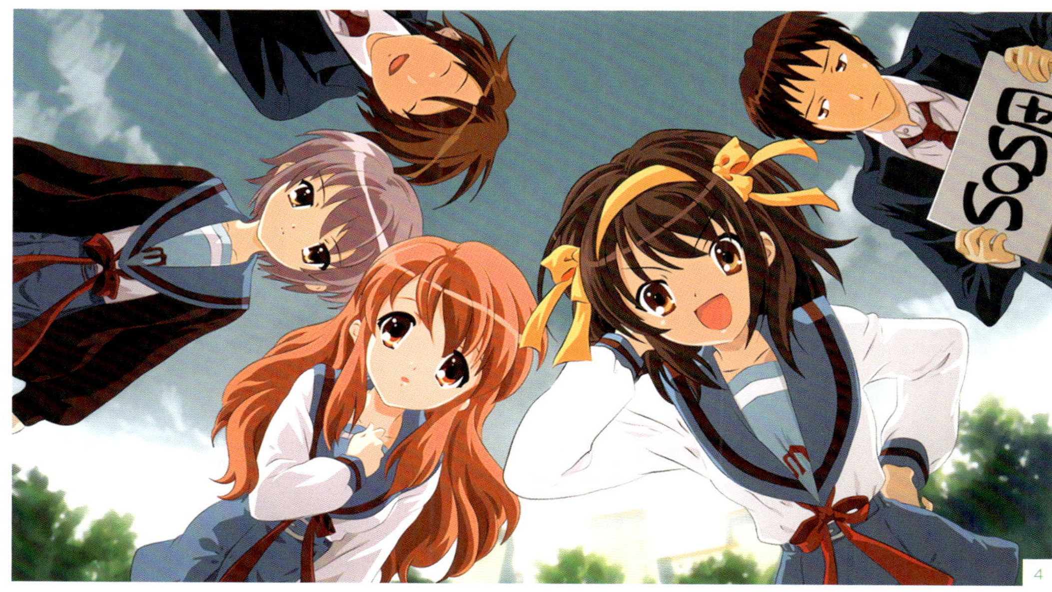

4
—
2006
Suzumiya Haruhi no Yūtsu (The Melancholy of Haruhi Suzumiya)

2011
The Idolmaster

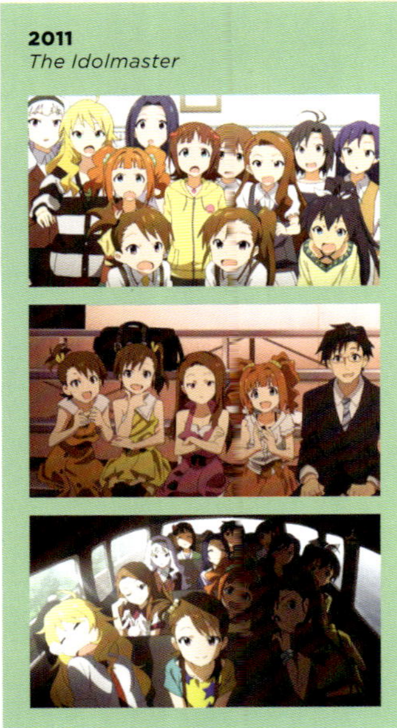

monomaniacs, right up there with giant robots, as evidenced by the very location of the AKB48 theater, adjoining a Gundam Café.

But this glittering universe was marred by numerous scandals, including an idol shaving her head to atone for a sexual act that was brought to light, another being harassed and then killed by a frustrated fan, and many singers continuing their careers in pornography. More than fifteen years on and *Perfect Blue* had never been so relevant!

These sorts of scandals didn't exist with the competition, **Vocaloid**. Vocaloid software programs, which enabled users to create their own songs and share them on the internet, took off in leaps and bounds in 2007 with the unveiling of Hatsune Miku's advanced voice bank and huge turquoise pigtails. She was the first successful virtual star, whose tens of thousands of songs were being played around the world. In 2009, developer Crypton Future Media responded to the web craze by organizing a concert that won over audiences with its 3D Vocaloid projected onto a transparent screen to create a holographic impression. It was the start of a true career, as she went on to produce a series of increasingly innovative performances and appeared in video games and commercials.

With her groundbreaking technology and interactive concept, Hatsune Miku became a twenty-first-century icon, cementing the strong bond that had united idol and otaku for over two decades. The concept of the virtual singer that had been pure fiction in *Macross Plus* (1994) was about to become very real. Idols had been around in anime for a long time, but now they could be the main subject. It was impossible to miss the phenomenon that was *The Idolmaster*, a rhythm-based video game developed over several platforms, including smartphones, in which players manage a pop idol agency. Whereas Sunrise freely adapted the franchise in 2007, A-1 Pictures (a Sony-owned subsidiary of Aniplex) took up the torch in 2011 with anime productions that were more faithful and complementary to the games, much to the delight of gamers!

In 2012, Satelight produced the sci-fi series *AKB0048*, in which the musical group is the last bastion against the prohibition of entertainment in

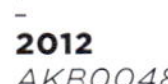

1
–
2012
AKB0048

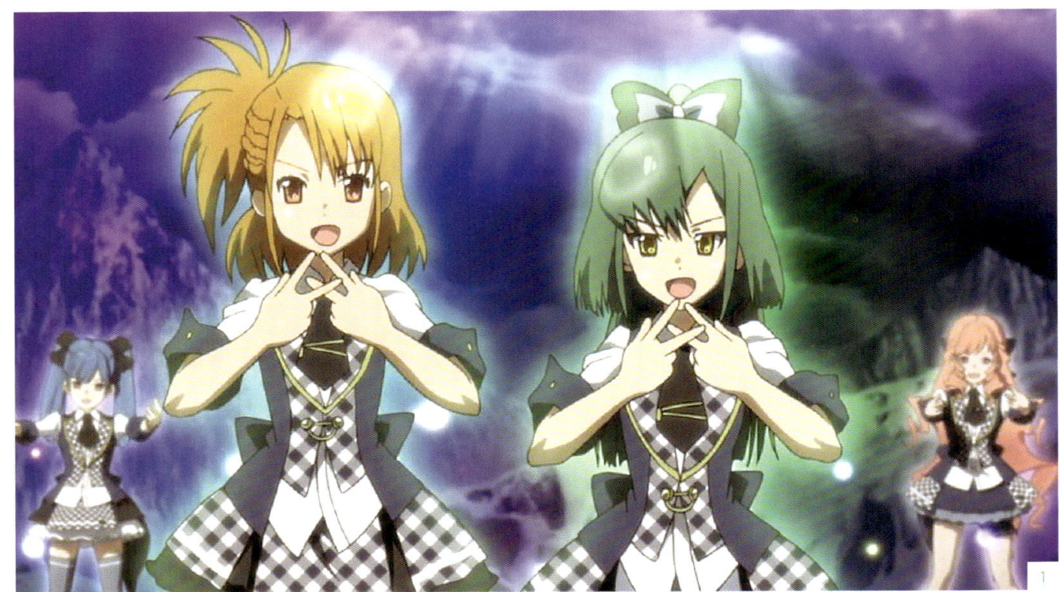

1

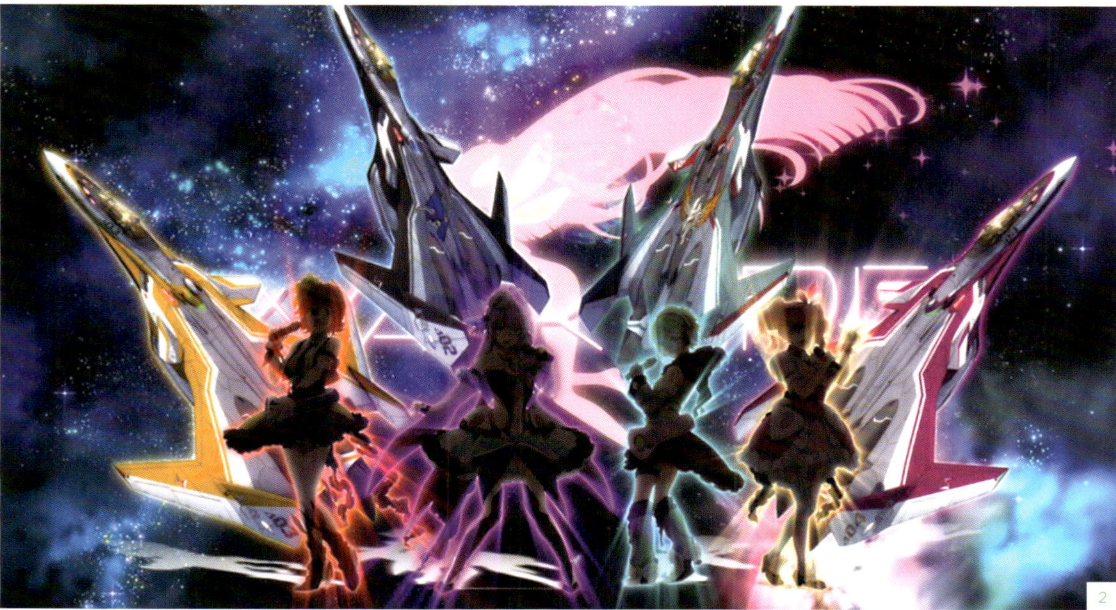

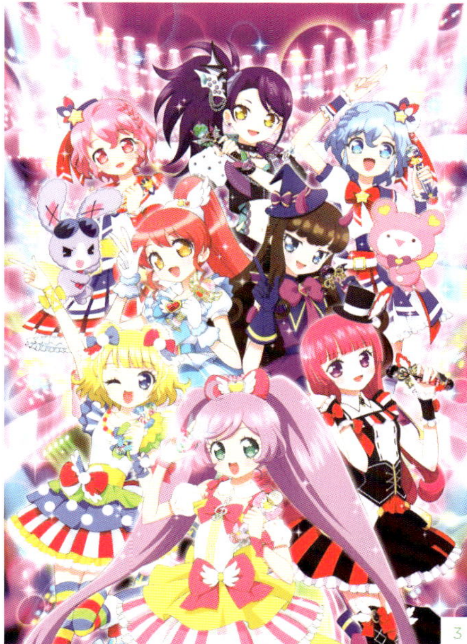

2
2005
Macross Delta

3
2014
PriPara

a world eaten away by industrialization. Directed by Shōji Kawamori, the series boasted high technical quality, with band members singing and voicing the many *moe* characters. The anime's success was hardly surprising, leading to a second season. And Kawamori bounced back with *Macross Delta*, which in 2016 incorporated the idol group concept into its series.

On Tokyo TV, the magical girl comedy *PriPara* kept female audiences entertained every week from 2014 to 2017. Tatsunoko Production adapted an arcade game into a long-running anime series, featuring a pop idol world where characters work their way up the performance ladder. Reality had caught up with fiction. And if the heroine is crazy about the singers, it's because fans now held their rightful place in the spotlight!

COOL OTAKU

Pop idols and the *moe* concept had an essential characteristic that the world of Hello Kitty was developing on a massive scale: *kawaii*, the hallmark of Cool Japan.

When Japan became the official host country for the 2020 Summer Olympics in 2013, it expanded this foreign policy by creating the Cool Japan Fund, with a cumulative capital of ¥63.3 billion ($526 million), 85 percent of which was financed by the State, with the remainder coming from private companies. The country was investing in many cultural events around the world to ensure that its international appeal didn't fade, especially as Korea and China were becoming major competitors. In addition to cultural promotion, the investment was expected to raise between ¥8 and 11 trillion ($79 and $113 billion) by 2020. With soft power dominating the international scene, it was hardly surprising that people were drawn to the many *kawaii* products, wanted to eat sushi, and see the most famous idol of them all, Hatsune Miku, who opened for Lady Gaga's 2014 tour.

There was no doubt that Cool Japan had also played a role in changing attitudes about the economic forces of manga and anime. Even in Japan, the pejorative term *otaku* was becoming milder and more widespread. Tarō Asō, who became prime minister in 2007, was known for his passion for manga, and some pop idols claimed to be otaku themselves, including the multitalented Shoko Nakagawa and the musical group Dempagumi.inc. Not only were otaku multiplying, as evidenced by more than half a million visitors at Comiket, but they were also being labeled cool, with their growing popularity coinciding with another pop culture term: *geek*.

When Bryan Singer and Sam Raimi adapted the *X-Men* and *Spider-Man* comics, respectively, in the early 2000s, they brought international audiences into the world of comic book superheroes, which previously had appealed only to children and insiders. At the height of the DVD golden age, with artists claiming their influences, filmmakers became spokespeople for a subculture, like the Wachowskis, who proclaimed their love for anime with *The Matrix*, or Quentin Tarantino, who created his ode to Hong Kong and Japanese exploitation films with *Kill Bill*.

Fans of these imaginary universes suddenly saw the world turn toward their passions, to the point where they became the storytellers themselves. In 2004, *Spider-Man 2* was a worldwide success, especially in Japan, where it grossed $59 million, the highest box office earnings outside the United States. Japanese fans were won over by Peter Parker, the awkward student torn between his love affair and his secret identity. The same year, the TV adaptation of the manga *Genshiken* defended the reputation of otaku fans. The series depicts the daily life of "The Society for the Study of Modern Visual Culture," which turns out to be nothing more than a group of manga and anime enthusiasts. They are particularly interested in the TV series *Kujibiki Unbalance* and analyze and debate each episode. In order to spend time with her boyfriend who is in the club, a "normal" classmate is forced to hang out with the band of otaku, who of course turns out to be lovable.

The image of the pimply, perverted virgin was gradually replaced with a fan who had undeniable human qualities. A case in point is the modern urban legend *Densha Otoko* (*Train Man*), in which an Akihabara devotee attempts to win the heart of a distinguished young woman with help from members of an online discussion forum. By 2005, the phenomenon had spread across several media, including a live-action romantic drama series that opened with Gonzo's animated opening credits, in homage to *Daicon IV*, the iconic music video of otaku culture.

At a time when the geeky quartet of the American sitcom *The Big Bang Theory* was entertaining audiences the world over, die-hard fans were becoming a hot topic. In Japan, the entertainment industry had never focused so much on its own target audience. The otaku heroines of *Lucky Star* and *Oreimo* weren't just a hot new trend on which to capitalize—they also broke the fourth wall, and fans were flattered to hear characters use their own jargon. This immediate connection also helped raise current social issues, like in *NHK ni Yōkoso!* (*Welcome to the N.H.K.*, 2006), one of the many series that focus on the *hikikomori*, recluses who stay at home with the internet as their only window to the outside world (there were more than 260,000 of them in 2015). But long gone were the days when Gainax staged morose interviews with adults consumed by their passion in *Otaku No Video* (1991); nowadays, anime conveyed positive social values. *Welcome to the N.H.K.*, for example, illustrates the absurdity of morbid phenomena such as collective suicide organized by internet users. There is also the feature *Summer Wars* (2009), which brings a computer geek into contact with a wealthy, long-standing family. The film attempts to strike a balance between the traditional (real life) and the modern (the digital world), without overlooking the fact that having a passion is also a way of asserting oneself in society.

Otaku had never felt so much a part of the entertainment industry, which responded to their every whim by getting them more involved. As a result, they were no longer just funny or endearing to watch, but the protagonists of great adventures. In *Gundam Build Fighters*, heroes battle it out with Gundam models from the various series of the

2007
Lucky Star

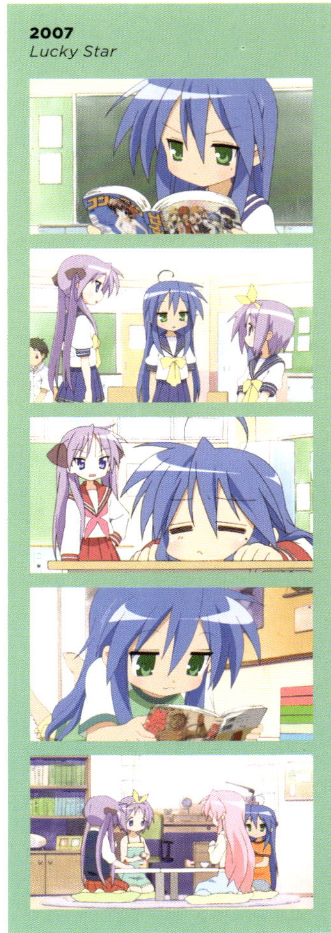

1
2004
Genshiken

2
2010
Oreimo

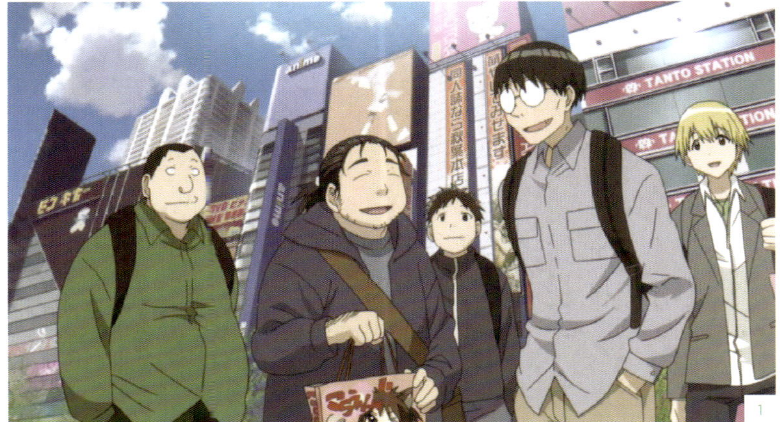

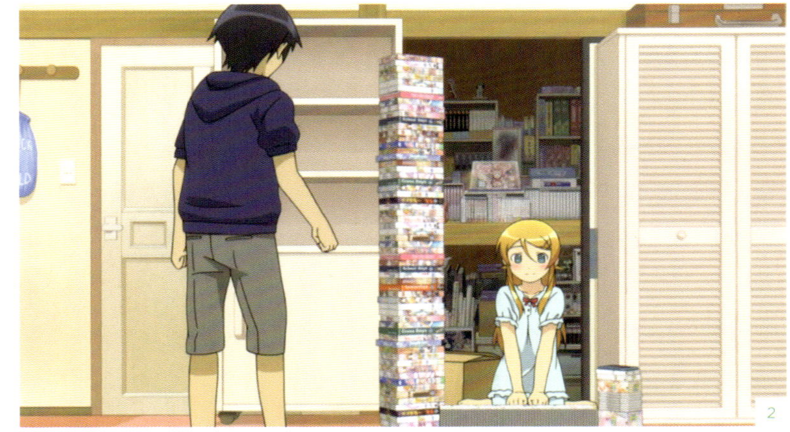

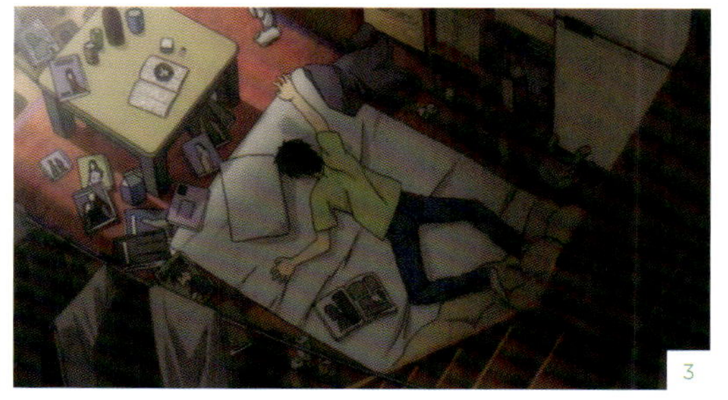
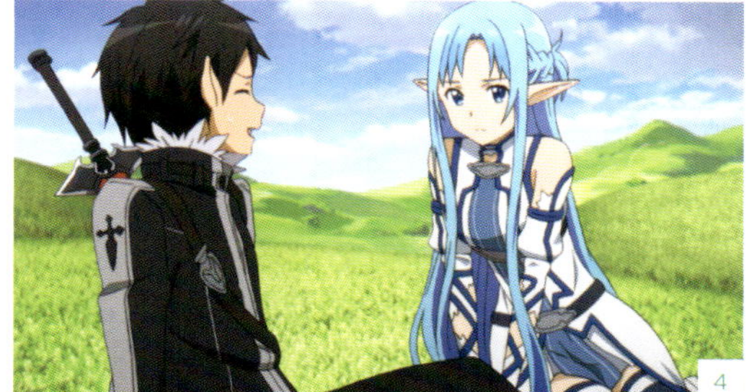
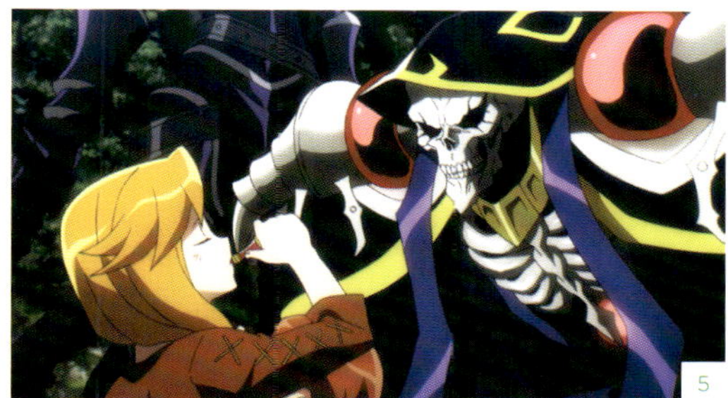

3
2017
Re:Creators

4
2012
Sword Art Online

5
2015
Overlord

franchise. As for MMORPG fans, they became warriors locked inside their favorite video game in *Sword Art Online* (A-1 Pictures, 2012), *Log Horizon* (Satelight, 2013), and *Overlord* (Madhouse, 2015). The heroes now had the mind of an otaku, with the fantasized physical abilities of otaku, in worlds adored by otaku.

The new generation had perfectly mastered the syntax of the moving image and the nuts and bolts of production. The relationship between creators and viewers went beyond the works themselves to reach a meta dimension! For example, in 2006, the creators of *Genshiken* made episodes of the fictional anime revered by the series' heroes, *Kujibiki Unbalance*, whereas in 2017, the Troyca studio merged fictional worlds with the real world in *Re:Creators*.

Climate of crisis

STARTING IN THE RED, ENDING IN THE BLACK

In 2006, Japan produced a record 135,530 minutes of anime—94 days! That's 20,000 more than in 2015, an increase of almost 20 percent. Oversaturated studios were in a constant race against time, to such an extent that veteran animators no longer had time to mentor young recruits. This training was an inherent, if unspoken, part of the contract signed by industry newcomers, yet it justified the meager salaries at the bottom of the ladder. New animators were paid on a per-drawing basis, with freelancer salaries varying between $340 and $1,130 a month. With the advent of digital technology and the new millennium, the industry had become too forward-looking, forgetting to pass on its archaic (but not obsolete) techniques to future generations.

Ironically, this know-how was exported to mainland Asia during the boom years of the late twentieth century. Subcontractors at the time, South Korea (*My Beautiful Girl, Mari*, 2002; *Oseam*, 2003; *Wonderful Days*, 2003) and then China (*Monkey King: Hero Is Back*, 2015; *Big Fish & Begonia*, 2016) began demonstrating their own industry's advancements on the big screen, slowly gaining recognition on the international stage. From that point onward, Japanese studios turned to Vietnam, India, and Thailand, where the labor force, while less expensive, was lacking the necessary skills, as viewers would soon notice.

The situation became so worrying that, after ninety years, the anime industry created a national union, the Japanese Animation Creators Association (JAniCA). No fewer than 500 members joined the association when it was launched in October 2007 at a press conference held by director Satoshi Kon and other animation directors, including Moriyasu Taniguchi and Akihiro Kanayama. JAniCA was responsible for successful changes right off the bat. In 2010, ¥215 million ($1.9 million) was raised to provide training sessions for animators outside of work, and in 2012, the Japanese government began sponsoring animation start-ups with grants and subsidies for short films. A faint glimmer of hope emerged with the arrival of talented young foreign artists who had been fascinated by Japanese production from an early age. A "French touch" became evident, in both the anime world and at the eponymous Japan Expo event, as roughly twenty French artists interested in venturing into the field were able to do so through the Furansujin Connection project. It would be impossible to name them all, but Thomas Romain, who designed the cover of this book, is flourishing as a designer (*Space Dandy*) and cocreator (*Basquash!*).

Human and financial resources were running low in a system that had become too greedy, and new partnerships were appearing on scene. *Tiger & Bunny*, created by Sunrise in 2011, is a clever example of the industry's new state of mind. The armor of the superheroes starring in a reality TV show in the futuristic megalopolis of Stem Bild City is adorned with the logos of their sponsors, like Formula One cars. Sponsors that were very real, including Amazon,

Pepsi, and Domino's Pizza, and that paid equally real yen to the production committee! Meanwhile, Gainax collaborated the same year with car manufacturer Subaru on four short films for an online release entitled *Wish Upon the Pleiades*. The studio, which had been struggling since Hideaki Anno left to develop the *Evangelion* brand at his own animation studio, Khara, also needed to recover from the departure of two key players, Masahiko Ōtsuka and Hiroyuki Imaishi. After their landmark series *Gurren Lagann*, which turned robot series upside down by following the hero's evolution from child to teenager to adult, they split from Gainax to create Studio Trigger in 2011.

This brain drain was a lesser evil compared to other, sometimes unavoidable, symptoms of the financial crisis. Bankruptcy, which hit small subcontracting companies such as Palm Studio (2007), no longer spared the bigger, more established companies. In 2010, Group TAC, famous for *Touch* and its *Street Fighter II* adaptations, went out of business. It was the liquidation of Manglobe in 2015 that had the greatest impact on the industry—the studio went out of business just as it was in the midst of producing *Genocidal Organ*, a feature film planned as part of a marketing strategy shared with two other studios. A last-minute entity, Geno Studio, was set up to complete the film, now a symbol of the ever-present crisis. Even Studio Ghibli, after the limited success in 2013 of *Kaze Tachinu* (*The Wind Rises*), Miyazaki's biography of the inventor of the Zero plane, and *Kaguya Hime* (*The Tale of the Princess Kaguya*), a traditional legend reimagined by Takahata, could no longer sustain its particular business model of animators on permanent contracts. It put its feature film department on indefinite hiatus in 2014.

THE SHORTER, THE BETTER

The additional 20,000 minutes produced in 2016 were all devoted to new titles, unrelated to preexisting licenses. However, the majority of these series now consisted of thirteen episodes. The disparate lengths of past series had given way to a gulf between the long-running classics and shorter, less ambitious projects carried out by production committees.

Those short series were suffering the consequences of their marketing-driven strategy, particularly in the late-night slots. By sticking strictly to otaku preferences, series ended up becoming more and more alike. It was hard to tell *Gakusen toshi Asterisk* (*The Asterisk War*) from *Rakudai Kishi no Calvary* (*Chivalry of a Failed Knight*) when they debuted in 2015—they both feature a hero with unsuspected power who defeats the universally respected student council president in a duel, even though she's in a rage after he sees her half-dressed. The two shows would suffer the same consequence for their lack of imagination: they were both abject failures.

Production committees were doing too many things at once but had no other choice. They would bet on four or five different series, and only one of them would be a big enough commercial success to pay off the debts of the others. When they got the numbers in order, accountants were clear: it was less risky to invest in four thirteen-episode series than in a single series of fifty-two episodes. It was up to the scriptwriters to adapt to this format and develop an open-ended finale in case of a possible sequel, which would also not exceed thirteen episodes. Faced with this hyperproductivity, studios were struggling to deliver finished products on time. The many defects that were still present at the time of the TV broadcast would be corrected later for the DVD or Blu-ray release, the lifeblood of the *shin'ya* anime war.

The unexpected triumph of *The Melancholy of Haruhi Suzumiya* added a new dimension to the anime market. The series originated not as a manga but as a light novel. The books weren't shorter, but the richly illustrated stories were aimed at a teenage audience and their style was very simple, similar to theater, with long series of dialogue.

Haruhi Suzumiya may not have been the first anime based on this medium, but it was the first

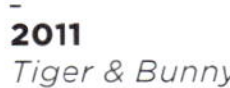
1
2011
Tiger & Bunny

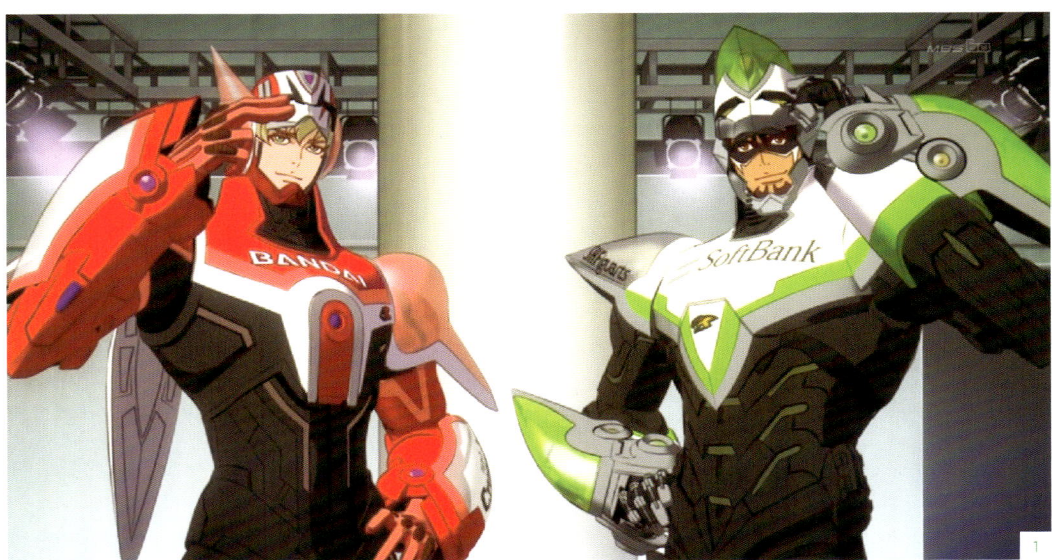

1

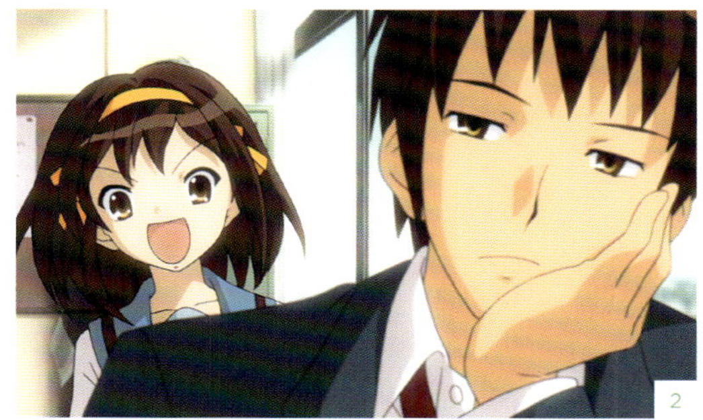

2

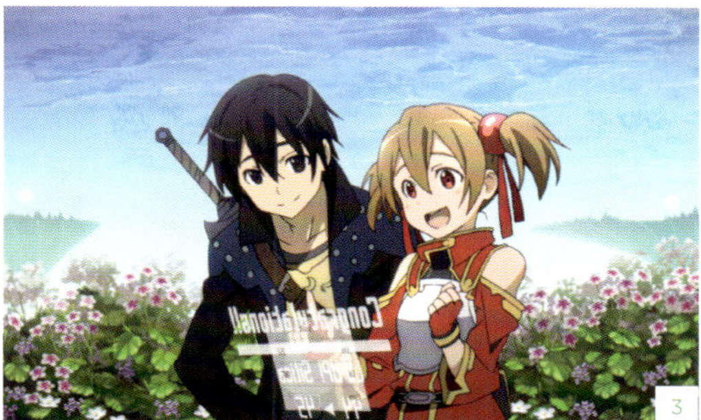

3

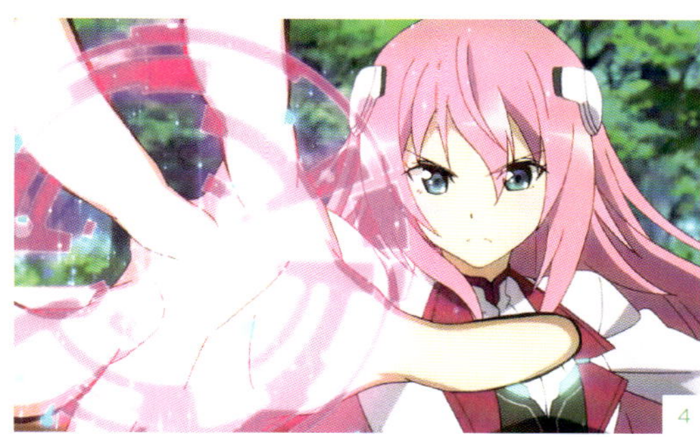

4

to achieve such great success! Light novels had become production committees' new gold mine, rivaling manga, and they cost less to produce. Kyoto Animation, the studio behind *Haruhi Suzumiya*, developed an editorial branch and handpicked the best titles for adaptation into animated series. Nevertheless, the publisher Kadokawa made the biggest contribution to this market's development, where (semi-)professional authors from the *dōjin* world were teaming up with illustrators discovered on the interactive website Pixiv. Launched in 2007, in 2016 over twenty million amateur and professional illustrators shared their creations on the site.

Light novels became the backbone of media-mix ventures, to which production committees added visual novels or *eroge* video games, manga, TV productions, movies and DVDs, and more. If the adaptation of the first volumes was successful, the next ones provided enough material to create one, or even several, additional season(s). If not, the title was abandoned for a new attempt with another novel. Little by little, the thirteen-episode format became the new standard in consumer habits. These short series were faithful to the original material with no filler episodes, dealt with themes in tune with the times, and had the potential to capture the attention of young viewers who were used to seasons of popular American series that lasted for three or six months.

For example, Reki Kawahara's *Sword Art Online* saga focused on the world of network games. The series, which he started in 2009 and reached twenty-eight volumes in 2024, conquered the world with a TV adaptation in 2012 (twenty-five episodes) and its sequel in 2014 (twenty-four episodes). Each season is divided into two or three distinct arcs corresponding to one volume of the novel and varies in storytelling quality. *Sword Art Online* falls into "damsel in distress" clichés, with shameless fan service, but also delicately tackles the theme of AIDS, a taboo subject in Japan. Although most of the stories are stereotypical, the bold storylines in some of these light novels have been passed on to the animation industry.

DESPERATELY SEEKING NEW HEROES

Creating the standard of a thirteen-episode series also disrupted the previously established pattern of manga adaptations, as it now took four times as many series to fill a yearlong schedule! The situation was made all the more serious by the fact that magazines no longer had a new flagship series. In 2009, *One Piece* and *Naruto* celebrated twelve and ten years, respectively, of market dominance, until a challenger finally overshadowed them.

Humanity's desperate struggle for survival against the Titans who had been devouring them for centuries, the brainchild of Hajime Isayama, became the only manga to rival the colossal sales of *One Piece*. But it was the TV adaptation, the first production of Production I.G's Wit Studio, that launched *Shingeki no Kyojin* (*Attack on Titan*) into the mainstream. Harnessing the best of both human (staging, 2D animation) and computer resources (rotating camera during action sequences, lighting effects), the series directed by Tetsurō Araki in 2013 made up for the manga's major shortcoming (poorly mastered graphics) while retaining its best aspects (an uncompromising story featuring one gruesome death after another).

The colossal triumph matched the human and financial efforts that Wit Studio invested, and they paid off due to an unprecedented marketing campaign. But there was another side to the coin—this level of quality took time. There were thirty-

2
2006
Suzumiya Haruhi no Yūutsu (The Melancholy of Haruhi Suzumiya)

3
2012
Sword Art Online

4
2015
Gakusen toshi Asterisk (The Asterisk War)

2013
Kaguya Hime (The Tale of the Princess Kaguya)

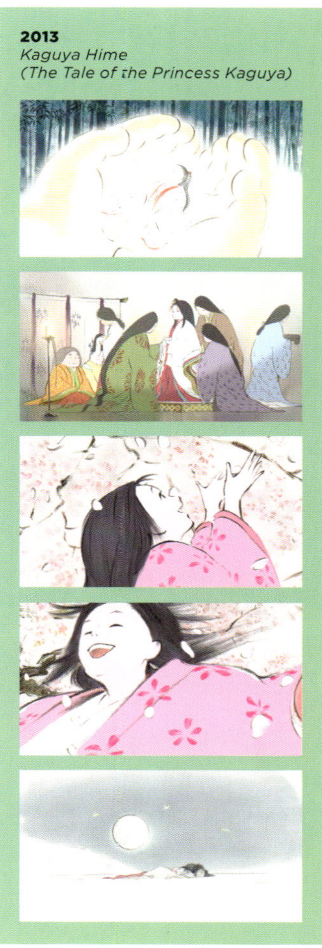

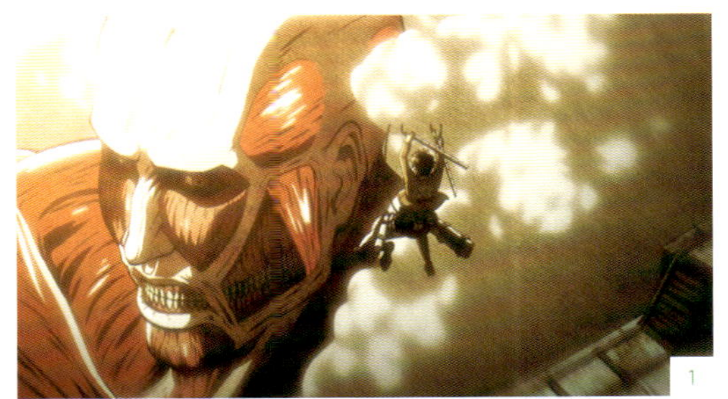

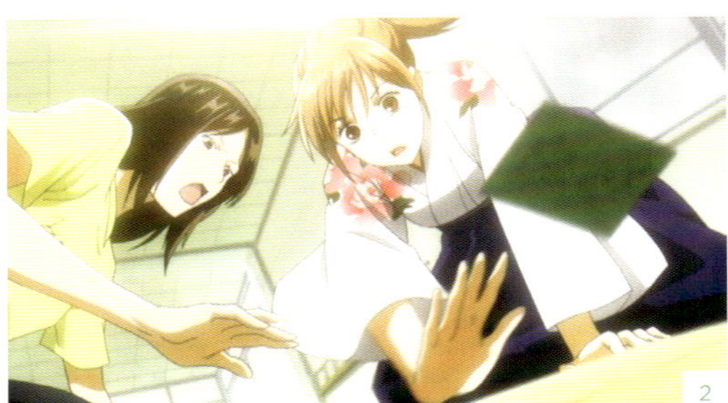

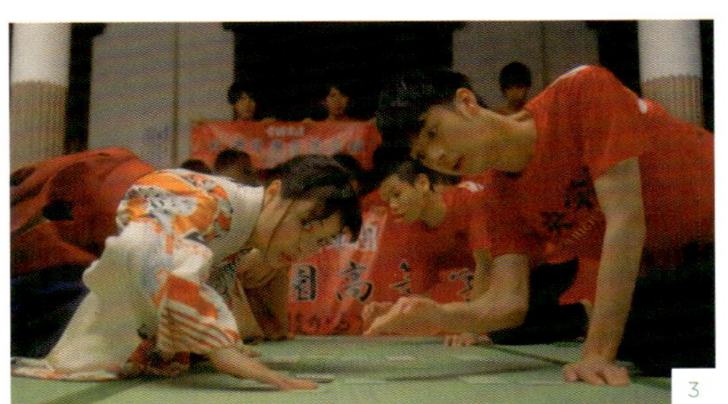

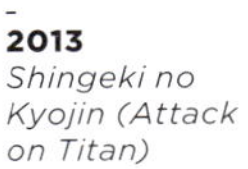

1
2013
Shingeki no Kyojin (Attack on Titan)

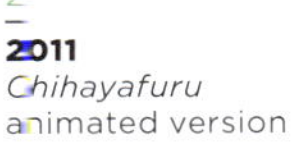

2
2011
Chihayafuru animated version

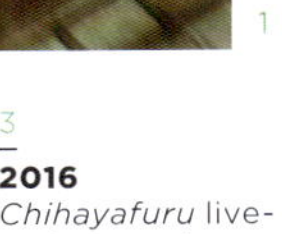

3
2016
Chihayafuru live-action version

four months between the 25th and final episode of the first season and the first episode of the second season (2017), which only has 13 episodes. And, without minimizing the intrinsic quality of *Attack on Titan*, the title also owes its success to a lack of competition. The absence of new, unifying heroes was all the more keenly felt as studios had no choice but to capitalize on their tried-and-true franchises.

Lupin III thus returned to TMS for a spin-off in 2012, but more importantly, for a fourth canonical series in 2015, thirty years after the last one. Although the same studio produced *Tetsujin 28-go FX* in 1992, it was the Eiken studio that brought the steel giant back in 2013 in *Tetsujin 28-go Gao!*, which accomplished the feat of lasting three years and 139 episodes! Toei, for its part, was forced dust off its heroes from the past millennium and update them in modernized versions that quickly caused a scandal! Animated in continental Asia, *Saint Seiya Omega* (2012), *Sailor Moon Crystal* (2014), and *Dragon Ball Super* (2015) suffered from the same syndrome as *shin'ya* anime—the TV versions were full of glaring defects absent from the DVD editions, which had been reworked by the Japanese before release. As for *Cobra*, the franchise celebrated its thirtieth anniversary with a new series in 2010 that was more faithful to the manga, produced by Magic Bus, a studio founded in 1977 by Osamu's older brother Satoshi Dezaki.

Only the fledgling David Production brought a semblance of freshness by daring to tackle a manga legend, *Jojo no Kimyō na Bōken* (*Jojo's Bizarre Adventure*). Since 1986, Hirohiko Araki had been unfolding the (mis)adventures of the Joestar family members over several generations in several specific story arcs. Sporadic attempts had been made, including six OAVs in 1993 and seven in 2002, but the manga seemed impossible to adapt given its scope (over 130 volumes to date), graphic style, and above all, its "Stands," astral beings with supernatural powers who fight in the heroes' place. These technical hurdles had disappeared with the rise of computer technology, and the new trend toward short series was a perfect match for these distinct story arcs! Director Naokatsu Tsuda respected the original format and adapted their length to the length of the manga: 26 episodes for the first season in 2012, 48 for the second in 2014, 39 for the third in 2016, and so on.

These icons were no match for an industry facing unexpected competition from live-action productions. Special effects had now evolved so much that even the most fantastic titles could be translated into feature films with flesh-and-blood actors on a green screen. The trend that started in 2004 with eight productions (including Hideaki Anno's *Cutie Honey*) had finally taken over the industry, with some twenty titles released annually since 2010. It was also invading the small screen, even if new dramas were mostly based on realistic manga, thrillers, or romantic comedies, to limit the cost of special effects. Sometimes they were successful, especially slice-of-life series like *Ore Monogatari!!* (*My Love Story!!*) in 2015 and *Chihayafuru* in 2016. However, they were often unsuccessful—half the viewers of the first part of *Attack on Titan* (2015) refused to inflict the torment of a sequel on themselves the following year! The flurry of adaptations reflected a new global trend: whether in Hollywood, where Marvel and DC heroes had taken over, or in France, with *Astérix*, *Michel Vaillant*, *Lucky Luke*, *Iznogoud*, and *Boule & Bill* movies, the comic book heroes of the last century were now prime material for nostalgic forty-somethings and their children on the big screen. They had been waiting for the past ten years for a new generation of heroes, who had yet to arrive.

Broadening targets

A DEPLETED RESERVOIR

During the economic boom of the 1980s, nobody had noticed the country's rapidly changing demographics. Everyone was paying attention to the economic meltdown on the horizon of the coming decade. With the new millennium, the demographic crisis became critical in Japan, whose population had been declining since 2010. The fertility rate was no higher than 1.4 per woman, with the number of births falling steadily since the 1980s. In 2016, it fell below the symbolic million mark, a figure not seen since the end of the nineteenth century!

The situation was all the more worrying given that, in contrast, Japan's population was a model of longevity: in 2014, people over sixty-five accounted for a quarter of the population. Their proportion was expected to reach 40 percent by 2060, posing a simple problem in the medium term—who would be able to look after all these senior citizens? In the short term, the situation was even more dire for animation studios who had to consider the opposite situation. If the proportion of elderly people increased, then the proportion of children decreased accordingly.

In 1965, youth under fifteen represented 25 percent of the population, a rate that stabilized until 1980 (23.5 percent) before stalling and then decreasing to 18.2 percent in 1990, 14.6 percent in 2000, and so forth. The latest official report to date (May 2024) announced the chilling figure of 11.3 percent. Although the total number of children had grown slightly in half a century from 99,209 in 1965 to 126,830 in 2017, their share of the population had been cut in half! The drastic reduction in the number of young people had far-reaching consequences for the animation industry on multiple levels.

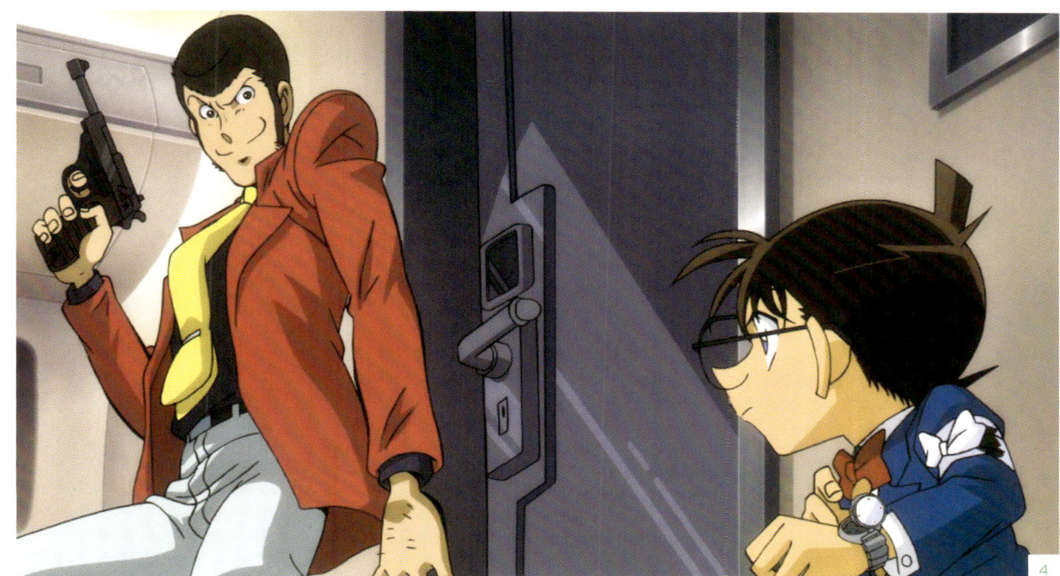

4
—
2009
Lupin III tai Meitantei Conan (Lupin III vs. Detective Conan)

The first seems obvious—lower ratings for series aimed at young audiences. This was particularly true for new titles, although it hadn't prevented carefully crafted media-mix franchises such as *Yo-kai Watch* (2013) from gaining the complete loyalty of children. The veterans, from *Doraemon* to *Crayon Shin-chan* to *Dragon Ball*, were doing just fine. Because people had watched these shows when they were five and eight years old, parents were familiar with their content and confidently left their children with these programs . . . when they weren't watching them together! Producers began creating cross-generational stories in which children's and parents' heroes showed up together—*Detective Conan* and *Lupin III* played cops and robbers in a TV movie in 2009, whereas *Dragon Ball* and *One Piece* characters came together in a crossover to promote the launch of *Toriko*, the Shueisha-Toei team-up's newest venture. Despite the support, this gourmet comedy adventure series would never reach their status, with 147 episodes between 2011 and 2014.

Similarly, the otaku target was becoming increasingly narrow. Die-hard fans of the 1980s were now in their fifties, and still swearing by nostalgic shows such as *Yamato*, which returned in 2012 (*Star Blazers: Space Battleship Yamato 2199*) and 2017 (*Star Blazers: Space Battleship Yamato 2202*). Viewers in their thirties and forties, on the other hand, were inundated by the return of their old favorites that were making use of the latest technology, such as *Mobile Suit Gundam Unicorn*, an OAV series commemorating the show license's thirtieth anniversary in 2010, made into a TV series in 2016, *Macross Frontier* in 2007, and *Macross Delta* in 2016. There were fewer and fewer "youngsters" in their twenties, and all they had were short-lived harem titles looking to make a quick buck rather than make history.

Even Trigger's 2013 manifesto *Kill la Kill*, directed by Hiroyuki Imaishi, couldn't help but ironize the ubiquitous fan service of otaku culture—the heroine's uniform shrinks as her powers increase, evocative angles abound, and on and on. Paradoxically, despite its offbeat humor, *Kill la Kill*'s reputation was partly built on this outrageous eroticism. Only in part, though, as the show's greatest quality is its exceptional technical level, which raised the bar by several notches at the expense of many sleepless nights. Following in the footsteps of the animation teams from *Astro Boy*, *Heidi*, and *Evangelion* in their day, a handful of enthusiasts out there were still pushing the medium to its limits.

They were increasingly rare, though, given the falling birth rate! Worse still, they were less invested because the poor working conditions, lack of training, and low pay had many animators packing it in after their first job. According to one JAniCA report, a novice animator worked an average of eleven hours a day for an annual salary of $9,600 in 2013! Three out of four newcomers gave up after their first try, preferring more lucrative day jobs, especially because they could break into freelancing through the amateur scene. There was no incentive for young people to join the industry, which was reacting to the scarcity of its two essential resources—children and otaku—by appealing to new audiences.

GIRLS ON FILM

Fuji TV was the first channel to embark on this exploration of other viewer categories. The channel was criticized for its lack of rigor when it came to *shin'ya* anime, with schedules and the number of episodes varying from week to week. It kept this bad habit, with the exception of a new time slot introduced on April 14, 2005. It was called Noitamina (Animation spelled backward, stylized as noitaminA), airing on Thursday and Friday nights at 12:45 a.m., a time usually reserved for sappy dramas for young women returning home late from work. It was this audience, long ignored by the industry, that Noitamina hoped to win over.

The first titles set the tone. Over twenty-four episodes, *Hachimitsu to Clover* (*Honey and Clover*) follows the careers of art school students, their friendships, their love lives, and the start of their working lives. *Paradise Kiss*, which was half as long, was more lighthearted with a more or less identical plot, except in this series, the heroes studied fashion design. Both series were adapted from manga (by Chica Umino and Ai Yazawa, respectively) that were a hit in *josei* magazines, targeting an older audience than the *shōjo* titles. Romantic drama was as prevalent as ever in these shows, but the relationships were no longer limited to just a few kisses, and they came with more serious consequences.

The rest of the industry seemed to have lost the bet and was quick to withdraw its criticism. Japanese young adults were fascinated by the modern romances set in dream worlds that were less excessively flamboyant than their predecessors *Love Me, My Knight* and *Glass no Kamen* (*Glass Mask*). For three years, Noitamina alternated between romances like *Nodame Cantabile* and *Antique Bakery*, and horror series based on the urban legends that Japanese women loved so much, such as *Ayakashi: Samurai Horror Tales*, *Mononoke*, and *Hakaba Kitarō*, a darker, more faithful adaptation of Mizuki's work.

The race was on! After *Paradise Kiss*, Madhouse adapted another manga by Ai Yazawa, *Nana*. Broadcast on NTV beginning in 2006, the series tells the story of two young women who meet on a snowbound train destined for Tokyo. They are as different as can be, but the tender-hearted young woman and the disillusioned punk rocker share the same name. Now roommates, Nana the coquette and Nana the musician support each other through life's rough patches but also tear each other apart. The phenomenon took the industry by surprise! Female viewers wanted nothing more than to imitate the looks of their idols, so particular attention was paid to the heroines' outfits (one of the strengths of the manga), especially those of the punk-rocking Vivienne Westwood fan. To have a rock star, they needed a song, which was sung by Anna Tsuchiya, a star on the rise, just like Mika Nakashima, who played the character in the two live-action films released concurrently in 2005 and 2006, at the height of the live-action manga boom. In short, media-mix projects (anime, live-action films, albums, fashion accessories, and more) were well matched to this new audience, as long as they were tailored to their needs.

As young women, former *Sailor Moon*, *Sakura*, and *Utena* viewers were now projecting themselves onto the two Nanas, mirroring their multiple personalities, both starry-eyed and surly. The new trend was being felt around the globe. In the minority during the earliest conventions, the number of girls participating steadily increased until their numbers were virtually equal to the boys—girls represented 46 percent of Japan Expo attendees in 2017! Two other factors also came into play over this decade . . .

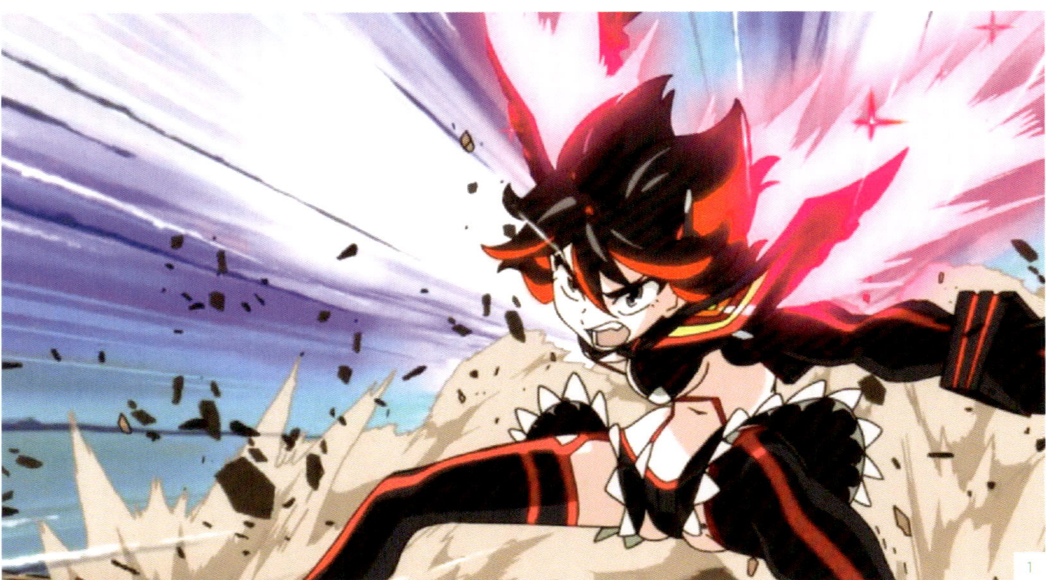

1
2013
Kill la Kill

WOMEN SPEAK TO FANS

Trained at Mushi Production, Yōko Hatta had moved to Kyoto to live with her Kansai-born husband. In 1981, she founded Kyoto Animation, which entered the big leagues with *Haruhi Suzumiya* in 2005 after two decades of subcontracting. The company, mostly staffed by women, quickly found a way to appeal to female audiences. With *K-On!* (2009) and *Tamako Market* (2013), director Naoko Yamada made a name for herself among fans and went mainstream three years later with the feature film adaptation of *Koe no Katachi* (*A Silent Voice*), Yoshitoki Ōima's deeply moving manga about deafness. Hiroko Utsumi made her debut with the swimming series *Free!* (2013), featuring young men in swimsuits—it was a guaranteed success!

The path for Sayo Yamamoto, a protégé of Shinichirō Watanabe, was somewhat more difficult. Manglobe gave her the first shot at directing in 2009 with *Michiko & Hatchin*, an adventure tale of a femme fatale and a kid on the run. She then focused on *Lupin III*'s cunning sidekick in the spin-off *Mine Fujiko to Iu Onna* (*The Woman Called Fujiko Mine*) for TMS in 2012, before finally giving free rein to her passions—figure skating and *yaoi*—in *Yuri on Ice* in 2016. The realism of the athletic sequences delighted experts in the field, but the ambivalence of the relationship between the young Japanese athlete Yuri and his coach Victor fascinated audiences the most. The emergence of these female artists coincided with the development of the female counterpart of the otaku market. The rise in access to smartphones and applications led to the development of **dating sims**, or dating simulation games, designed for young women. More sophisticated than *eroge*, these dating sims worked on the same principle, only the genders were reversed: the player decides which stereotypical hunks to seduce in an imaginary or realistic universe. A new, wider audience now joined the *fujoshi* ranks!

It wasn't until 2015 that a new phenomenon caught on with the general female public. Half a century after the first black-and-white adaptation (1965), and twenty-seven years after the color version (1988), Fujio Akatsuka's manga *Osomatsu-kun* returned to the screen, but this time the sextuplets were their twenties. The unemployed virgin loser heroes of *Mr. Osomatsu* raked young Japanese men over the coals. And Japanese women were relishing it, even those who didn't watch cartoons before! Especially since the production, after two years of trying to get their schedules to coincide, had lined up six highly reputed voice actors to play the siblings, guaranteeing that at least their six fan bases would be in front of the TV late into the night.

VARYING PLEASURES

Censored for daring to shamelessly bash popular shows from *Anpanman* to *Attack on Titan*, the humor in *Mr. Osomatsu* knew no bounds; its scriptwriters had carte blanche. Likewise, *Free!!* and *Yuri on Ice* started to explore female fantasies, which were handled with appropriate subtlety by directors who shared the same fantasies as their female viewers. Directors were given unprecedented levels of creative freedom thanks to Noitamina. From 2008 on, Noitamina programming abandoned its female target audience (now prey for the competition) to take a more experimental approach. This initiative continued in 2010, when it broadcast two series instead of one, leaving more room for original, non-manga-based projects.

Directors became preoccupied with social themes, such as terrorism in *Higashi no Eden* (*Eden of the East*) in 2009 and *Zankyō no Teroru* (*Terror in Resonance*) in 2014, adoption in *Usagi Doroppu* (*Bunny Drop*) in 2011, twenty-first-century agriculture in *Gin no Saji* (*Silver Spoon*) in 2013, and criminal behavior in *Psycho-Pass* in 2012. They were gradually carving out a niche for

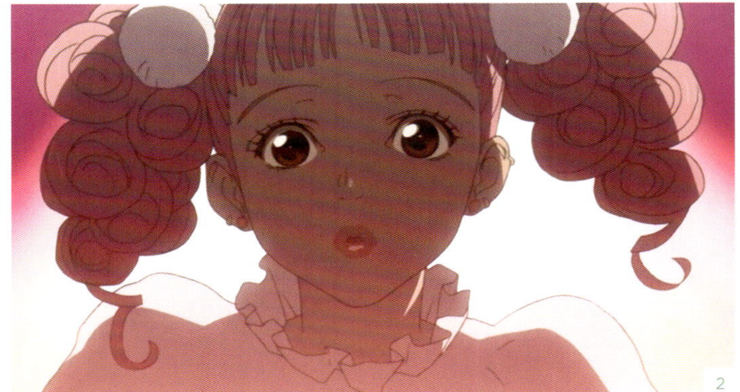

2

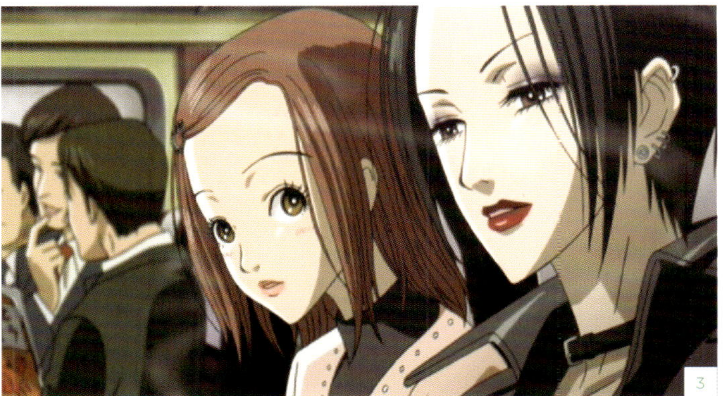

3

2
2005
Paradise Kiss

3
2006
Nana

themselves in the studios best suited to their vision of the profession, like Shinichirō Watanabe, who flourished at MAPPA, where he directed *Kids on the Slope* (2012), a jazz-filled friendship between an introverted high school student and an outgoing one in 1960s Japan, and *Terror in Resonance*. The approach mirrored the model that had taken root in the film industry, where each director was surrounded by production companies designed around their own specific working methods.

Thanks to diverse genres, both in theaters and during late-night programming blocks, creativity was reclaiming ground from the preformatted titles that had dominated the market a decade earlier. This variety was the missing ingredient enabling studios to finally move away from the thirty-year distribution pattern inherited from OAVs and turn to a business mode that was already widespread in the rest of the world.

ANYTIME, ANYWHERE

Whereas Japanese studios cringed at the development of YouTube (where illegal fansub quickly circulated), they welcomed Nico Nico, its Japanese counterpart, in 2006. The video platform became an ideal springboard for amateur creators, particularly with the development of Vocaloid voice synthesizer software—animation could bring these virtual singers to life!

Although they were hesitant, professionals gradually turned to this new mode of distribution, which until now had only been considered from a promotional angle. For example, the four short episodes of *The King of Fighters: Another Day* produced by Production I.G were included on the bonus DVD accompanying the rerelease of the video game *The King of Fighters 2006*. In 2008, the Yahoo! Japan website finally took the plunge and released the six episodes of *Eve no Jikan* (*Time of Eve*), breaking free from the time constraints imposed by television as episodes ranged from fifteen to twenty-seven minutes. The market for original net animation (ONA), videos designed for the communication tools of the new millennium, was emerging. Available free of charge, they were primarily used to test the viability of a potential series (the twenty-three-minute short *Cat Shit One* in 2010), or to develop a game universe for Japanese smartphones (*Keitai Shōjo* in 2007) or worldwide consoles (*Brotherhood: Final Fantasy XV* in 2016). Whether for promotional or corporate purposes, short films such as *Toki wa Meguru: Tokyo Station*, commissioned from A-1 Pictures for the 100-year anniversary of Tokyo station in 2014, still retained the artistic freedom often demanded by their financiers.

The internet also provided creative freedom to animators, who didn't have to manage high-stakes projects. In 2013, Trigger animators, working with Hiroyuki Imaishi and Akira Amemiya, had a great time playing with the constraints of the shoestring budget for *Inferno Cop*'s thirteen three-minute episodes. They used vocal sound effects, inlays of

1
2009
Michiko & Hatchin

2
2016
Yuri on Ice

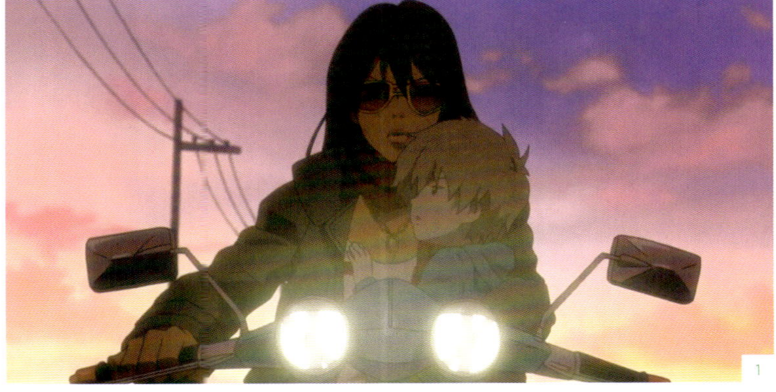

1

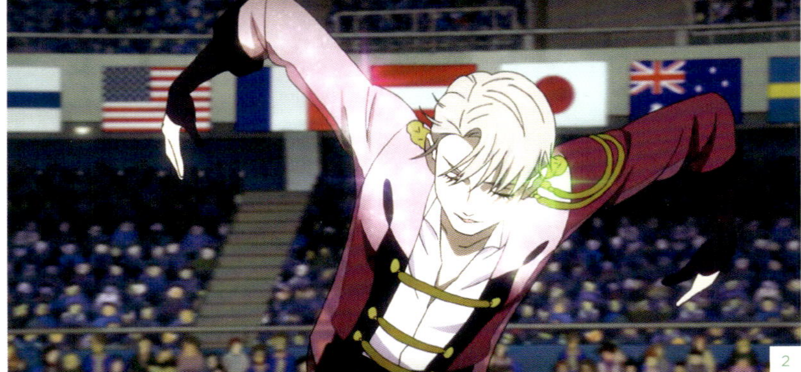

2

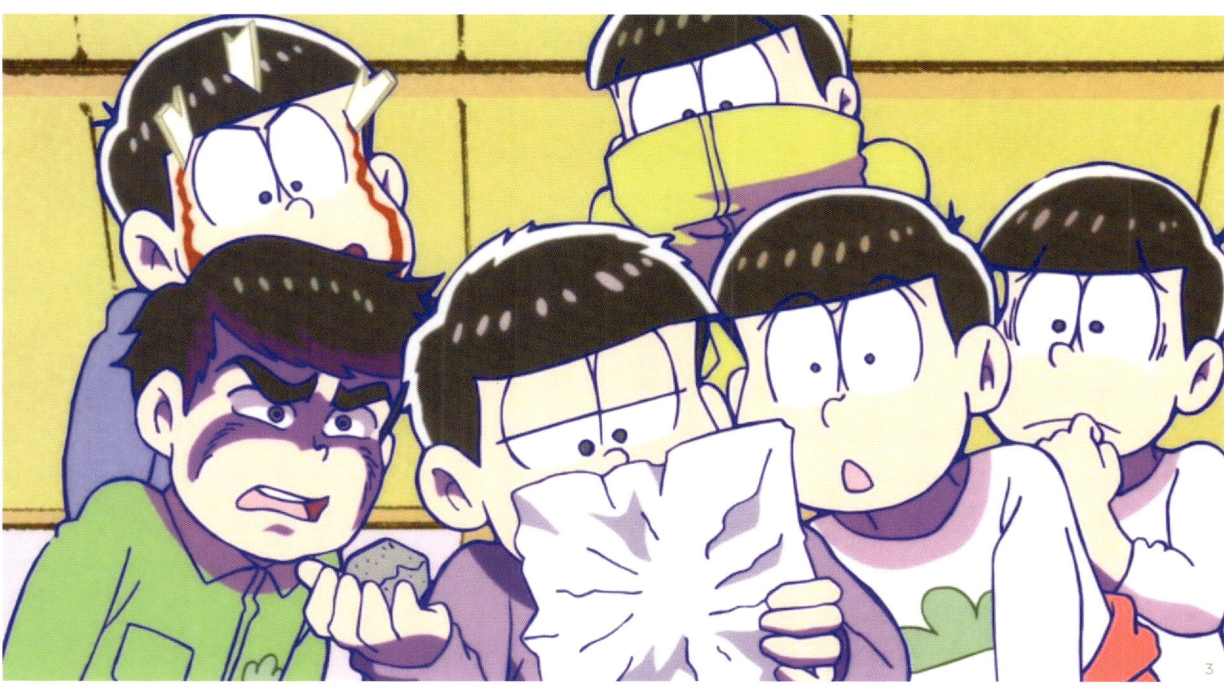

3
2015
Mr. Osomatsu

2012
Sakamichi no Apollon (Kids on the Slope)

live explosions, and absurd twists and turns. The web series was reminiscent of the stories children invent when they're playing with their toys and recaptured an uninhibited freshness sorely lacking in the crisis-ridden industry. Amemiya would take this minimalist style a step further, contrasting it with sumptuously animated scenes in his follow-up ONA, *Ninja Slayer*, in 2015.

The real turning point came in 2014, driven by Hideaki Anno and Kazuya Tsurumaki, who were tired of seeing the anime industry languish. As was Hayao Miyazaki, who designed the mascot for Nihon Animator Mihon'ichi (Japan Animator Expo). The directors of each of the short films added weekly to this Niconico channel (formerly Nico Nico) had only one instruction: to experiment and let their imaginations speak for themselves! The incubator that was the Khara studio enabled new directors to make their mark, such as Hibiki Yoshizaki with his *Me!Me!Me!* short, a dreamlike, psychedelic journey between lust and terror that could not have been broadcast on television. But Japan Animator Expo's primary objective was achieved after it ended in 2015 with its thirty-fifth title. Some of the short films, picked up by producers or broadcasters, took on a new dimension as series (Sayo Yamamoto's *Endless Night* was the basis for *Yuri on Ice*) or TV movies.

More than anything, 2014 finally marked the industry's transition to digitization. Cellular and internet provider Docomo launched its "anime store" service, a video-on-demand (VOD) platform accessible "anytime, anywhere" (according to its slogan) on their tablets and smartphones. Its rival SoftBank jumped on the bandwagon with *Anime Hodai* (Unlimited Anime), based on the same principle: a constantly growing catalog of several thousand titles, including new releases, for ¥400 a month (around $3.60). Although limited to animation, these offers were in line with the economic model that the rest of the world had adopted. In fact, giants such as Netflix were increasingly turning their attention to the profitable niche sector of Japanese cartoons.

Globalization

FROM FANSUB TO SIMULCAST

In 2002, international revenues accounted for 50 percent of anime's profits, a figure that had increased fivefold since 1995 when it had been only 8 to 10 percent. The ubiquitousness of DVDs around the world was benefiting animation, which was increasingly showing up in media stores internationally. Fansub, however, had hit the video market, rapidly making a wide range of anime available. The fact that this phenomenon spread so quickly in the early 2000s was partly due to the passivity of Japanese rights holders with regard to the foreign market. As a result of this lax attitude, the industry saw its revenues plummet and its titles freely distributed across many websites.

As the international market became uncontrollable, the 2008 financial crisis hit animation studios from all sides, such as Gonzo, which tried to broaden its target using the VOD platform Crunchyroll, previously known for its pirated content. This is how the site legally distributed the fantasy series *Doruāga no Tō: The Aegis of Uruk* (*Tower of Druaga*), while offering fansub in parallel! Crunchyroll ceased its illegal activity in 2009, when it struck gold with *Naruto Shippuden*. That year was a turning point in the fight against piracy, with the launch of VOD platforms specializing in anime. While Funimation was competing with Crunchyroll using Toei Animation hits, in France, companies specializing in DVDs were taking the internet by storm with streaming platforms, such as Dybex with Dailymotion and Kazé through its KZ Play platform (which would become Anime Digital Network in partnership with Kana Home Video). A major new player was also making its debut: Wakanim, which would gradually extend its services to the UK in 2013.

There was only one way to counter the fansub that had produced millions of anime devotees—make episodes available as soon as possible after their Japanese TV broadcast. Channels could still sell advertising slots while attracting web audiences with temporary free access. **Simulcast**, short for simultaneous broadcast, emerged as a new way of legally consuming anime abroad. The concept of near-simultaneous broadcasting was shaking up the commercial habits of Japanese producers, who weren't used to dealing with foreign markets until after releasing their work in Japan.

In the end, the loss of revenue generated by fansub was a shock to the system in Japan, which had adapted to the foreign market by becoming a simulcast provider in 2013 with Daisuki, a platform created by several prestigious studios. One of those studios was Aniplex, which also acquired Wakanim two years later.

Between 2010 and 2015, total profits from online anime almost tripled, going from ¥14.9 billion to ¥43.7 billion. This increase demonstrated that the public had adapted to this form of media consumption, as evidenced by Crunchyroll's 20 million worldwide subscribers in 2017. However,

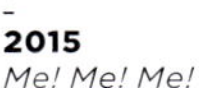
1
2015
Me! Me! Me!

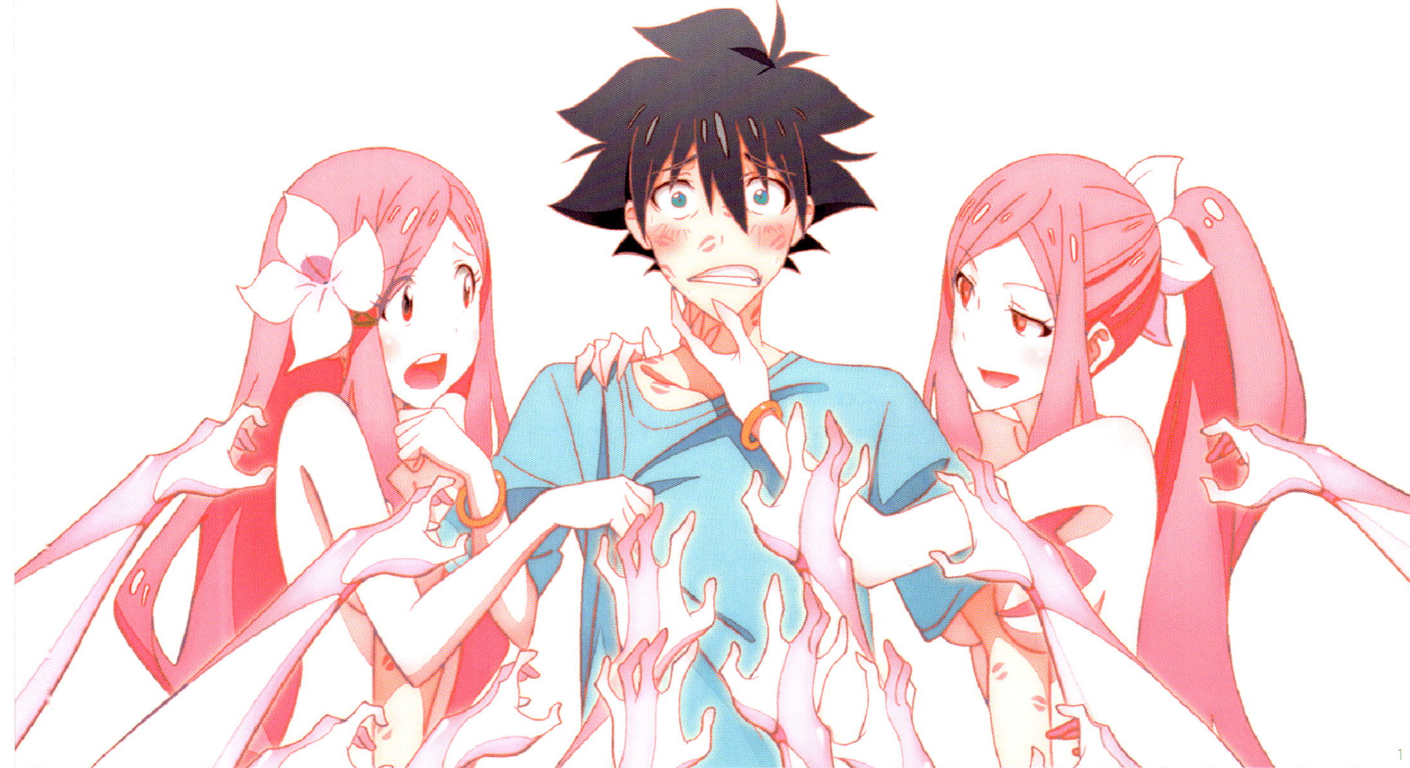

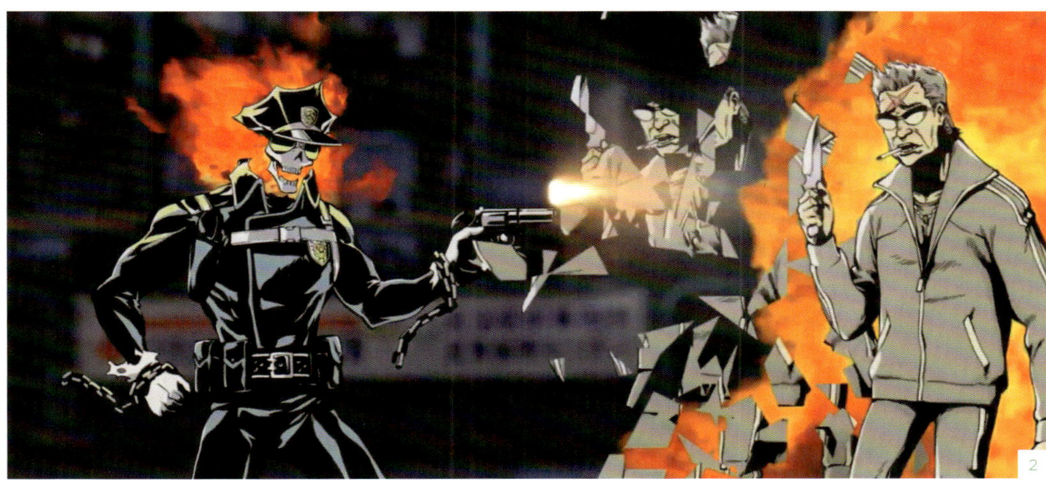
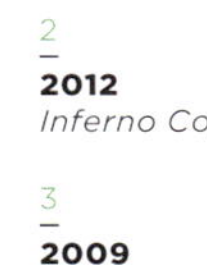

2
2012
Inferno Cop

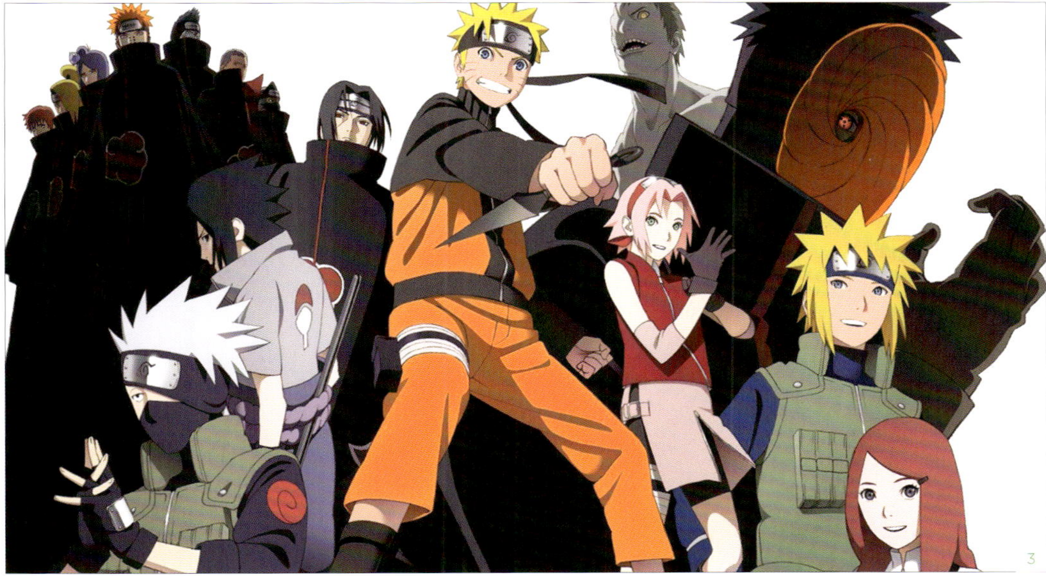

3
2009
Naruto

the main driver for this increase was the Chinese market. The most prominent Chinese platforms like Youku Tudou had taken a strong interest in anime and were gradually building up a substantial catalog. Media giants Amazon and Netflix had also arrived on scene, revitalizing the market and shaking up anime heavyweights Crunchyroll and Funimation, who had partnered up in 2016. Each platform was fighting hard for exclusives (the best way to stand out), to the point of coproducing or financially sponsoring anime.

A PIXELATED MASTER KEY

Anime and manga can be considered the keystones of the worldwide craze for Japanese culture. They have inspired creatives all over the world to draw on their graphic codes, such as the American channel Nickelodeon in the series *Avatar: The Last Airbender* (2005) and the French company Ankama Games in its various games and series, starting with *Dofus* (2006) and *Wakfu* (2008). In addition, live-action adaptations of anime and manga, already abundant in the Land of the Rising Sun, were beginning to be major features abroad, notably in Hollywood with *Speed Racer* (2008), *Dragonball Evolution* (2009), *Edge of Tomorrow* (2014), *Ghost in the Shell* (2017), and *Death Note* (2017). The West was trying to reappropriate the universal subjects addressed by Japanese works that had already been marketed abroad by transposing the themes from one culture to another.

Increasingly present in Japanese productions, 3D CGI enhanced this universality. By using computer graphics, producers were free from the visual and budgetary limitations of traditional animation, which the Japanese compensated for with excessively stylized graphics that became their identity. Visually, only the character design in a fantasy film like *Hottarake no Shima: Haruka to Mahō no Kagami* (*Oblivion Island: Haruka and the Magic Mirror*, 2010) makes it clear that the work is Japanese. CGI also facilitated international coproductions, like the American-Japanese remake of *Astro Boy* (2009) and *Yona Yona Penguin* (2009), which was animated in Japan, France, and Thailand. This children's adventure was Rintaro's first original feature, showing that even veteran animators were embracing the new way of filmmaking.

Several ambitious feature films were produced in 3D CGI, but they were quickly overshadowed by the mass of American films that maintained their technical and budgetary supremacy in the field. How could anime stand out in the crowd? By using well-known figures who were only too happy to return to the forefront for wider distribution. In 2012, Production I.G released Kenji Kamiyama's *009 Re:*

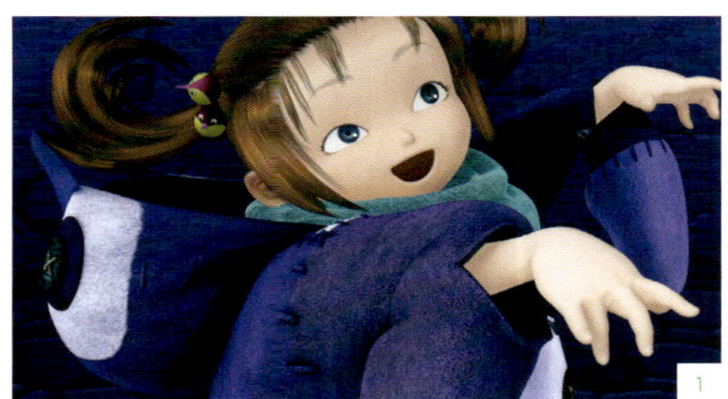

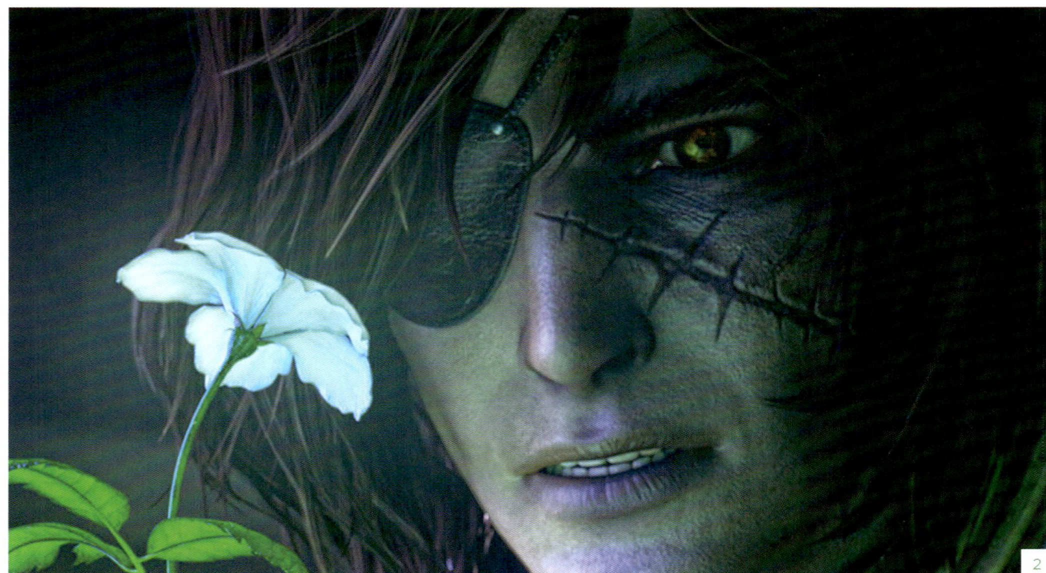

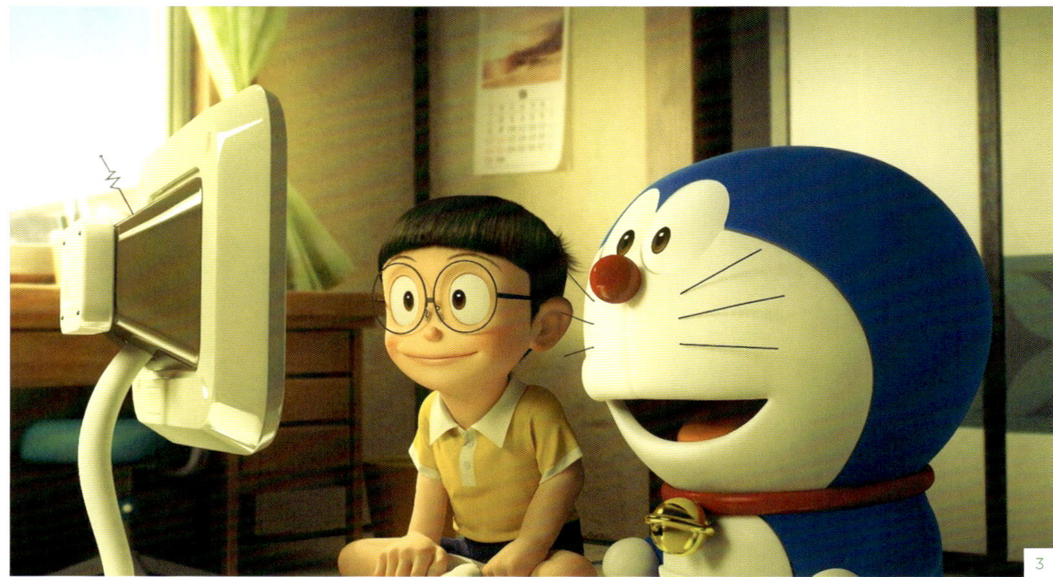

1
2009
Yona Yona Penguin

2
2013
Uchū Kaizoku Captain Harlock (Harlock: Space Pirate)

3
2015
Stand By Me Doraemon

Cyborg, a complex and depressive sequel to Shotaro Ishinomori's manga. The following year, Shinji Aramaki revisited *Captain Harlock*, swapping the toon shading of *Appleseed* for photorealism. The director made Leiji Matsumoto's universe his own, delivering a tormented film that deconstructs the hero's journey. Toei Animation was back with *Saint Seiya: Legend of Sanctuary* in 2014, a feature film that modernized the original story to try to appeal to teenagers of the 2010s.

Very different from the original works, these reboots were commercial failures at home and sold best internationally, notably *Harlock: Space Pirate* ($30 million budget), whose box office earnings in France ($5.8 million) and Italy ($6.6 million) far exceeded those in Japan ($4.4 million). It was the Chinese market ($5.7 million) that saved *Saint Seiya*, along with Brazil, Mexico, and France, which all exceeded the measly $2.1 million that the movie earned in Japan. In 2017, Toei went one step further by releasing the 2D-3D feature *Mazinger Z* in Italy and France ahead of its Japanese release.

Even Shin-Ei Animation's robotic cat of the future got its own 3D version in 2014. *Stand by Me Doraemon* wasn't a traditional annual film but a remake perfectly suited to international audiences. The feature film was an obvious success at home, but it made the most money in China, with worldwide box office sales quintupling the initial $35 million.

This return of major titles in CGI didn't seem to be a phase but rather a graphic revival that was gradually taking hold in an industry rooted in 2D animation. Polygon Pictures animation studio was making a name for itself with a number of productions directed by Hiroyuki Seshita, such as *Gojira Kaijū Wakusei* (*Godzilla: Planet of the Monsters*), the *kaiju* icon's first animated feature in 2017! It was perfect timing—between the 2014 American blockbuster directed by Gareth Edwards and the Japanese hit directed by Hideaki Anno and Shinji Higuchi in 2016 ($75 million at the Japanese box office, twice as much as *Rogue One: A Star Wars Story*), the international stage was primed to welcome the toon-shaded claws of the king of monsters.

NEW PILLARS

With the new millennium upon them, young filmmakers had no intention of hiding in the shadow of their blockbuster mentors. With *Dead Leaves* (2004), *Trava: Fist Planet* (2001), and the award-winning *Mind Game* (2004), directors Hiroyuki Imaishi, Takeshi Koike, and Masaaki Yuasa, respectively, broke through the graphic limits set by their predecessors. They used high-energy staging, unusual angles, and distorted perspectives to accompany their eccentric characters on outlandish adventures. In 2009, Koike showcased this emancipatory spirit in *Redline*, a futuristic racing film in which the numerous mechanical devices are traditionally animated—a feature that took seven years to produce in an industry where computers reigned supreme.

Mamoru Hosoda had a more realistic and mainstream style with a focus on continuous movement, obscuring his characters' shadows to concentrate on the fluidity of the animation. The director learned from his failure at Studio Ghibli and developed his style in the sixth *One Piece* film (2005) and *Toki o Kakeru Shōjo* (*The Girl Who Leapt Through Time*, 2006). In 2009, Hosoda established himself in the eyes of the world as a creative pillar in the making with the original *Summer Wars*. The film is about a traditional family's battle against an artificial intelligence that has hacked into the OZ system, a virtual social network used by institutions the world over.

Animator Sunao Katabuchi used a more understated style and directed *Arete Hime* (*Princess Arete*, 2001), Studio 4°C's first digital production. His film is poetic and feminist, a formula inherent to his filmmaking, and one he repeated in 2009 in the dreamlike *Mai Mai Miracle*.

There was also freelance director Keiichi Hara, who had numerous episodes of *Doraemon* and *Crayon Shin-chan* to his credit and had mastered the theme of the family. He put that skill to good use in his feature films *Kappa no Coo to Natsuyasumi* (*Summer Days with Coo*, 2007), *Colorful* (2010), and *Sarusuberi: Miss Hokusai* (*Miss Hokusai*), all three of which won the Best Animation Film Award at the Mainichi Film Festival.

Among this new wave of studio directors, a young video game company employee turned

2004
Mind Game

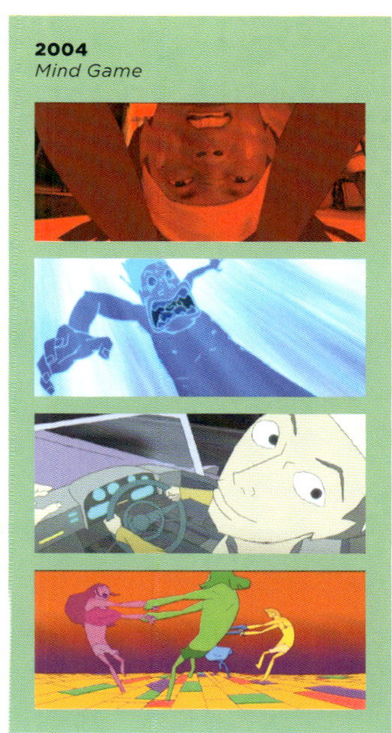

4
—
2009
Redline

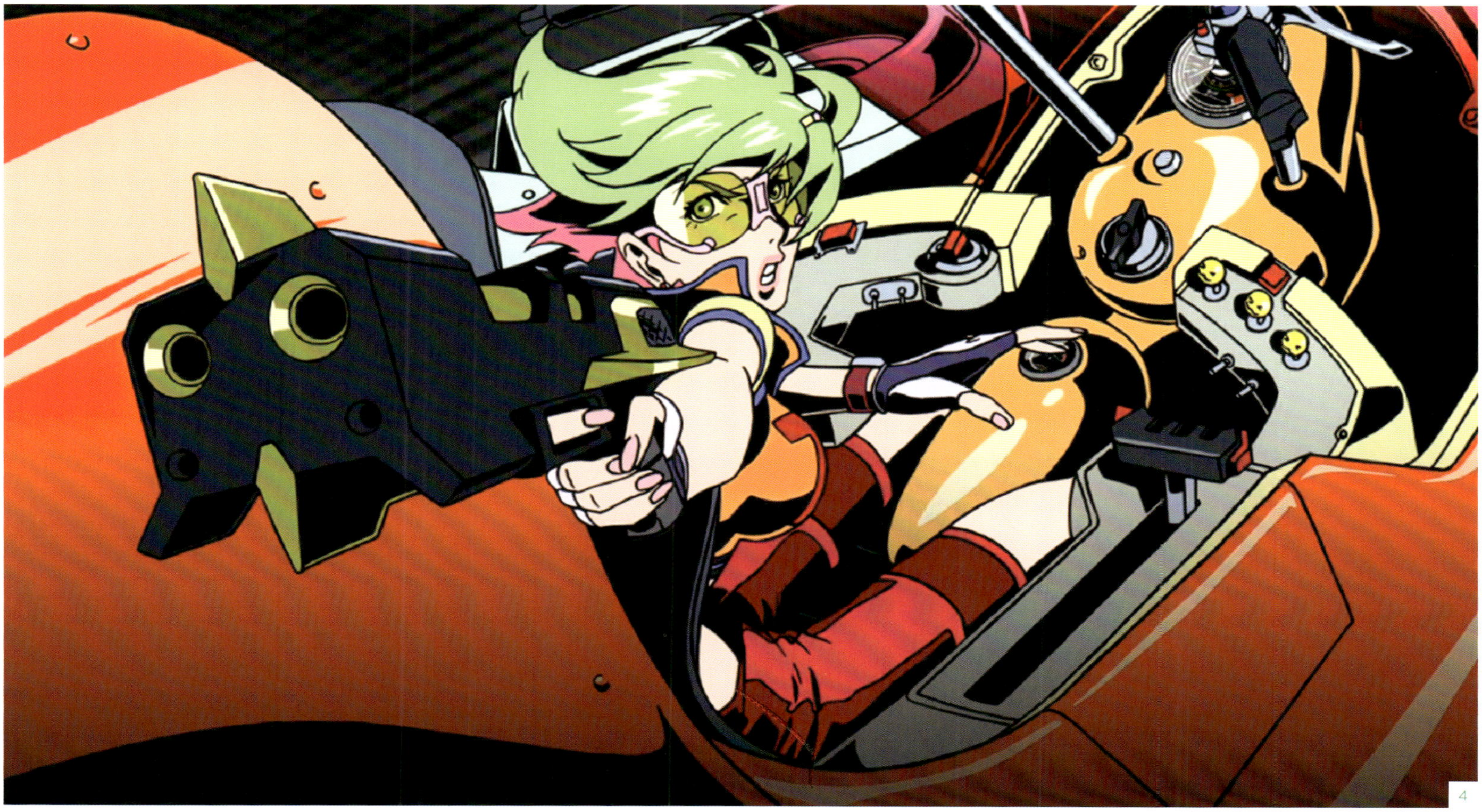

4

2002
Hoshi no Koe
(Voices of a Distant Star)

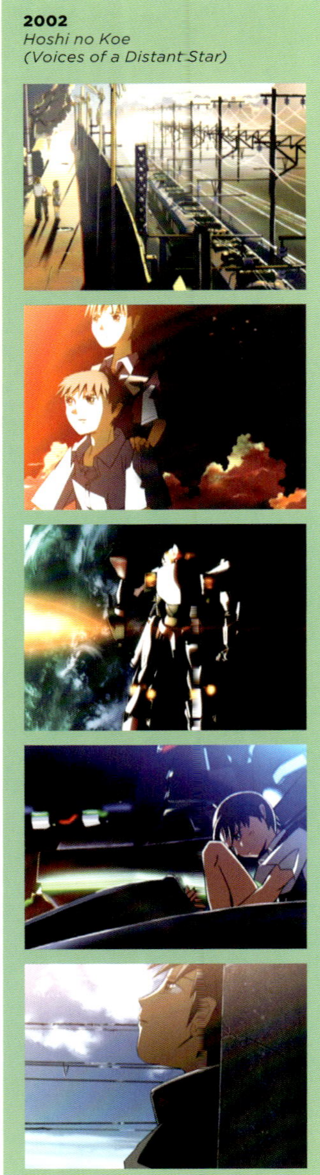

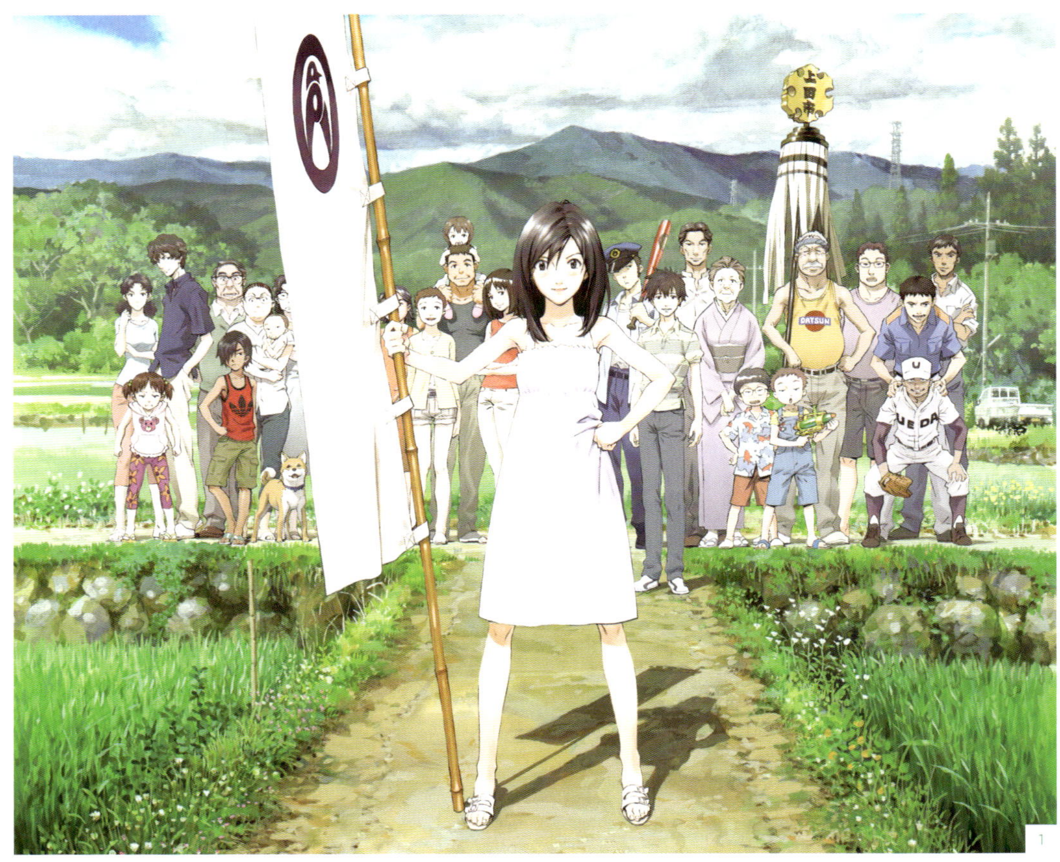

1
2009
Summer Wars

everything upside down in 1999 with *Kanojo to Kanojo no Neko* (*She and Her Cat*), a five-minute short he made at home alone! The widespread availability of computer hardware and graphic design software enabled Makoto Shinkai to develop an entire film himself. He did it again in 2002 with the short film *Hoshi no Koe* (*Voices of a Distant Star*), which took seven months to complete. This twenty-minute film laid the foundations of his style—a romance buffeted by space and time, melancholy characters, and extremely detailed backgrounds that use lighting effects to enhance reality. The film's DVD success led to a number of short productions like music videos and commercials, and feature-length films, including *Kumo no Mukō, Yakusoku no Basho* (*The Place Promised in Our Early Days*, 2004) and *Byōsoku 5 Centimeter* (*5 Centimeters per Second*, 2007). Although he now had to delegate, his natural versatility meant he retained total mastery of his style, which he incorporated into each of these films, except for *Hoshi wo Ou Kodomo* (*Children Who Chase Lost Voices*), a tribute to Miyazaki's filmmaking that proved to be his least personal work.

Yasuhiro Yoshiura went down a path similar to Shinkai. He began in 2000 with a number of short productions, which led to his directing *Pale Cocoon* in 2004, a twenty-minute film in which he developed his passion for depth of field, virtual camera movements, and futuristic science fiction. He used this effective combination in his ode to Isaac Asimov, the ONA *Eve no Jikan* (*Time of Eve*, 2008), and in his feature film *Sakasama no Patema* (*Patema Inverted*, 2013).

Like the Hatsune Miku concept, Shinkai and Yoshiura were the result of a web generation that drew its distinctive style from self-education, the very essence of DIY. Backed by their own production companies, CoMix Wave Films Inc. for Shinkai and Studio Rikka for Yoshiura, they expressed the same need for independence as other directors with a

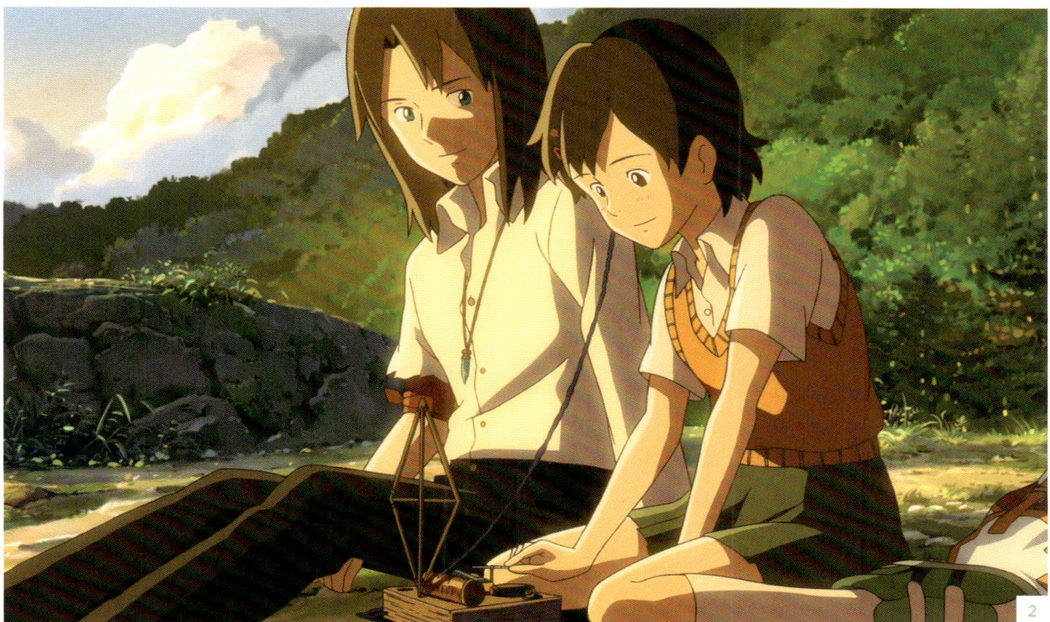

of Miyazaki, the figurehead of an industry that capitalized as much on the box office revenue from his films as on the image of anime that he presented to the world.

All eyes were on these up-and-coming directors, who were dubbed "the new Miyazaki" by the international press as soon as one of their films met with success. At Studio Ghibli, the eternal problem of passing the torch never found a suitable solution. Miyazaki's son Goro's *Kokuriko-zaka Kara* (*From Up on Poppy Hill*, 2011) was only a minor success, as was Hiromasa Yonebayashi's gothic *Omoide no Marnie* (*When Marnie Was There*, 2014), despite his international success with *Karigurashi no Arrietty* (*The Secret World of Arrietty*, 2011). Following a restructuring at Studio Ghibli, producer Yoshiaki Nishimura (*Howl's Moving Castle*, *When Marnie Was There*) left to create Studio Ponoc in 2015, taking with him animators and director Yonebayashi, who immediately started on his film, *Mary to Majo no Hana* (*Mary and the Witch's*

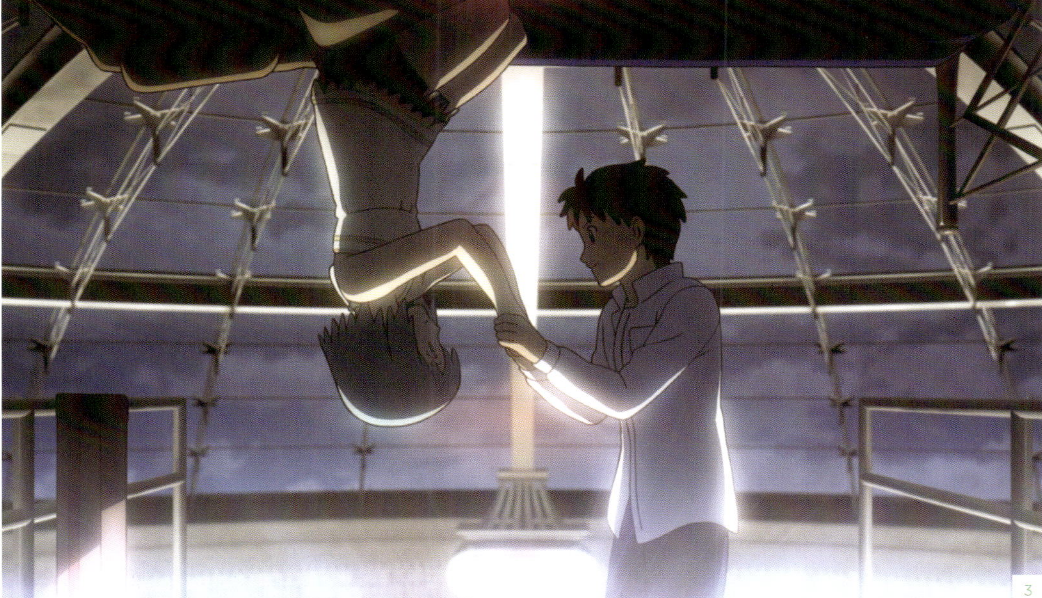

2
2011
Hoshi wo Ou Kodomo (Children Who Chase Lost Voices)

3
2012
Sakasama no Patema (Patema Inverted)

4
2009
Mai Mai Miracle

5
2015
Sarusuberi: Miss Hokusai (Miss Hokusai)

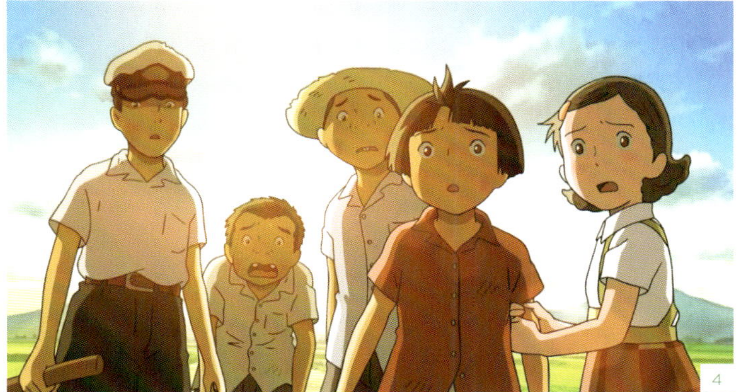

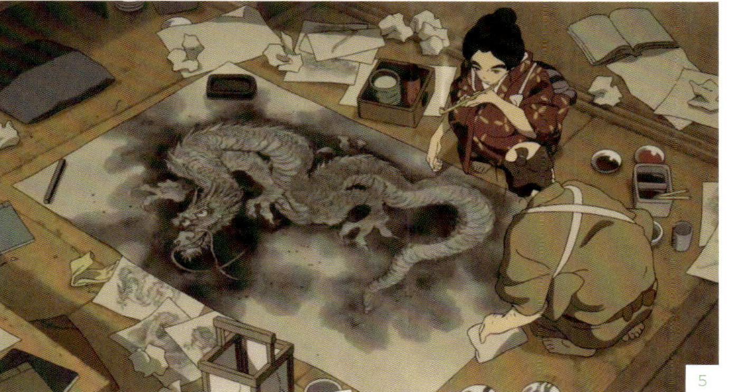

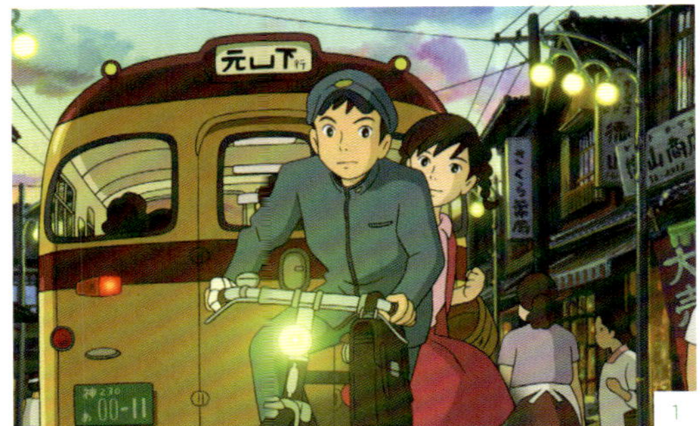

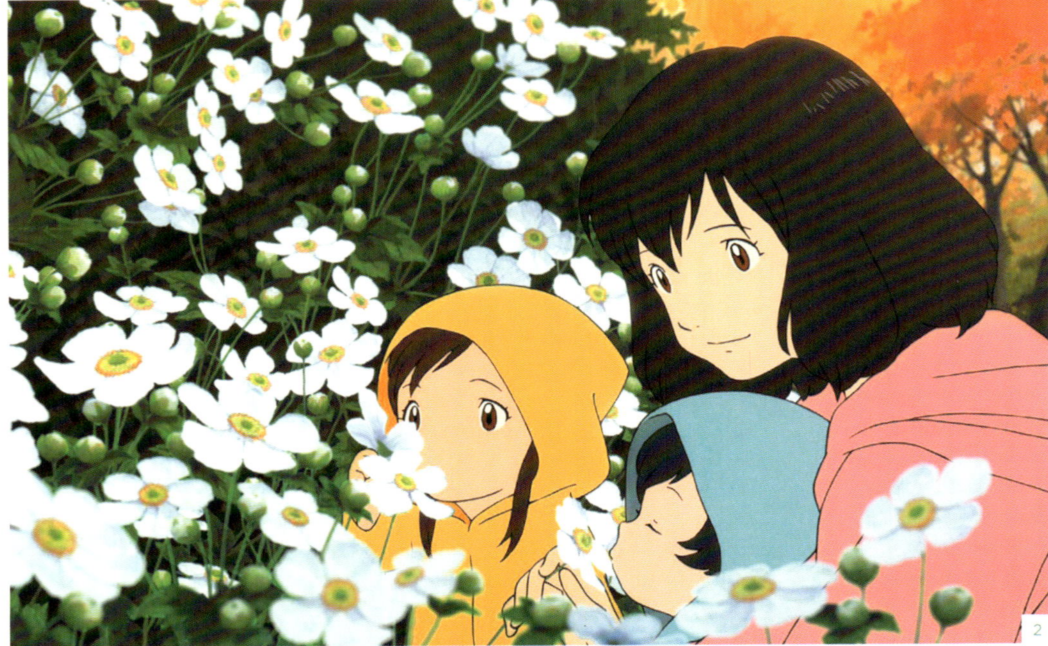

1
2011
Kokuriko-zaka Kara (From Up on Poppy Hill)

2
2012
Ōkami Kodomo no Ame to Yuki (Wolf Children)

3
2017
Yoaketsugeru Rū no Uta (Lu Over the Wall)

Flower). If Studio Ghibli's legacy wasn't commercial success, it would undoubtedly be recognized for its distinctive style!

Financially, Mamoru Hosoda set himself apart with *Bakemono no Ko* (*The Boy and the Beast*, 2015), which grossed ¥5.8 billion in Japan, making Studio Chizu one of the most profitable independent companies. Audiences became accustomed to Hosoda's themes and cinematic techniques, just as they had grown familiar with the filmmaking of Makoto Shinkai, who released his fourth feature the following year, *Kimi no Na wa* (*Your Name.*). The film was a smash hit!

A technical and narrative manifesto of Shinkai's filmmaking, *Your Name.* tells the story of two high school students, Mitsuha, a country girl, and Taki, a city boy, who have switched bodies in their dreams, only to realize that the exchanges are real. To everyone's surprise, the film was so popular that it topped the 2016 Japanese box office with more than 18.9 million admissions, making it the fourth most successful film at the Japanese box office after *Spirited Away*, *Titanic* (1997), and *Frozen* (2013). A veritable phenomenon, *Your Name.* benefited from anime's international popularity to become the biggest foreign Japanese box-office success of all time, raking in ¥40 billion (around $366 million), compared with ¥25 billion for *Spirited Away*.

Would Makoto Shinkai become the new Miyazaki? Not likely, given how much the two directors' works differ in form and content. First and foremost, *Your Name.* is not aimed at children, as evidenced by its twisted romance and post-Fukushima

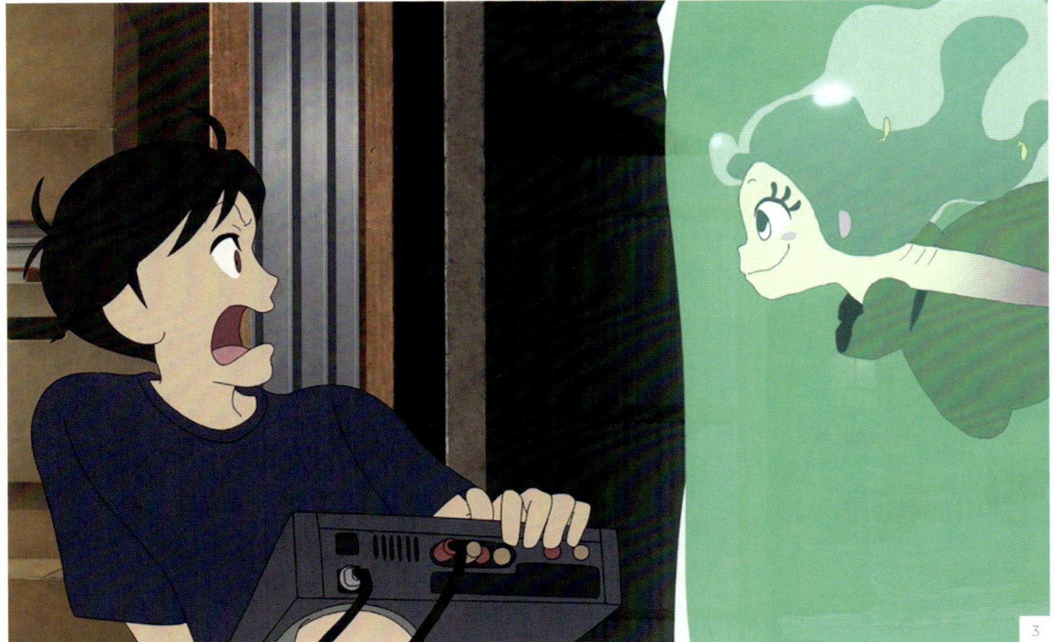

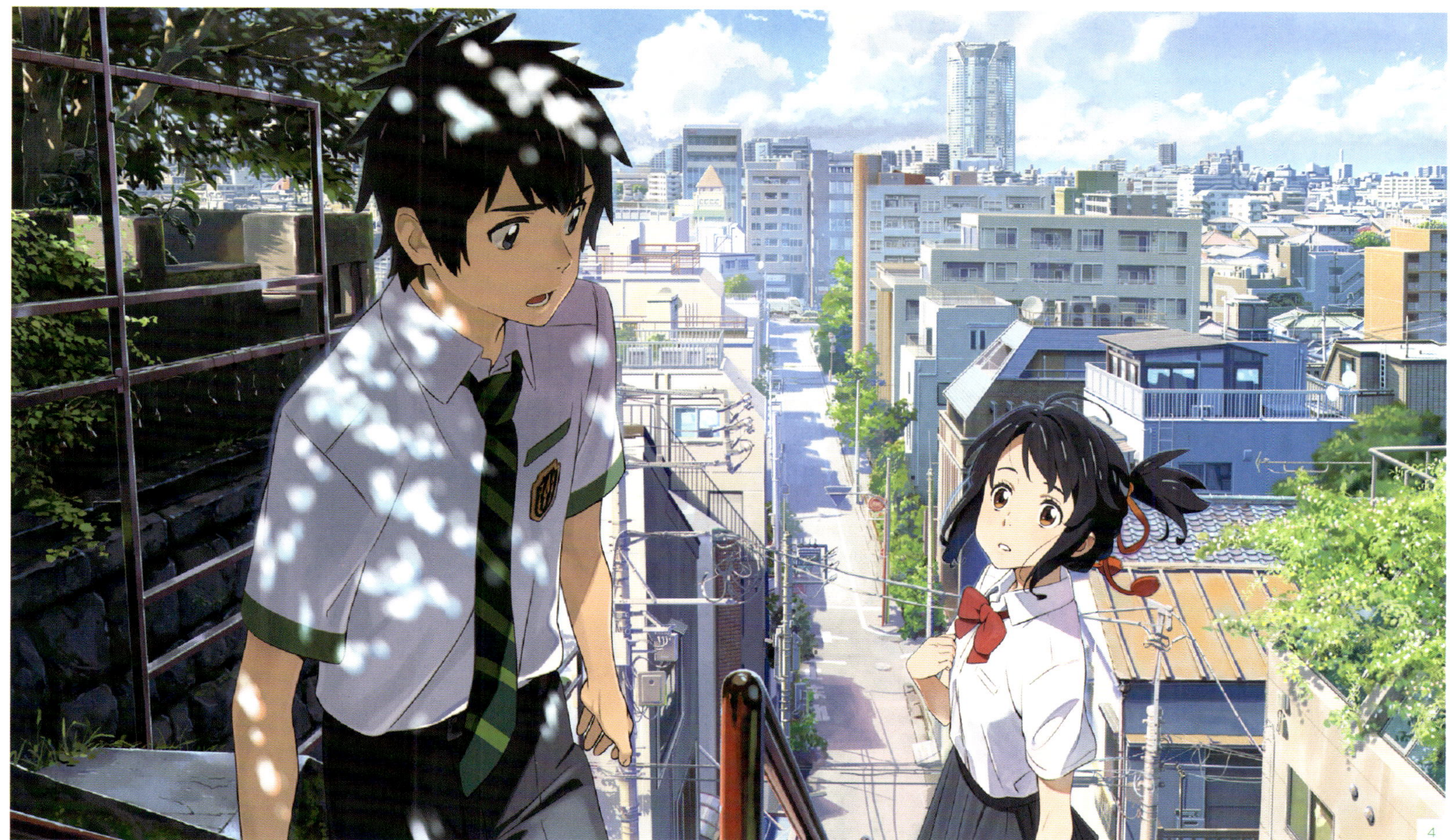

4
—
2016
Kimi no Na wa
(Your Name.)

message, the ghost of which haunts the entire film. Instead, Makoto Shinkai positioned himself as the driving force behind a generation that is excessively connected yet more grounded in reality than previous generations, who had taken refuge in visceral imagery to express their grievances. In contrast, this new generation eschewed graphic violence (on-screen visions of death had been avoided since the tragic earthquake in 2011) in favor of positive human values.

This is clearly illustrated through the cinematic releases of 2017. In Kenji Kamiyama's futuristic *Hirune Hime* (*Napping Princess*), only the blind trust between a father and daughter can overcome a multinational corporation. Sunao Katabuchi's *Kono Sekai no Katasumi ni* (*In This Corner of the World*), MAPPA studio's first feature film, follows the day-to-day survival of a Japanese family during World War II. Finally, a music-loving mermaid gives a disillusioned teenager back his zest for life in Masaaki Yuasa's *Yoaketsugeru Rū no Uta* (*Lu Over the Wall*). The last two titles won awards at the 2017 Annecy International Animated Film Festival—*In This Corner of the World* won the Jury Award and *Lu Over the Wall* won the prestigious Cristal for a Feature Film, more than twenty years after the last Japanese winner, *Pom Poko*!

After a century of emancipating itself as technology and local markets evolved, anime was finally receiving the recognition it deserved on the world stage. But as part of the cultural globalization that began with the internet, it needed to redefine its identity to better assert itself on international screens, whether in cinemas or on smartphones. And, above all, anime needed to resolve the crises that were eroding it from within, threatening to turn its plans for conquest into defeat.

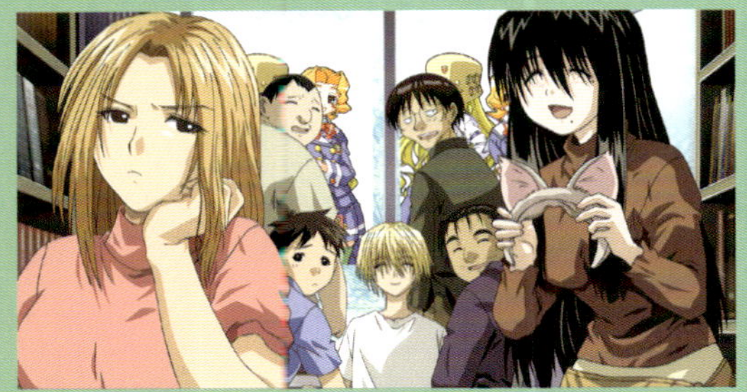

GENSHIKEN

Genshiken
Year: 2004
Category: TV
Director: Takashi Ikehata
Animation Studio: Palm Studio

AT A GLANCE:
While they had been ostracized until the end of the twentieth century, otaku became cool with the advent of the internet. This series, which presents them in a positive light to the general public, is full of hidden references to their culture.

YOU MAY ALSO LIKE . . .
The female otaku portrayed in *Princess Jellyfish*. *Gintama*'s many pop-culture references. *Welcome to the N.H.K.*, which focuses on homebound recluses.

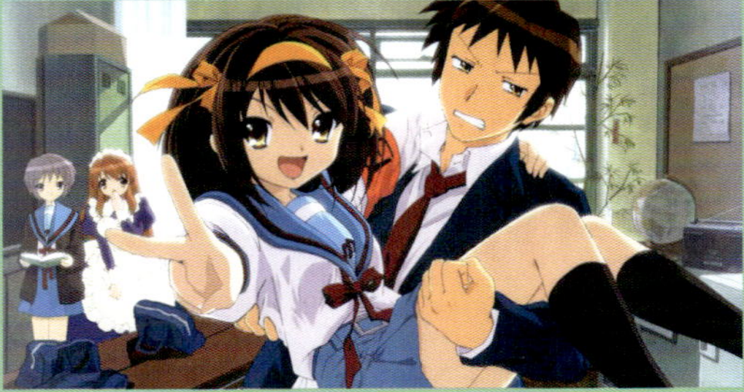

SUZUMIYA HARUHI NO YŪUTSU

The Melancholy of Haruhi Suzumiya
Year: 2006
Category: TV, film
Director: Tatsuya Ishihara
Animation Studio: Kyoto Animation

AT A GLANCE:
This series was an international success that introduced the world to Kyoto Animation and its uncompromising technical standards while launching a new wave of light novel adaptations.

YOU MAY ALSO LIKE . . .
Lucky Star with its otaku heroine and *K-On!* with its pop *moe* band are two direct descendants of *Haruhi Suzumiya*. Both series were also produced by Kyoto Animation.

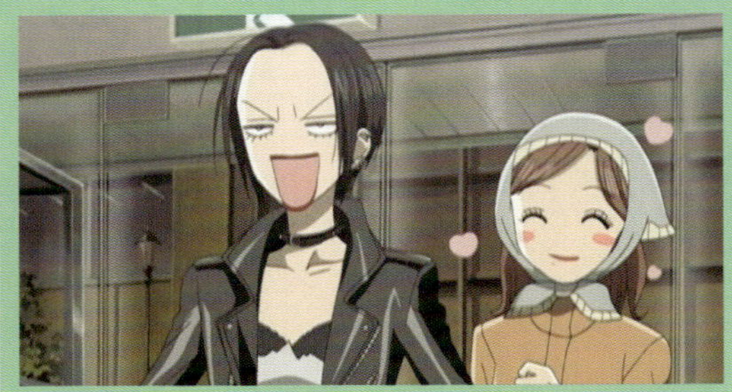

NANA

Nana
Year: 2006
Category: TV
Director: Morio Asaka
Animation Studio: Madhouse

AT A GLANCE:
The everyday experiences, triumphs, struggles, romances, and heartaches of two trendy Tokyo residents who appear to have nothing in common. Anime finally learns to appeal to women.

YOU MAY ALSO LIKE . . .
The atypical heroine in *Peach Girl* who struggles to fit into conventional society. *Skip Beat!*, in which thwarted love meets show business. *Paradise Kiss*, by the same *mangaka*.

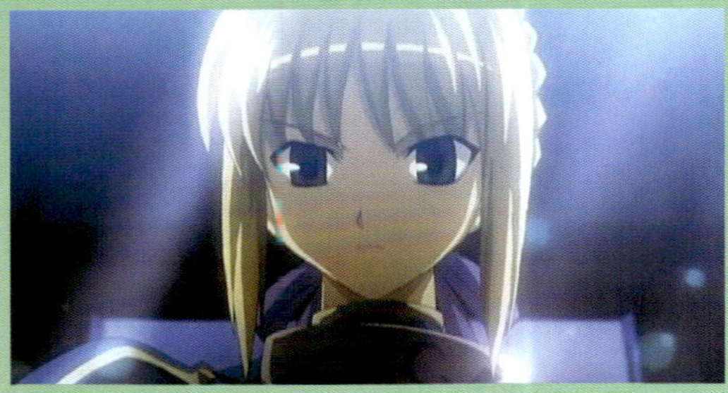

FATE/STAY NIGHT

Fate/Stay Night
Year: 2006
Category: TV, film
Director: Yūji Yamaguchi
Animation Studio: Studio Deen

AT A GLANCE:
Companies in charge of the often erotic visual novel video games, such as Type-Moon, are becoming crucial drivers in the animation industry.

YOU MAY ALSO LIKE . . .
Tsukihime from a game by the same publisher. The fateful confrontations between the heroines in *My HiME*. *Shakugan no Shana*, whose dark tone has also been adapted for video games.

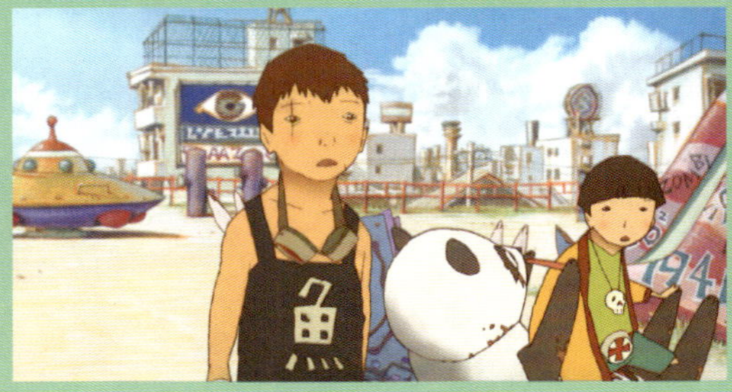

TEKKONKINKREET

Tekkonkinkreet
Year: 2006
Category: Film
Director: Michael Arias
Animation Studio: Studio 4°C

AT A GLANCE:
The first anime film made by a foreigner! The industry is experimenting with new, unprecedented possibilities thanks to globalization.

YOU MAY ALSO LIKE . . .
Mind Game, a unique film that frees itself from the usual constraints of animation. The short *Noiseman Sound Insect* by the same production company. The characters and their fractured psyches in *Paprika*.

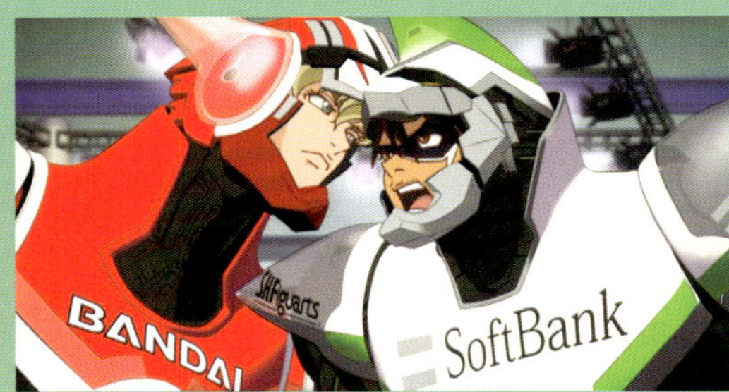

TIGER & BUNNY

Tiger & Bunny
Year: 2011
Category: TV
Director: Keiichi Sato
Animation Studio: Sunrise

AT A GLANCE:
Product placement within the plot of a series to finance its development is just one of the avenues being explored by an industry plagued by the financial crisis.

YOU MAY ALSO LIKE . . .
Hōkago no Pleiades, a massive advertisement for Subaru made by Gainax. *Samurai Flamenco*, a new mix of superhero categories. *One-Punch Man*, whose hero overturns the usual narrative codes.

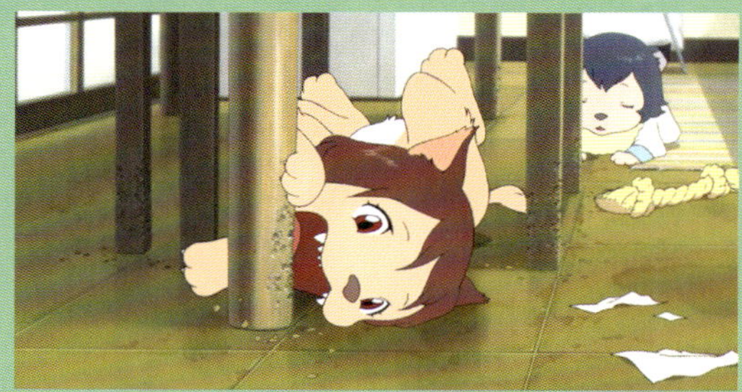

ŌKAMI KODOMO NO AME TO YUKI

Wolf Children
Year: 2012
Category: Film
Director: Mamoru Hosoda
Animation Studio: Studio Chizu

AT A GLANCE:
This feature film dedicated to motherhood is the first by Studio Chizo, a production company tailor-made for the director, an approach that will be extended to many artists.

YOU MAY ALSO LIKE . . .
The Boy and the Beast, a similar film about fatherhood. *Napping Princess* and *A Letter to Momo*, in which family ties carry over into dreams and beyond death.

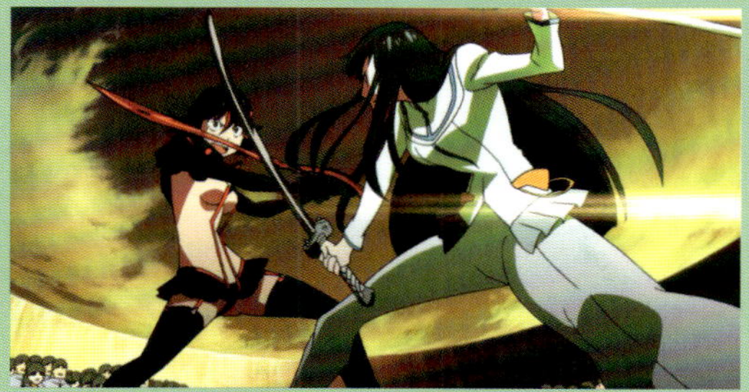

KILL LA KILL

Kill la Kill
Year: 2013
Category: TV
Director: Hiroyuki Imaishi
Animation Studio: Trigger

AT A GLANCE:
Kill la Kill is a technical manifesto of Trigger studio, recapturing the same defiant spirit of the early 1980s in both plot and production.

YOU MAY ALSO LIKE . . .
Project A-Ko for its many similarities. *Gurren Lagann*, which transcends the codes of the "giant robot" genre. The animated experiment *Dead Leaves*. *Redline*'s mad racing.

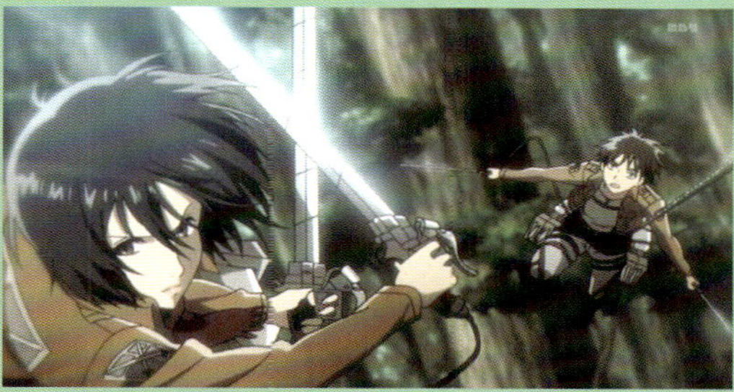

SHINGEKI NO KYOJIN

Attack on Titan
Year: 2013
Category: TV
Director: Tetsurō Araki
Animation Studio: Wit Studio

AT A GLANCE:
This new social phenomenon instantly became a financial windfall, verging on advertising overdose—a rare series that brought people together were heavily targeted by industrial marketing.

YOU MAY ALSO LIKE . . .
Knights of Sidonia, a space opera about humanity's survival in the face of colossal predators. *Kabaneri of the Iron Fortress*, produced by the same team.

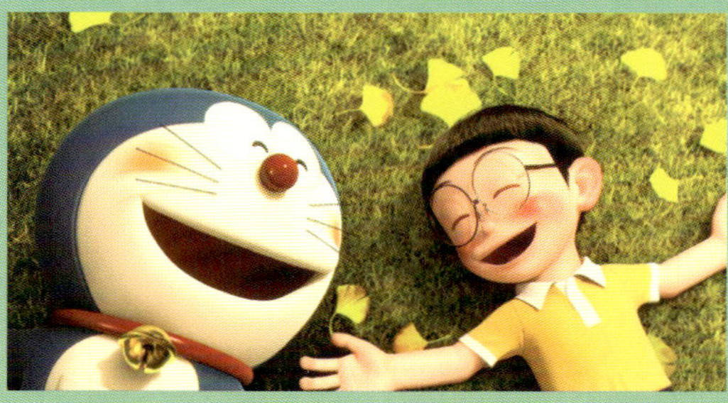

STAND BY ME DORAEMON

Stand by Me Doraemon
Year: 2014
Category: Film
Directors: Ryūichi Yagi and Takashi Yamazaki
Animation Studios: Shirogumi, Robot Communications, and Shin-Ei Animation

AT A GLANCE:
Historic icons adapt to CGI animation! Twenty years after *Toy Story*, anime gives in to a technology already adopted by the rest of the world.

YOU MAY ALSO LIKE . . .
Appleseed, first major project in 3D toon shading. *Saint Seiya: Legend of Sanctuary*, which modifies its original material to meet the demands of a twenty-first-century audience.

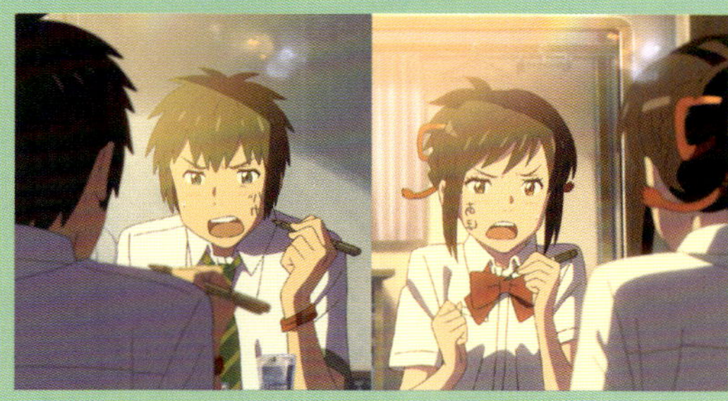

KIMI NO NA WA

Your Name.
Year: 2016
Category: Cinema
Director: Makoto Shinkai
Animation Studio: CoMix Wave

AT A GLANCE:
A triumph that rivals the box office success of Studio Ghibli productions, *Your Name.* is proof of the public's appetite for animation that is in tune with the times.

YOU MAY ALSO LIKE . . .
Voices of a Distant Star and *5 Centimeters per Second*, the director's previous bittersweet productions. *The Girl Who Leapt Through Time* for its similar themes.

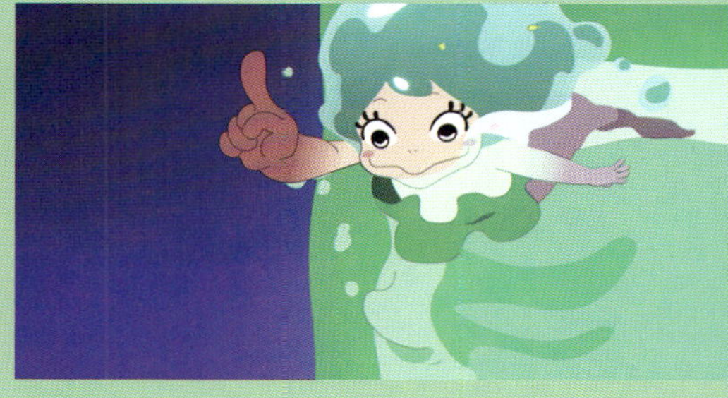

YOAKETSUGERU RŪ NO UTA

Lu Over the Wall
Year: 2017
Category: Film
Director: Masaaki Yuasa
Animation Studio: Science Saru

AT A GLANCE:
Produced entirely with Flash software, this magical tale opened the door to other production methods. The bold approach received worldwide acclaim.

YOU MAY ALSO LIKE . . .
Ponyo is a similar film in terms of content, allowing viewers to appreciate the stylistic gap between two generations of filmmakers. *Kaiba* and *The Tatami Galaxy*, two series that highlight Masaaki Yuasa's creativity.

Conclusion

In May 2015, with televised anime having reached a new record of 322 series broadcast, Hideaki Anno predicted the end of Japanese animation. According to him, the medium would decline for five years before collapsing entirely, undermined by a lack of resources and manpower, and be overtaken by international competition. But the director of *Evangelion* was not pessimistic—this inevitable end of the cycle would be followed by anime's rebirth.

Later, during the closing ceremony of the Rio 2016 Summer Olympics, Prime Minister Shinzo Abe arrived on scene dressed as Nintendo icon Mario to promote the next Summer Olympic Games in Tokyo. Pop culture was undoubtedly the central theme for the 2020 sporting event, whose mascots included the heroes of *Dragon Ball*, *Sailor Moon*, *Astro Boy*, *Naruto*, *Crayon Shin-chan*, *One Piece*, *Yo-kai Watch*, and *Pretty Cure*. Yasushi Akimoto, a member of the organizing committee for the opening ceremony, planned to showcase his musical group, AKB48, even though the Japanese general public, when polled, said they preferred fifteen or so other artists to represent their music scene to the world.

A financial engine designed for the international market, Cool Japan stubbornly promoted the *kawaii* trend, the only exportable "made in Japan" label, according to officials. However, the plethora of carefully calibrated media-mix titles, backed by production committees, only targeted a shrinking otaku fringe audience. At the same time, the general public in Japan had fully adopted animation as an omnipresent medium in their daily lives in commercials, music videos, pachinko, smartphone apps, and more, and was clamoring for creative, original content. This was illustrated by the triumph of *Your Name.* in Japan, and even more so abroad. The otaku target may have been just a small part of the Japanese public, but it paled in comparison to the massive international consumer base that arose with the internet. In 2015, revenue generated abroad (¥583 billion) exceeded merchandising revenue (¥579 billion), the industry's mainstay, for the first time!

The online network also consolidated the otaku community, which had become increasingly critical and demanding. Disappointing such a foundational group was off the table for many of the 430 studios in Japan—a spontaneous boycott of their productions by furious fans would be fatal to their cash flow. In this race to the bottom, which was partly responsible for the decline predicted by Anno, their efforts seemed so far removed from the expectations of international fans that they were in vain. Those fans were willing to invest in outside-the-box productions by crowdfunding, showing up in force to raise 10 percent of the budget for *In This Corner of the World* on Kickstarter. This fan enthusiasm persuaded several companies to provide financial support for Katabuchi's film. Without their contributions, producer Masao Maruyama would not have been able to complete this unconventional project, which would have required years of fundraising.

As global audiences clamored for anime, entertainment heavyweights reacted in their own way on every continent. In China, Haoliners Animation League expanded by opening a branch in Korea and another in Japan. Its Japanese studio, employing Japanese artists, aimed to create productions for the Japanese market—Chinese investors capitalized on local expertise to recoup costs in a field well-known to the Japanese. In Europe, Monaco-based Shibuya Productions announced the release of *Astro Boy Reboot*, a remake of the first weekly series in the history of anime with Western graphics, a collaboration between Tezuka Productions and French production company Caribara Animation. Banking on the nostalgia of thirty-somethings, Shibuya Productions also prepared for the return of *Cobra* in the fan-favorite story arc *Cobra: Return of Joe Gillian*. In the United States, VOD giant Netflix was involved in producing thirteen Japanese animated series for 2018, including remakes of *Devilman* and *Saint Seiya: Knights of the Zodiac*, along with innovative projects such as an adaptation of the manga *Children of the Whales*. Similarly, Amazon Prime Video offered an anime streaming service called Anime Strike, a catalog of a thousand titles for five dollars a month, which it gradually expanded with exclusive content following a contract with Fuji TV over their Noitamina late-night programming.

International support for the animation industry wasn't just financial—dozens of passionate artists whose careers had begun with a love for anime went to Japan to try their luck. There were so many vacancies and such a shortage of qualified workers, including in 3D animation, that in October 2017, the government announced it would be easing visa rules for foreign animators. However, there were still many constraints for incoming animators: they needed to understand Japanese, put up with long hours, and have a large financial cushion because entry-level salaries were so low. Despite all this, these foreign workers didn't start at the bottom of the ladder, thanks to their training. As uncompromising as it may be, the industry rewards the most tenacious, such as animator Eddie Mehong, who successfully launched Yapiko Animation in Tokyo in 2012.

A perfect example of this meritocracy is Makoto Shinkai, who started at the bottom and produced the short film *She and Her Cat* in 1999, going on to become a box-office superstar with *Your Name.* in 2016. But in that span of less than twenty years, how many beginners sacrificed their artistic ambitions for a side job more likely to pay the bills? All the more so as the mentoring aspect of the industry disappeared with the advent of computers and increased production. Age-old expertise was in danger of dying out for lack of successors. If the industry didn't reconsider its salary model, Japanese animation could, once again, suffer the disastrous fate predicted by Hideaki Anno.

What does the second half of the prophecy entail, the revival? In the short term, the arrival of a new hero whose commercial appeal will reinvigorate the economic and creative machine. Apart from *Attack on Titan*, which is unsuitable for children, *Pokémon*, *One Piece*, and Detective Conan in *Case Closed* haven't found a successor in more than twenty years! Rather than playing the role of a cheap Nostradamus, we can anticipate the future on a grander scale by looking back over the past century. Technological advancement has always been the catalyst behind the evolution of anime, as seen with film, television, video recorders, computers, 3D, and the internet. It's time to innovate, to be bold like Hayao Miyazaki! Miyazaki, who had refused to use 3D, decided to experiment with it for a short film initially scheduled for release in 2018. Inspired by the digital tool, he prepared to make a comeback in 2019 with a feature-length film in CGI. At the age of eighty-six, he rediscovered the enthusiasm of his early days as a novice in a new medium. Will it be holography to Hatsune Miku? Or augmented reality like *Pokémon Go*? Or perhaps virtual reality, which the *Kizumonogatari* franchise tried its hand at in 2017? It's hard to know which of the many current experiments will be the future engine boost of an ever-rising rocket—and why not all of them?

One thing remains certain: whether it's abrupt or gradual, the evolution of anime will have considerable repercussions on several fronts. First, economically, as the expanding simulcast market, which grew by 50 percent between 2009 and 2015 from ¥1.25 trillion to ¥1.82 trillion, comes to a halt as the number of subscribers stabilizes. But the real consequences will be mainly sociocultural! For anime, which is attempting to redefine itself, is now part of the world's collective subconscious, as the Olympic mascots reminded us. Furthermore, Japan's selection by the Olympic Committee sparked reactions from anime fans around the world, as, prophetic in retrospect, *Akira* set the 2020 Olympics in Neo-Tokyo. Will that global event prove to be the final tipping point for the birth of neo-animation?

Glossary

A

Anime: Term used to refer to cartoons in Japan and used in English to designate Japanese animation.

Atemi: Unarmed blow with the foot or hand.

B

Benshi: Master of ceremonies who first explained the technological principles of cinema to the audience before voicing the characters in the film, still silent at the time.

Bunraku: Japanese puppet theater.

C

Chanbara: Sword fight films.

Character design: Standardizing the graphic traits of a character.

Character designer: Artist in charge of creating the character design. Sometimes shortened to *chara designer.*

Chiyogami: Japanese patterned paper used for paper art.

Computer-generated imagery (CGI): Graphics or designs produced with computer assistance.

Cosplayer: Person who dresses up as a character in a cartoon, movie, video game, or book. (“Cosplay” is a contraction of “costume playing”.)

D

Dating sim: A dating simulation game.

Dōga: Moving picture.

Dōjin (or dōjinshi): Self-published Japanese fanzine. Mainly parodies, sometimes erotic.

Drama: Asian TV series or audio story based on a book.

E

Eroge: Erotic video game.

F

Fan base (or fandom): Refers to all the fans of a particular subject.

Fan service: Behavior designed to play into the fantasies of fans.

Fansub: Fan-made subtitles.

Fujoshi: Literally “rotten girl,” a term for singles over twenty-five years of age. Also used by female otaku as a nickname for themselves.

G

Game system: Rules defining how a video game is played.

Gekiga: Adult manga characterized by darker, more complex stories rooted in reality.

Gunpla: Plastic models from the *Gundam* franchise.

H

Harem anime: Term used to talk about works in which the main character is surrounded by many protagonists of the opposite sex.

Hentai: Refers to erotica and pornography in anime and manga.

I

Idol: Japanese starlet whose career rarely lasts more than a few years.

J

Josei: Manga designed for young adult female readers.

K

Kaiju eiga: Monster movies.

Kamishibai: Literally “paper theater,” involves telling a story by scrolling drawings through a frame one by one.

Kawaii: Literally “cute.”

Kojiki: Collections of legendary stories about the divine creation of Japan.

L

Layout: Detailed drawings containing all the information needed to shoot a film, from animation to camera movements to the location of sets and props.

Light novel: Novel for young adults, usually consisting of simple text and a few illustrations.

Lolicon: Abbreviation for “lolita complex.” Refers to a fan of eroticized little girls.

M

Magical girl: Young girl with magical powers.

Maid café: Café where servers are dressed in maid costumes.

Manga: Japanese comic book.

Manga eiga: “Cartoon films.” Term used to designate animation when it was still considered a subgenre of cinema (*eiga*).

Mangaka: Manga artist.

Mecha: Armor, robot, or cyborg whose function is generally to fight. Shortened from *mechanics.*

Mecha designer: Artist responsible for creating mecha designs.

Moe: Concept or type of female character who inspires a desire to protect them.

N

Nekketsu: Literally “hot blooded.” Subgenre of *shōnen* manga that emphasizes going beyond one’s limits, with strong characters who have an iron will.

O

Original animation video (OAV): Animated production intended to be sold directly on video.

Office lady: Salaried working woman.

Otaku: Japanese word to describe someone with is obsessed with one particular area of anime or manga and may exhibit asocial or neurotic behavior. There are otaku of anything and everything.

P

Pachinko: Japanese vertical pinball machine.

Persocon: Japanese abbreviation for *personal computer* or *PC*.

Pinku eiga: Erotic film.

R

Rakugo: Comedy performed on stage, originating in the seventeenth century.

Robot anime: Genre of Japanese cartoons featuring mainly robots.

Role-playing game (RPG): Includes tabletop games and those played on video game consoles or computers.

S

Salaryman: White-collar businessman.

Sailor fuku: Female school uniform inspired by sailor uniforms.

Seiyū: Japanese voice actor.

Shin'ya anime: Late-night anime broadcast on television between 11 p.m. and 4 a.m.

Shōjo manga: Means "teenage girl" in Japanese. Refers to manga for young girls.

Shōnen (manga): Means "teenage boy" in Japanese. Refers to manga for young boys.

Shōnen-ai: Subgenre focused on homosexual love and romance between androgynous male characters.

Simulcast: Shortened form of *simultaneous broadcast*. Episodes are made available as soon as possible after their Japanese TV broadcast.

Sonosheet: Or "flexi disc," denotes a flexible vinyl disc of lower quality than the 33 rpm. Later renamed "punch sheet."

Story manga: Manga based on cinematic processes and themes.

Super deformed (SD): Animation in which a character is depicted with a small body and a huge head.

Super sentai: An iconic genre of Japanese superheroes, in which fighters in different-colored outfits fight together against evil.

T

Tanuki: *Yōkai*, a supernatural creature from Japanese folklore, inspired by the Japanese raccoon dog, which resembles a badger or raccoon.

Tengu: Creature from Japanese folklore elevated to the rank of *kami* or *yōkai*, traditionally depicted as humanoid with raptor-like features (beak or long nose).

Terebi manga: "Television manga," as opposed to "cartoon films" (*manga eiga*).

Tokusatsu: Japanese audiovisual productions rich in special effects.

Toon shading: 3D technique that resembles traditional 2D animation but accentuates contours and simplifies colorimetry. Also called cel shading.

Visual kei: Japanese category of musicians often associated with hard rock, characterized by artists with distinctive makeup, extravagant outfits, and androgynous looks.

Visual novel: Visual story somewhere between a book and a video game, in which the reader generally has a choice about how the story unfolds.

Vocaloid: Voice bank and computer-generated singer created by a voice synthesis software.

W

Wakamono sports eiga: Youth sports film.

Yakuza eiga: Gangster film.

Yaoi: Manga for women featuring explicit relationships between homosexual men.

Yōkai: Name given to supernatural beings in Japanese folklore.

Yonkoma: Four-panel comic strip.

Index

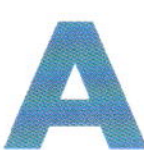

Adachi Mitsuru (1951–): *Mangaka*. Author of *Touch*.

Akai Takami (196[illegible]–): Animator, illustrator, co-founder of Gainax studio.

Akatsuka Fujio (1935–2008): *Mangaka*. Author of *Tensai Bakabon* and *Osomatsu-kun*.

Amano Yoshitaka (1952–): Artist, character designer for *Gatchaman*, *Amon Saga*, and the *Final Fantasy* video game franchise.

Amemiya Akira (Unknown): Animator, storyboard artist, and episode director on *Gurren Lagann* and *Kill la Kill*.

Anno Hideaki (1960–): Director of *Nadia: The Secret of Blue Water* and *Neon Genesis Evangelion*. Founder of Studio Khara.

Aochi Chūzō (1885–1970): *Mangaka* and animation pioneer. Collaborated with Yasuji Murata and worked on the *Norakuro* film series.

Aoyama Gosho (1963–): *Mangaka*. Creator of *Case Closed*.

Arai Wagorō (1907–1994): Early director specializing in cutout silhouettes. Directed *Ochō Fujin no Genso* and *Princess Kaguya*.

Araki Hirohiko (1960–): *Mangaka*. Creator of *Jojo's Bizarre Adventure*.

Araki Shingo (1939–2011): Character designer and animator for *Goldorak*, *The Rose of Versailles*, *Ulysses 31*, and *Saint Seiya*. Collaborated closely with Michi Himeno.

Araki Tetsurō (1976–): Director of *Death Note* and *Attack on Titan*.

Aramaki Shinji (1960–): Mecha designer and pioneering director in 3D with *Appleseed* and *Harlock: Space Pirate*.

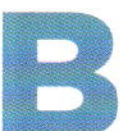

Buronson (1947–): Manga writer. Creator of *Fist of the North Star*.

C

CLAMP: Artist collective of four female *mangaka*. Creator of *X* and *Cardcaptor Sakura*.

D

Daikubara Akira (1917–2012): Toei's pioneering animator and director. Worked on *The Tale of the White Serpent* and *Magic Boy*.

Dezaki Osamu (1943–2011): Disciple of Osamu Tezuka, director of *Ashita no Joe*, *Nobody's Boy: Remi*, and *Cobra*.

Dezaki Satoshi (1940–): Osamu Dezaki's older brother, director of *Captain* and *Urusei Yatsura* (OAV and film).

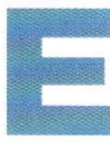

Endō Makoto (Unknown): Director specializing in 3D, which he supervised on *Blood+*, *Ghost in the Shell: Stand Alone Complex*, and *Eden of the East*.

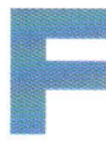

Fujioka Yutaka (1927–1996): Puppeteer. Founder of Tokyo Movie Shinsha (TMS).

Fujikawa Keisuke (1934–): Scriptwriter on most of the sci-fi series of the 1970s to 1980s, including *Mazinger Z*, *Galaxy Express 999*, and *Space Battleship Yamato*.

Fukazawa Kazuo (1933–): Scriptwriter for *The Great Adventure of Horus, Prince of the Sun* and *A Thousand and One Nights*.

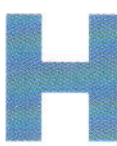

Hara Keiichi (1959–): Director of several *Crayon Shin-chan* films, *Summer Days with Coo*, *Colorful*, and *Miss Hokusai*.

Hara Tetsuo (1961–): *Mangaka*, illustrator of *Fist of the North Star*.

Hattori Tadashi (1908–2008): Composer, known for his collaborations with Akira Kurosawa.

Hayashibara Megumi (1967–): Voice actress, known for voicing the heroines in *Magical Princess Minky Momo*, *Cowboy Bebop*, and *Paprika*.

Himeno Michi (1956–): One of the first women recognized as a character designer. She collaborated closely with Shingo Araki and worked on *Saint Seiya*.

Hirano Toshiki (1956–): Character designer and director. Worked on *Fight! Iczer One* and *Megazone 23*.

Hisaishi Joe (1950–): Hayao Miyazaki's official composer since *Nausicaä of the Valley of the Wind*.

Hiwatari Saki (1961–): *Mangaka*. Creator of *Please Save My Earth*.

Hōjō Tsukasa (1959–): *Mangaka*. Creator of *Cat's Eye* and *City Hunter*.

Hongō Mitsuru (1959–): Director of the first seasons of *Crayon Shin-chan*, *Outlaw Star*, and *World Trigger*.

Hosoda Mamoru (1967–): Director trained at Toei and Studio Ghibli before flourishing at his own Studio Chizu with *Summer Wars*, *Wolf Children*, and *The Boy and the Beast*.

Horie Mitsuko (1957–): Singer and voice actress with a prolific career after her debut at twelve years old, which includes *Love Me, My Knight*; *Sailor Moon*; and *Lalabel, the Magical Girl*. Nicknamed "Queen of the *Anison* World."

I

K

Kon Satoshi (1963–2010): *Mangaka* and director. Directed *Perfect Blue*, *Millennium Actress*, *Tokyo Godfathers*, and *Paprika*. Member of the Japanese Animation Creators Association (JAniCA).

Kondō Yoshifumi (1950–1998): Animator expected to succeed Hayao Miyazaki. Director of *Whisper of the Heart*, who died of exhaustion during the production of *Princess Mononoke*.

Kotabe Yōichi (1936–): Animator and character designer. Worked on Miyazaki and Takahata's early works (*Heidi*, *Panda! Go Panda!*) and *Pokémon*.

Kōuchi Junichi (1886–1970): Director of the oldest archive in the history of Japanese animation dated 1917, *Hanahekonai: A New Sword Chapter*. Left animation for manga in 1930.

Kumagawa Masao (1916–2008): Animator trained by Kenzō Masaoka. Worked on *The Spider and the Tulip*, directed *The Magic Pen* and *The Carefree Station Manager Poppoya-san** before joining Toei when it was created.

Kuri Yōji (1928–2024): *Mangaka*, independent animator, international festival favorite, and teacher.

Kuroda Yoshio (1936–): Director of productions, including *Wolf Boy Ken*, *Monarch: The Big Bear of Tallac*, *The Dog of Flanders*, and *Peter Pan: The Animated Series*.

Kurosawa Akira (1910–1988): Japanese director and major influence on cinema worldwide.

Kurumada Masami (1953–): *Mangaka*. Creator of *Saint Seiya*.

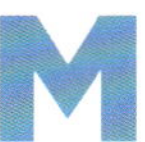

Maeda Mahiro (1963–): Director of *Blue Submarine No. 6*, *Gankutsuou: The Count of Monte Cristo*, and *Evangelion: 3.33 You Can (Not) Redo*. Cocreator of Gonzo studio.

Maeda Toshio (1953–): *Mangaka* specializing in erotic horror. Creator of *Urotsukidōji*.

Maejima Kenichi (Unknown): Director of *A.LI.CE*, the first 3D feature-length anime.

Maruyama Masao (1941–): Producer trained by Osamu Tezuka. Cofounder of Madhouse, founder of MAPPA.

Masaoka Kenzō (1898–1988): Pioneering director of *Chikara to Onna no Yo no Naka*, the first film made with cel animation, and *The Spider and the Tulip*.

Masaki Mori (1941–): Director of *Barefoot Gen* and *Time Stranger*.

Matsumoto Leiji (1938–2023): *Mangaka* and designer. Creator of *Space Pirate Captain Harlock*, *Galaxy Express 999*, and *Interstella 5555*.

Minekura Kazuya (1975–): *Mangaka*. Creator of *Saiyuki*.

Mitsunobu Hiroyoshi (1937–): Director specialized in sports on episodes of *Dokaben* and the *Captain Tsubasa* series.

Miura Kentaro (1966–2021): *Mangaka*. Creator of *Berserk*.

Miyazaki Goro (1967–): Architect by training and creator of the Ghibli Museum. Director for Studio Ghibli whose films include *Tales of Earthsea* and *From Up on Poppy Hill*, and the *Ronja, the Robber's Daughter* series. Son of Hayao Miyazaki.

Miyazaki Hayao (1941–): Oscar-winning director and cofounder of Studio Ghibli. His films include *My Neighbor Totoro*, *Porco Rosso*, *Princess Mononoke*, *Spirited Away*, and *The Wind Rises*.

Miyazawa Kenji (1896–1933): Author whose texts have frequently been adapted into animation, such as *Night on the Galactic Railroad*.

Mizuki Ichirou (1948–2022): Singer. Recorded more than 1,200 songs for films, series, and cartoons in his fifty-year career. Nicknamed the "Emperor of *Anison*."

Mizuno Ryo (1963–): Author and game designer. Imported fantasy to Japan and created *Record of Lodoss War*.

Mochinaga Tadahito (1919–1999): Director specializing in stop-motion animation. Collaborated with the American studio Rankin/Bass.

Mochizuki Tomomi (1958–): Director and sound specialist. Productions include the only Studio Ghibli TV movie, *Ocean Waves*, series such as *Ranma ½*, and films like *Kimagure Orange Road*.

Mori Yasuji (1925–1992): History's first animation director on *The Little Prince and the Eight-Headed Dragon*. Trained Hayao Miyazaki and Isao Takahata at Toei.

Morimoto Kōji (1959–): Animator and director with a clear preference for music videos. Cofounder of Studio 4°C.

Motohashi Kōichi (1930–2010): Producer and founder of Nippon Animation.

Mukuo Takamura (1938–): Art director. Worked on *The Dog of Flanders*, *Devilman*, and all the *Sailor Moon* series.

Murata Yasuji (1896–1966): Pioneering director and expert in paper cutout animation. Worked on the short film series *Norakuro* and *Momotarō*.

N

Nagahama Tadao (1936–1980): Puppeteer and director. Directed the Toei-Sunrise coproduction *Romance Robot Trilogy* (*Chōdenji Robo Combattler V*, *Chōdenji Machine Voltes V*, and *Tōshō Daimos*).

Nagai Go (1945–): *Mangaka*. Creator of the "giant robot piloted from within" genre with *Mazinger Z*. Author of *Cutie Honey*, *Devilman*, and many more.

Nagaoka Akinori (1954–): Director of *Anpanman*.

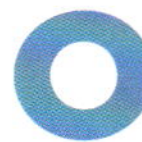

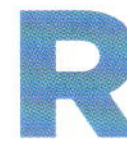

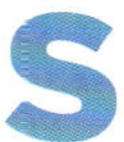

Serikawa Yūgo (1931–2000): One of the main directors at Toei Animation when it moved to the small screen. Works include *Wolf Boy Ken*, *Mako-chan*, and *Meg the Witch*.

Seshita Hiroyuki (1967–): Director and producer specializing in 3D at Polygon Pictures. Directed *Ajin*, *Blame!*, *Knights of Sidonia*, and *Godzilla: Planet of the Monsters*.

Shibayama Tsutomu (1941–): Director eternally associated with the *Doraemon* franchise.

Shidara Hiroshi (1936–): Director of series for younger audiences, such as *Lady Lady!!* and *Hello! Sandybell*.

Shimokawa Ōten (1892–1973): Pioneering director. Creator of *Imokawa Muzukō the Doorman*, the oldest known cartoon whose archive has yet to be found.

Shinkai Makoto (1973–): Self-taught director. Directed *Your Name.*, the biggest international success in Japanese cinema.

Shirow Masamune (1961–): *Mangaka*. Creator of *Ghost in the Shell* and *Appleseed*.

Shudō Takeshi (1949–2010): Scriptwriter. Worked on *Magical Princess Minky Momo*, *Legend of the Galactic Heroes*, and *Pokémon*.

Sonoda Kenichi (1962–): *Mangaka* and character designer. Creator of *Bubblegum Crisis* and *Gunsmith Cats*.

Suda Masami (1943–2021): Character designer and animator. Worked on many Tatsunoko series before his breakthrough hit *Fist of the North Star* at Toei.

Sugii Gisaburō (1940–): Director who worked on *The Tale of the White Serpent*, the first *Astro Boy* series, *Touch*, and *Street Fighter II*.

Sugino Akio (1944–): Animator and character designer. Collaborated with Osamu Dezaki on *Nobody's Boy: Remi*, *Cat's Eye*, *Treasure Island*, *Ashita no Joe*, and *Cobra*.

Suzuki Toshimichi (1923–2008): Producer and creator of *Gall Force* and *Bubblegum Crisis*.

Suzuki Toshio (1948–): Producer and president of Studio Ghibli until 2014.

T

Tagawa Suihō (1899–1989): Pioneering *mangaka*. Creator of *Norakuro*, whose hero, a clumsy black military dog, became a propaganda mascot during World War II.

Tajiri Satoshi (1965–): Producer and video game creator. Created *Pokémon*.

Takachiho Haruka (1951–): Sci-fi writer. Creator of *Crusher Joe* and *Dirty Pair*.

Takada Akemi (1955–): Illustrator and character designer. Worked on *Urusei Yatsura*, *Kimagure Orange Road*, and *Magical Angel Creamy Mami*. Member of the artist-writer collective Headgear, creator of *Patlabor*.

Takahashi Rumiko (1957–): *Mangaka*. Creator of *Urusei Yatsura*, *Ranma ½*, and *Maison Ikkoku*.

Takahashi Ryōsuke (1943–): Scriptwriter, producer, and director. Worked on *Votoms*, *Cyborg 009*, *The Cockpit*, and *Blue Gender*.

Takahashi Yōichi (1960–): *Mangaka*. Creator of *Captain Tsubasa*.

Takahata Isao (1935–2018): Director. Cofounder of Studio Ghibli. Worked on *Wolf Boy Ken*, *Heidi*, *Grave of the Fireflies*, *Pom Poko*, *The Tale of the Princess Kaguya*, and many more.

Takeuchi Naoko (1967–): *Mangaka*. Creator of *Sailor Moon*.

Tanaka Yoshiki (1952–): Writer. Creator of the sci-fi series *Legend of the Galactic Heroes* and the fantasy series *The Heroic Legend of Arslan*.

Tanaka Yoshitsugu (1907–1982): Pioneering director. Worked on various propaganda films, including *Picture Book 1936*.

Taniguchi Moriyasu (1945–): Animator. Cofounder of Anime R studio. Worked on *Aura Battler Dunbine* and *Dream Hunter Rem*. Founding member of the JAniCA association.

Tezuka Osamu (1928–1989): Legendary *mangaka* nicknamed the "God of Manga." Animation pioneer behind the first weekly TV series in black and white (*Astro Boy*) and color (*Kimba the White Lion*).

Tomino Yoshiyuki (1941–): Tezuka-trained director. Creator of the *Gundam* series.

Toriumi Hisayuki (1941–2009): Screenwriter and director. Supervised the *Gatchaman* series.

Toriyama Akira (1955–2024): *Mangaka* and character designer. Created *Dr. Slump* and *Dragon Ball*.

Tsuda Naokatsu (Unknown): Director of the TV series *JoJo's Bizarre Adventure*.

Tsutsui Yasutaka (1934–): Writer. Author of *Paprika* and *The Girl Who Leapt Through Time*.

Tsurumaki Kazuya (1966–): Director, Hideaki Anno's right-hand man. Directed *FLCL* and *Gunbuster 2*. Head of the Japan Animator Expo project.

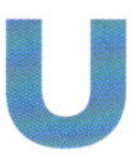

Umetsu Yasuomi (1960–): Animator, character designer, and director. Worked on *Robot Carnival*, *Mezzo Forte*, and the *Kite* series.

Umino Chica (Unknown): *Mangaka*. Creator of *Honey and Clover*. Character designer for *Eden of the East*.

Bibliography

English

Anime: A History by Jonathan Clements (BFI Palgrave)
Jonathan Clements turned his in-depth thesis into a book that is accessible to the most curious readers. The fruit of meticulous research and interviews, *Anime: A History* remains today's essential, reliable, and well-documented anime reference.

The Anime Encyclopedia by Jonathan Clements and Helen McCarthy (Stone Bridge Press)
Over 2,000 titles are meticulously detailed, both technically and artistically, in this encyclopedia designed by two world-renowned experts. Frequently updated, the book is more than just an academic compendium and includes wealth of anecdotes and analysis.

Anime Explosion! The What? Why? & Wow! of Japanese Animation by Patrick Drazen (Stone Bridge Press)
Patrick Drazen uses an impressionist method to describe the expansion of Japanese animation. By exploring a theme, genre, studio, title, or artist in detail, he gradually paints a picture of the industry today.

French

L'animation japonaise: Du rouleau peint aux Pokémon by Brigitte Koyama-Richard (Flammarion)
This large-format book's origins are in Japanese prints, which, unfortunately, overlooks a number of important periods in the history of animation. However, the university lecturer's immersive look into the Toei studio gives it exclusive added value.

Capter le moment fuyant: Osamu Tezuka and l'invention de l'animation télévisée by Samuel Kaczorowski (L'Harmattan)
How was the first weekly animated series in Japanese history created? Through an examination carried out with the rigor of a university thesis, director and researcher Samuel Kaczorowski deciphers a founding myth while avoiding the pitfall of many specialists—the posthumous idealization of Osamu Tezuka.

L'animation japonaise en France: Réception, diffusion, réappropriations written by a collective, under the direction of Marie Pruvost-Delaspre (L'Harmattan)
Avoiding any value judgment, this academic essay takes a discerning look at the assimilation of Japanese animated culture by the French public. An ideal read for breaking down preconceptions and gaining a better understanding of a genre still plagued by misconceptions.

WEBSITES

English

Japanese Animated Film Classics
http://animation.filmarchives.jp/en/index.html
Now in the public domain, the first short Japanese animated films can be viewed online thanks to the National Film Archive of Japan in Tokyo.

The Association of Japanese Animations
http://aja.gr.jp/english/japan-anime-data
The Association of Japanese Animations provides the public with key figures on the market economy, year after year. It is the perfect tool for measuring the industry's evolution in Japan and internationally.

Motion Picture Producers Association of Japan, Inc.
http://eiren.org/index.html
The MPPAJ lists the commercial success of Japanese films, both live action and animated, from 1980 to the present day.

French

AnimeLand
http://www.animeland.fr
The leading French magazine dedicated to anime with its first issue dating back to April 1991. *AnimeLand* is the ideal bridge between newbies and dedicated enthusiasts. In addition to its news and features, the community forum will guide beginners in their first steps.

Planète Jeunesse
http://www.planete-jeunesse.com/
Contrary to what its name suggests, Planète Jeunesse covers a wide selection of animated works for audiences of all ages. Its detailed fact sheets and helpful commentaries are what make it so special.

Catsuka
https://www.catsuka.com/
This website specializes in animated films, keeping you up to date with the latest news while helping you discover new favorites through video links. Catsuka ran as a bimonthly TV show on the French Nolife network from 2010 to 2018.

Acknowledgments

The two authors of this book didn't even know each other until a year before the book was written. Both longtime fans of anime, we realized how complementary our respective knowledge was during a meeting organized by Émilie Jollois, a publishing director in search of the right duo to bring Ynnis Éditions' new project to life: a book commemorating the 100-year anniversary of anime in 2017.

A two-person writing team requires a third party to act as referee and supervisor, someone who can separate the wheat from the chaff among the authors' various ideas. A captain who is as kind as she is unwavering, our editor Marichka Besse always stayed the same course—to provide a book rich in information, sometimes highly specialized information, but accessible to as many people as possible.

The book's layout was crucial to this mission and evolved in parallel with the writing process. Through continual improvements, Élise Godmuse was able to manage our requirements along with the technical constraints imposed by the quality of certain archives. The whole thing is wrapped up in a cover designed in Tokyo by Thomas Romain, a tribute to the works that led him to his profession as an anime designer.

Thank you to this cutting-edge quartet—without their contribution, 100 Years of Anime would never have seen the light of day. But without you, who are reading this now, it wouldn't exist. So, thank you for joining us on a journey through the history of a medium that is now an essential part of pop culture. May this experience prove useful to you the next time you watch a Japanese cartoon. Which one? The choice is yours.

We would also like to thank Ilyes Rahmani, Marion Cochet-Grasset, Sonia Jensen, Steve Naumann, Laurine Delaporte, Fabien Mauro, Romain Serir, Béatrice Larmine, Sylvie Hellot Brevignon, and Timothy Killian (All the Anime France), Méko, Charlock, Alexis Francomme, Adrien Leclère, and the Ermont-Eaubonne media libraries.

Matthieu Pinon and Philippe Bunel

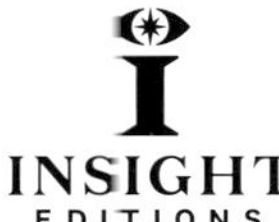

PO Box 3088
San Rafael, CA 94912
www.insighteditions.com

Find us on Facebook: www.facebook.com/InsightEditions
Follow us on Instagram: @insighteditions

Originally published in French by Ynnis Éditions in 2017 under the title
Un siècle d'animation japonaise
Legal deposit: November 2017
2nd printing. Printed in May 2022 by Imago Publishing in Slovenia.

English translation by Ambrosia Noyes.

ISBN: 979-8-3374-0055-6

Publisher: Raoul Goff
SVP, Co-Publisher: Vanessa Lopez
VP, Creative: Chrissy Kwasnik
VP, Manufacturing: Alix Nicholaeff
Editorial Director: Lia Brown
Art Director: Matt Girard
Senior Editor: Stephen Fall
Editorial Assistant: Audrey Salo
Executive Managing Editor: Maria Spano
Senior Production Manager: Greg Steffen
Strategic Production Planner: Lina s Palma-Temena

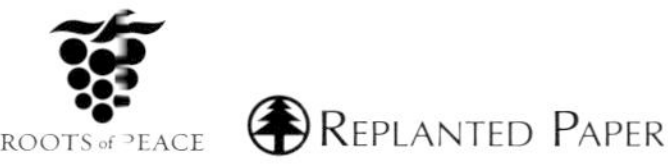

Insight Editions, in association with Roots of Peace, will plant two trees for each tree used in the manufacturing of this book. Roots of Peace is an internationally renowned humanitarian organization dedicated to eradicating land mines worldwide and converting war-torn lands into productive farms and wildlife habitats. Roots of Peace will plant two million fruit and nut trees in Afghanistan and provide farmers there with the skills and support necessary for sustainable land use.

Manufactured in China by Insight Editions

10 9 8 7 6 5 4 3 2 1

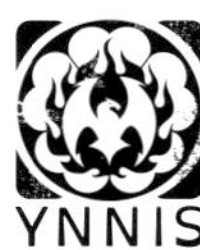

Publishing Manager: Cedric Littardi
Authors: Philippe Bunel and Matthieu Pinon
Editor: Marichka Besse
Graphic Design: Élise Godmuse
Layout: Élise Godmuse
Cover Artwork: Thomas Romain
Proofreader: Sonia Jensen

Ynnis Éditions
38 rue Notre-Dame-De-Nazareth
75003 Paris, France
www.ynnis-editions.fr
Instagram: @ynnis_editions

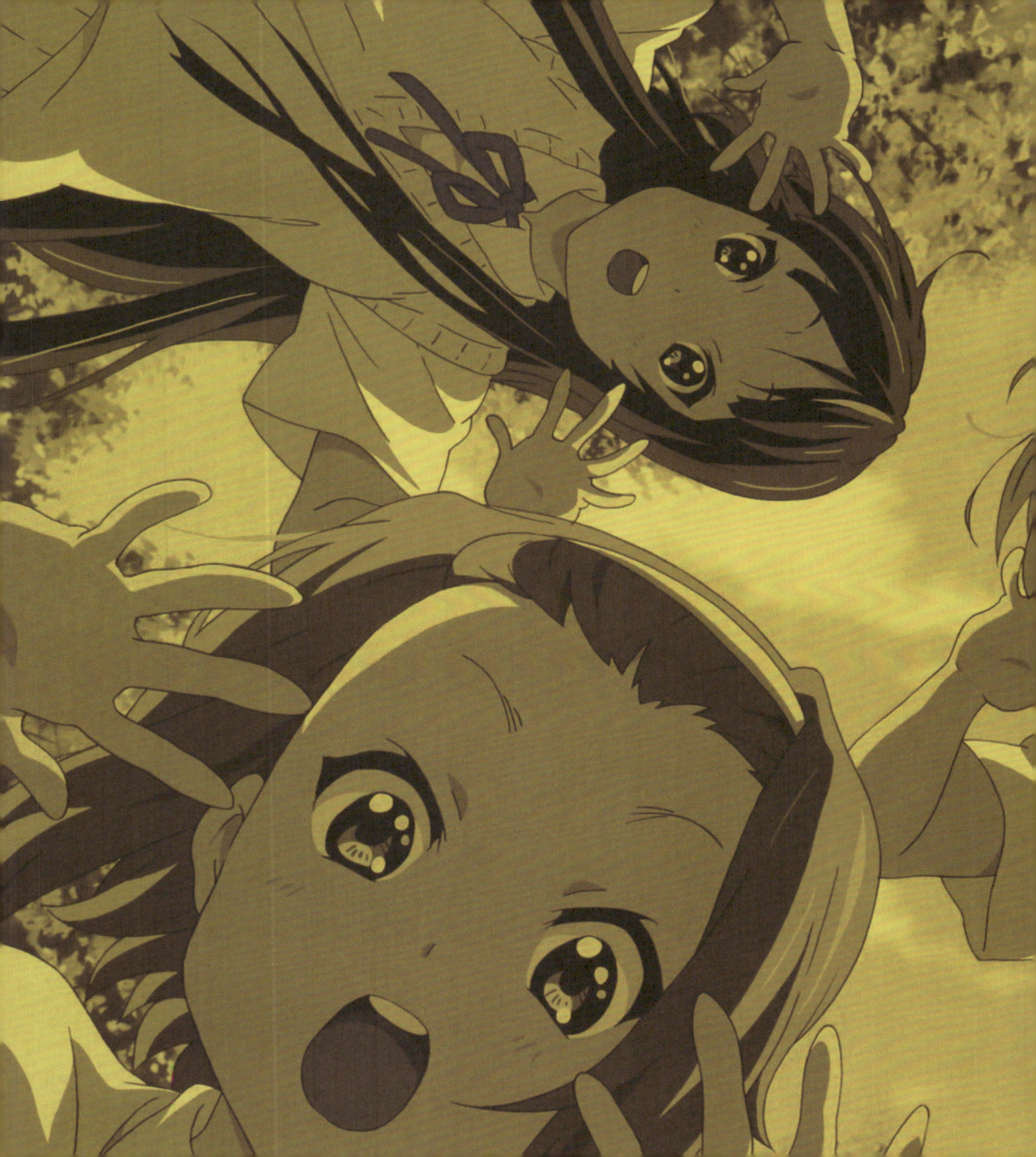